IN PRAISE OF THE HUMAN FORM

IN PRAISE OF THE HUMAN FORM

Arts of Africa, Oceania and America

JOSETTE AND JEAN-CLAUDE WEILL COLLECTION

edited by
Charles-Wesley Hourdé and
Jean-Pierre Weill

with a text by
Philippe Dagen

photographs by
Vincent Girier-Dufournier

5 CONTINENTS

Entries'authors
Pierre Amrouche [PA]
Viviane Baeke [VB]
Harry Beran [HB]
Maëva Chanoine [MC]
Jean-Paul Colleyn [JPC]
Eric Coote [EC]
Marie Yvonne Curtis [MYC]
Aurélien Gaborit [AG]
Bertrand Goy [BG]
David Henrion [DH]
Hélène Joubert [HJ]
Alisa LaGamma [ALG]
Hélène Leloup [HL]
Bettina von Lintig [BVL]
Constance de Monbrison [CDM]
Sean Mooney [SM]
Michel Orliac [MO]
Philippe Peltier [PP]
Constantine Petridis [CP]

TABLE OF CONTENTS

INTRODUCTION

Charles-Wesley Hourdé

The art market is a small world where one's private life and professional life are constantly interwoven. In this microcosm, I was fortunate to make the acquaintance of Josette and Jean-Claude Weill. I can never thank their son Jean-Pierre enough for the confidence he showed by allowing me to work with him on this project, which in my view deals with one of the most extraordinary collections of African, Oceanic, and Amerindian artworks in private hands.

Over the years, I have often had occasion to bump into the Weills: Josette, Jean-Claude, and Jean-Pierre used to visit the galleries in Saint-Germain-des-Prés and the auction houses on a regular basis. We would also meet at important events dedicated to the art of distant lands. I knew about their collection by reputation, and I had heard only wonderful things about it among the small circle of initiates who had had the privilege of seeing it.

It was through an object—an exceptional nail fetish, illustrated in *Utotombo*—that I had the opportunity almost ten years ago to get to know this fascinating couple better, along with their entire collection. I was working for Christie's at the time and I volunteered to bring them the object they had just bought. I realized as soon as I arrived at the flat in avenue Foch just why I had heard so many enthusiastic accounts of the objects I would find there.

The first I came across was Robert Burawoy's large *nkisi*, which acted as a magnet, surrounded as it was by a myriad of other smaller but equally exquisite sculptures. These were followed by a delightful Maori figurine, placed on a stand by the cabinetmaker Kichizô Inagaki (I was just preparing an article on his work at the time), a group of works from Mali that I seemed to recall from Hélène Leloup's catalogues, and an extraordinary Yoruba head, which had already struck me when I saw it in my godfather's flat in Avenue Pierre I de Serbie . . .

The calm radiance of the Weills, immediately apparent in their warm welcome, was reflected in each of the objects in their collection. Indeed, its function is to act as a coherent whole in which each piece contributes to the overall effect, while at the same time accentuating the uniqueness of its fellows. This collection would not exist without the Weills and in my view it constitutes a direct extension of their nature as human beings. The unforced sureness of their choices is not the result of long deliberations. They choose. And once chosen, a work captivates them by its beauty, its power, the variations and nuances in its materials. They have fallen in love with it and continue to feel a deep and sincere attachment to it.

The unmistakeable taste that distinguishes them derives from their confident knowledge of the classical aesthetic canons on which the market is based and on their unparalleled eye for art. As a result, their collection contains a fair number of works that could be described as iconic—in the sense that they perfectly embody the aesthetically aware early generations of twentieth-century collectors and art lovers. The stunning *Nimba* statue from the former Vlaminck Collection, Paul Wirz's elegant Senufo horseman, or Paul Chadourne's wonderful *Ciwara* headdress are good examples.

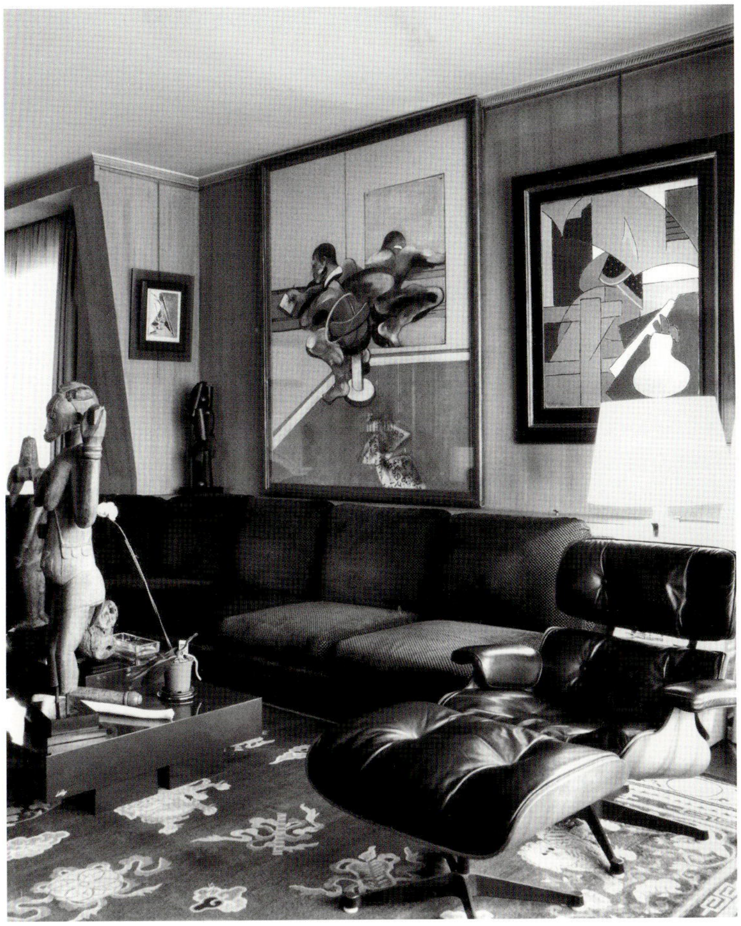

These classic pieces take on a fresh flavour in juxtaposition with sculptures that are otherwise atypical, or at least more intimate compared with traditional tastes. The Weills' apartment, bathed in a subtle, mysterious half-light, majestically reveals the expressive power of their Bamileke, Bangwa, and New Guinea artworks. The beauty of the materials—textured patinas, grooved wood, polished ivory, metallic encrustations—are imbued with a special resonance. So it is that an imposing *Nimba* shoulder mask and a hieratic Mboye statue happily co-exist.
The Weill Collection includes several masterpieces of tribal art. However, an assemblage of a number of iconic pieces does not make a collection: the decisive, synthetic, even organic beauty of the Weill Collection is entirely due to the eye and the personality of its creators.

At this first visit I spent a long time chatting with the Weills, surrounded by all their treasures. Enchanted though I was by these artistic (re)discoveries, I was certainly not blind to the equal charms of my kind and unaffected hosts. The conversation ebbed and flowed naturally, aided by the reassuring presence of the works all around us. When the door at last closed behind me that day, I had the sensation that we had spent these few happy hours together as a family.
I hope this book will convey to the reader something of the exceptional, stimulating and indeed eye-opening nature of this double encounter. Firstly, with a pair of passionate and delightful collectors; secondly, with a unique assortment of works silently engaged in the most fertile of dialogues.

SECRET CONVERSATION

Jean-Pierre Weill

There was no music in the apartment at 45 Boulevard Lannes we moved out of in 1958, nor in the one on Avenue Foch.
There were paintings. Contemporary artworks that were beginning to decorate the walls filled this void and became our daily companions.
My sister Viviane, my brother Bernard, and I sometimes joined our parents on trips to exhibitions. I enjoyed these outings more and more as I grew older and my curiosity was awakened. I asked many questions to try to understand things better, but the answers I got were always brief, not to say terse. They boiled down to "this is good" or "this isn't."
I was dismayed by this reaction but I accepted it and above all I made the most of what I got. I regarded it as perfectly normal and decided that it was up to me to follow things up and find my own way to the truth. I knew I had my work cut out to acquire my mother's knowledge, taste, and daring and my father's sharp eye, so that one day I would have confidence in my own judgment and make my own discoveries.
This was how at a very young age I came to choose the essentially solitary strategy to find my way through museums in quest of my own answers to these questions. In August 1969, when I was fourteen, I accompanied my parents on a trip through Normandy, where we went from one antique dealer to another, hunting for bargains to furnish the house they were building, having hired Paul Dupré-Lafon, the great architect-cum-decorator who is now out of fashion, to design it. There was a small African art department on the first floor at Dodier's in Avranches and I fell head over heels for a Dogon dance mask, which I asked to have as a present for my forthcoming birthday. I had found a fresh, vast, and unexplored territory for my adventures. The whole world of tribal art opened up for me.
Five years later I had the good fortune to meet Hélène Kamer, then Jacques Kerchache, who were enthusiastic and enthusing dealers. Hélène's gallery in Quai Malaquais and Jacques's house at la Poterne des Peupliers were each in their own way the entrance to an Aladdin's cave and, to me, whole new worlds to explore. They were both effervescent and skilled raconteurs. They showed me hundreds of objects, explaining where they came from, the ethnic groups that made them, and the function they fulfilled. I was enchanted by the highly personal way they had of looking at them and the way they spoke about them.
I came to realize that an object's chief and essential attribute was its authenticity. Statues speak to those who know how to look and understand.

This was the moment when my path once again crossed my parents' and I was able to resume what was an awkward relationship during my teens. They loved paintings and their beautiful collection was full of very personal, strong, and ambitious choices: De Stael, Dubuffet, Bacon, Schiele (who was virtually unknown in France in 1974) . . .
They knew very little about tribal art and fifteen years previously a dealer on Boulevard Raspail, who was well known but also unscrupulous, had put an end to their early enthusiasm. But their great friend Jean-Claude Bellier, who already had a fine collection of his own, was able to rekindle their interest in this field. That's how our adventure lasting almost fifty years began.

I accompanied them to Hélène's gallery and to Jacques's apartment den. I was very much under his spell at the time and I loved it when he showed us some highly original pieces of great quality. They bought their first objects from them, as well as from Jean-Claude and Bob Burawoy.
Through my parents I got to know the leading dealers and their treasures. In this way I was able to extend my experience and acquire first-hand knowledge of these objects. We gradually built up a strong complicity, and it became more and more compelling for us to seek and discover new objects to pursue. We often succeeded.
When it came to choosing, there was no real method or logic, just a great freedom and extremely high expectations. We didn't concentrate on any particular ethnic group. We were looking for strong, unusual, original pieces.
What attracted us in these African and Oceanic cultures was the extraordinary diversity of form and the astonishingly inventive approach to sculpture they displayed. It was this unique relationship between an object's functionality and its aesthetic qualities.
We didn't talk much amongst ourselves but we almost always agreed when it came to choosing. My parents soon acquired greater self-confidence in their choices and started expanding their circle of dealers, adding Bernard Dulon, Alain de Monbrison, and Lance Entwistle in particular.
Then my parents discovered Eskimo ivories, which completed their ivory collection.
With this eclecticism and a boundless field of activity, the apartment on Avenue Foch was turning into a cabinet of curiosities. Statues from faraway lands found their place in this assortment and entered into the on-going dialogue. These creatures moulded by the hands of sculptors, blacksmiths, soothsayers, witch-doctors, or sorcerers interacted with others created by the great Western artists of the twentieth century. Invisible worlds stood face to face, mingled, expressed their curiosity, and spoke to each other.
The collection grew and spread all over their apartment. But far from becoming scattered and in spite of the most disparate geographical provenances and multifarious styles, it gained a greater sense of identity and coherence.

I accompanied my parents on these enthralling adventures for forty-five years and the time has now come to leave a record of it. The record of a shared passion, a taste, a sensibility, and a special quest.
This book bears witness to this journey and in it one can perhaps detect the echo of the enigmatic dialogue which developed between these sculptures, but beyond this, more personally, the echo of the secret conversation between my father and I.

CONCERNING THE WEILL COLLECTION

Philippe Dagen

Gaining access to a collector's rooms is one of the chief pleasures of a critic and art historian. The first reason is obvious: being able to approach the sometimes exceptional quality of what he finds there, famous or little known works which he is able to enjoy better than at an exhibition or in a museum, exploiting an intimacy that is only possible in this type of context, with its surprises and discoveries. The second reason has less to do with delectation than study: each visit, every experience adds observations and evidence to build a fuller picture of the different types of collectors and their interiors which grows over the years.

I have had the professional privilege, so to speak, of getting to know several places and collections of this type located in various countries—Germany, the United States, and France in particular. It would certainly be inadvisable to establish a classification on the basis of these visits. But one can distinguish the main categories easily enougH. apartments where the collections are arranged as if in a parade so as to produce a carefully calculated and rather theatrical effect; those that have reached a saturation point so that the collection has taken over virtually the whole of the available space, with the risk that one can neither move around easily nor even look at the works satisfactorily; those that have something of the total artwork about them, each item in the collection being linked to the others by subtle intellectual associations that only the owner or owners of the collection appreciate.

Without going into details, there are some astonishing and even spectacular examples of the first of these in Park Avenue, New York, and in the streets around the Metropolitan Museum, and others that are second to none in Quai Malaquais, Quai Voltaire, and in the neighbourhood of Rue de Varenne and Rue de l'Université. Instances of the second type of collection can be found in these same areas in the big cities, as well as in less aristocratic districts, the pinnacle probably being reached by a New York couple who built a kind of freestanding structure made up of framed works in the middle of the living room of their apartment, so that their elegant sofas and armchairs were lined up against the walls, walls where other works hung, frequently overlapping. The historical example of the third category is undoubtedly André Breton's apartment, which has become a legendary benchmark of its kind. In this case, which usually applies to collections amassed by artists and writers, the result amounts to a self-portrait and an autobiography created through the choice and arrangement of objects that have to do with artistic creation, natural history, or something else altogether. In the interests of comprehensiveness, I'm obliged to include a fourth group whose development I have witnessed over the past few years: collections cobbled together for essentially speculative purposes and displayed in houses or apartments that have more in common with a showroom or dealer's gallery than a private residence.

Josette and Jean-Claude Weill's collection certainly does not fall into this last, regrettable category, nor even in the first, less questionable but nonetheless irritating, which could be described as financial exhibitionism. It is closest to the second type, with aspects of the third. All along the corridor and in the various rooms, the works are simply there, so to speak, arrayed unostentatiously, just as the architecture and furnishings are unpretentious. On the other hand, they are everywhere. They are arranged on shelves, on the furniture and, in the case of the larger pieces, on the floor. There are no heavy theatrics, no stunning visual effects, unlike a similar collection not far from the building where the Weills live, where monumental sculptures from New

Guinea form a kind of shrine at the end of a long, broad gallery and are illuminated so as to increase still further their striking appearance. There is nothing of this here: no breathtaking spectacle, no straining after effect. The works are simply there, together. All together: sculptures from Africa and Oceania, sculptures by contemporary artists, paintings and works on paper by other twentieth-century artists. They aren't arranged in any particular order, neither on the basis of cultural geography nor chronologically.
Your first impression is that you have suddenly been surrounded by all these works and that they all get along perfectly, in a manner of speaking. They aren't merely arranged in juxtaposition to each other, but appear in a certain sense to be related and allied. Without at first knowing exactly why, this brings to mind two verses from a sonnet by Baudelaire:

> *"Man passes through forests of symbols*
> *which watch him with familiar glances."*

It is not so much the symbols that are interesting here as the curious reference to "familiar glances": the sculptures watch the visitor as he looks at them and is influenced by their presence, a familiar presence that is neither ostentatious nor exhibitionistic. It would be presuming too much to explain exactly why Baudelaire wrote "familiar glances." But what these lines suggest, namely the sense of finding oneself in the presence of living beings in a welcoming environment, might—it is perhaps not too fanciful to imagine—have been experienced by Baudelaire himself when visiting a collection, a cabinet of curiosities or an artist's studio. It is no accident that the sonnet is entitled *Correspondances*: for what is a truly personal collection, if not an assemblage of correspondences? These form one or several networks. Indeed, a net seems the most appropriate metaphor. It can be interpreted in several ways. The collector is a fisherman who catches works in his net and the collection is a net in which each piece is a knot connected to the others: a structure with its own inner coherence. That is exactly what one feels on first entering the Weills' apartment: there is a sense of unity whose governing principles, or logic—a word that here doesn't necessarily stand for a rational arrangement or method, but a certain way of choosing—need to be understood. The task now is to perceive clearly and explain this logic—these correspondences.
Now, while it is absolutely clear the moment you cross the threshold of their home that this is the type of collection you are dealing with, you quickly come to realize that actually describing this logic is no easy matter. The first reason for this conviction is that no sooner have the introductions been made than Josette and Jean-Claude Weill invite you to look round the apartment, starting with the large room where we are and which ordinary would be referred to as the living room, if it were not for the fact that it is partly an office and partly Jean-Claude Weill's smoking room—where he indulges his taste for cigars—and especially because it is inhabited by numerous human figures made of wood, ivory, bone or bronze. The wooden and ivory objects are mostly African. The bronzes are by Germaine Richier and Louise Bourgeois: once again human figures, contemporary statues among ancient statues come from afar.
The visit continues in various other rooms, including the dining room and even the bathroom. Unlike the other apartments mentioned above, where one has to squeeze and snake past objects and even step over them in some instances, this is an apartment that positively invites you to wander around. At the same time, the walls are almost entirely the domain of paintings—Vieira da Silva, Nicolas De Staël, Jean Dubuffet, Gaston Chaissac, Sam Szafran, Pierre Soulages, and Bernard Dufour. Wherever it is possible to stand a small artwork on a piece of furniture or a shelf, the Weills have done so. Is there any room left for fresh acquisitions? It's unlikely. And then there's the matter of finding works that are easy to match with those gathered over a period of almost half a century. For—and here we return to the matter of correspondences—the other pieces confirm what the "living room" immediately makes apparent: the homogeneous nature of the collection. What one might call the "Weill taste."
The question now is how to define it. So far the words associated with it have been familiarity, unity and homogeneousness. These cannot be explained in terms of cultural geography—the non-Western works have multiple provenances, including Africa, South-East Asia, India, and New Guinea—nor as a result of history, since several contemporary paintings and sculptures form part of this uniform effect. There is

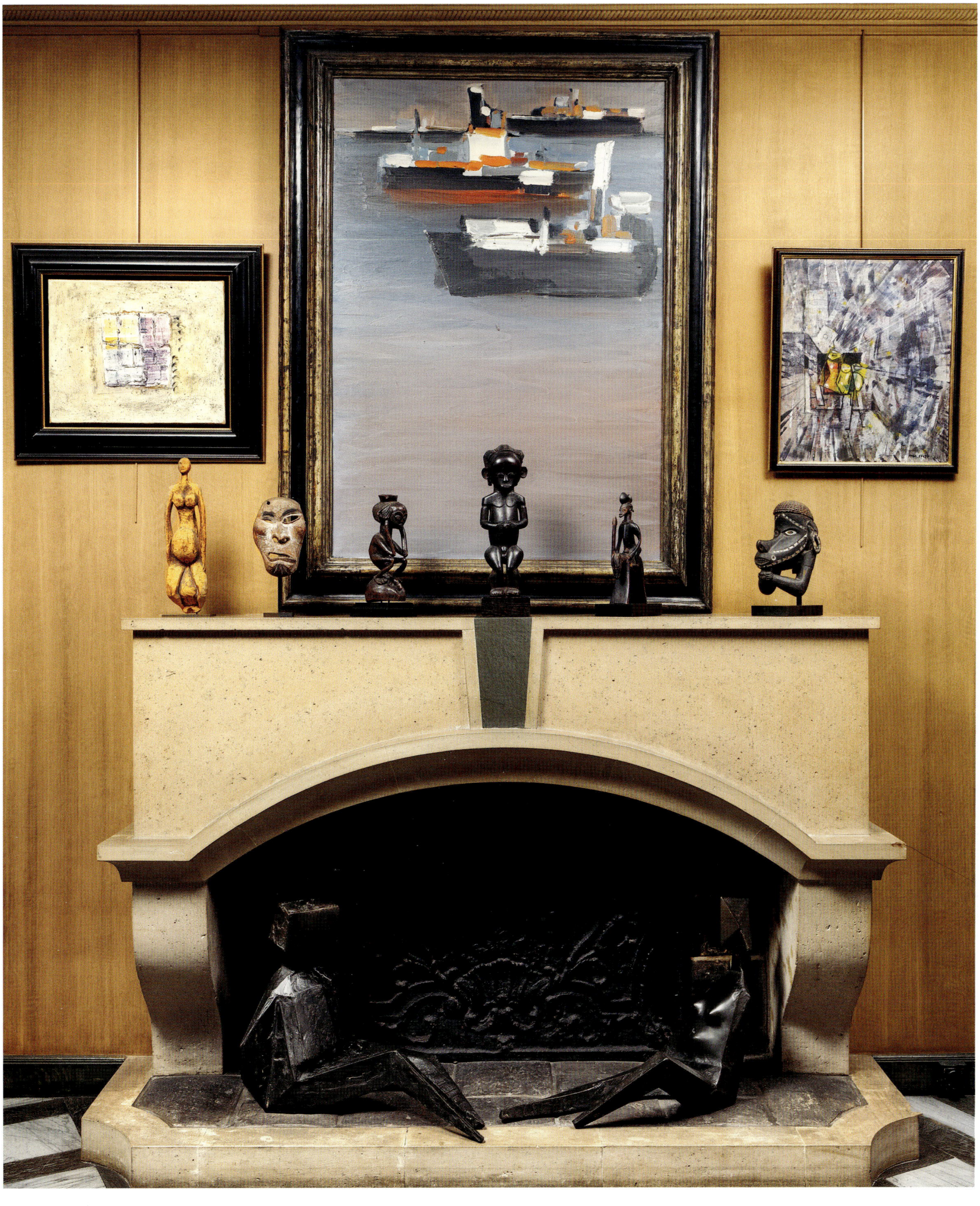

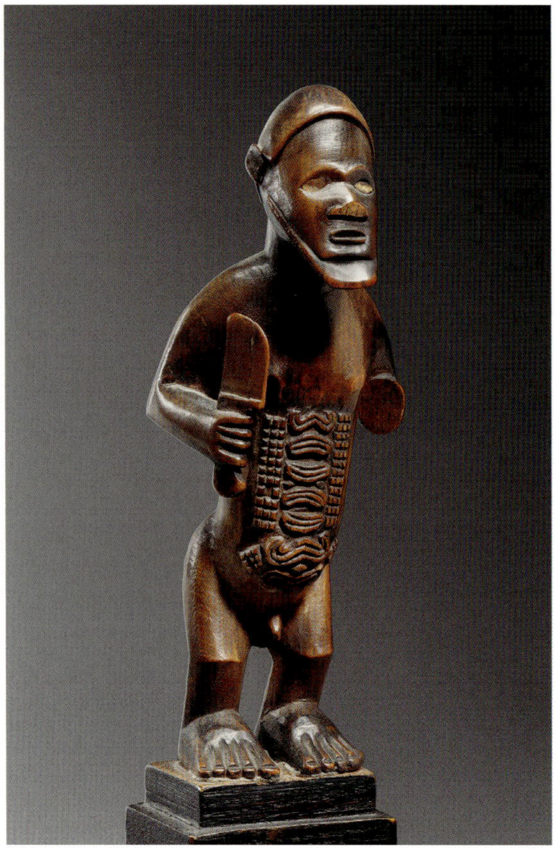

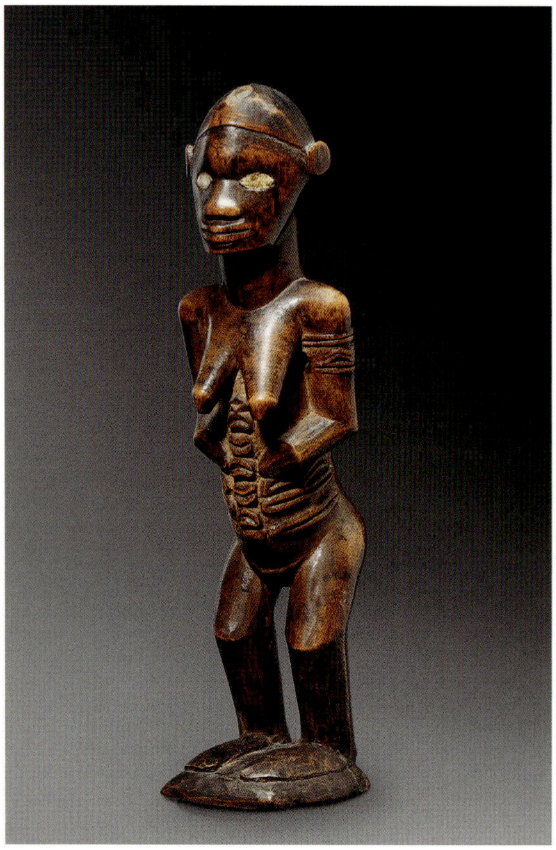

Three bembe objetcs given as a present to Jean-Claude Weill by his mother in 1945

nothing systematic, neither the desire to create long series according to styles or regions, nor an obsession with a single material—ivory for example—nor the search for what for the sake of convenience we call masterpieces—exemplary pieces in pristine condition with an instantly identifiable origin. There are undoubtedly masterpieces of this kind here, but also works that have seen better days and are now incomplete; pieces that can be categorized as what one might call court art—the art of a princely or royal court—and others that have a distinctly less aristocratic origin and function; very large objects and miniatures. What then? How and why was this assemblage put together? The simplest thing, obviously, is to ask those who put it together.

But asking this question out of the blue, without leading up to it in any way, is probably not the best way to get an answer, I reasoned. Much too brutal, far too much like a TV interview, where everything is simplified and reduced to just a few minutes at the cost of jettisoning any nuances. You need time to understand, which is not the way of today's ubiquitous helter-skelter system of communication. I therefore suggested making a second visit a few days later, when we could take our time—a proposal accepted with alacrity. I had this conversation with Jean-Claude Weill alone at first and his wife joined us later. Rather than discussing the works themselves, I preferred to build up the overall context—the Weill fashion house—first, for it seemed important to establish how we got here, so to speak, sitting face to face in the company of so many sculptures.

The main details regarding when the firm was founded and how it evolved have long been known, at least by those in the fashion business. I shall recall just the bare essentials of the story here: Jean-Claude's grandfather is born in Alsace in 1867; Alsace becomes German territory after defeat in the Franco-Prussian War, in 1870; as a young man this same grandfather travels to Paris, where his uncle gives him a job in the clothing industry; uncle and nephew fail to see eye to eye on several matters, with the result that the younger man decides to set up his own business, "in a servant's room, in 1892." The room soon has to accommodate a wife, "grandma," who offers her own criticisms of her husband's products. So, probably through gritted teeth, he suggests she show what she can do and try to design models that would be more appealing. The outcome is a triumphant success and the company begins to flourish.

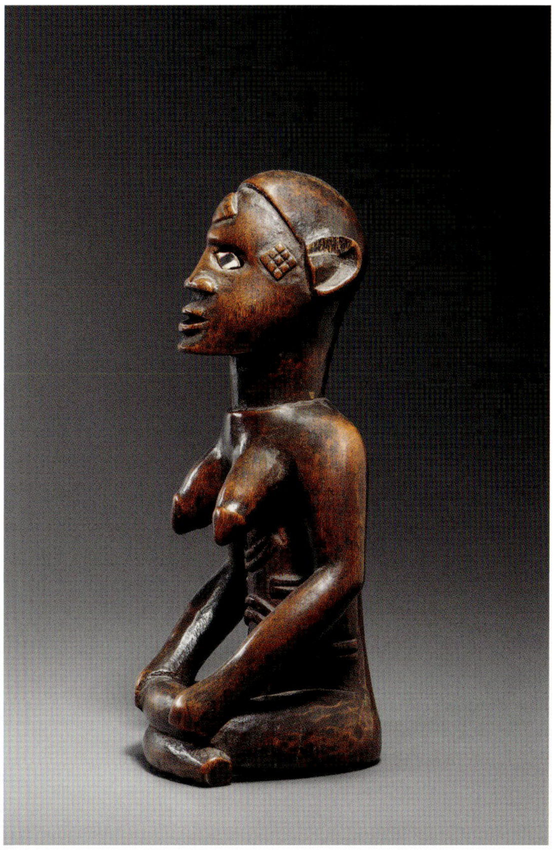

The firm was "Aryanized," to use the appalling terminology of the period, during the Occupation. The Weills took refuge in Vichy, of all places, and later moved to the spa resort of Challes-les-Eaux, near Chambéry. This area was under Italian occupation at the time, which Jean-Claude Weill calls "a joke." When the Wehrmacht took over from the Italian army, which capitulated in September 1943, the situation took a turn for the worse and by Easter 1944 the family had to move once again, this time to Saint-Bonnet-en-Bresse, where they were hidden by the family of Jean-Claude's mother's chambermaid. In few words he evokes "hovels along a road," machine-gunned by German soldiers making their way north after the Allies' Provence landing. At the same time, the woman who was to be his wife, Josette Ullmo, who in her words was born into a "lower-middle class family in Besançon," was lying low in Château de Peyrins, a children's home in the Drôme. The head of the institute, Germaine Chesneau, gave refuge to over one hundred Jewish children during the war, saving them from deportation to Nazi concentration camps. When the Wehrmacht troops passed through the area in August 1944, the children—sixty-four at the time—were hidden in the woods around the castle, then put up in the barn of a nearby farm. The castle was ransacked, but fortunately that was the worst that happened. Josette Ullmo's father had an even closer shave: he was captured in Nîmes and spent time in the camps of Compiègne and Drancy, but avoided being loaded onto an eastbound train. "He did not leave," his daughter says, adopting the same concise, matter-of-fact attitude to these episodes as her husband.

After the Liberation, the Weills took control of their business once again, in accordance with an understanding they had reached with three clients who had agreed to hold onto the company's shares until the end of the war. "My father revived it," says Jean-Claude. In 1948, when Jean-Claude was twenty-three, the Fédération du Vêtement Féminin organized a study trip to the United States. "I went with one of my cousins, who worked in tailoring." They acquired first-hand knowledge of American society and its factories, as well as witnessed the early days of what was to become consumerism. This experience and an introduction to Marcel Bleustein Blanchet—the founder of Publicis and a pioneer of the mass advertising industry—convinced him that the Weill house would have to change the way it did business. "In 1950, we launched a mass advertising campaign, with around ten films and newspaper announcements. Then we opened a shop in Paris, with great pomp and adds in all the editions of France Soir. I have to say that it took off immediately. A few years later there were queues on Saturdays. Our great success was to get the Weill brand recognized. We were the first to put a label with our name on it on our clothes . . . No question, what we learned from the Americans was key."

The firm still exists; it's still a family-run company and its offices and workshops are in the same building in Rue Livingstone in Montmartre, near Marché Saint Pierre, as they were in 1924. The building was restored recently; its upper floors were completely gutted and the rooms enlarged, but Jean-Claude Weill's office was left untouched, as was a dining room. It is no exaggeration to say there is a strong sense of professional and family continuity from one generation to the next—something of a rarity nowadays. Paying a visit and being shown round by Josette and Jean-Claude's son Jean-Pierre Weill means meeting a number of other Weills, the next generation, in their thirties. It also gives you the chance to notice that art has a place here, too: there are several paintings and Jean-Pierre Weill's office in particular contains an extraordinary self-portrait of Bernard Dufour in

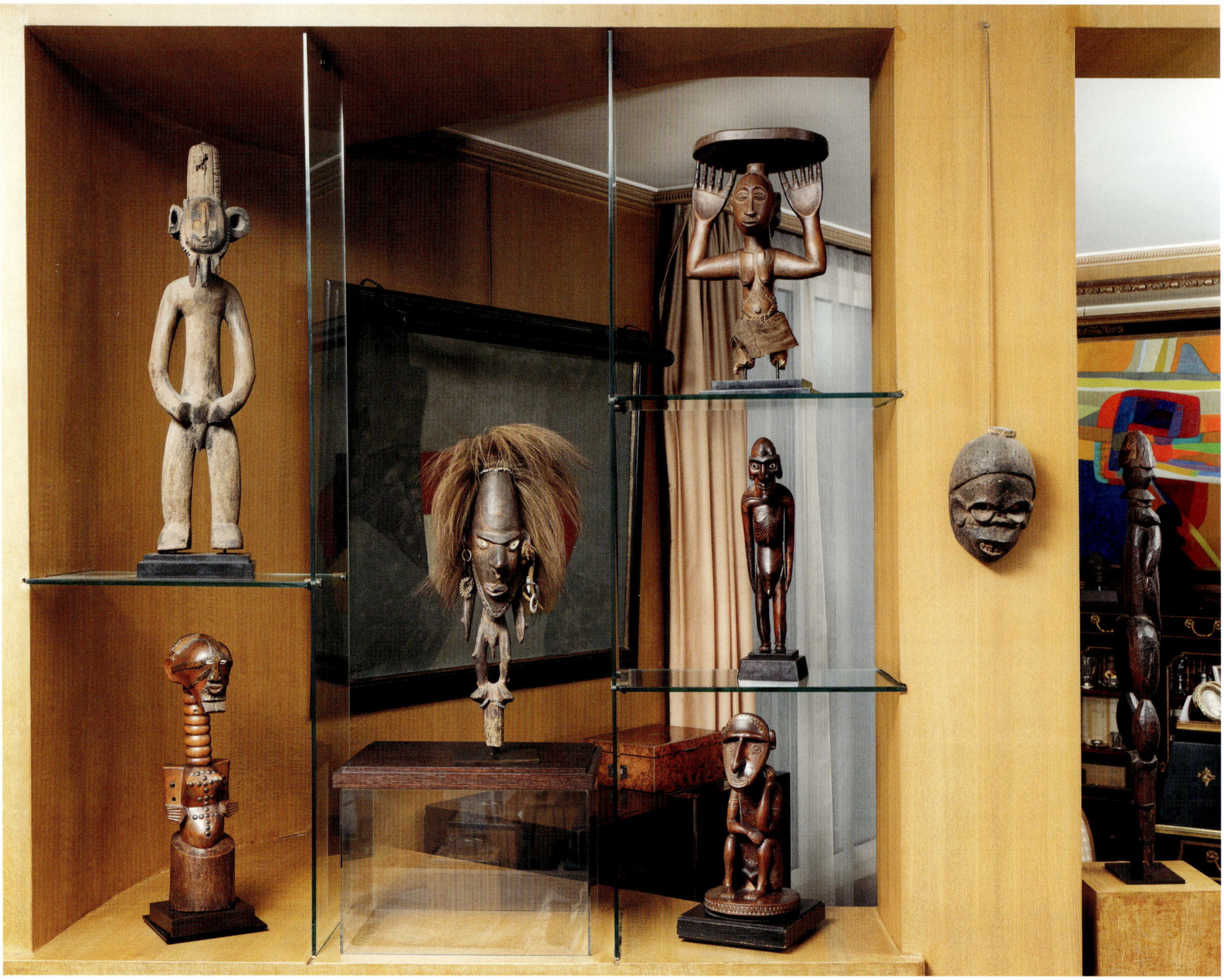

the nude. In this instance it also gave as the opportunity, since we had both seen it, to describe the house at Pradié and its master, a figure larger than life, a painter, photographer, and writer of the first rank. Dufour had a private collection of what he called, jokingly, his "negro objects." There is no comparison with the number and rarity of the works in the Weill Collection, except in one regard: the real link is the Loeb family.
The Loebs? What's the connection? Unexpected, in the case of the Weills: Robert, Jean-Claude's father, was friends with the Loeb twins, Pierre and Edouard. More precisely, they were comrades in arms during World War I. For the record, Pierre and Edouard Loeb were born in Paris in 1897. Pierre opened his first gallery in Rue Bonaparte in 1924, where he exhibited works by Picasso, Miró, and the Surrealists, including Ernst, Masson, Man Ray, and a few others; moving to Rue des Beaux-Arts, he added a number of new artists to his stable: Braque, Dufy, Balthus, Paalen, and so on. Galerie Pierre had become one of the beacons of avant-garde art in Paris by 1939, better known even than Galerie Simon and the gallery run by Daniel-Henry Kahnweiler, who failed to match Pierre Loeb's instinct for appreciating Surrealism's intellectual and artistic impetus. Although less well known than his brother, Edouard also ran a gallery and had tastes that were very similar to his brother's. Pierre's son Albert continued the family tradition until 2015.
One of the artists Pierre Loeb exhibited was Bernard Dufour, which is a way of making the Weill connection. However, there is a more direct one: Pierre Loeb was one of the most active dealers in African and Oceanic

art in Paris between the wars and right up to the late 1950s, and his contacts among the Surrealists certainly contributed in this respect. Among other finds, he has been credited with the discovery of the statues produced around Lake Sentani. It was Pierre Loeb who financed Jacques Viot's journey to this region in New Guinea in 1929, during which he came upon an important group of sculptures. Although the territory was under Dutch administration at the time, its art was largely unknown. Crates of mostly African sculptures were still being delivered to the gallery years later—I owe this detail to Bernard Dufour—and Loeb sometimes agreed to swap the contents for works by "his" artists.

It thus seems that art entered into the Weill family through these wartime friendships. But it also appears not to have been either quick, or easy. "I loved art, but my parents had no time for it," quips Jean-Claude Weill in no uncertain terms. But his father still entrusted the design of the company building to the architect Paul Dupré-Lafon, who was only twenty-four at the time, having been born in 1900. Dupré-Lafon duly fulfilled the commission in what was then the modern style and subsequently specialized in designing elegant townhouses and residences in west Paris: his imprint can still be seen in the furniture in the Weills' apartment. Therefore, if Robert Weill really was uninterested in the arts, as his son says, he certainly took a risk in seeking out a young man who, although undoubtedly not given to experimenting in the manner of Le Corbusier, was nonetheless much taken by modern architecture between the wars, just as Robert Mallet-Stevens was. Why mention him in particular? Because between 1921 and 1923, the year his patron was ruined, Mallet-Stevens devoted himself to the villa that the couturier Paul Poiret wanted to build at Mézy-sur-Seine. Architects renewing their profession, couturiers renewing fashion: it isn't hard to see what they had in common.

Here, digressing from the main subject—at least the reader might view it as a digression—there would be enough material for an analysis of a more general nature. It would go into the considerable part played by couturiers in the history of the avant-gardes in art, architecture, and literature, especially in France. It was no accident that Jacques Doucet, Paul Poiret or his sister Nicole Groult took part in the artistic avant-gardes of the first third of the twentieth century, through their acquisitions and various initiatives. Nor that Yves Saint-Laurent and Pierre Bergé were the kind of collectors they were. Relations were close between the fashion industry and writers—Doucet paying Breton and Aragon—and painters—Poiret finding work for Dufy and posing for Derain, Saint-Laurent posing for Warhol—throughout the century. It simply won't do just to put it down to chance: there have been far more couturiers involved in the arts of their time than bankers or industrialists taking a similar interest. It is highly likely that the desire to experiment and the willingness to take risks were decisive factors; they all took the view that repeating what had already been done was just a waste of time. In their discreet way, the Weills also played their own part in this story. When they bought a painting by Francis Bacon in the 1970s, he was certainly not the famous artist he is now. The same goes for Egon Schiele, who was far from being as highly regarded as he is today. End of the digression.

So the Loebs were friends of the family. Jean-Claude Weill's first purchase was a Max Ernst. "My parents were more into Renoir, Degas, Marquet. I think we appreciated better than they what the Loebs represented." Ernst was followed by De Staël. "I see one of his pictures in the gallery's basement. 'It's not for sale,' says Pierre Loeb. But I won't take no for an answer and in the end he gives in and sells it to me. I'd have bought many more, but he wasn't De Staël's main dealer. I'm not even sure he liked him very much. I later bought some Vieira da Silvas and several Dufours from him. And he also had a few African pieces . . . " Here we are at last: Africa, the heart of the Weill Collection. No doubt unintentionally, our conversation followed the natural course of events, in chronological order: the fashion house, the acquisitions of modern paintings, then the first African works.

Jean-Claude Weill provides further details:

"We bought from a very restricted number of dealers: Hélène Leloup, Jacques Kerchache, Bernard Dulon, Alain de Monbrison, and the Entwistles, to whom we were introduced by Jean-Claude Bellier, who was a friend."

"How did you approach things, in practice?"

"Methodically. We're methodical collectors. We went to auctions. And every Saturday we would visit these galleries, my wife and I. And we would also go round to Claude Bernard's . . . that's where we bought our

Bacon. Then there were the Szafrans, too."
"Both of you would go?"
"Of course."
"So you chose pieces together?"
"It was a shared decision. Actually, we always eyed the same piece, my wife and I. We have the same taste."

Later on Josette Weill adds a few details, on the humorous side, about the often vague, generic "we." On Pierre Loeb: "He didn't take us seriously, at least not at first. He wouldn't explain anything." On collecting sculptures produced by cultures that had for so long been saddled with the adjective "primitive": "We were the butt of many people's jokes: 'How could you spend your money on stuff like that?' That was roughly what they were thinking, and even what one or two actually said to us." They wouldn't dare say anything of the kind today. African and Oceanic art have at last been recognized for what they are: just art, and as such worthy of the same respect as any other. As a sign of this evolution, which has been especially slow in France, Jean-Claude Weill now sits on the board of the Friends of Musée du quai Branly.
In another conversation, Jean-Pierre Weill added a few personal details concerning his period at Laurent Dodier's gallery in Avranches and his trips to the ostentatious Palais de la Porte Dorée housing what was then the Musée des Arts Africains et Océaniens, the former Musée des Colonies, to see and learn what he could from the exhibits. He also mentioned his discussions with Jacques Kerchache. "He would show me objects and tell me about them. His house was a fantastic cabinet of curiosities, full of objects to do with witchcraft, anatomical figures and works by Jean Benoit, too. He introduced me to Surrealism. It was fascinating. I think I can say quite honestly that I was under his spell for years." He also described Hélène Leloup, still Hélène Kamer at the time, Jean-Claude Bellier and Alain de Monbrison, that Paris coterie of lovers of art from distant lands (an expression borrowed from Félix Fénéon and more appropriate than most that are generally used), whose history is yet to be written—a task both necessary and problematic. A number of names do not appear in this chronicle of the Weills' view of things, although they might be expected: Charles Ratton and René Rasmussen, for instance. Others are mentioned but coupled with such scathing judgments that they are best avoided here.
This might be the place for a second digression, concerning the history of the art of distant lands in the twentieth century: the awareness and understanding of these works was not yet very widespread in Paris in the 1960s and 1970s. The collections in the Palais de la Porte Dorée and in the Musée de l'Homme were weighed down by old-fashioned displays and few, or inadequate descriptions—which I can corroborate, having seen them in the late 1970s. The typical art lover's bookshelves were not well stocked, whereas today they sag under the weight of exhibition catalogues, catalogues of private and public collections, monographs arranged by type of objects, peoples, or styles and studies examining the history of ethnography and colonization, which are inseparable. There was nothing of the kind yet in around 1970: perhaps a few works, most of which in black and white, and very few exhibitions, one of the most important being *Arts primitifs dans les ateliers d'artistes*, held at the Musée de l'Homme in 1967. For collectors who regard themselves as "methodical," not without a certain bashful irony, no doubt, introduction into this world required a discipline and application that might discourage some. They didn't discourage the Weills and it is probably not too much to say that they were probably not too upset to find themselves at odds with the prevailing taste of the French bourgeoisie of those years.
So here is this question of taste—and its associates—choice, logic and coherence. How does one pin it down? By describing its unique features? Jean-Claude Weill's initial reply is rather evasive: "I don't know. I wouldn't know how to define it, if it exists. When you buy something, you don't ask too many questions. You look closely and then you buy. We just trust our eye, our instinct when we choose things." Be that as it may, one need only sit in that room, looking at the statues, to realize how strongly they are bound to each other by a common thread that is neither geographic nor stylistic. "Yes, perhaps . . . But what is undeniable is that we have never had the slightest interest in masks. Basically, we don't have any at all, except for a 'sickness mask.' Actually, we regard masks as being a rather predictable kind of taste, a bit too obvious. Everyone interested in Africa was looking for straightforward, graceful pieces—beautiful masks."

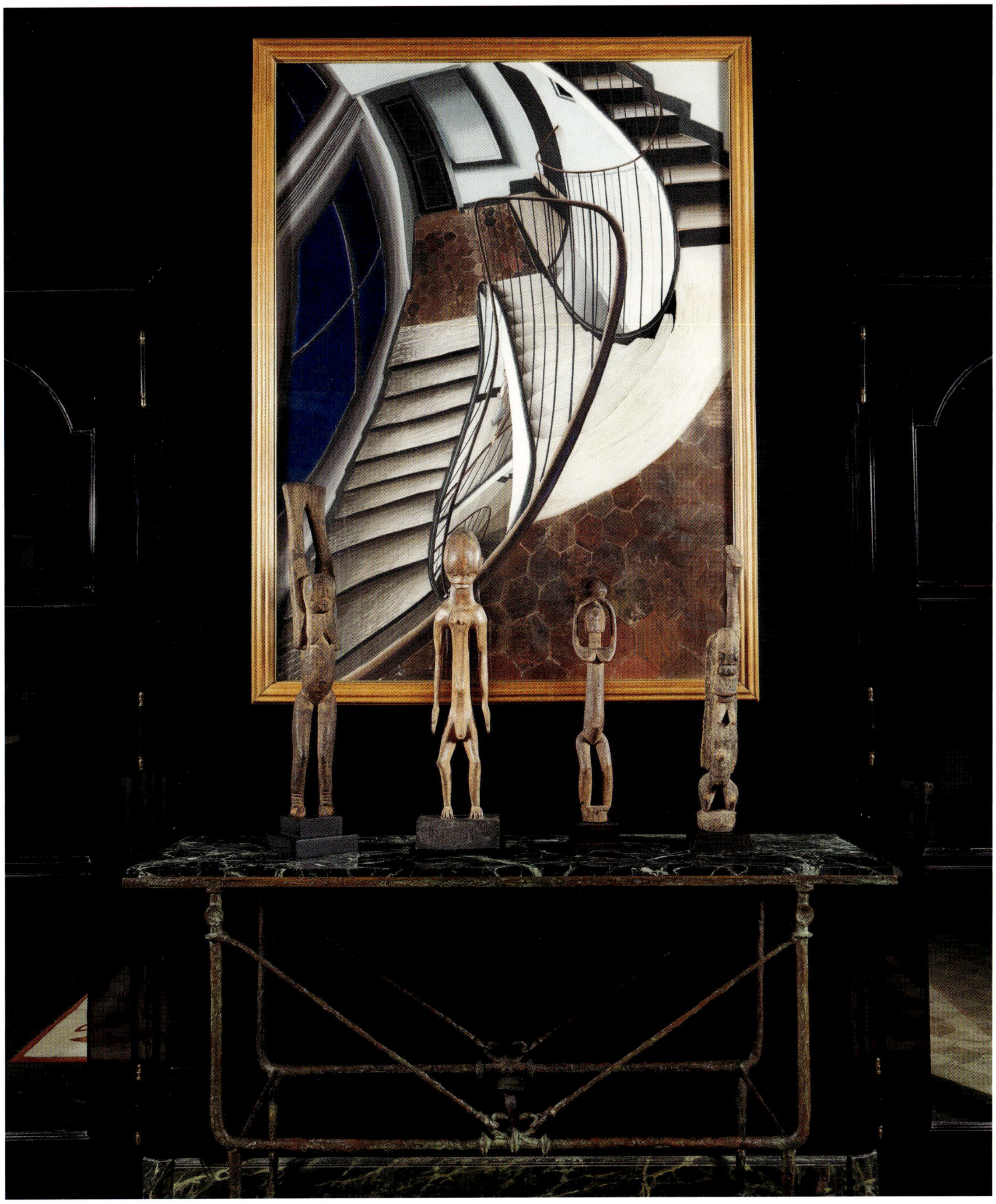

"The beautiful masks with a fine black patina and skilled carving that you find in sale catalogues?"
"They were all the rage when we started out. A lot of highly skilful works, while we preferred to buy pieces from Cameroon, which were harder and for that reason less in demand. Strong, not wishy-washy, works . . . I only like harder things."
Josette Weill is in full agreement. "We have never been interested in questions of rarity. What matters is what the work conveys. And if the work has been knocked about a bit, if it's a little damaged, it doesn't matter much, as long as there's something about it." This "something" is made up of physical and mental components. Physical because it is patently clear that the collection is built around a central, omnipresent theme, the naked human, chiefly female figure. Mental because it is equally obvious that the Weills respond to the emotions, passions, desires, and anxieties, too, that have been instilled in the material by the sculptors: what one might call a charge, which is what each sculptor, according to his makeup, projects and incorporates in his works, with their gestures, proportions, and volumes. It is clear that this charge is what a man or woman

with a modern European background discerns and will differ from what the maker of the object had injected into it previously, following an assortment of mythological tales and special religious and social rules. This is not unique to the art of distant lands. A museum visitor does not look at a fifteenth- or sixteenth-century religious painting in the same way as its patrons and the faithful in the church for which it was created. The history of a work is the history of the constant changes in the way it is perceived and understood over time and of the mental and social changes influencing that perception, as well as the effect of transferring a work from the chapel to the museum or from one continent to another. In this regard, there is no difference between a Virgin Mary from Rome and a Senufo figure. Created within a certain world, by and for that world, they now exist in a completely different context, in which they are perceived in a manner that is totally different from the moment of their creation.

This belongs to the realm of the intimate, the autobiographical and possibly the secret. What a work of this kind means to a collector in his heart, only he can say, supposing he understands it clearly himself and is able to express it—and here again personal experience teaches that more often than not the collector does not have a very clear idea of exactly what attracted him to the pieces in his collection—what they mean to him. I remember Bettina Rheims claiming that she felt protected by a number of African and Oceanic objects in her studio. It's not rational, if one takes a straightforward view of rationality, and the photographer certainly doesn't believe in spirits, whether benevolent or evil. But her comment is perfectly reasonable if it's differently interpreted: these objects have now been an integral part of the artist's life for such a long time—they are in a workshop and not in her home—that their familiar presence keeps at bay time's passing and the anxiety that accompanies it. The relationship each person has with these objects is inevitably different and personal, indeed so personal that it is impossible to say very much more in analysing the relationship. When Jean-Claude Weill replies that, "we just trust our eye, our instinct" when choosing a piece, he really cannot say much more about his reasons for pausing in front of a particular object and feeling the urge to take it home with him. When his wife states that, "we have never used middle-men; we've always bought things ourselves," she says just that. These "methodical" collectors are actually subjective collectors.

Just the same, it is still possible to flesh out their choices a little more, firstly by looking more closely at the history of the collection and then making a broader analysis. A little history: when Jean-Claude Weill admits his predilection for "harder" works, in contrast to "beautiful masks," he takes a stand against what was standard French taste between the wars in what was then "negro art." Why French? Because masks and statues came mainly from French West African colonies, areas gathered together in a single French West Africa and since broken down into separate countries, such as Côte d'Ivoire, Gabon, or Mali. Contact between these colonial territories and metropolitan France was eased by the presence of numerous colonial administrators, missionaries, members of the armed forces, and traders. These regions were home to the Baule, the Guro, and the Fang, as well as other societies whose sculptural styles are often distinguished by a preference for long and complex procedures, stylizations involving curves and symmetry, surfaces that are highly polished and covered with a patina and decorative elements. Loom pulleys and spoons: a whole array of decorative art thus enjoyed virtually unalloyed popularity in France from the 1920s onwards—except for the Surrealists, who soon grew tired of so much prettiness. This fine French-style "negro art" stood out from the works, chiefly from the Congo, to be found in the Tervueren Museum and in the Belgian collections, as well as from those from present-day Nigeria exhibited in the British Museum. The main supplier of this art was Paul Guillaume, who contributed greatly to its spread through his photography, although he has not escaped criticism for identifying, in Baule masks for example, the signs of a "classicism" that was said to be the acme of artistic sophistication—a very French quality, of course. The various versions of Man Ray's 1926 *Noire et Blanche* photograph, illustrate this concept. During these years—and for many years to come—the works of the Lega, Bakongo, Yombe, or Bembe were kept at arm's length and not considered fit to sit at high table in Paris; the same went for Bangwa, Bamileke, and Bamum art. These works were not entirely unobtainable on the market, being stocked mainly by Ratton, but he himself was generally supplied through Germany, either by dealers or directly by museums in German cities in meltdown after the 1929 stock market collapse and forced to sell part of their collections. One can still see in the Musée du quai Branly traces of this fondness for the so-called

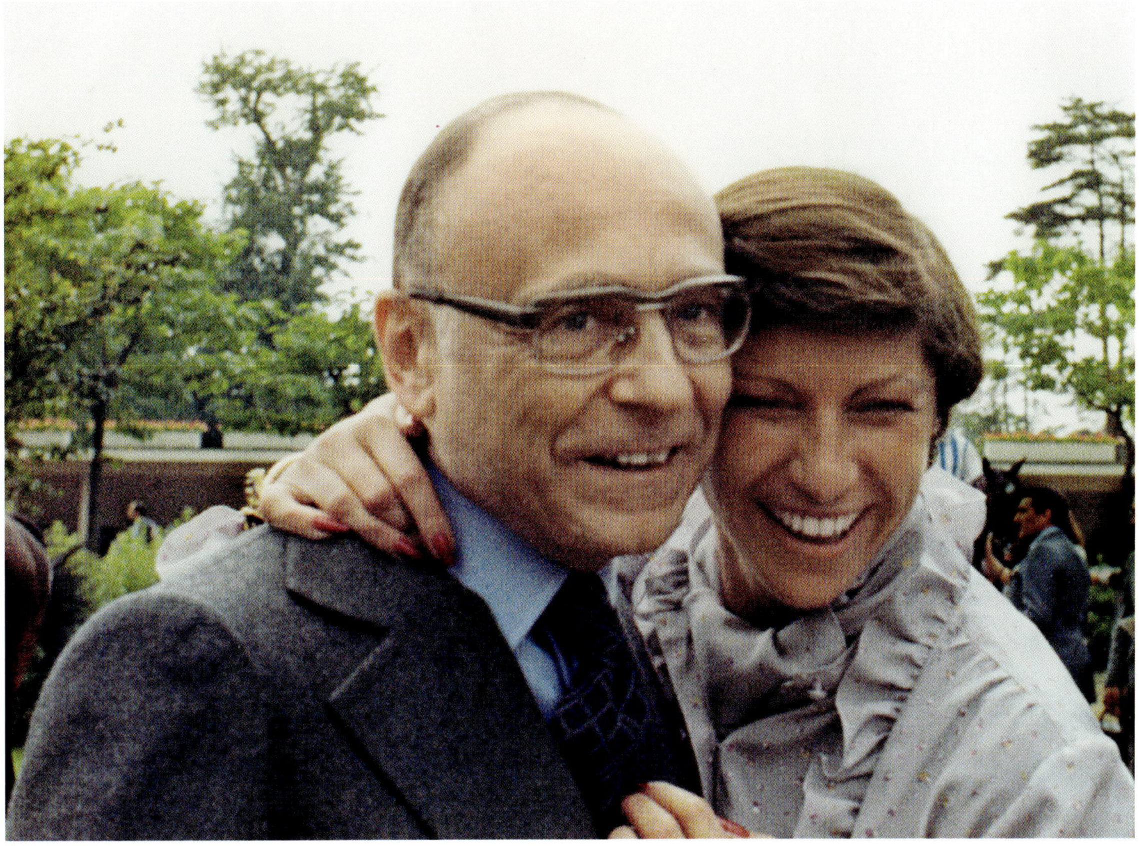

Guro, Baule, or Senufo "classicism" between the wars, a pre-eminence that was never really questioned until after World War II and that was further accelerated by the discovery of Dogon sculpture. In this survey of the history of taste, the Bembe, Lega, or Luba pieces of the Weills testify to the unusual nature of their preferences in view of this prevailing penchant for a neat and well-fashioned "classicism."

In conclusion, I would like to expand on a point: I have already mentioned above how interested the Weills are in both contemporary art and the art of distant lands. They have bronzes by Richier and Bourgeois, paintings by Picasso, Dubuffet, and Chaissac. The bronzes: bodies, kneaded or stretched, distended or squashed. Picasso, Chaissac: human figures facing the viewer. And Africa and Oceania everywhere amongst them. Assemblages of this kind are typical of a particular moment in the history of collecting, what one might call the modern period, during which intimacy was the main factor shared by both modern Western painting and non-Western statuary. The common feature? Expressiveness without relinquishing elegance, the need to get to the heart of things without endeavouring to please or to pander to popular taste. A Lega head, like a head by Chaissac, is a living presence in a form that doesn't reproduce a physiognomy but expresses an emotion, a passion, a mental state. This is undoubtedly why the Weills' apartment, huge as it is, seems too small and overcrowded. The point is that it is not inhabited only by a pair of collectors, but by many living presences they have welcomed into their home.

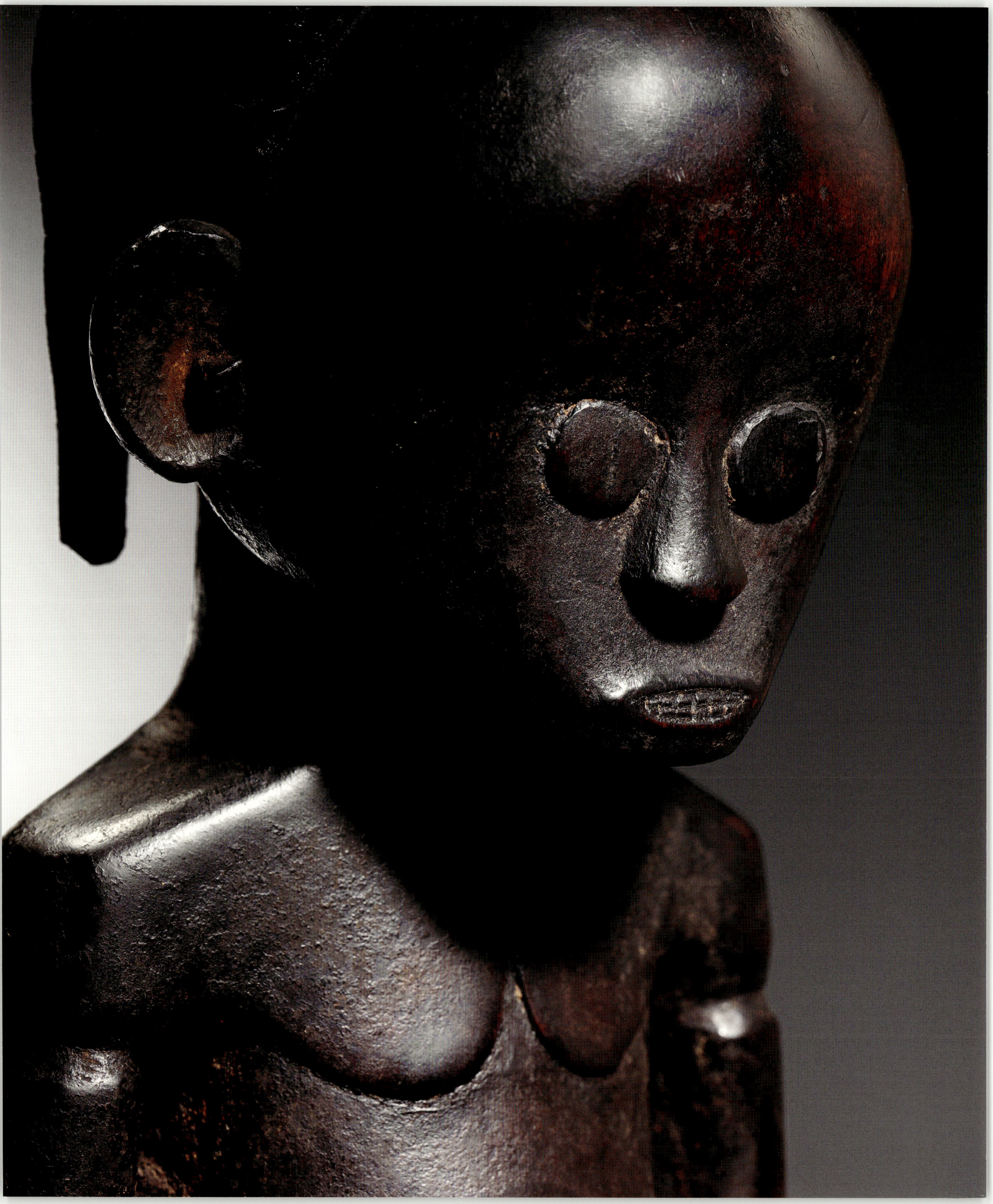

AFRICA

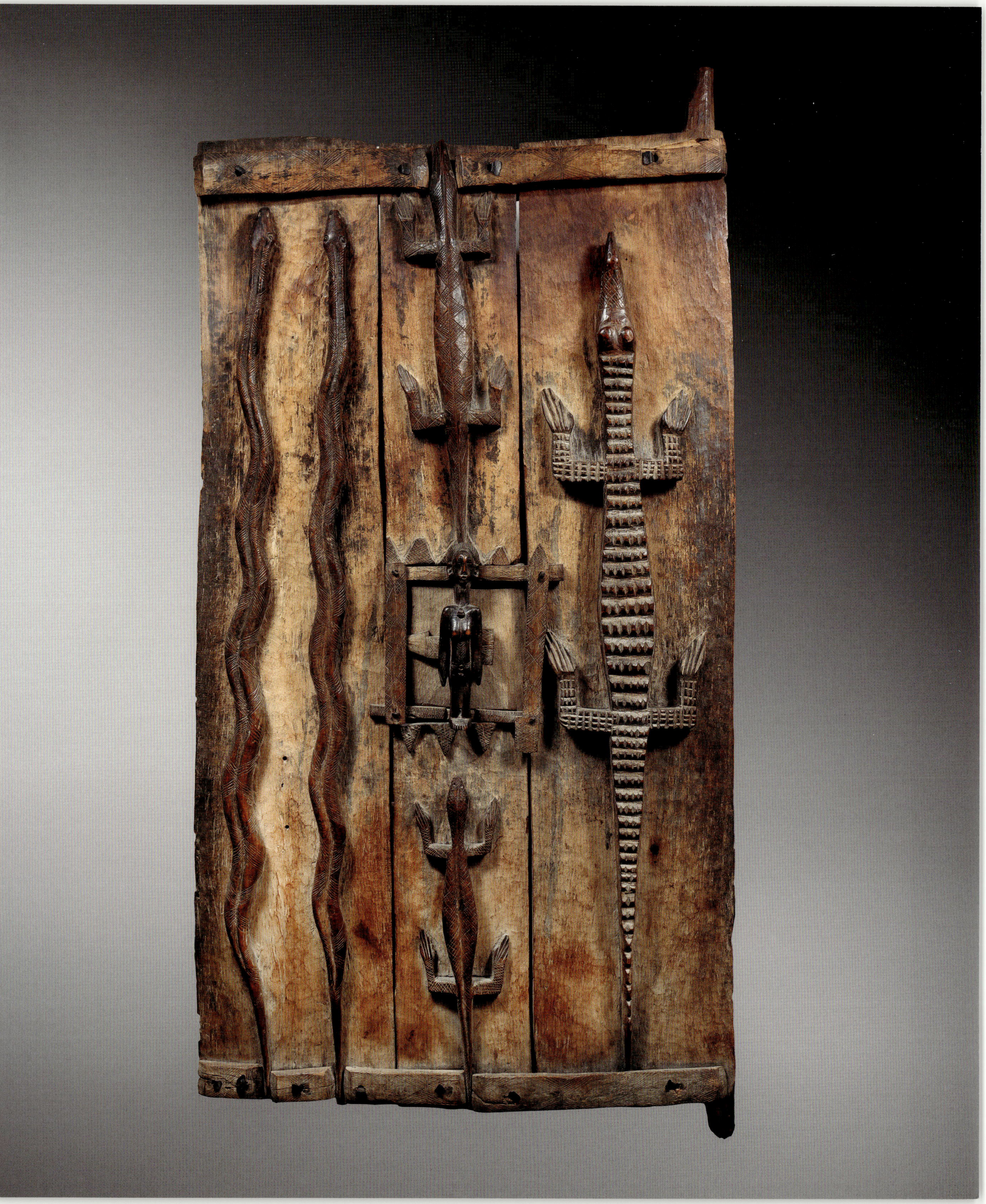

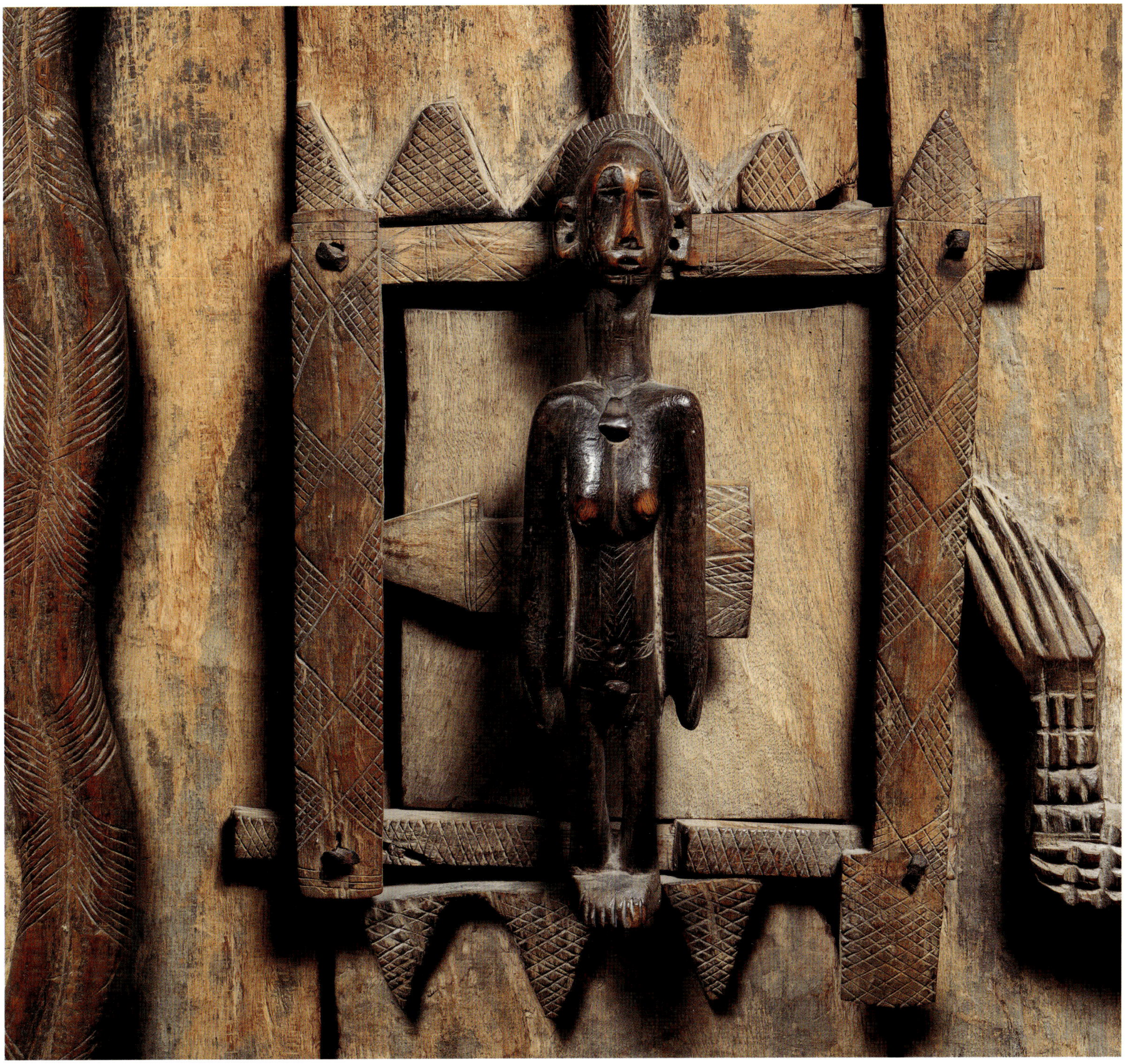

Bamana door
Mali, H. 185 cm

The bas-reliefs sculpted on this door depict snakes (*saa*), lizards (*koro*), crocodiles (*bama*), and a hermaphroditic human figure. There is another probably by the same hand, hypothetically originating from the San neighborhood, in the Museum of Primitive Art, in New York (ref.50.310, see Goldwater, 1960). The animal motif often represents the *tana*, the family's personal taboo or the animal form of a spirit who has granted the head of the family farming rights to a patch of land. These doors (like almost all sculptures) were carved by blacksmiths (*numuw*) commissioned by the head of the family. A woman's parents would often give her a fine door as a wedding present, which she would then put on her house in her husband's plot where she would henceforth live. [JPC]

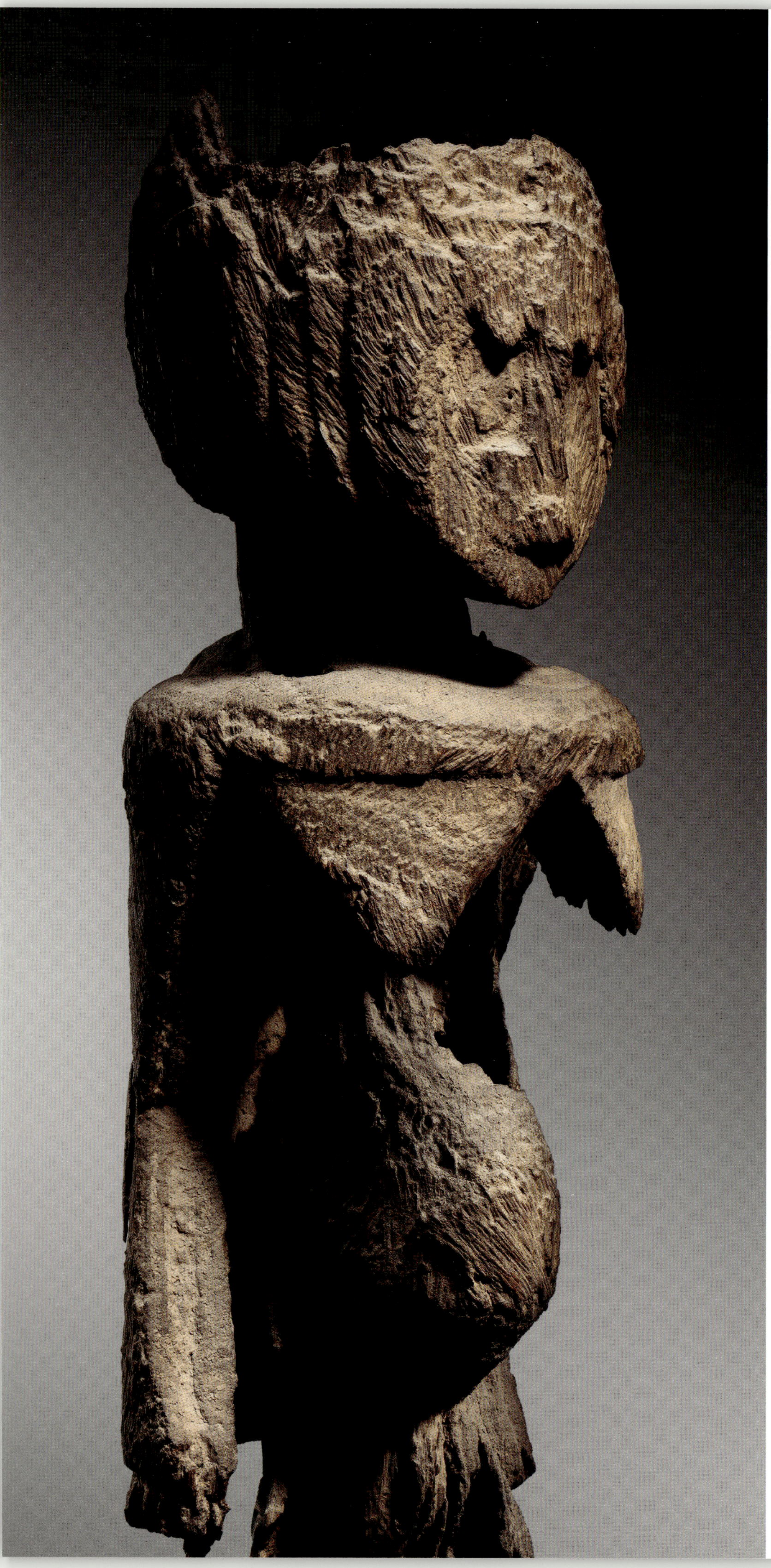

Niongom bust
Mali, H. 76 cm

This piece highlights the touching contrast between the promise of life inherent in this young woman and her body disfigured by the ravages of time. The use of the same hardwood handled in a similar manner and the distinctive rendering of the breasts enable this statue to be compared with works identified as examples of Niongom art, sculpted over 400 years ago by artists probably belonging to the first wave of Dogon settlers in the southern cliffs of the Bandiagara Escarpment. The elements and various parasites have together burrowed right into the figure's very entrails, without however affecting its emotional impact. The oldest of these sculptures, now one of the icons in the Musée du quai Branly, was described as a "masterpiece in the full sense of the term" by Mmes Paulme and Lifchitz when they unearthed it in 1935. [BG]

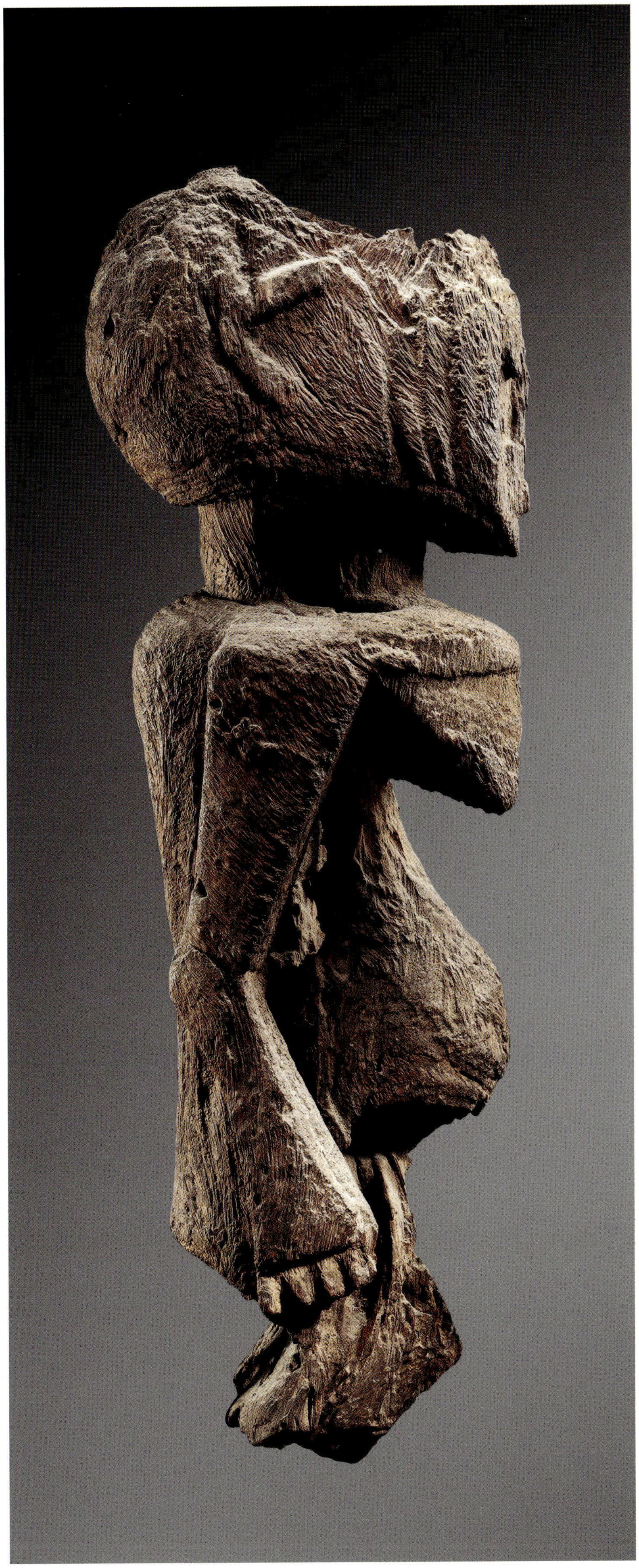

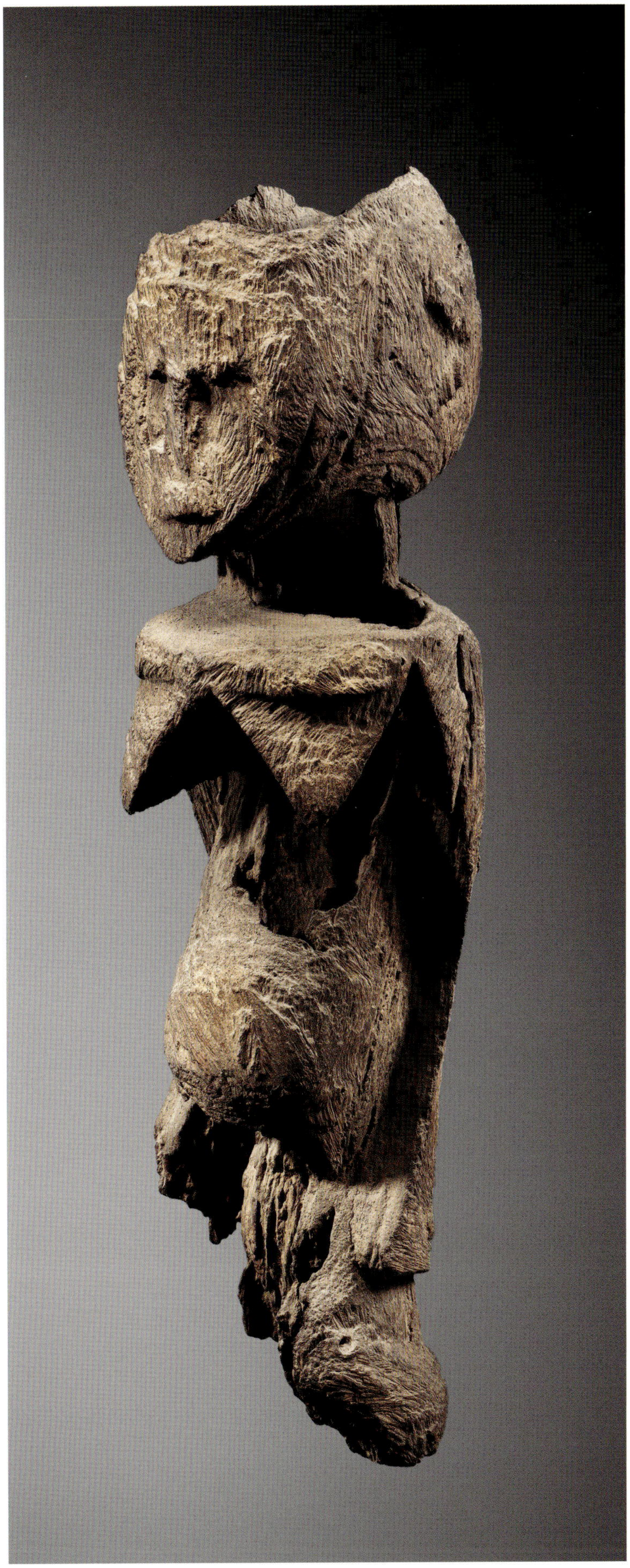

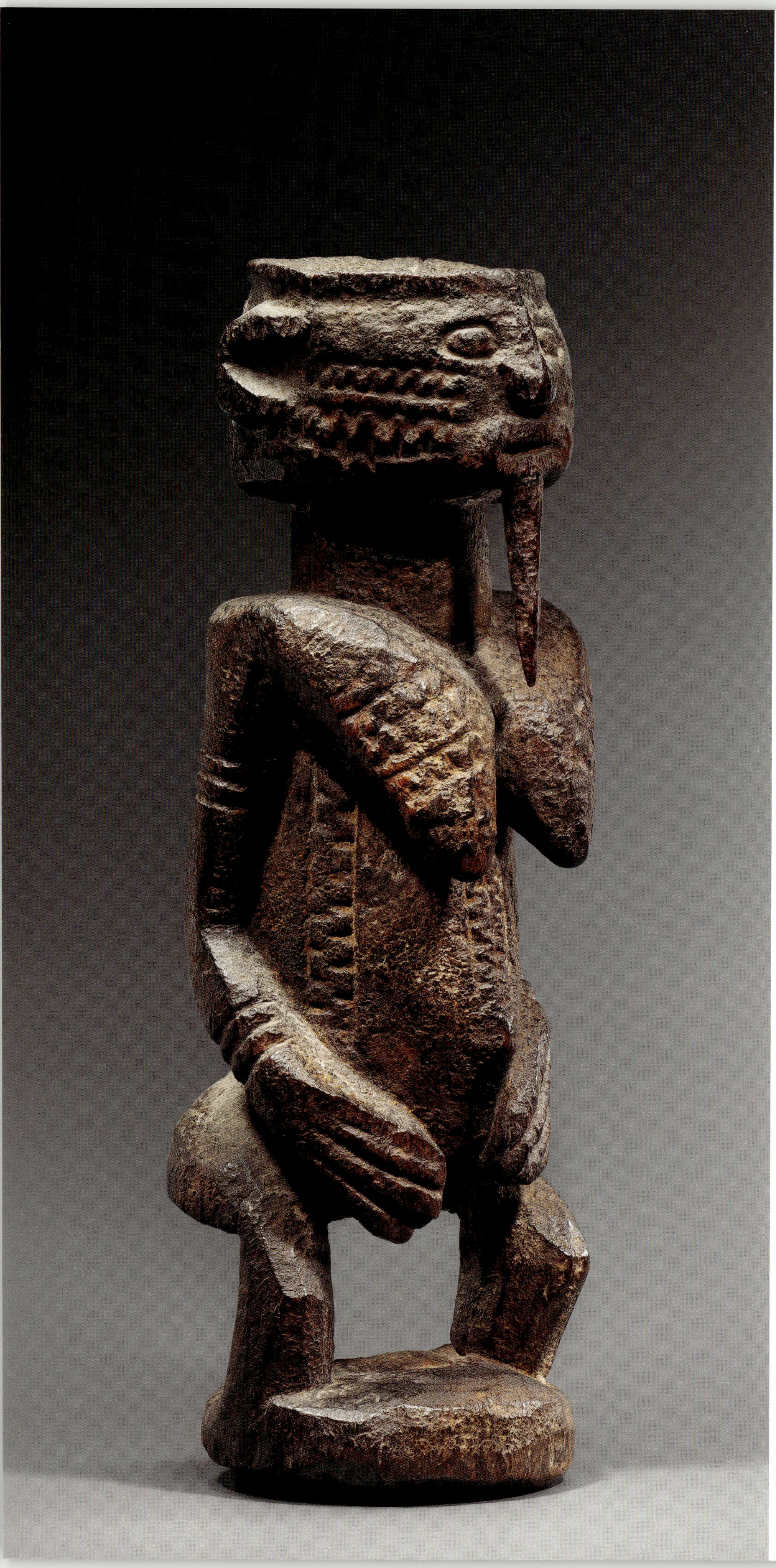

Djennenke statue
Mali, H. 29.5 cm

This piece, with its assertive pose and expression, powerful body softened by the undeniable femininity of its generous breasts, provides a synthetic vision of the selection of Dogon and Tellem sculptures in the Weill Collection; the closely-packed network of scarifications on its skin underlines the importance of these body markings during the entire Sudanese period.
The rows of chevrons, stripes or buttons distributed throughout its body, especially on the temporal region, suggest the work might be associated with Djennenke wooden statuary and Djenne terracotta anthropomorphic works whose origins probably lie in the ancient Soninke culture in the Kingdom of Ghana. [BG]

Bombou Toro statue
Mali, H. 37.5 cm

This statue of a seated female figure is a traditional example of works from a corpus identified by Hélène Leloup as Bombou Toro, the first specimens of which were discovered by Marcel Griaule on the southern cliff at Bandiagara, in the Ogol-le-haut quarter of the Sangha commune. A thick dark patina covering the entire figure testifies to its age and its long use, but it fails to completely cover the arrow-shaped nose and the long, thin labret that are typical of the style. The upper plateau of the ritual stool blending into the figure's buttocks and the unusual gesture made by the arm to reach the vessel on the head enliven the work's classicism with a touch of originality. [BG]

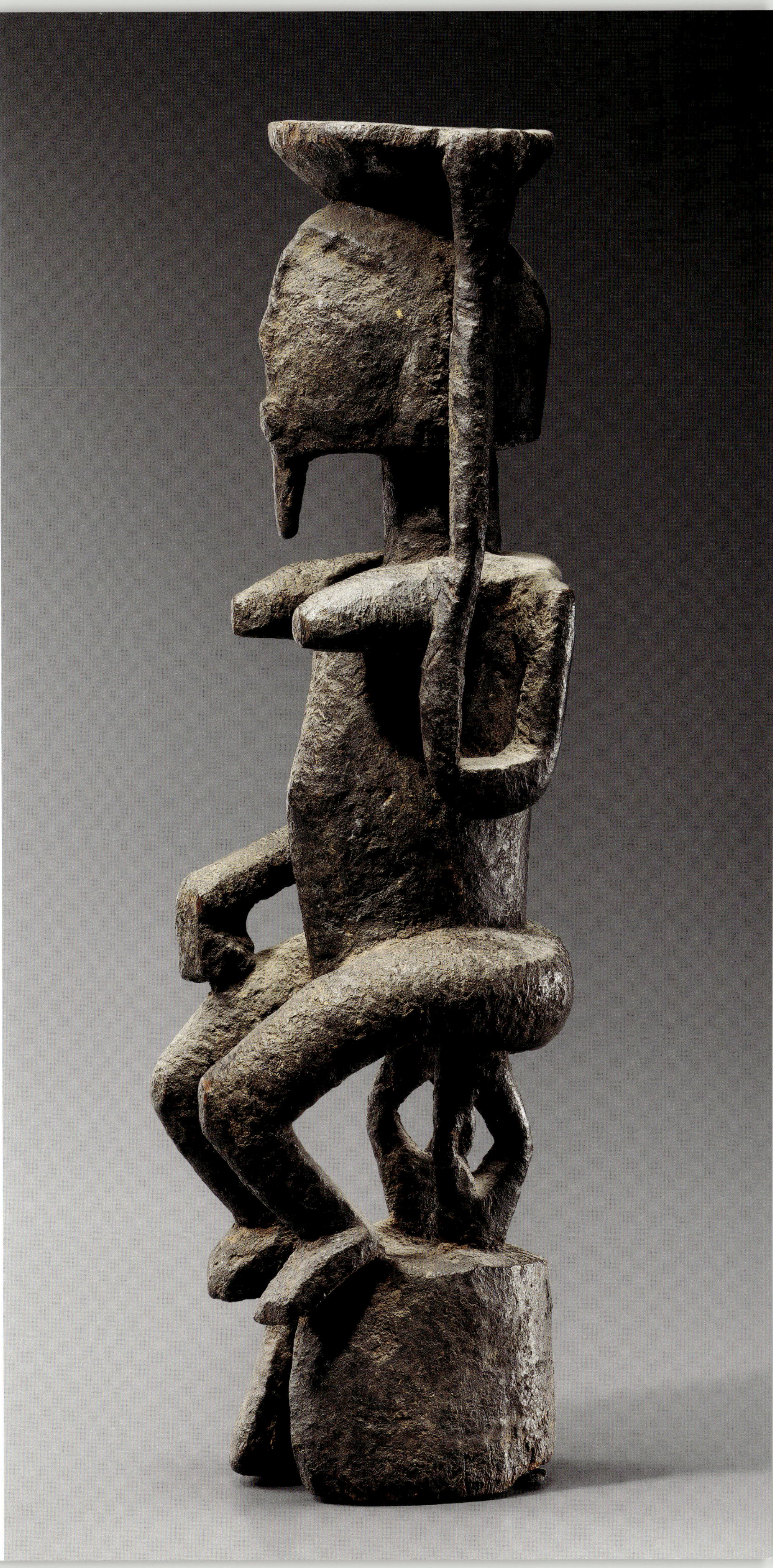

Tellem statue
Mali, H. 74 cm
1304–64 (70.2%, C14 test by CIRAM, Bordeaux)

Dating back to bygone times, this poignant image of unconditional submission irresistibly suggests a "Christ in another form and of another belief," as well as another gender. At a time when Giotto was laying the foundations of the Italian Renaissance, well before Cosimo de' Medici took an interest in the art of distant lands, no one imagined there might be another glittering culture, far from the Mediterranean, on the margins of the Kingdom of Mali and known only to Arab caravan drivers. And yet an artist fashioned this supplicant, her arms stretching up to the sky, hands joined together in hope that the gods will heed her prayers and restore life to nature and grant her fellows a few drops of rain. At the opposite extreme from a bustling Florence shimmering in a thousand colours, her richly apparelled crowds thronging the streets and the walls of her buildings glowing with all the warm Siennas of her bricks and plaster, the Tellem sculptor, in the calmness of his hut, had only the immensity of the Seno plain at his feet, the powdery blue of the sky, the green of the tree-dotted savannah and the ochre of the rock for inspiration. Using a crude tool and exploiting the gnarled contours of a handy tree trunk, he managed to express with moving economy all the physical and psychological pain endured by this imploring woman, her arms on the verge of being torn away, her body contorted and, in an unstable and involuntary *contrapposto*, her legs buckling under the effort of keeping her balance. This exceptional work, identifiable as Tellem owing to its posture and age and outstanding in the skill displayed in the carving in the round and the shape of the face, contributes to the mystery that attaches to a people whose origins remain as uncertain as the circumstances of their disappearance. [BG]

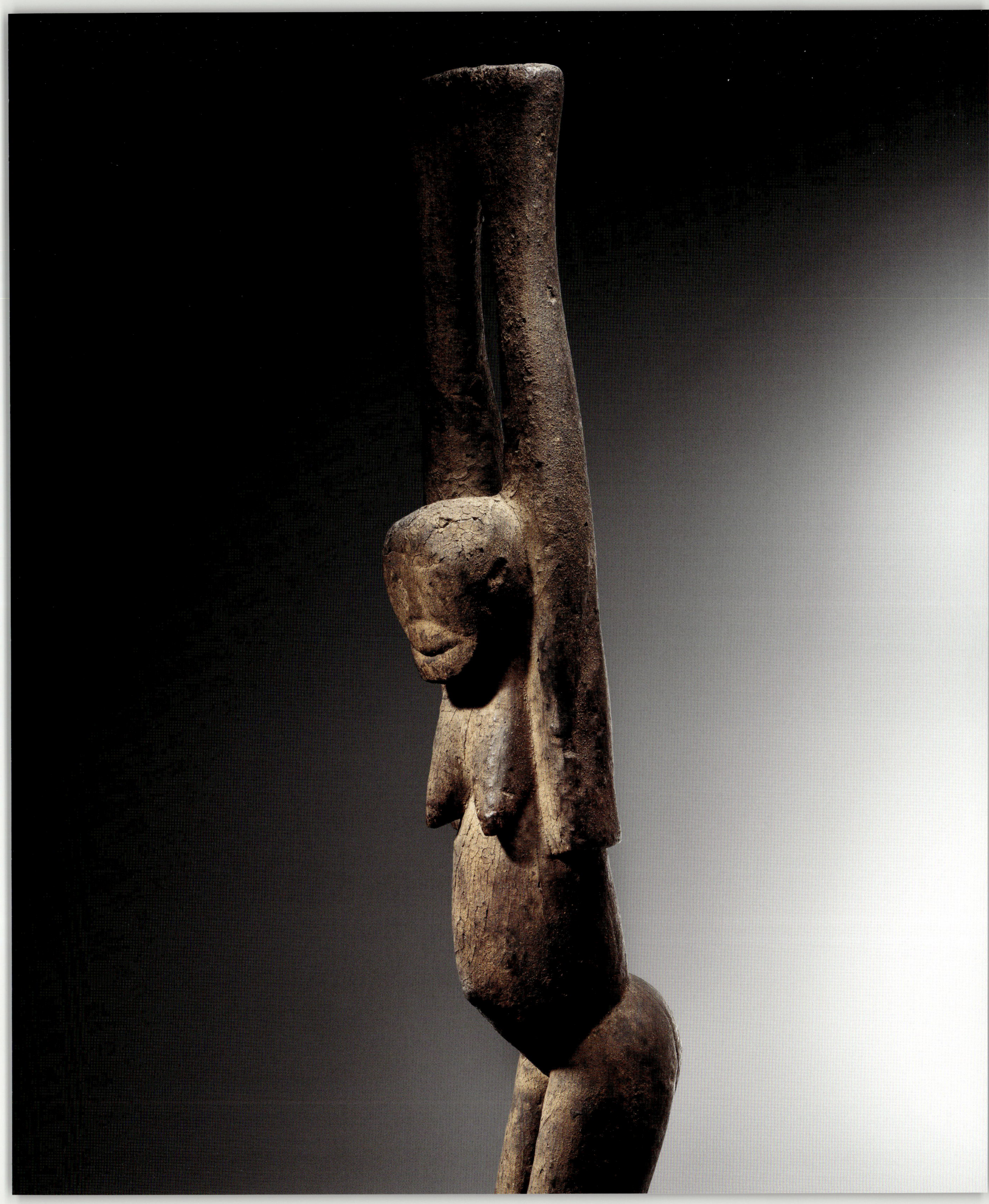

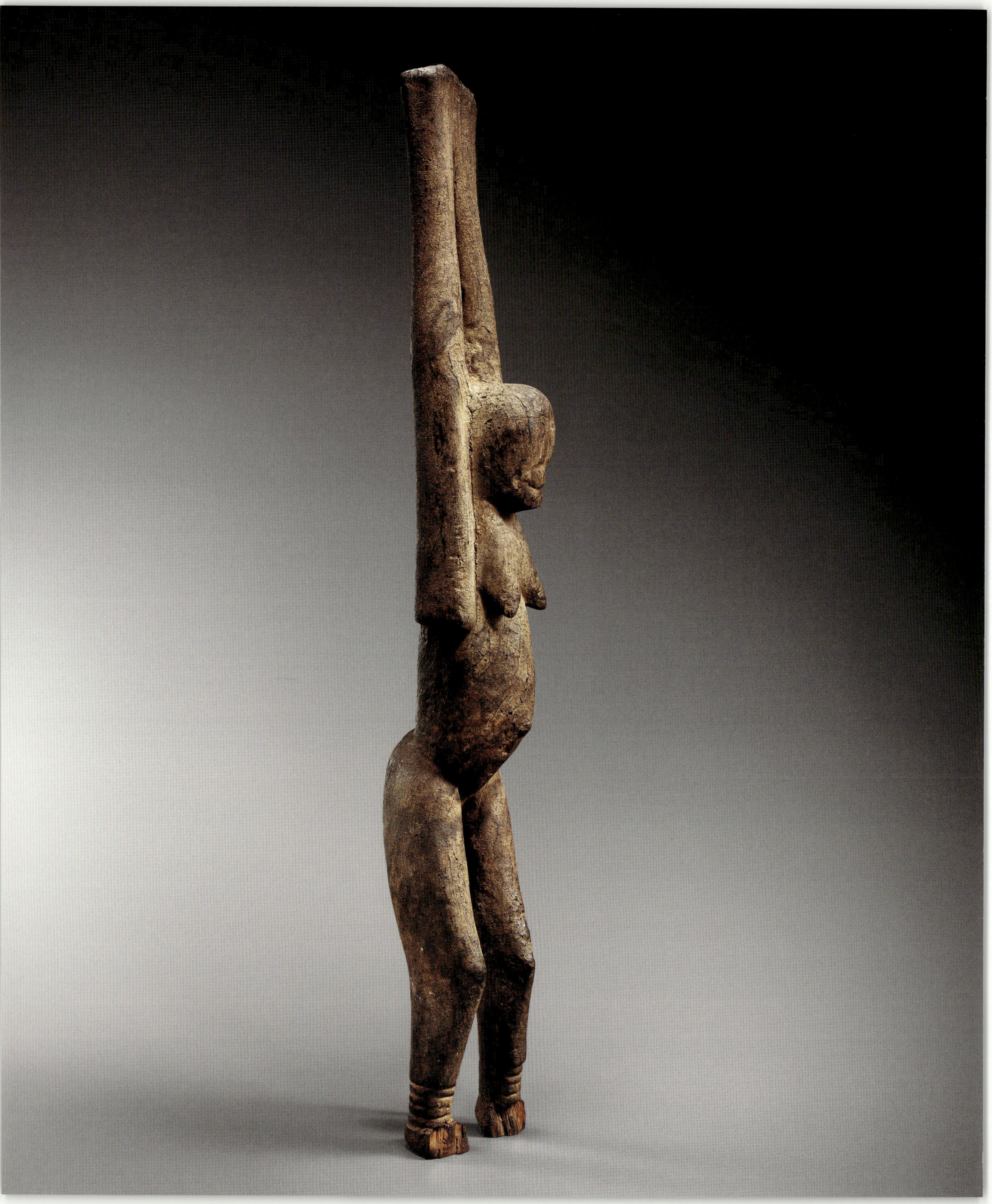

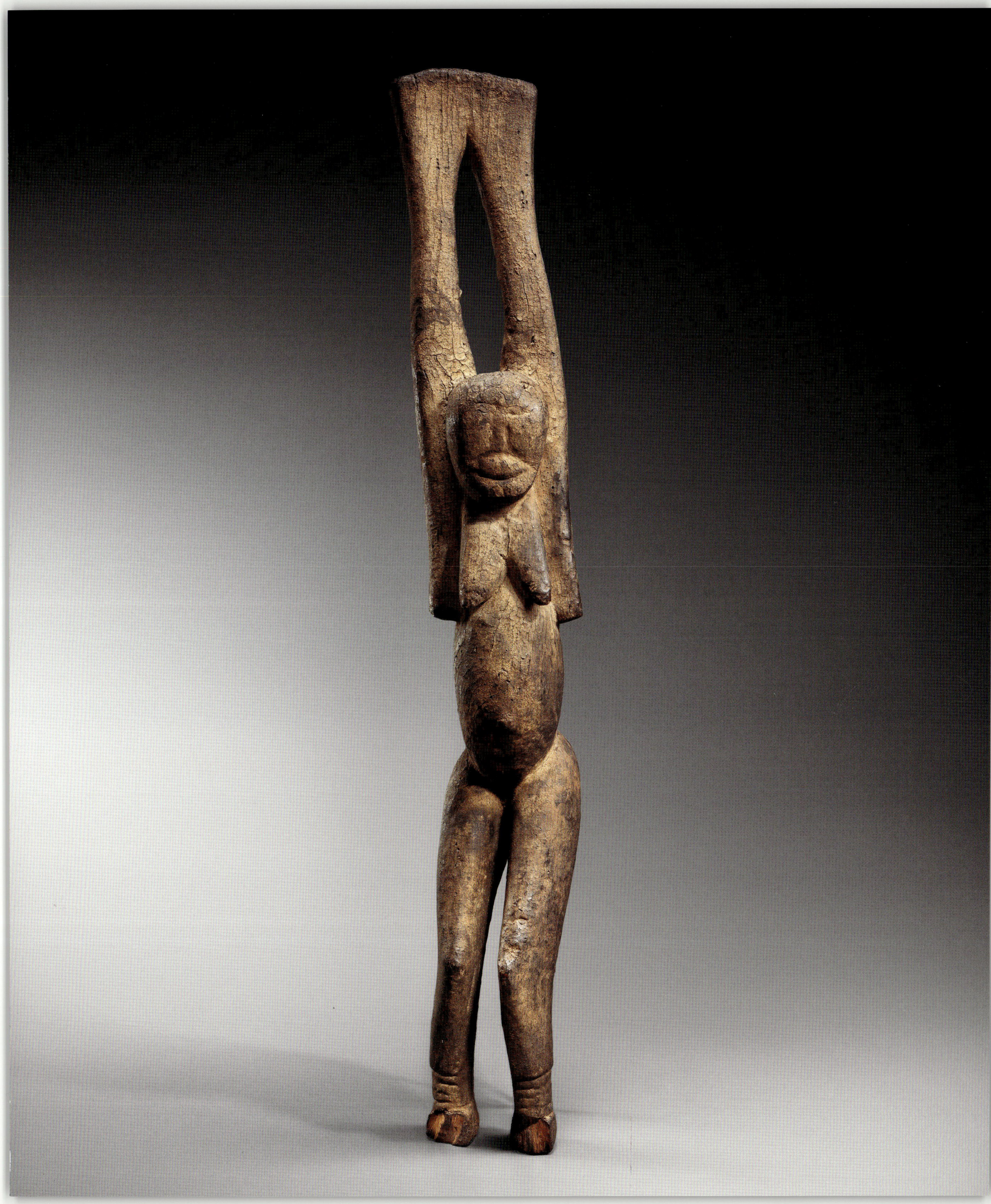

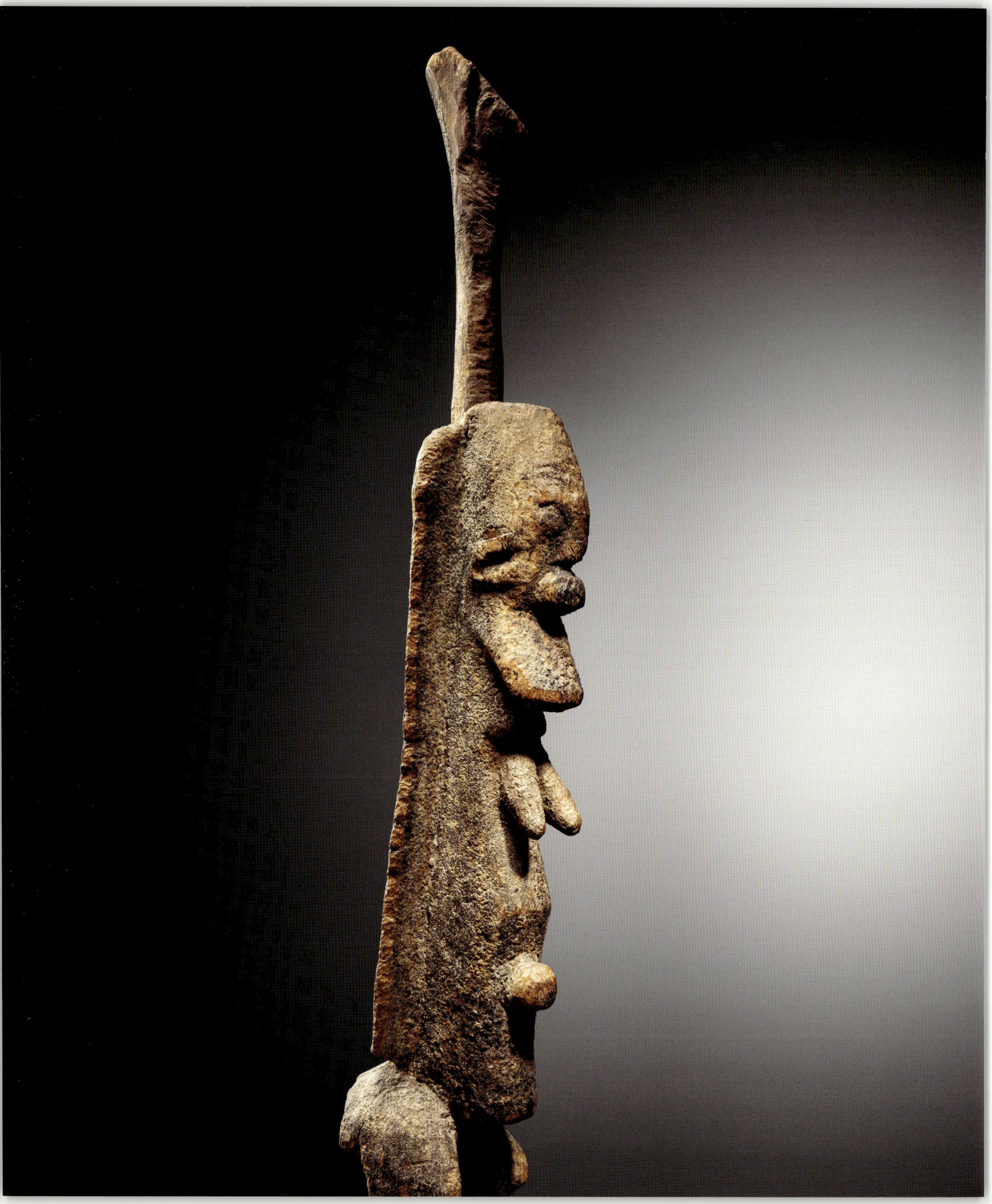

TELLEM

Helène Leloup

After several years of field research and studies it can now be said that the Dogon left the Middle East and travelled through Egypt (Meroë) before settling along the Niger, the source of life. The Dakar-Djibouti expedition (1931–33) led by Marcel Griaule caused a sensation in Paris and triggered lasting interest in the region.

Henri Kamer and myself organized our first expedition in 1956. We found an old American army lorry and loaded it with four trunks (containing film equipment, photographic equipment, pharmacy, foodstuffs, weapons from Gastine & Reinette), thanks to which we felt ready to take on the mountains.

I kept my maps and the few guides to the region in a bag at my feet, along with my personal handbag with sundry useful tools. And of course there were hats.

When we reached Dakar, we took the road to the interior as far as Tanbacounda, where we were caught by an extremely rare occurrence: a rain of small frogs that luckily stopped before we continued on our way towards Guinea. We had planned the journey in stages that would enable us to buy some magnificent objects. Guinea was already being governed by Sékou Touré, who, as a good Marxist, was intent on stamping out religious practices. We then turned northwards in the direction of Mali and Mopti, before heading toward Sanga.

In Sanga, we travelled along narrow, precipitous tracks in the mountains to explore the Dogon territory and try to acquire statues of the ancestors known as "Tellem." We gained the confidence of the villagers and together we began hunting for likely tombs in the area where we would dig out pieces of wood carved into human form. We haggled with the heirs of the entombed over the price of the objects we found before moving on to the next village.

Nowadays, scientists can date these statuettes thanks to the carbon-14 method. In addition, recent research has shown that African countries actually traded across the Mediterranean, which explains some of the objects we found in the tombs. For example, the Italian merchant Antonio Malfante (1409–50) visited Mali and must have heard about the inhabitants of the mountains, an encounter that is borne out by the extremely fine Tellem (see opposite page—from 1416 to 1446, 95.4%, C14 test) in the Weill Collection, which I sold to Jean-Claude and Josette Weill, good friends and enlightened art lovers.

Tellem statue
Mali, H. 63.5 cm
1416 –46 (95.4%, C14 Test by CIRAM, Bordeaux)

This work could be taken as being the archetypal Tellem sculpture, so perfectly does it match the criteria distinguishing this culture: its considerable age, the flat back found in a high-relief, the arms raised to the sky, the elongated torso and the encrustations that have accumulated on the patina over the centuries it was kept hidden away in a cave in the cliffs in central Mali where the Dogon now live. The hermaphroditic character of the figure and its beard recall the depictions of Mesopotamian kings, linking it to a regional style stretching from the Bandiagara Escarpment to Djenne, between two branches of the Bani, a tributary of the Niger. While the extraordinary Soninke statue created in around the year 1000 that welcomes visitors to the Musée du quai Branly is still regarded today as the official doyen of this stylistic family, there is no clue as to which, of the Tellem living along the cliff from the tenth century and the Soninke, who lived in the Kingdom of Ghana at the same time, lay behind the creation of this touching representation of a human being. [BG]

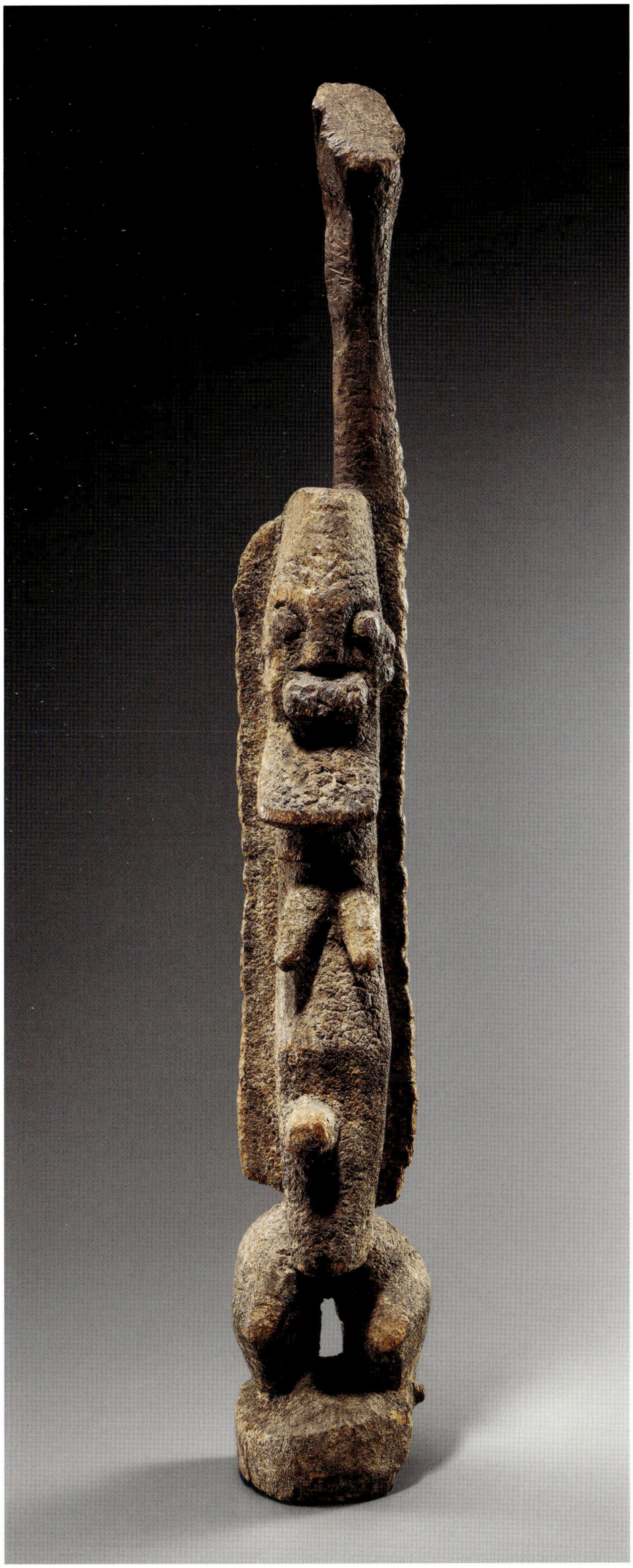

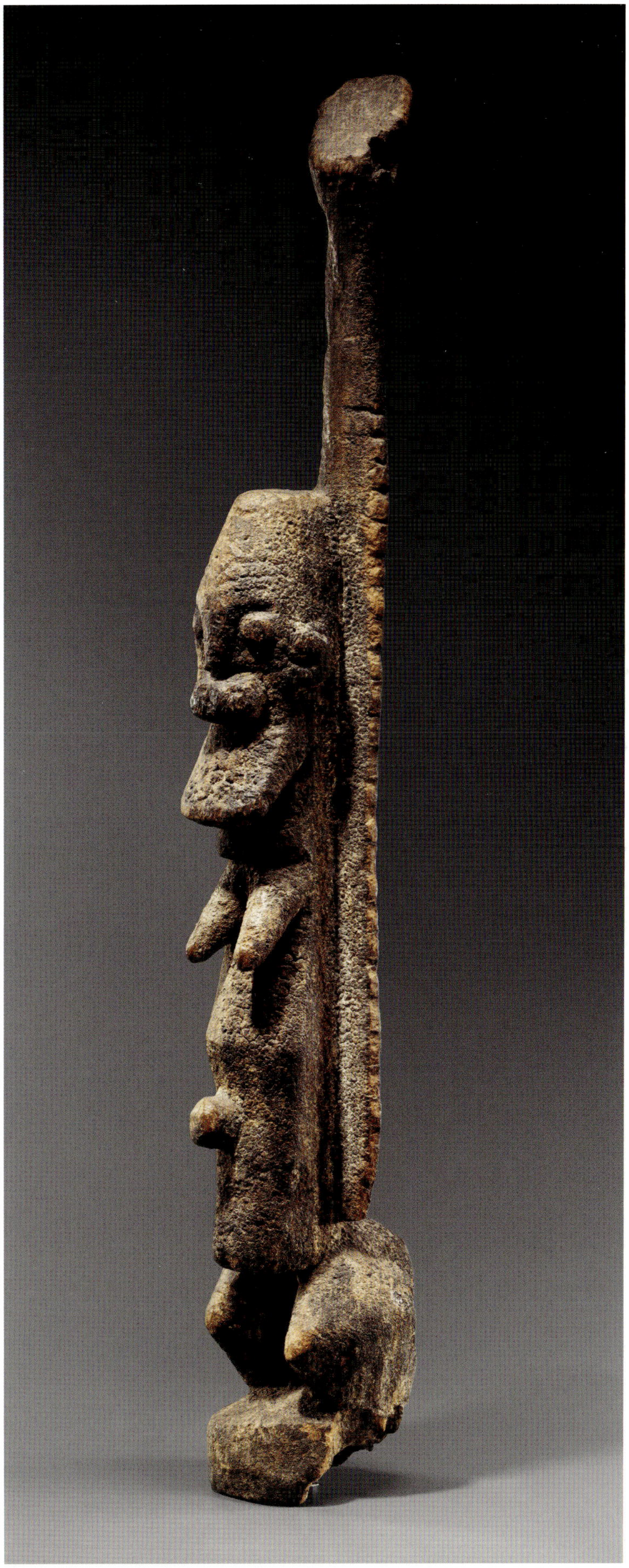

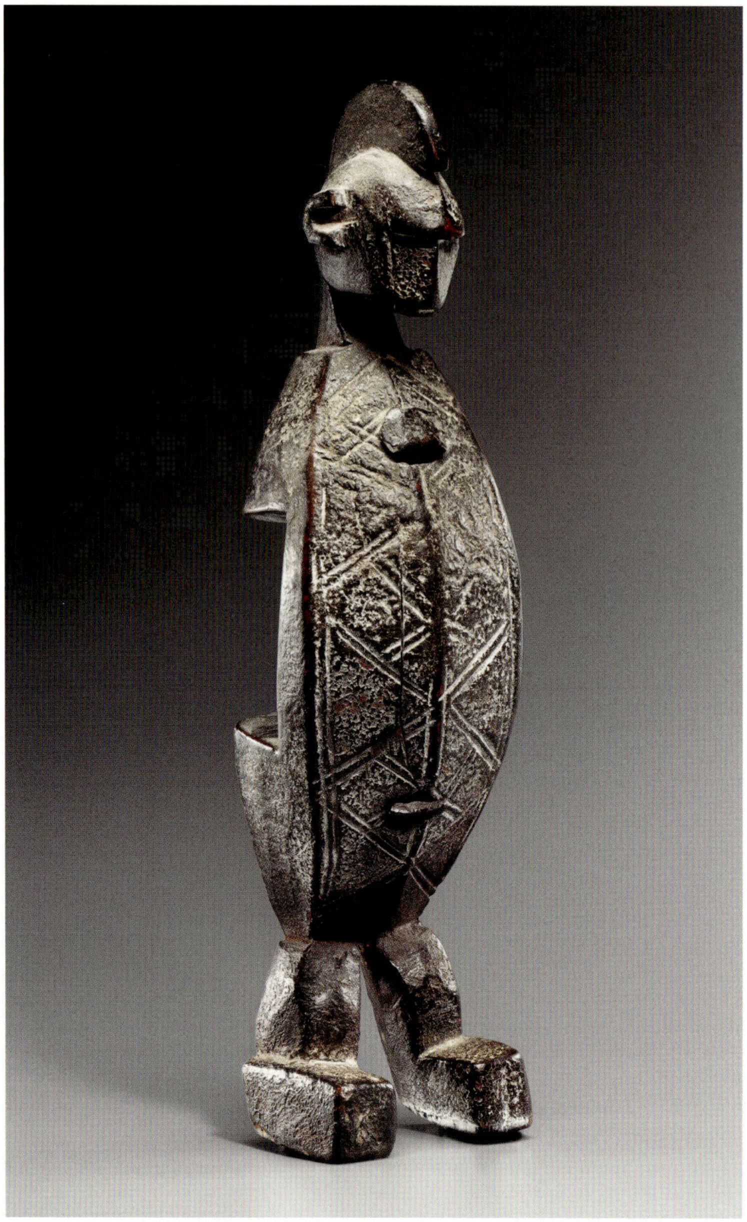

Part of a Bamana doorlock
Mali, H. 25.5 cm

This is the vertical part of a doorlock that was probably used on a granary or a woman's room. This kind of doorlock was made of three distinct parts, the most important of which is the present element. Like the chimera, this doorlock section is double, depicting simultaneously a standing figure and a tortoise. The animal figure in these locks is often the owner's clan taboo, but it can also be a votive offering, the tortoise symbolizing longevity. These doorlocks are tending to disappear since belief in their magic properties is waning (on account of the spread of Islam) and they have now acquired a certain value in the art market. Up until the 1960s they were still a prestigious wedding gift. The sublte, geometric, pyrographic patterns adorning this doorlock indicates its high degree of quality.[1] [JPC]

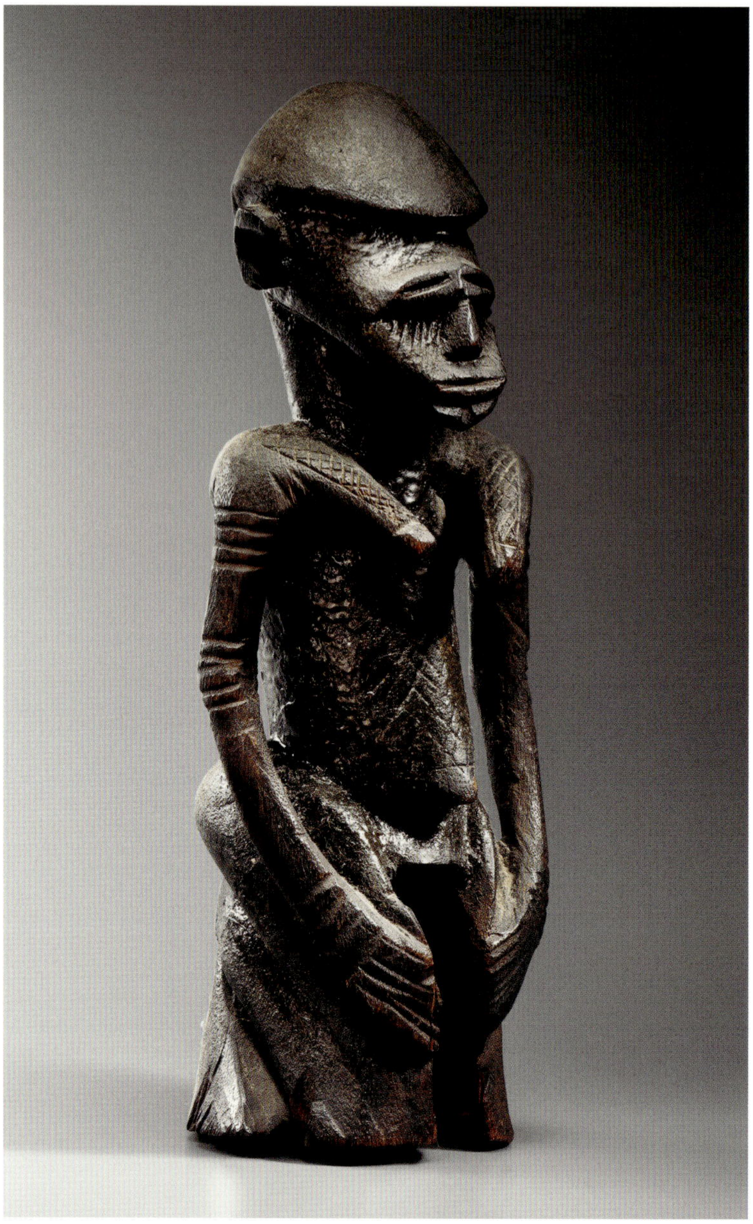

Turka statue
Burkina Faso, H. 27.5 cm

The Turka are one of the numerous small ethnic groups living in the Falls region of Burkina Faso, near the Banfora Cliffs. Their statues follow the style typical of the Sudanese savannah, to the extent that observers after the period between the wars attributed them by turns to the Bambara, the Bobo or, more recently, the Senufo culture. However, its own distinct identity is now recognized and is wonderfully illustrated in this figure, with its highly "cubist" face marked by scarifications that extend down the torso. The figure has been sculpted in a kneeling posture in the manner of the Dogon, neighbours living on a nearly cliff. Its slick patina made of endless coats of ritually applied unguents has survived and testifies to its frequent use and the care taken over its proper storage in a protected space, in view of its importance. [BG]

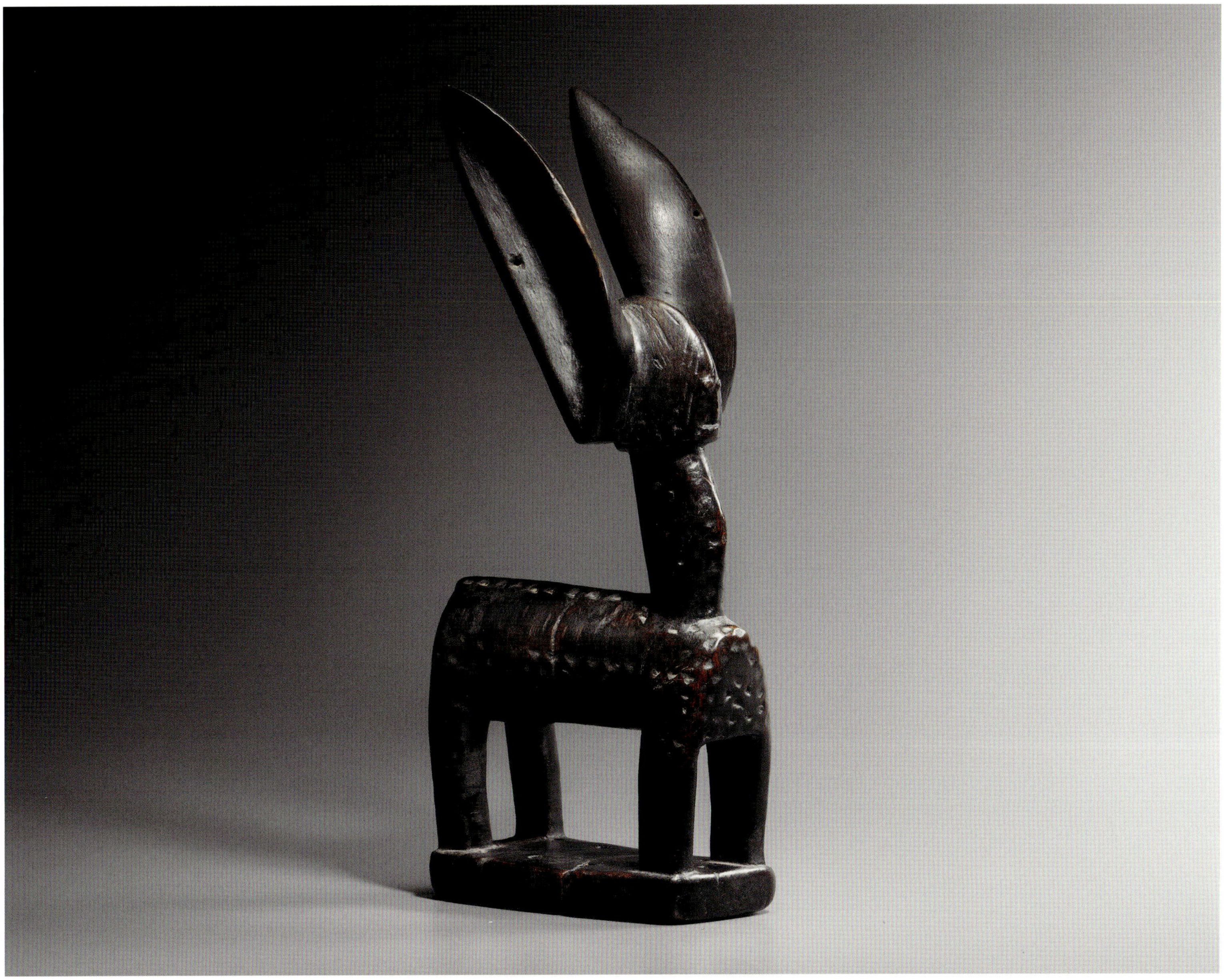

Bamana head crest
Mali, H. 24.5 cm

The word literally stands for the head (mask) of a small bush animal (game). *Sogonikun* head crests are attached by pieces of string to woven caps in the same way as the *ciwara*. They still exist, although they have become very rare. They belonged to cultural associations (*ciketonw*), which could be defined as extra-familial cooperative societies designed to help boost the family's manpower at hoeing and harvesting time. Some of these village associations also act as itinerant entertainment troupes. This piece's shape puts a premium on vigilance, symbolized by the large ears, probably based on antelopes' ears. [JPC]

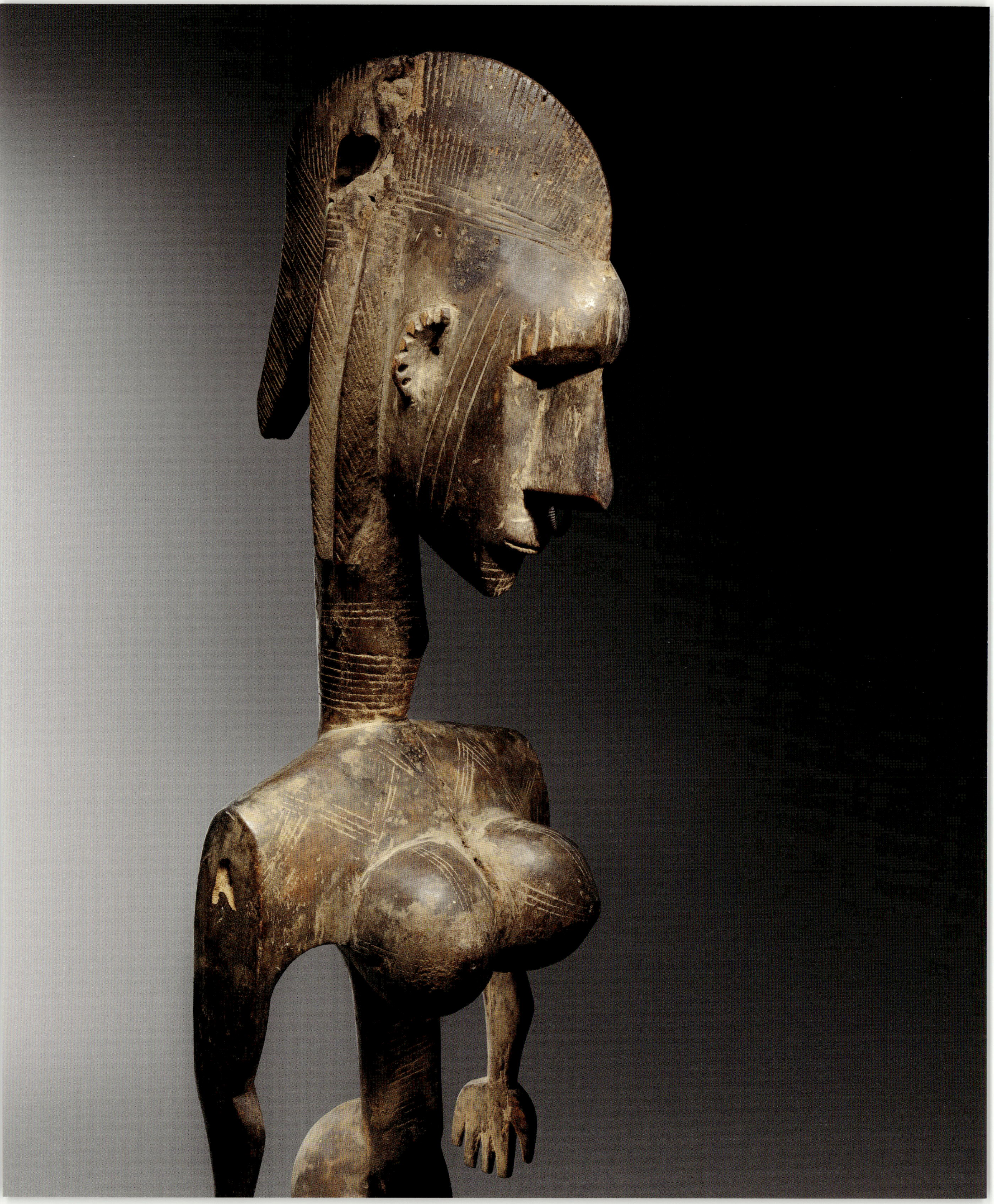

Bamana statue
Mali, H. 70 cm

Nyeleni means "little Nyele," a very common first name for the first daughter, and *Jonyeleni* means "little Nyele of the *Jo*," which is the representation of the ideal young woman whom young men who are *Jo* initiates can legitimately court after their initiation. Curiously, without there being any question of artistic influence between the cultures, the sculptors of the valley of the Niger and European avant-garde artists were both at the same time involved in experiments in form that would express a vision rather than describing the external world. [JPC]

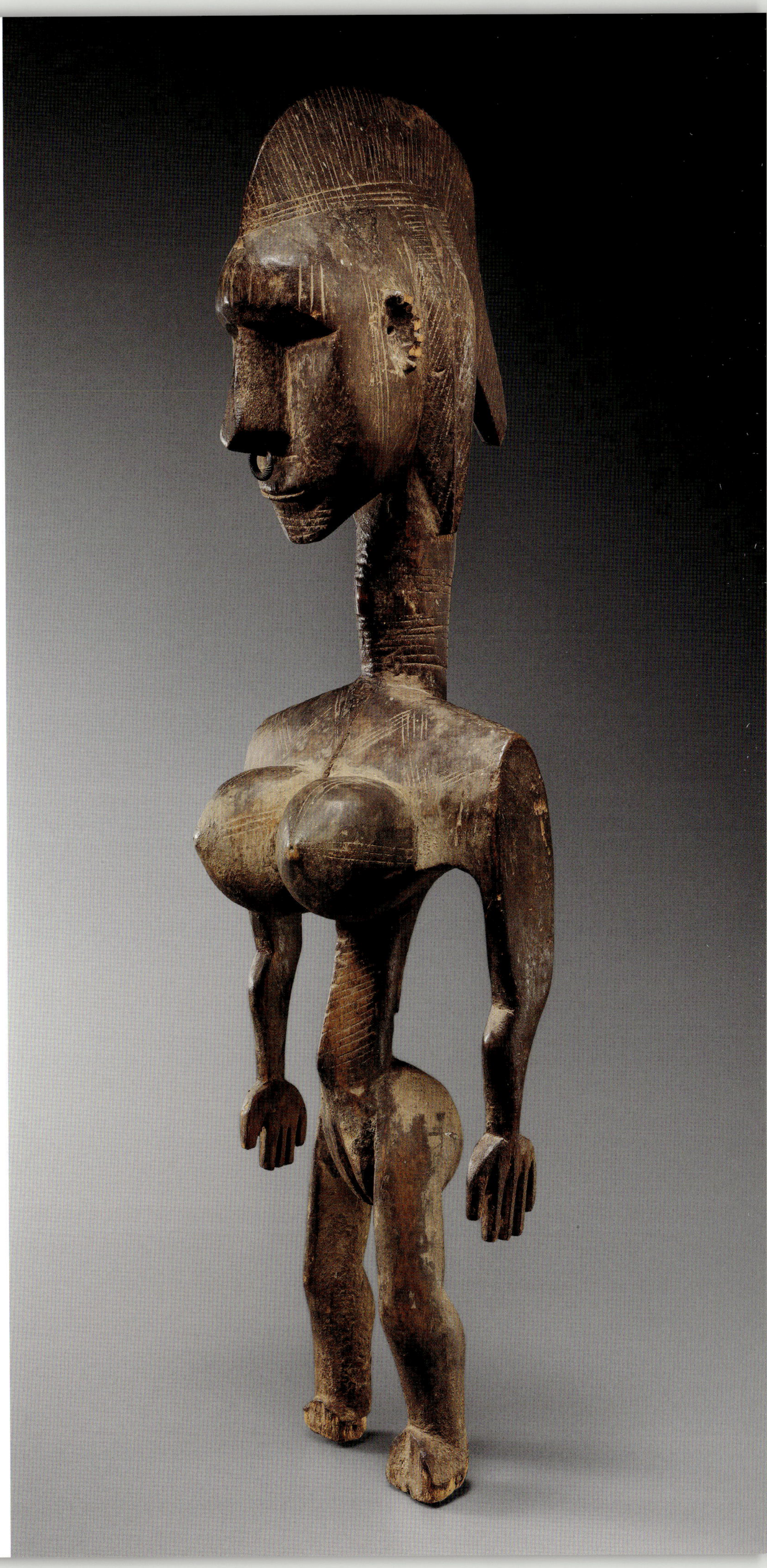

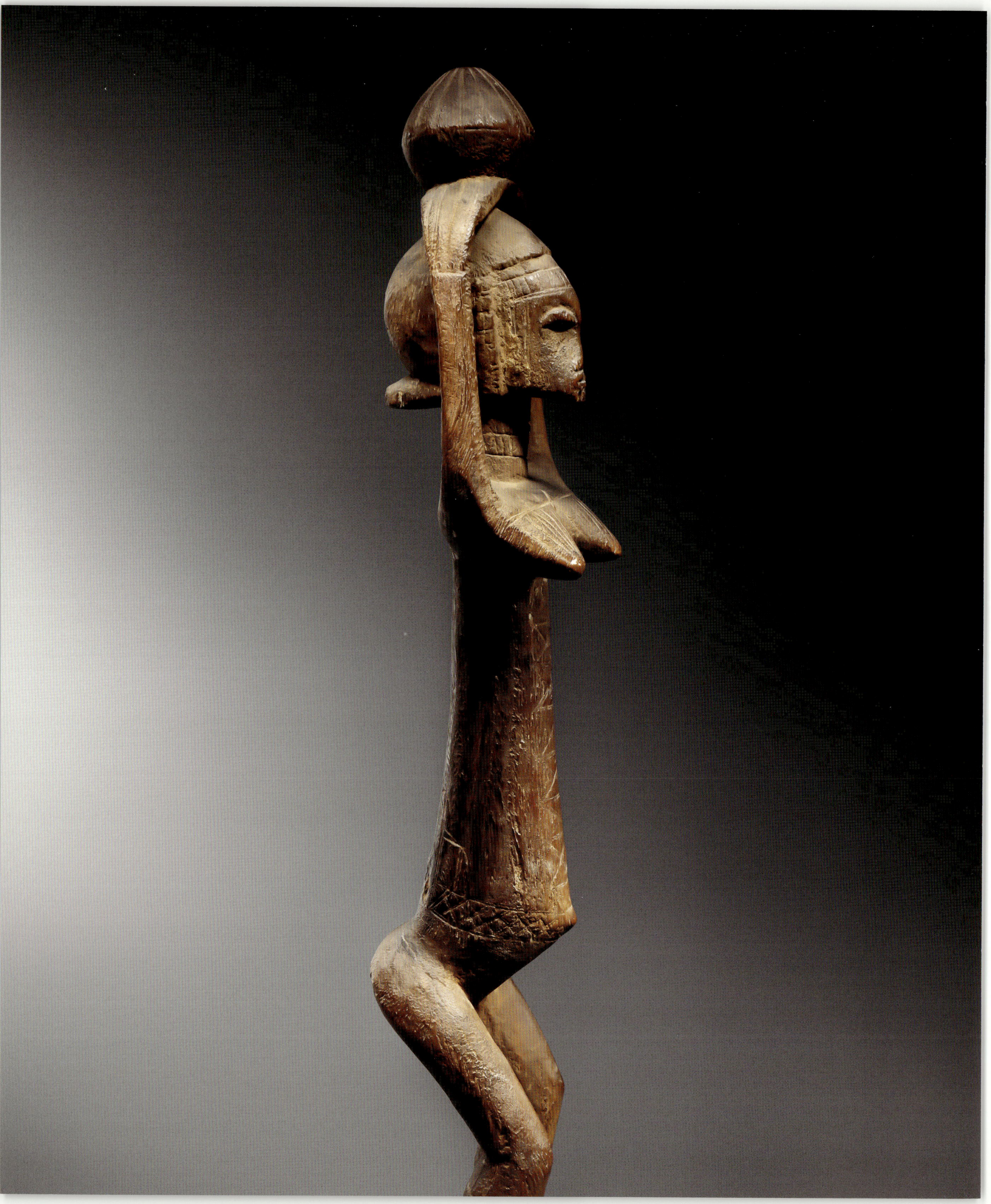

Bamana statue
Mali, H. 54.5 cm

These sculptures appeared on the art market in the 1960s. Known as *jomogoni, jomooni*, or *jomaani*, "little people of the *Jo*," they are part of the *Jo* performance, a male and female cult whose observance used to be mandatory in many villages in southern Mali. These are "visibles," things to look at (*mafilè fènw*) and they were usually arranged in a group. They depict men and women in all sorts of poses and bearing various objects. A little like the *Kore*, to the north and west, the *Jo* initiation marked the passage to adulthood and possible marriage. These cults were protected by a very solemn oath of secrecy, numerous taboos and extremely demanding ritual commitment, but they have been gradually abandoned after Mali's independence and the re-Islamization that followed. They survived far longer in Baninko (around Dioïla), but they have virtually disappeared today.[1] [JPC]

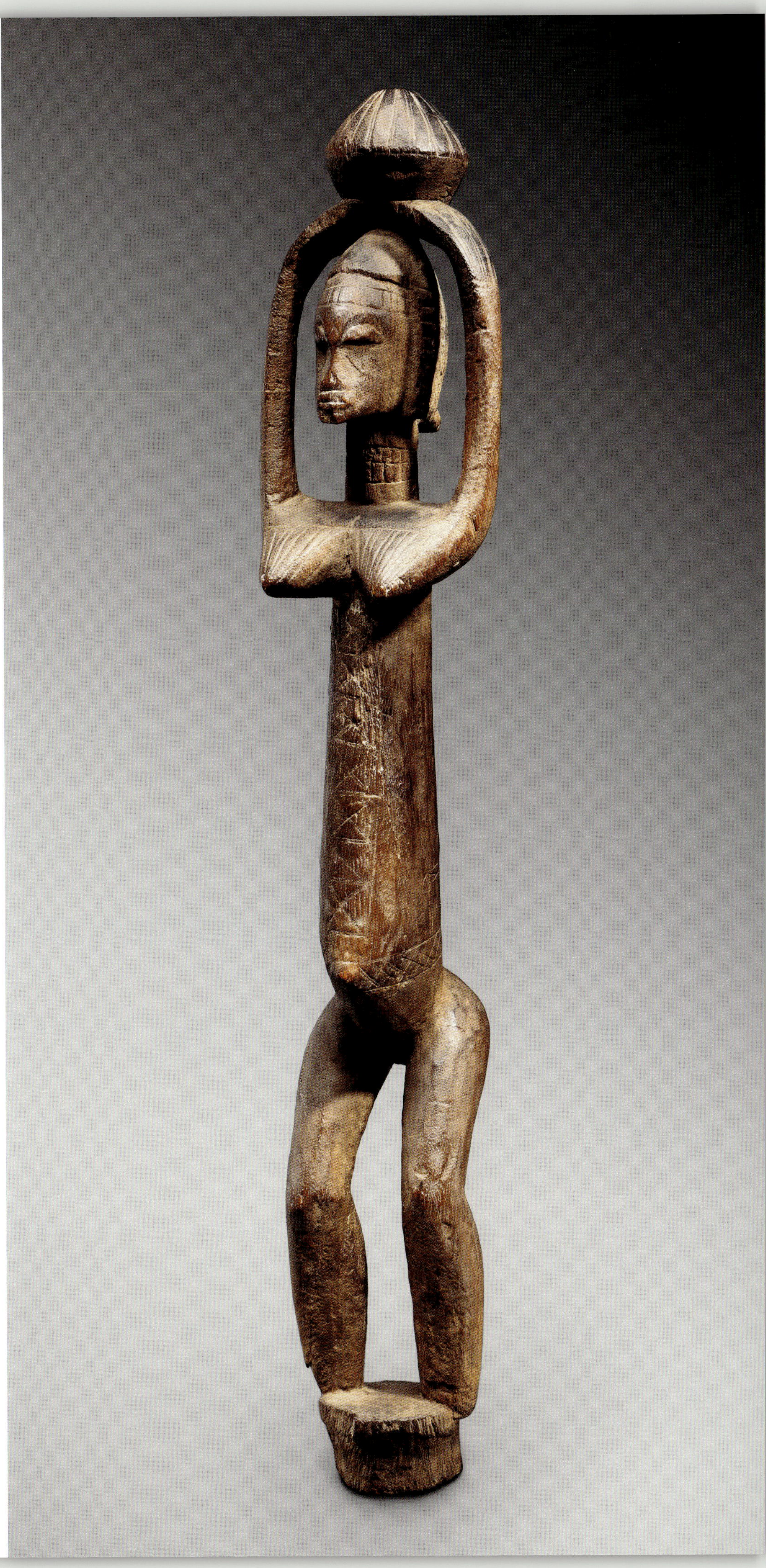

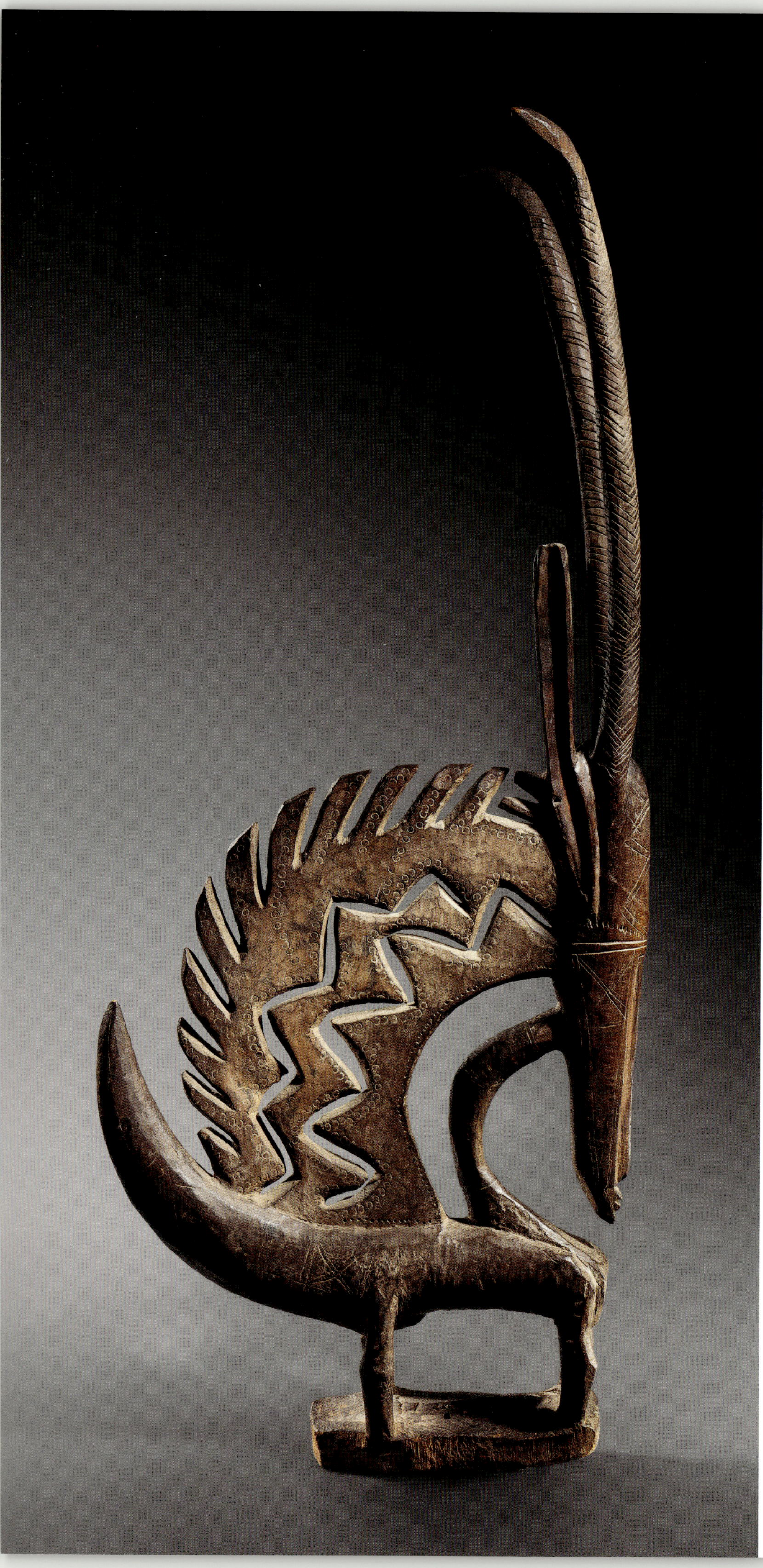

Bamana head crest
Mali, H. 112 cm

This stunning Bamana head crest belongs to the "vertical" style later named by Dominique Zahan and Pascal Imperato the "Segou style." In fact, this style was so popular in the valley of the Niger that it spread throughout the Sikasso region among the Senufo-speaking community. The piece itself comes from Kénédougou. The handling of the curves in the tail and crest, in a certain sense "against the grain," is particularly striking.

The *ciwara*, a miraculous being (at once a wild beast and an antelope), as well as an association and a cult, highlights the complementary nature of the male and female sexes. One of its main functions was to escort farmers to their work in the fields with singing and dancing. The "manifestation of the *ciwara*" at hoeing time took the form of an agricultural contest during which the best farmer, the one who completed his furrows first, was proclaimed a sacred "farming beast." During this performance, the solo singer, male or female, would declaim a laudatory verse at the *saamoo*, the tireless farmer, which would be answered by a choir of girls and the audience. These sculptures, which are all the more astonishing for often being made of a single piece of wood, would be hard to carve nowadays on account of the extensive deforestation and the loss of the tradition and its associated artistic skills.[1] [JPC]

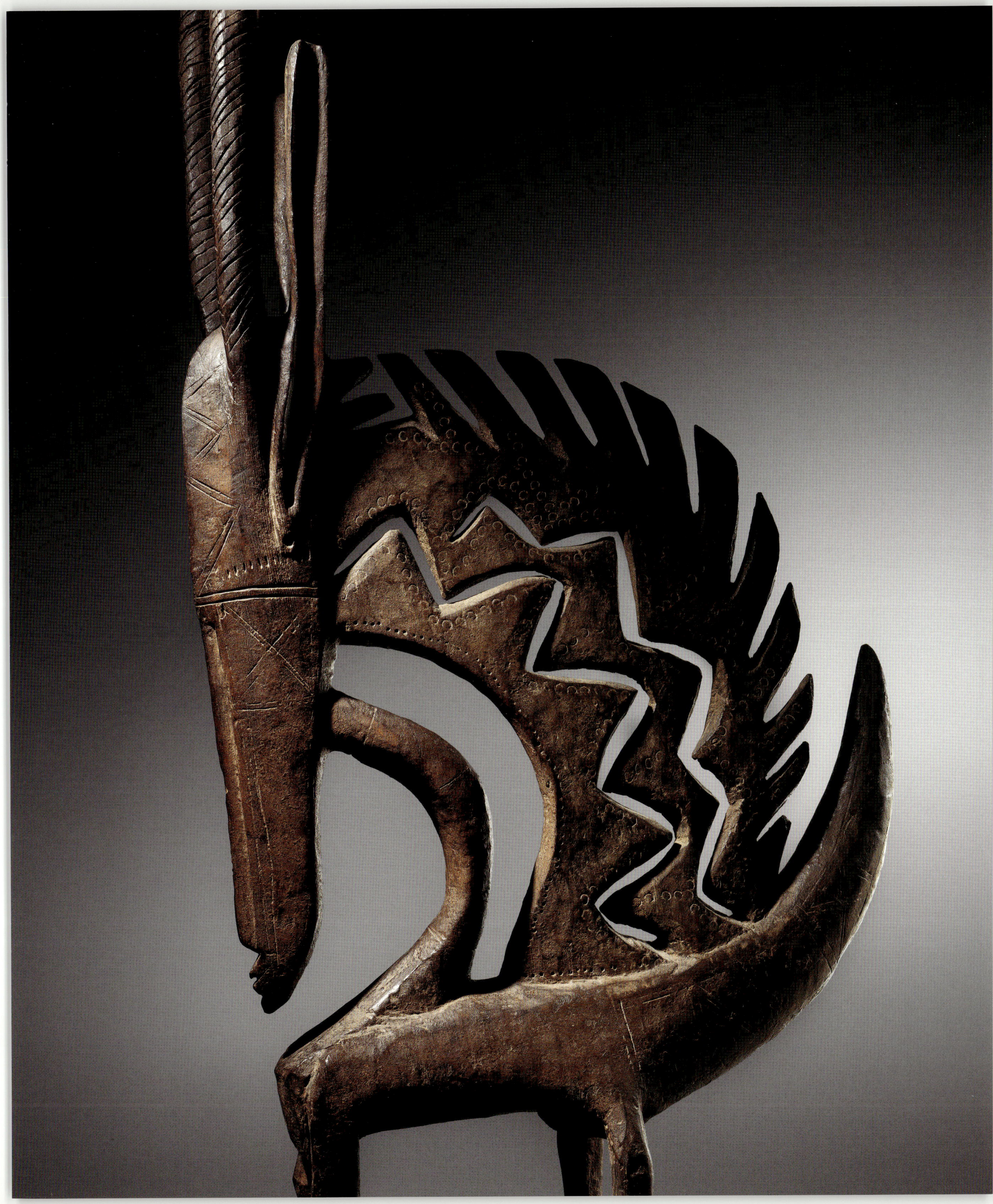

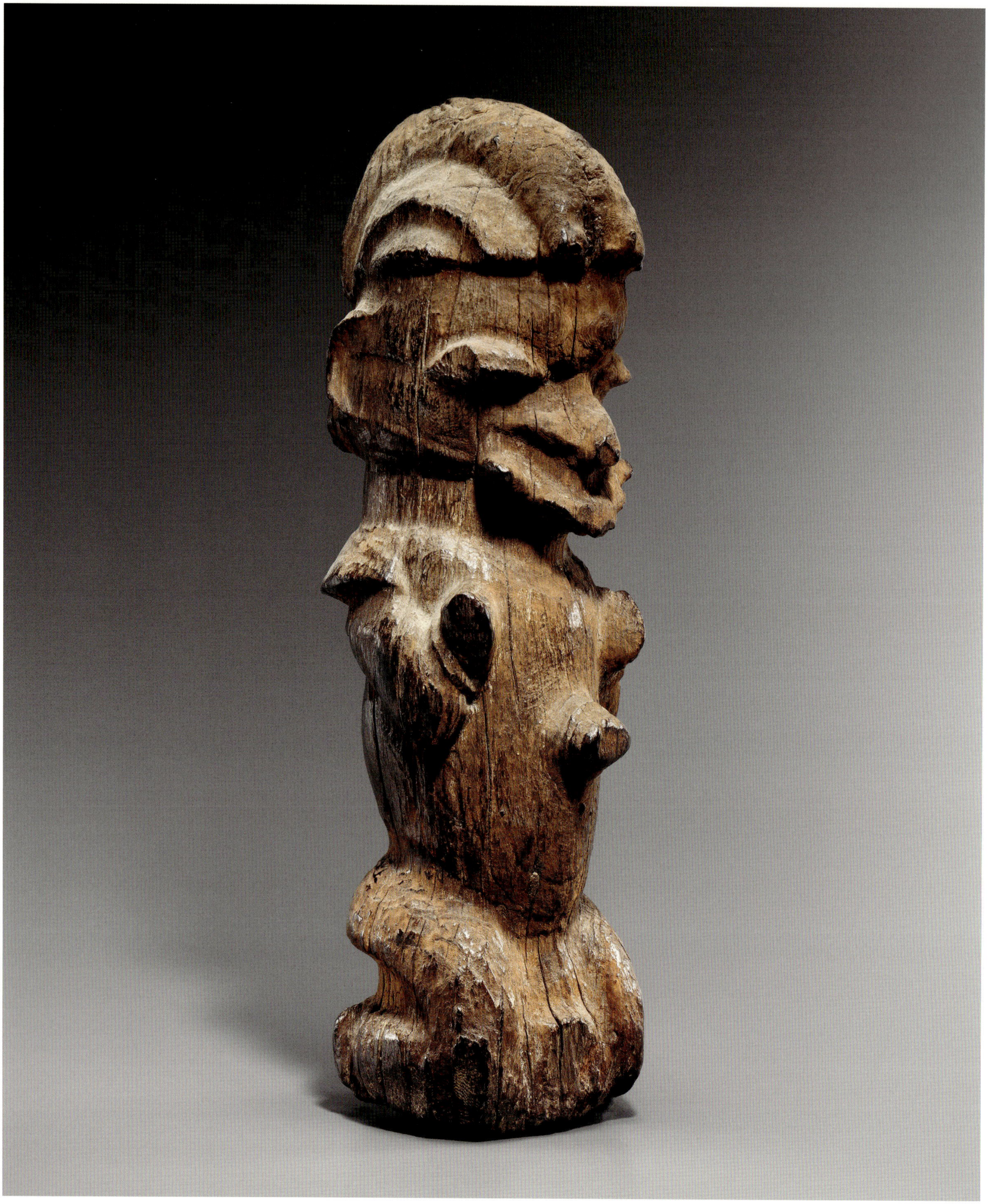

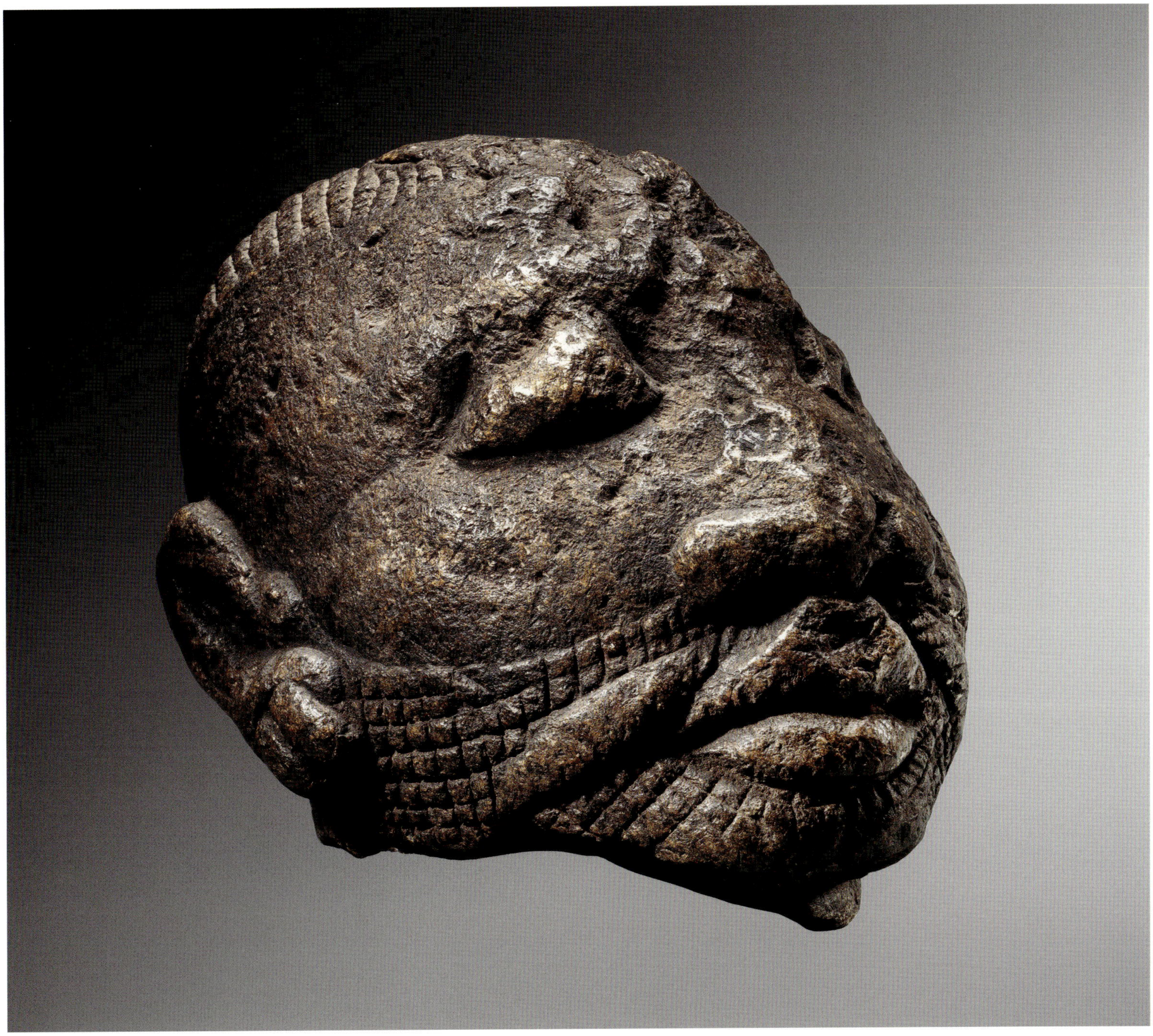

Kissi statuette
Sierra Leone, H. 24 cm

This is one of the earliest known wooden figures from Sierra Leone. The damage it has suffered and general wear and tear have not affected its impact as a piece of sculpture, which has enabled it to be linked to two great African sculpting traditions: the handling of the face is very close to what can be found in well-known ivory pieces created for Europeans during the sixteenth century. The hairstyle–or headdress–the pose, and the proportions are similar to those found in *nomoli* soapstone statuettes produced before the seventeenth century and which the Mende, Temne, Kissi, or Sherbro peoples still find buried in the earth. [AG]

Kissi head
Sierra Leone, H. 15.5 cm

While stone sculptures are rather rare in Africa, soapstone statuary from the coastal regions of West Africa are an interesting exception and include a small group of carved heads from southeastern Sierra Leone. Each head is thought to represent the spirit of a chief, *mahen yafe*. They were made as a tribute to a dead chief and/or used during divination ceremonies within the *Poro* initiation society. Although the beard and hair are highly stylized, the facial features are idealized and naturalistic, the desire to provide a realistic portrayal being confirmed by the earrings. [AG]

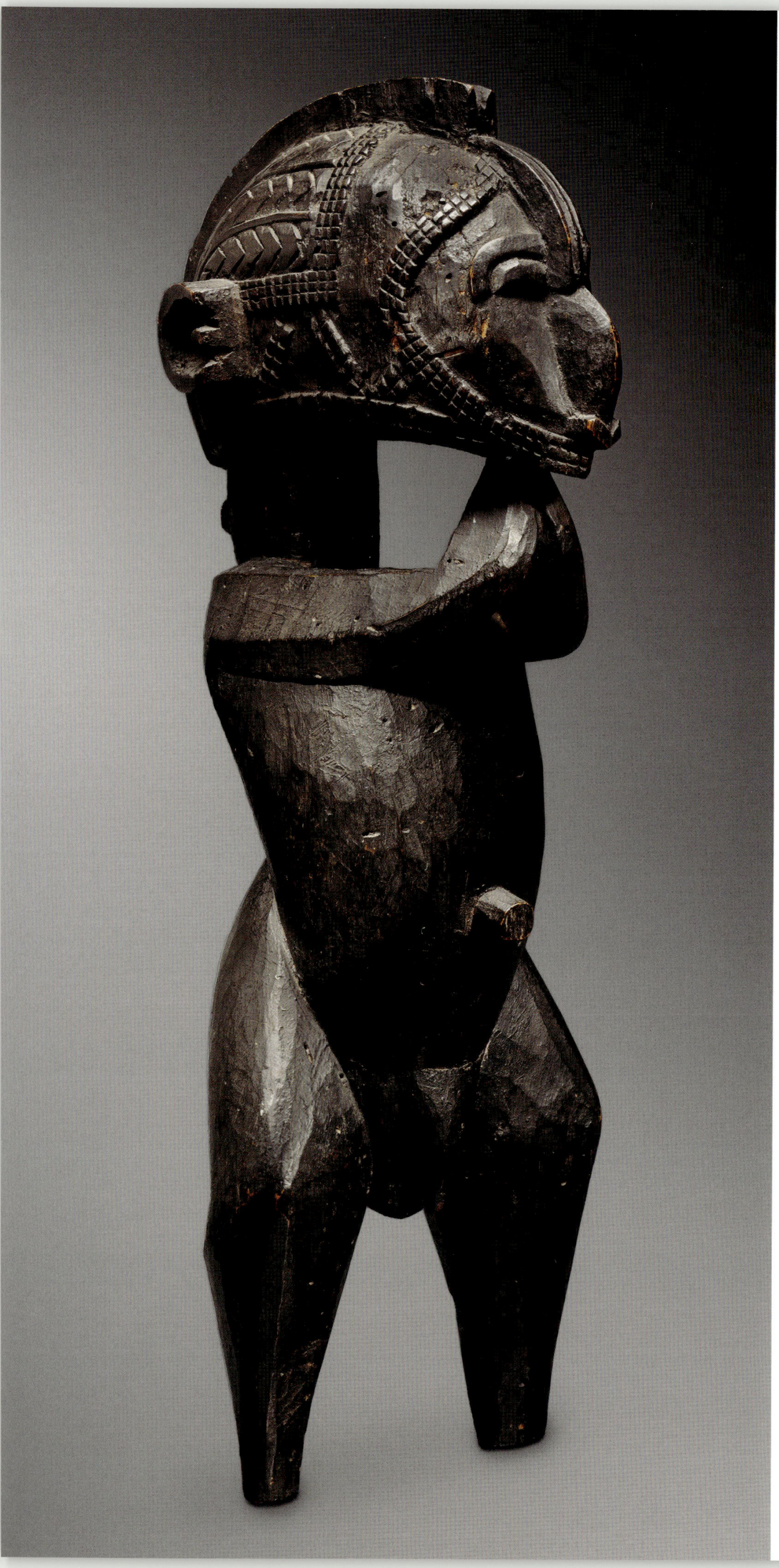

Baga statue
Republic of Guinea, H. 57 cm

This wooden statue displays similarities with the head of the great *nimba* shoulder mask, but is associated with both a male or female body. In this case, the body is male.

Although there are few records of how these statues were used, old documents confirm their existence in the Baga villages in Tshalbunto in 1885,[1] when Captain Coffinières de Nordeck explored the area. The Fathers of the Holy Spirit in Boffa noticed it in the sacred hut of the old Kamfori Youla of Boffa in the early twentieth century (photo shot in around 1920).[2] Similarly, the colonial administrator A. Chevrier received a large chief's drum supported by this type of statue "in poses that were all alike" in 1906; the author recorded that they, "represent the spirits that live in the neighbourhood and need to be looked after with great care . . . "[3] Lastly, when the campaign of forced Islamization of the Baga Sitem village of Mare got underway in 1957, two examples of this type of statue with a *nimba* head turned up among the various objects seized.[4]

Field studies carried out from the 1990s[5, 6] show that these statues were used by the Baga Pukur, Sitem, and Bulugnit as cult guardians to evoke the spirits of the lineage ancestors. Known as *terenka* (pl. *kerenka*), they were kept in sacred huts (*kulo kupon*) where they were honoured and received offerings of rice, kola nuts, sacrificial chickens, and libations. The head of the family would bring it out for various purposes, such as soothsaying, communicating with the ancestors and for protection against disease and bad luck.

These *nimba*-headed male and female statues are emblematic figures in Baga art and can also be found as accessories for other objects—as caryatids on large drums (*timba*), supports for chiefs' seats during rituals held in the sacred forest[7]—and as such are important elements in Guinea's cultural heritage. [MYC]

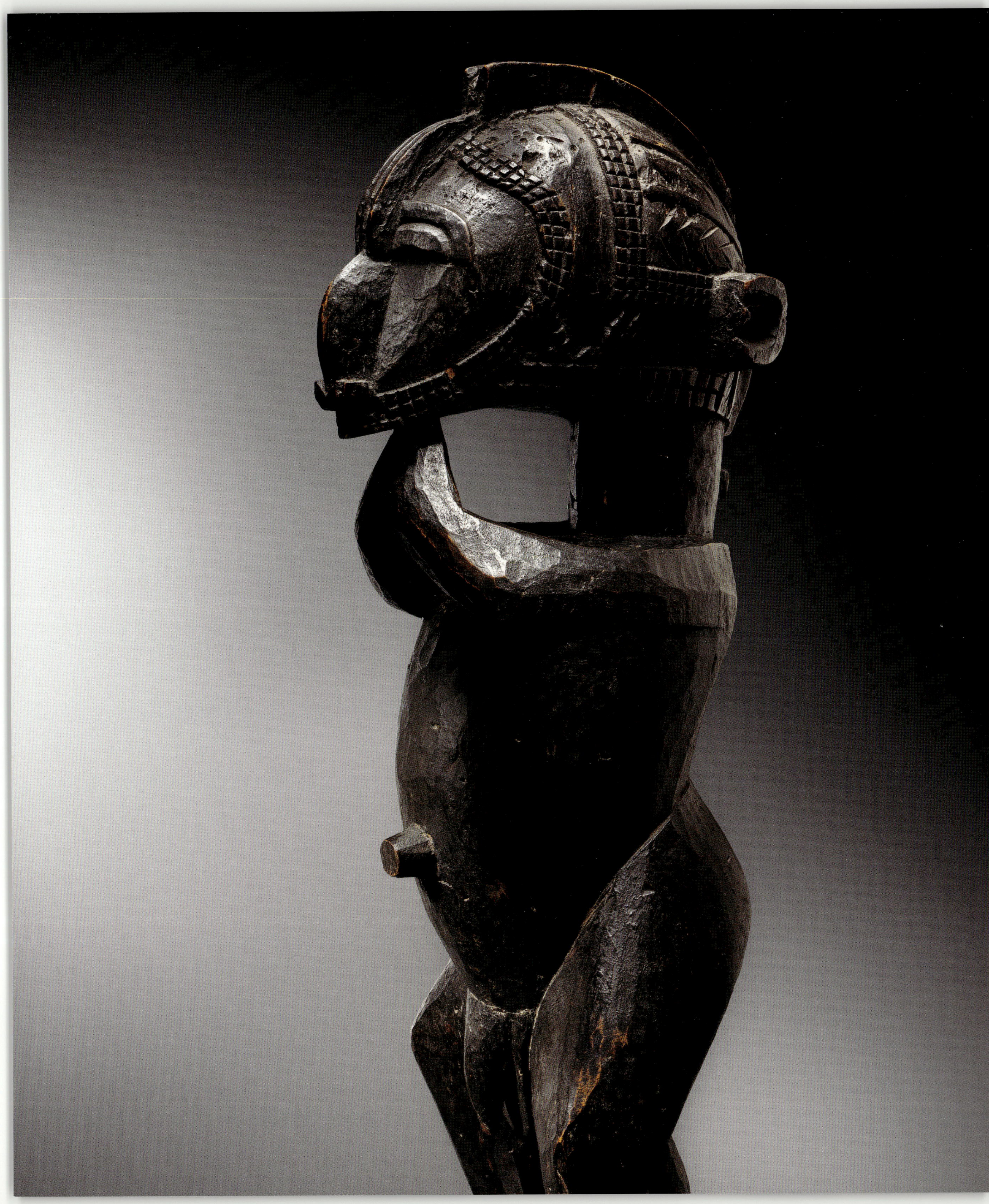

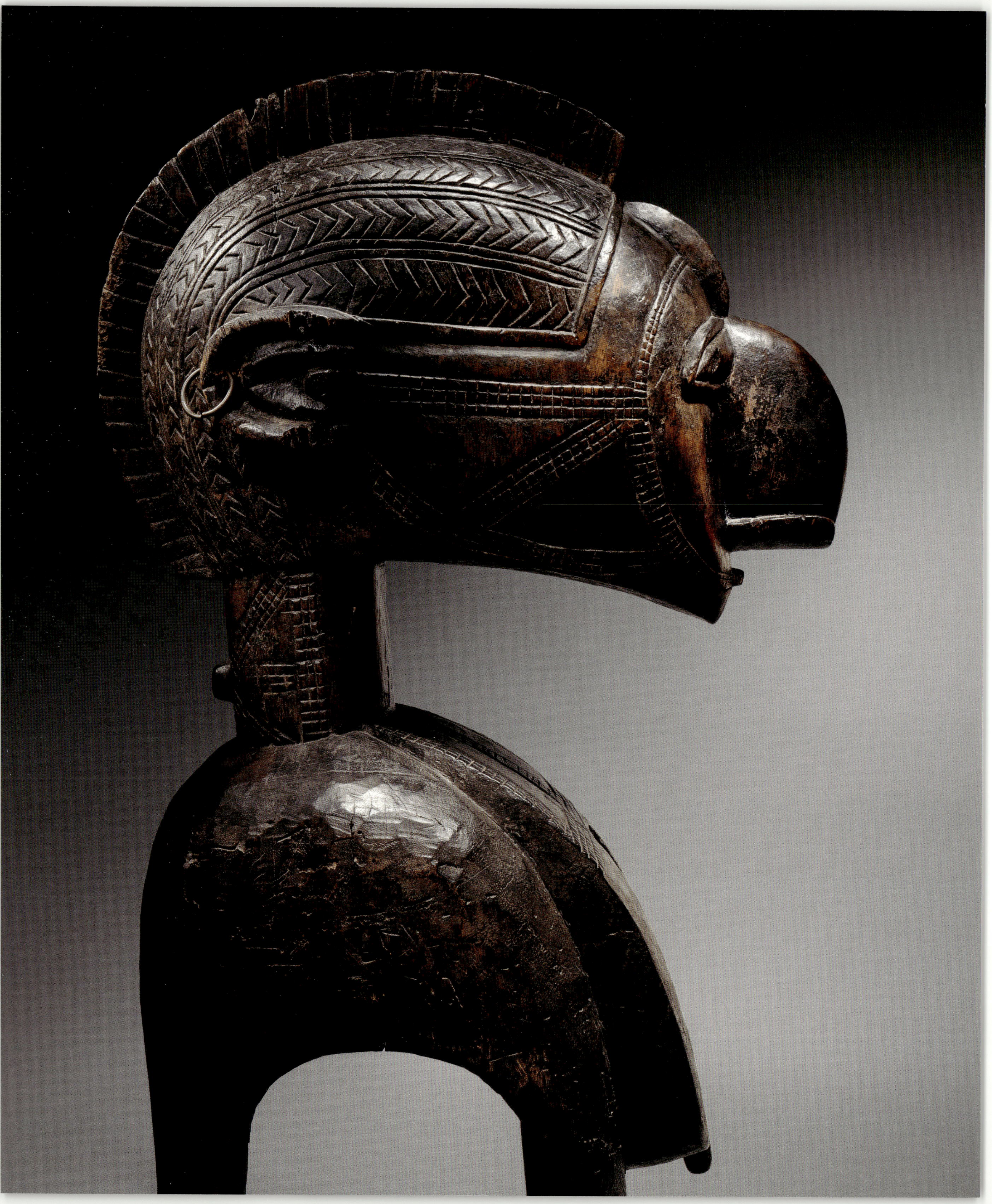

Baga shoulder mask
Republic of Guinea, H. 116 cm

This mask, whose feet show signs of wear, combines both anthropomorphic and zoomorphic (hornbill beak) characteristics. The head is extremely large and decorated with beautiful braids and the oval face features protruding eyes, tubular U-shaped ears set flat against the head, a very small mouth, and a pointed chin. Supported by four long feet and shaped like a large hollow bell, the bust has a mother's large drooping breasts at the front, with two holes in between to enable the wearer to see out. The head and bust are decorated with incised geometric patterns. The whole piece is black and coated with oil, lending the mask a lustrous sheen.

In 1885, Captain Coffinières de Nordeck was the first to describe and illustrate this type of *penda* mask, which he saw in the village of Tshalbunto.[1] A photograph of a "female idol of the Baga Fore," reproduced on a postcard of the period, was taken by A. Chevrier in the first decade of the twentieth century.[2] In addition, this mask's striking appearance caught the imagination of modern European painters at the beginning of the century, such as Derain, Matisse, and Picasso, and they set about collecting Baga objects.[3] Picasso bought a *nimba* mask in 1928 which he kept for the whole of his life and is today in the collection in the Musée Picasso. In 1938, Béatrice Appia of the Musée de l'Homme photographed a *nimba* mask accompanied by a row of tambourine players and dancing girls in the village of Monchon.[4] Asekou Sayon's[5] forced Islamization of the Baga at the end of the 1950s led to the destruction of a large number of Baga objects, mainly by fire. As a result, this type of mask was much sought-after by collectors and a number of *nimba* masks were sold to the art dealer Hélène Leloup in 1957.[6] So it was that these pieces found their way to various public and private collections in Europe and America. The "classic" *nimba*, as described by Van Geertruyen,[7] spawned a series of masks with different shapes, sizes and styles. It also gave rise to the creation of standing statues whose head is a replica of the *nimba*, which acted as caryatids for large chiefs' drums[8] and supports for ritual stools.

Majestic and spectacular, the great Baga mask has now become the emblem of the modern state of Guinea (bank notes, tourist advertising . . .). It is known as *d'mba* by the Baga Sitem, *yamban* by the Baga Pukur and *nimba* by the Baga Bulugnits, the Nalu, and the Susu, but it was actually created over three centuries ago in a small Baga Pukur village called Mnar (Binari in Susu) located close to the mouth of the River Kapachez, on the northern coast of Guinea.[9, 10, 11] The Baga are a small rice-growing and fishing community who became famous during the nineteenth century following the discovery of their extraordinary sculptures. This great mask was also used by the neighbouring Nalu and Landuma.

The *nimba* mask's main function was to ensure the women's fecundity and the fertility of the land that was cultivated. When it was time for the rice to be sowed or the crop harvested, the Baga *Sitem* (elders), aided by adults, youths, and women would organize a *d'mba* dance in the main square in the village. It was always preceded by some twenty young musicians, who advanced while beating energetically on double-headed drums (*sengbe*). The wearer, hidden behind a raffia skirt, needed to be very strong (as he had to carry an object weighing over 50 kg) and he would advance in step with the music accompanied by the singing of the soloist, echoed by the chants of the women. When the dancers entered the scene, he would rock the mask from side to side in the middle of the crowd that had gathered to greet the mask's spirit and thank it for granting their wishes: abundant crops, wealth, health, and progeny. When the people's joy was at its height, the dancer would show off some acrobatic moves, lifting the mask up high, at which the crowd would cry "Ayo." Some men would come up to touch the *d'mba*'s breasts in recognition of women's central role in the Baga community.[12]

The *nimba* mask is even now taken as the ideal of beauty and goodness for Baga posterity. Masquerades of this kind are staged by groups of young people to introduce an extra thrill in village dances or outside to welcome visiting dignitaries and foreigners, as well as during special festivals, thus helping to preserve the memory of their ancestors. [MYC]

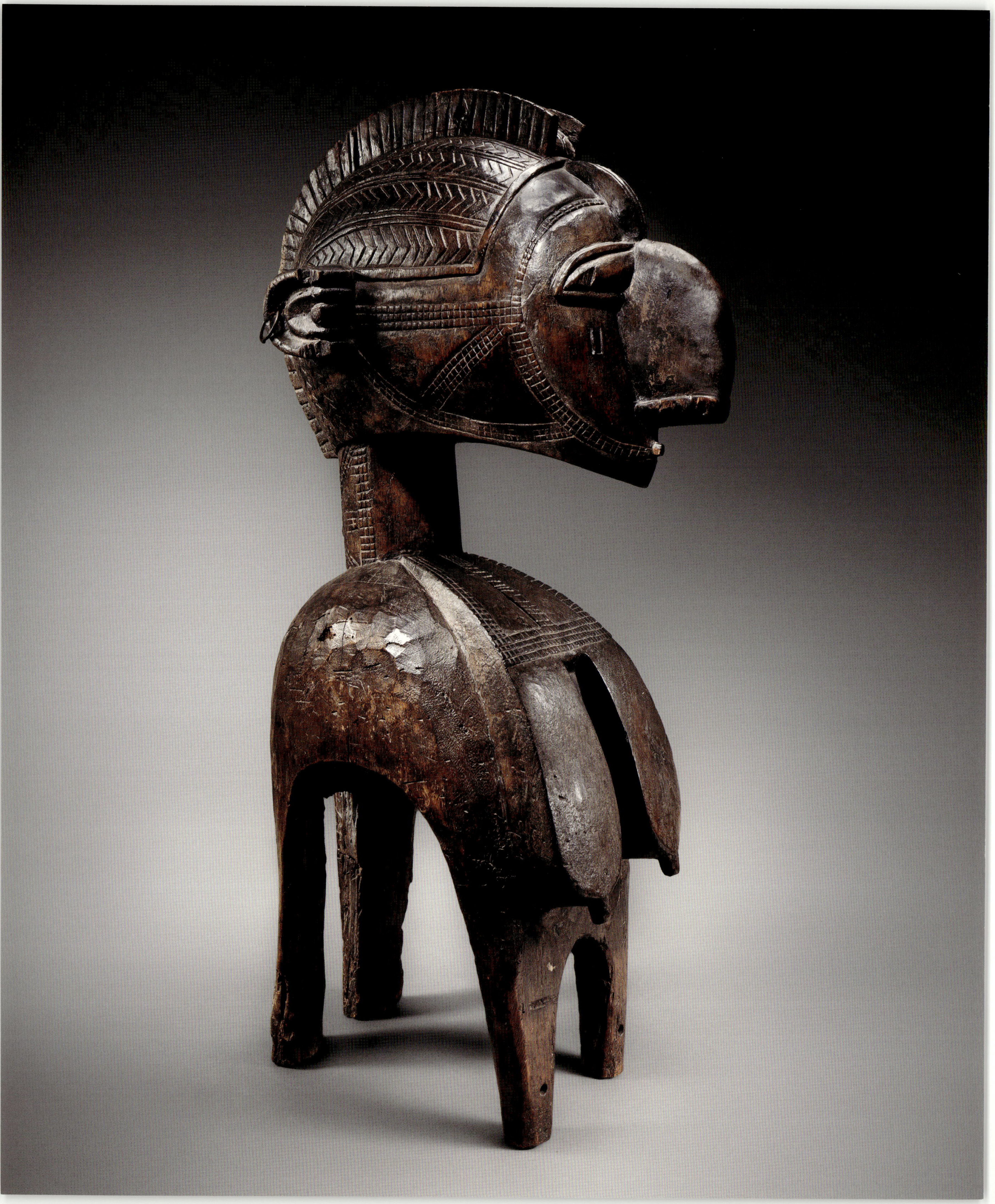

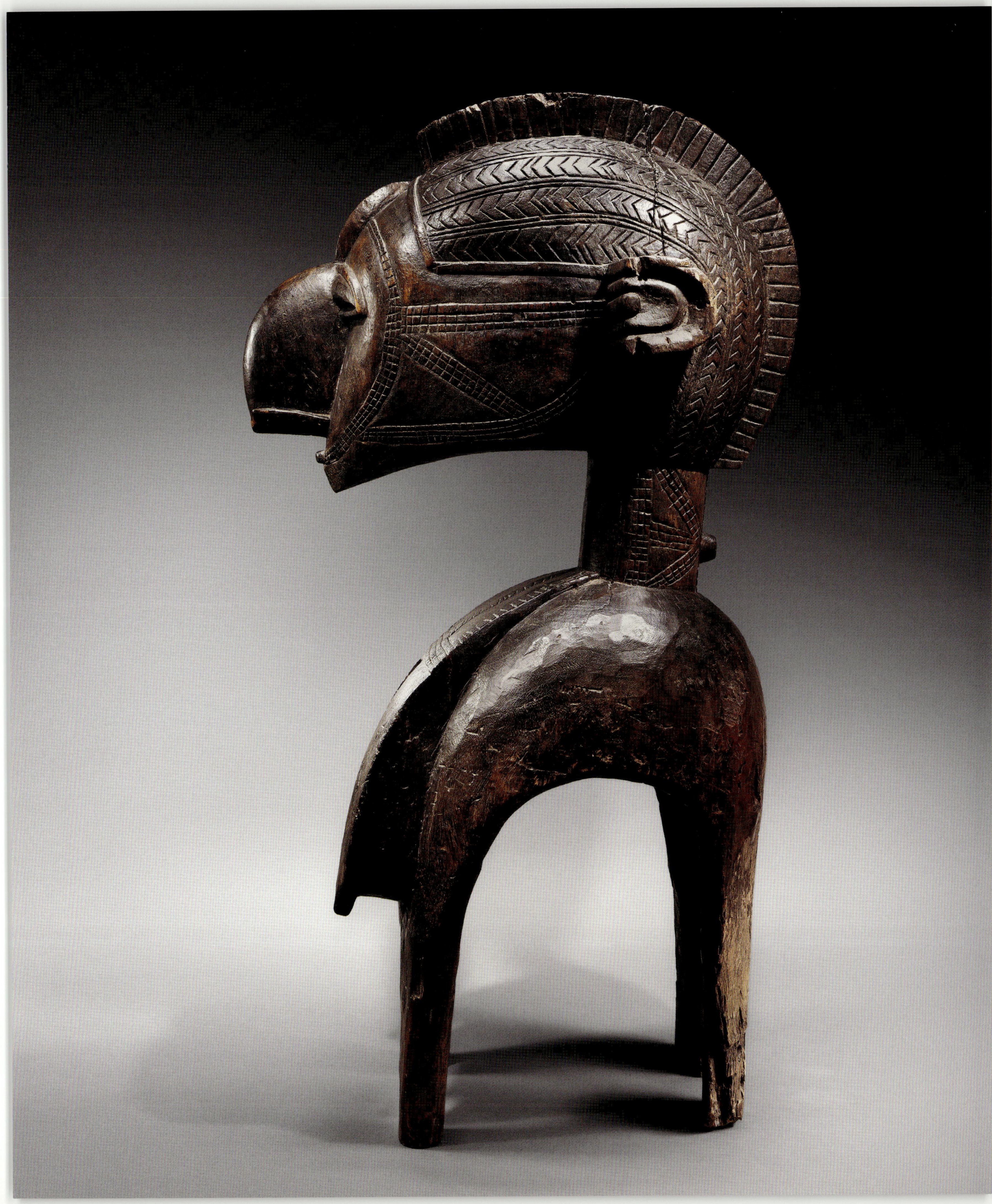

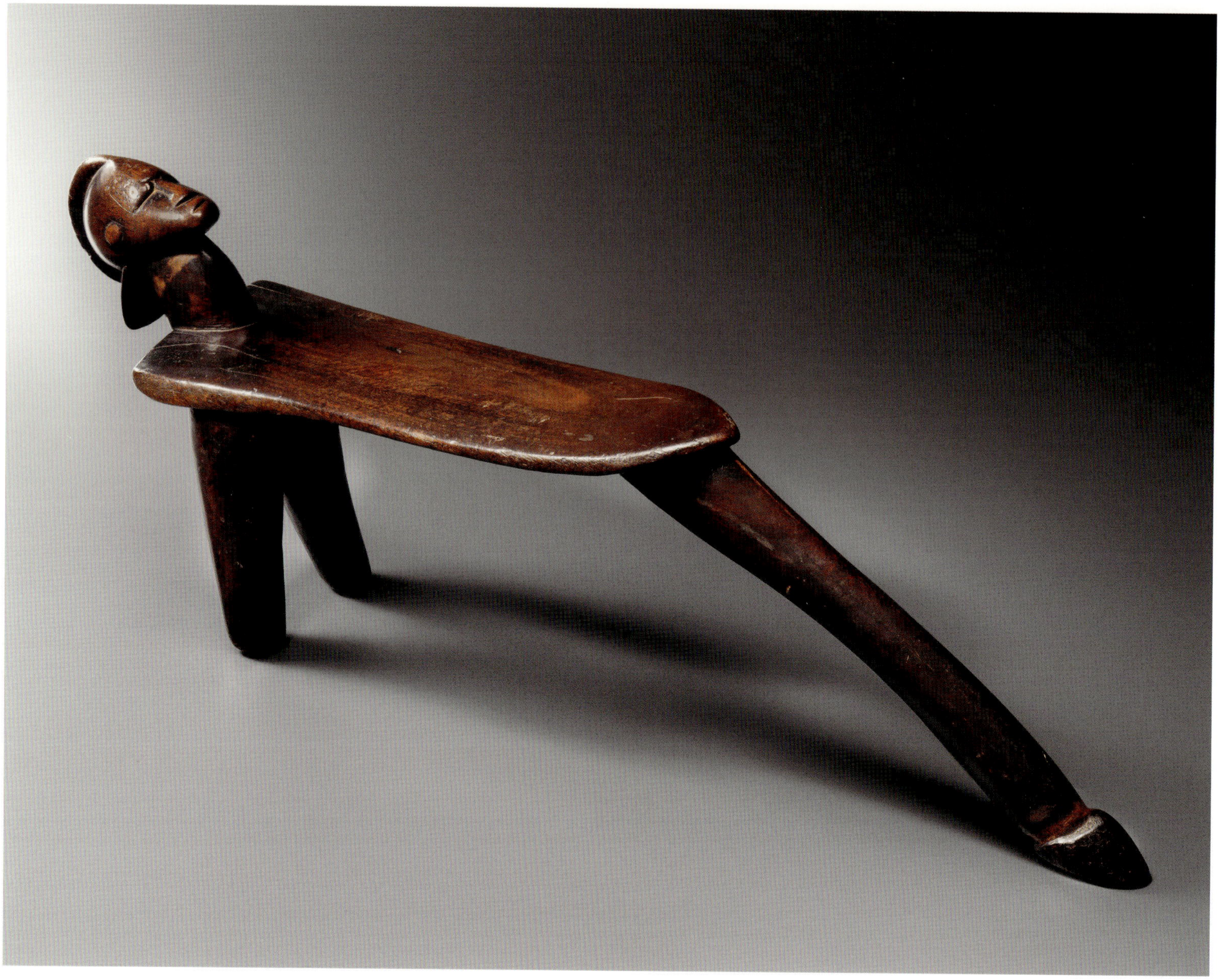

Lobi stool
Burkina Faso, L. 62 cm

The designer of the Lobi three-legged stool (*bitebo*) ought to have a place among the great masters of design: the model shown here is a spectacular example of this skill in combining functionality and aesthetic appeal. The sculptor has embellished an object in daily use with a skilfully carved head in the purest style of his ethnic group without sacrificing the sturdiness required of an all-purpose article in constant use. In addition to providing the stool's stability, the front leg could also double as the ergonomic handle of the fearsome club that no self-respecting warrior or hunter would ever be seen without, as the first Western travellers to the region observed in the early twentieth century. [BG]

Mossi statue
Burkina Faso, H. 94 cm

Arms held slightly away from the body, hands stretched out to match the tensed hips and face raised ecstatically to the sky, this figure seems to be performing a propitiatory dance. This stunning *ninande* is exceptional in its size, expressiveness . . . and gender. Mossi statuary is very rarely hermaphrodite, whether the figures pay tribute to the ancestors or are designed as guards for a councillor's residence to protect against evil spirits. The women's *gyonfo* crest, borrowed from the Foulani, contrasts with the beard framing the highly expressive face, while the undeniably virile base of the belly clashes with the majestically callipygian rear. The female aspect predominates in the end thanks to the figure's comely breasts and "three vertical stripes, with the navel at their centre," which was typical of women's decorations, as Lucien Marc pointed out in 1904, the three facial scarifications being sexually neutral. [BG]

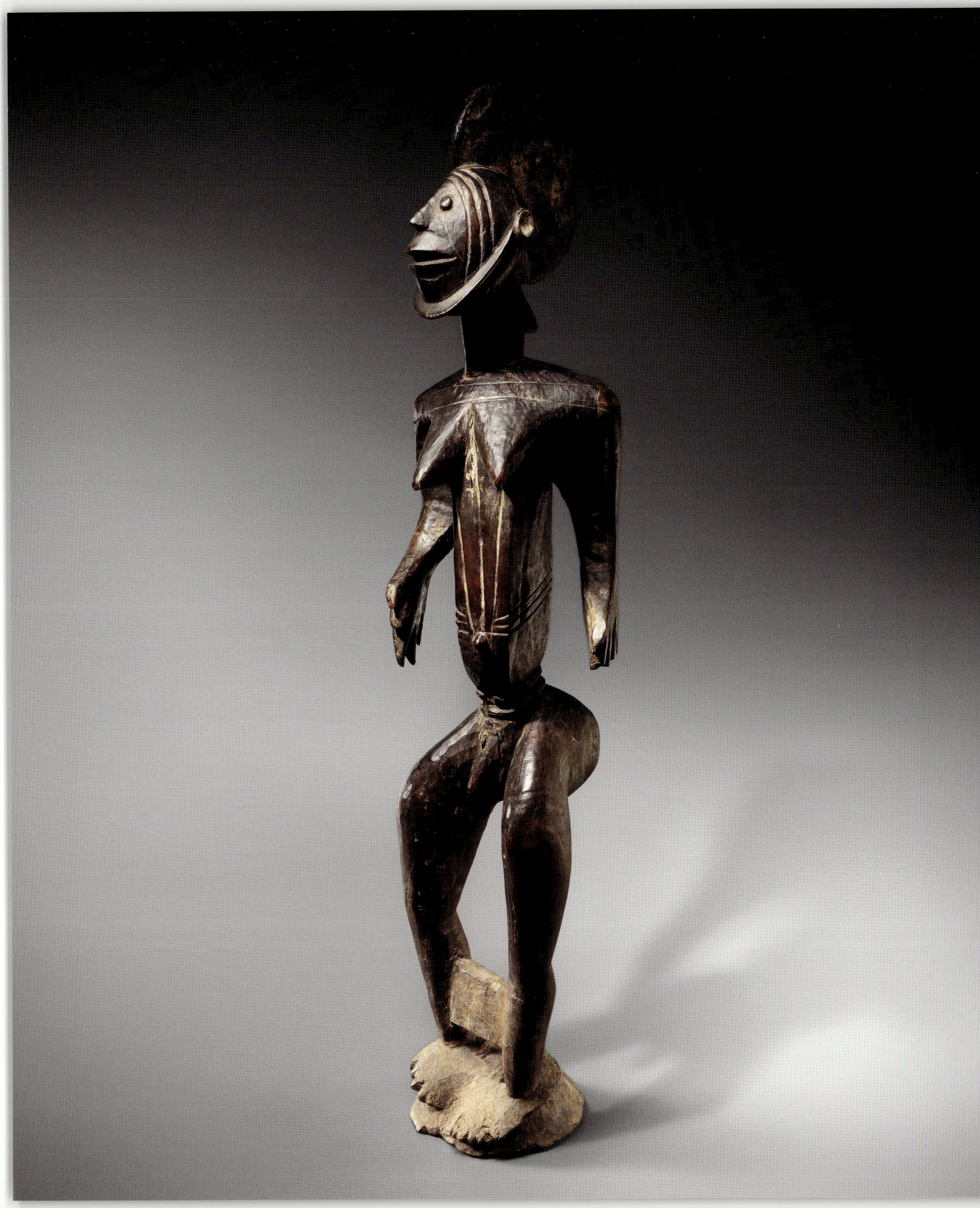

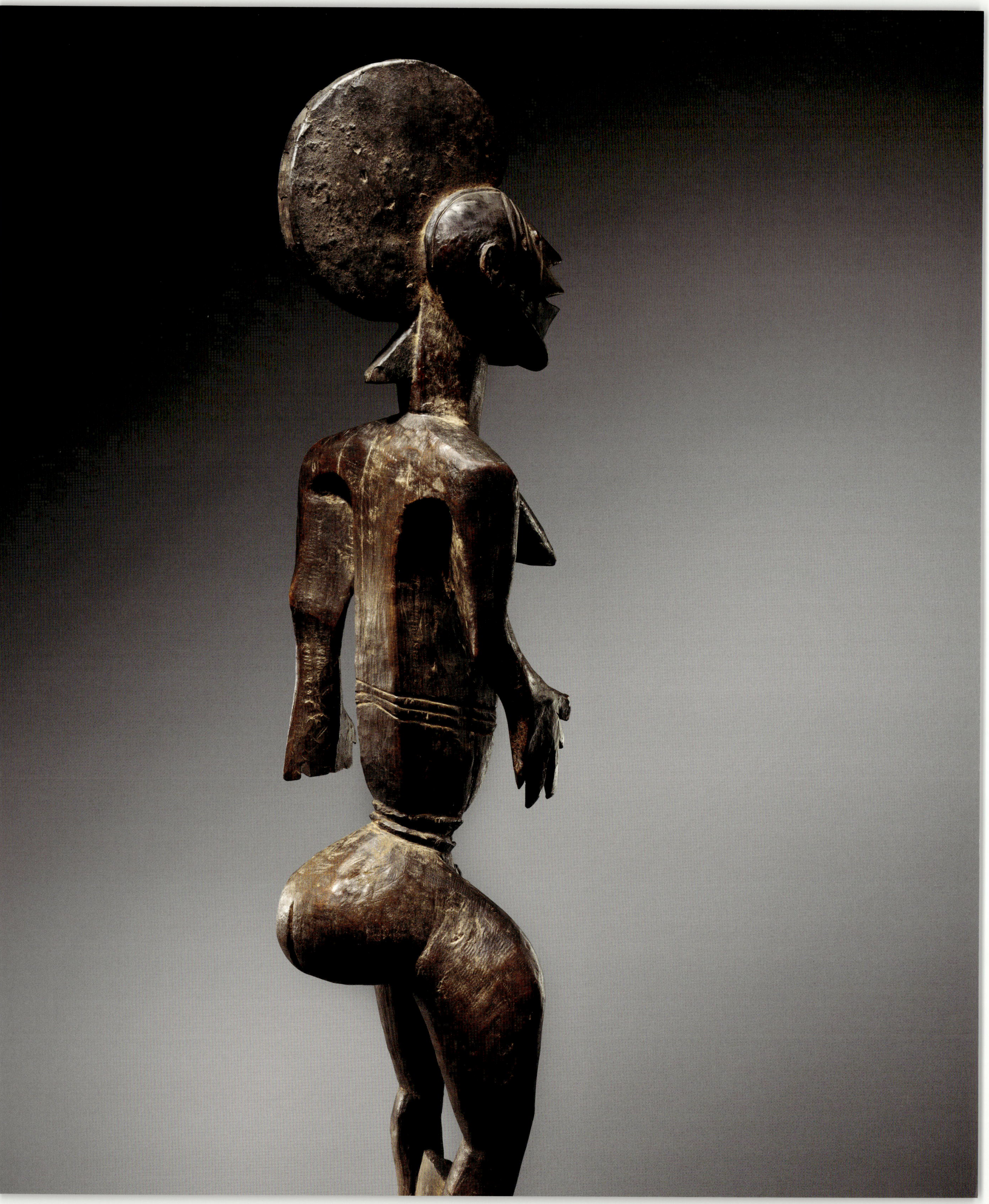

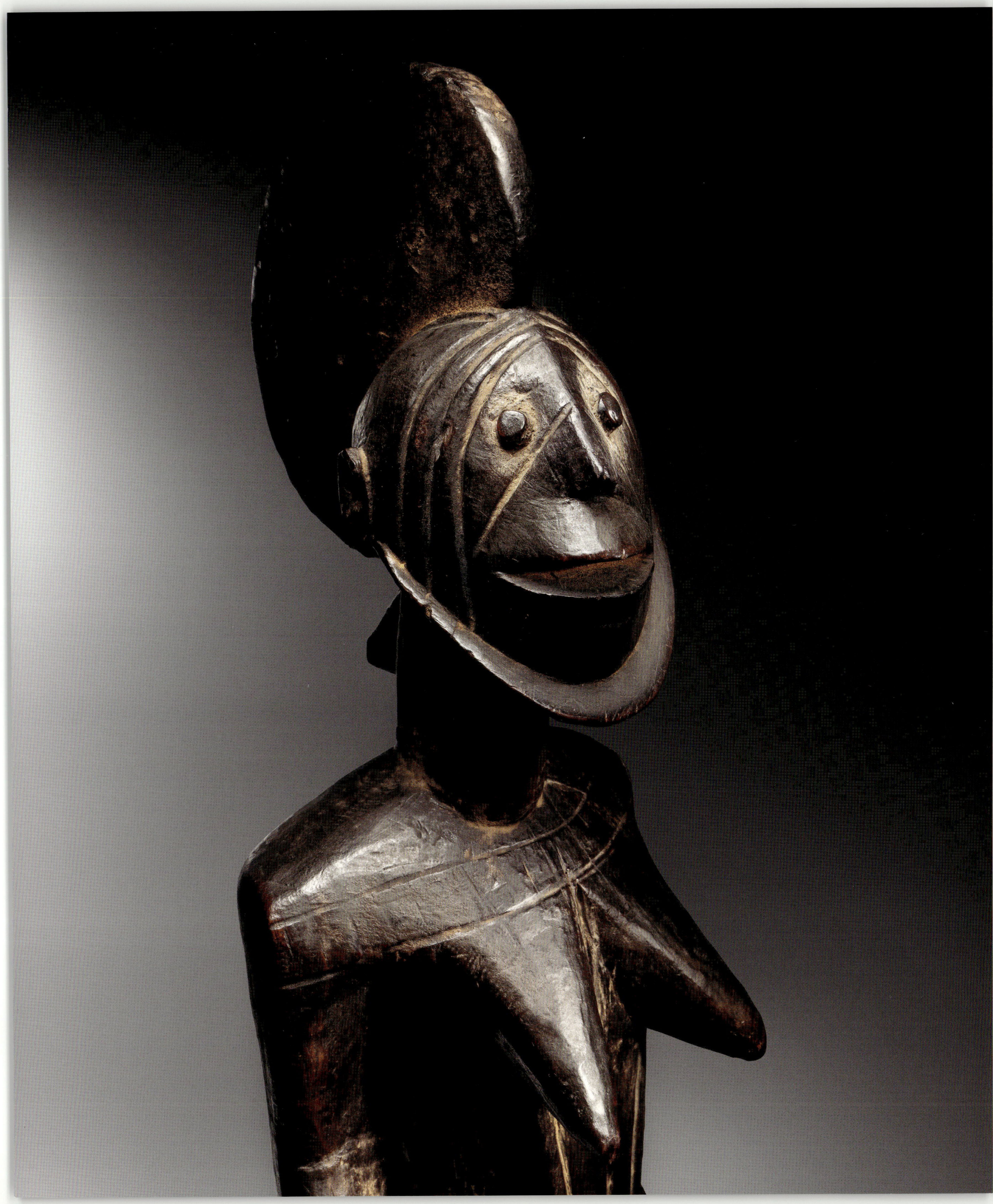

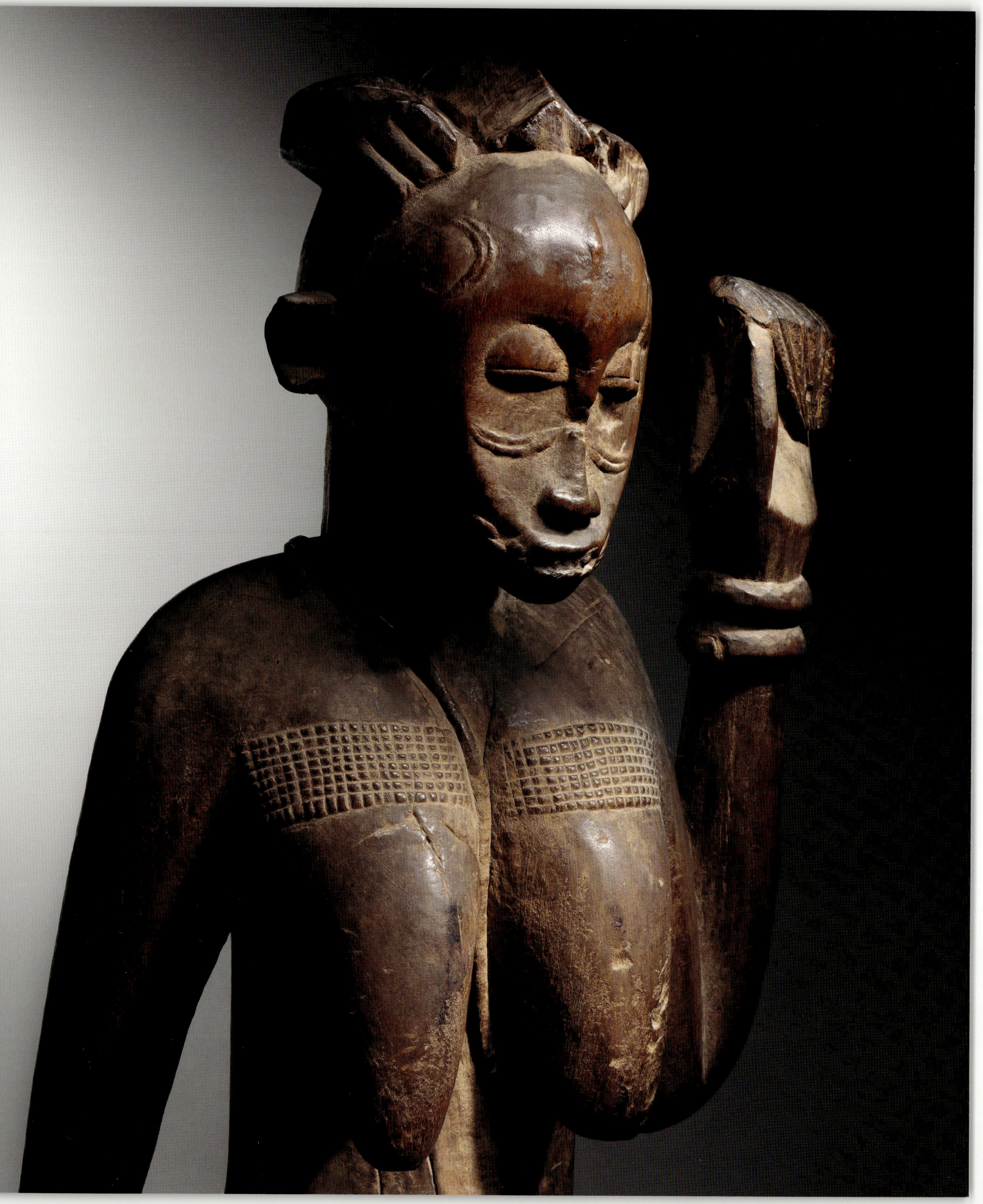

Senufo statue
Côte d'Ivoire, H. 102 cm

The Senufo statue in the Weill Collection is exceptional from all points of view. Peacefulness, abundance, sensuality, and harmony are the words that immediately spring to mind to describe the beauty of this future mother. She holds her left arm raised to the sky, with the palm outwards and the fingers folded as if in a friendly greeting, adding a unique, enigmatic flavour to a work that nonetheless is entirely faithful to the canons of traditional Senufo art. The meaning of this gesture, which lies completely outside all codes and conventions, will forever remain the secret of an inspired artist who has long since disappeared. The subtlety of the facial features and the care taken over the smallest detail, from the *bila* modestly covering the pelvic area, to the string of "Marabout" amulets unusually worn over the shoulder rather than around the neck, suggest this is the work of a *kulebele* sculptor rather than a plain blacksmith.
The work was probably commissioned by one of the secret societies around which the spiritual life of the Senufo was built, the *Tyekpa*, the counterpart of the *Poro*, which was mainly concerned with fecundity and fertility under the auspices of the ubiquitous original mother, Katyeleo. Although these themes usually take the sculptural form of a woman and child, this image—to our knowledge unique—of a manifestly pregnant young woman, also falls under the protection of the "divine mentor"; this is made explicit through her heavy breasts, rounded belly and swollen navel highlighted by keloids shaped like a Templar cross, the symbol of the womb carved on the doors of huts, the mother's realm *par excellence*. The decorations on the breasts and the perfectly oval face are typical of the works of the central Senufo, those from Sinematiali or those from the mythical Lataha wood, from which the *deble* masterpieces in the Rietberg or the Barbier-Muller Museums were spirited away when the iconoclastic sect of the prophet Massa began their burning frenzies in the 1950s. [BG]

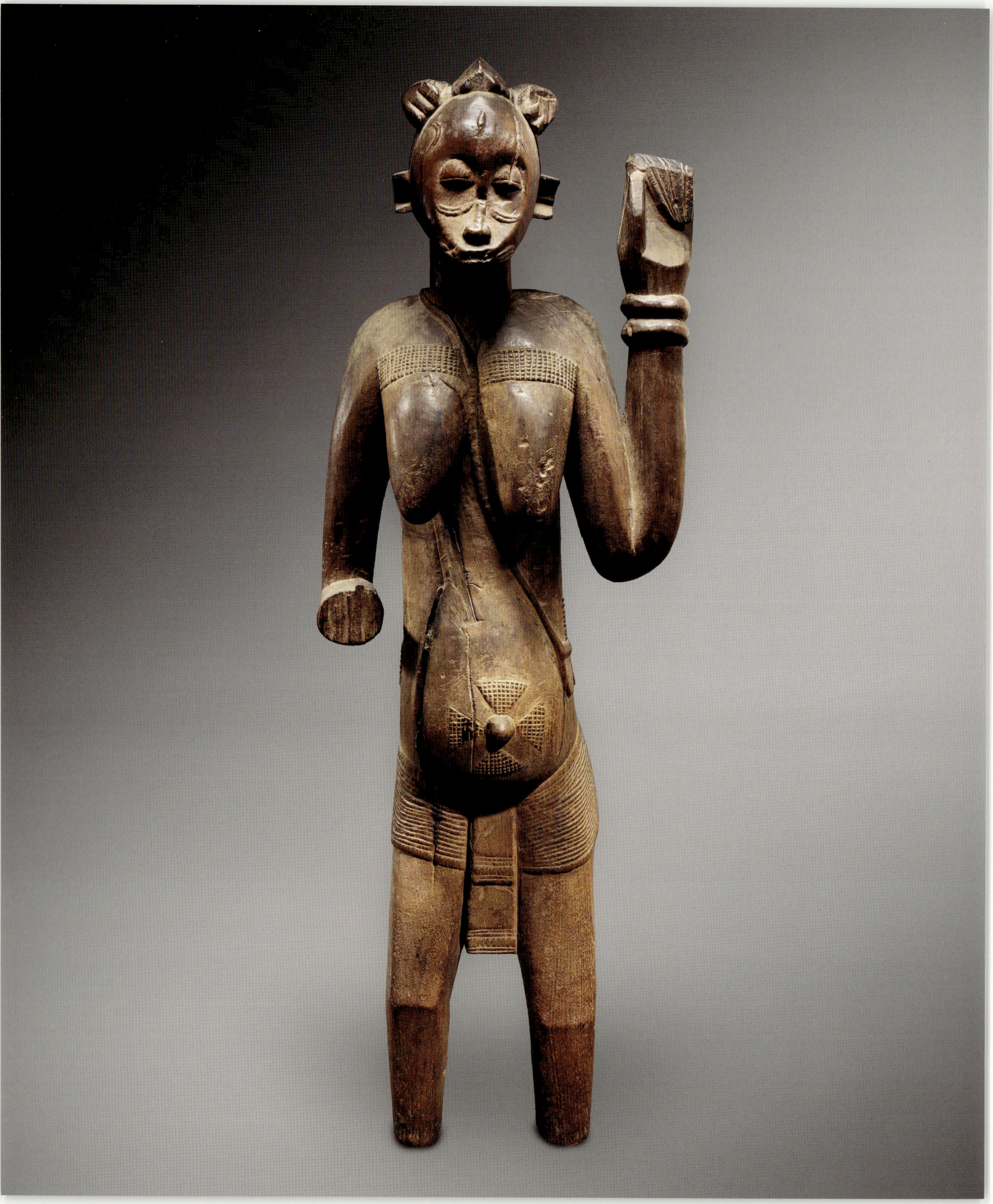

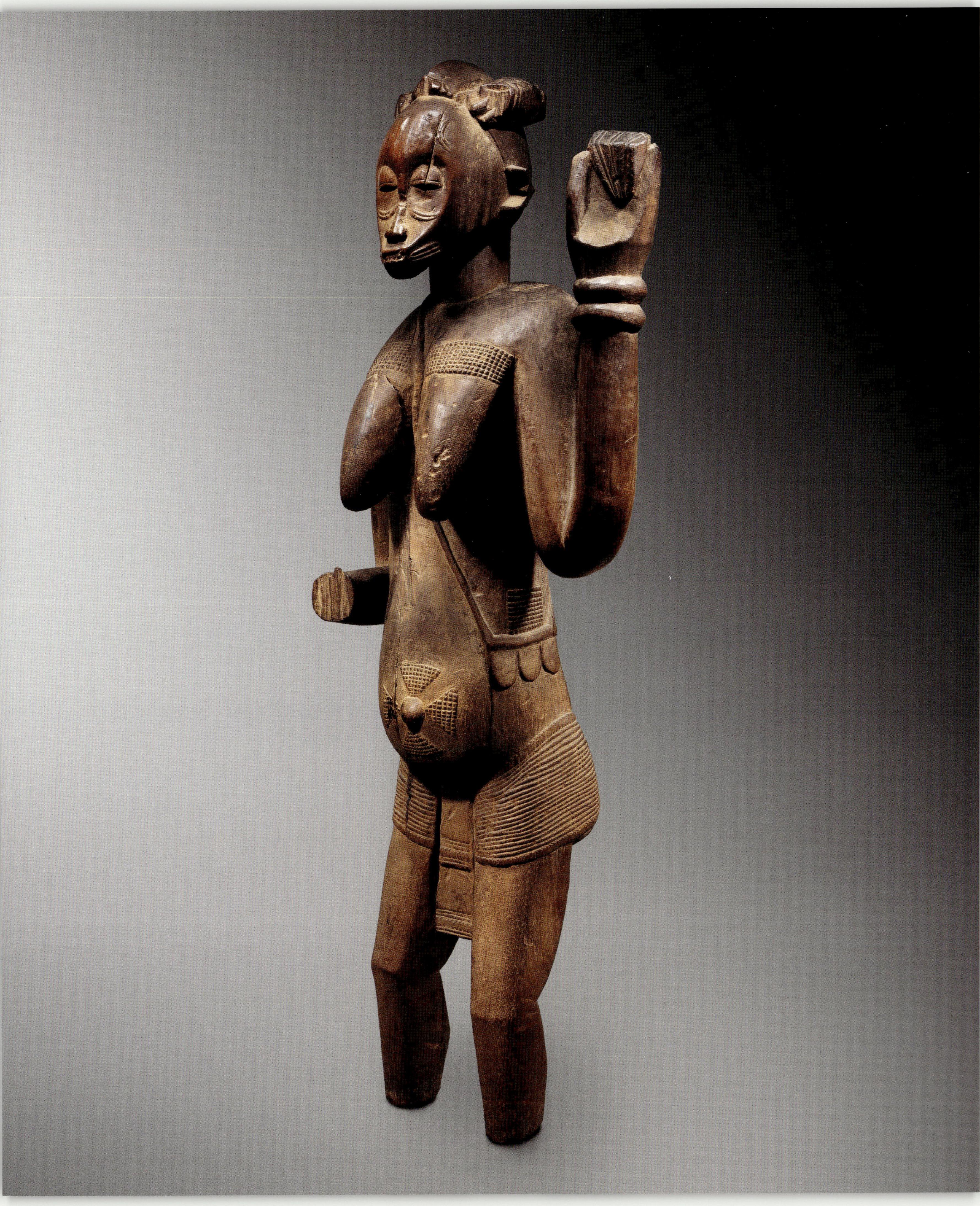

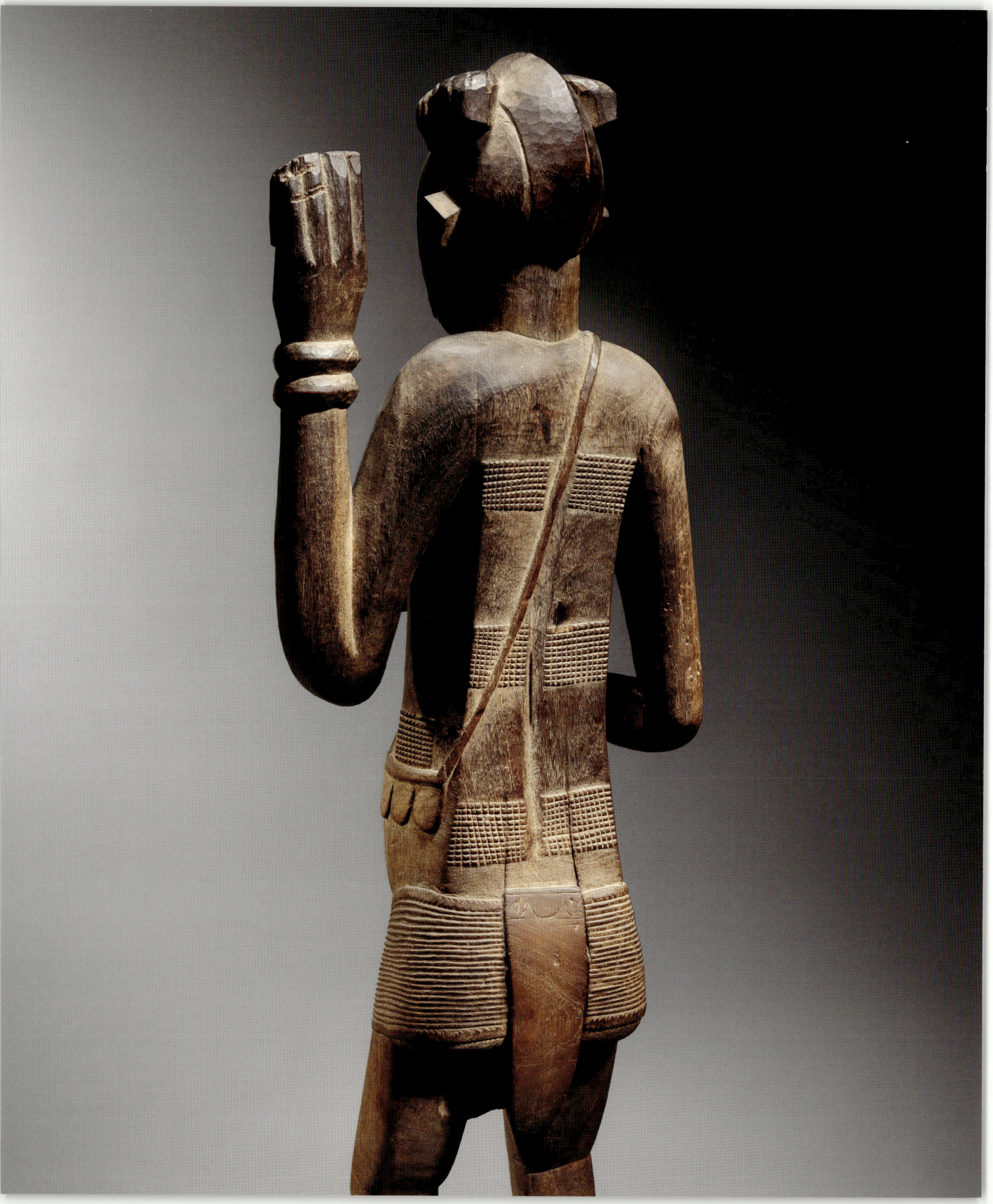

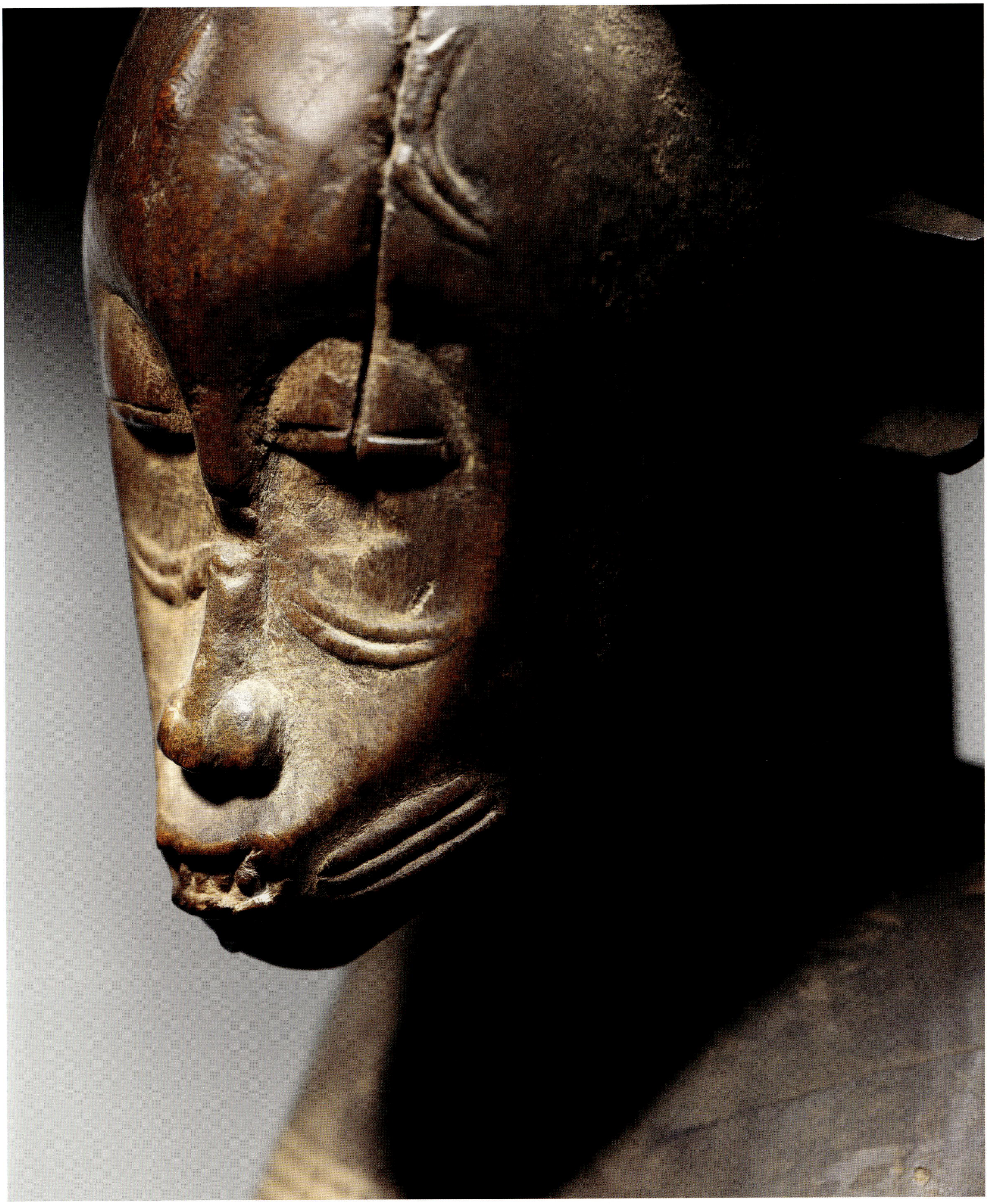

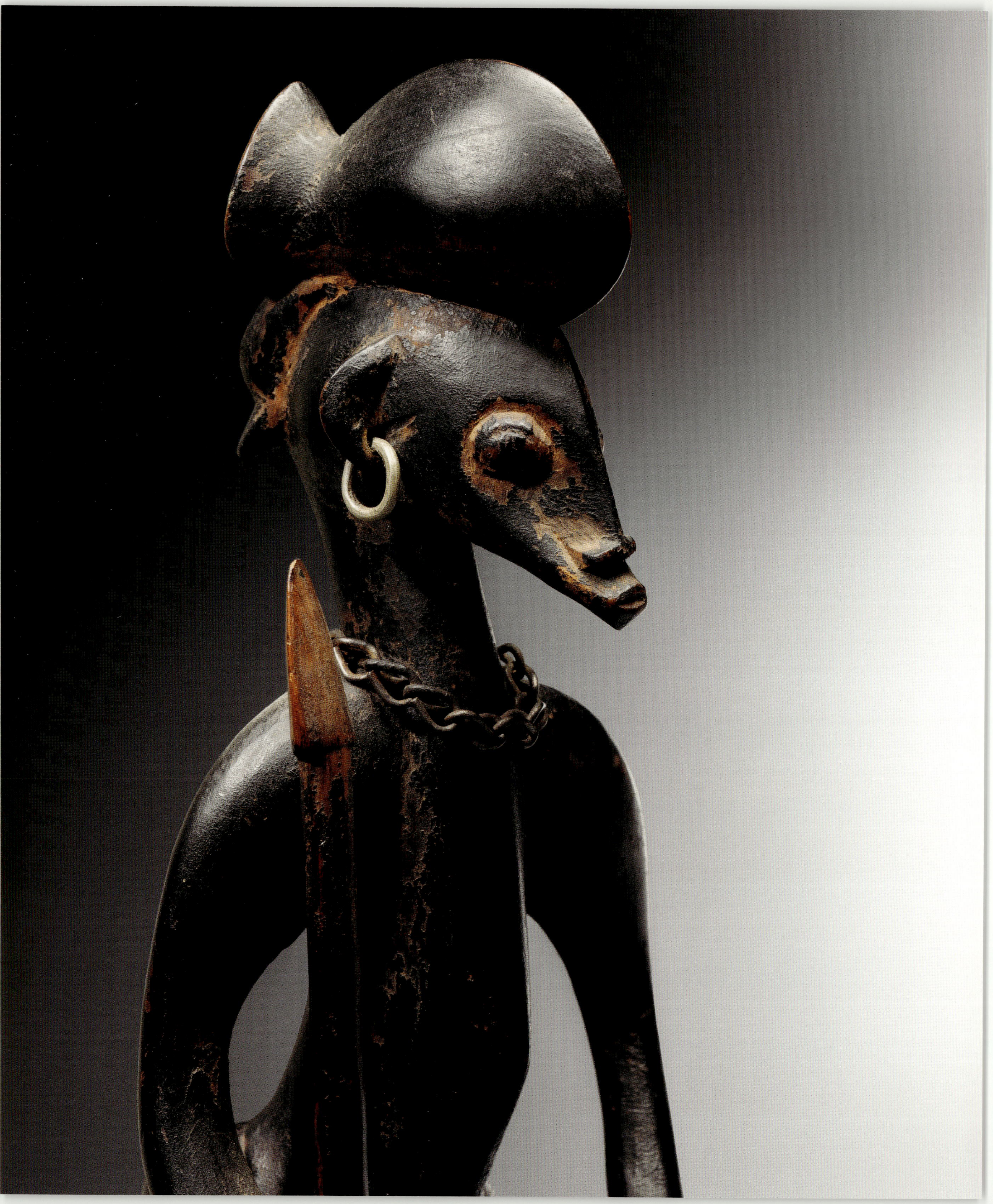

Senufo horseman
Côte d'Ivoire, H. 29 cm

The Senufo of Côte d'Ivoire are arable rather than livestock farmers; horses are rare and reserved for dignitaries/councillors. Captain Binger caused a sensation when he rode one through the area in 1887, as his effigies modelled in low relief on the mud walls of Senufo huts attest. However, the explorer was among the Senufo of present-day Mali, in Fourou in the region of Minianka, where the eponymous Barbary pony was able to adapt to the challenging environment of the Sudanese savannah without falling prey to insect-borne diseases. The equestrian statue illustrated here probably comes from this border area, where over half a century ago Karl-Heinz Krieg found an identical statue in the Ivorian village of Kanakoro, a few kilometres to the south of Fourou, when he was collecting for the Linden Museum in Stuttgart.

These works are often described as *bandeguele* spirits, "minor beings with a grotesque appearance," according to the description by Bohumil Holas, a pre-eminent, although also controversial guide to Ivorian material culture. In this case it seems more likely the figure is simply a "master horseman"—*syonfolo*—a kind of hero rooted in local history, such as the story of the of Almamy Samory Toure's "sofas," who are said to have ridden all the way to the land of Kong to quell a revolt.

The artist has undoubtedly created a masterpiece of balance, a perfect symbiosis between man and beast, in which the former is larger, symbolizing humanity's dominion over the animal. The figure has been carved with the greatest skill and matches the canonical requisites for the statues of the region—a narrow oval face jutting forwards, hair arranged in buns and protruding navel. The arms held straight along the body, the bare shoulders, the gaze focused on a distant horizon, the arched lower back, the heels pointing down towards the ground are all signs of an expert horseman. An instructor at the Cadre Noir de Saumur riding academy would have appreciated the impeccable posture of such a recruit as he holds his sword strictly vertical in spite of the horse's gait. The talented sculptor has been able to seize the passing moment when the horseman relieves the burden on his mount by just raising his lower back from the saddle. This unmistakeable sense of movement is amplified by the position of the slightly arched legs, depicted in a perfectly controlled minimalist style. [BG]

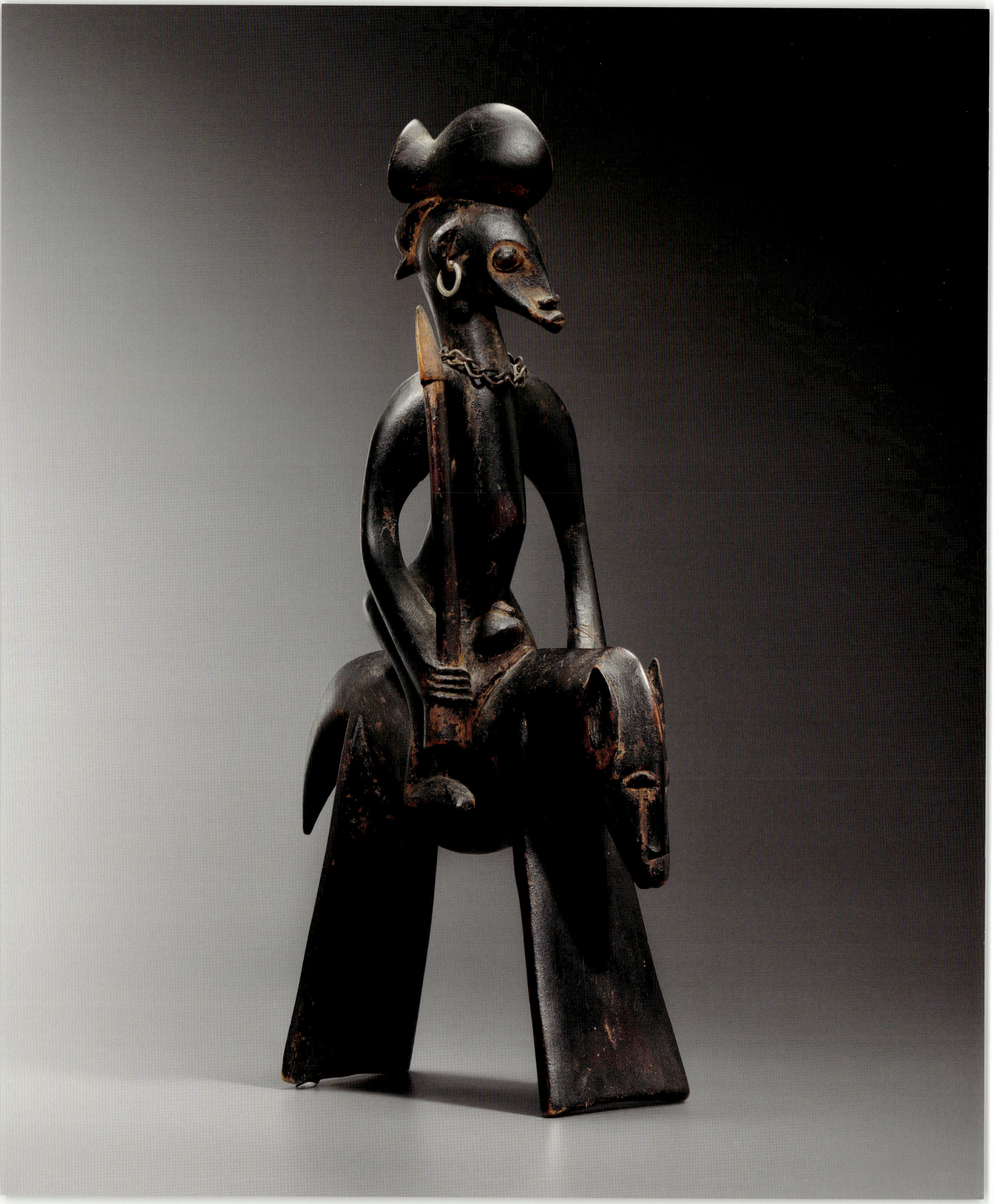

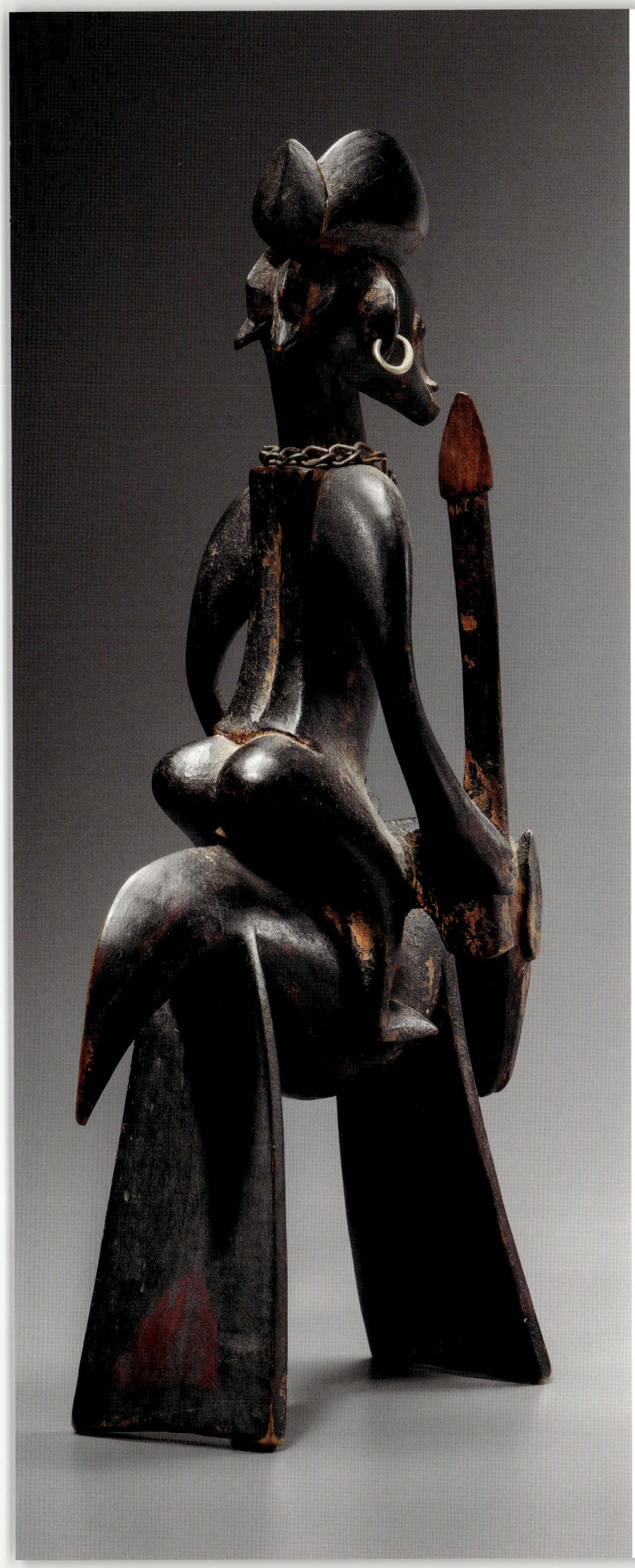
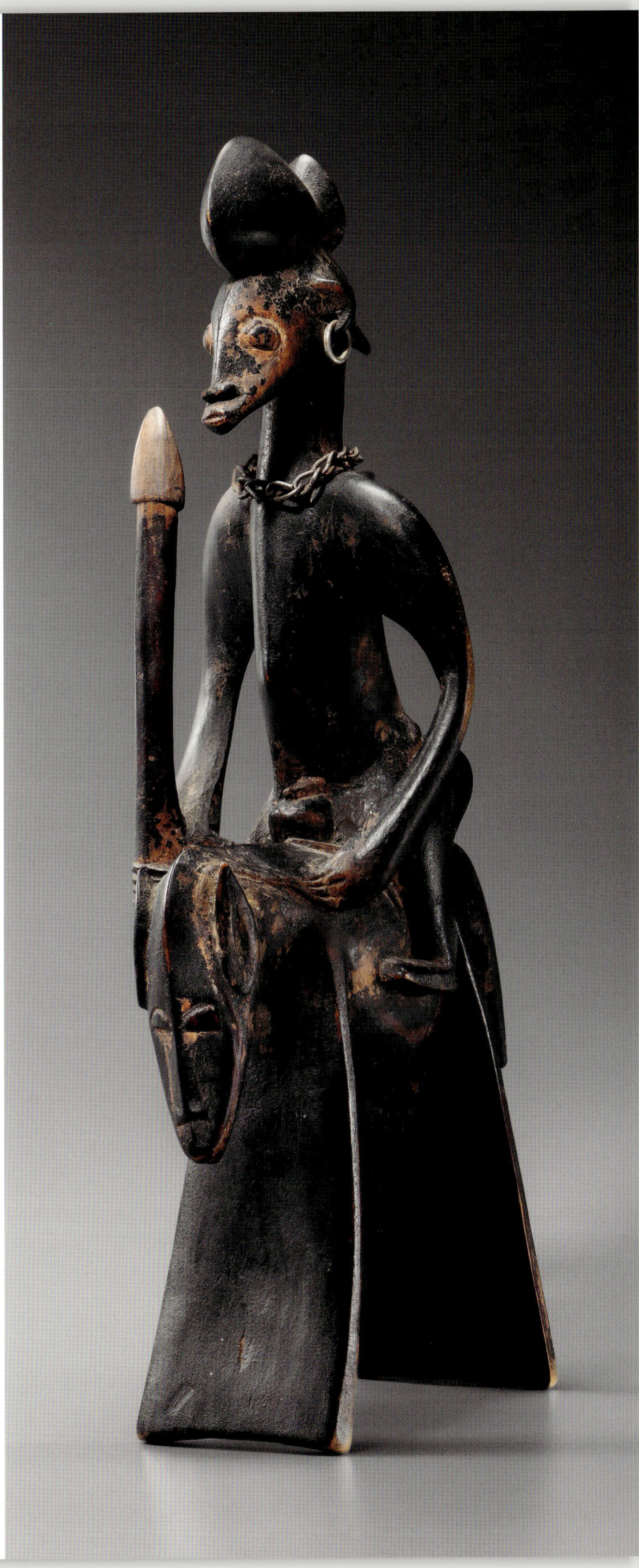

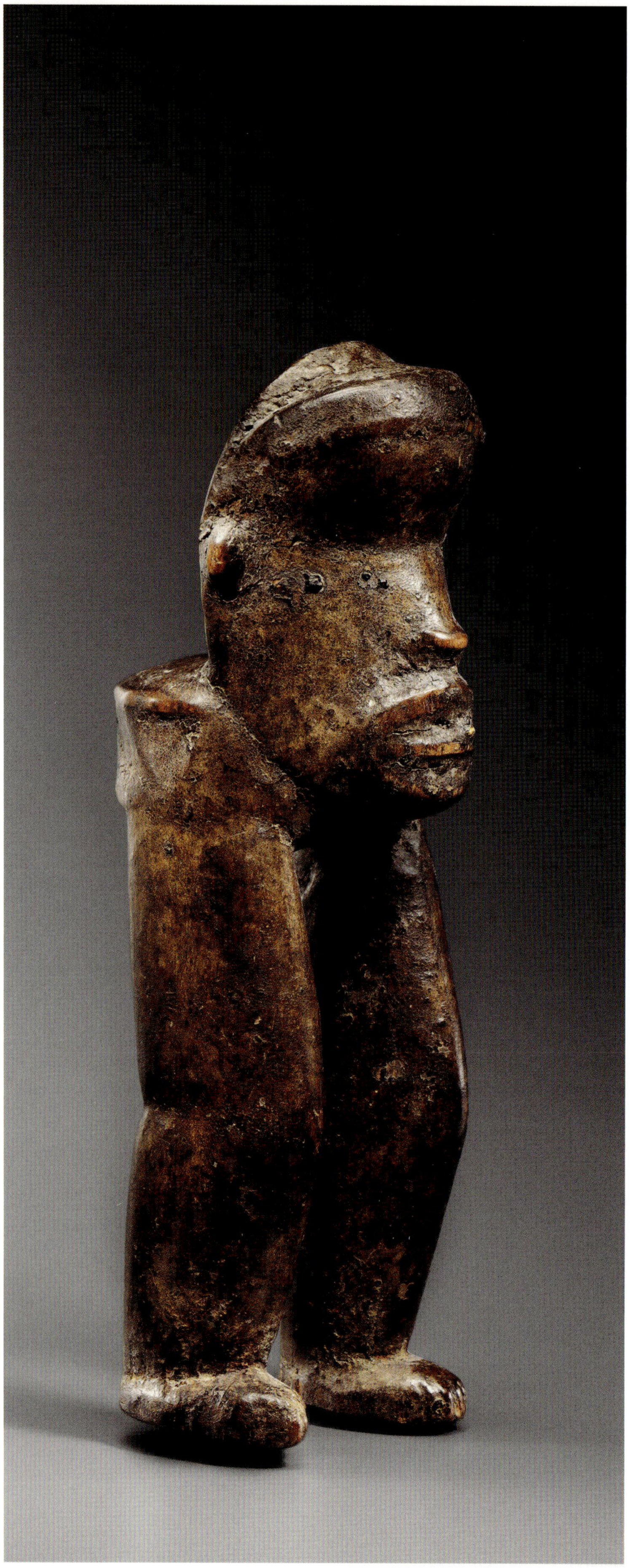

Dan sculpture
Côte d'Ivoire, H 18.5 cm

Dan sculptors and their neighbours on the other bank of the Cavally have sometimes carved the handles or bases of everyday tools in the shape of women's legs. In contrast, the enigmatic association of lower limbs and a miniature mask, *Ma go*, is an outright rarity: only two specimens are known to exist and they come from the same workshop in Mano territory in Liberia. While the fine sacrificial patina coating the moving little face illustrated here confirms its ritual use as a portable substitute for the large masks, no tradition explains why it appears to emerge from a pubis. Has the artist fulfilled the dream of providing a voice to an organ that is normally silent, in "mystical correspondence" with Diderot and his "indiscreet jewels" conjured up for the Congolese king Mangogul? [BG]

Koulango statue
Côte d'Ivoire, H. 55 cm

The female statue shown here is intriguing in its rarity, originality and careful balance of its forms, as well as the mystery that surrounds its origins. What is known is that the piece comes from a large region in northern Côte d'Ivoire—now a crossroads between four nations—whose history is distinguished by the endless migrations of peoples crossing it in search of fertile land or escaping from conquering hordes. The arched posture of this extremely rare statue, with its long neck resting on shoulders thrown backwards, arms held tight against the body, hands joined at the navel, closely resembles bronze amulets that have been present in France since the eighteenth century and attributed to the Koulango. On the other hand, the figure's face, surmounted by a crested headdress, recalls the statues of the Lobi, who were the Koulango's vassals in the ancient pre-colonial Kingdom of Bouna. [BG]

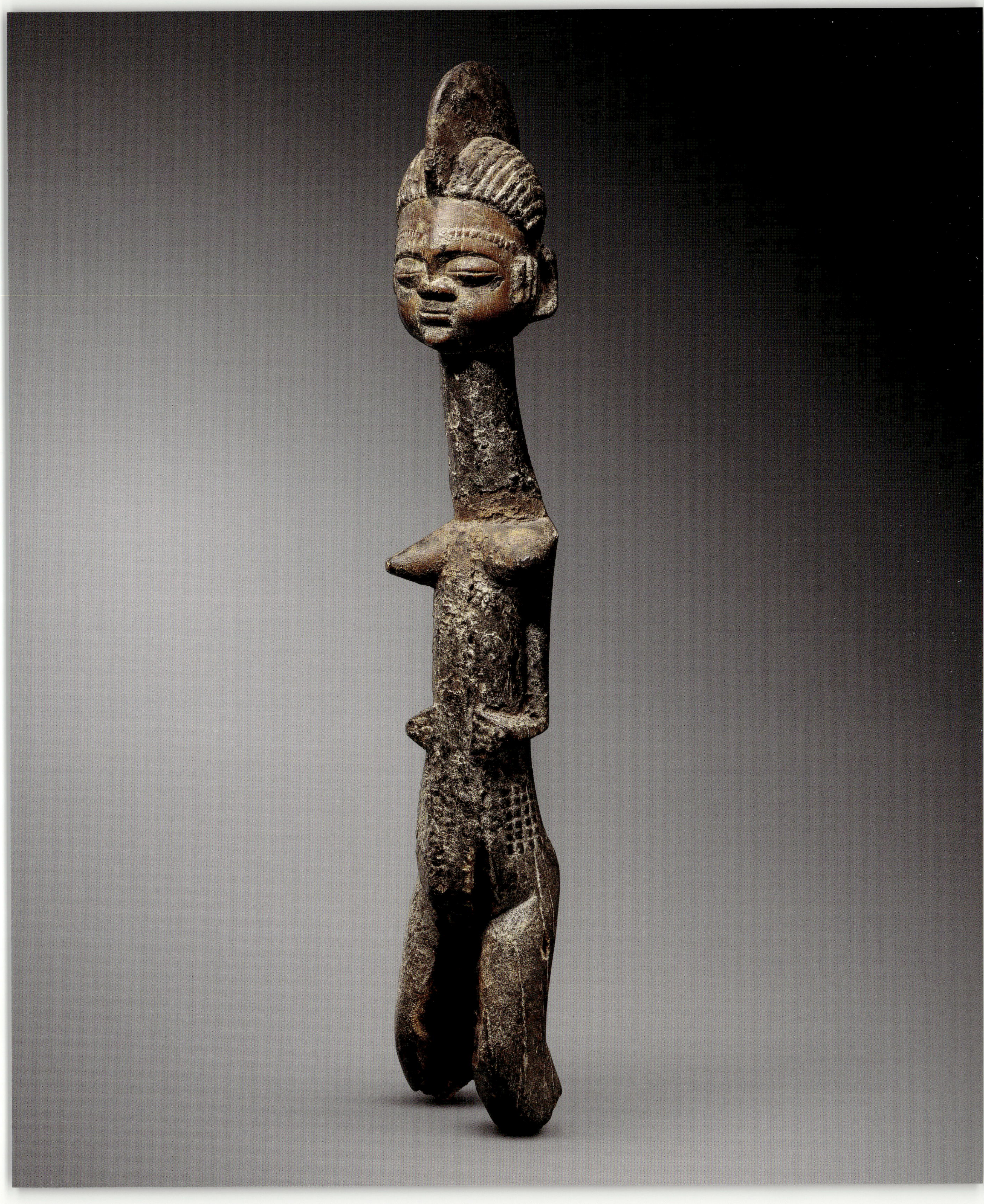

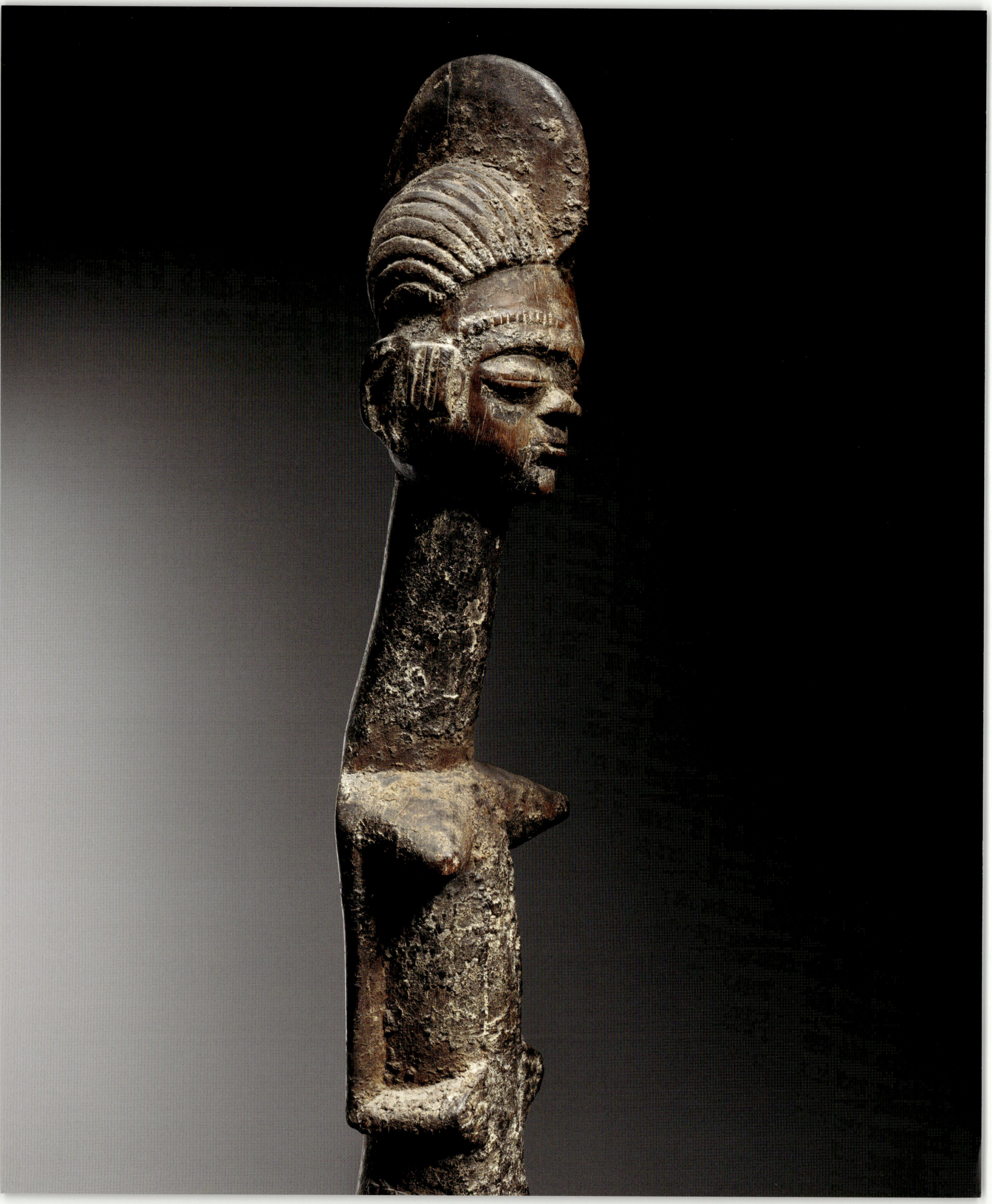

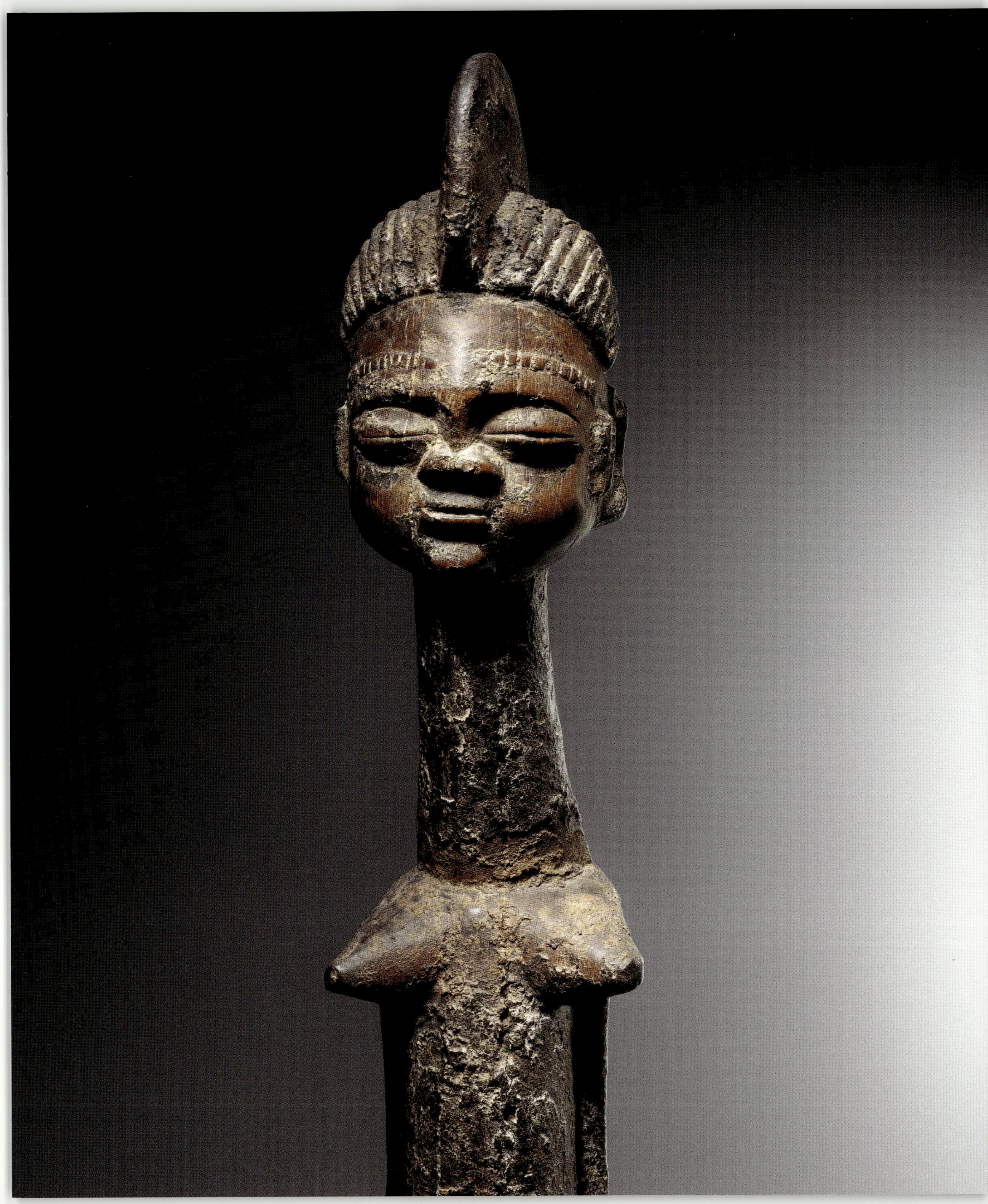

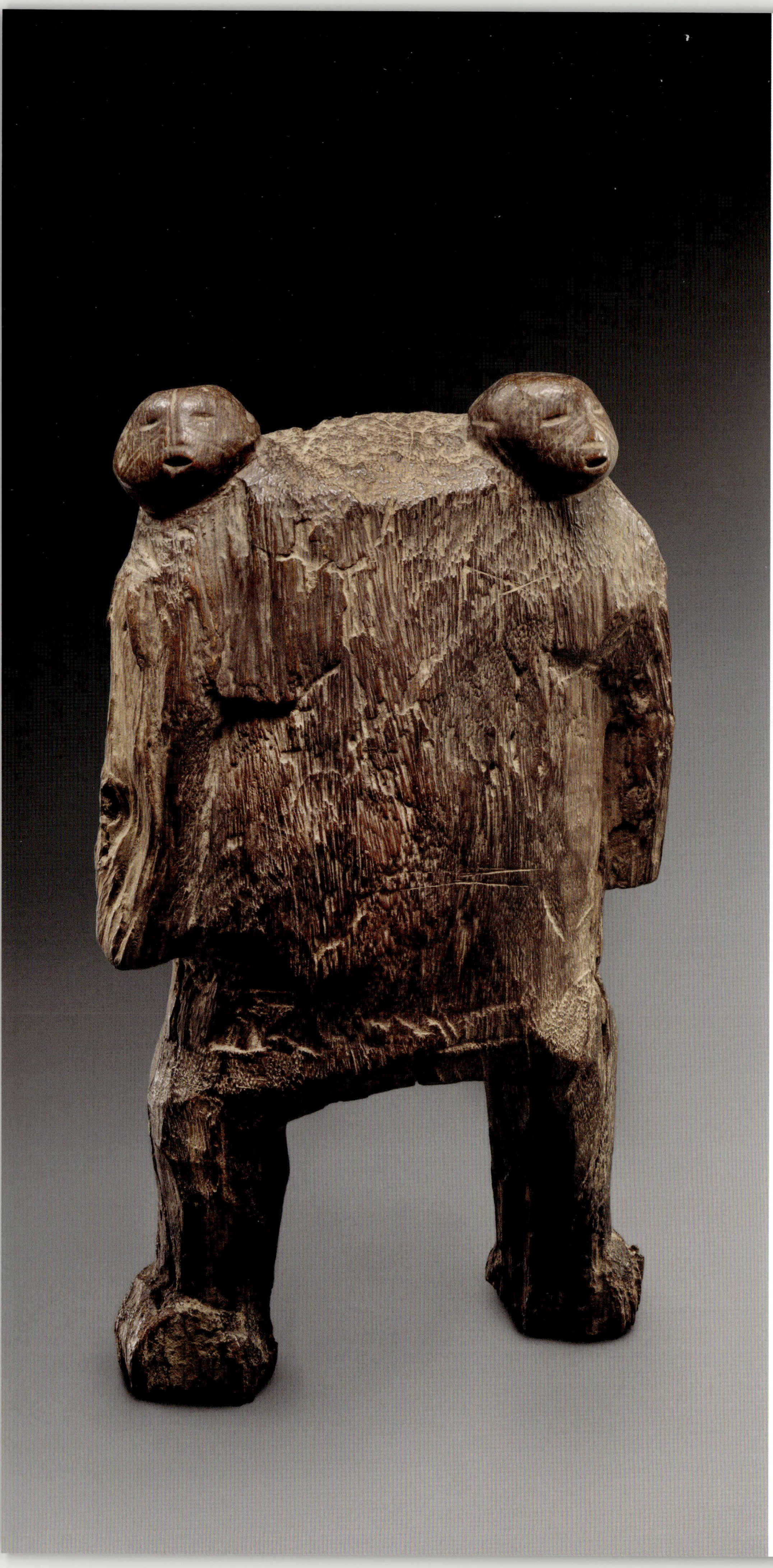

Lamba-Naodem statue
Northern Togo, H. 31 cm

The Lamba and the Naodem-Losso live in the Kante region to the north of Kara. They have kept the tradition of making figurines to record the frequent birth of mostly non-identical twins in the area. This statue discovered around twenty years ago is probably a condensed version of one of these representations, a single body surmounted by two heads. According to some, the piece actually portrays a couple, or is simply an object depicting good and evil in a single body. [PA]

Bamana sculpture
Mali, L. 35 cm

Unlike many classical objects that are given the form of bovids and have become well known since the Dakar-Djibouti expedition, this *boli* sporting two sharp blades on its back has the appearance of a menacing animal to ward off or to cast magic spells. It is meant to depict a guard dog or other protecting animal, whose keen sense of smell can detect sorcerers and their evil charms, such as the bakongo dogs used by the *nganga* witchdoctors among the Kongo. The constant libations poured over the object have created an exceptionally smooth lacquered patina. This sculpture is comparable to certain Fon objects known as *tron* found along the former Slave Coast, which have an identical coating. [PA]

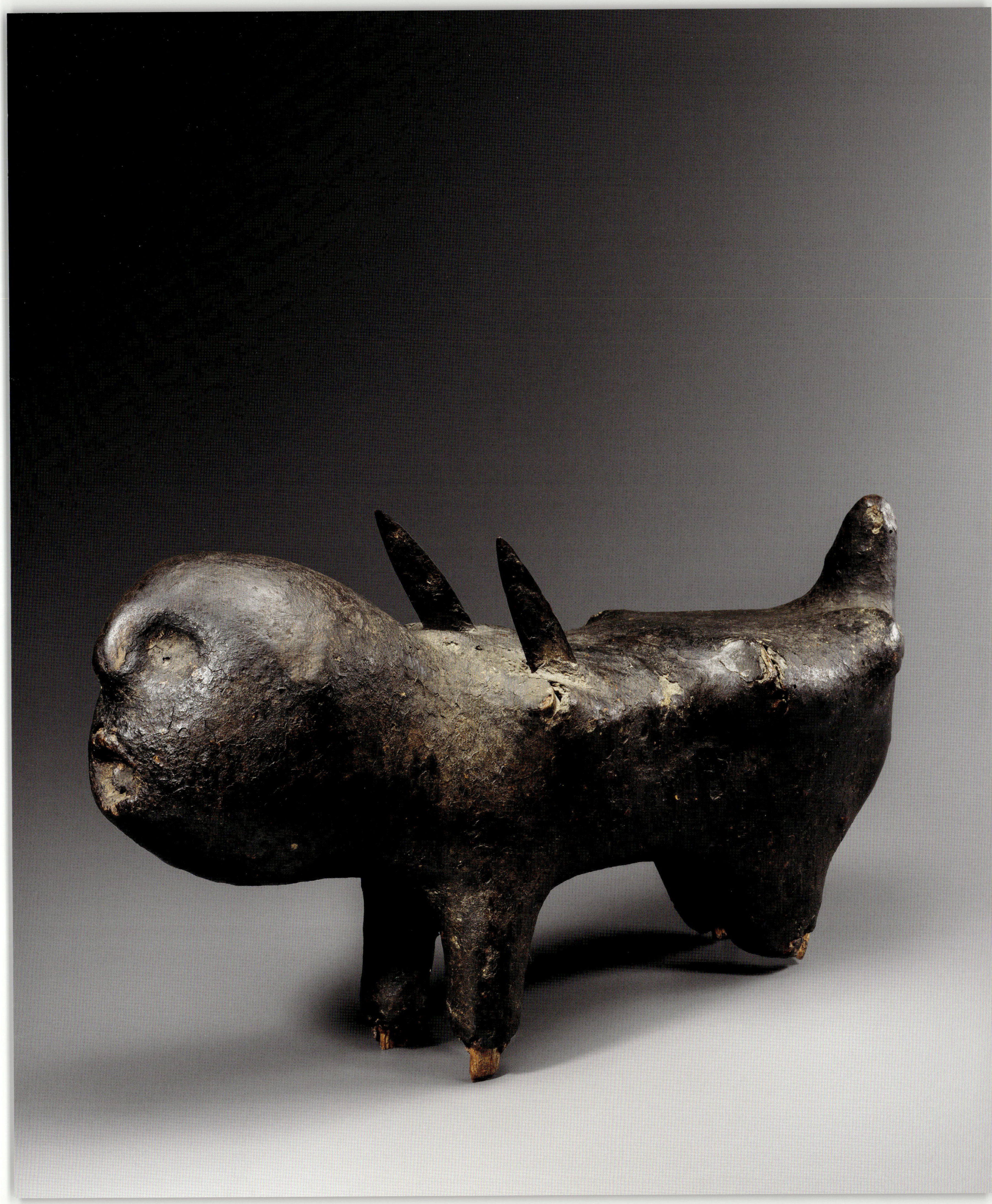

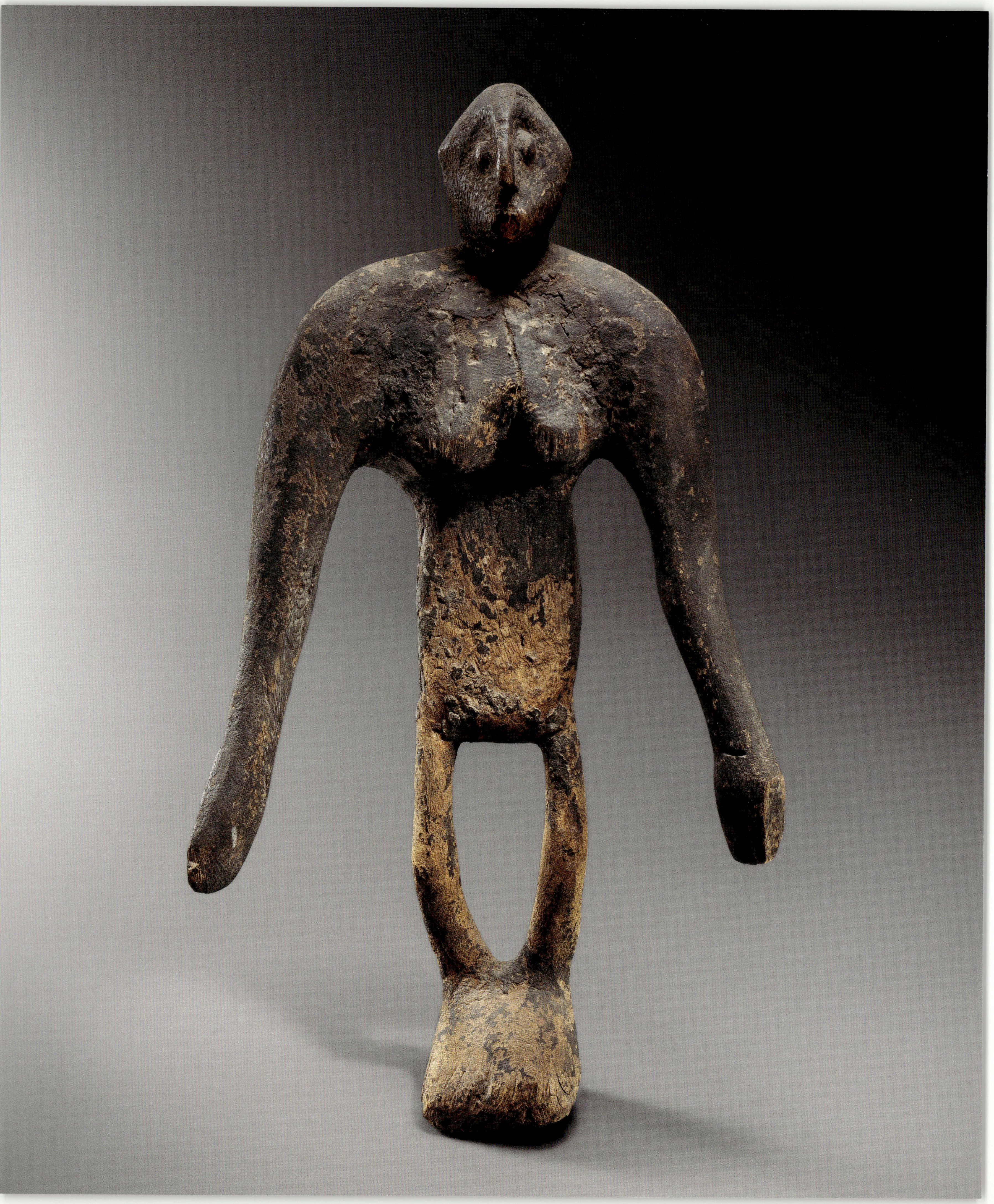

Statue
Nigeria (?), H. 58 cm

This female figure is completely covered with a thick brown coating created by libations poured during ritual sacrifices. The underlying form, with its highly expressive face and broad chest, creates a powerful effect. The feet are not visible, having blended into the base of the statue. The general style of this untypical object brings to mind certain Montol statues from Nigeria that also often have broad shoulders and similar simian features, as well as being made of a comparable type of fibrous wood. Attributions are always tricky when we have no information regarding where a piece was collected, which is the case here. Ethnic groups in the sub-Saharan region enjoy close relations and often share rituals, according to their geographic distribution. For instance, different styles are frequently interwoven among the Bamana, Mossi, Lobi, and Gurunsi and further south along the border with Ghana. [PA]

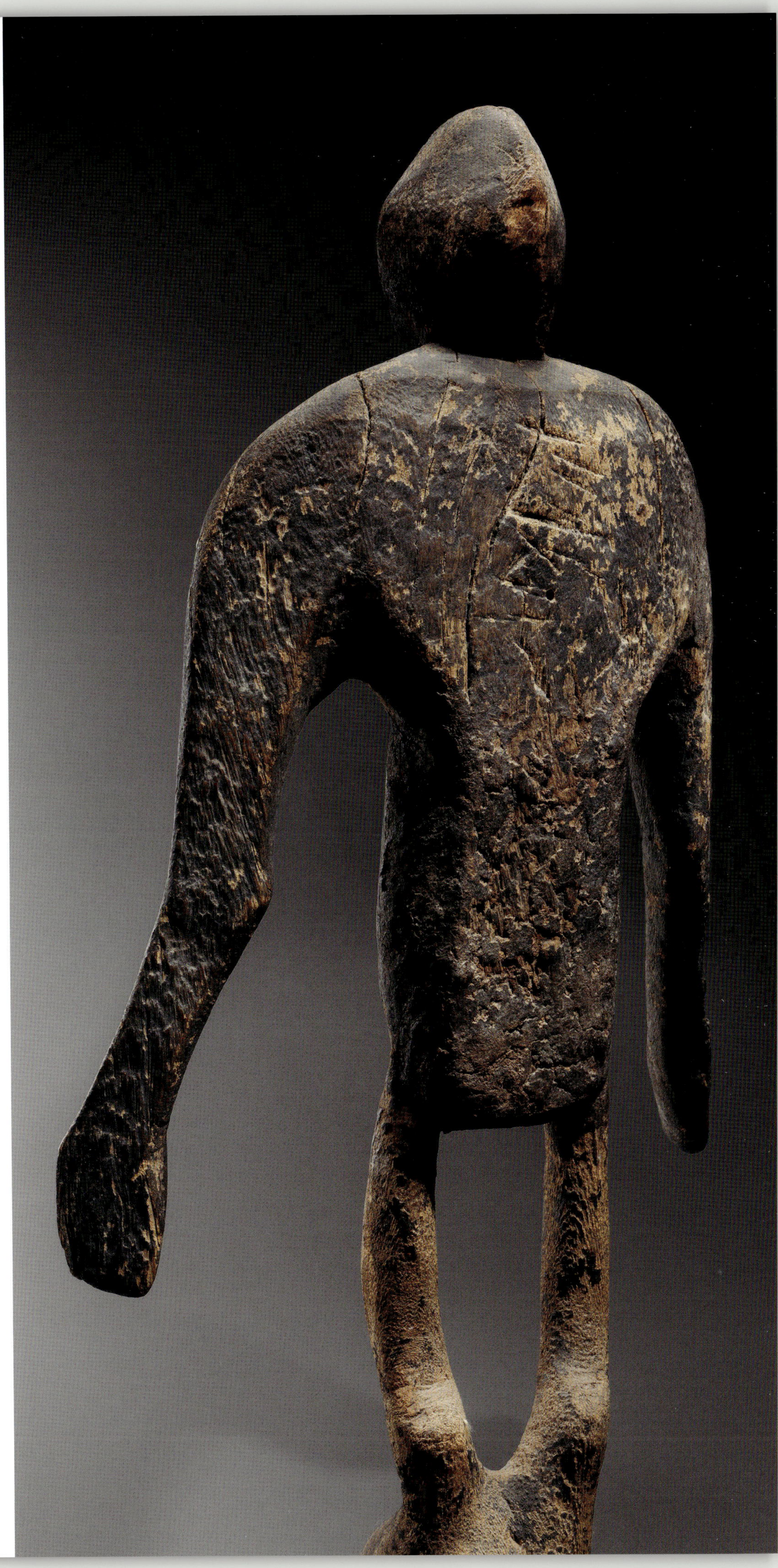

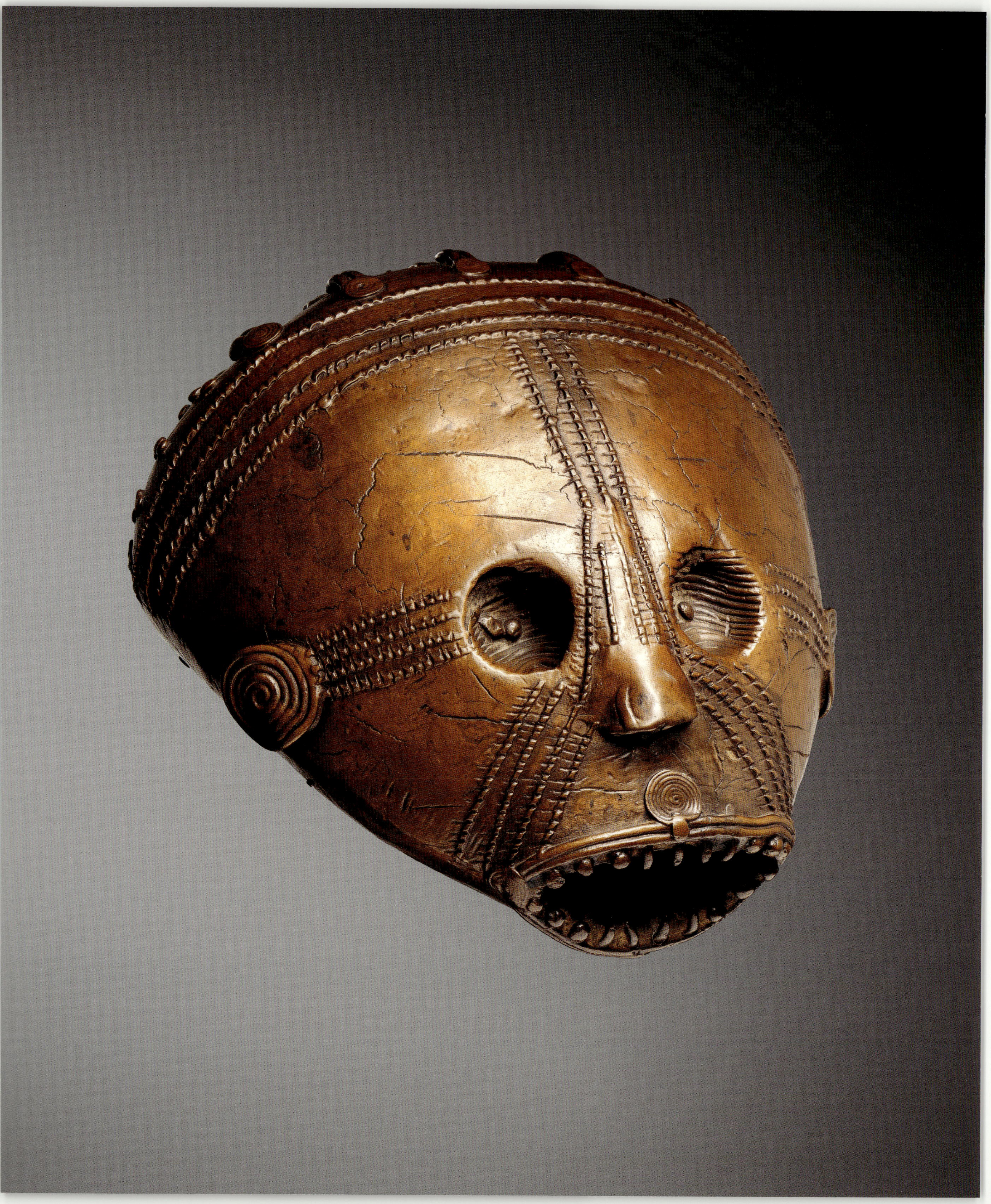

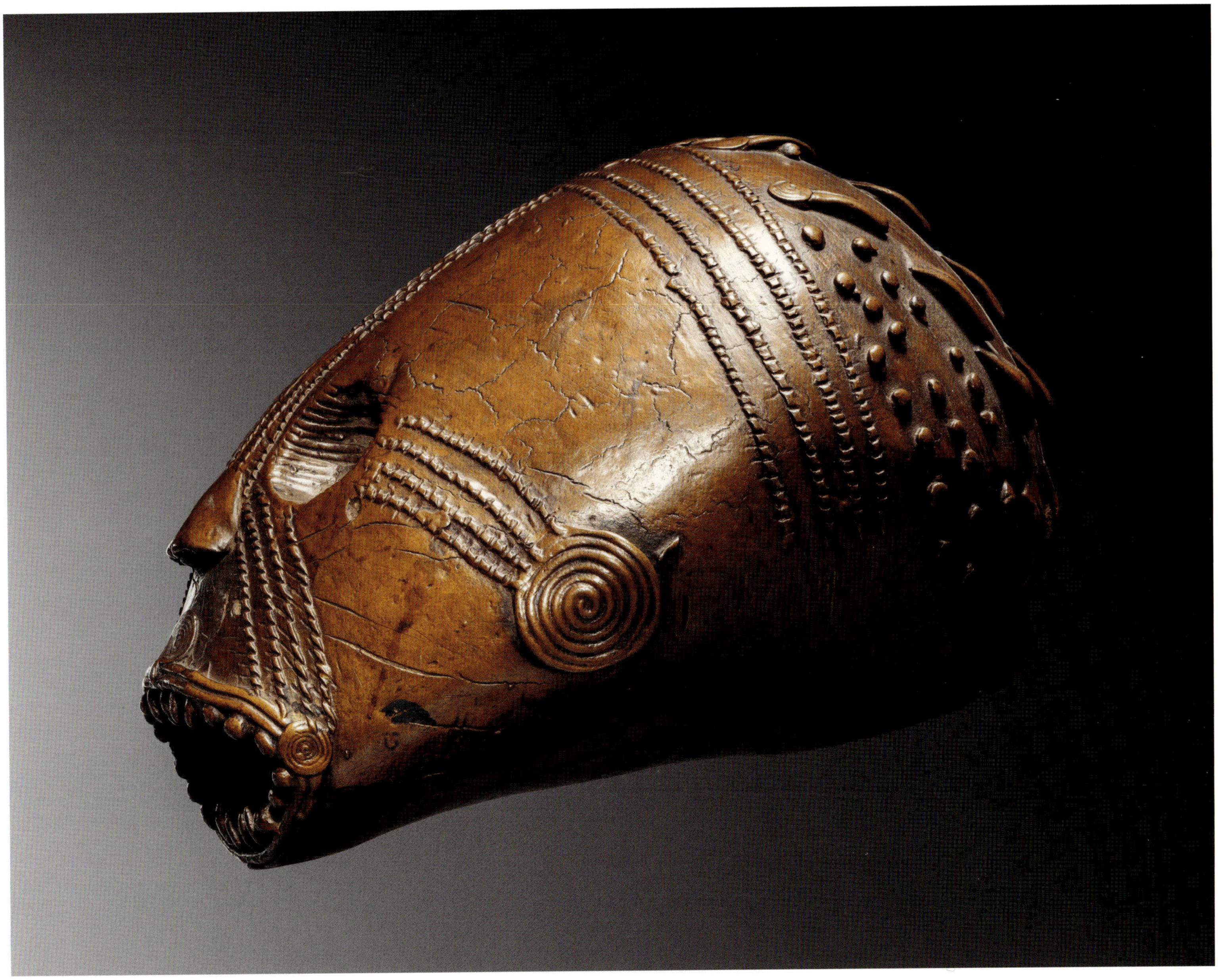

Votive head
Cross River, Nigeria, H. 17.5 cm

The secret Efik *Ekpe* (*Ngbe* among the Ejagham) male age grade society, placed under the tutelary aegis of the spirit of the leopard, was once an important feature of the ancient city of Calabar, where it was employed in business activities from the end of the seventeenth century, especially the slave trade, ensuring peace and equality among its members. The *Ekpe* material to which only initiates have access was kept in its lair: reference to the fierce, voracious leopard guaranteed its aspect would remain secret. [HJ]

>
Tiv (?) statue
Nigeria, H. 30.5 cm

Metalworking, particularly involving copper alloys, has spread throughout the region of the middle reaches of the Benue. Figurative axes, sceptres, rings, and several types of small statues cast using the lost wax technique are examples of the art of the itinerant art casters, notably among the Abakwariga, one of the cultures along the Benue corridor, which were encountered by the first travellers in the region (Balkie, 1856). It is not easy to attribute a function and a precise origin to such an original figure, but one can hazard a guess that it served as protection against evil forces, accentuated by the powerful gesture of the hands held wide open. [HJ]

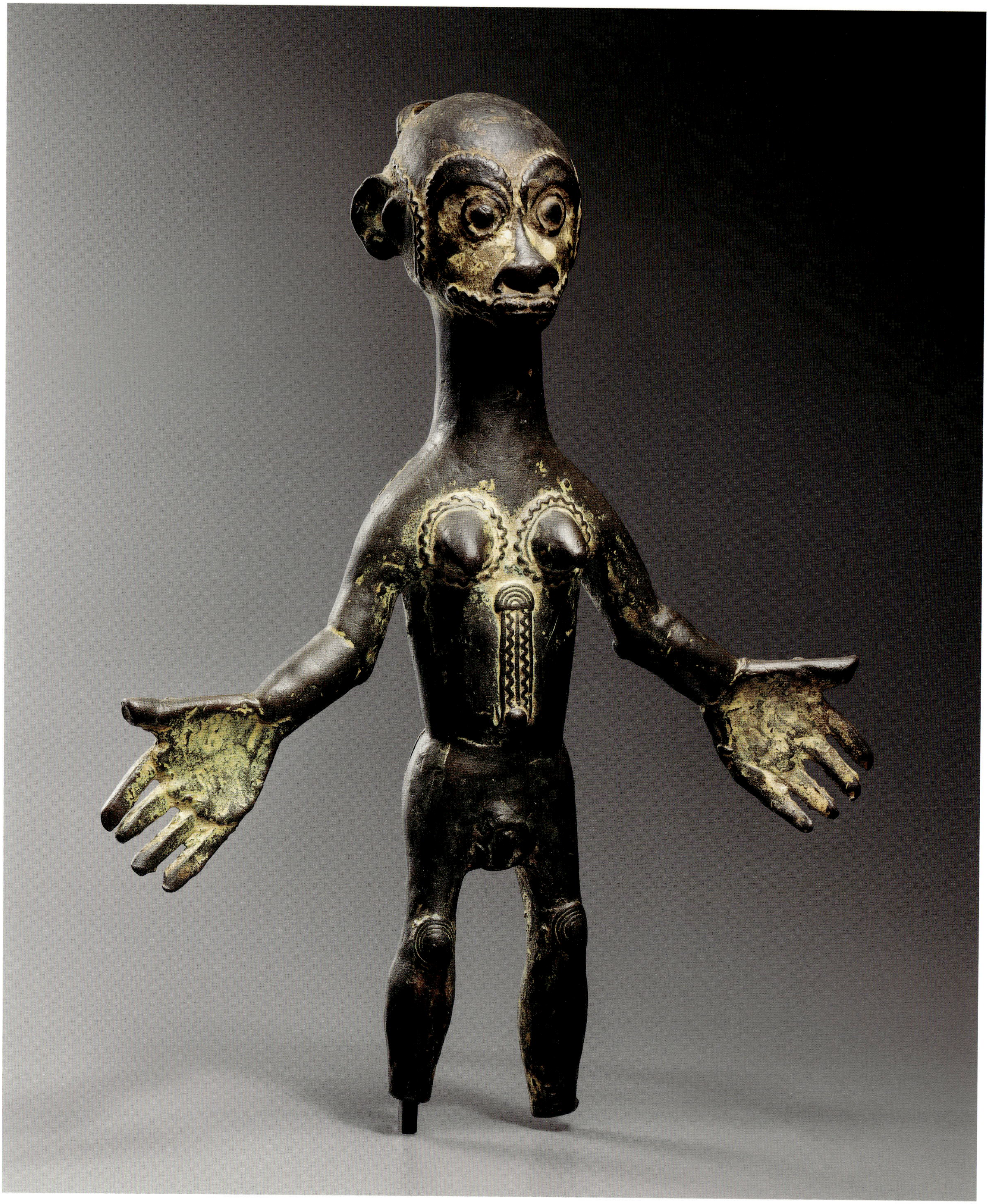

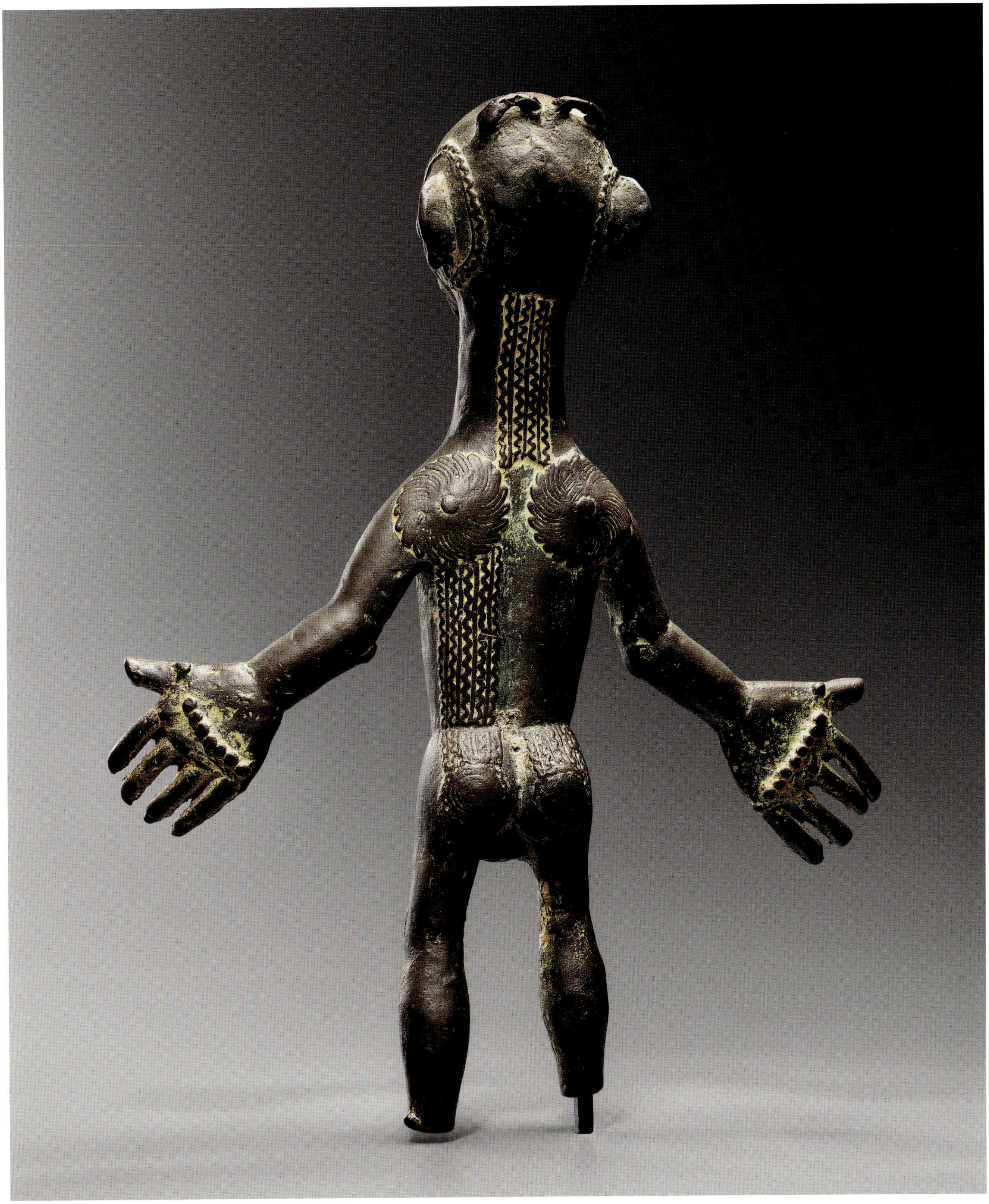

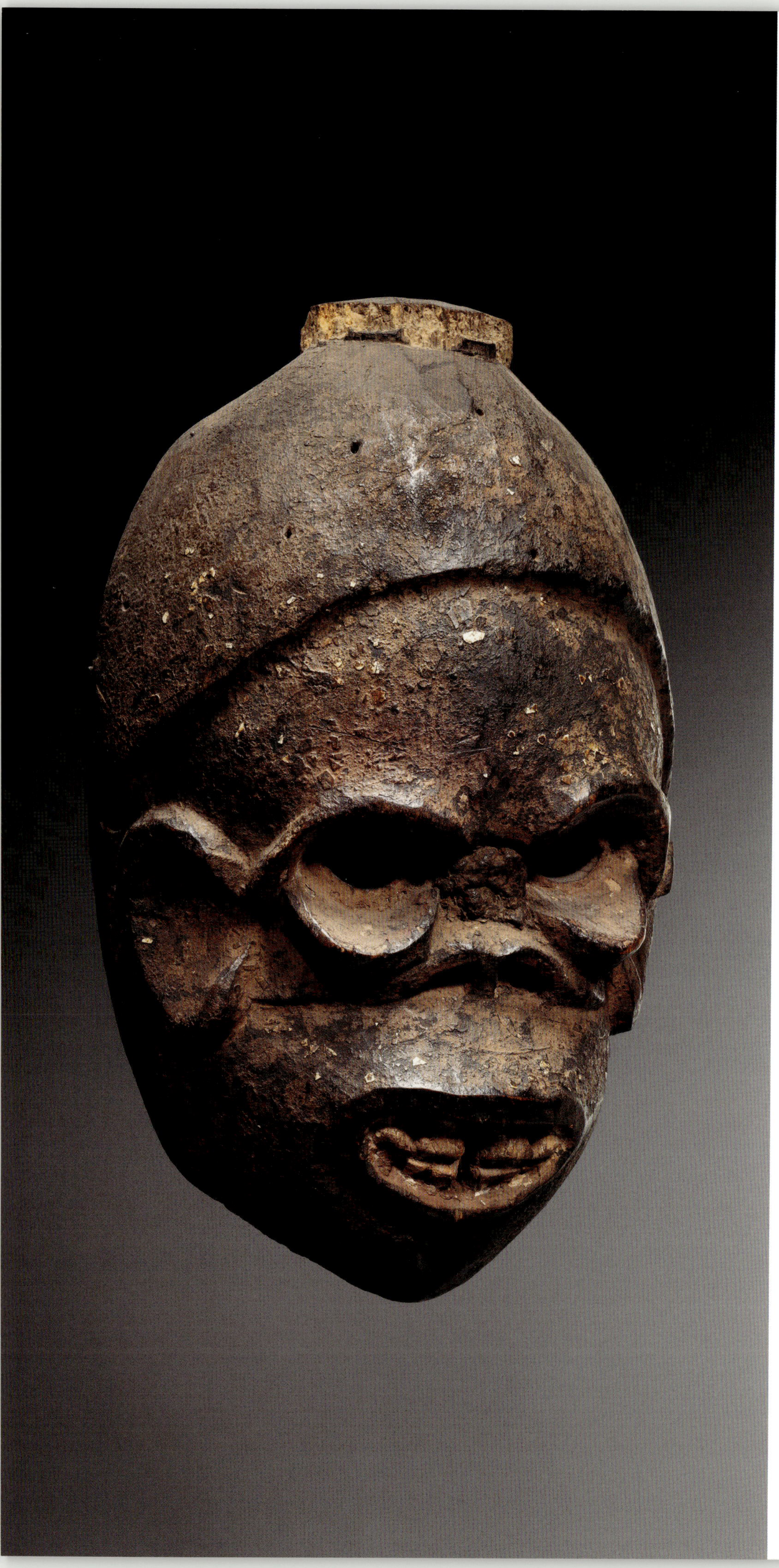

Ibibio mask
Nigeria, H. 25.5 cm

Multiple characteristics of this face, from its empty round eye sockets, nose summarily suggested by just the nostrils modelled in relief and the mouth open to reveal metal teeth, combine to blur the boundary between an example of unhealthy facial features and an expressive depiction of a living person suffering from a disease. Drawing upon the most devastatingly disfiguring tropical diseases, such as leprosy and yaws, this mask was a protection against the negative and anti-social forces that threatened to cause personal and collective harm in Ibibio communities. [HJ]

Mask
Middle Benue (?), Nigeria, H. 41.5 cm

This enigmatic mask made up of an oblong skull whose jaws look like a long beak and a double set of empty eyes set on either side of a nasal ridge depicts a supernatural spirit that has emerged from the bush and is endowed with a subtle combination of powers. Both its origins and function are unknown. Its smooth and unusual appearance—from the formal point of view it shares features with the *sura* bird-beak masks covered in ochre and embellished with jequirity beans that are found in the plateau region, or the Montol *gugwon* crocodile masks, or even the Jukun *Aku-Ma* mask, a hybrid mask consisting of a half-open beak with buffalo horns. These masks are used by the village communities of this rugged area during farming rituals. They are carried horizontally and combine anthropomorphic and zoomorphic features. [HJ]

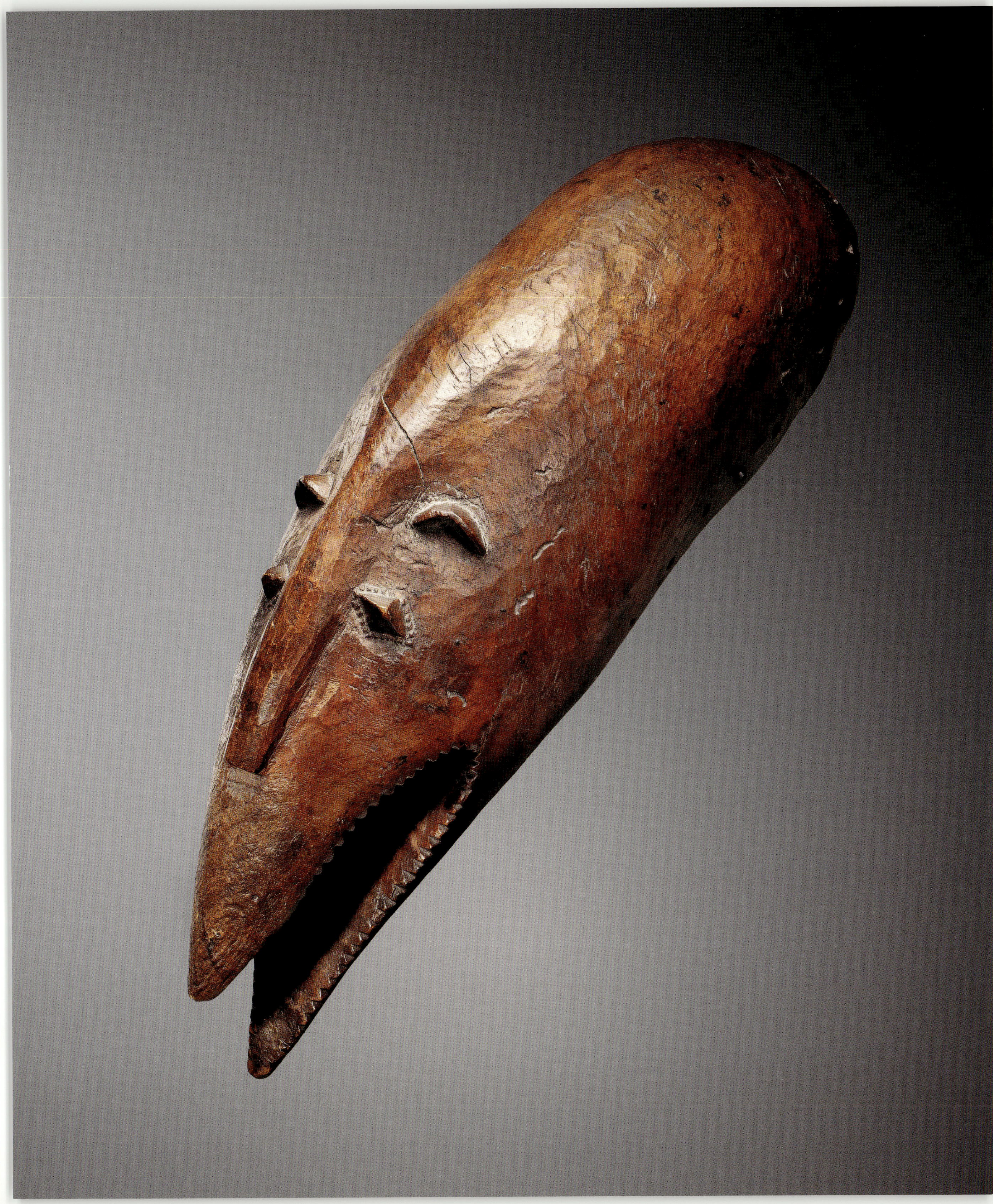

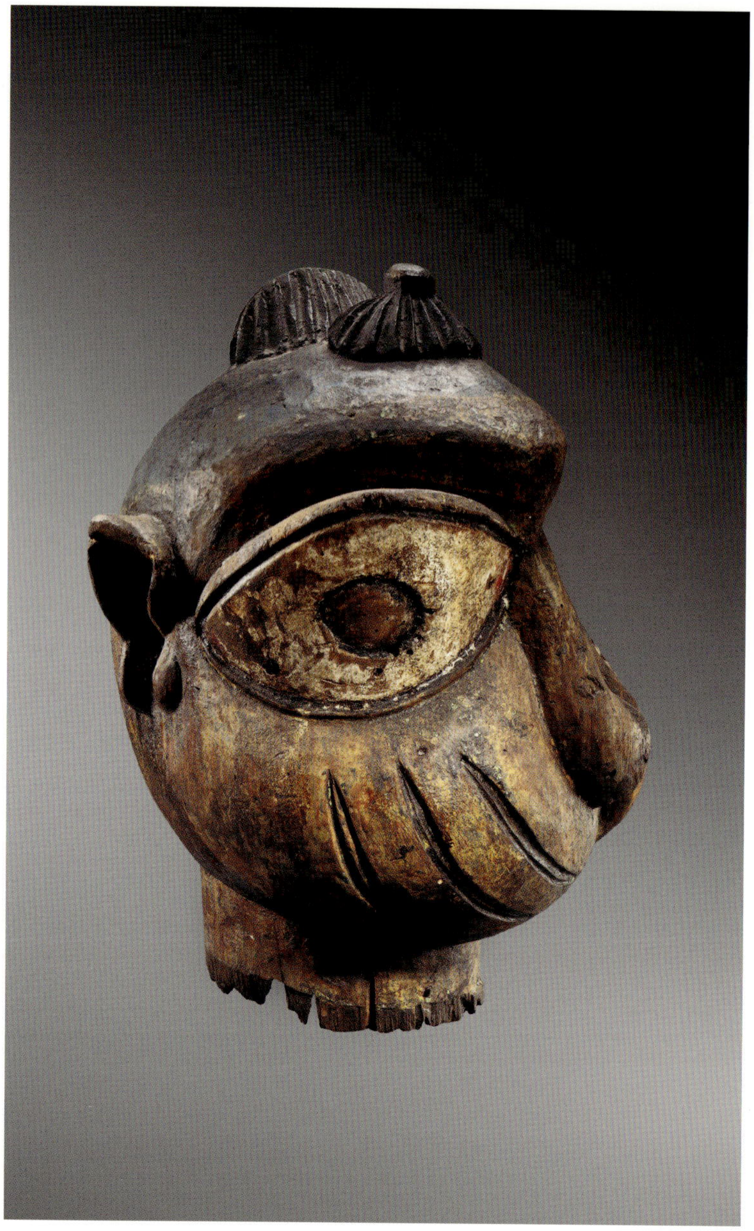

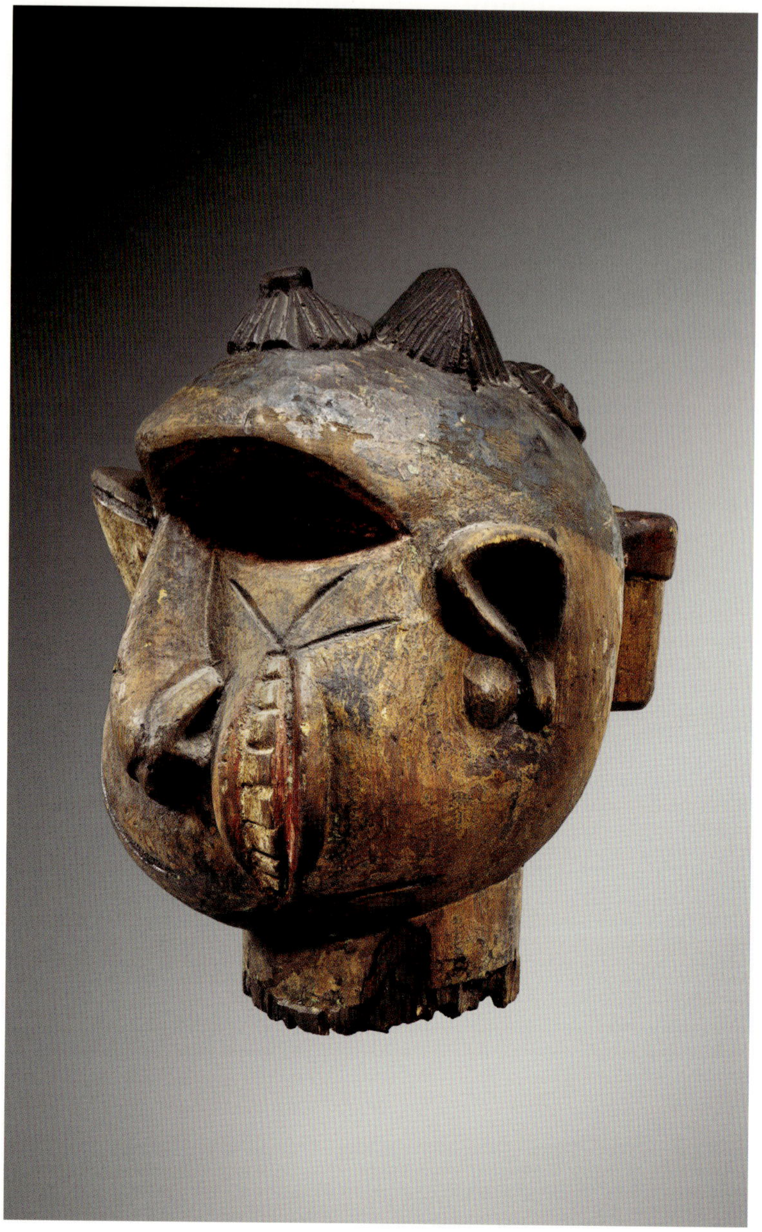

Yoruba head
Nigeria, H. 33 cm

So-called "sickness" masks and crests often allude to diseases or accidents that permanently alter a person's appearance: in this case, facial paralysis is depicted particularly powerfully. This Yoruba head, whose huge left eye juts out of its socket, while the mouth is almost vertical, could have been a source of inspiration for Picasso. In an iconographic repertoire that celebrates life, it serves to draw attention to the needs and the ambiguity of the ancestors, who are both benevolent and malicious at the same time.[1] [HJ]

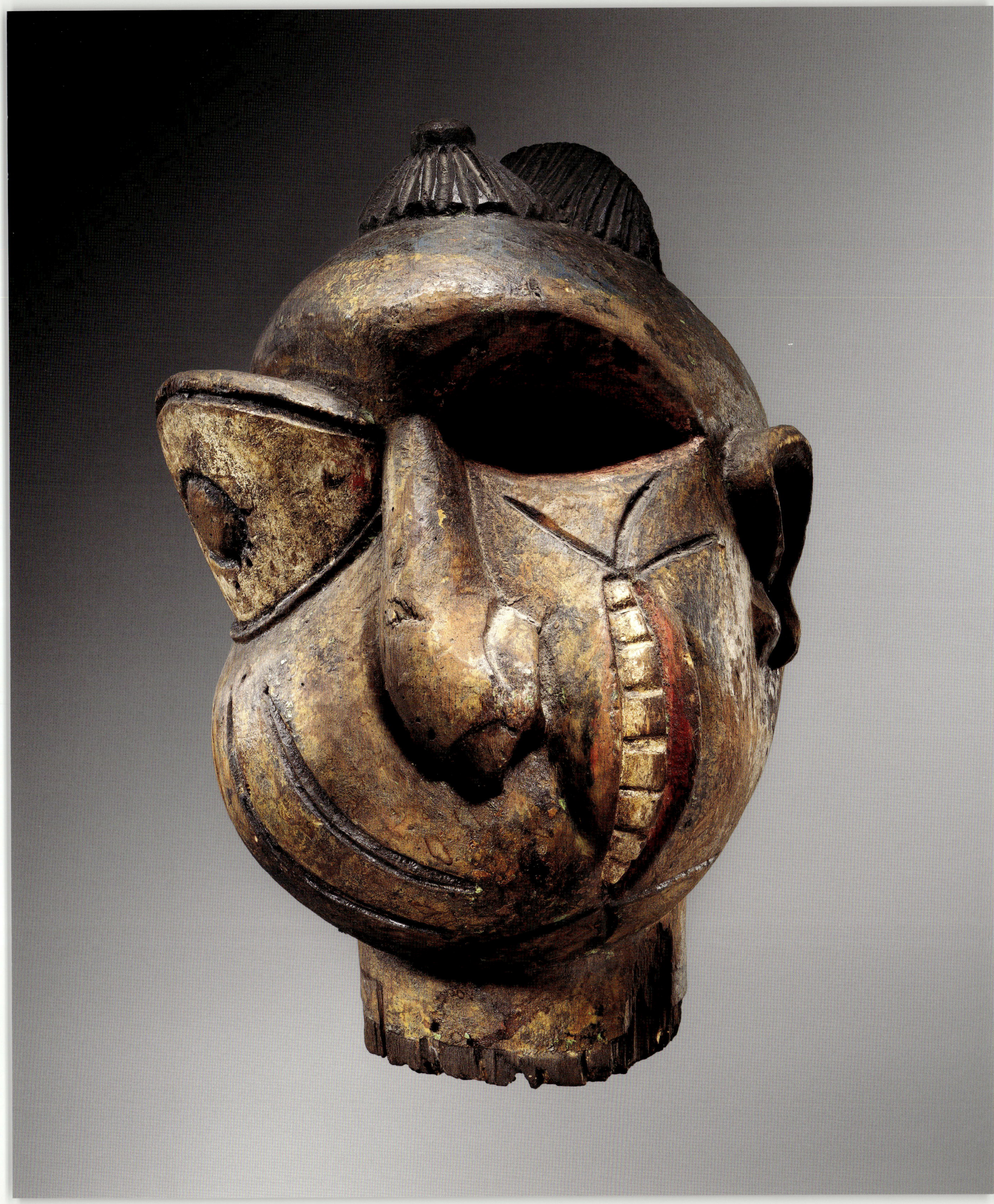

Jukun Wurbo statue
Middle Benue, Nigeria, H. 82 cm

The Jukun of the Taraba and Wase valleys in the northeastern part of Jukun lands have developed a statuary art for their shrines. These statues were attributed to the Wurbo by Arnold Rubin[1] and display remarkable morphological symmetry, coded gestures, stretched earlobes fitted with plugs, crenelated hairstyle and beard shaped into three braids in the male figures. Depicted standing upright, with hands resting on their hips, these figures have a curious flat face that projects forwards at the end of a long neck, usually adorned with rings. It has been suggested that the oldest depict a mask wearer.[2] In their natural context, they were coated with red and white pigments and covered with various decorations, a cloth covering the lower body, a headband, plumed headdress, and pearl necklace. Many of these formed husband and wife couples, although they tend to court sexual ambiguity, which would probably have ensured greater spiritual effectiveness. They were sometimes gathered together in a group to represent an extended family, or were kept inside a container used in worship, which would protect them from the ravages of wood-eating insects.[3] While there, they would receive offerings and prayers would be addressed to them. People might carry them around in their arms and dance with them during healing rituals, partly hiding the holder's body and face, or they might witness the initiations of the young at harvest time. The figures embodied the spiritual principles of the *Mam* healing cult and as such would be present during the witchdoctor's trance. [HJ]

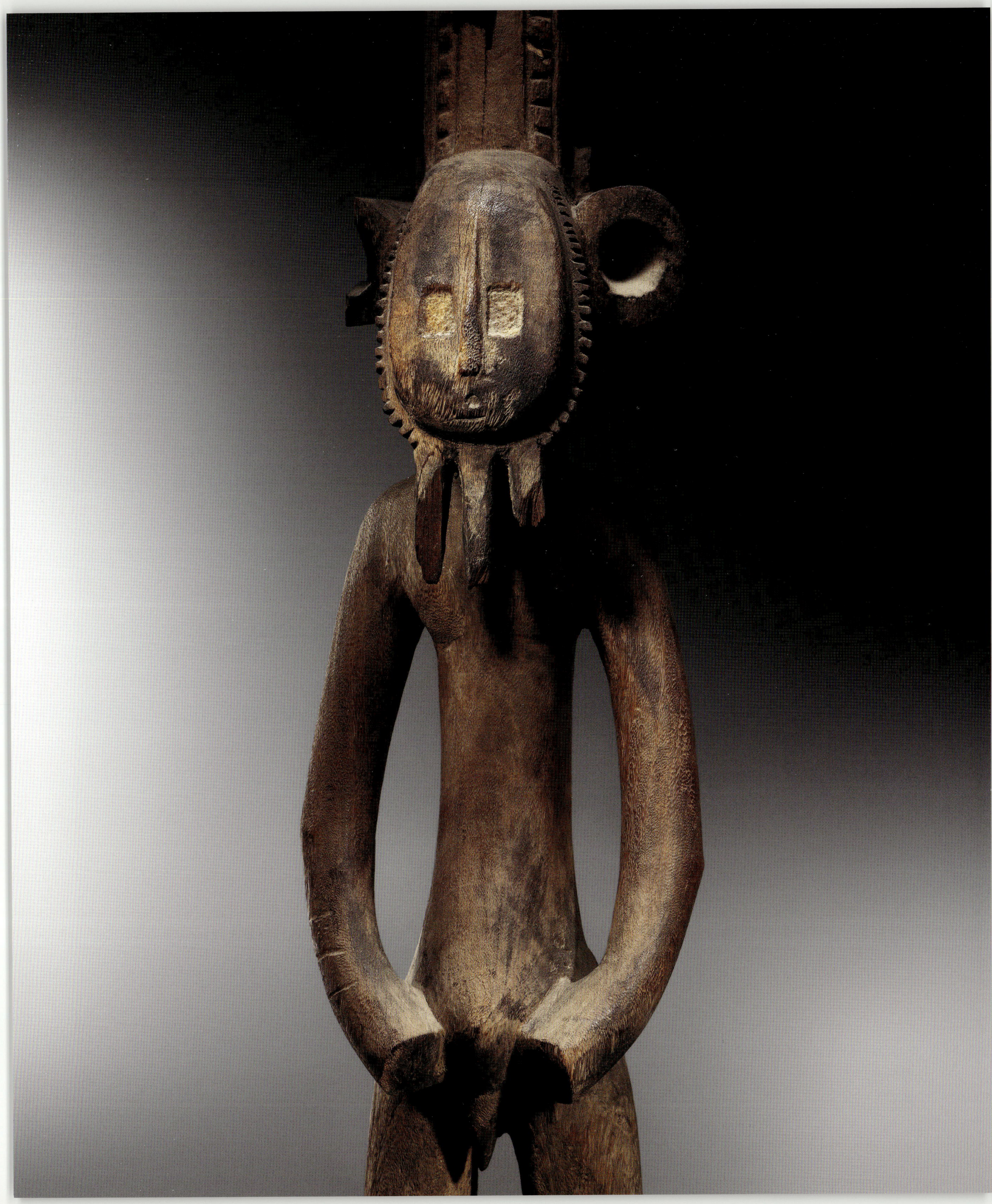

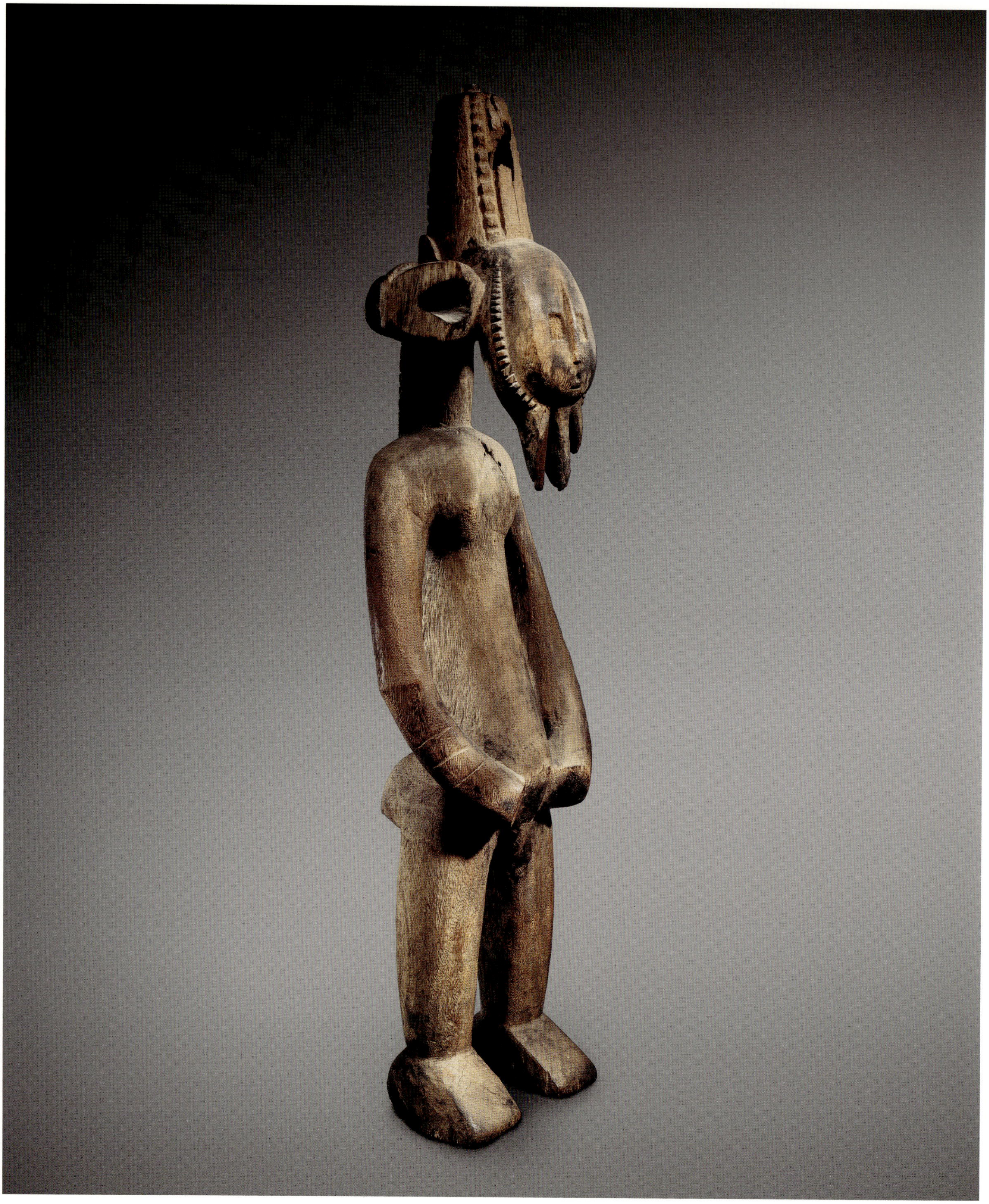

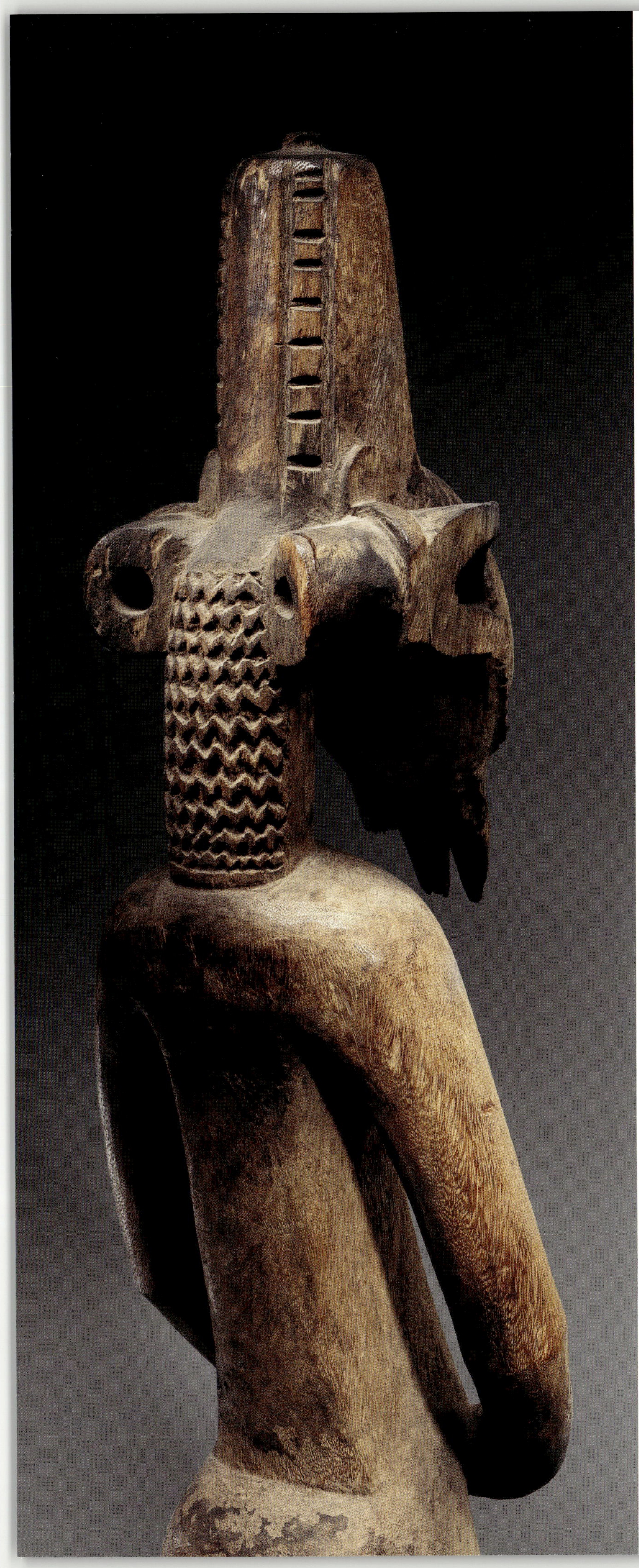
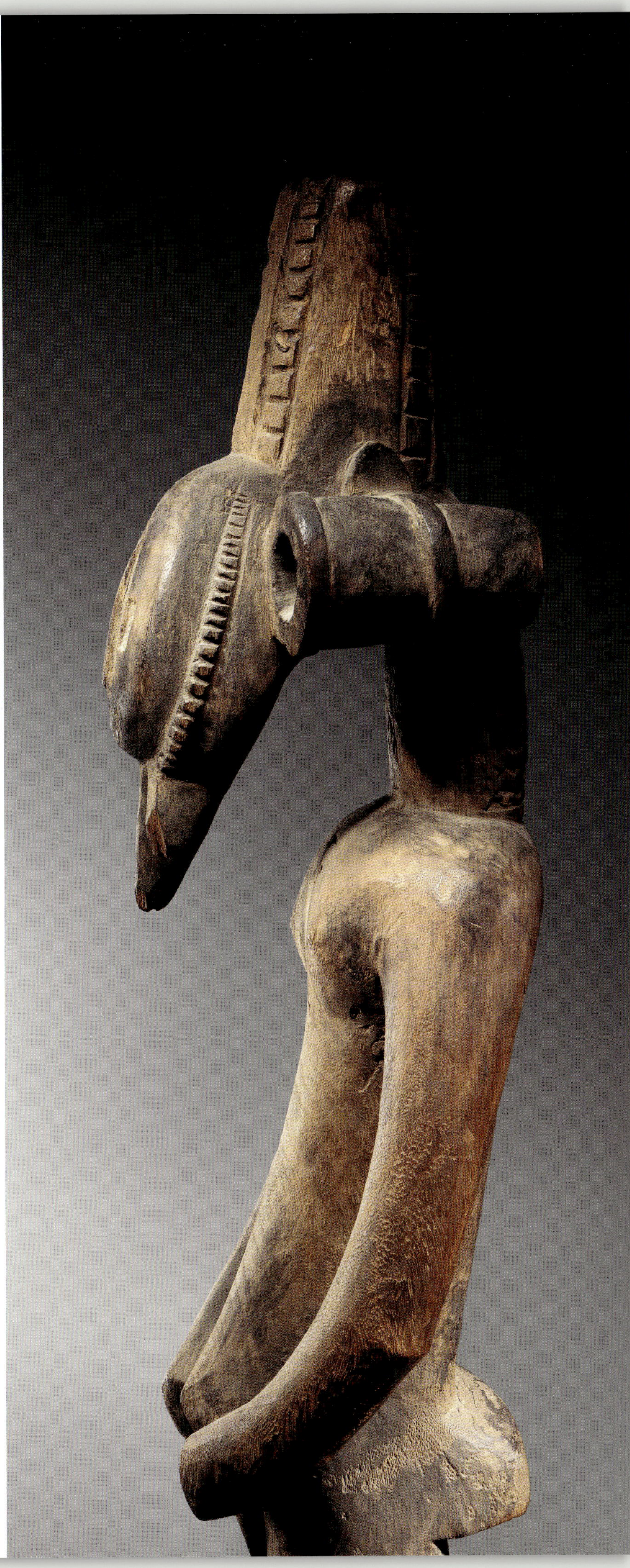

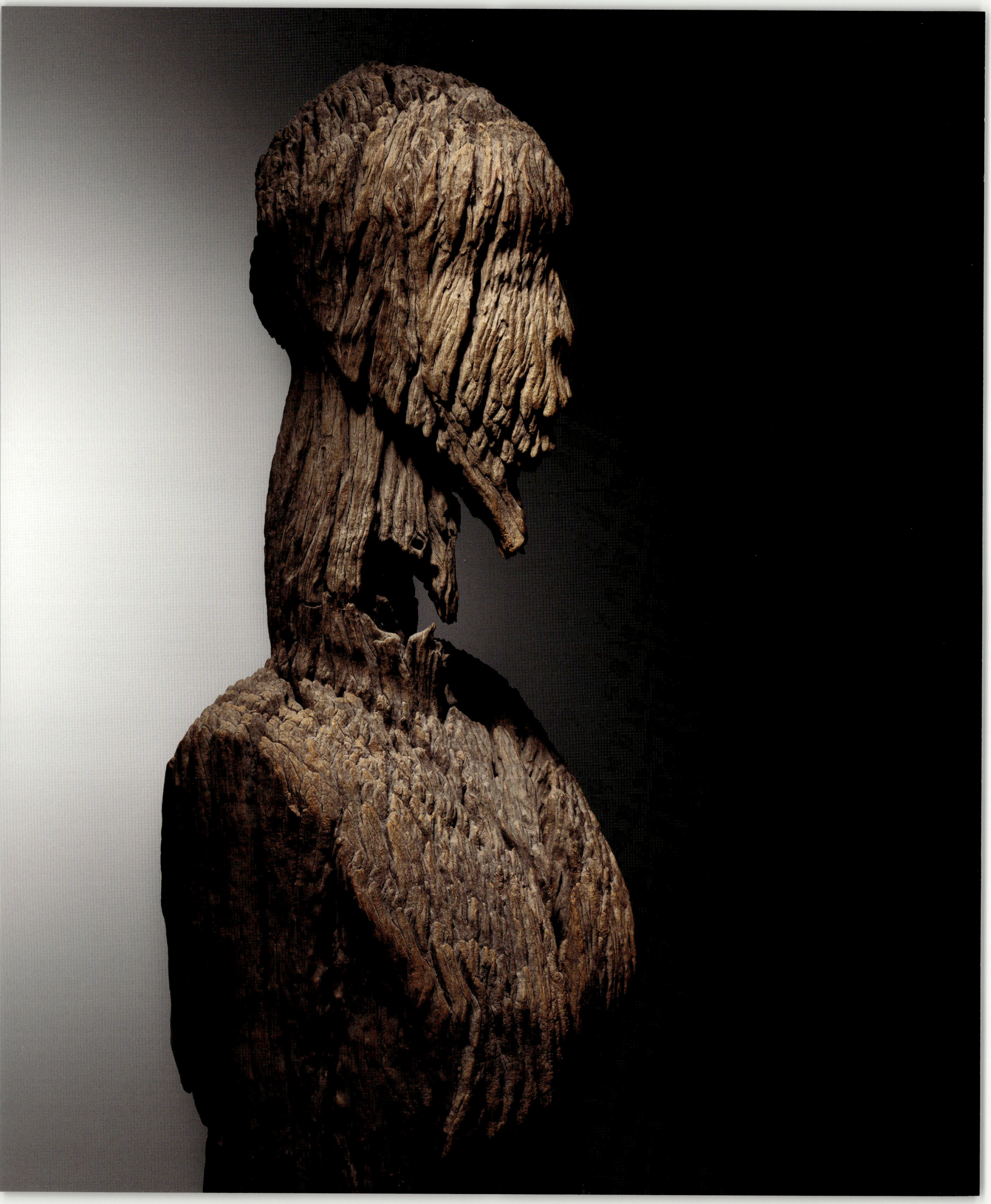

Mboye statue
East of the Gongola valley, Nigeria, H. 118 cm
1309–61 (64.8%, C14 test by CIRAM, Bordeaux)

A small corpus of large male figures made of heavily weathered wood revealing several centuries of use, confirmed by a number of C14 tests (fourteenth/sixteenth centuries), has been identified and attributed to the upper reaches of the Benue, more precisely, the eastern part of the Gongola valley (Mboye/Yungur). These pieces reached the art market in the late 1960s and their hieratic poses and naturalistic proportions immediately attracted attention. The elegant handling of the thighs, arms and pectorals can be clearly seen in spite of the heavily eroded surface. The broad shoulders and powerful muscles are highlighted, even exaggerated,[1] in order to stress the figure's strength and maturity. The hair is always very carefully picked out, as is the small triangular beard, ending in a characteristic point, which is echoed in the figurative ritual bowls of the Yungur. Pearl necklaces or body scarification are occasionally added. The figure has a long neck and the face seems calm and concentrated, with the mouth closed and the eyes picked out under the eyelids. As in this example, the figures are generally viewed frontally, the arms being held straight down, close against the body to suggest vigilance. The life-size dimensions of these figures are unusual for this region and are a throwback to a time when standing statues of deceased chiefs were erected for the whole community to see; relations with the spirits of the ancestors were maintained through offerings and libations of ochre poured over the statues. E. Meek suggests these figures are in fact portraits of "earth-priests" who were in charge of rituals in those distant times. The Mboye kept up the tradition until the end of the twentieth century. The practice of holding a second funeral in Mboye lands, in which the deceased are evoked through a carved wooden effigy that is then kept in a consecrated place, along with skulls and ritual pots, was still current in the 1980s, as Maria Berns saw during a field trip.[2] [HJ]

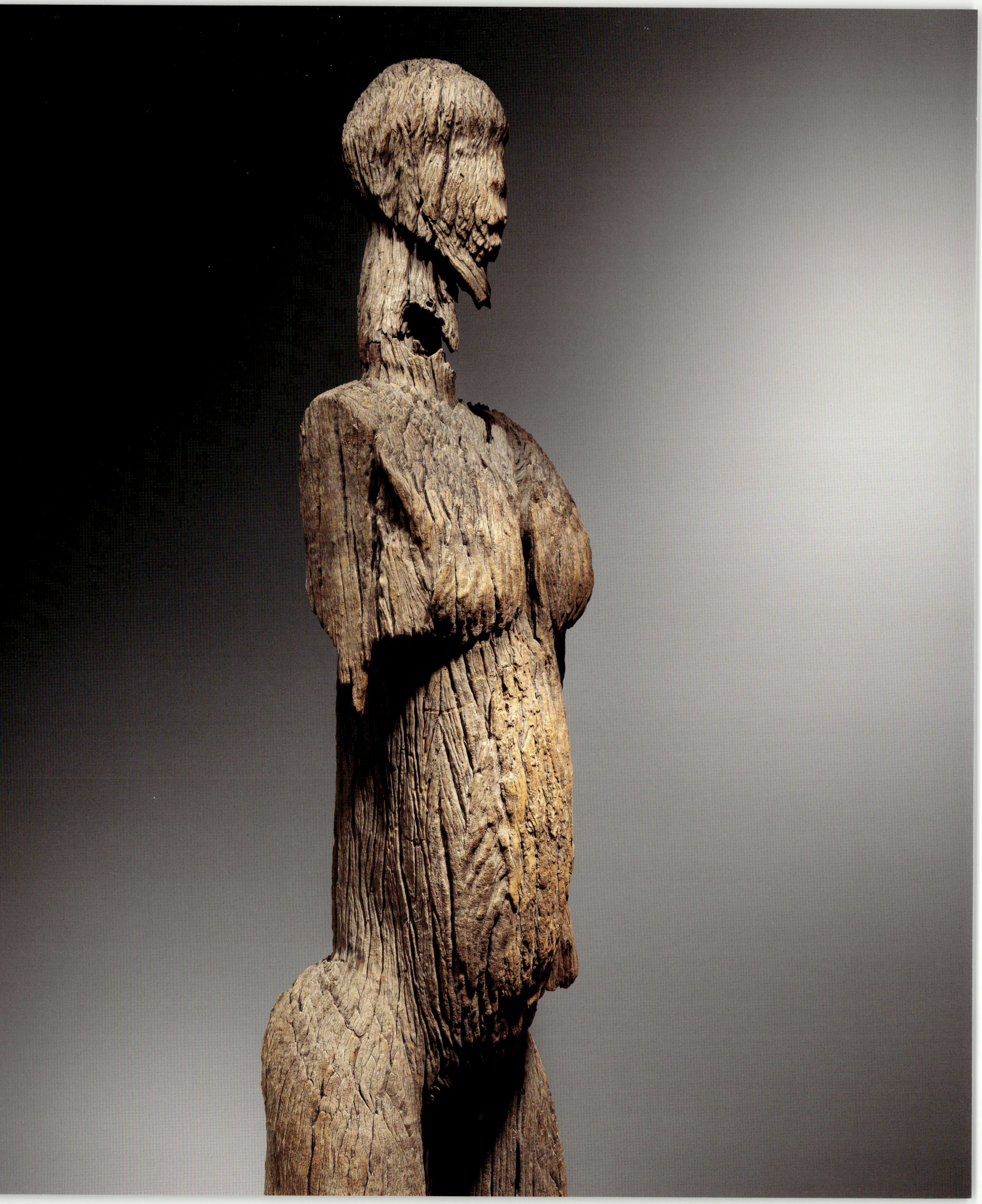

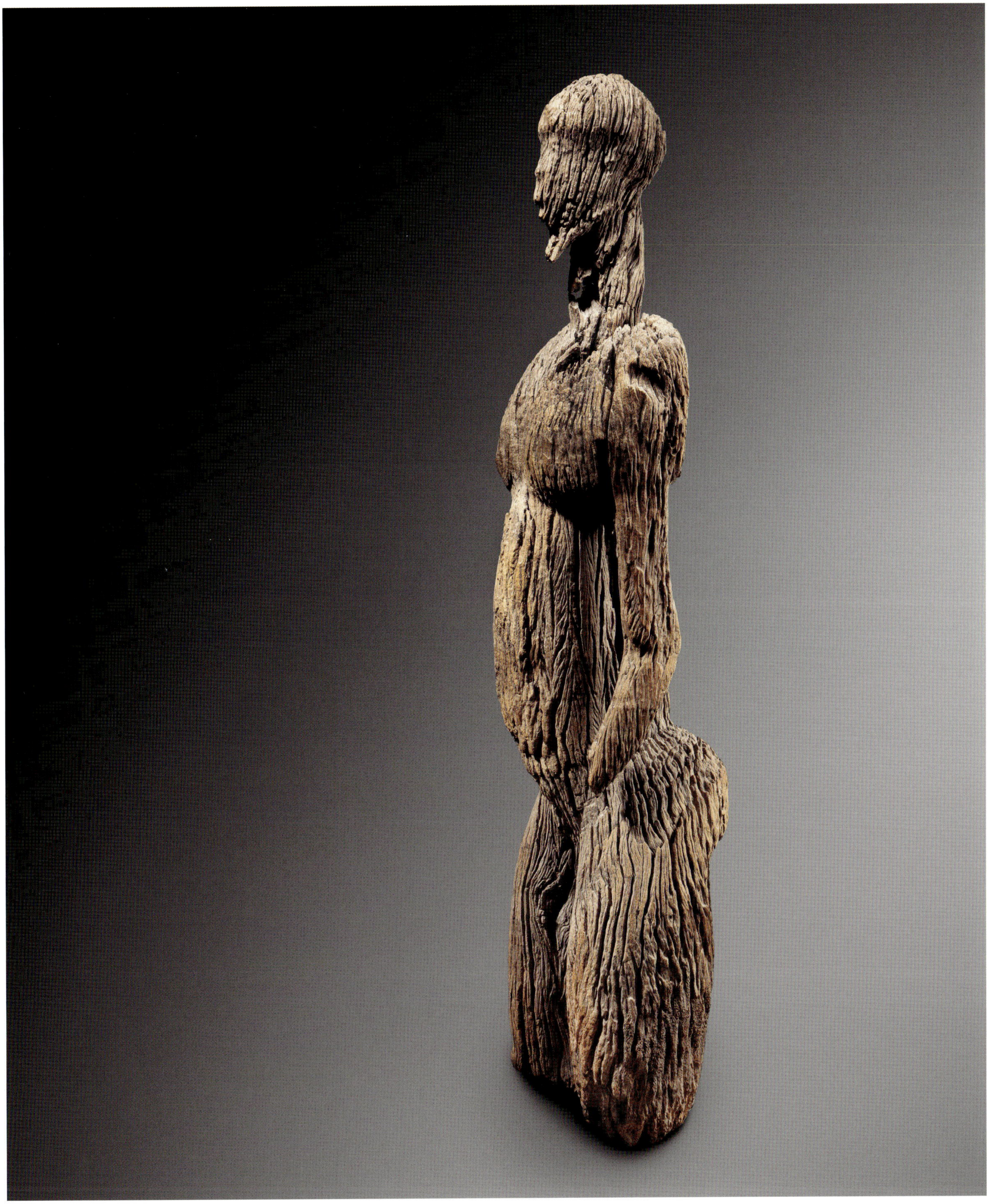

Mbembe drum figure
Nigeria, H. 71 cm
seventeenth–eighteenth century

The *ikoro* is the monumental sacred drum of the Mbembe, who live in the region of the River Ewayon. The drums are five metres long and were placed under the tutelary authority of lineage founders depicted as drum fronts.[1] Two seated figures, a warrior and a mother and child would be depicted on a platform projecting from the slit drum cylinder, which could be heard over ten kilometres away.[2] These instruments of assembly were associated with societies wielding power, on the model of male age grade societies where each level was reached on payment for the right of access. They were used during rituals, especially the warrior society rite, which consisted in presenting the head of a defeated foe to the drum, a practice that was banned by the British colonial authorities at the beginning of the twentieth century, leading to the rapid fading away of the use of these instruments. [HJ]

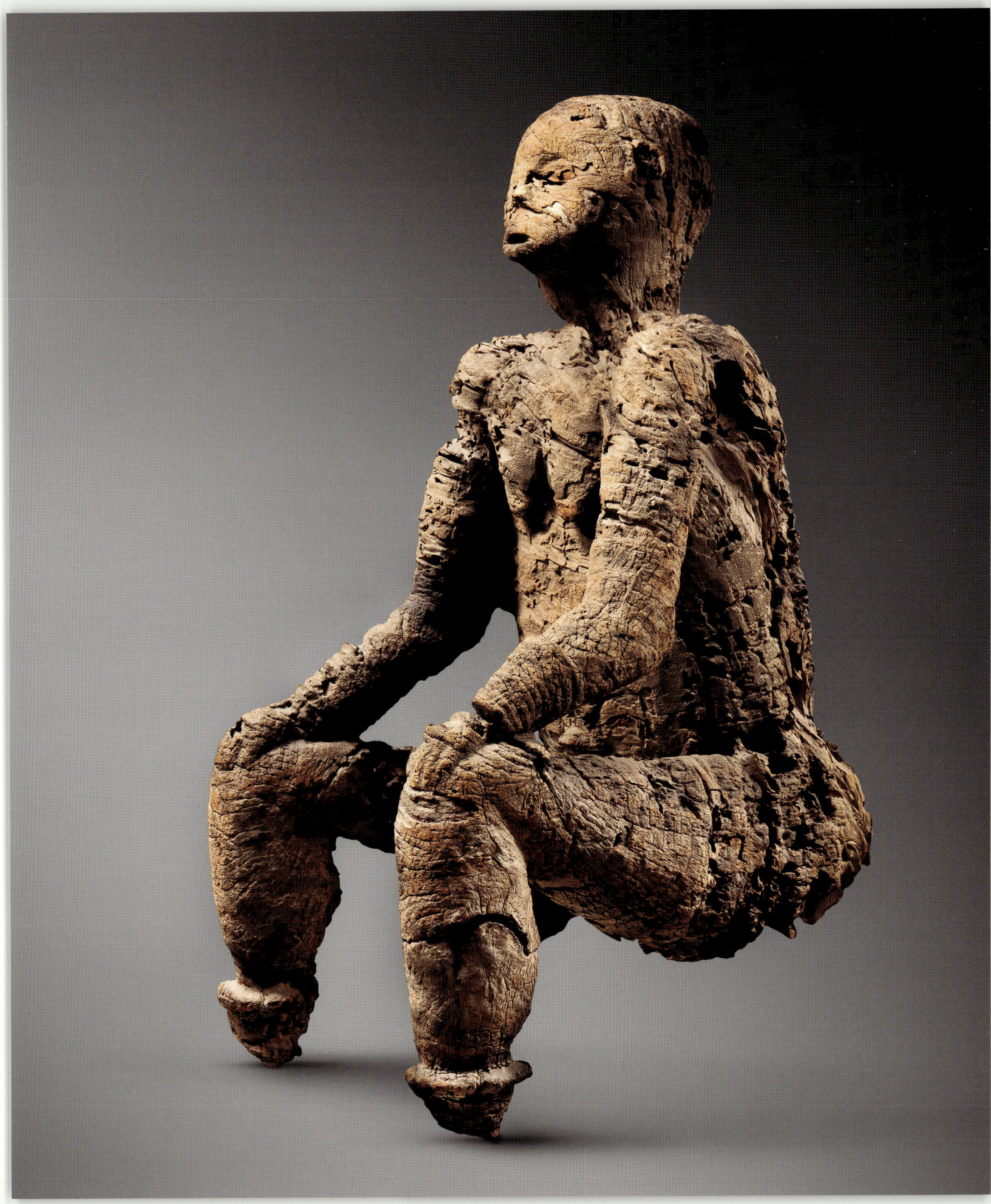

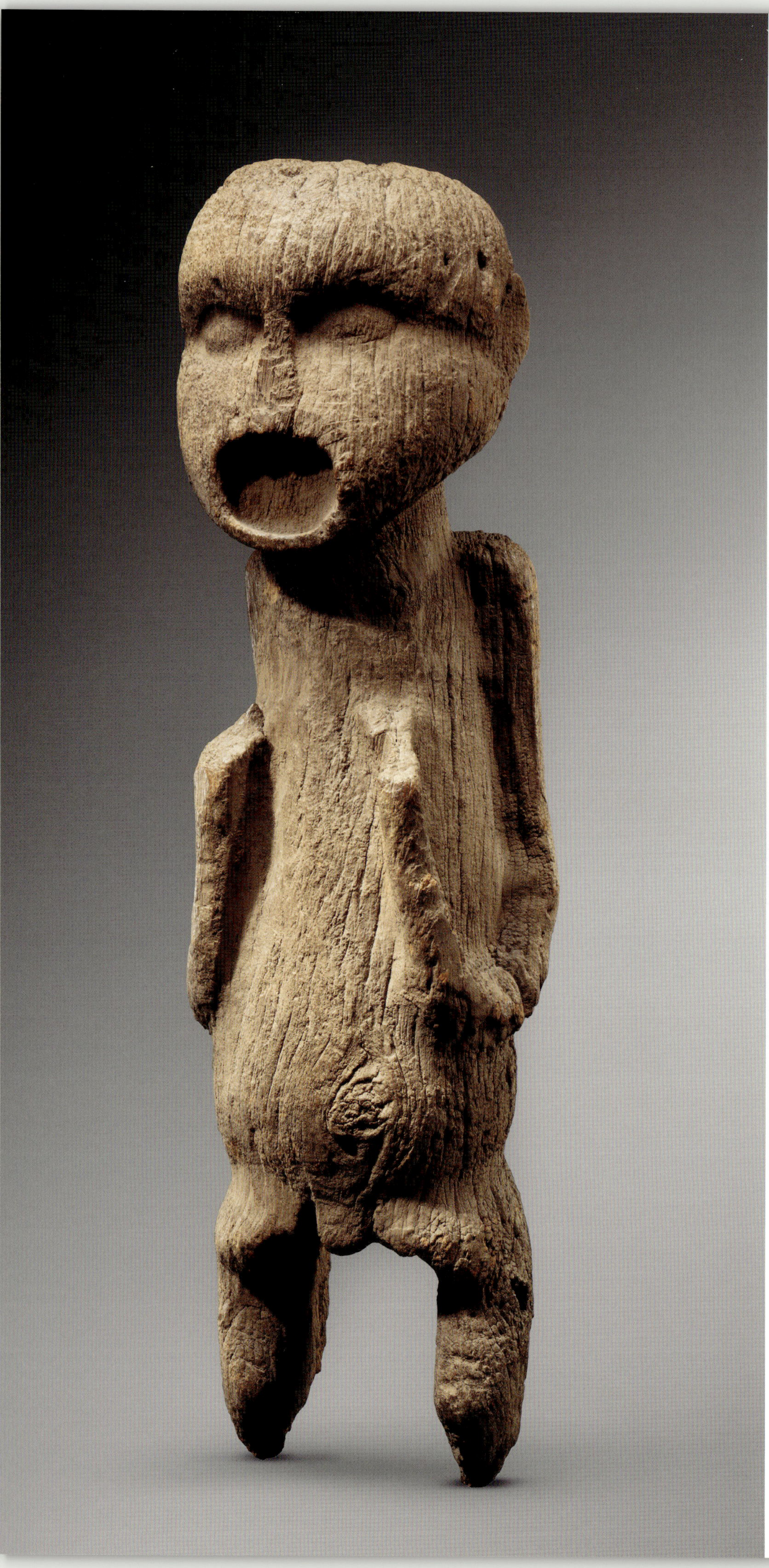

Mbembe statue
Nigeria, H. 62 cm
1646–1800 (84.7% – Test C14 by CIRAM, Bordeaux)

This expressive male figure shown standing upright, with arms folded and hands against his chest, illustrates one aspect of the art of the Mbembe, a small ethnic group divided into some ten independent statelets governed by an elected chief. The wide-open mouth seems to be making an impassioned speech. The figure's general appearance, ovoid head, and bulging belly resemble the style of the Mbembe living in the Cameroon Cross River area. The scant information we have suggests these figures, of which few examples survive, portrayed exceptional chiefs and had a commemorative function.[1] [HJ]

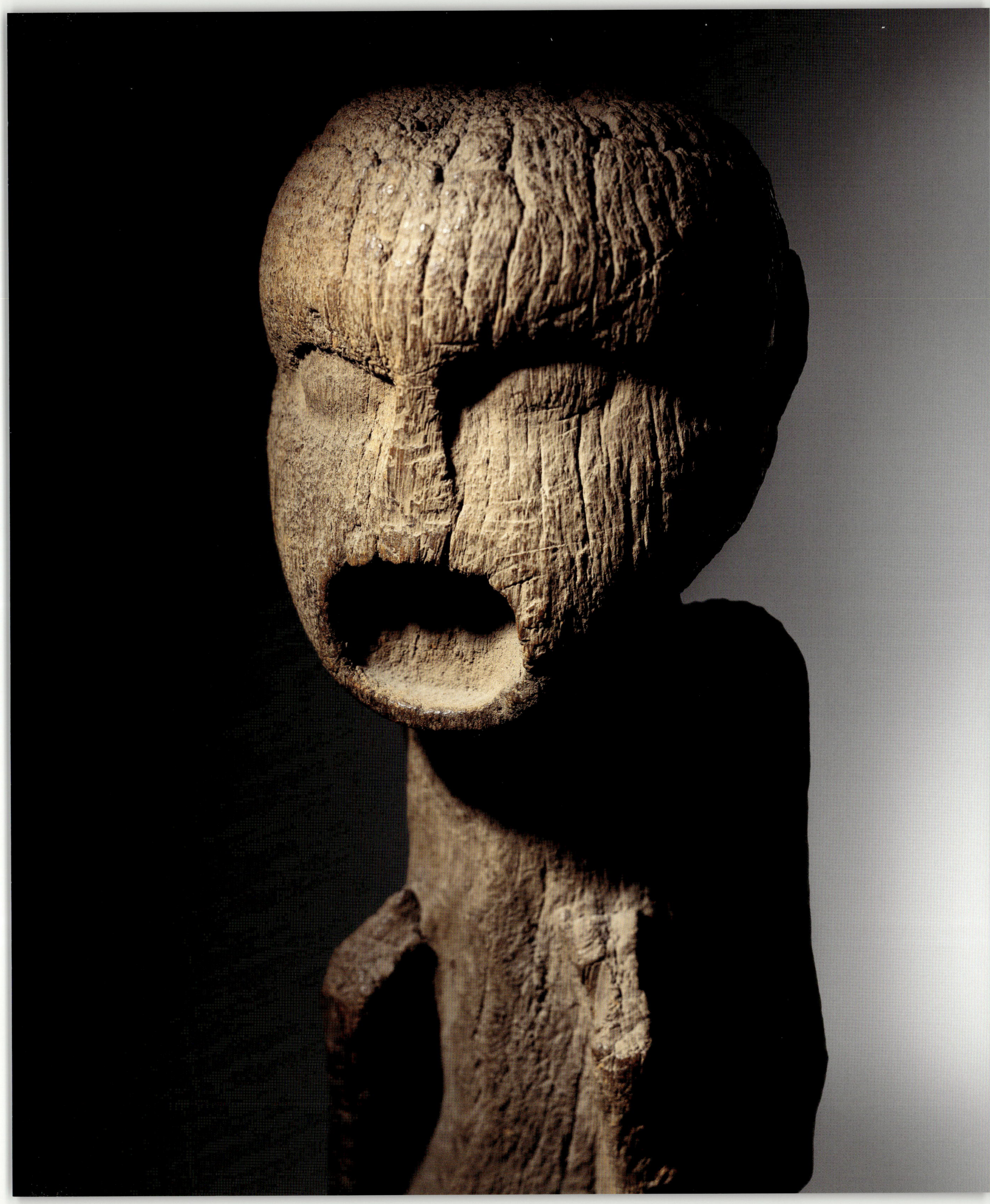

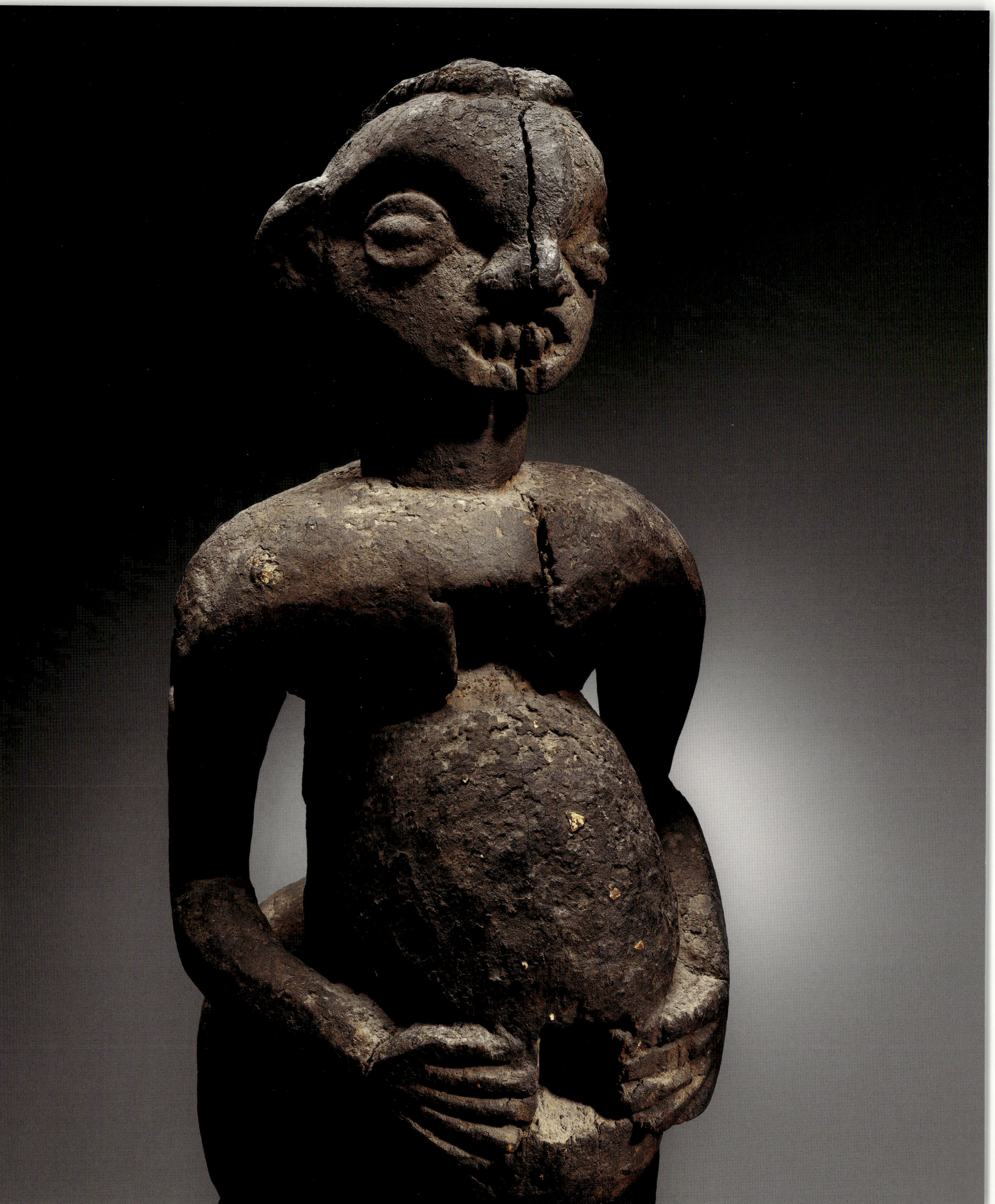

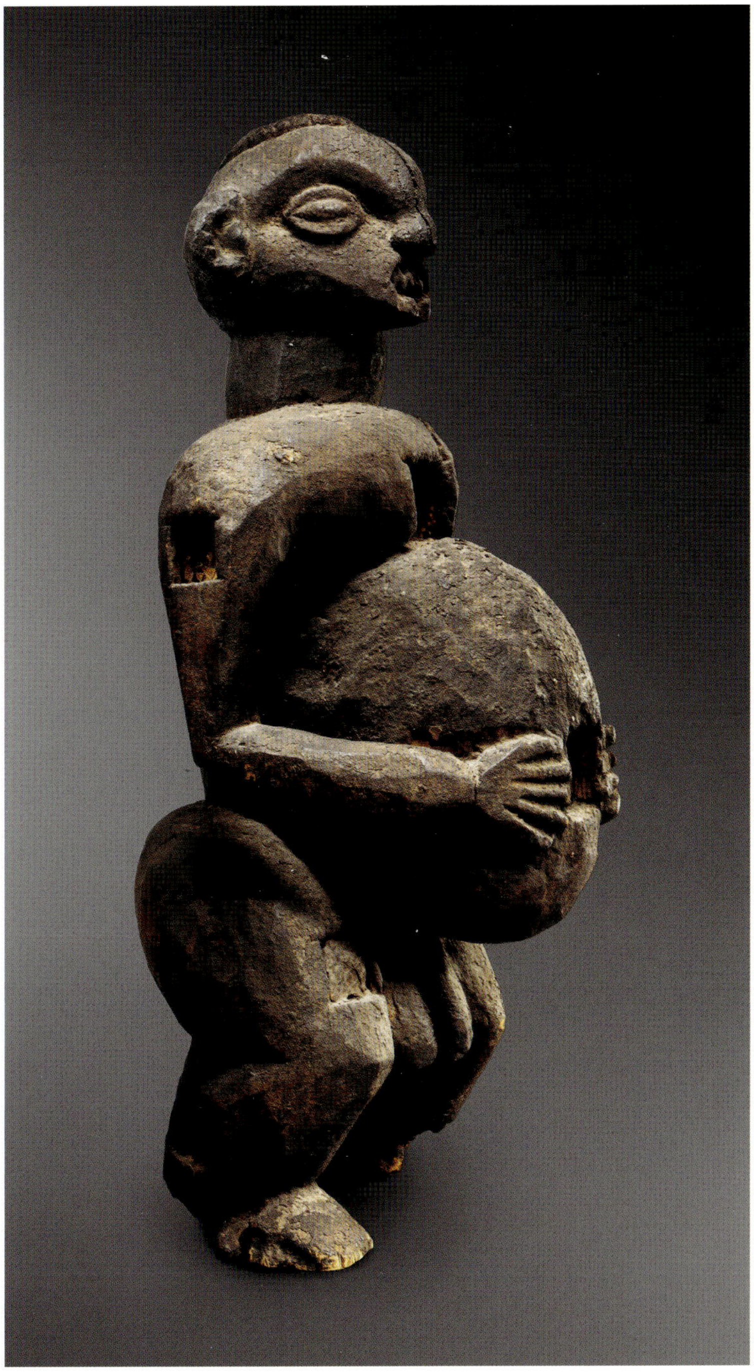

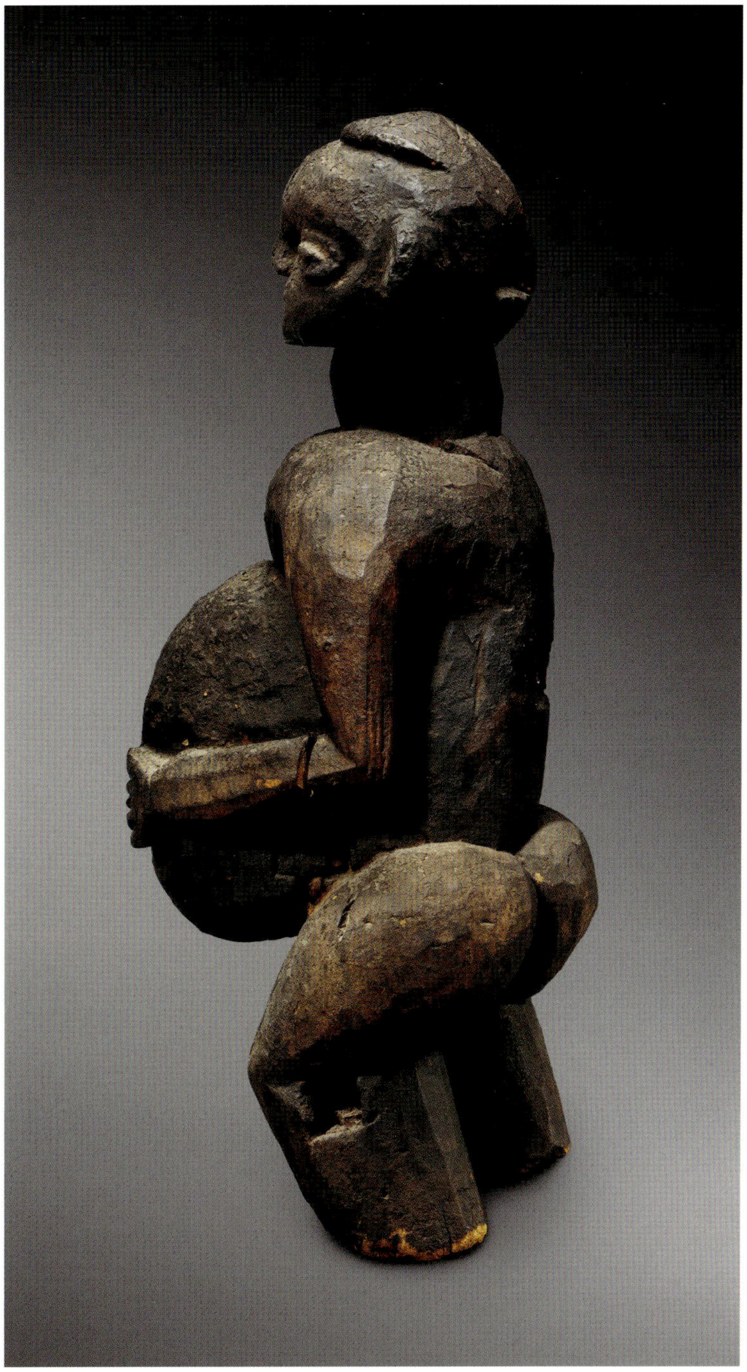

Bangwa statue
Western Bangwa, Cameroon, H. 68 cm

This expressive stocky statue was once the agent of the *Ku'ngan,* an autonomous society of rite experts under the aegis of a chieftain. The potent figure has cavities on several parts of its body; this is where the figure was charged with secret ingredients and was then intended to have an effect through sympathetic magic. *Lekat* is the name given to depictions of this kind by the Western Bangwa and it must be understood in the context of the Bangwa's concept of witchcraft. Such figures were used in attempts to ward off crises from the society. [BVL]

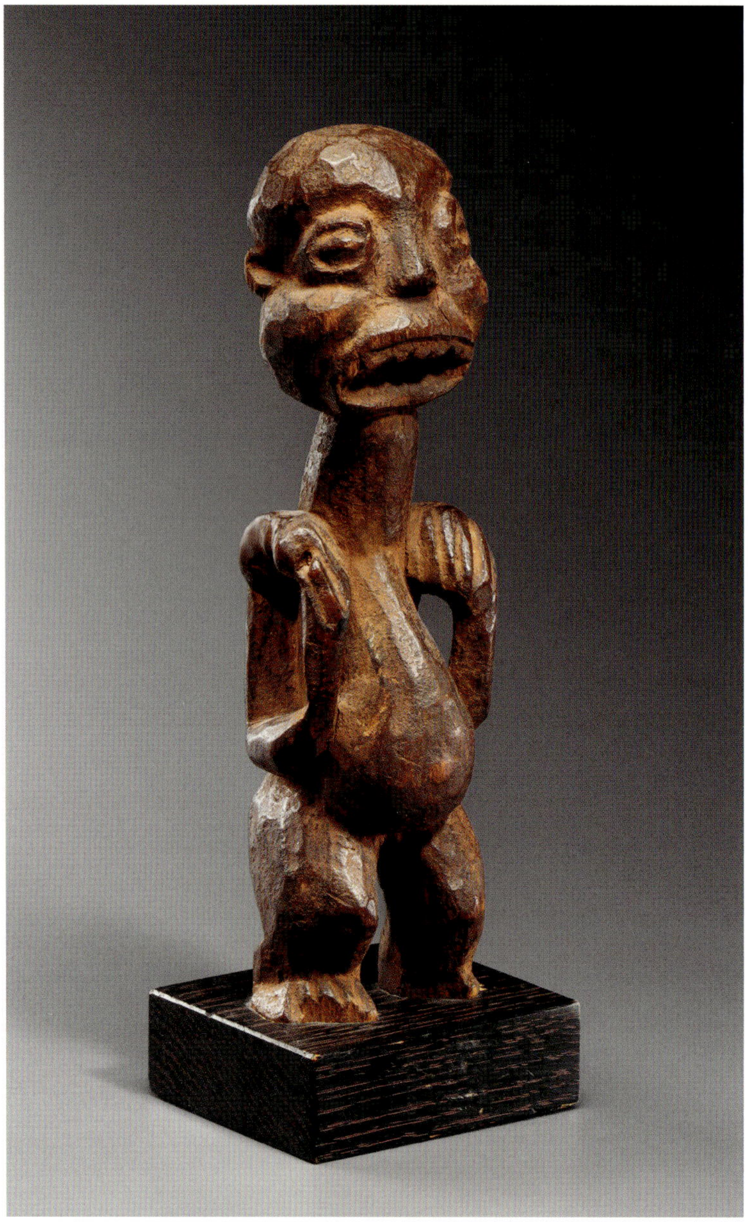

Bangwa statuette
Eastern Bangwa, (Bangwa-Batoufam Bamileke region),
Cameroon, H. 19 cm
Stand by Kichizô Inagaki

The protruding belly of the statuette can symbolize children that have not yet been born and represent fertility. Similar to some other protective figures, the hands are resting above the breast. A powerful figure (161 cm, inv. no. 79–300–919) held in the Museum Five Continents, Munich, represents a woman in pain shortly before giving birth. This miniature statue shares the same expression. Small-sized *Mu Po* were worn as amulets and masked members of the *Ku'ngang* also had them with them when they danced.
The finely faceted figure is covered with a softly shining patina; it has been mounted on a base created by the Japanese craftsman, Kichizô Inagaki (1876–1951) who lived in Paris. [BVL]

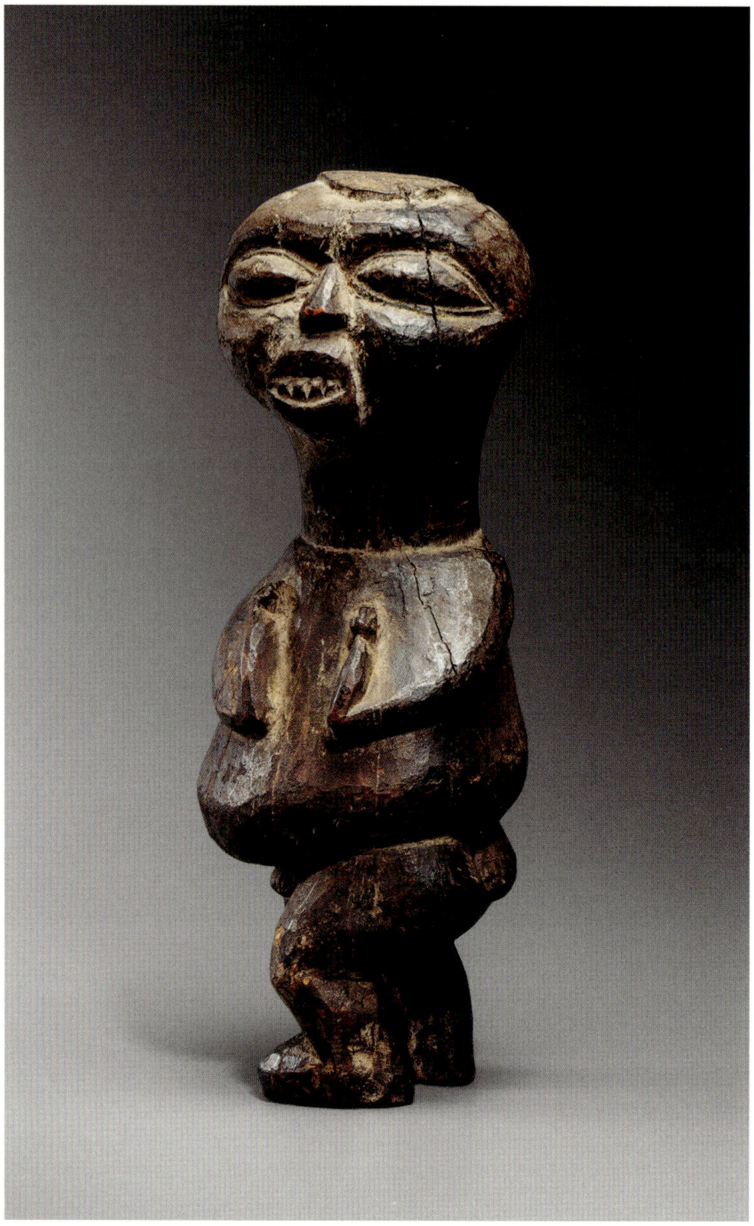

Bamileke-Batie statuette
Cameroon, H. 19 cm

We are aware of small amulets with "rolled-up" arms and relief-like limbs, whose bodies are made of a block of wood, steatite or ivory, from the Tikar, Bamileke, or Mambila (ca. 5–7.5 cm). Larger *Mu'Po* are more articulated.
There is a similar figure to the one shown here in the collections of the Ethnological Museum in Berlin Dahlem (inv. no. III C 40080); with the exception that it is facing the front.
The curved arms lie directly on the body on top of the enormous belly; on the one hand, this is a symbol of feminine fertility and, on the other, of a magical potential. The twisting of the *Mu'Po* from the Weill Collection is in keeping with the art of the Cameroon grasslands that is so rich in meaningful gestures and dynamic movement. [BVL]

Bamileke-Batie statue
Cameroon, H. 38 cm

The female portrayal has cavities on the rear side into which the "magic medicine" could be inserted. Franz Thorbecke brought a similar *Mu'Po* from Bamunam—not far from Batié—back with him from his 1911/12 expedition (Reiss-Engelhorn-Museum Mannheim; IV Af 7420). Figures of this kind were in the possession of the *Ku'ngang* society. The protruding belly that embodies magical potency and fertility is especially striking. Larger *Mu'Po* figures (25–50 cm) are meant to be placed at the ceremonial site before the annual *nggu* purification rites take place. [BVL]

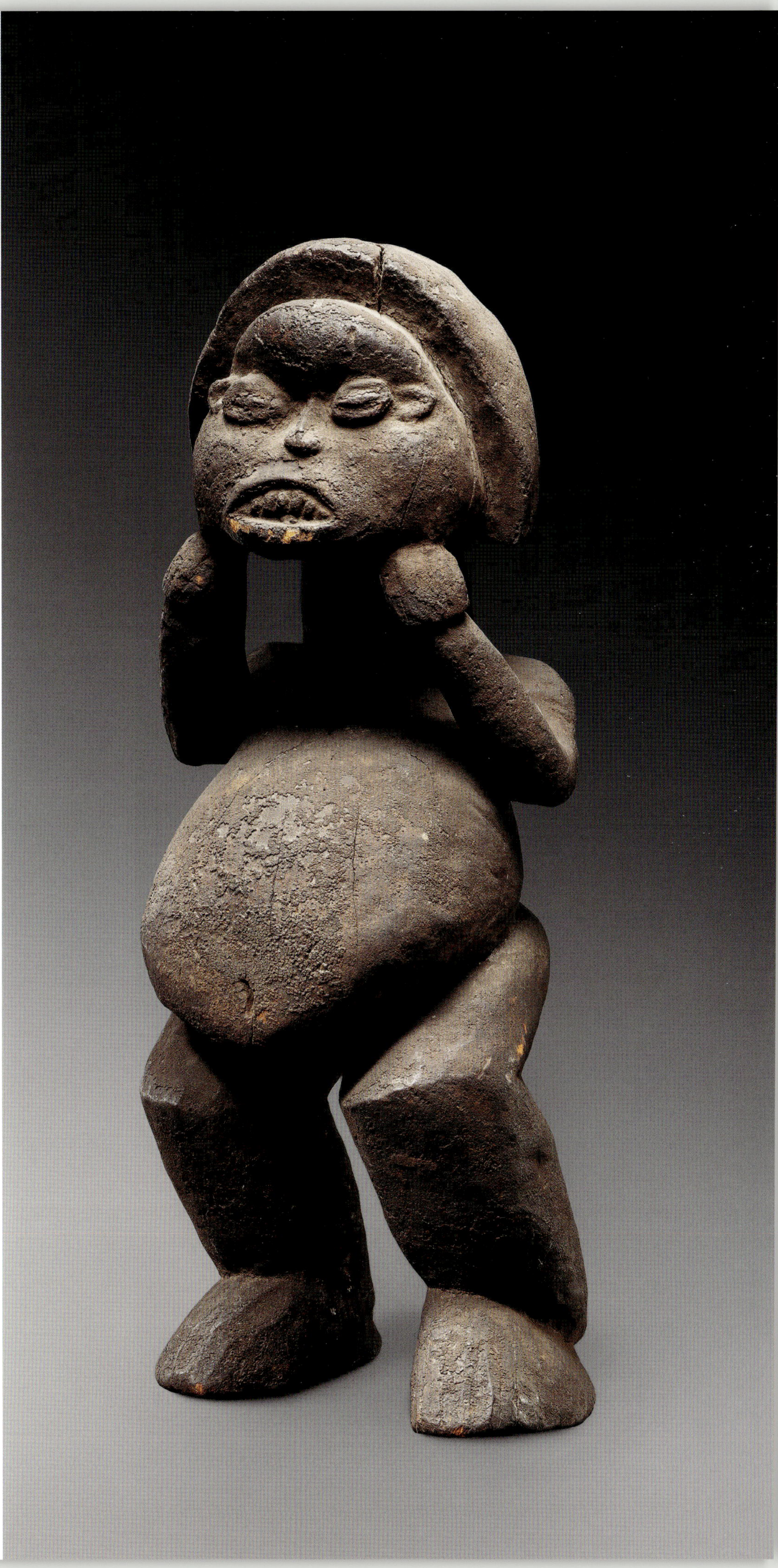

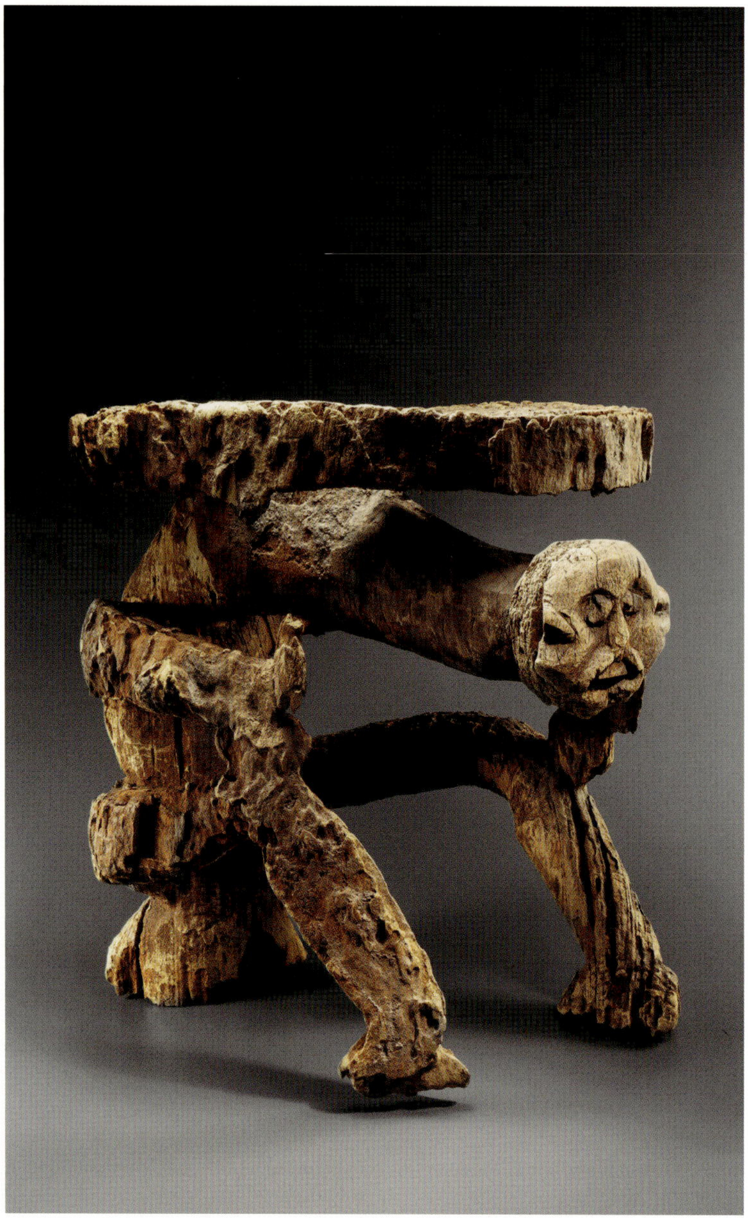

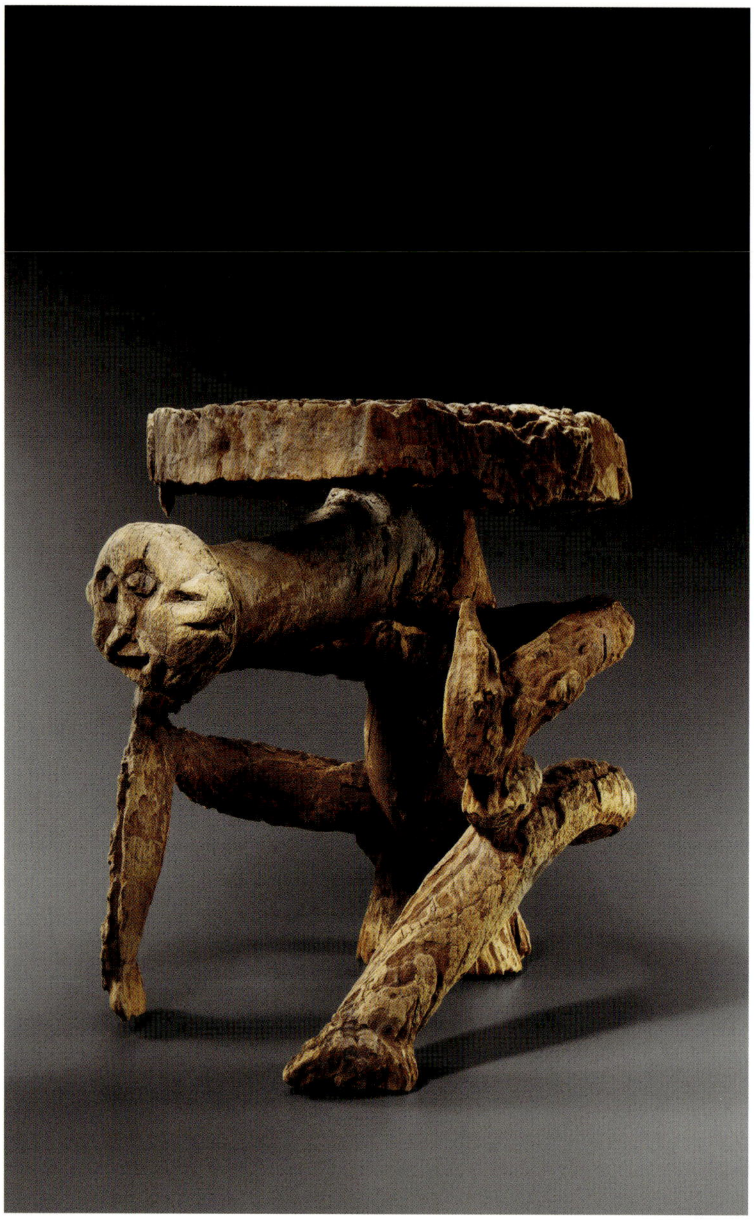

Fragment of Bamileke-Batie throne
Cameroon, H. 46 cm

Large seats of the Bamileke are hewn out of massive trunks. The sculptors adapted the motif they had in mind to suit this circumstance. It either took a circular course around a hollowed-out interior or the artist cut its "knobby" way diagonally across the trunk as in this case. A crouching supporting figure with a formidable neck, which appears extremely phallic on account of its small face, was created. Erosion also played a creative part in this unusual object. A photograph taken *in situ* sometime around 1950 still shows the complete *Kuo Ketuok*. [BVL]

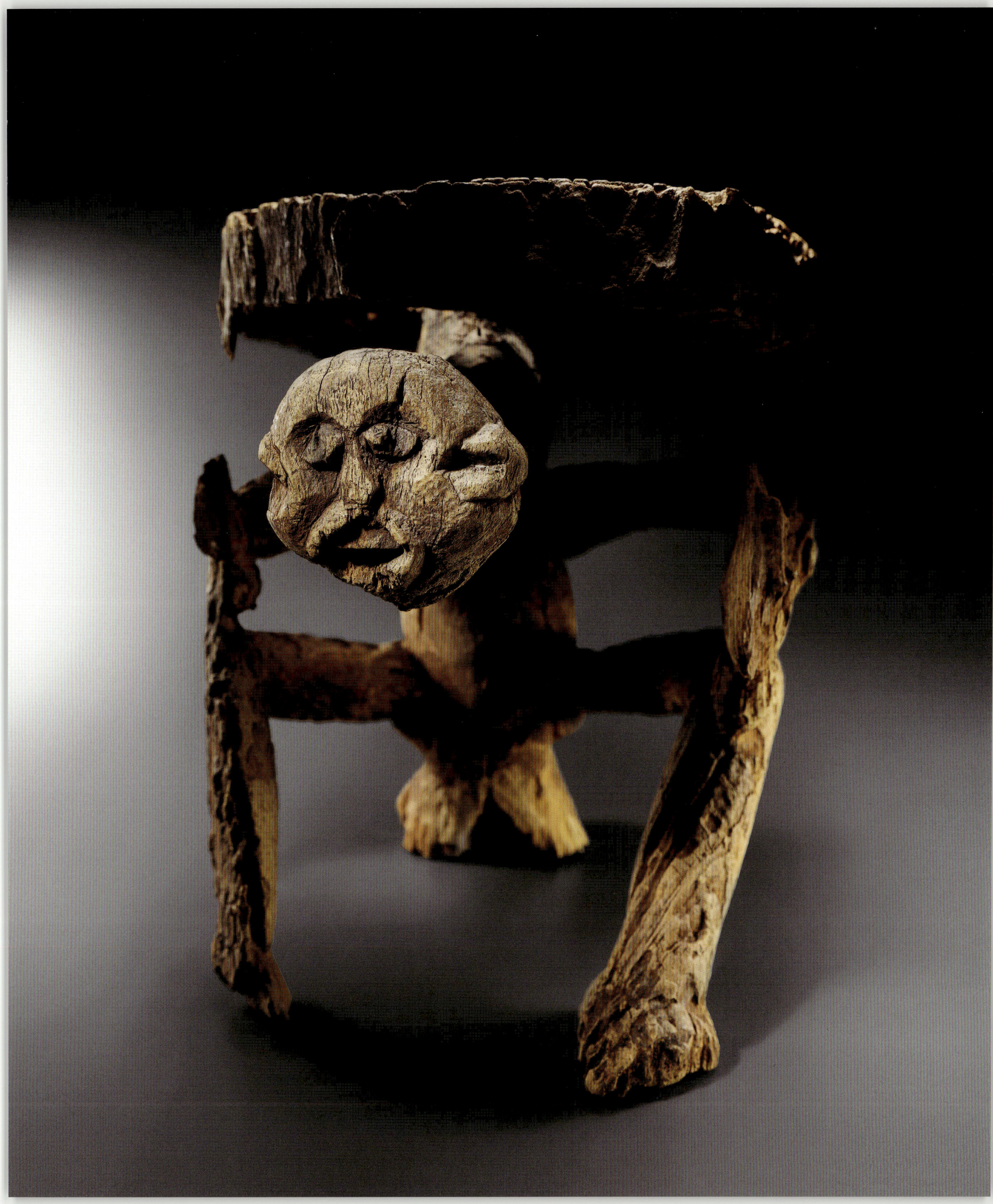

Bangwa crest
Bangwa occidental, Cameroon, H. 42 cm

Troh "masks" are characterized by a black patina and a fiercely expressive face, with globular eyes, spherical cheeks reminiscent of cubism, and a mouth showing threatening teeth. The accumulation of soot and libations gave these artefacts, attributes of the members of the first circle of the secret society *Troh*, a growing magical power. For this reason, even insiders wore these masks on their shoulders and never on their heads, to prevent any harmful magical influence. The *Troh* society had a reputation as a "kingmaker." [BVL]

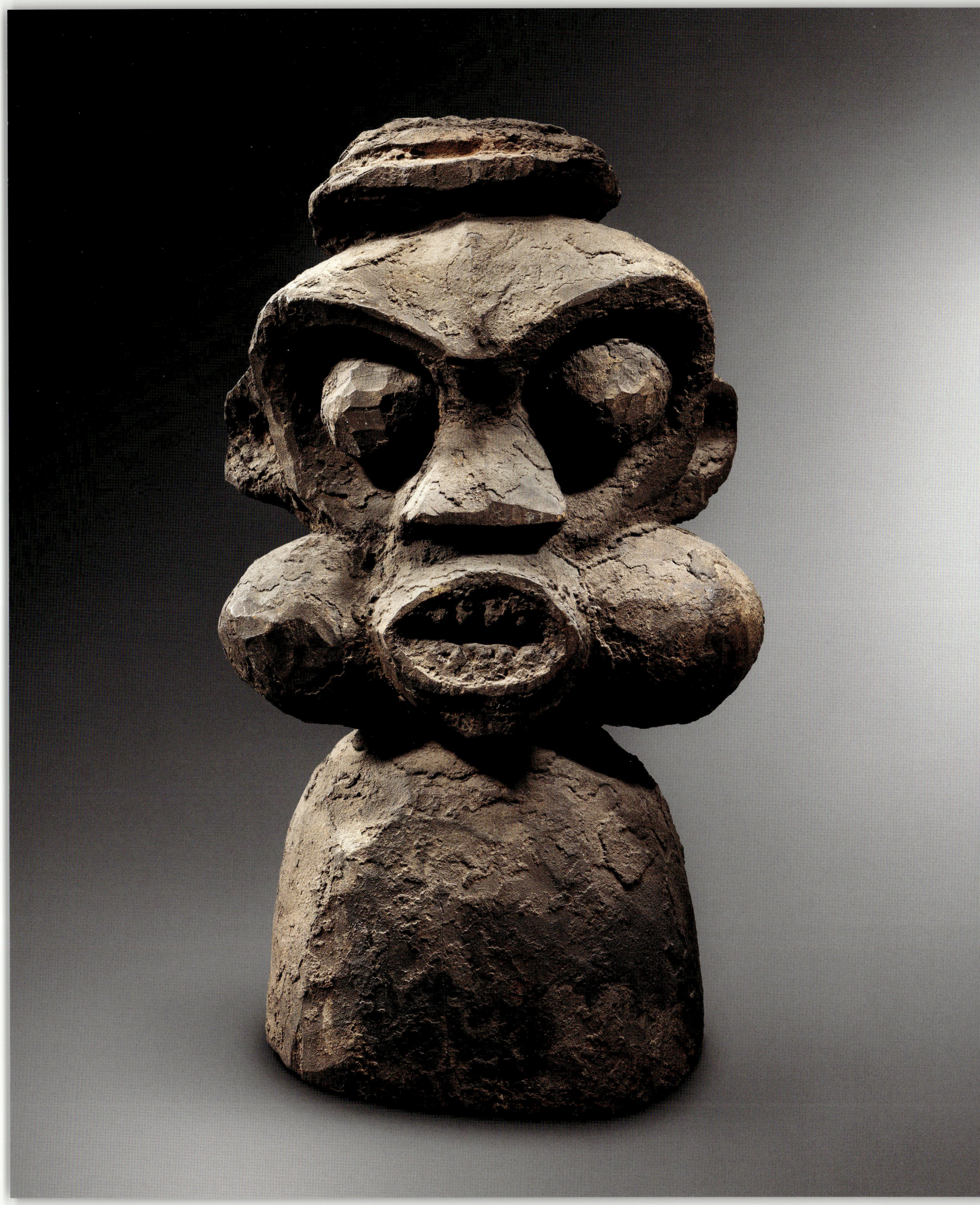

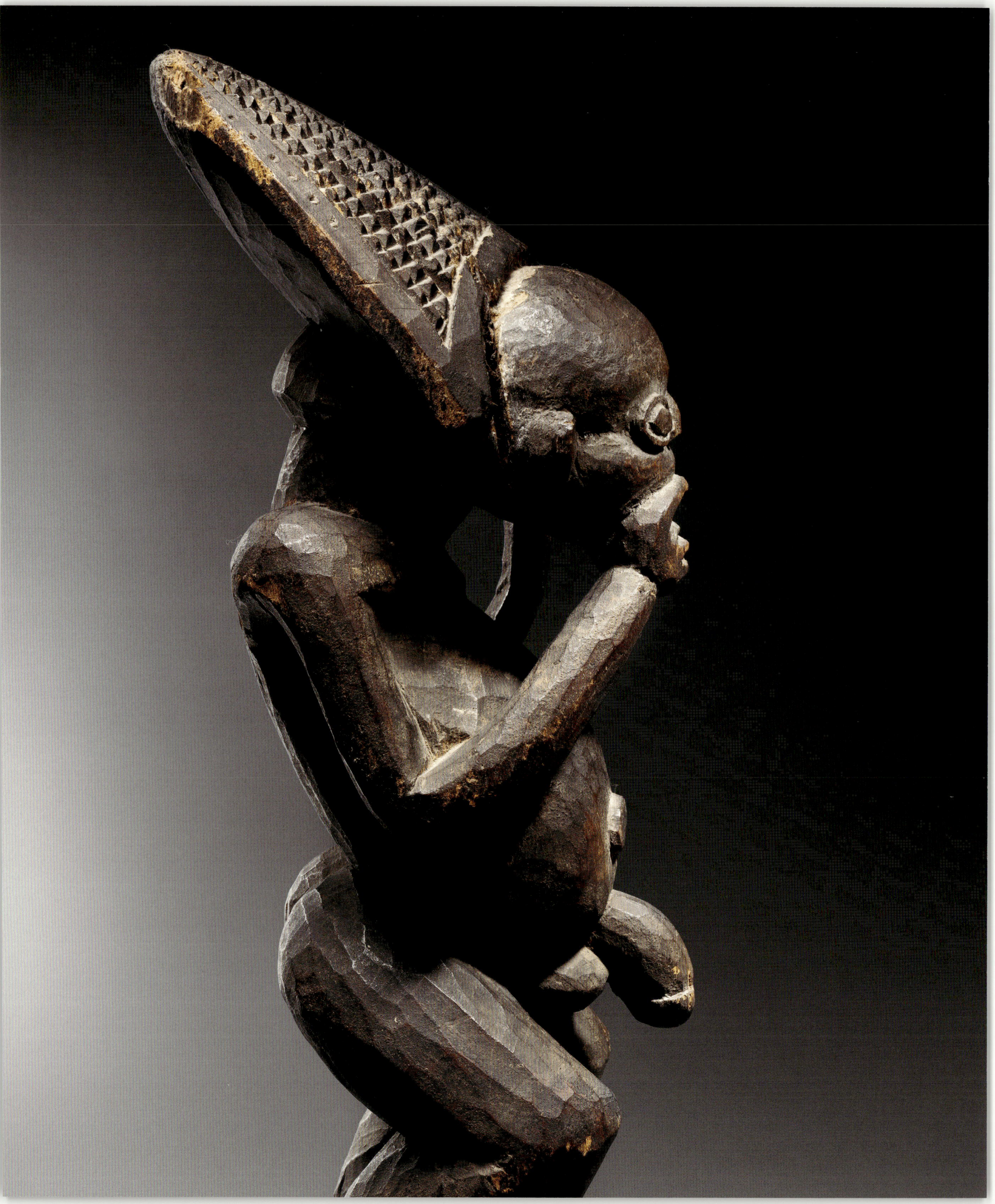

Bamileke statue
Cameroon, H. 51 cm

An insignia—namely, a high burled cap—shows that this figure represents a chieftain. The motif of a stout man who is grasping his head is unusual in this artistic environment. The other hand touches his chin; this gesture is frequently found in commemorative figures but, here, a finger that covers and replaces the mouth is a significant characteristic. The body is constructed out of articulated volumes as is common in many Bamileke figures. Could the chief possibly come from the Dschang region (Bafou Fondong)? This is difficult to determine without any more precise details. [BVL]

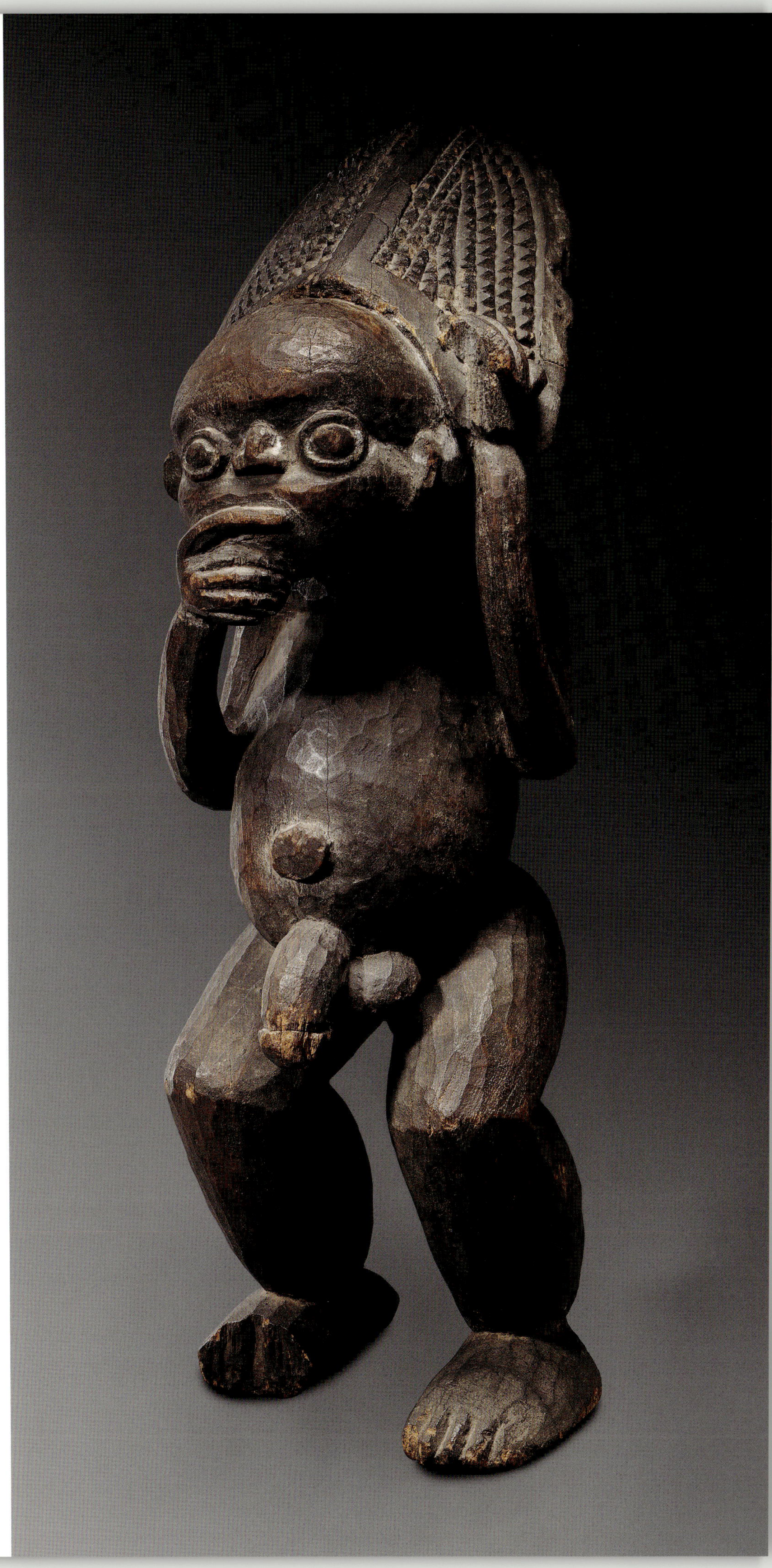

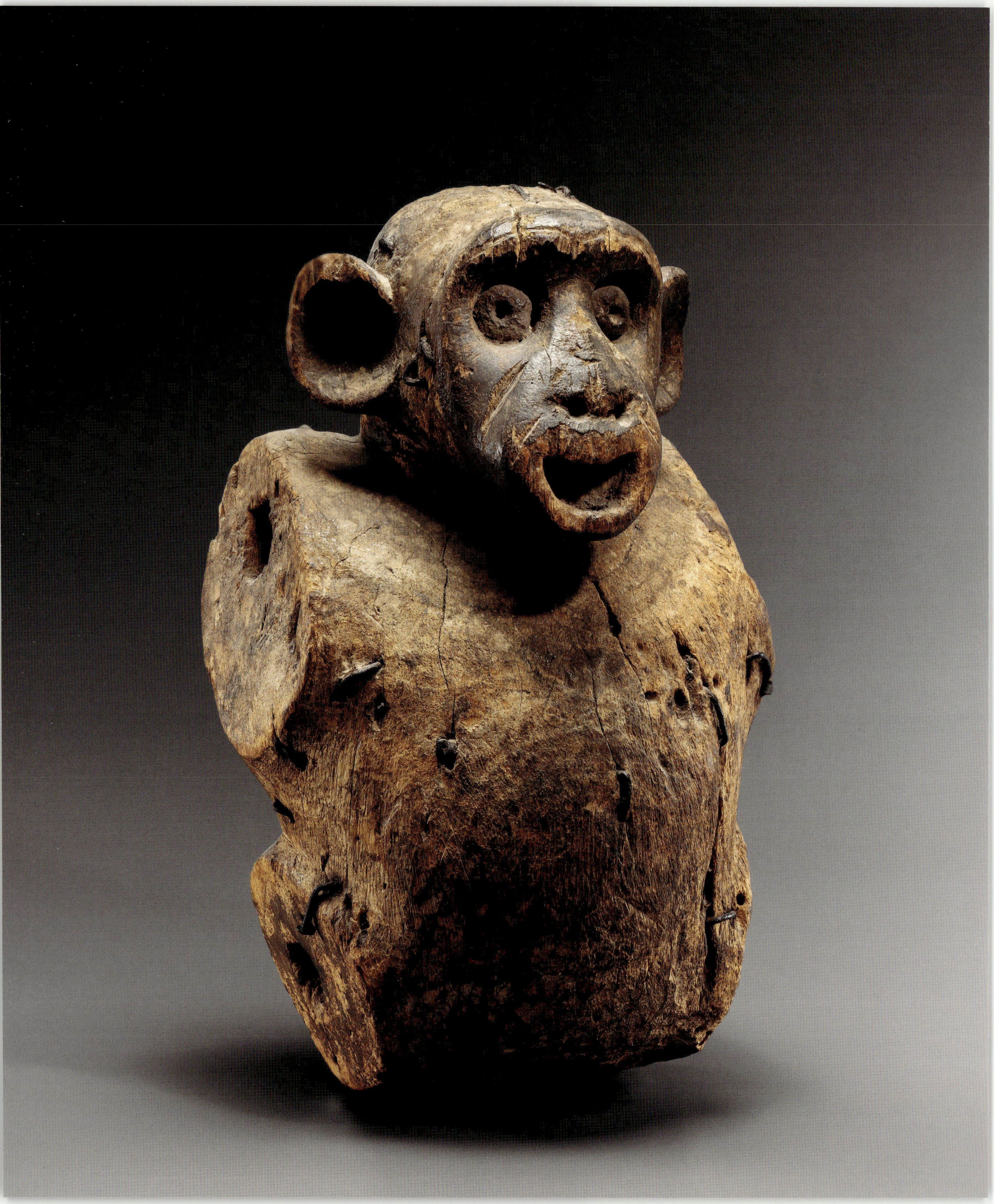

Fang bulu-beti monkey
Ebolowa region, southern Cameroon-northern Gabon, H. 32 cm

This important bust of a monkey, a sculpture that was originally not made from a single piece of wood, has lost none of its power even though it has lost its four limbs. Originally, it must have been covered with material that looked like fur, which was attached to the iron staples that are still visible here and there on the head and body. Only fifteen or so examples of these Bulu-Beti monkeys are known to exist and have been published to date. These statues were connected with the worship of the *ngil* or *ngi*, the gorilla, which featured greatly in the ritual pantheon of the Fang, of which the Bulu-Beti are a sub-group. Louis Perrois has analysed these objects and the cults associated with them in a thorough study carried out for Christie's in June 2014, when a Bulu monkey collected around 1920 by Leon Truitard, a colonial administrator in Cameroon, was auctioned. This Truitard monkey was particularly realistic and had the peculiarity of still having a reliquary housed in its head, proof of the figure's magical/religious function. This Bulu community counts around one hundred thousand souls and has a very sophisticated religious culture, in which the belief in hidden powers embodied in certain animal sculptures plays an important role. A number of different species of animal have this ability, but it seems that apes are the most respected of all, very likely owing to their similarity to humans. Whether a chimpanzee or a gorilla, the animal is considered to be a link between the real world and the spirit world and depending on the circumstances it can trigger visions in its possessor, who must be an initiate or a sorcerer, since being in possession of such a powerful object is not without danger. The monkey in the Weill Collection is particularly spectacular, with its face that is at once human and animal, and is of considerable age (probably dating from the nineteenth century), which its aspect immediately suggests. Objects of such importance were obviously kept hidden away in a secret place, where they would not risk being seen by non-initiates and especially not by Europeans. [PA]

>
Bamileke statue
Cameroon, H. 37 cm

This nude male figure is depicted squatting, with his long arms curving down to his hands carved in relief placed on his knees. This statue has human hair and is notably naturalistic.
It is not possible to determine with any certainty the function of this figure based on any iconographic characteristics. For example, the familiar status insignias of commemorative figures are missing. And, on the other hand, there is no clear identification for its use as a "magical figure." With its fine patina and signs of usage, it can be assigned to the Bamileke. [BVL]

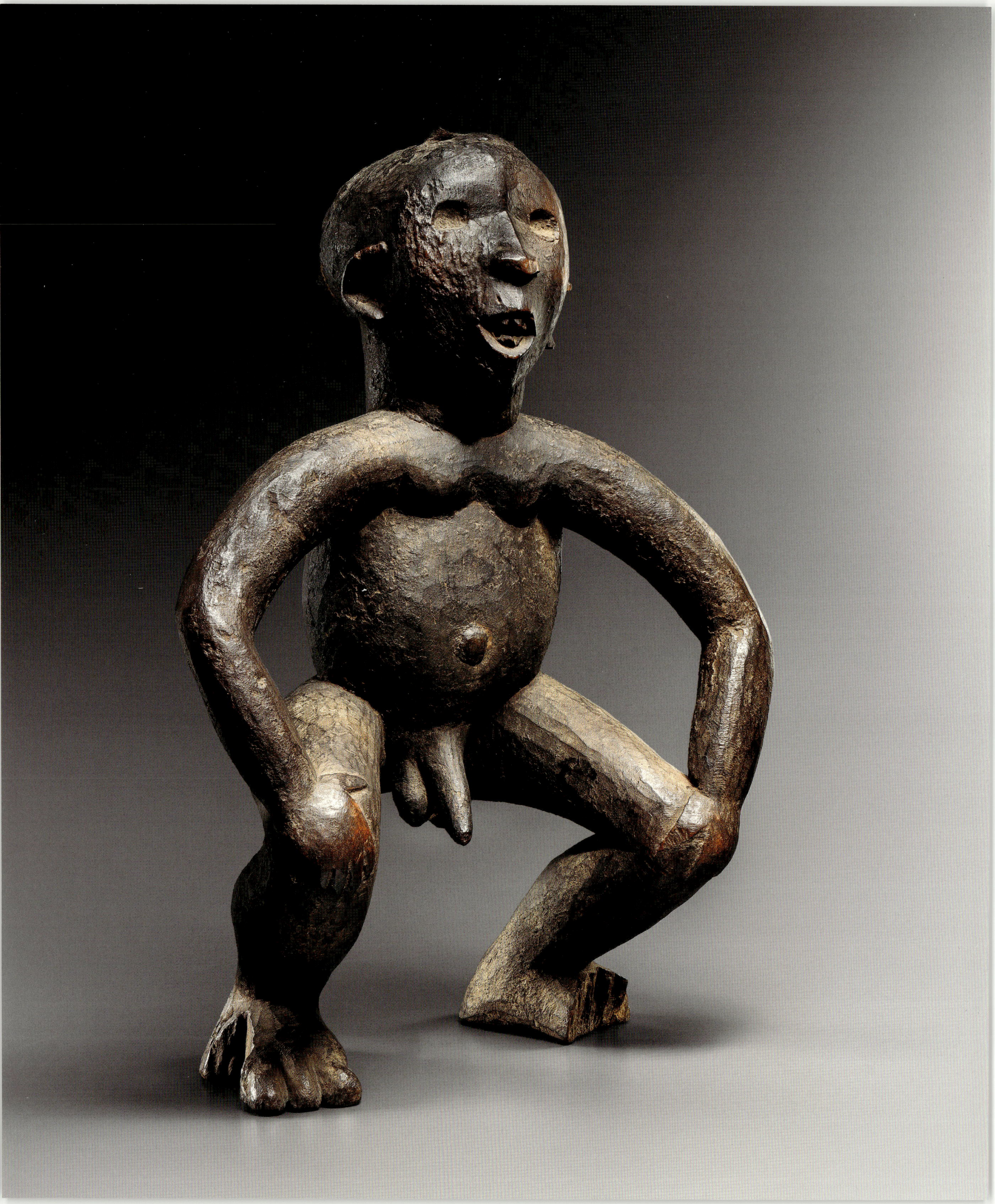

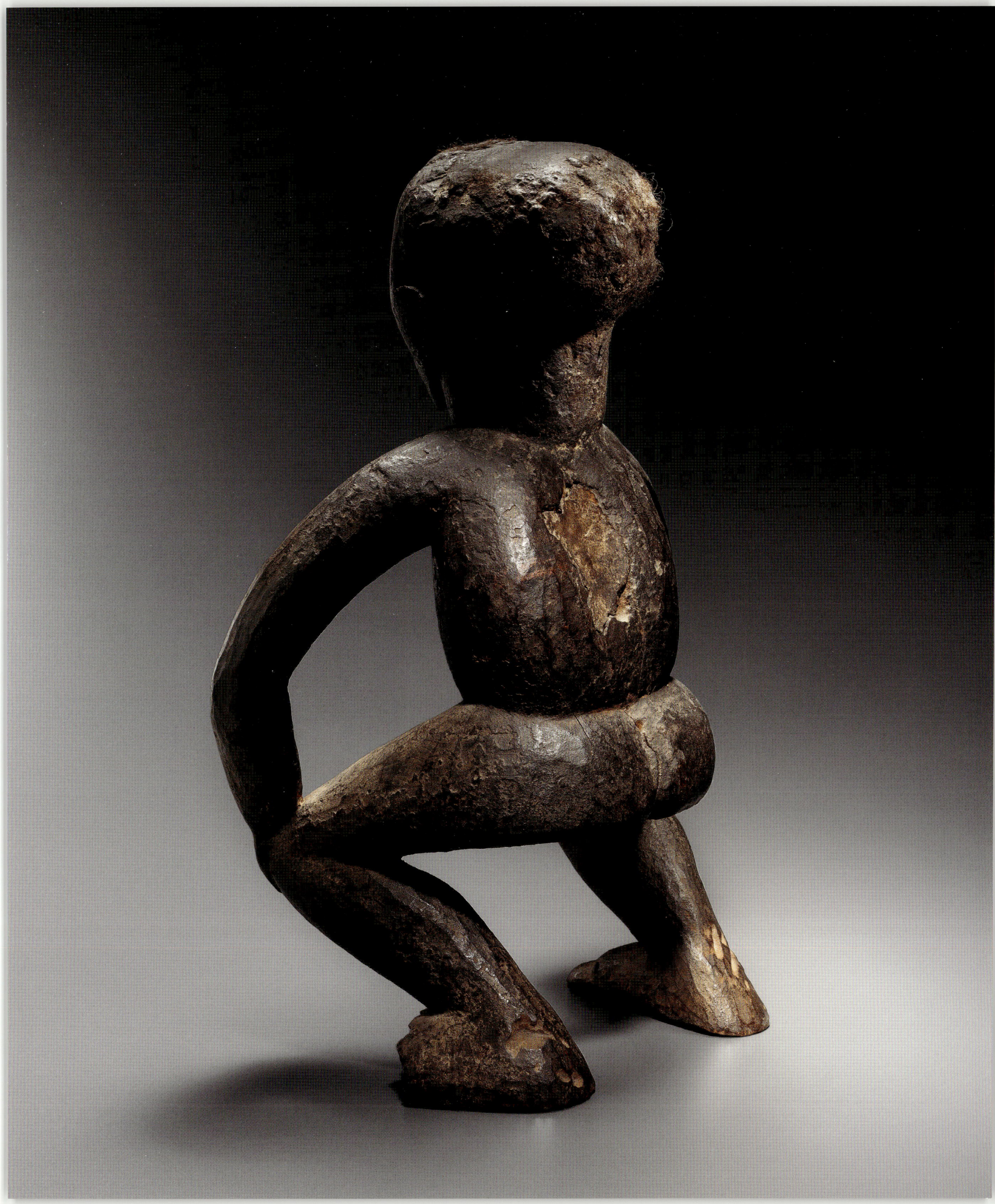

Fang reliquary figure
Ngumba or Ntumu group, South Cameroon, H. 51 cm

The lyrical elongated definition of this figure reflects a bodily ideal embraced by Fang sculptors from southern Cameroon. The intensity of the gaze of the simply hewn face has been accentuated through the addition of metal discs to the eyes. The vertical form of a strong neck intersects the horizontal of broad shoulders at a right angle. At that level, the slender body is subdivided into a series of three parallel vertical columns defining the torso and arms that are continuous with the legs.
In Fang communities, such works were integrated into *byeri*, the spiritual practices devoted to assuring the flow of ancestral protection to the living (Fernandez, 1982, p. 253). As the figurative element of a Fang extended family's reliquary ensemble, this sculpture constituted a simulacrum or effigy of the contents of the sacra it originally accompanied. *Byeri* shrines were generally kept in an intimate chamber by the titular family head who addressed it when invoking the ancestors. The sculptures were also detached from the altar on occasion to be manipulated in performative re-enactments of a family's history animated by music and dance. [ALG]

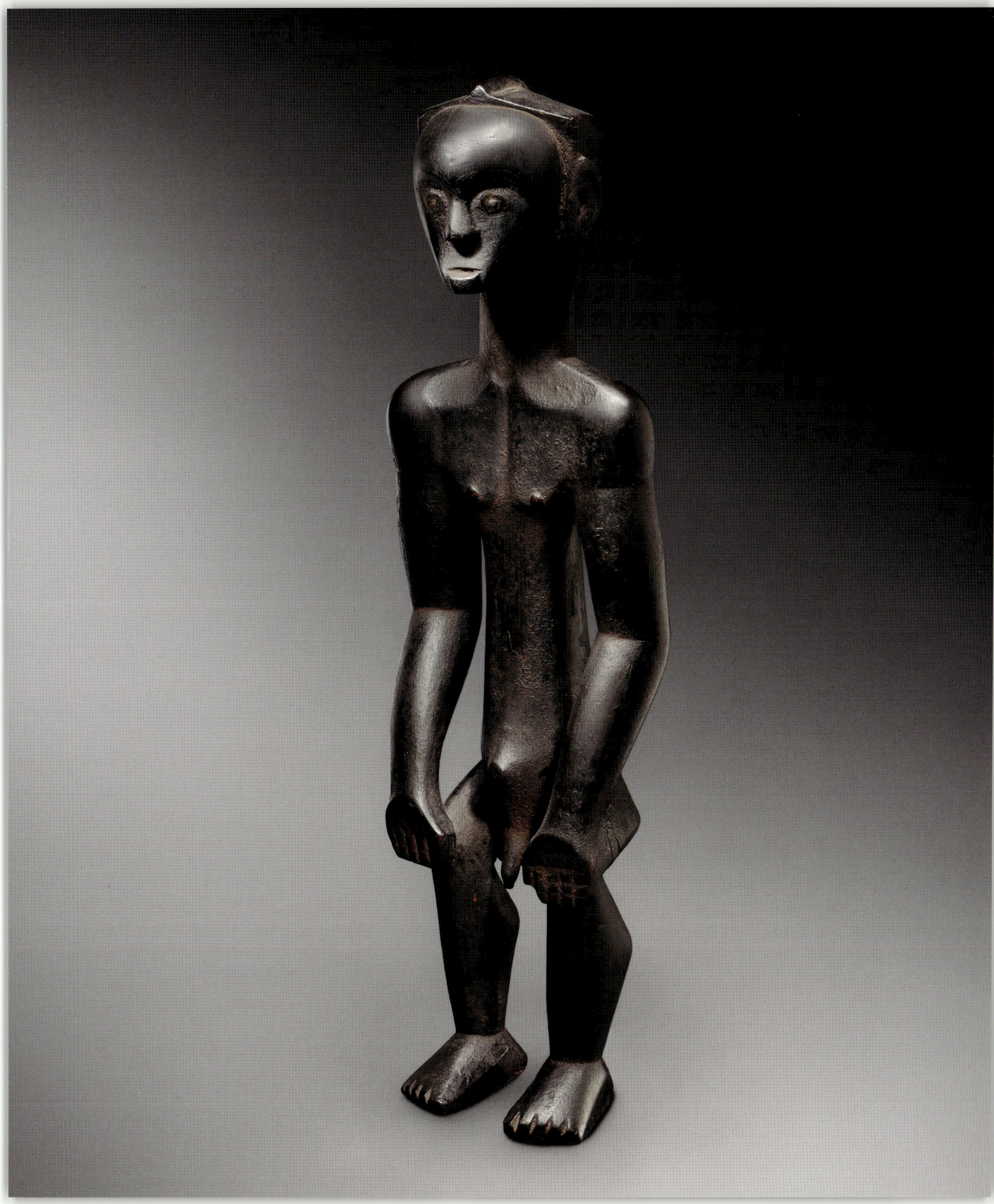

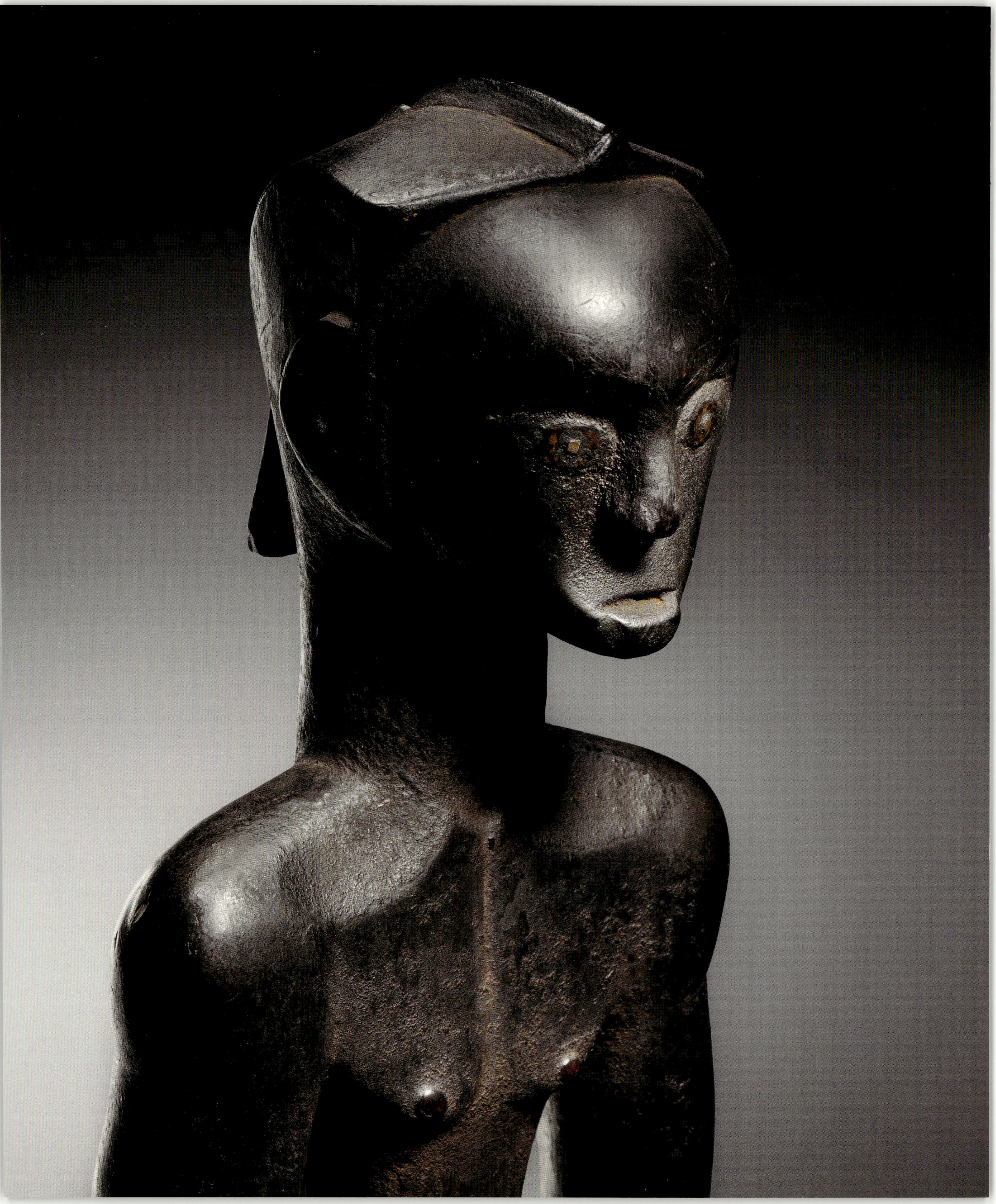

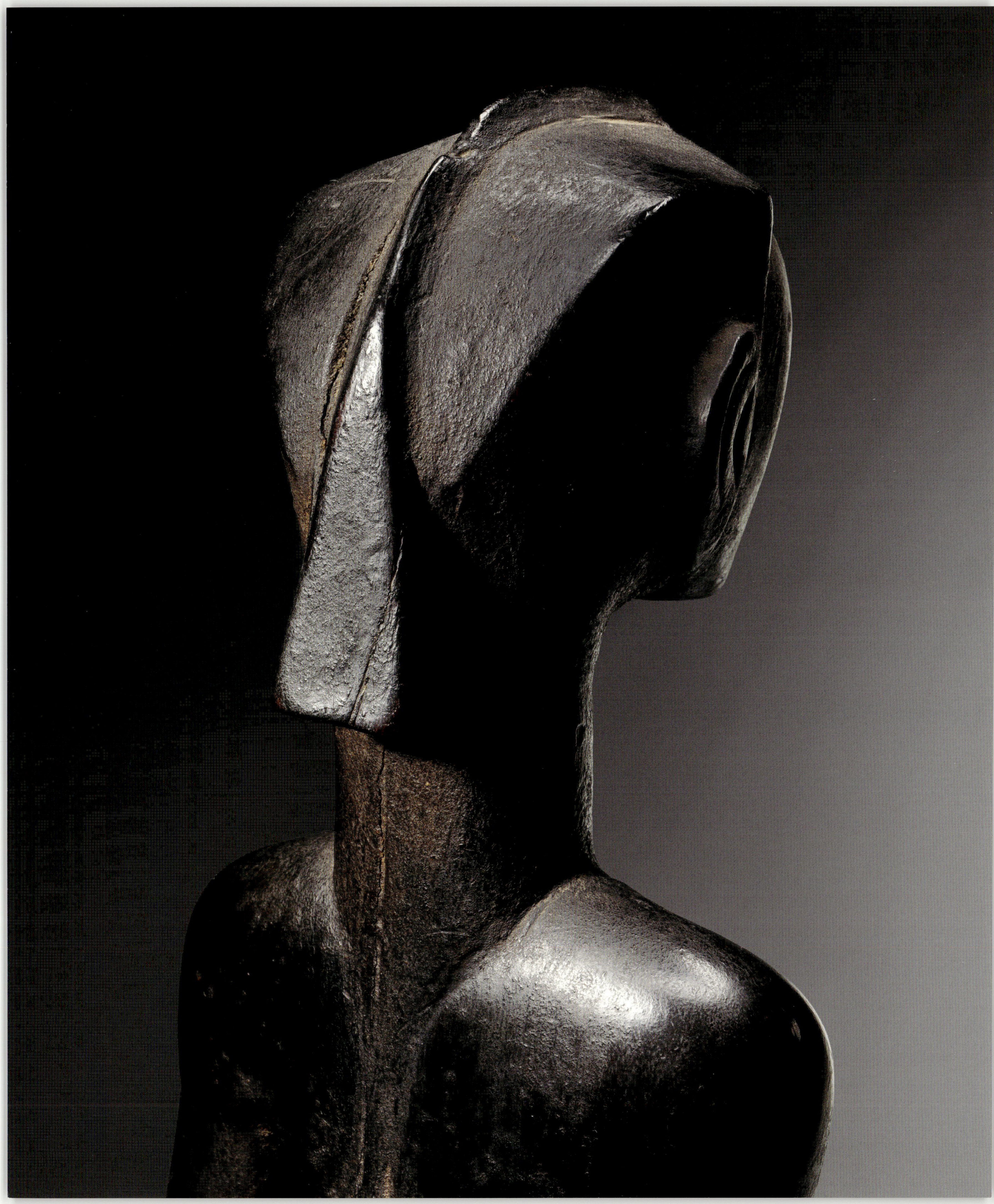

Fang reliquary figure
Betsi-Nzaman group, South Cameroon, H. 43.5 cm

Equatorial communities were historically transitory. Given their physical mobility from one generation to the next, genres of familial altars were developed that allowed the essence of venerated ancestors to be carried with their descendants. Among the Fang of present-day southern Cameroon, northern Gabon, and Equatorial Guinea, these took the form of cylindrical bark containers for the relics of influential members of an extended family. Wood figurative sculptures were positioned at the summit of the lid. While the sacra within were accessible only to those initiated Fang elders, the sculpture was a profane decorative element that at once suggested the idea of a guardian of the vessel's contents and expanded upon their significance for the uninitiated.

The elder appointed as custodian and historian of his familial altar addressed prayers on behalf of its members followed by the anointment of the sacra with libations. A critical part of imparting a mastery of knowledge relating to one's genealogical forbearers was the removal of their relics to accompany and bring to life recitations invoking the major protagonists of past generations. As the memory of certain ancestors became increasingly remote, the relics associated with them were replaced with those relating to more recently departed familial leaders.

Through their sculptural representations Fang carvers created a dynamic tension between an altar's interior and exterior dimensions. The vessel's contents combined particles of potent bodily matter relating to many distinct generations of an extended family. In contrast, the physiognomy of a single figure at once conceptually evoked its founder and its membership at large. This is reflected in the approach developed to define the body as a series of distinct volumes fluidly integrated into a bilaterally symmetrical form.

In this interpretation the proportional relationship of vigilant guardian's head, torso, and lower body are relatively naturalistic. The head is extended at either side by prominent ears and defined by a broad convex forehead with facial features of raised disc-like eyes on either side of the raised ridge of the nose above an abbreviated horizontal mouth. The one detailed passage of adornment is the elaborately dressed coiffure that extends from the back of the head arranged in a series of parallel vertical ridges. At once intensely alert and still in a posture conceived to accommodate the figure's placement seated at the summit of the receptacle lid, he places its hands on either side of a raised navel. This gesture underscores the compositional centre of the representation and amplifies the significance of the umbilicus as the point of connection across generations that is also the role of the altar itself. [ALG]

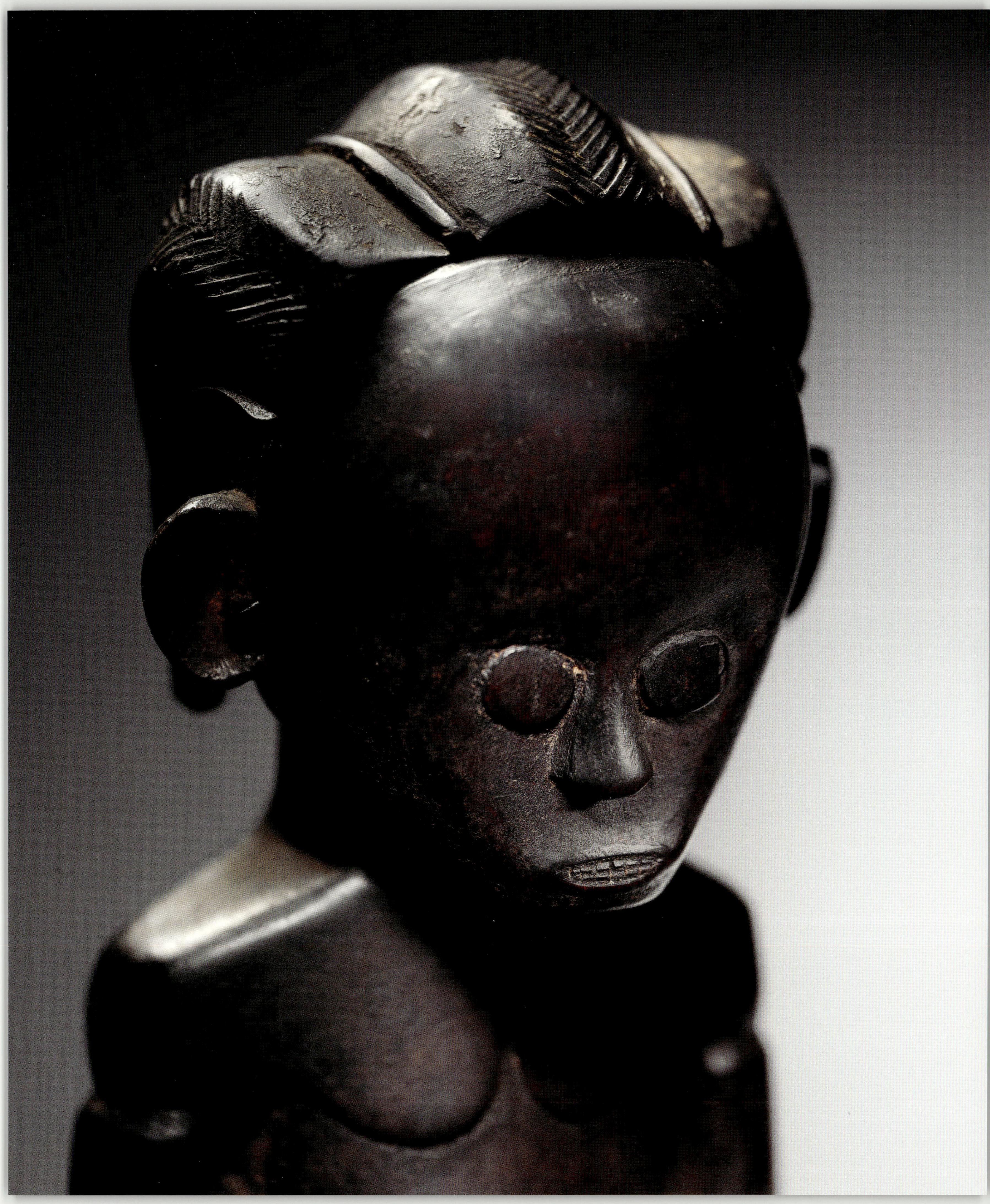

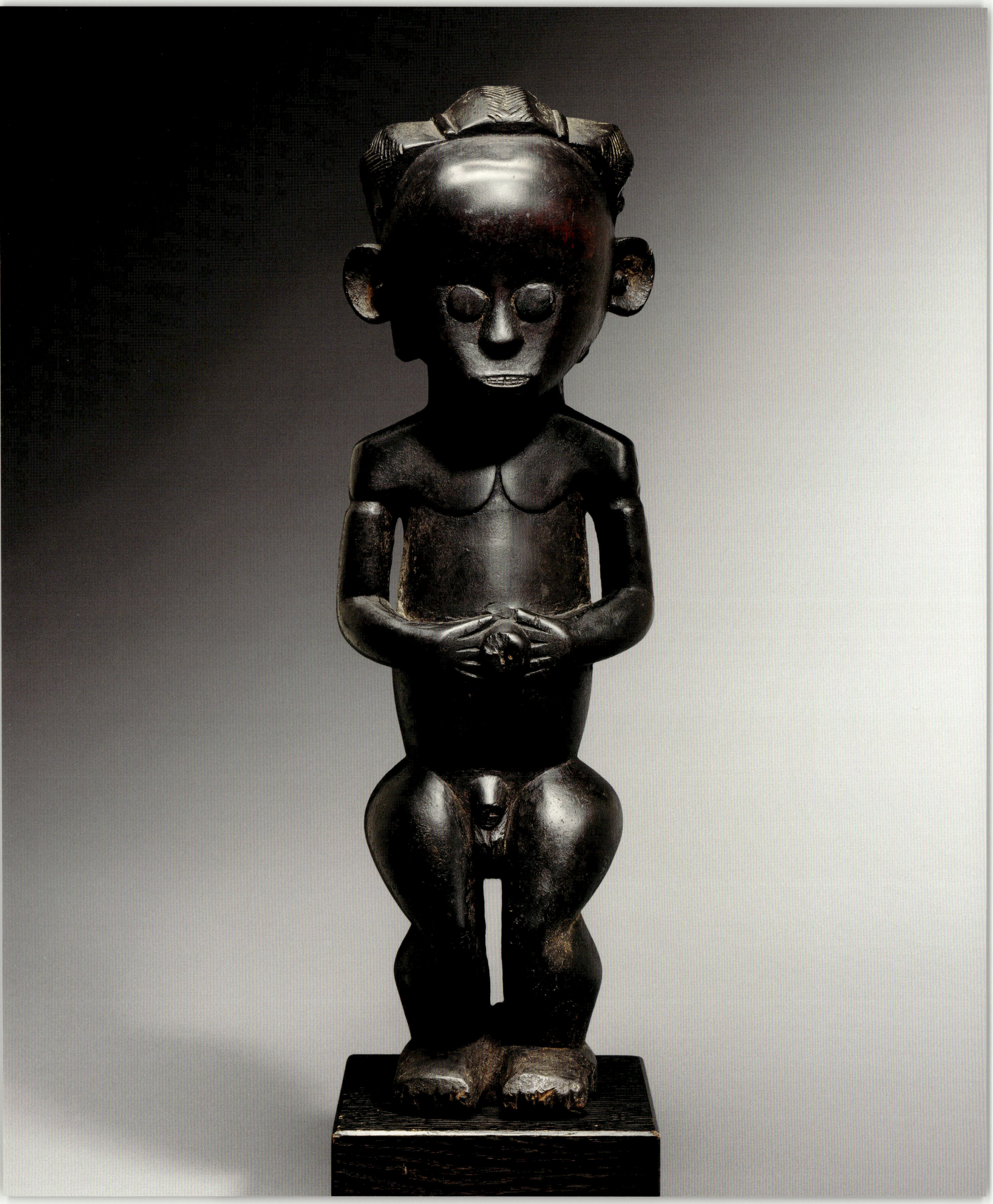

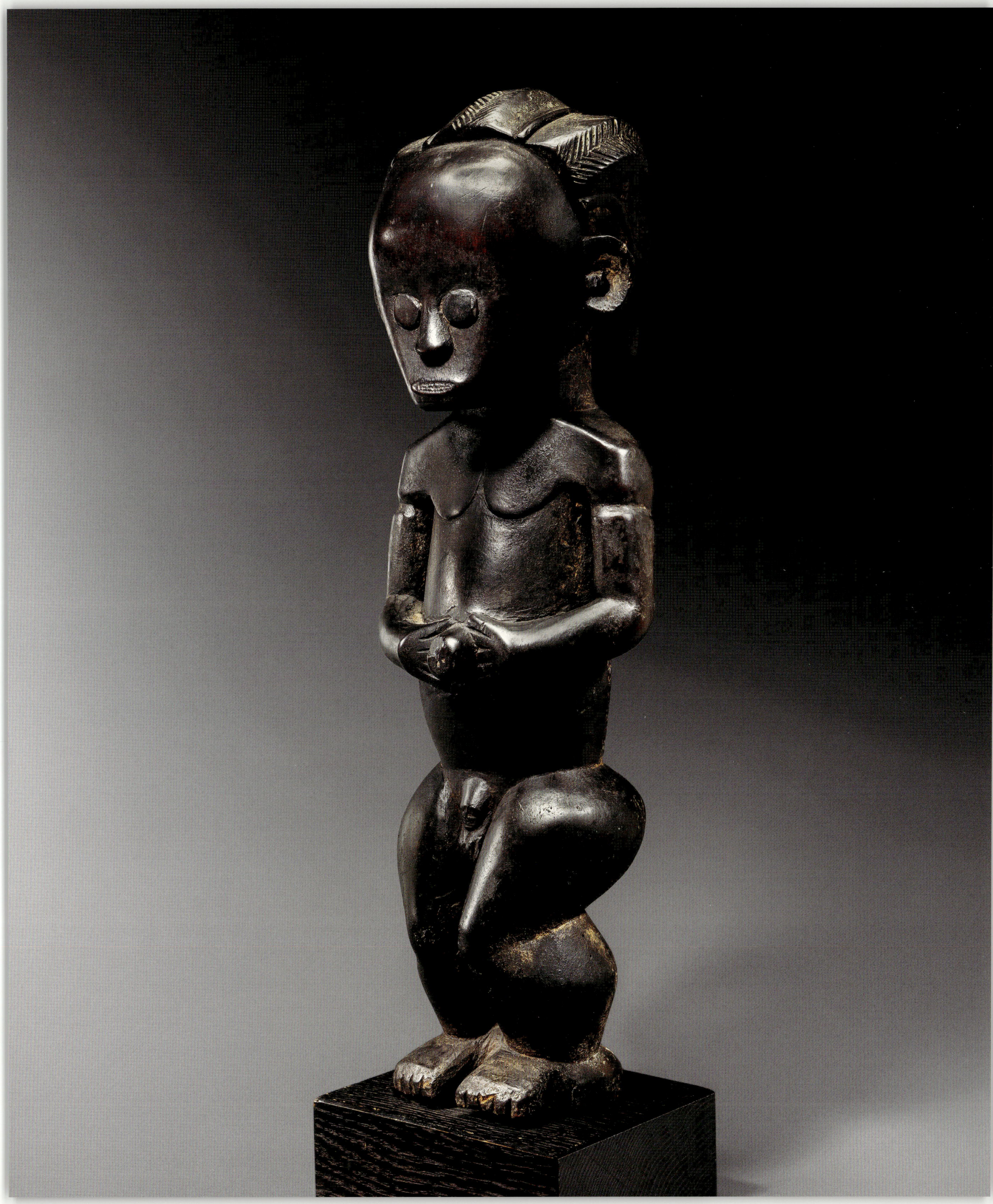

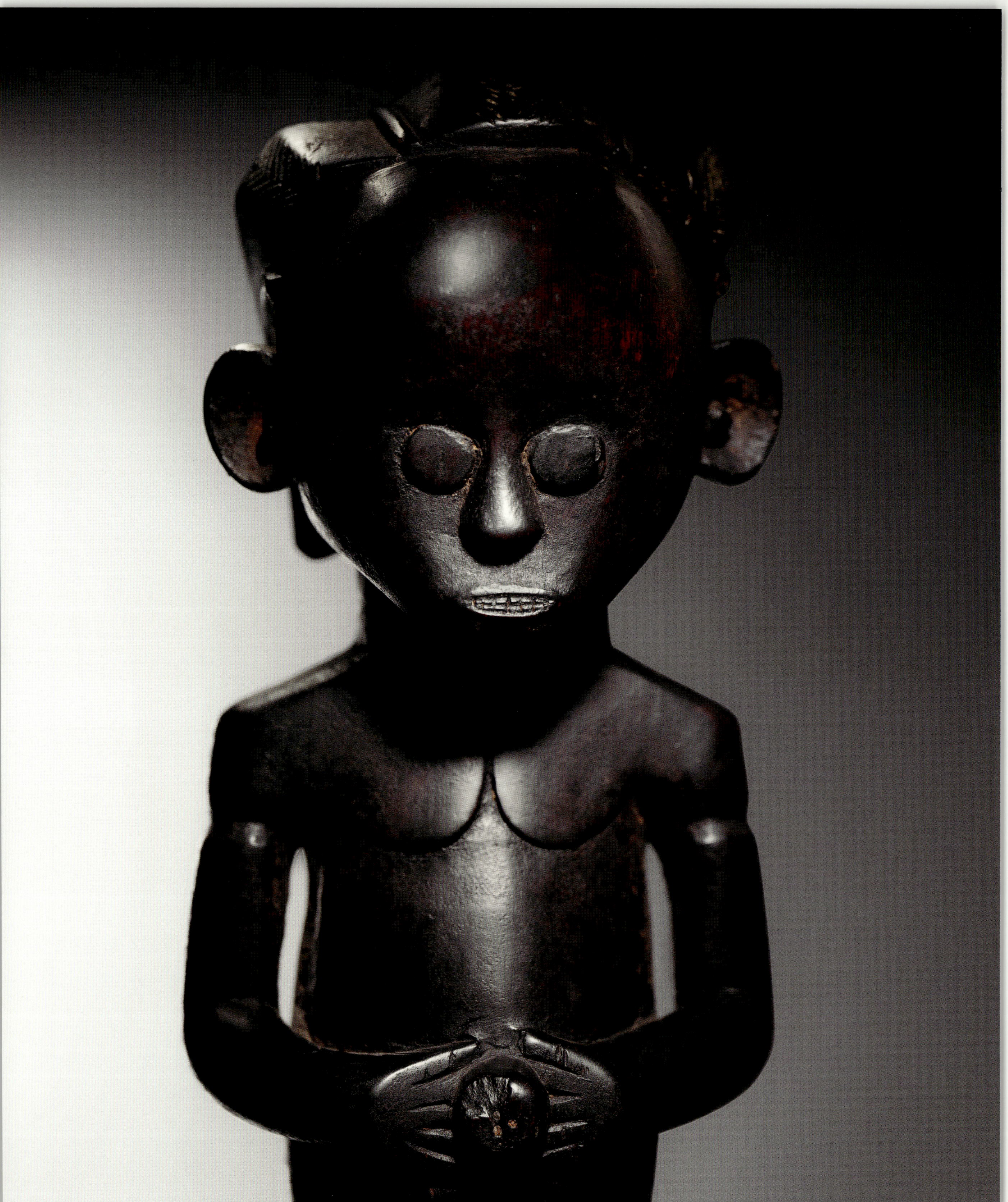

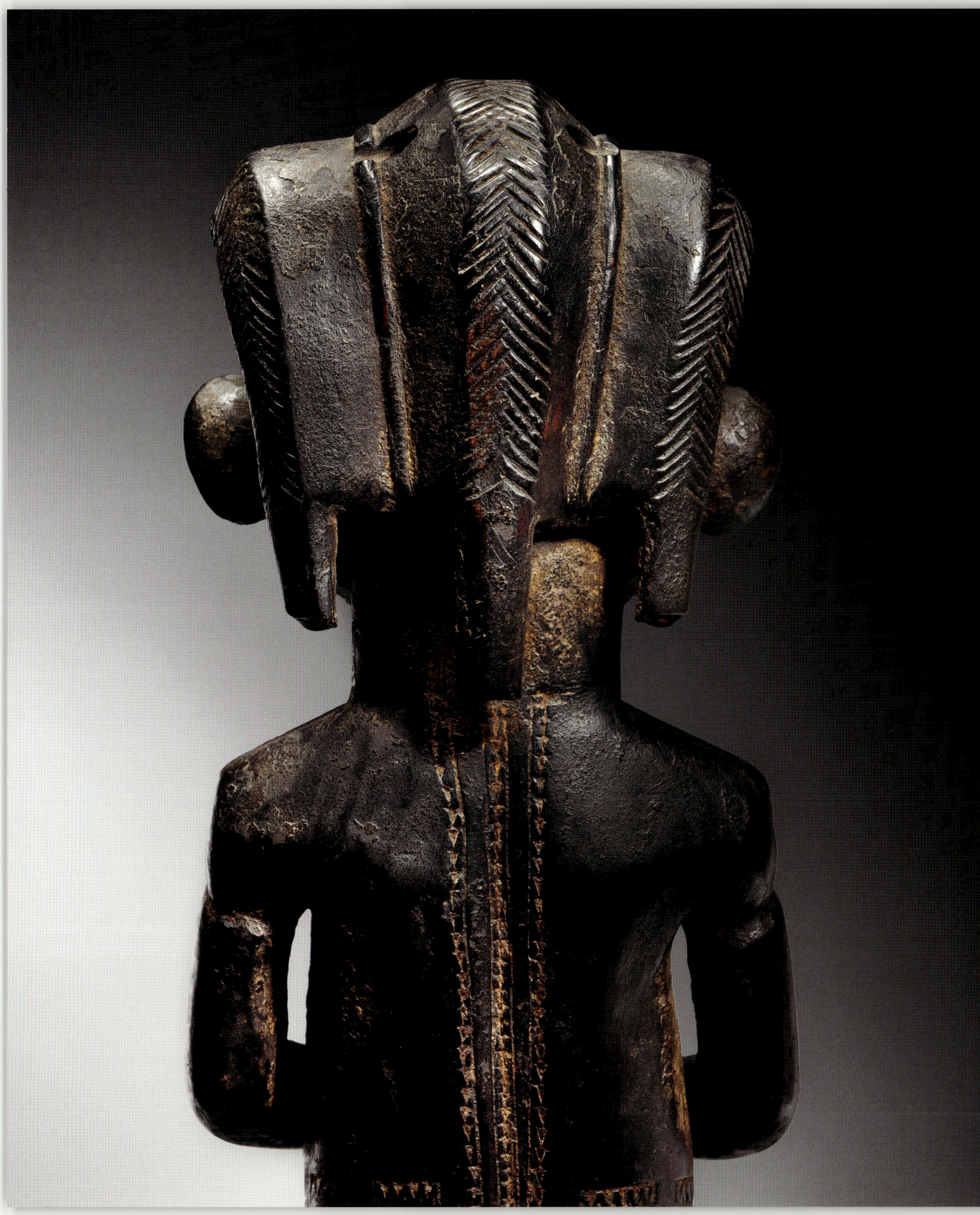

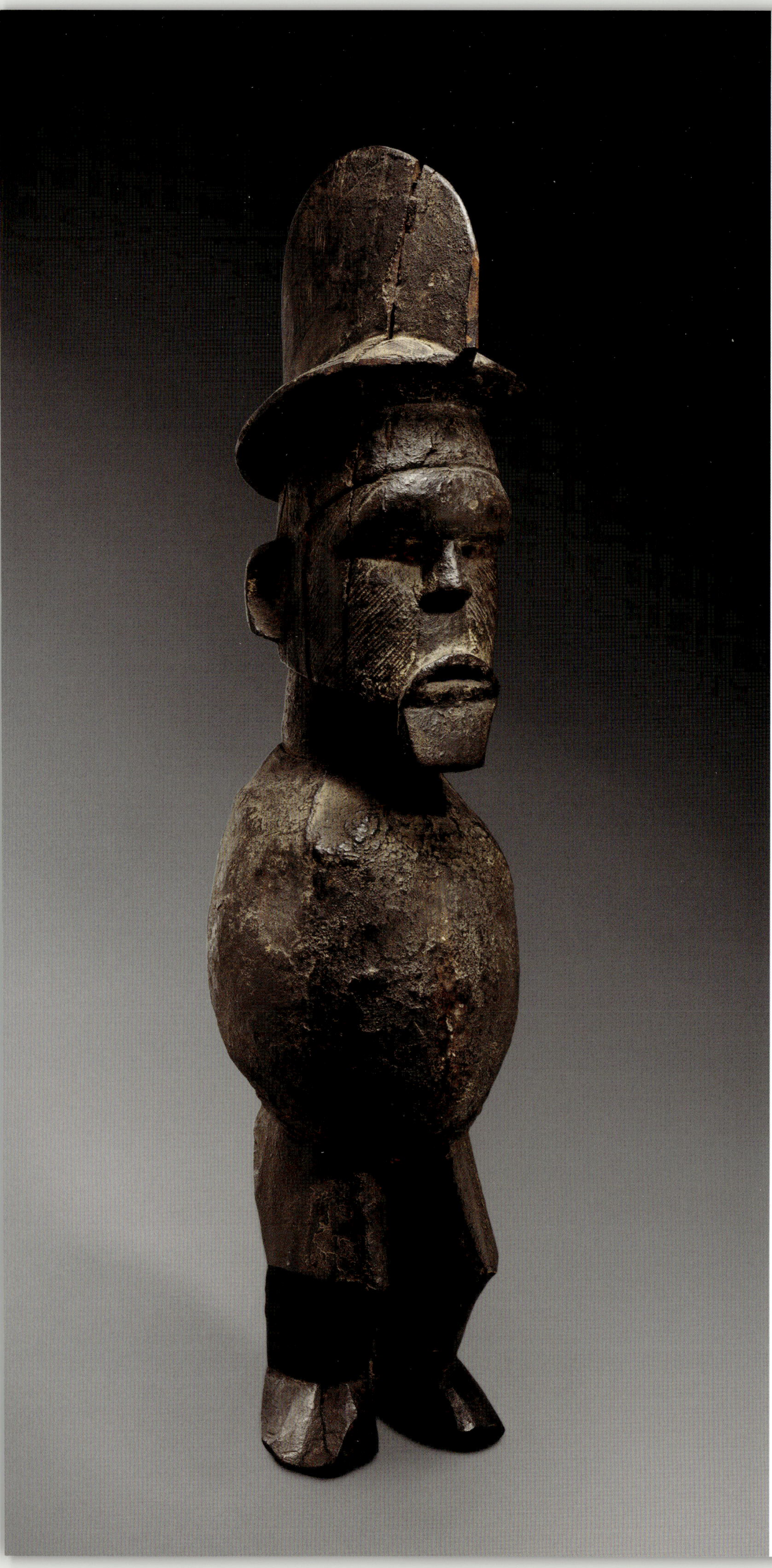

Teke statue
Malebo Pool region, Democratic Republic of the Congo, H. 56 cm

This figure, whose torso and belly have completely disappeared under a ritual coating, is decorated with striped tattoos and a headdress that Lehuard calls *imwu/mupani* and which I, following Marc Felix, view as being based on the shape of an upturned dugout canoe.[1]

In the absence of information gathered in the field, it is impossible to ascertain this figure's function or even its name, for its ritual characteristics depend entirely on the nature of the ingredients used in the unguents comprising the coating—something only the *ngàà* who made it knows.[2]

Among the Teke on the right bank of the river, where the statues have the generic name *itio*, the figure might depict a deceased person and enclose his *ikwii* spirit, whom the head of the family would worship in the family shrine.[3] On the left bank of the river, it might be a *ntswo* statue as part of a lineage healing cult and harbour an important *nkir* spirit, which would have been that of a *mukur*, an agnatic ancestor. On the other hand, it might be a type of *mati* (plur. *buti*) magic charm containing the *mupfu* spirit of the deceased, who, captured by a special ritual, did not achieve the rank of ancestor.[4]

Between ancestor worship, healing ritual practices and magic flirting with sorcery, the true purpose of this figure is now forever lost among the most arcane magical ingredients that fill it with mystery. [VB]

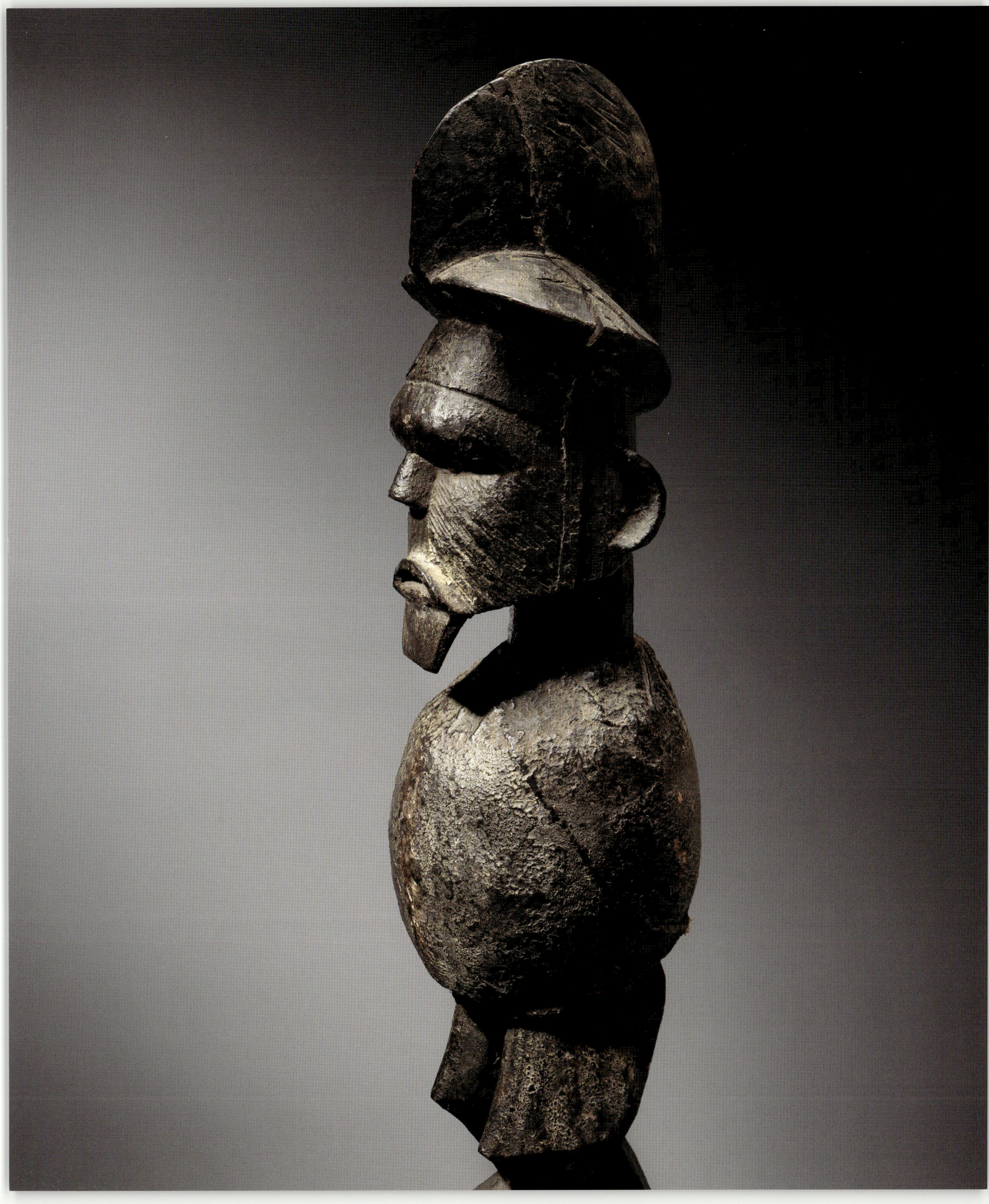

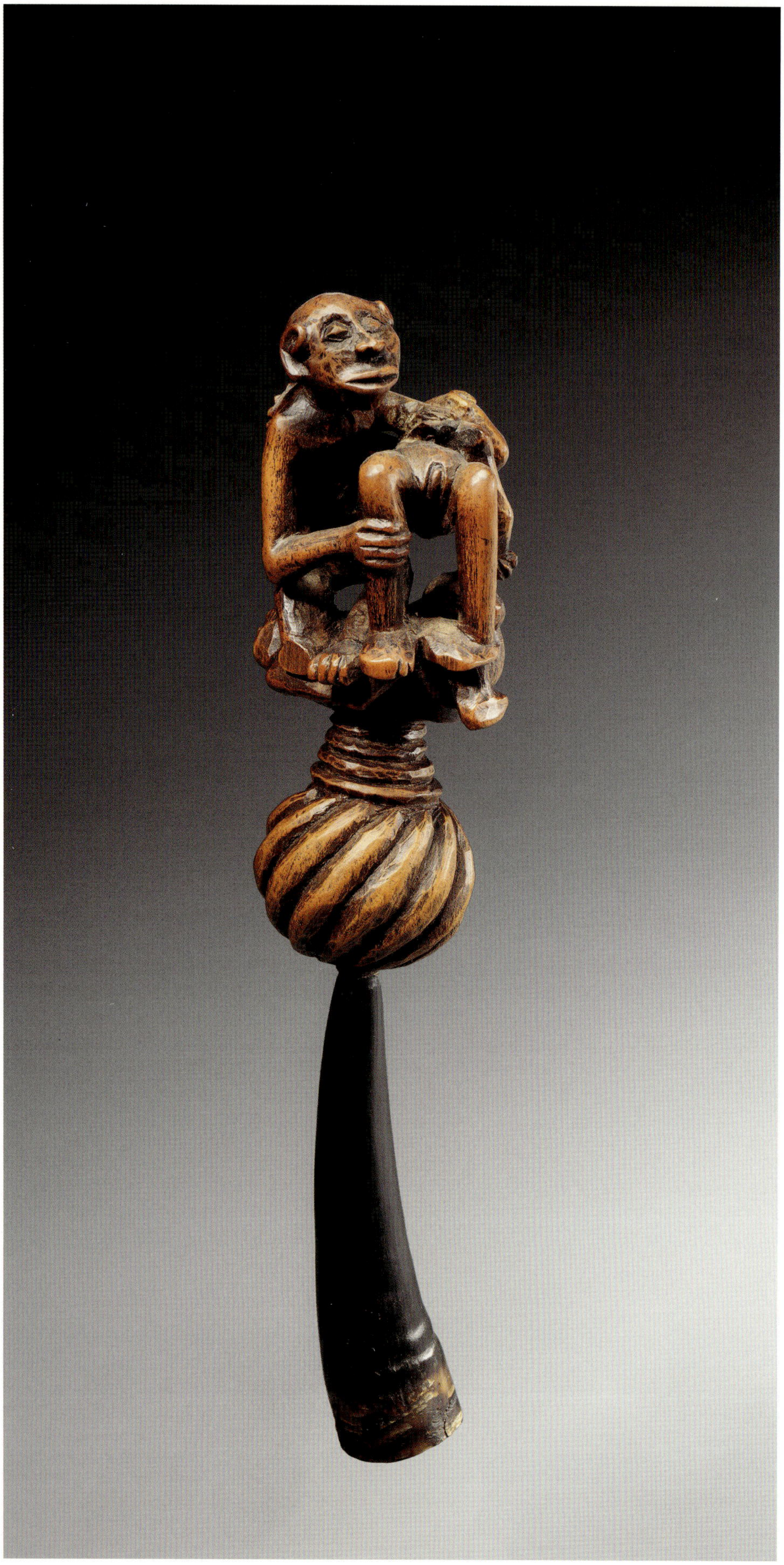

Kongo whistle
Democratic Republic of the Congo, H. 18 cm

This Kongo wooden miniature depicts a couple engaged in an unidentified sexual ritual: the man, on his knees and leaning forwards, seems to be presenting the woman's sexual organs to the audience. His left hand rests on the woman's belly, while the right grasps her right shin. There is another miniature depicting a similar scene in a work published by André Portier and François Poncetton (*Les Arts Sauvages d'Afrique*, 1956, pl. XXII, no. 35): in this case a naked boy is shown lying across a woman's left thigh, with his raised feet resting on a rectangular stone, exposing his genitals.
The sexual practices of the peoples of Central Africa have powerful symbolic connotations, being associated with initiation rituals and fertility rites and serving to create a link with the spirit world (Rachewitz (de) B., *Eros noir/Black Eros*, 1963/1964, p. 104). Designed as a decoration for the *nsimba* whistle, this particularly finely carved wooden miniature plays an essential role in the object's ritual power as it was employed in a hunting context or in medical treatments (Brincard M.-T., *Sounding Forms. African Musical Instruments,* New York, 1989, p. 165). Associated with the *nkisi* figures of power, *nsimba* whistles were an integral part of the instruments of magic of the *nganga* ritual specialist. [MC]

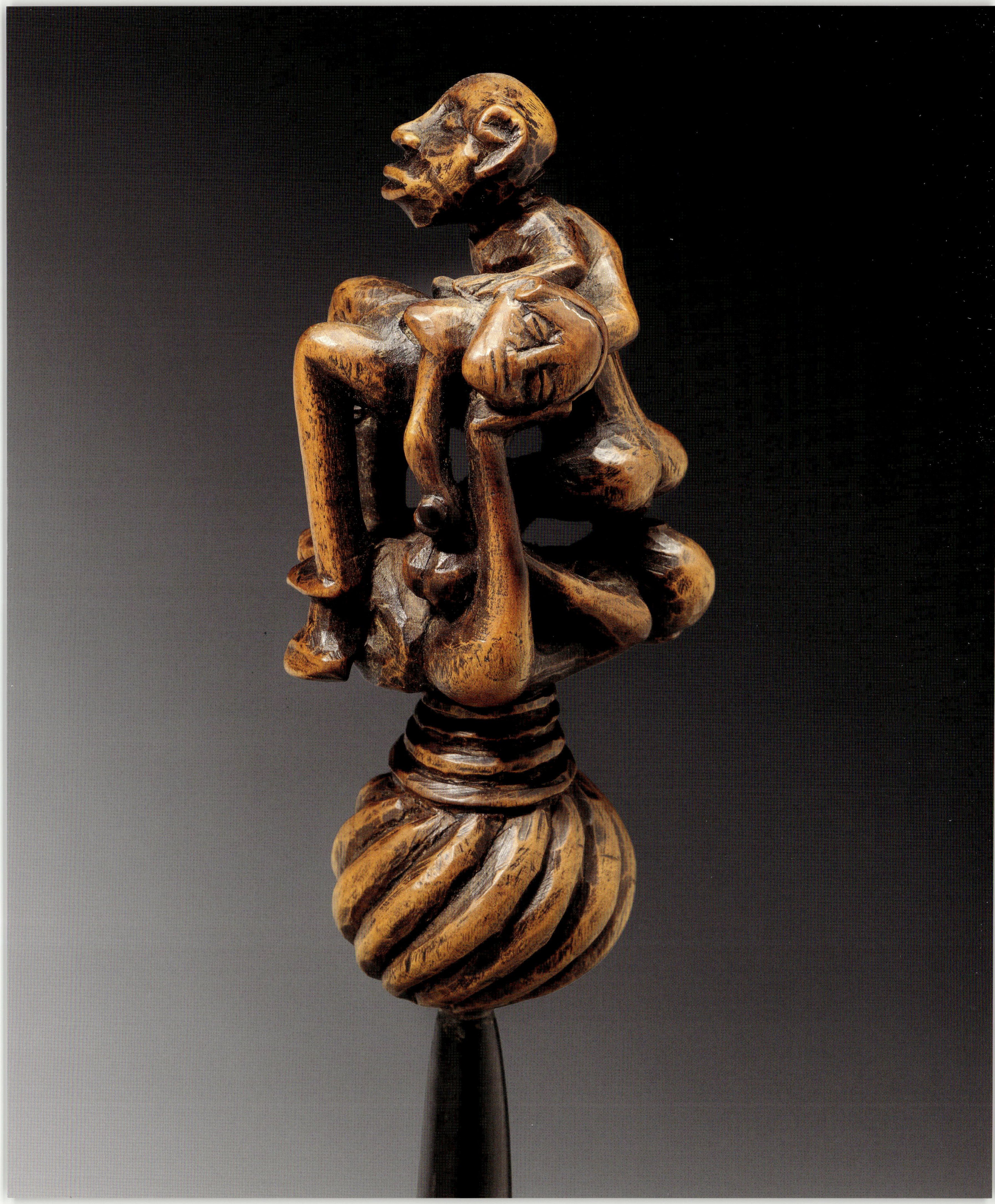

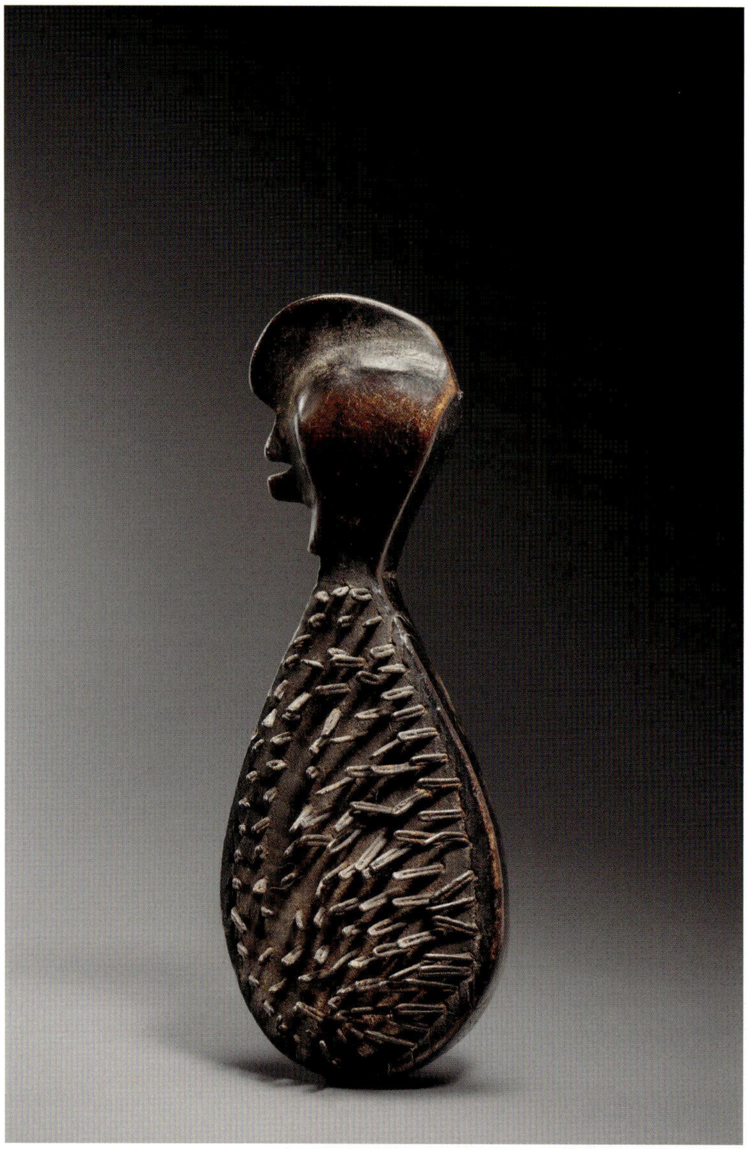

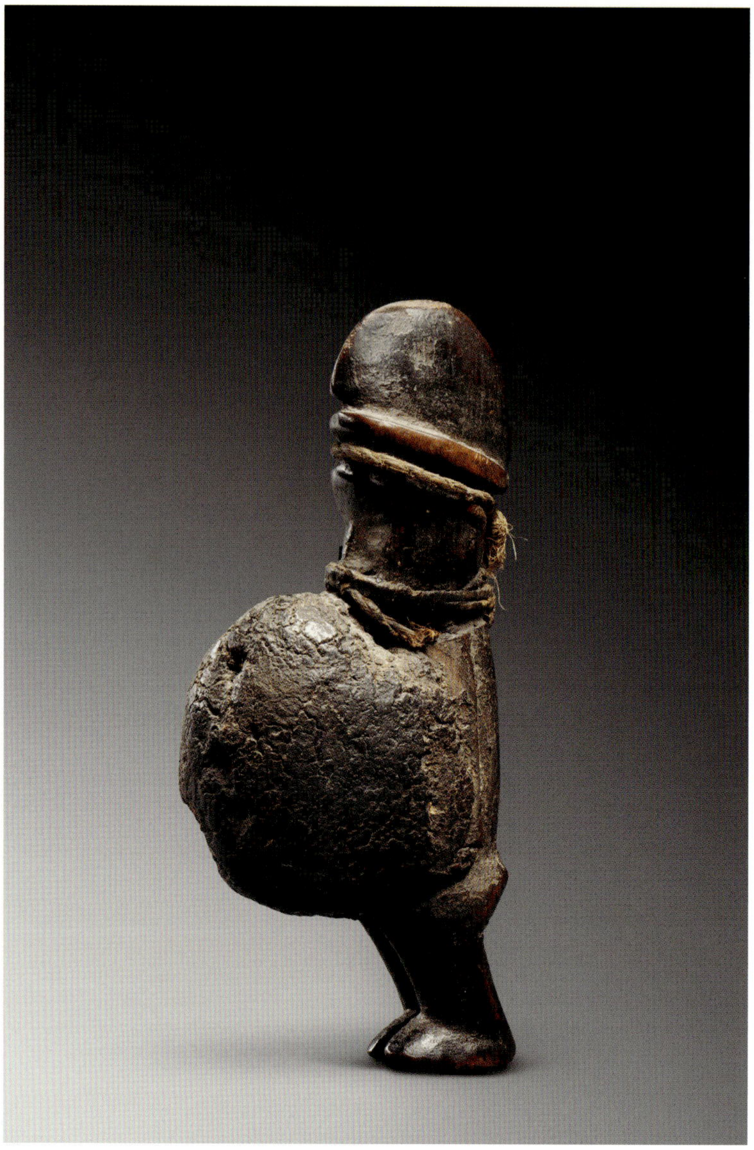

Songye comb
Democratic Republic of the Congo, H. 11 cm

The small sculpted head surmounting this object looks like the Songye's *kifwebe* masks. Indeed, they share the same jutting mouth, straight nose and large characteristic crest, which the male examples of this type all display. The precise function of this little object remains unknown. However, the fine reddish brown patina the piece has accumulated over the years leaves no room for doubt as to its age and its considerable use. The object's pure lines and its undeniable charm have enchanted several generations of collectors, the first of whom, significantly, being the artist John D. Graham, a major figure in the New York art scene of the 1920s, who introduced Jackson Pollock, among others, to African art. [MC]

Teke statuette
Malebo Pool region, Democratic Republic of the Congo, H. 11 cm

A witchdoctor (*ngàà*) has endowed this tiny but imposing figurine with magic powers. A small claw, held in place by a piece of string tied around the figure's neck, is barely visible among the other details. This clue, as well as its tiny size,[1] suggests the figurine was used in a hunting context,[2] possibly as a *mbyuu*.[3] On the right bank of the river, in the Mbe region, his type of charm, or *āti*, belonged to the *oseel'bene* category of objects, charms designed to bring luck to their wearers (in this case a hunter), as opposed to healing charms (*imiõ*) and charms worn for protection (*kaa*).[4] [VB]

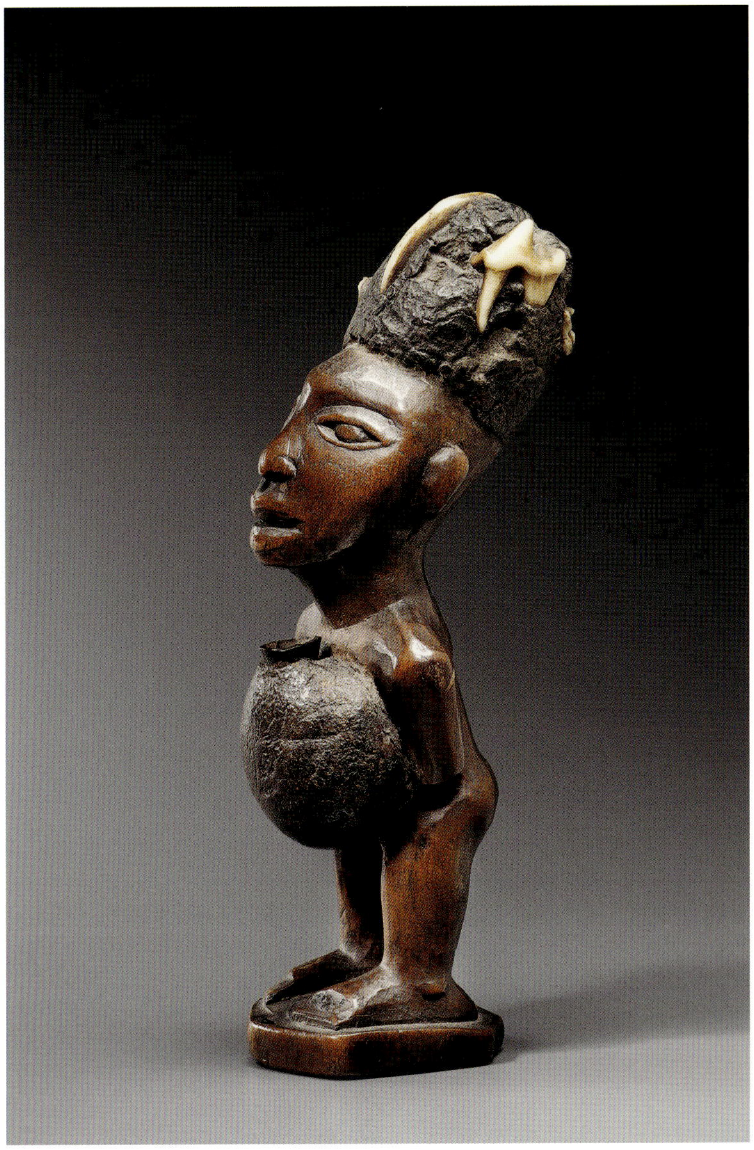

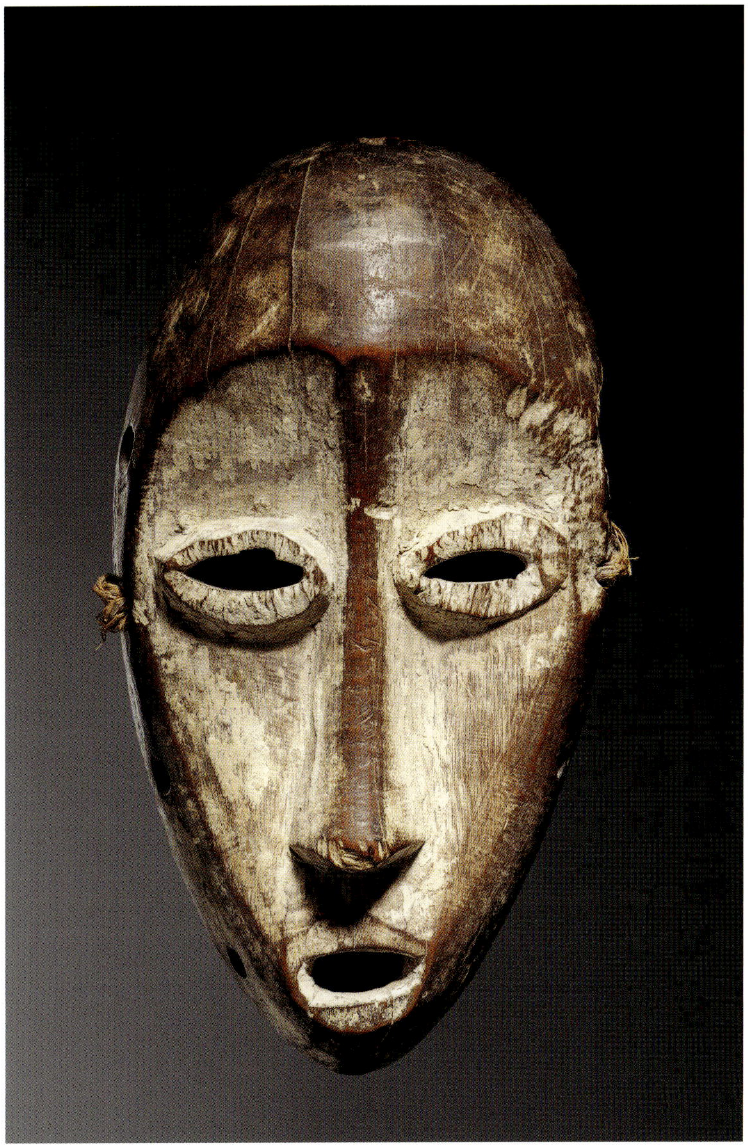

Vili statuette
Democratic Republic of the Congo, H. 14 cm

Most *minkishi* are plain baskets, pots or shells filled with various substances, each serving a particular therapeutic or protective purpose. When the *nkisi* is in the form of an anthropomorphic figure (*teki*, plur. *biteki*), these substances are generally concentrated within a resinous wad called a *bilongo*. This little figurine has two, one on the belly and another on the head.
An antelope horn has been set into the charm on the belly, while the *bilongo* on the head is filled with teeth and pieces of jaw, two clues suggesting this particular specimen was meant to bring luck in the hunt. [VB]

Lega mask
Democratic Republic of the Congo, H. 16 cm

The *bwami* society regulates the entire social and spiritual life of the Lega and features an extremely precise hierarchical structure that includes five initiation grades for both men and women. The small *lukwakongo* masks belong to fourth grade initiates—*lutumbo iwa yananio* (the *bulonda* is the female equivalent)—of which they are one of the most prestigious emblems. Initiates would wear these objects with pride and dignity on the forehead, on the temples and on the arms during collective ceremonies. They might even be attached to a carrying frame (*pala*), on either side of the large masks owned by higher ranking initiates, the *kindi*. This eminently symbolic grouping alluded to "the continuity within the *bwami* and kinship groups, a continuity that binds the living to the dead" (Biebuyck D.P., *Lega, Éthique et beauté au cœur de l'Afrique*, 2002, pp. 71–2). [MC]

Hemba caryatid stool
Nkuvu or Muhona, Tanganyika, Democratic Republic of the Congo,
H. 45.5 cm

The powerful Luba Kingdom extended its influence to the western part of Hemba territory, where this stunning caryatid stool was made, during the reign of King Kumwine Ngombe (ca. 1840–70). It is undoubtedly one of the finest examples of a shared cultural history, as this type of seat originally belonged to the Luba tradition. Known in this kingdom as a *kihona*, it symbolizes women's role as privileged intermediaries between the living and the spirits of dead kings and chiefs. It was one of the key emblems of royal power and was believed to contain the *vidye* spirit of a dead king, a spirit that possessed one of his wives, who then became his *mwadi*. When not used during enthronement ceremonies, this seat was (and still is) carefully kept hidden from prying eyes.[1]

The Hemba have always ignored the institution of royalty or sacred chiefdom and by adopting this stool that properly speaking belongs to the formal language of the Luba, they have certainly given it a whole new meaning. According to François Neyt, however, the northern Hemba groups have developed a hierarchical society divided into *twite* and *bafumu*; the chiefs, or *balohwe* (sing. *mulohwe*),[2] at the pinnacle of the hierarchy in the latter group, are invested by the *twite*. Only a *mulohwe* could own a *kihona* stool like this and sit on it when dispensing justice.[3]

The Luba *kipona* caryatid stool stepped outside the sacred, secret, spiritual sphere to enter the realm of conspicuous political and judicial power when it became a Hemba *kihona*. Perhaps because the religious and magical domain, devoted entirely to the ancestors, was already occupied by male *singiti* ancestor figures and the formidable *kabeja* Janus figures.[4]

But it might be that the sculptor who created this particular stool was not so preoccupied with the respective functions that the Hemba society attributed to male statues and female caryatids. By lending this figure the same serene expression found on *singiti* ancestor figures, with mouth closed in an enigmatic smile and *úbatízha* expression turned towards the contemplation of an inner world,[5] the artist seems to have opened the gates to the world of the ancestors. [VB]

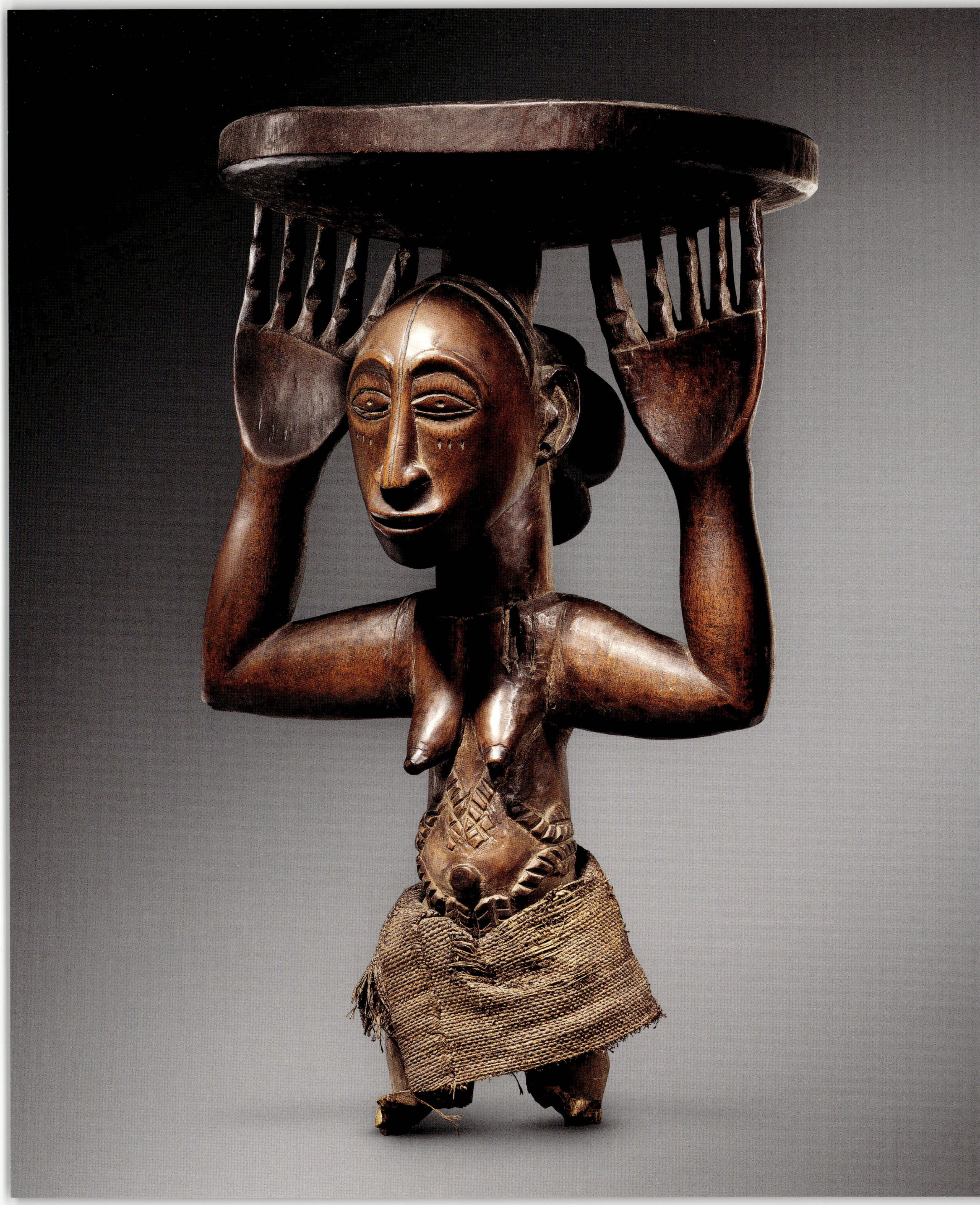

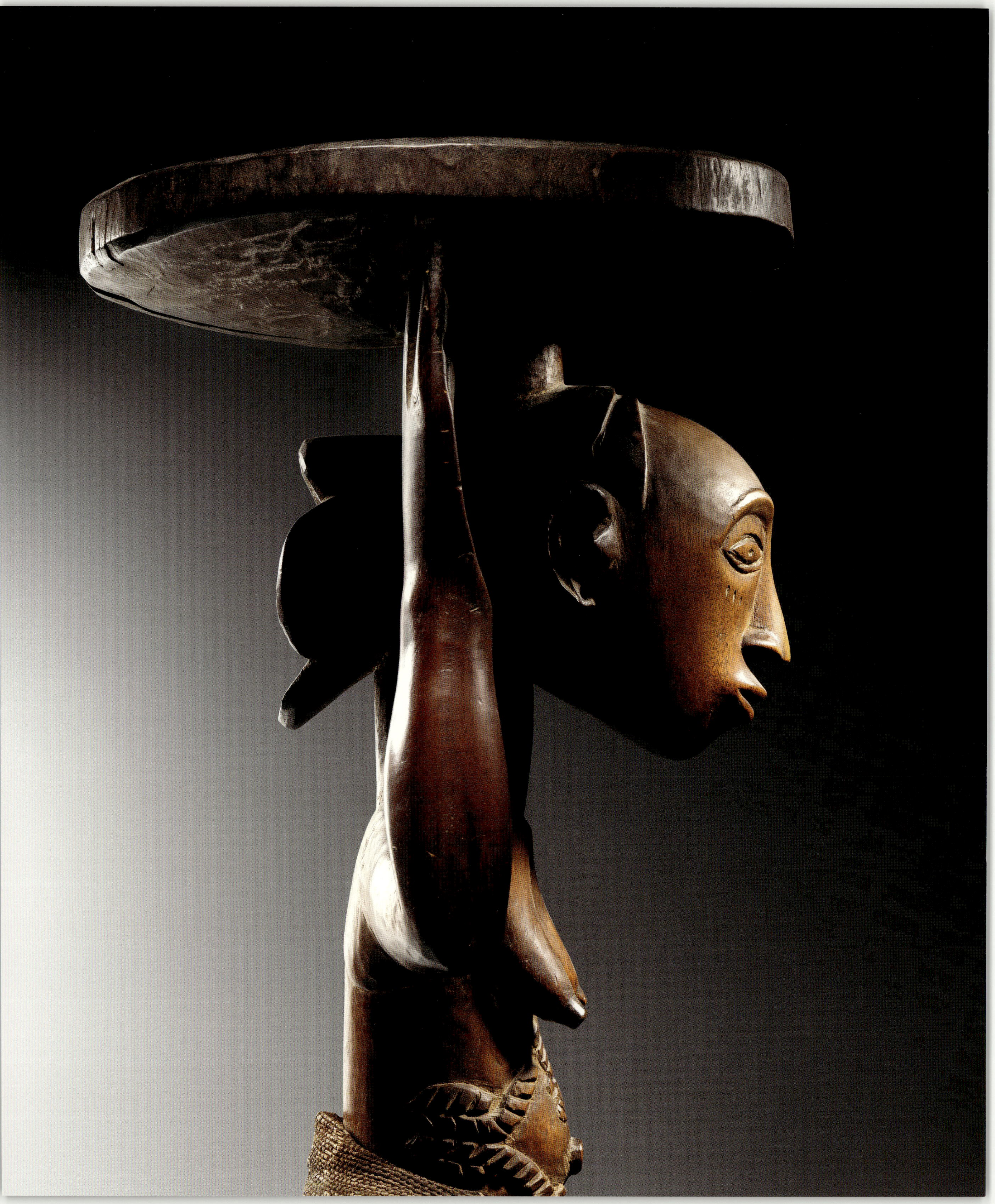

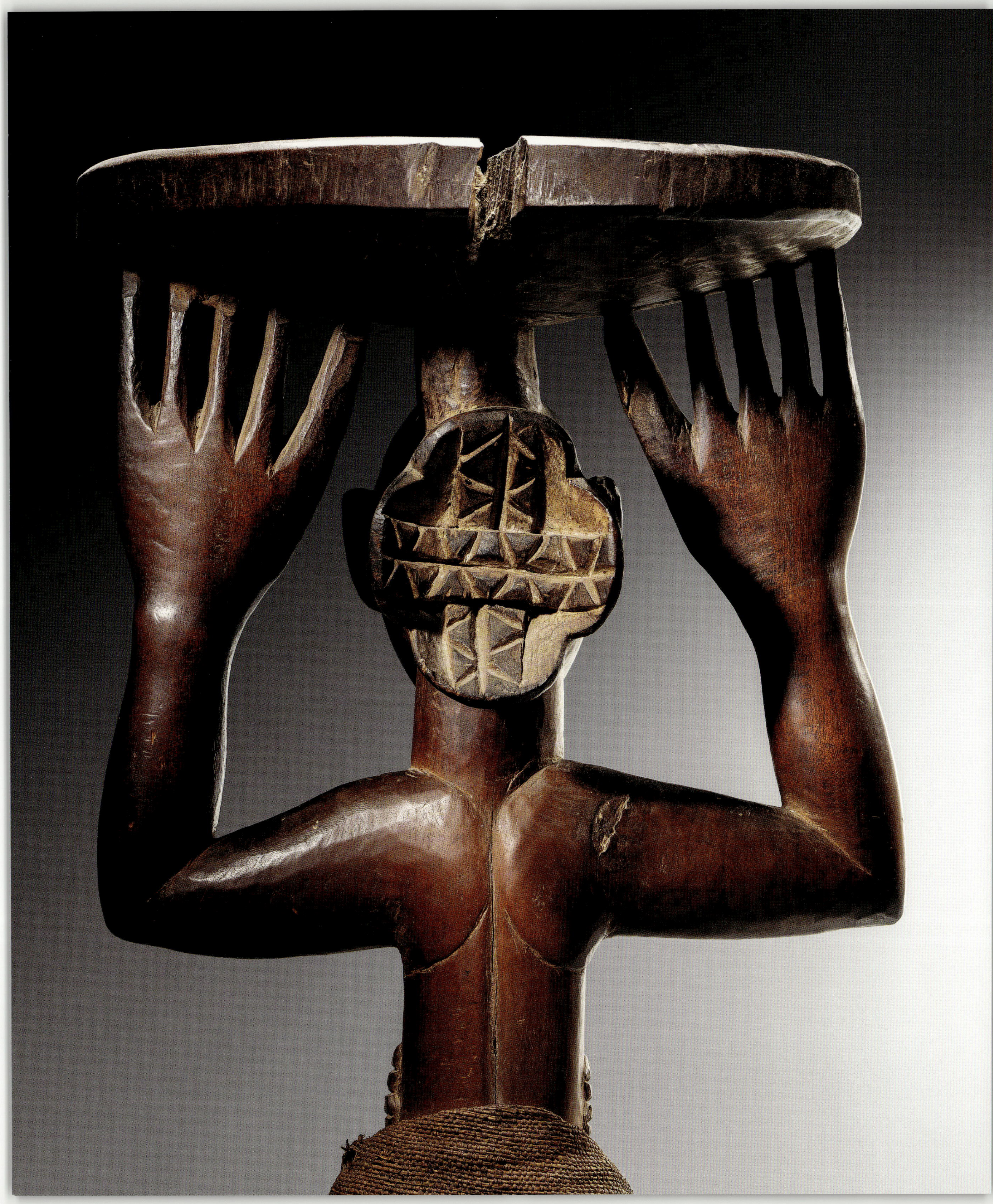

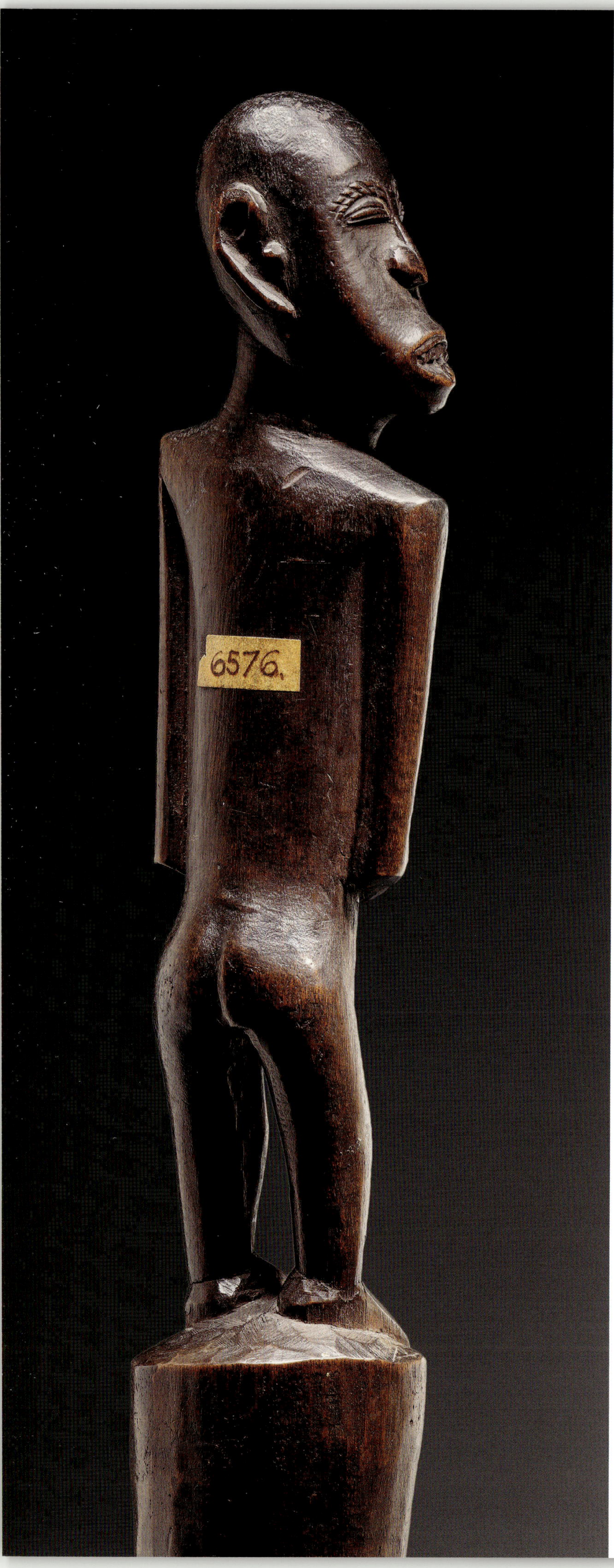
6576.

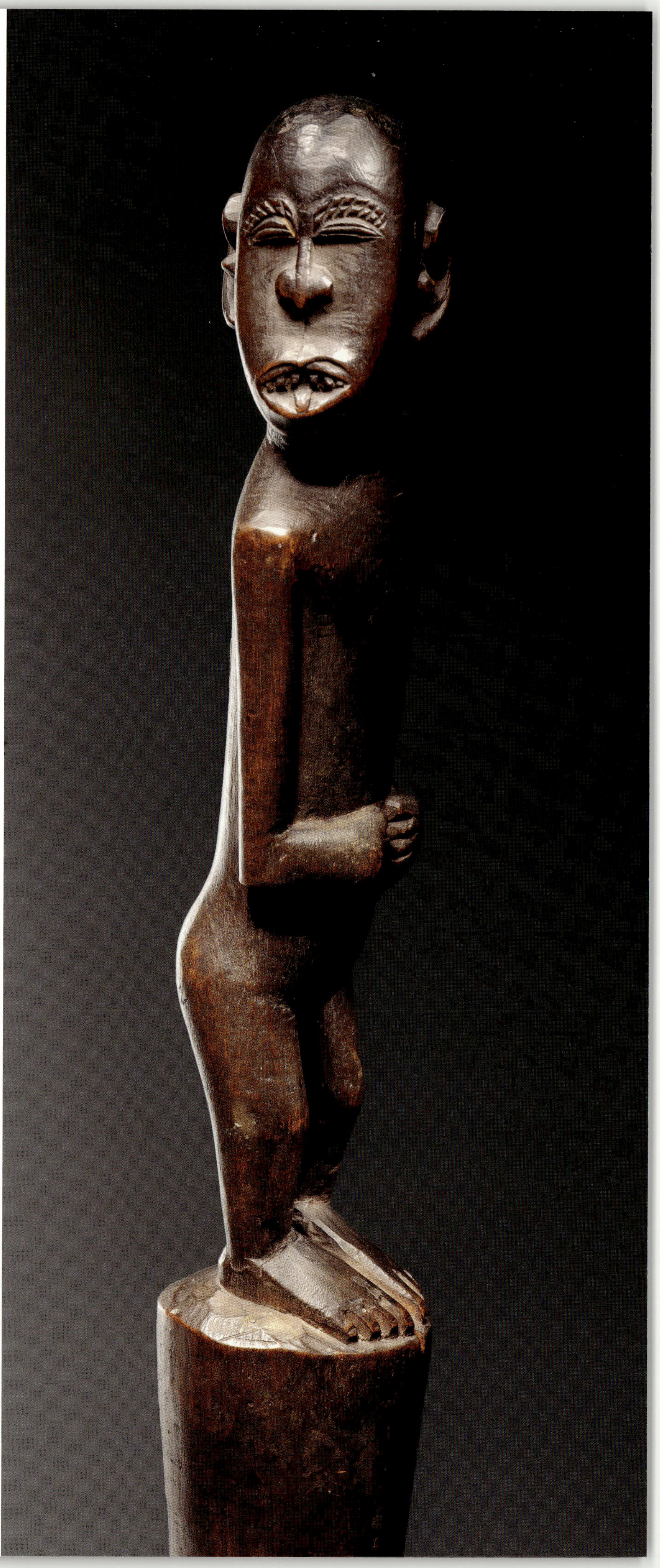

Vili sceptre
Democratic Republic of the Congo, H. 38 cm

Sculpted at the top of a sceptre, this effigy was probably planted in the ground during certain ceremonies, especially initiations (Cornet J.A., *Kongo: objets de bois, objets d'ivoire*, 1998, p. 10). Depicted standing upright, with hands joined over the belly, the feature of this male ancestor figure is the extreme economy in the handling of its clean, sober lines. The head is gracefully elongated and turned to the right, the eyes squinting and the mouth open to reveal the tongue and teeth. This conspiratorial expression reinforces the effect of the figure's stance, which stresses his vigilance and discernment.
The figure is believed to come from a Kongo-Vili workshop and, in particular, is an excellent example of the D4 Vili style, as identified by Lehuard (Lehuard R., *Art Bakongo. Les Centres de style*, vol. I, 1989, pp. 236–39).
[MC]

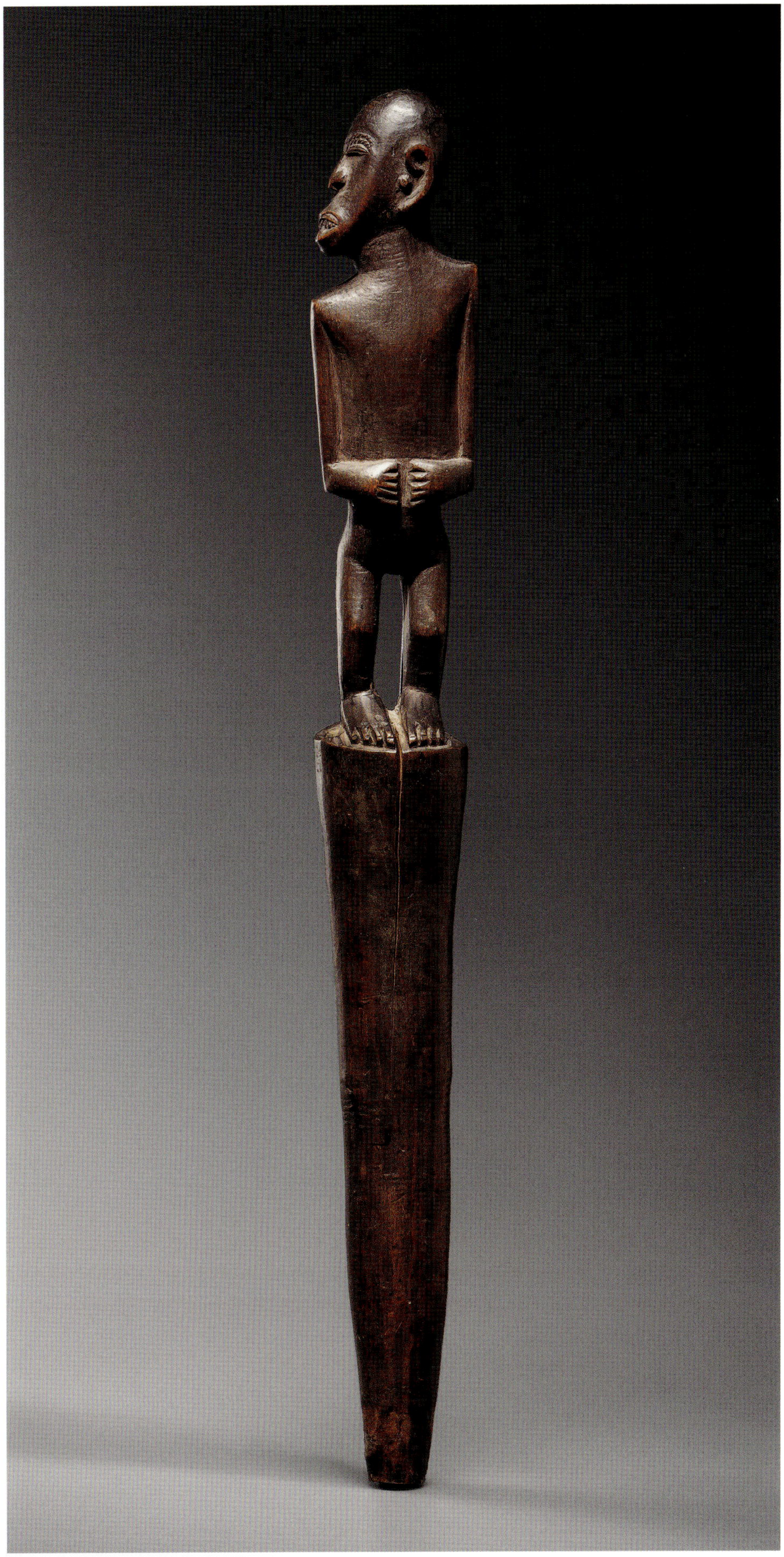

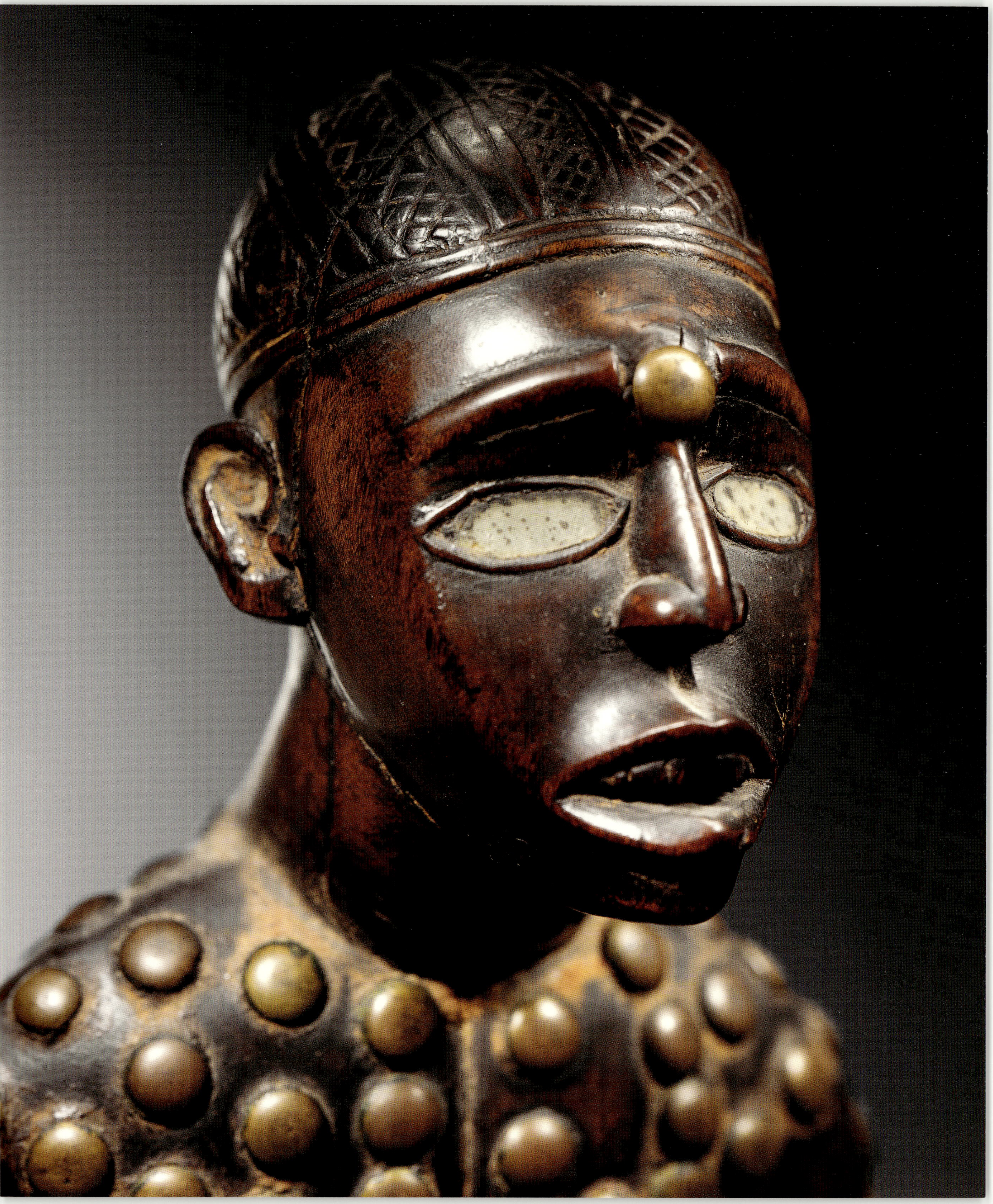

Yombe statue
Central Kongo Province, Democratic Republic of the Congo, H. 34 cm

A *nkisi* consists of a physical container (*ntinu*, body) within which is placed (or imprisoned) an invisible being, which among the Yombe would have been a *simbi* spirit; various animal, mineral, or vegetable ingredients were added in order to give it a specific purpose. These charms, known as *bilongo*, were mixed with resin and shaped into a wad that was placed on the belly and/or head of a statue, where they formed the heart, *ntima*, of the *nkisi*. This *nkisi*, whose style is similar to that of the master of Kasadi, is unusually adorned with several brass nails. It once had a *bilongo* receptacle, nailed (in a symbolic sense) on the belly, signs of which are clearly visible. This powerful accessory was undoubtedly removed for aesthetic reasons when the object reached Europe. [VB]

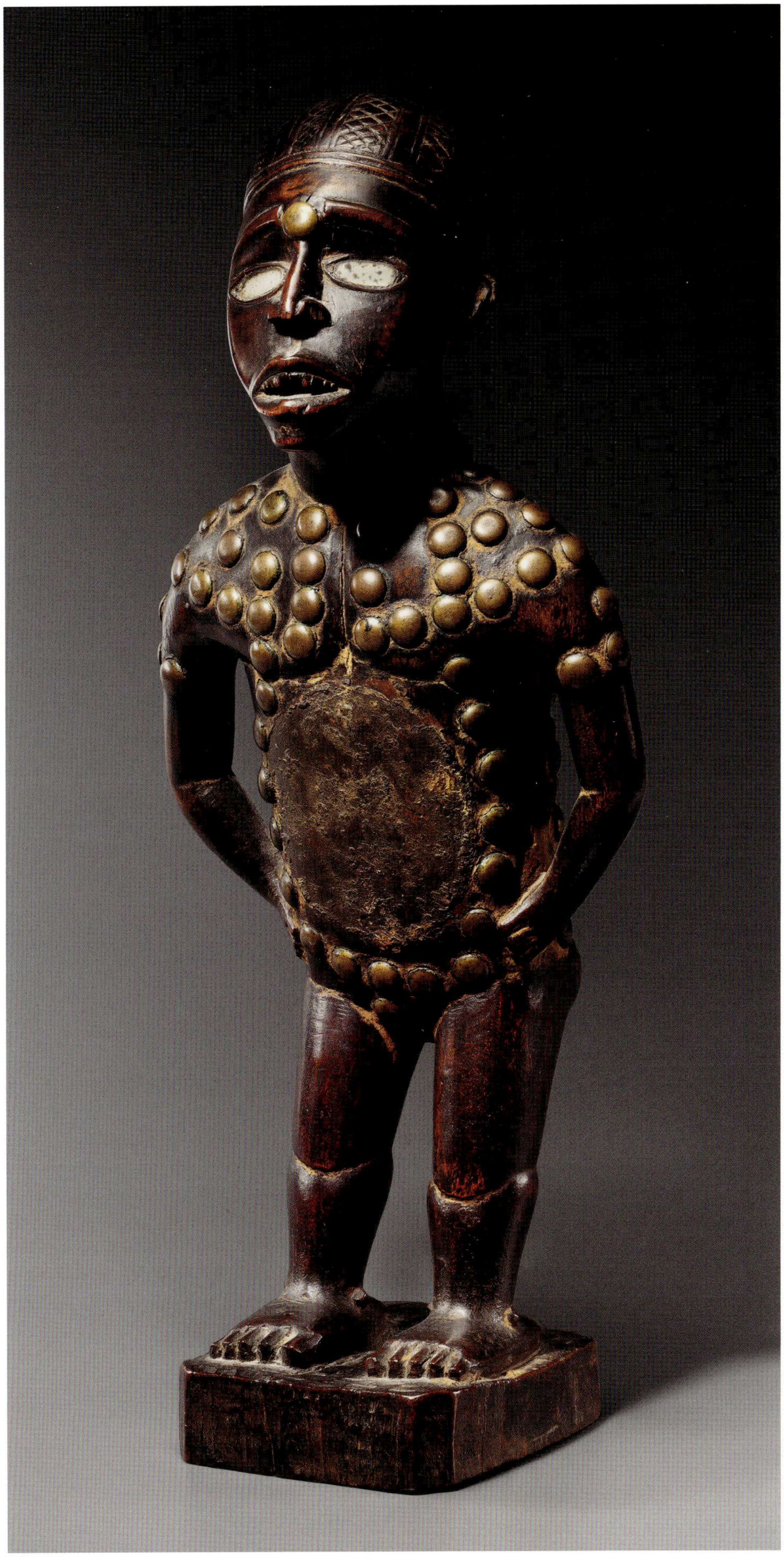

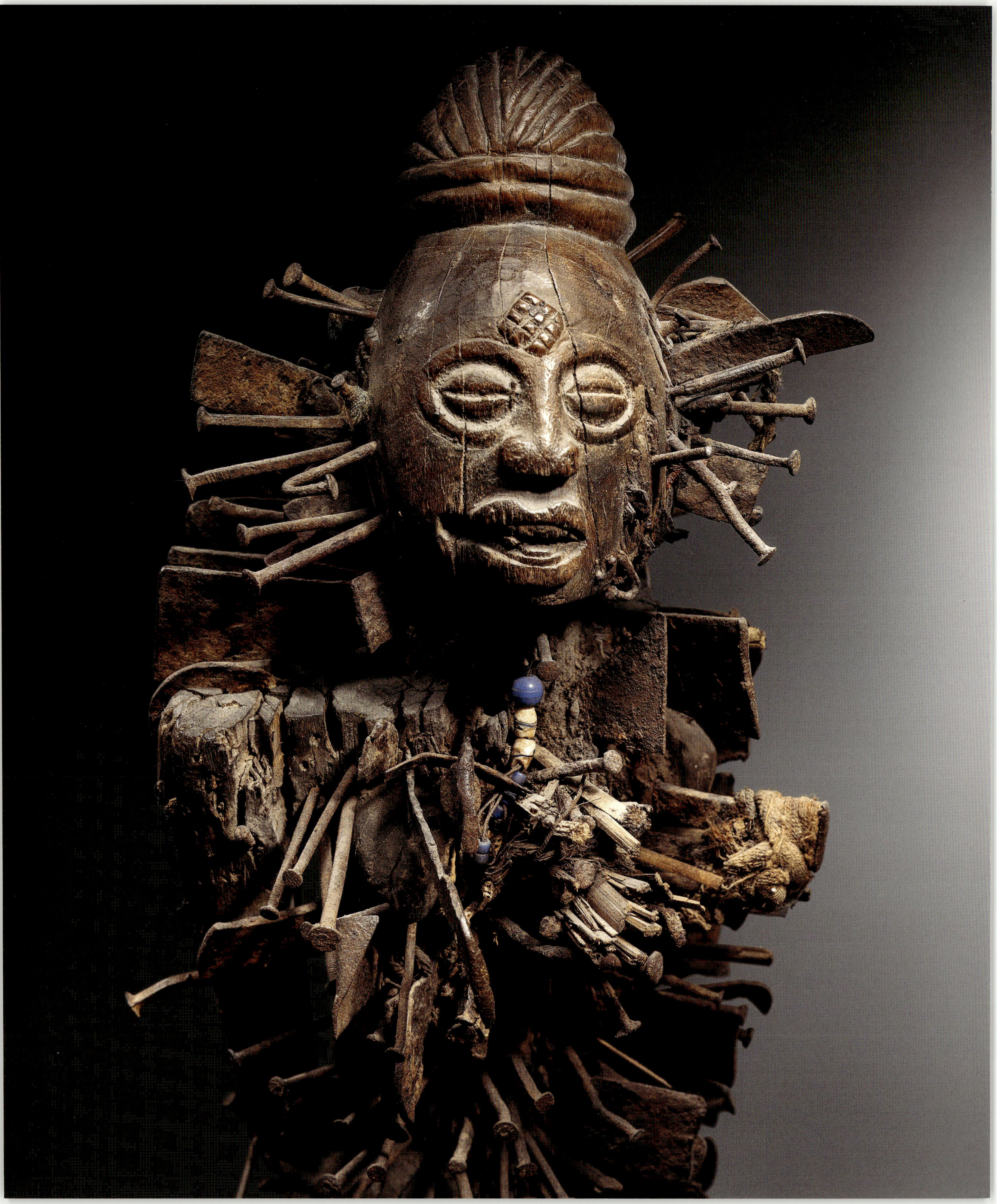

Kongo-Mayanga statue
Central-Kongo Province, Democratic Republic of the Congo, H. 51 cm

According to Raoul Lehuard, this powerful statue studded with iron spikes was created by the Mayanga, who live to the northeast of the Yombe. Upturned faces, diamond-shaped tattoos on the forehead, and a very high, piled-up hairstyle, sometimes reaching down to the nape of the neck, as here, are typical of the Mayanga style.[1]
Karl Laman's[2] informers claim that among both the Yombe and the Mayanga the *minkisi nkondi* belonged in the higher *minkisi* (*ku zulu*, heaven and celestial waters) category when their function was to help chiefs in their ventures, while statuettes used for healing and soothsaying purposes were part of the lower *minkisi* (*ku nsi*, earth and terrestrial waters) category.[3] The latter were used in treating conditions affecting the women's body in its lower part, such as sterility, while the *nkisi nkondi* were associated with mainly upper body male afflictions causing nightmares, migraines and pneumonia. [VB]

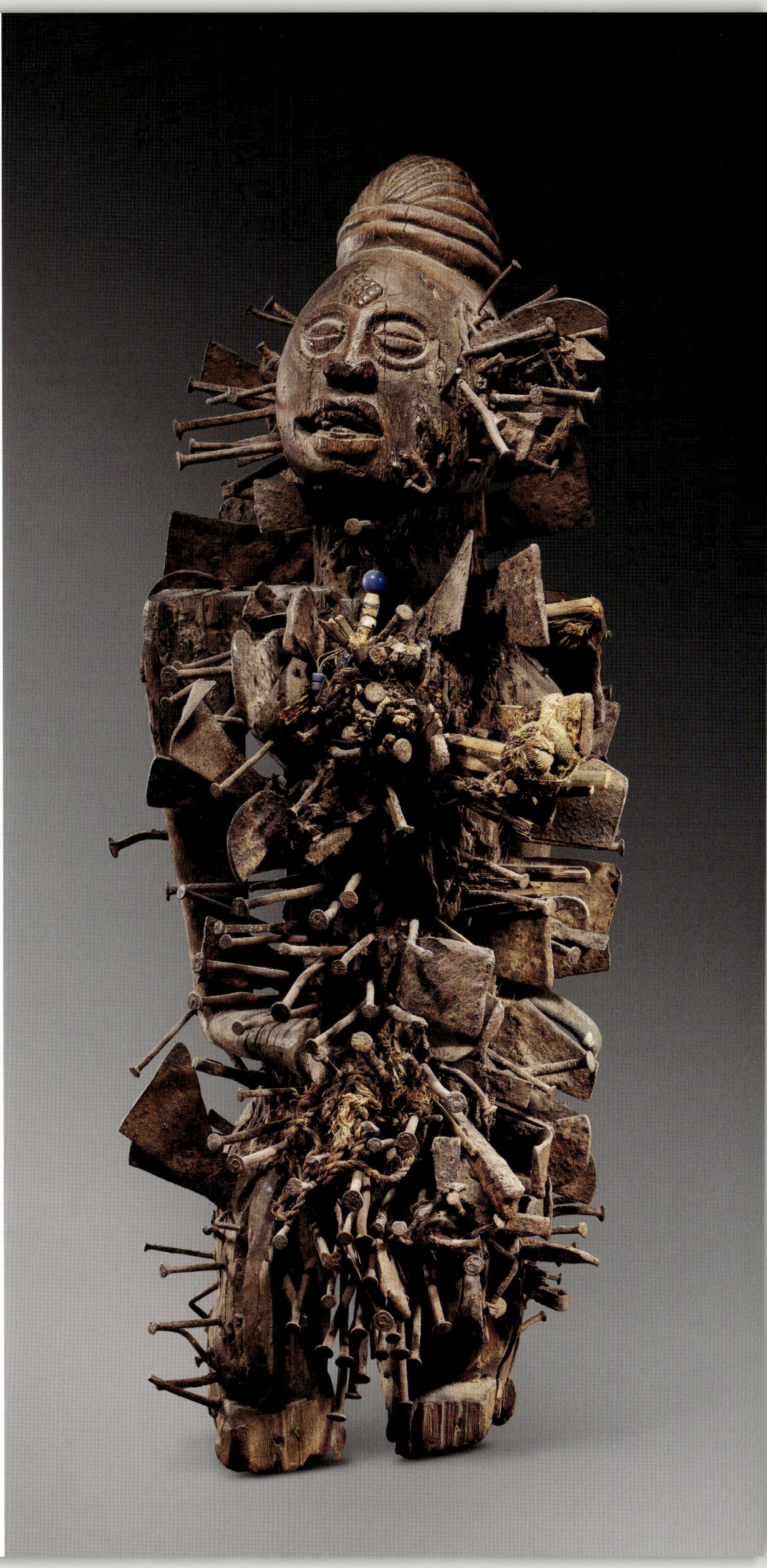

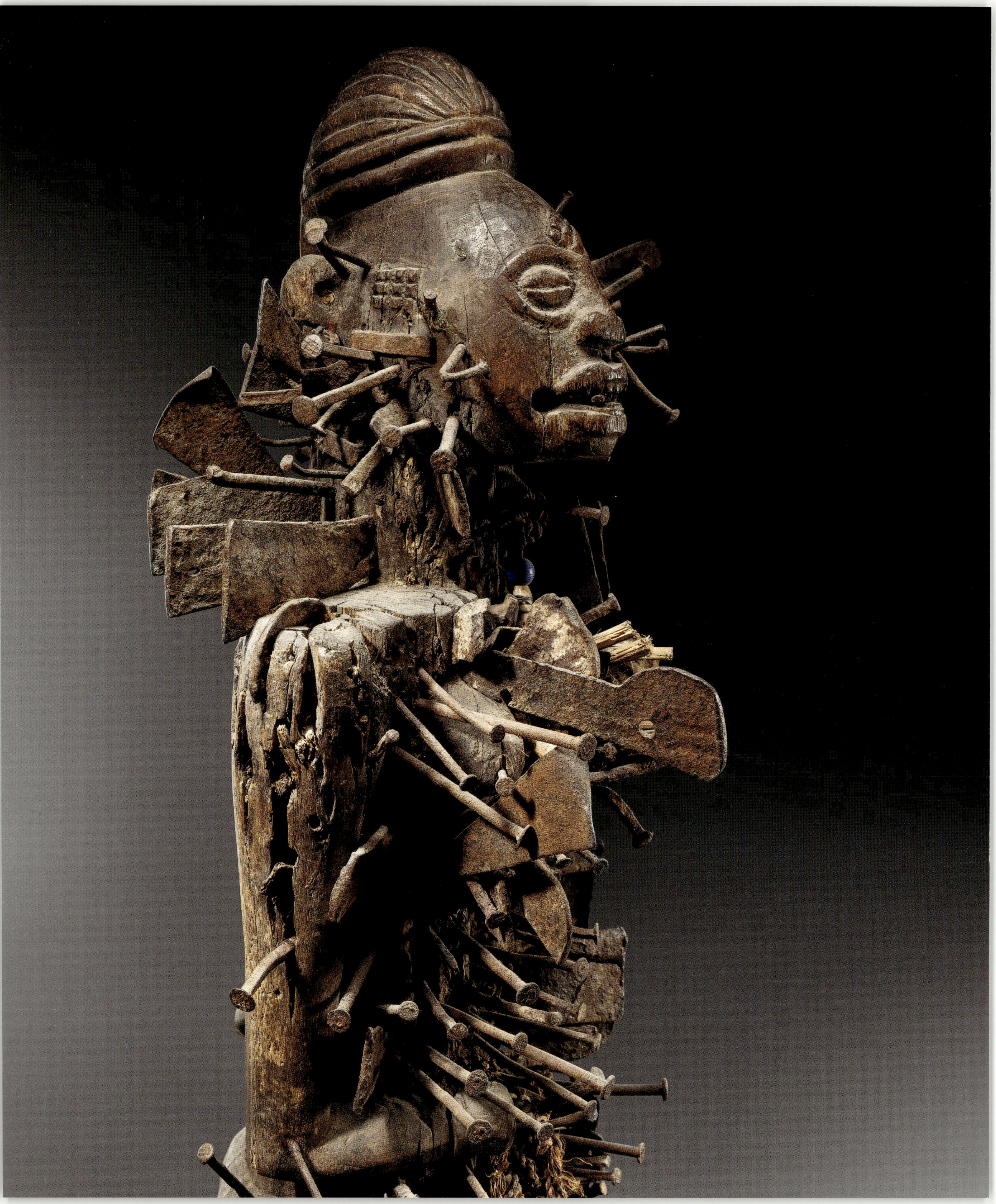

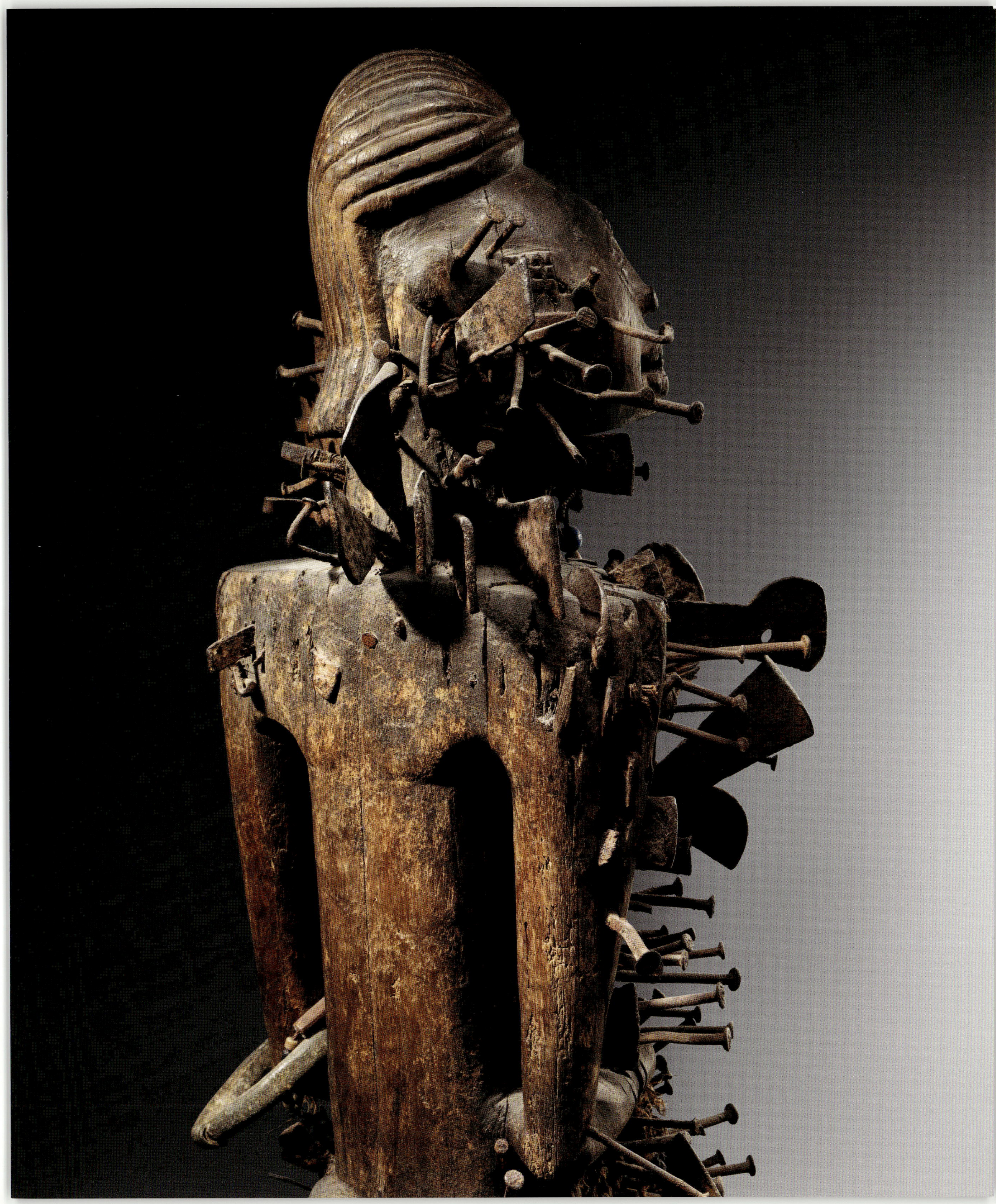

Vili statue

Democratic Republic of the Congo/Cabinda, H. 76 cm

Despite the fact that the various Kikongo-speaking populations, ranging from Gabon to Angola, accommodate quite a wide variety of religious beliefs,[1] they do share a reliance on the specific magical powers of the *minkisi* (sing. *nkisi*).

A protective or healing *nkisi* generally housed a supernatural being; in contrast, the large *nkisi nkondi* (from the verb *konda*, to hunt), such as the object illustrated here, was designed to be used in witchcraft and necessarily contained the spirit of someone who died badly (through suicide, murder, etc.), ensuring an appropriate degree of aggressiveness. The wad of empowering substances attached to the belly (*bilongo*) would direct its magical influence as required. When its powers were needed, the ritual expert (*nganga*) would activate it by piercing it with a nail or iron spike, hence the numerous spikes covering this example. The tongue resting on the lower lip is a reminder that the *nganga* had to lick the iron spike before sticking it into the figure so that it would follow his instructions and be suitably activated.

The statue is fashioned in the Vili style and was probably made in a workshop in "the Chiloango valley," from the name of the river that flows through the territory of the Vili. But in a linguistic irony, although many nailed statues were made in the coastal region where the Vili live, the generic term *nkondi* itself is unknown there and only other Kongo groups actually call them *minkisi nkondi*.

This male figure is wearing a *mpu* cap decorated with various incised symbols (*zinga* shells) and objects set physically into it (leopard teeth, bent iron spikes). These motifs, arranged in a ring around the top of the head, strongly resemble the pictogram arranged in a rosette that is the symbol of the *Lemba* initiation society and that adorns the lids of its *tukobe* ritual baskets made of tree bark. This important society exercised its authority in the former kingdoms of Loango (Vili) and Ngoyo (Woyo), as well as Mayombe, for almost three centuries.[2] The male figure in a sculpture portraying a couple of *Lemba* initiates wears a cap with the same initiation symbols.[3] This headdress and the little *ngongi* bell the figure wears around its neck, indicates that this *nkondi*'s powers belonged to a chief, while its *mpu* headdress suggests this chief was a *Lemba* initiate, as were all the great dignitaries engaged in the trading networks of the nineteenth century.

The figure's wide-open eyes staring at the invisible world and its hands resting on its hips in the arrogant *pakalala* pose still and forever invite us to take advantage of its powers. [VB]

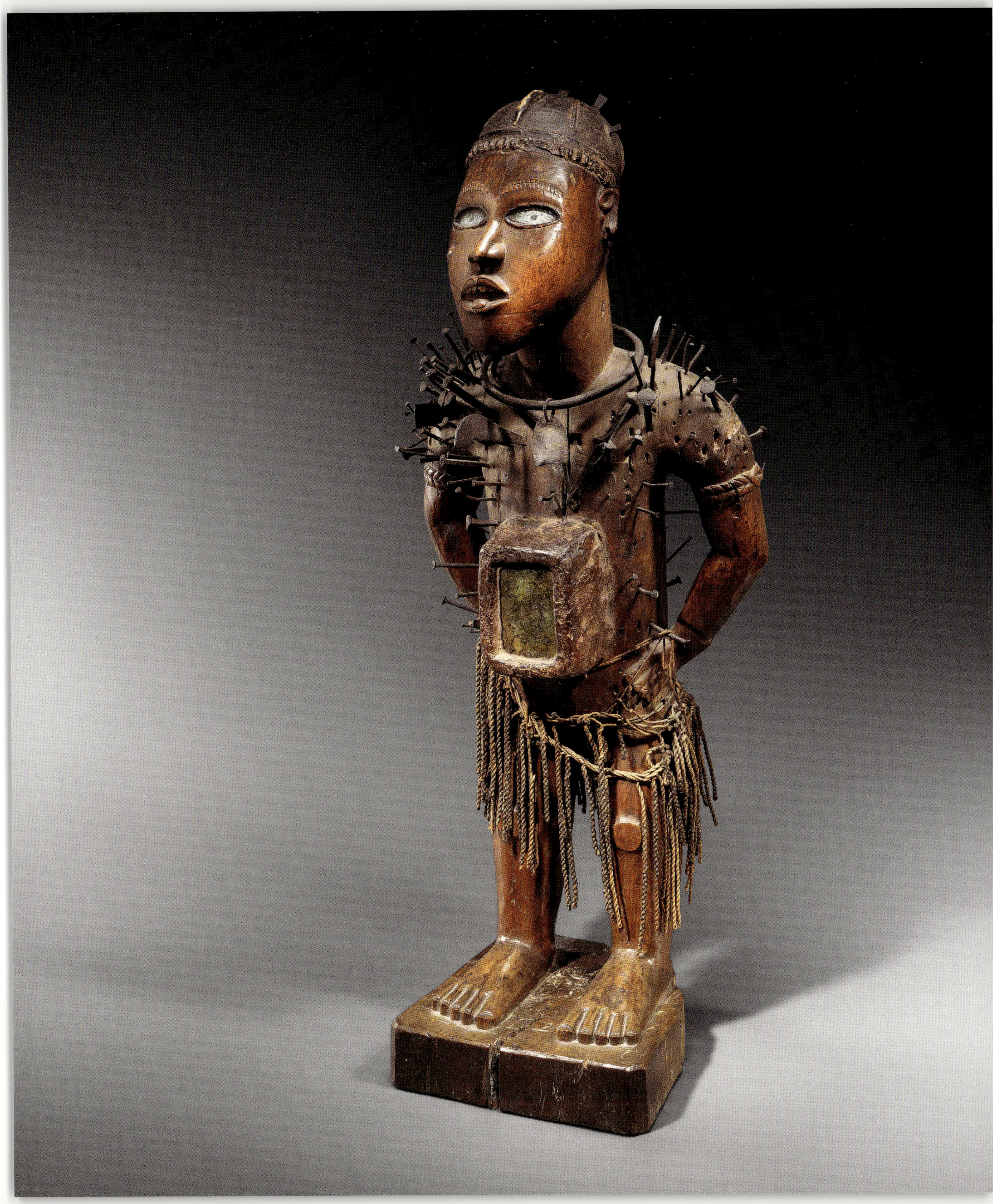

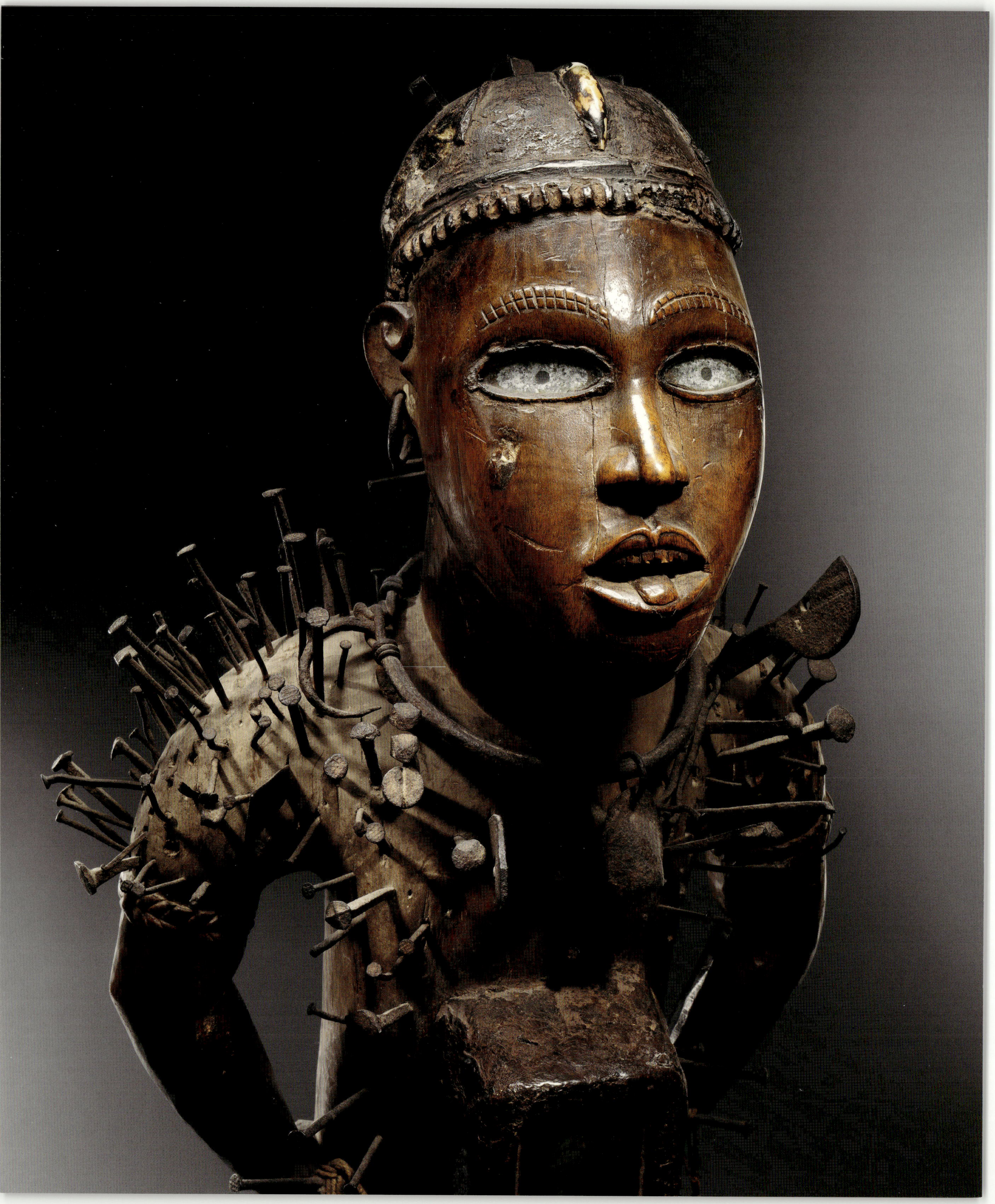

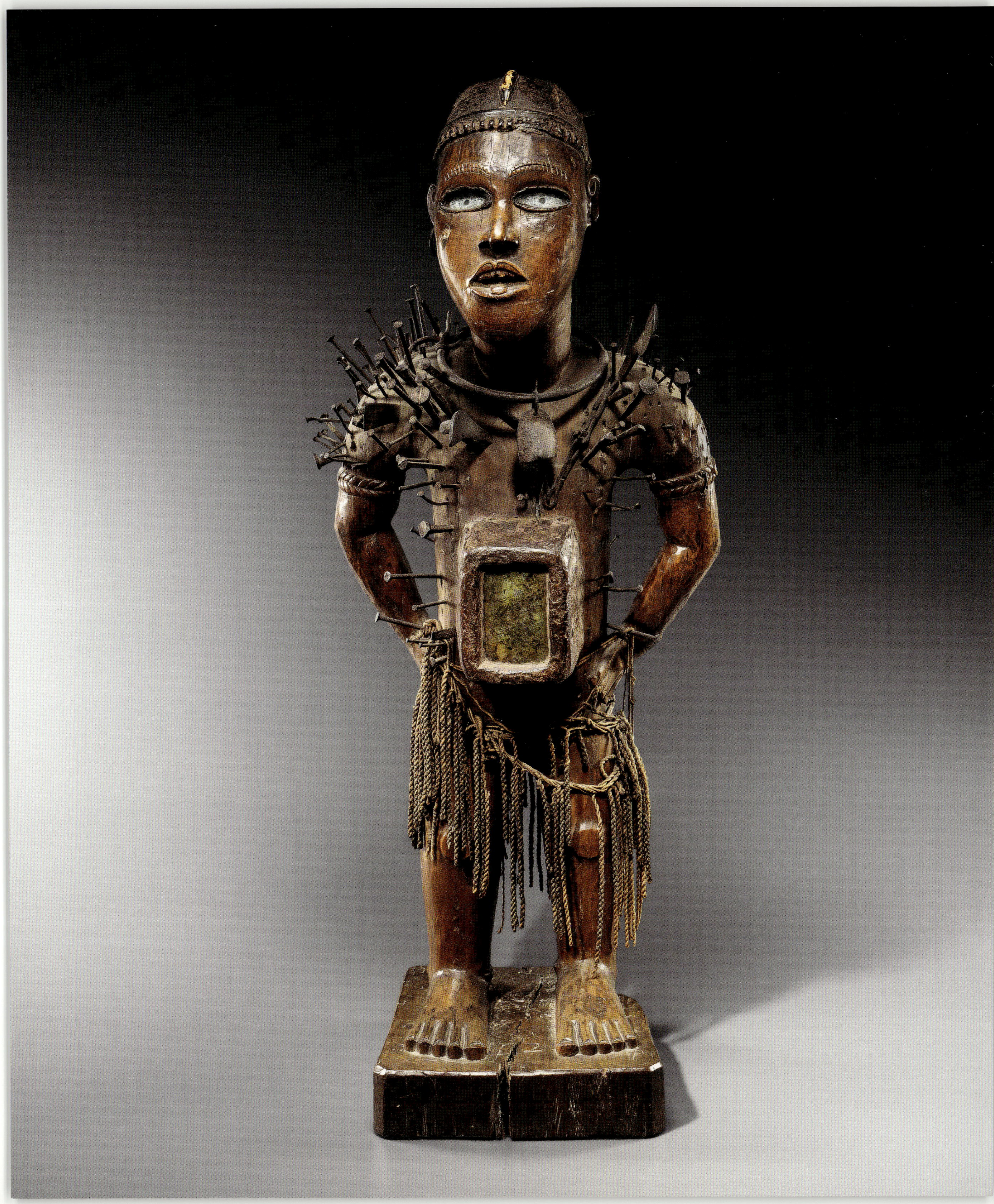

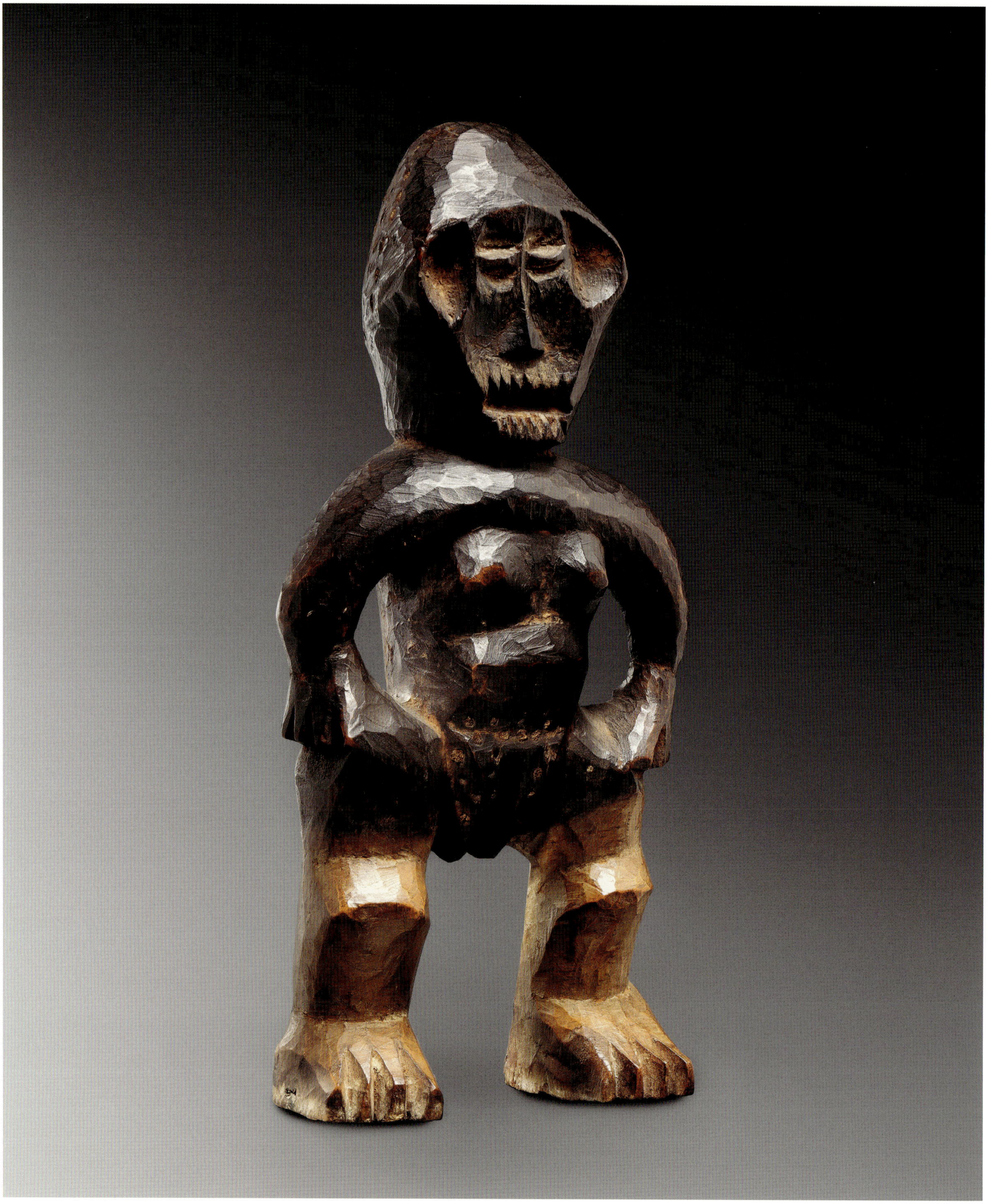

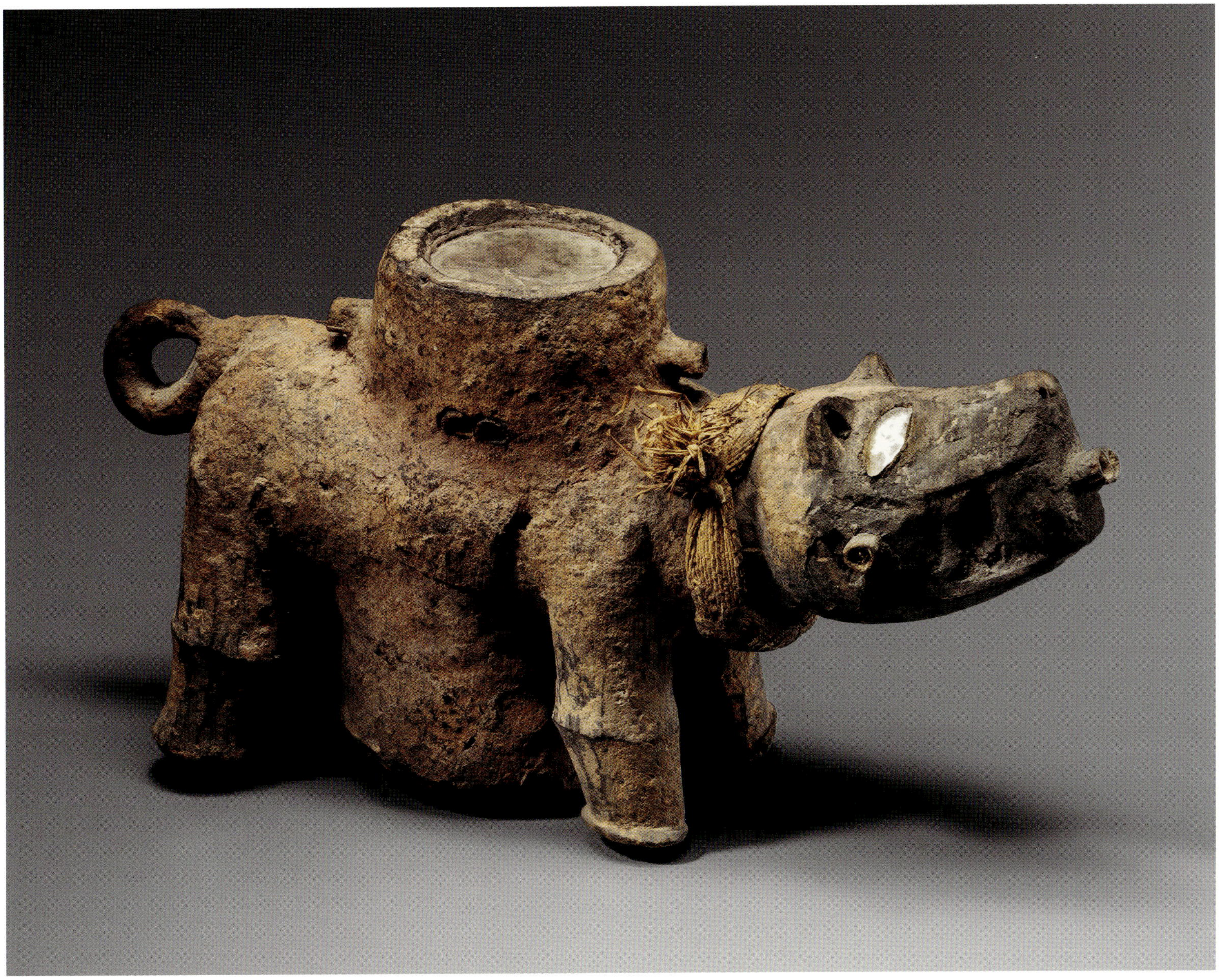

Metoko (?) statue
Democratic Republic of the Congo, H. 29 cm

This extraordinary statue seems to be a blend of cultural influences centred in the Maniema province. Clusters of figures with a similar appearance have been identified from the Lega area to Mbole territory on the west bank of the Lomami. The face of this particular example is not unlike certain *nsembu* or *ibole* Kumu masks, distinguished by open mouths displaying the teeth and ears placed in front of the temples. The contrast between the area blackened by wood fire and the paler unaffected sections is typical of the art found from the south of the Central African Republic to Ubangui (Felix M.L., personal correspondence, 2019).
The overall composition and the handling of the volumes in this effigy suggest a close relationship with the art of the Metoko, or Mituku, whose territory, located between the Lomami and the Lualaba, adjoins that of the Lengola and the Mbole (Leloup H., *Féminité. Sa diversité dans l'Afrique traditionnelle*, 2003, p. 93, no. 44). [MC]

Kongo dog
Democratic Republic of the Congo, L. 23 cm

Endowed as they are with a highly developed sense of sight and smell, dogs are indispensable companions for both the Kongo hunter and the *nganga*, whom they help root out anyone casting evil spells. "Those who stand by tradition believe these animals have four eyes—two for this world and two for the other world . . . During certain ceremonies, a ritual expert collects liquid from the corner of a dog's eye and rubs it into the eyes of a *nkisi* so that he may acquire some of the dog's acute vision. This substance is called 'dog sight,' *bweno a mbwa*" (Felix M.L., *Le Geste kôngo,* 2003, p. 50). It is therefore particularly significant that the *nkisi* in the Weill Collection has eyes made of slivers of glass—the reflecting material being thought to provide a contact with the hereafter. The animal has two impressive pads of magic substances sealed with mirrors and holds in its clenched jaws several pieces of wood that might allude to the hallucinogenic roots that the *nganga* use in their soothsaying rites. [MC]

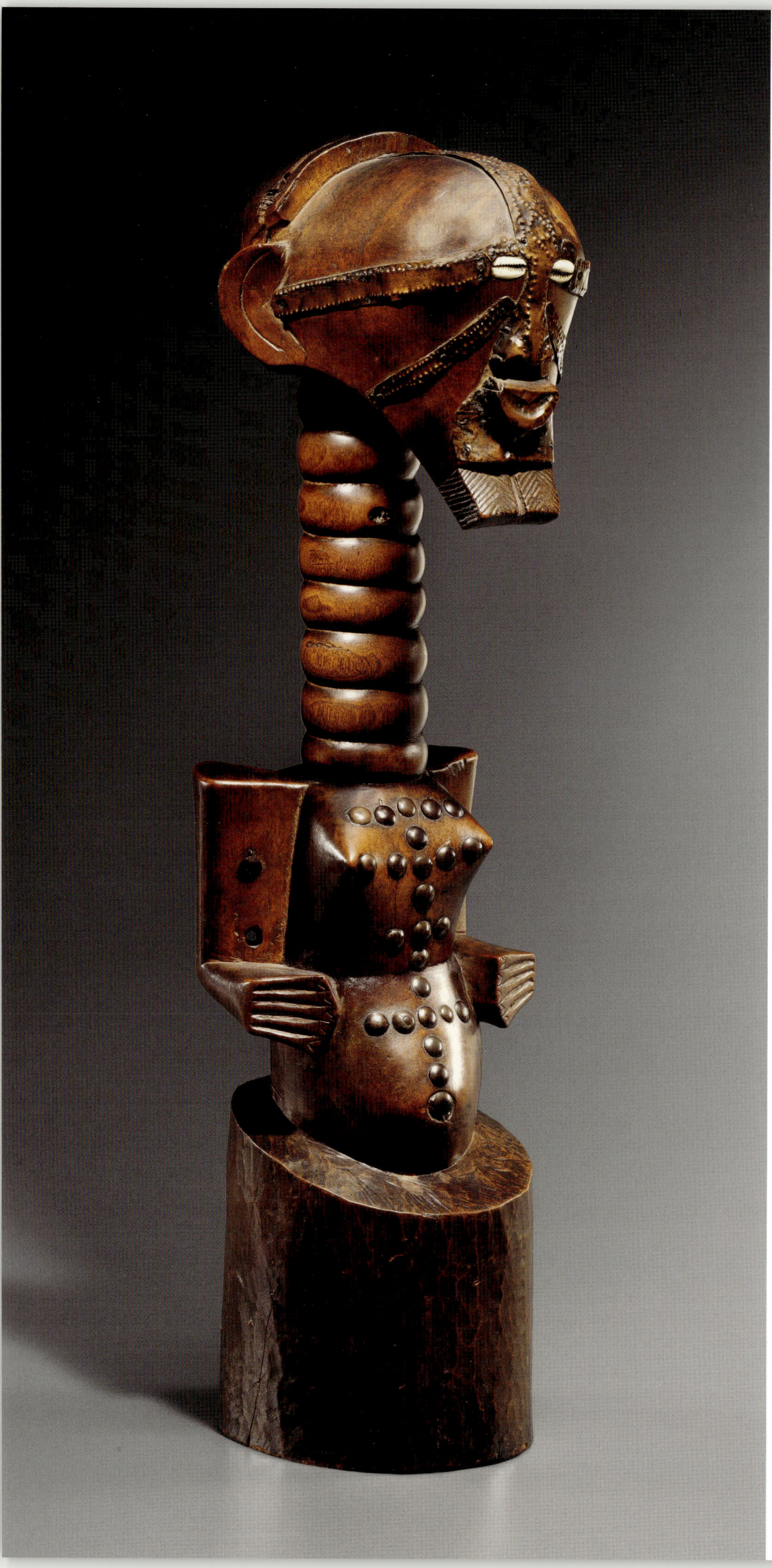

Songye statue
Lomami Province, Democratic Republic of the Congo, H. 53.5 cm

The striking features of this superb figure are its long neck made up of a series of rings and a body whose bottom portion is set into a cylindrical base. Although it is large enough to once have been a protective effigy for an entire community, it is not equipped with a *bishimba* receptacle, neither in the navel, nor on the head or elsewhere. The clearly delineated breasts and beard highlight this extraordinary figure's androgynous nature. Now, the Songye's myth of origin says that only Efile Mukulu, the demiurge creator, possesses the attributes of both sexes.[1] When a statue with a ringed neck is adorned with necklaces, the bead or skin decorations usually collect in the creases in the neck.[2] In this case there are seven folds, a symbolic number since a new initiation session of the *bukishi* society would begin every seven years, at the same time as the *yankole* political chief handed power over to his successor.[3] In the final stages of the ritual, those organizing the initiation placed a statue, the *Mukulu a Bukishi*, before the novices.[4] The *bukishi* disappeared from Songye rituals around the 1950s, but Stappers stresses that statues were still used during it.[5] Might it be that this androgynous figure was once designed to be part of this initiation rite where the creation myth was played out every seven years?
[VB]

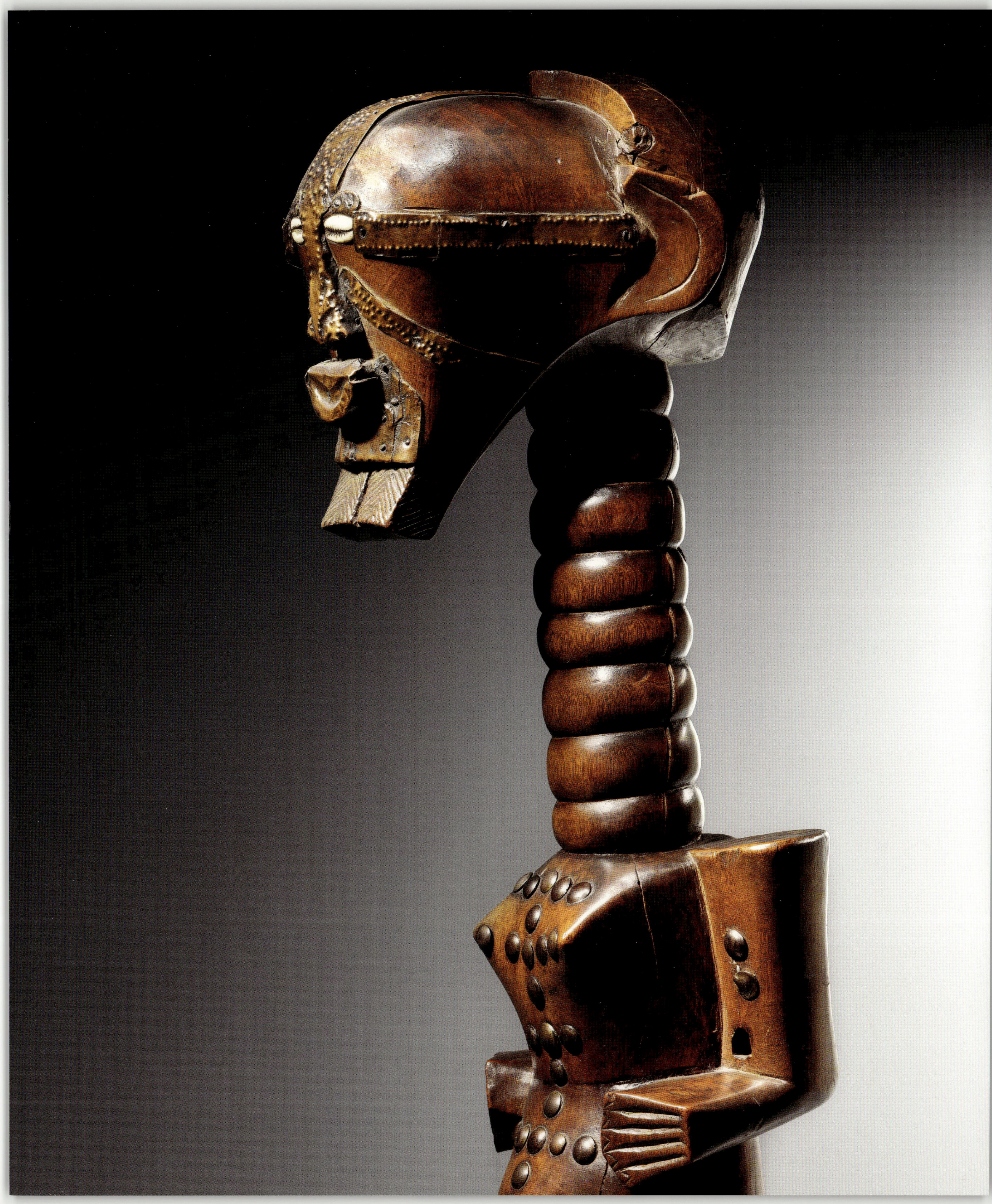

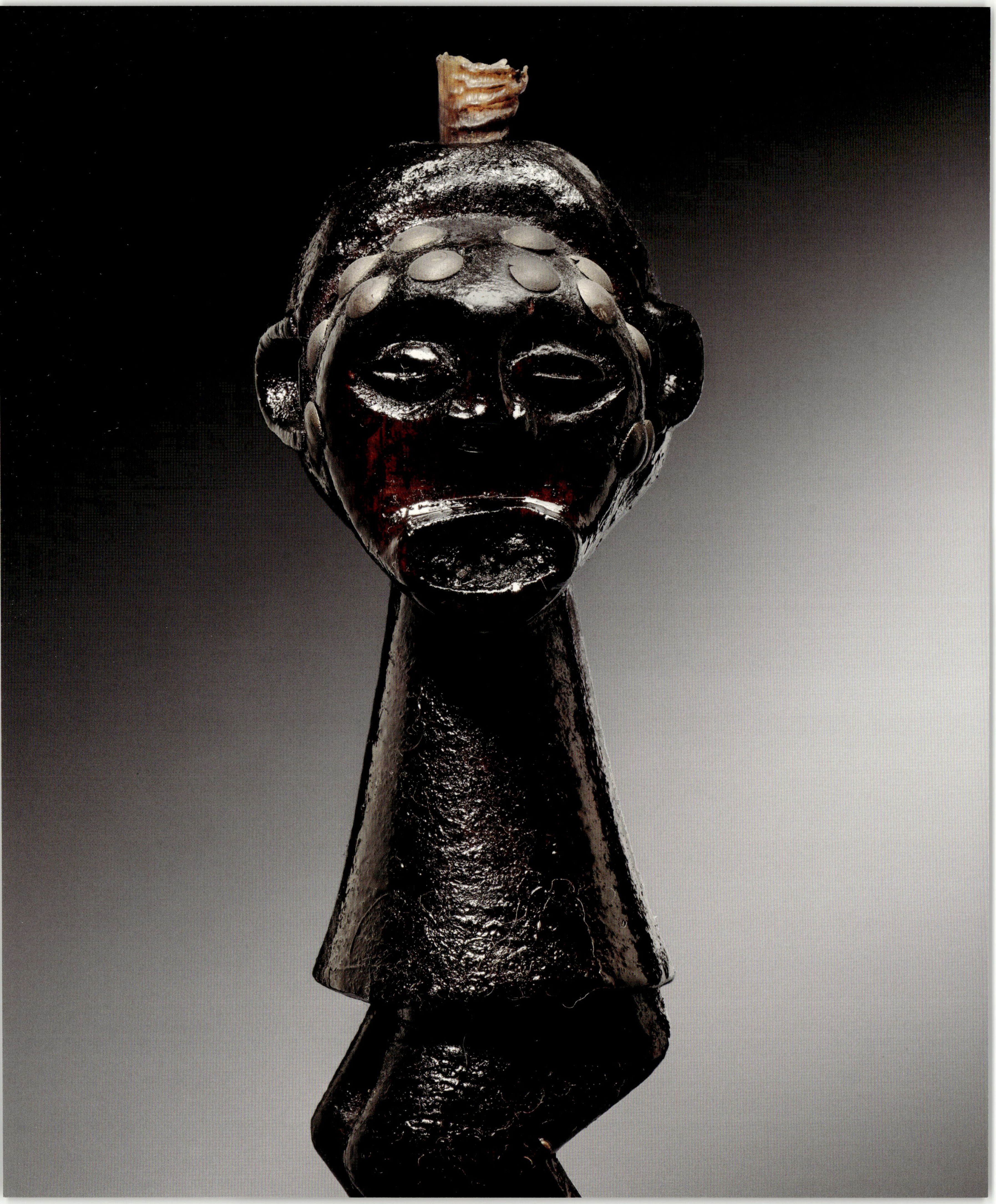

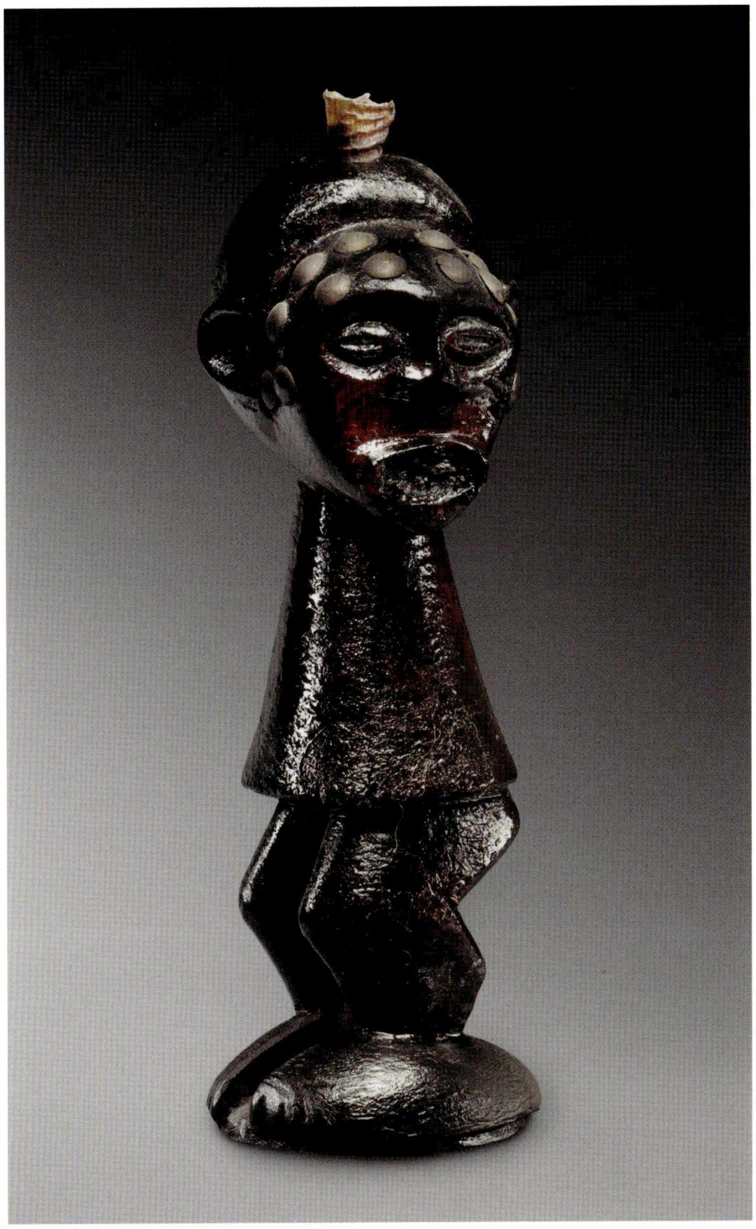

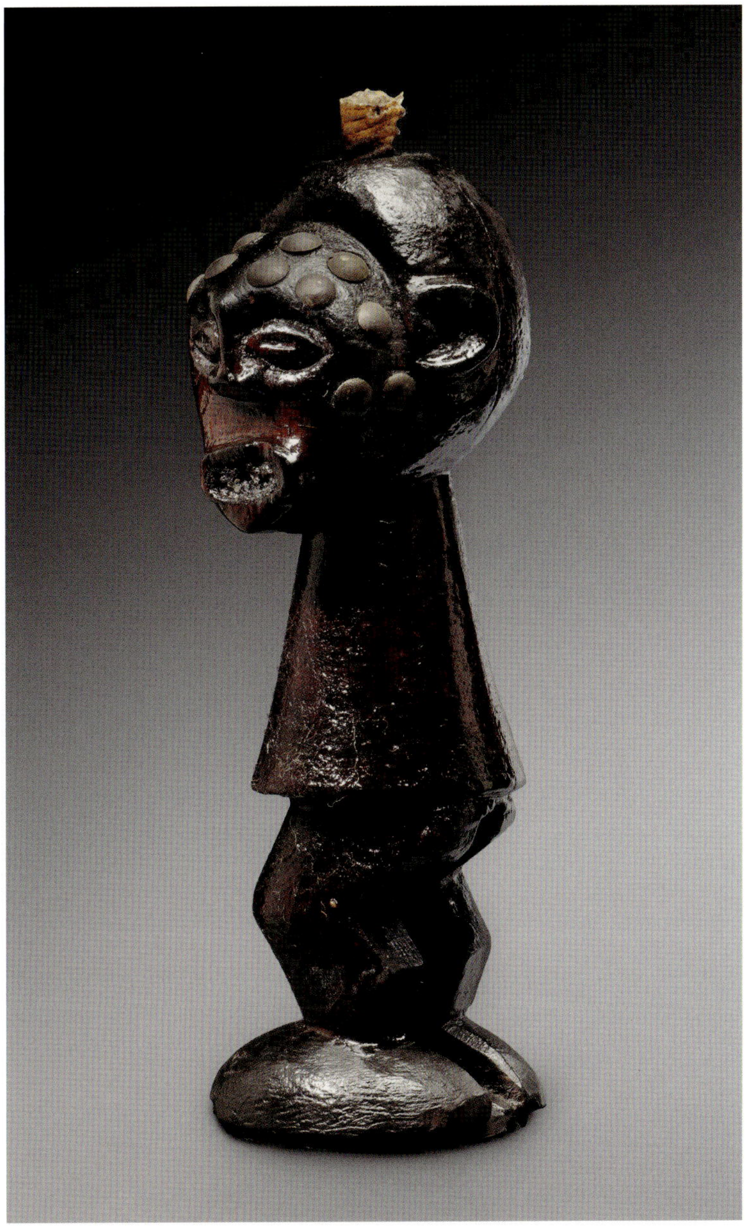

Songye statuette
Ilande or Milembwe region, Lomami Province, Democratic Republic of the Congo, H. 24 cm

All objects, pots, shell and bags among the Songye can become a *bwanga* or protective charm when the *nganga* ritual expert instils in it the appropriate therapeutic or magic power by attaching to it a wad of animal, vegetable or mineral substances known as *bishimba*. But it is only when a *bwanga* takes the form of an anthropomorphic sculpture that it can be called a *nkishi* (plur. *mankishi*). This stunning figure, in which the *bishimba* has been put in its mouth and in the antelope horn stuck on the top of its head, is part of a set of works that are all turned to face the side, a peculiarity that is found especially among the statues of the Ilande and Milembwe. It might refer to the way some *bandoshi* sorcerers, who appear as a bright light in the night but do not kill, are supposed to attack their victims by twisting their necks; the bewitched is completely paralysed as a result.[1] In addition, these witches could also target the unborn child, causing it to be born deformed. This particular *nkishi* has its head turned and is armless,[2] and for these reasons might have been designed to protect its owner from these two specific dangers. [VB]

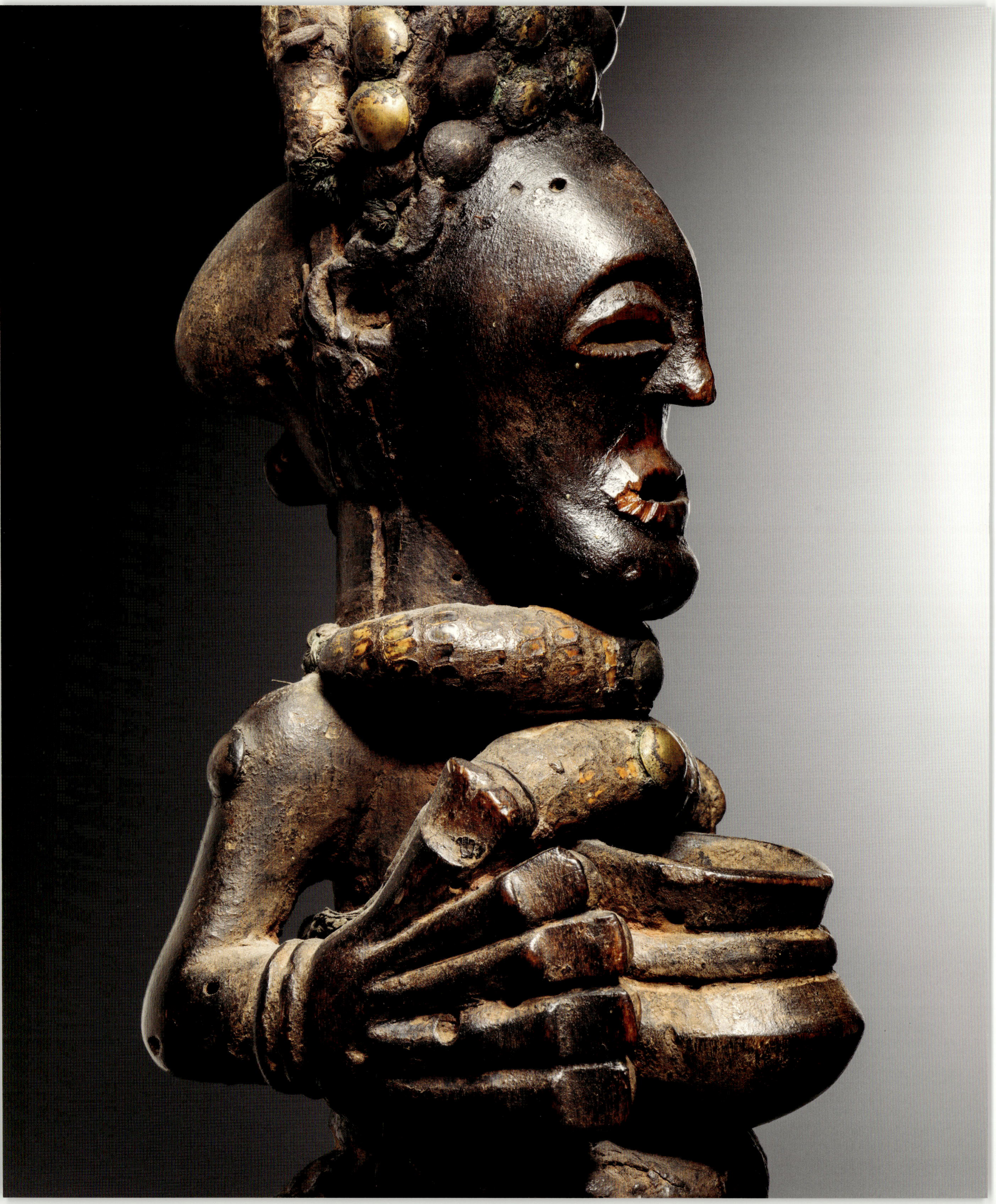

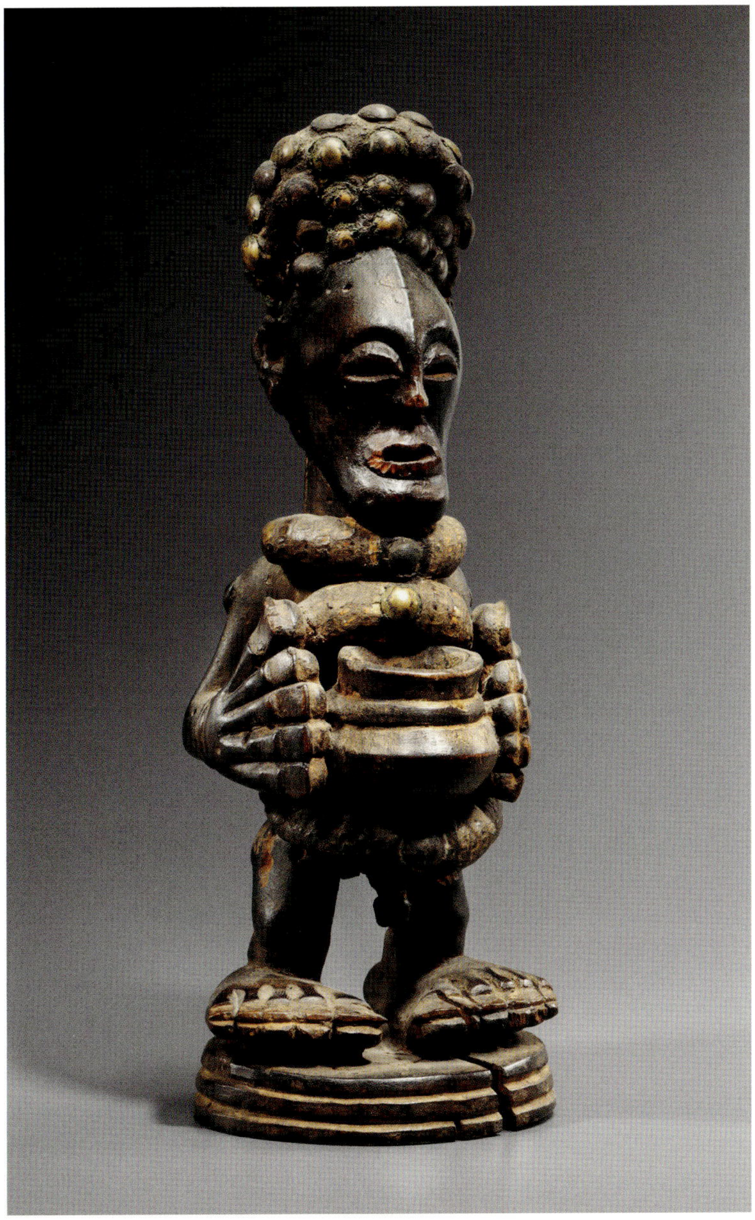

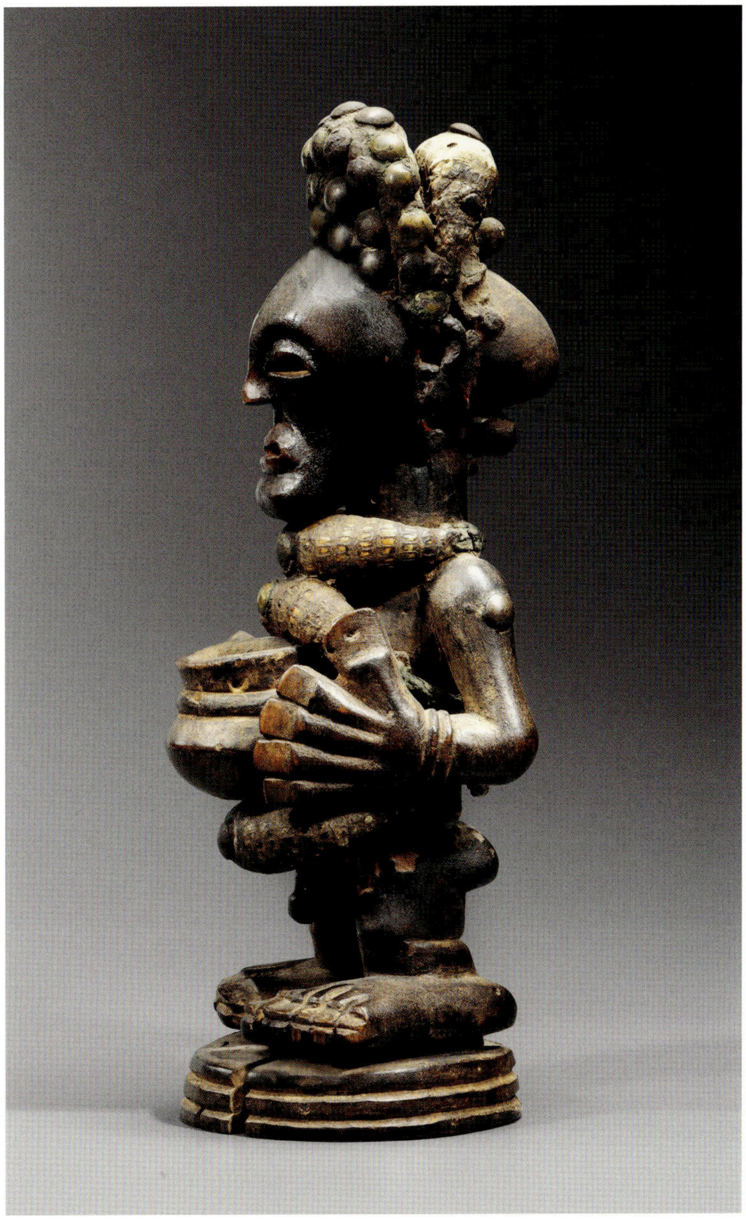

Kalundwe statuette
Democratic Republic of the Congo, H. 25 cm

As a fine specimen of the production of a Luba-Kalundwe workshop, this statuette shows a longilineal silhouette with paneled volumes and an elongated face with hollow cheeks. Holding a ceremonial bowl, the male character also multiplies power attributes, just like Songye *mankishi* do: reptile skin necklaces loaded with magic substances, upholstery studs punctuating the coiffure and the overall finery. The carving of the hands—enlarged, nails and knuckles carefully designed—recalls the Chokwe's sculptural technic, evidencing the creative vivacity of this geographical area as a whole. [MC]

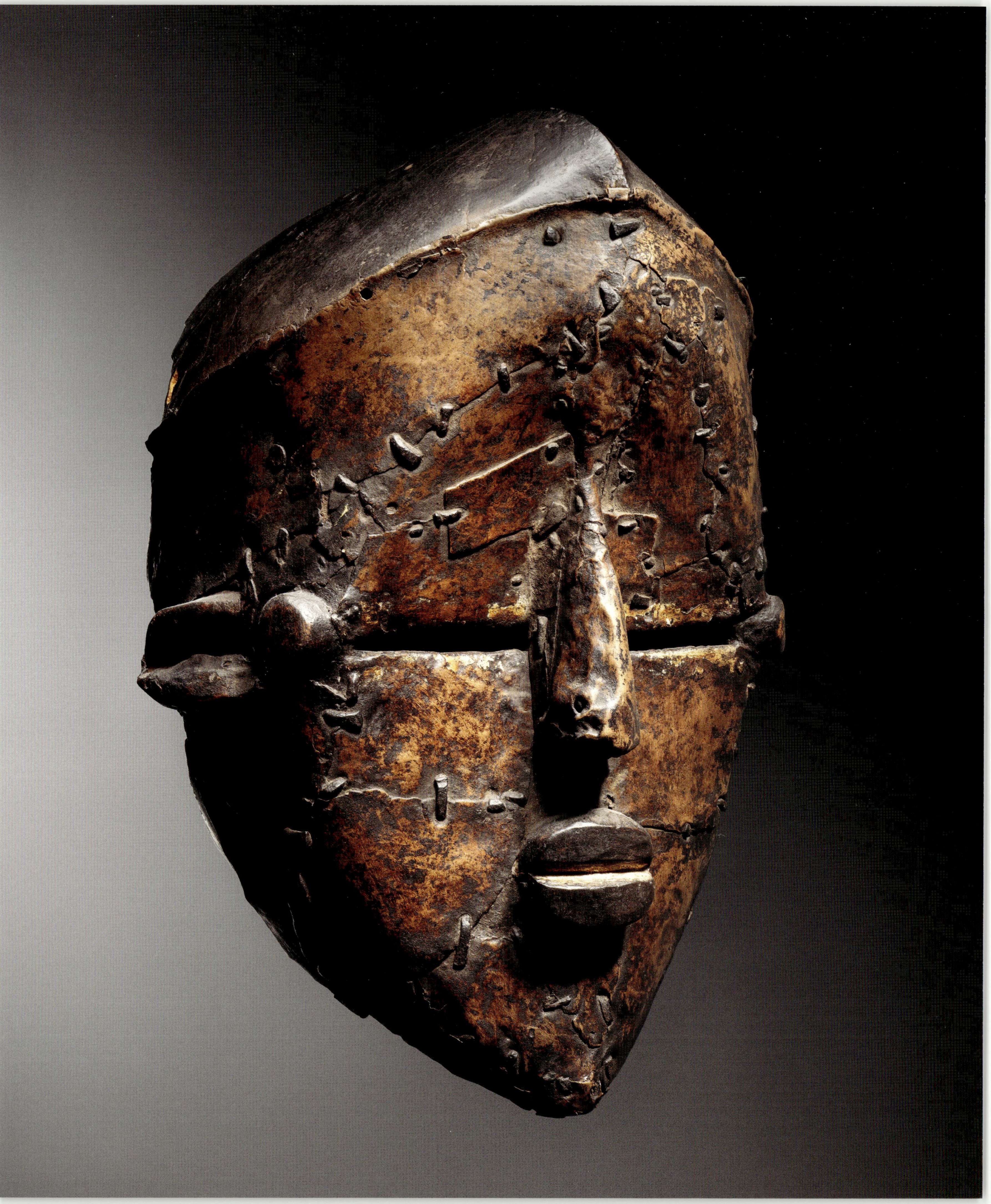

Lwalu mask
Democratic Republic of the Congo, H. 29 cm

The copper-covered mask in the Weill Collection belongs to a group of extremely rare works whose geographical provenance—located on the left bank of the River Kasaï between Angola and the Democratic Republic of the Congo—was identified in 1961 by Marie-Louise Bastin (Bastin M.-L., *Art décoratif tshokwe,* 1961). It was Rik Ceyssens who eight years later discovered a cluster of ten masks covered with copper plates in the same area but on the opposite side of the river and identified an artistic tradition shared by the Kongo-Dinga, the Kata, the Lwalu, and the Salampasu (see Ceyssens R. *in* Herreman F., Petridis C. (eds.), *Face of the spirits: Masks from the Zaire Basin,* 1993, p. 97). Partly relying on field notes taken by Albert Maesen, Paul Timmermans pursued the identification of the different Lwalu masks, publishing a dedicated study in 1967 ("Les Lwalwa", in *Africa-Tervuren*, vol. XIII 3/4, Tervuren, 1967, pp. 73–90).
The stylistic features of this distinctive set of works have also been described by François Neyt in 1981, completed later by Rik Ceyssens, who provided the *Treasures from the Africa-Museum* exhibition catalog with several insightful entries on the subject (Verswijver *et al., Treasures from the Africa-Museum*, Tervuren, Tübingen-Berlin/Tervuren, 1995). Known as *ngongo wa shimbungu*, these masks display an overall structure that resembles the wooden masks of the Lwalu, with their diamond-shaped face in which the gently concave surface is broken by the sharp nose ridge. At the same time, within the larger category, it is important to distinguish male masks (whose long noses look like the beaks of forest birds) from female masks, whose more dainty lines more closely resemble an owl (Neyt, *Arts traditionnels et histoire du Zaïre*, 1981, p. 205).
The Weill mask is striking in the contrast it provides between the careful handling and precision of the well-observed lines and the tough, not to say coarse, texture of the material it is made of. Indeed, the work is completely covered with copper plates that are arranged asymmetrically and held in place by big metal staples. The whole surface has been meticulously rubbed, polished, and coated with palm wine by generations of users. This type of irregular plate construction is only found in the earliest examples of this style. This specific Lwalu mask in the Weill Collection is called *shabaaba* and was photographed by R. Ceyssens in the village of Kangambu in 1971 (Ceyssens, *Ibid.*, p. 98, ill. 1).
We would like to thank Constantine Petridis for sharing with us precious insights about the Lwalu culture. [MC]

Luluwa statuette
Democratic Republic of the Congo, H. 27 cm

Previously attributed to the Holo of southwestern Congo, the figure's style—with its hallmark curvilinear facial scarifications in high relief—leaves little doubt that it originated in a workshop among one of the various subgroups of the Luluwa people. The crouching position is common among several neighbouring art traditions in southern Congo but most typically associated with the Luluwa. It appears quite frequently in those miniature carvings where the figure serves as a caryatid supporting a container for finely pounded tobacco used to be snuffed or smoked. However, in this particular example, the crouching figure carries a receptacle that instead would have served to contain a mixture of ingredients with medicinal and magical qualities called *bishimba* in the Luluwa language. As such, the sculpture belongs to the category of "power objects," once known as "fetishes," which the Luluwa label as *manga* (plural of *bwanga*). Most likely, it represents a genre called *bwanga bwa cilembi* that is used as a luck-bringing and protective device to ensure a successful and safe hunting expedition. The prominent depiction of enhanced genitalia should be interpreted as a symbol of male fertility, and as an expression of the Central African belief that there is a metaphorical connection between the life-sustaining activities of childbirth and the hunt.[1] [CP]

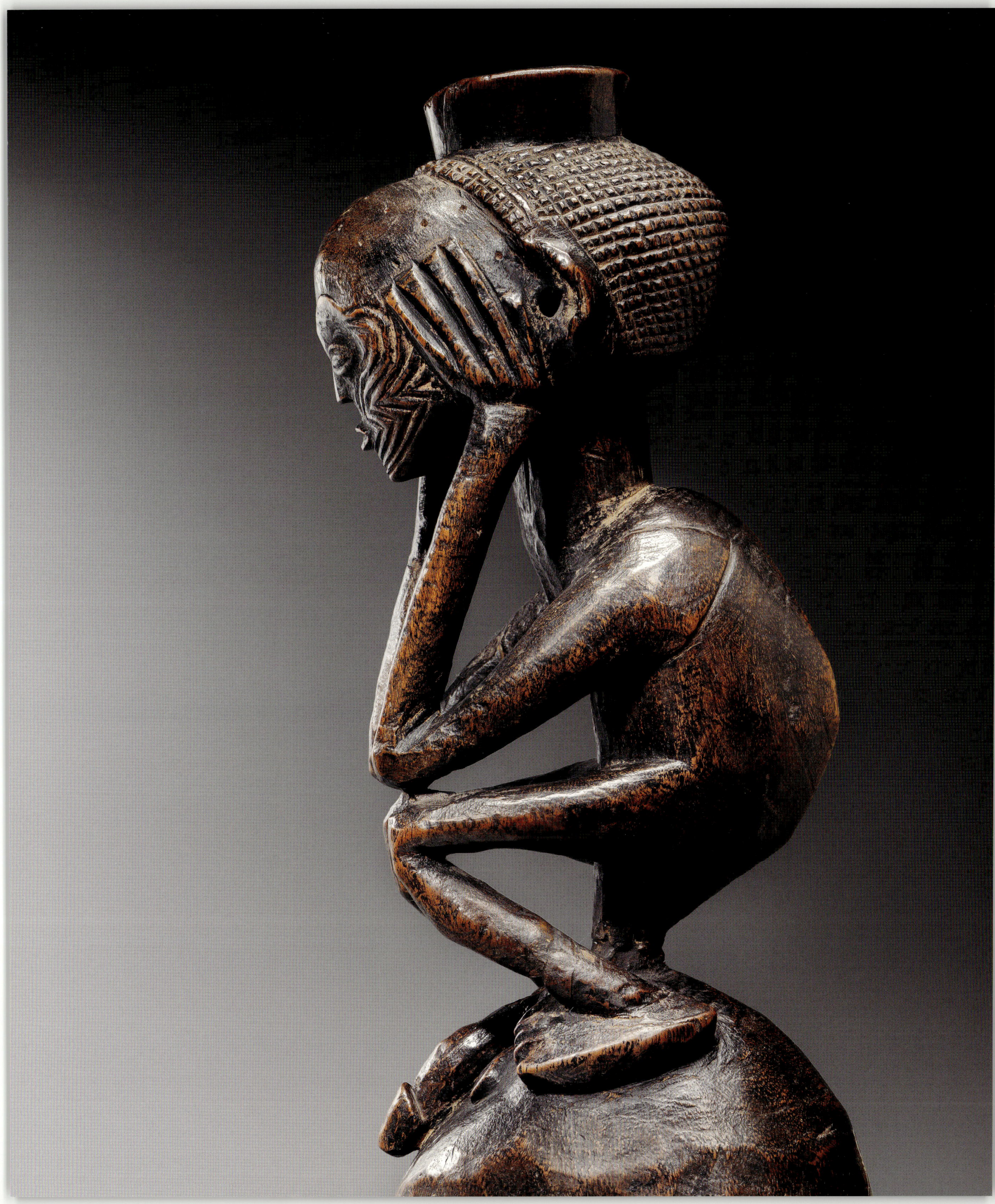

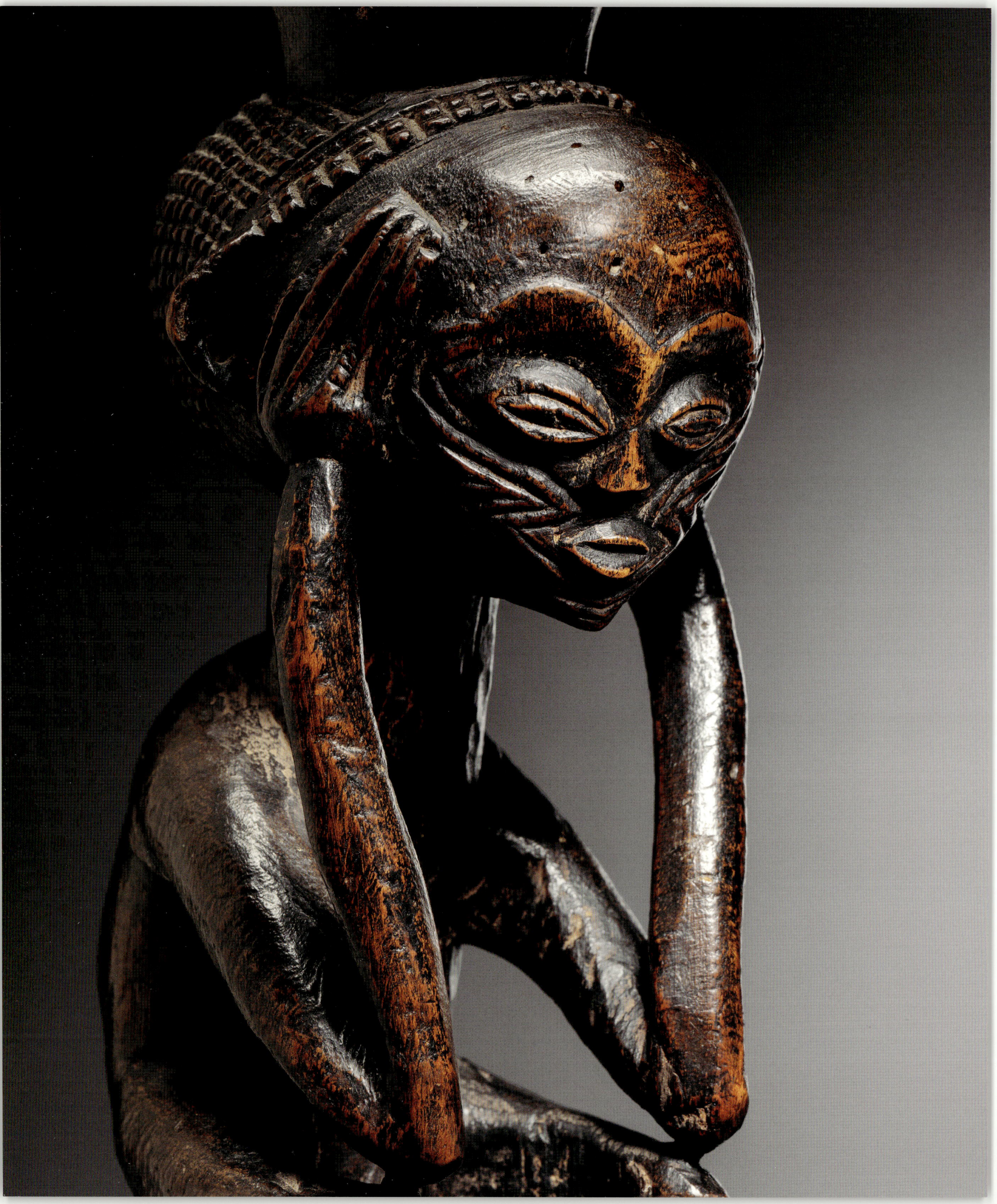

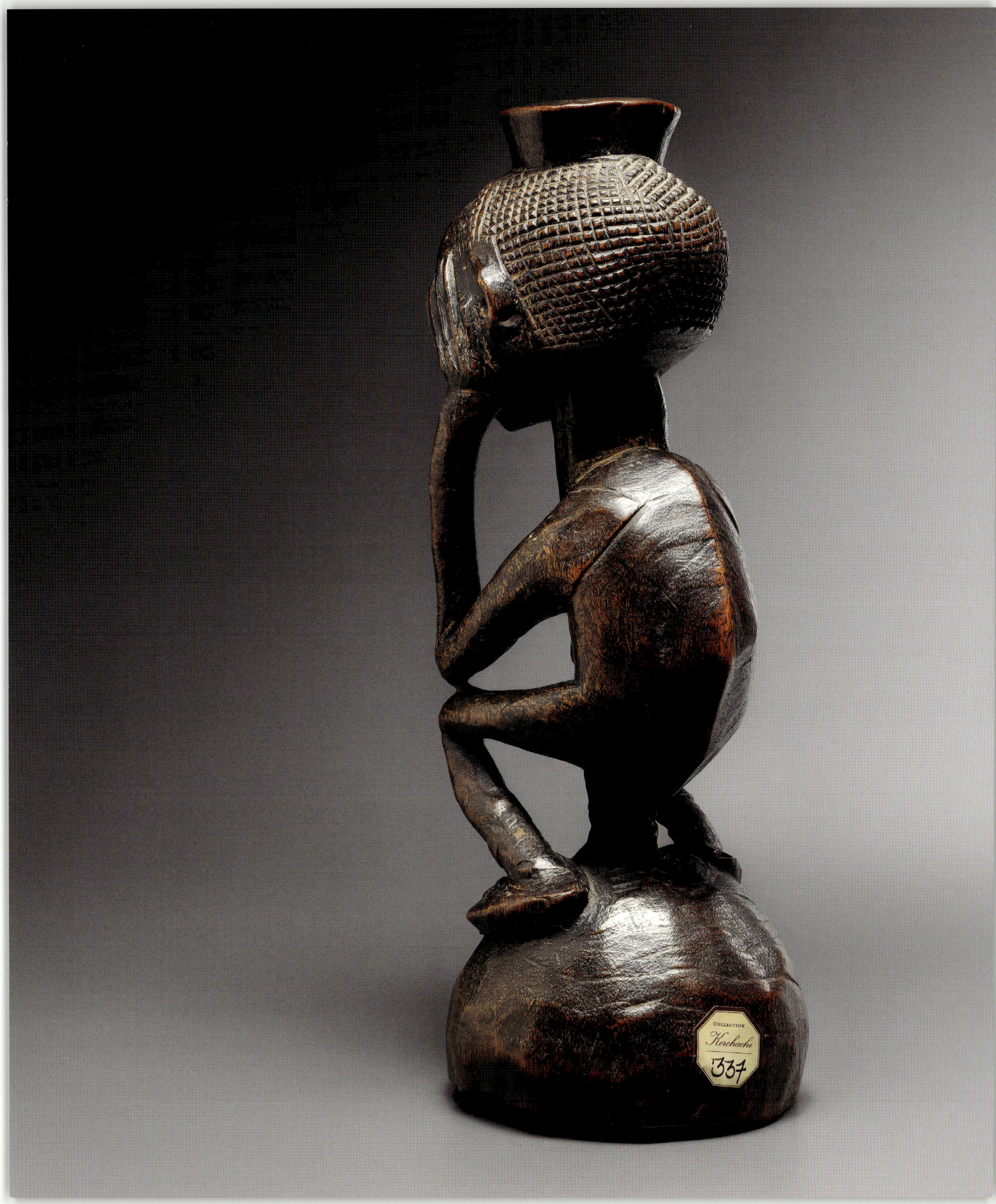
Collection
Kerchache
337

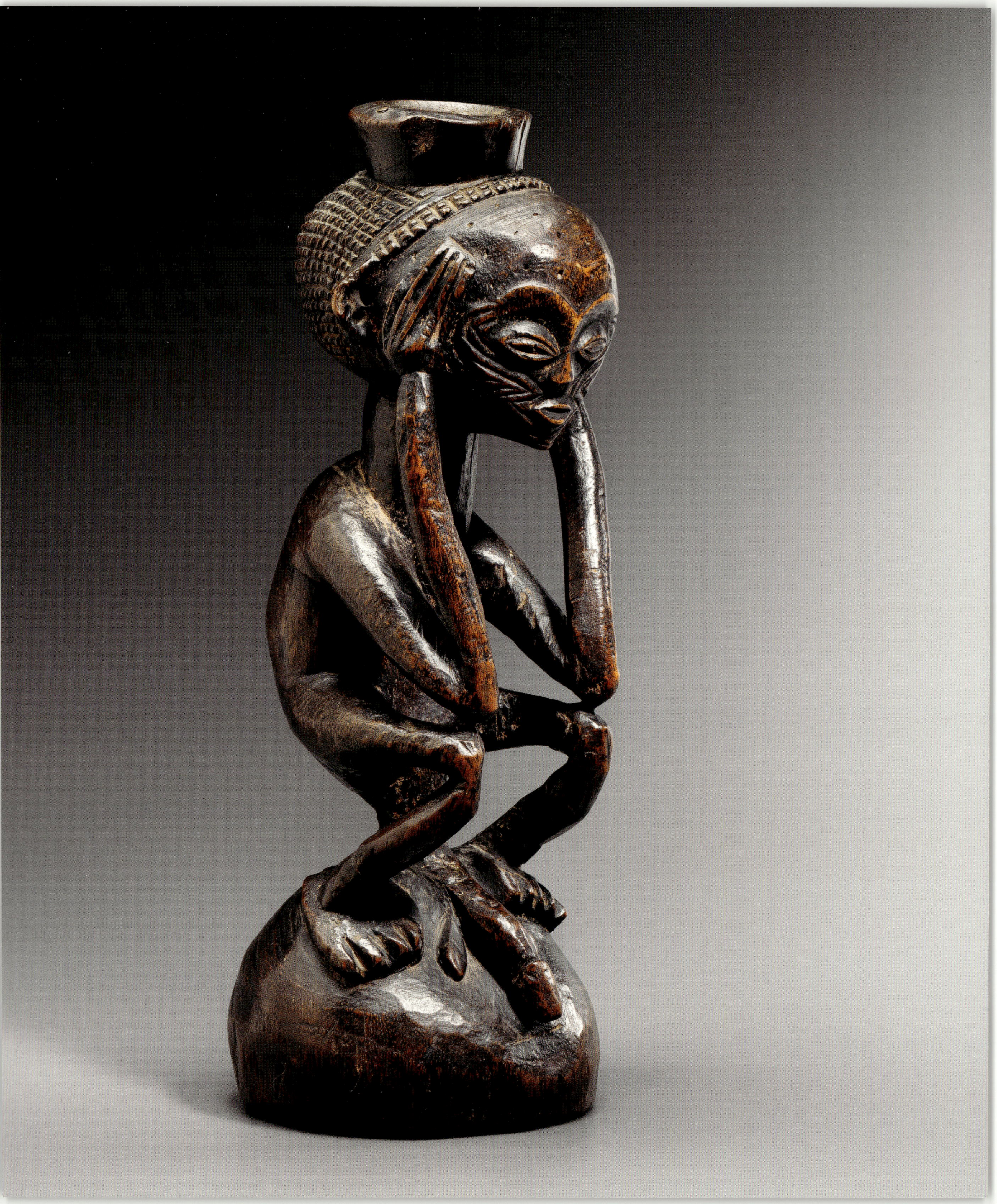

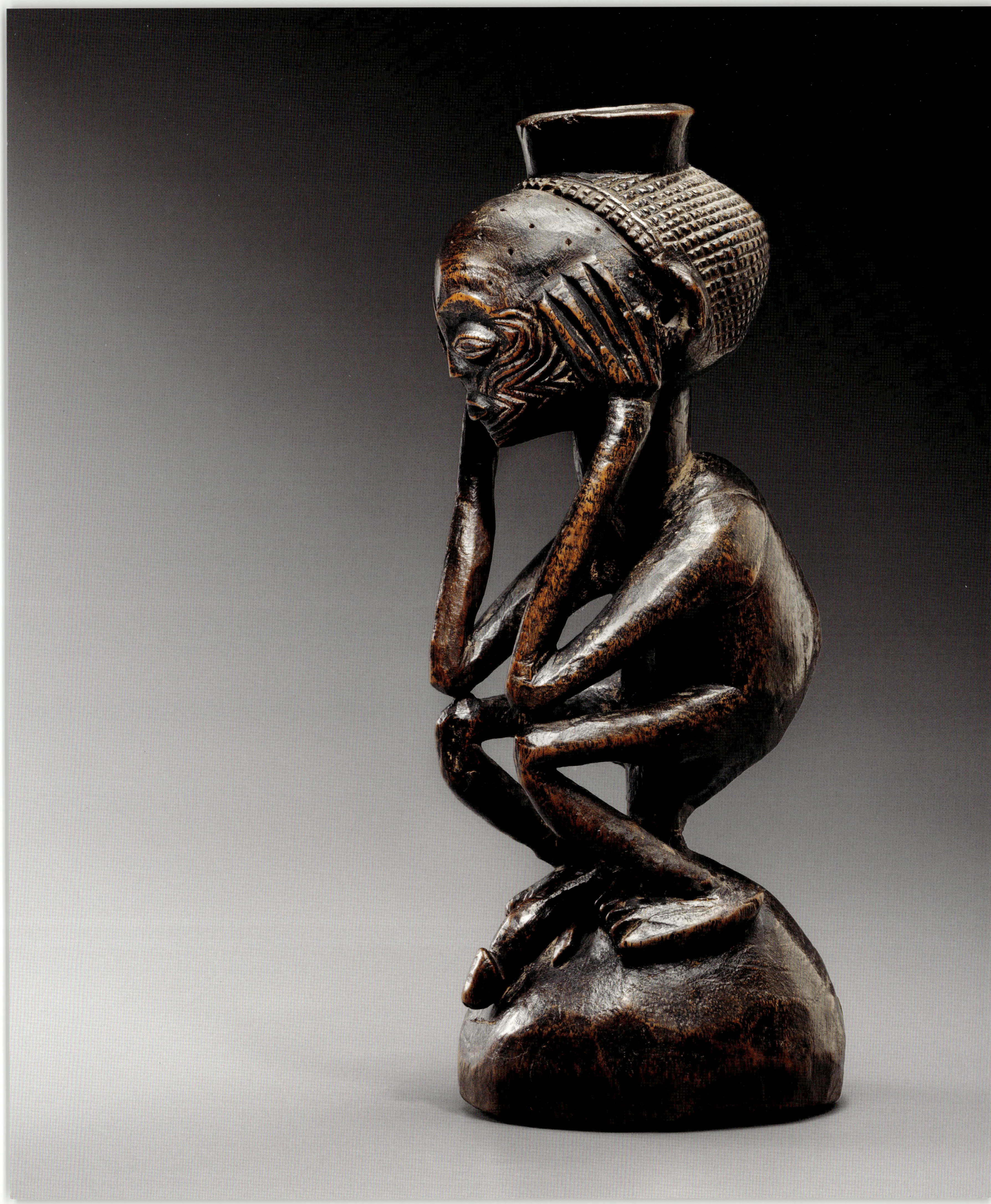

Songo statue
Angola, H. 26 cm

This singular object, which might have topped a staff or the back of a chair, displays the stylistic characteristics of the art of the Chokwe area, more specifically of Songo or Lunda craftsmen. The figure depicted is notably slim and fine-featured, with the limbs arranged symmetrically in a mirror image of each other, and an enlarged head in which the slit eyes and half-open mouth stand out. With the elbows firmly planted on its knees, the figure's hands are holding a large bowl under its chin. This striking posture is held in perfect balance by the exuberant net-like hairstyle that crowns the figure. While it is common in Angolan sculpture to see hairstyles and even heads that are elongated or accentuated for the sculptor's purposes, it is tempting in this case to suppose that the artist has from the start attempted to depict the long raffia visor that decorates certain types of masks in the region. [MC]

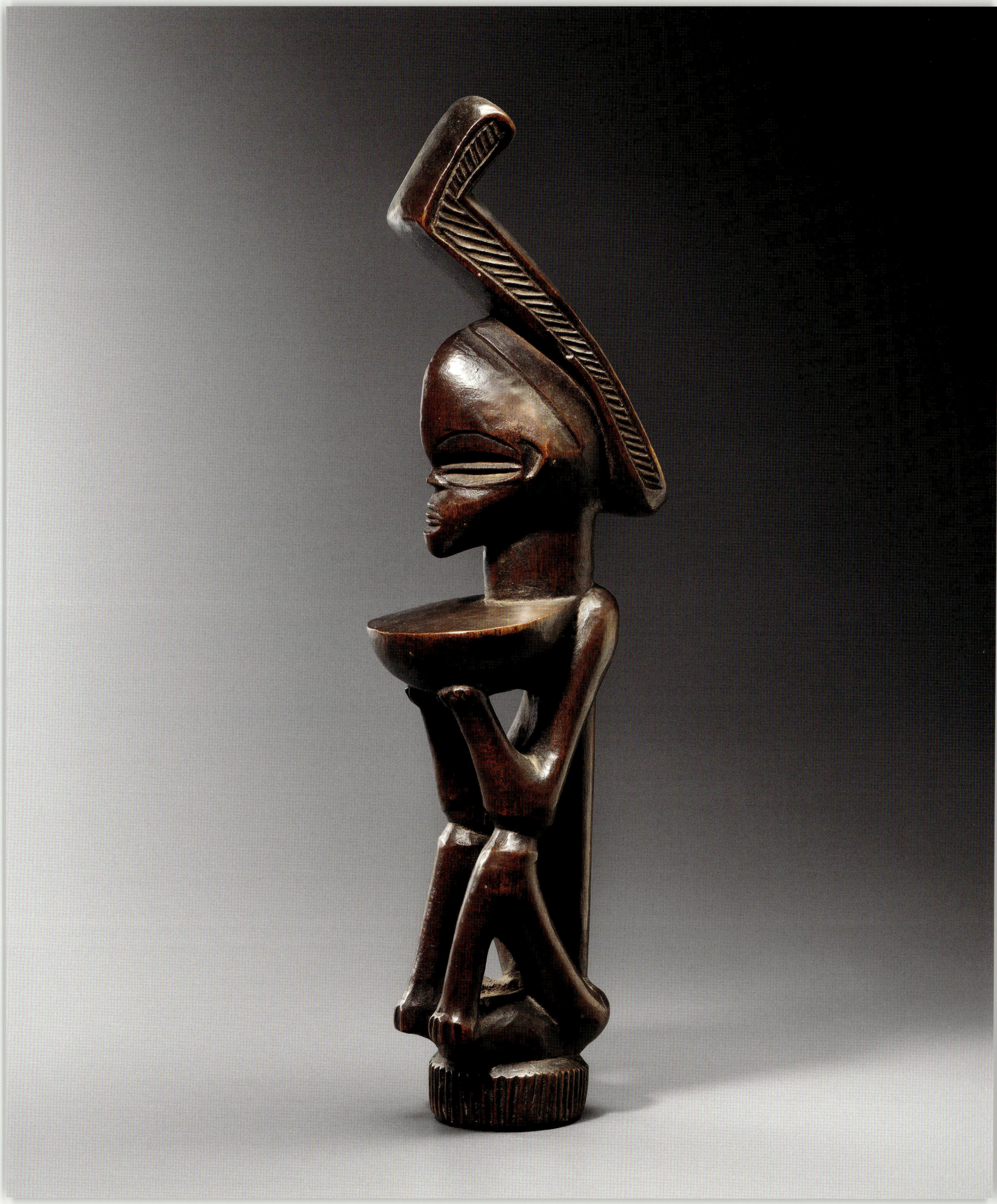

Bari statue
Sudan, H. 63.5 cm

Statues from the White Nile area (Bari, Shilluk, Dinka . . .) are talked of in tones of hushed respect in antiquarian circles from Bujumbura to Dar es Salaam and from Paris to New York.

I like to think that aside from their beauty and rarity, these objects enjoy privileged status on account of their origin along the Nile. These works were fashioned by proud tribes of Nile warriors and like their sculptors they are viewed with considerable respect.
The high reputation the populations living along the Nile enjoy as the manufacturers of superb forged iron weapons is unquestioned. The beauty and effectiveness of their shields, skilfully covered with stretched crocodile or buffalo skins, is also well-established, as is the magnificence of their ivory jewellery or the quality and astonishing variety of their wooden headrests.
Although Nilotic from the linguistic point of view, the Bari are regarded as a semi-Nilotic people and are made up of one hundred and fifty clans living along the White Nile (especially to the west) in the southern part of present-day South Sudan, but also to some extent in Uganda and Congo. The Bari were originally herdsmen but have since adopted a semi-settled lifestyle and have taken to arable farming, although animal husbandry remains their main occupation.
Groups of Bari migrated in the past from Somalia and Ethiopia, working their way down the valley of the Homo and especially the Nile valley. They now number around seven hundred thousand.
Their territory encircles Juba, the capital of South Sudan since 2011. Although in fact the youngest capital in the world, the town has been a local capital for centuries, which certainly explains why Bari statues are easily the best represented in museum collections in Eastern Europe, which were supplied by nineteenth-century Western adventurers.
The iconic specimen of Bari statues is to be found in the Ethnographic Museum of Berlin. It stands out from the other works of its kind by the extraordinary dynamism of the torso as it thrusts forwards and the unusual shape of its elongated head, making it look as if the figure is wearing a pharaoh's tiara. My surprise was unbounded when, knowing that I have harboured an interest in this cultural area for years, my friend Olivier Klejman told me a statue that was very similar to this famous benchmark object had just arrived from Israel. Its former owner, a French diplomat, was said to have acquired it *in situ*. I imagined the journey it must have taken, following the Nile from the middle of Africa all the way to Alexandria and from there across the Sinai to Judaea just as in the Bible story.
He also told me I would be able to admire the statue that very evening at the opening of the Paris Biennale des antiquaires. When someone raves about an object, the natural reaction is to build it up in one's imagination, only to be disappointed when confronted with the real thing. On this occasion I can honestly say that I was bowled over by the statue when I saw it at the Alain de Monbrison stand, with a little too much champagne already inside me. The power and solemnity of its face, the tension created by its lower limbs, bent as if ready to leap, and at the same time the balance achieved by the powerful arms created an enchanting effect. The whole space was built around this object, as if all the other pieces were paying tribute as arranged by the organizer of the occasion—a great spectacle!

African sculptors have tended to depict their ancestors or deities in a static pose, standing upright, with their feet rooted to the ground. Bari statues often look like sticks that have been slightly pared down, with long legs reaching down from a roughly outlined body with short arms. The phallic-looking head is often shaped with three strokes of a tool to define the nose and the mouth, while two little holes with a bead in each are enough to suggest a pair of eyes. The beautiful couple in the Vienna museum clearly reveals Ethiopian Konso and Gato influence. The coarse appearance of some statues conceals treasures of subtlety—a well-directed blow with an adze perfectly creating a volume, the sculpting of a figure elegantly following the natural twist of the stick used in making it. Some Bari, much like certain Mumuye artists in Nigeria or Pare in Tanzania, are among the few African sculptors to include a sense of movement in their works, seizing a particular moment and giving it a sculpted representation. When watching Bari sculptors at work, I often feel I'm watching someone make an inspired sketch, the anatomical errors if anything underscoring and emphasizing the power of the movement.
The sculptors restrain their enthusiasm, not believing that nothing succeeds like excess and working according to the principle that less is more. They like to leave their works coarse, which often gives them a greater sense of dynamism. In the case in point one has the impression that the statue is ready to spring to life and dance before one.
Among their Dinka neighbours, whose tribes blend into the Bari in some places, many statues are on tiptoe, which can be interpreted as a dance step caught in mid-air, a snapshot of soaring movement.
I learned from M. Joseph Mastaki that the Dinka would dance with their statues during ritual ceremonies, which leads me to think that perhaps the Bari statue in the Weill Collection and its pair in the Ethnographic Museum of Berlin are actually depictions of dancers in action, possibly even in a trance. [DH]

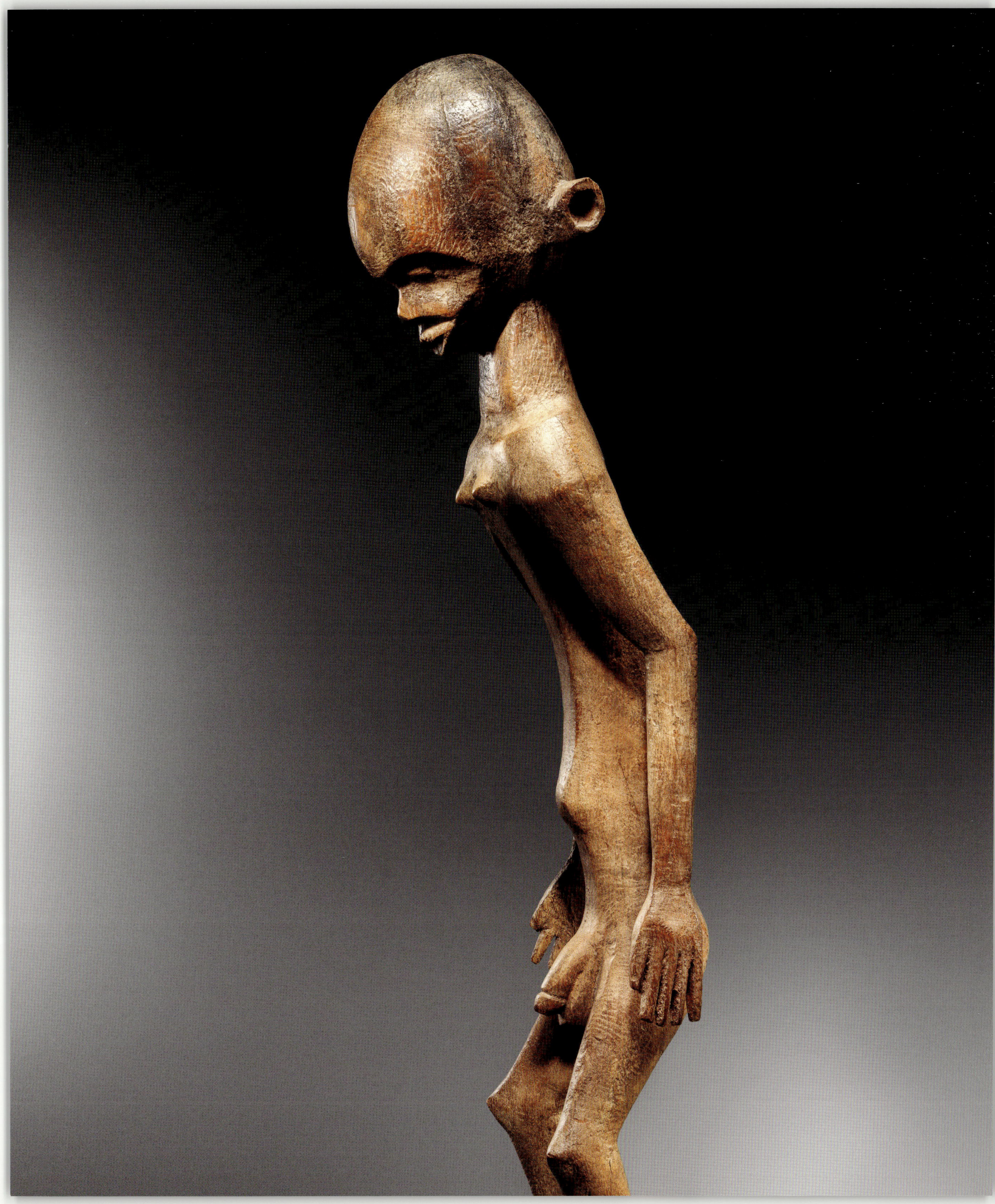

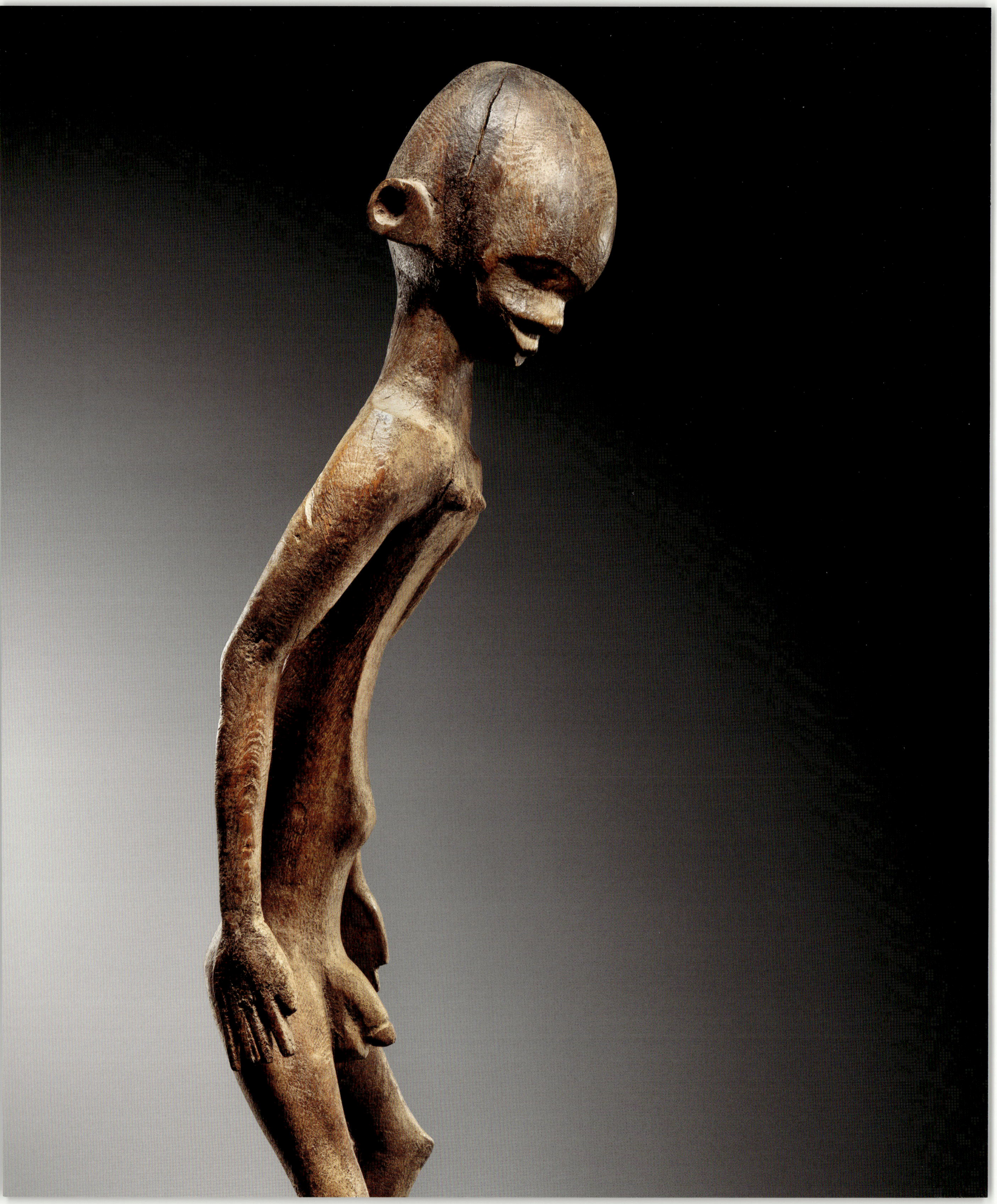

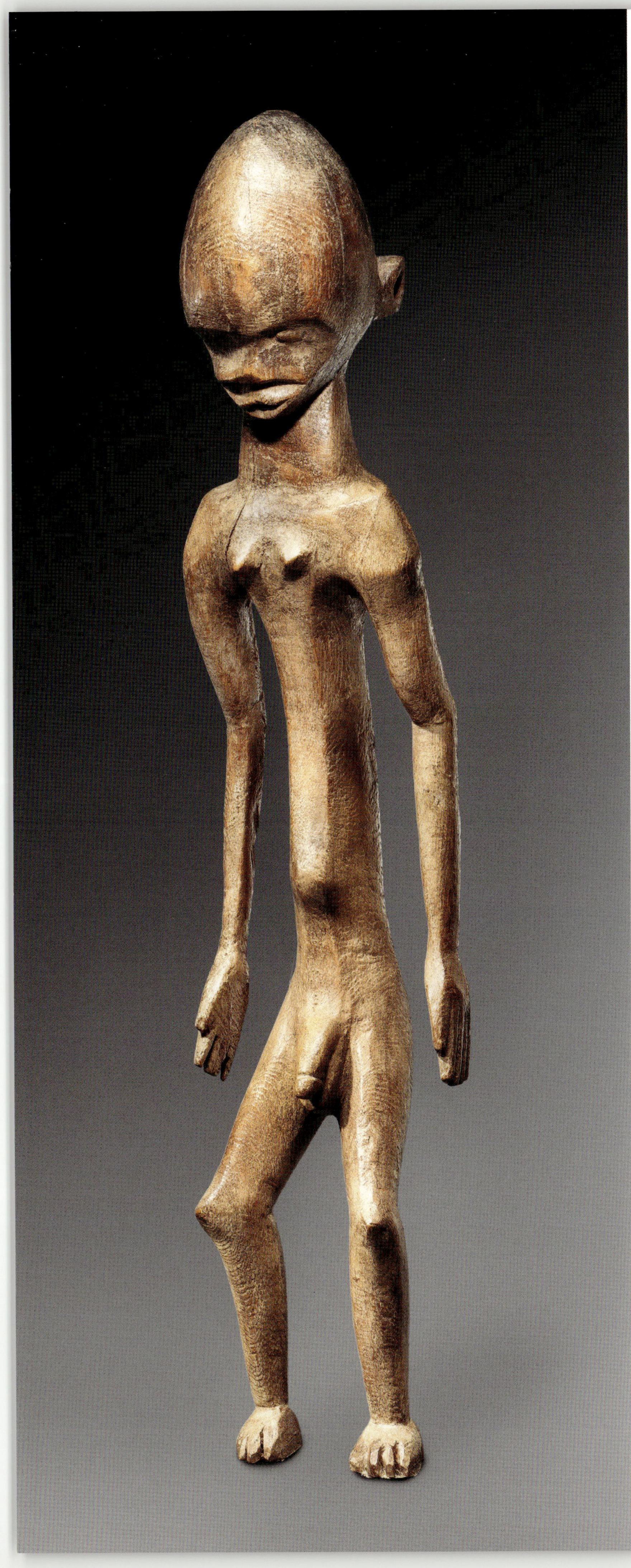

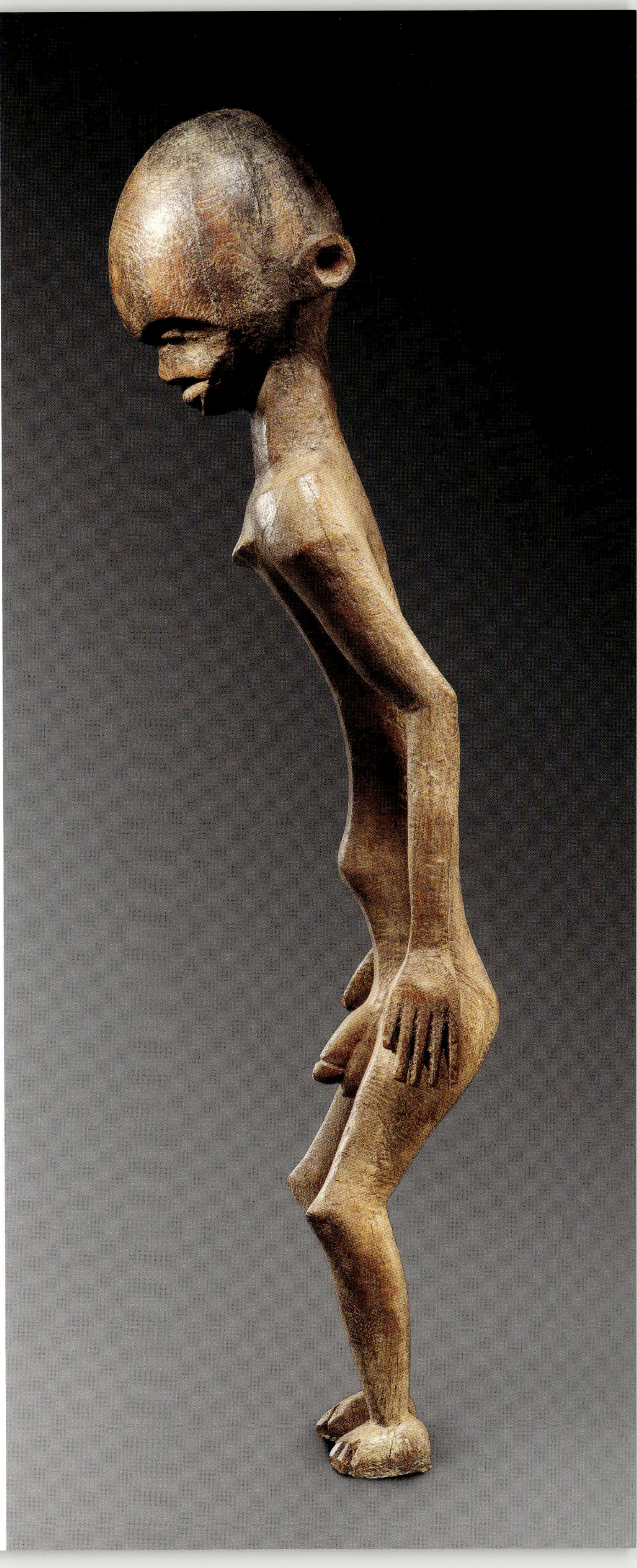

OCEANIA

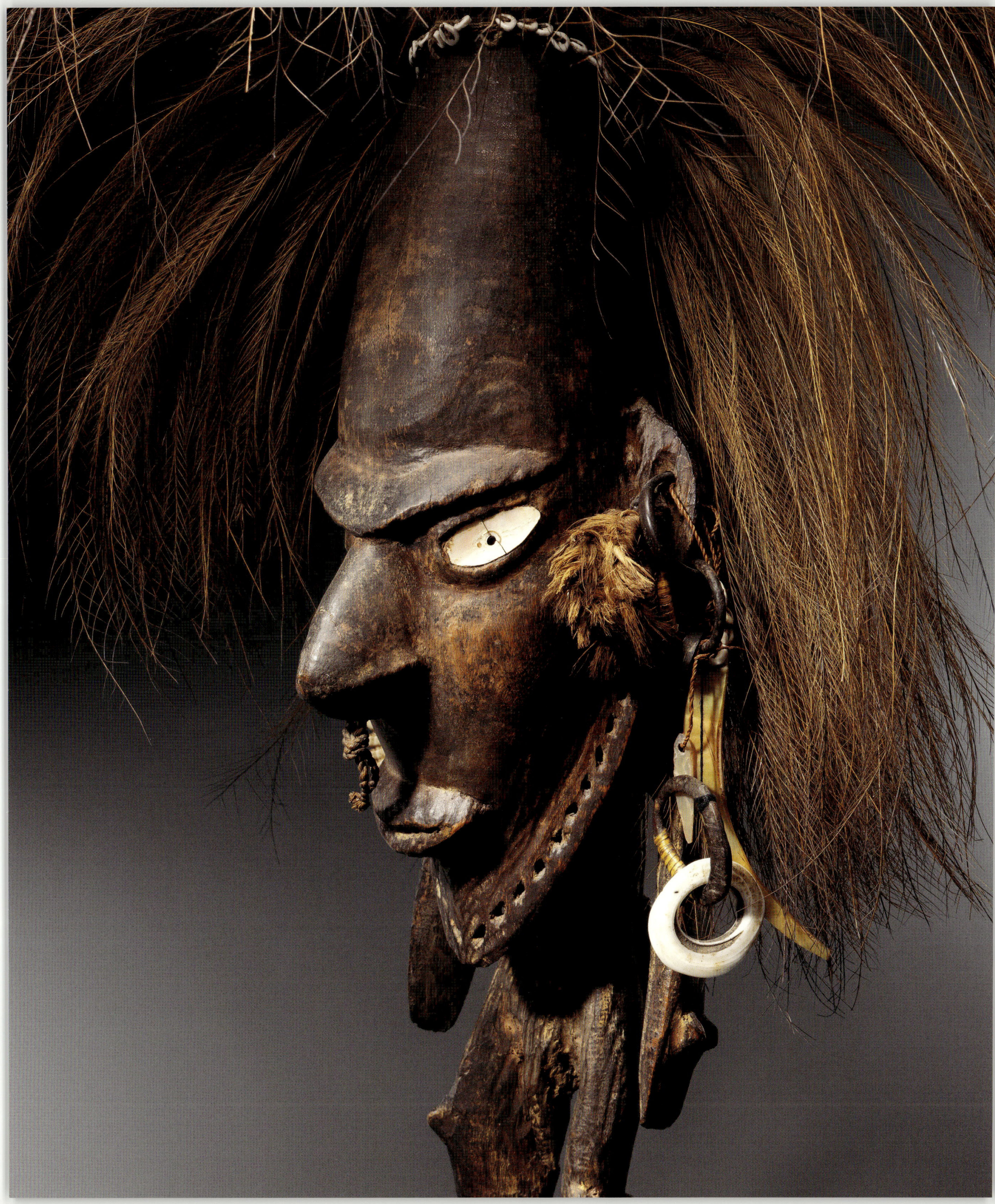

Massim Statue
Sculpted by Mutuaga, Dagodagoisu village, Suan Region,
Papua New Guinea, H. 39 cm

This human figure sculpture is clearly by Mutuaga, a Massim artist who was active from about 1880 to about 1920. I published a book about Mutuaga and his woodcarvings in 1996. Mutuaga lived in the village of Dagodagoisu, in the area where the Suau language is spoken, on the mainland of Milne Bay Province opposite Suau Island.

We know about Mutuaga because he was befriended by Charles Abel, a missionary who served on Kwato Island in Milne Bay Province from 1891 to 1930. The missionary's son, Sir Cecil Abel (1903–94), also knew Mutuaga personally and was given some carvings by him, which the carver had made himself. He remembered Mutuaga often came to the Kwato Mission Station to present carvings as gifts to Charles Abel for which he would receive Western goods in return. Cecil Abel shared his knowledge of the carver with me between 1987 and 1994. Further information about Mutuaga comes from Weibo Mamohoi from the village of Mogiriu. Weibo knew Mutuaga was a respected woodcarver and man of standing from a nearby village. According to Weibo, Mutuaga carved lime spatulas, free-standing figures, axe handles for the presentation of axe blades used as valuables, crescent-topped handles for the presentation of shell discs used as valuables, and house boards for important persons. Mutuaga had a son, Saliwowo, who was born in around 1915. When I interviewed villagers about Mutuaga in 1993, they said they remembered Saliwowo carved lime spatulas and a wooden replica of a shotgun, but none of these have been located.

My book about Mutuaga attributes eighty-eight woodcarvings to the artist, including the Weill sculpture (Beran H., 1996, pl. 79). Some of these are known to be by Mutuaga because they were given by the artist to Charles Abel and other members of the Abel family (*Ibid.*, pl. 38–43). Carvings of another group were collected by P.G. Black and are attributed to Mutuaga by him in the Black Collection of Melanesian and Australian art catalogue compiled in 1914 (*ibid.*, pl. 22–7 and pl. 29–31). Both the collection and the catalogue are in the Buffalo Museum of Science. Other carvings are attributed to the artist on a stylistic basis.

Since publishing the book, I have become aware of another thirty-four carvings that can be attributed to Mutuaga on a stylistic basis. My attention has been drawn to twenty-two of these by my readers. These readers' ability to identify carvings by Mutuaga on a stylistic basis shows that his style is indeed highly distinctive and described well enough in the book to be identified.

Massim carvings of human figures on lime spatulas range from the highly stylised to the semi-naturalistic (*Ibid.*, pl. 1–19). Mutuaga's carvings are at the naturalistic end of the range. His style is described as follows in my book on the artist (*Ibid.*, p. 13):

> "The human figures are sculpted three-dimensionally . . . The carvings are the only ones among Massim anthropomorphic sculptures that indicate the musculature of the limbs, the ankle bones, the bony prominence of the ulna near the wrist joint (the ulna prominence), the vertical groove between nose and upper lip (the philtrum), and the groove that runs down the middle of the back (the spinal sulcus)."

The Weill sculpture in the present entry has all of these characteristics. It has a well-sculpted body and striking head with a powerful nose.

As indicated above, Mutuaga was active for some forty years as a woodcarver and over the decades his style became increasingly naturalistic (*Ibid.*, pp. 74-85).

The Weill sculpture's first port of call was Britain, which it reached from Australia before 1920 (*Ibid.*, p. 146). It has circular eyes, which are an aspect of the earliest of Mutuaga's carvings, and was probably carved in the early 1890.

Douglas Newton included two lime spatulas by Mutuaga in his Massim exhibition catalogue (Newton D., 1975, fig. 15–6). He recognized that these carvings in a "particularly robust and ornate" style could be the work of a single hand but did not know the identity of the carver. The 122 carvings attributed to Mutuaga are recorded and illustrated in my 1996 book and in an unpublished essay of mine.

Cecil Abel told me that when his father saw Mutuaga's spatulas with human figure handles he told the artist that if he carved such figures on a stand, they would definitely be attractive to Westerners (Beran H., 1996, p. x and 17). And so Mutuaga did carve them and in considerable numbers. Two of the carvings (*Ibid.*, pl. 78 and 81) are approximately 60 cm high and, although made for Westerners, are among the finest Massim artworks.

Some of the leading figures in the Western community at a time when New Guinea was governed by the British collected works by the artists. These include Reverend William Lawes, who, with his wife, became the first European resident on the Papuan mainland in 1874 (*Ibid.*, pl. 78); Commodore James Erskine, who proclaimed the British Protectorate over Papua in 1884 (*Ibid.*, pl. 52); Reverend George Brown, who led Methodist missionaries into what is now Milne Bay Province in 1891 (*Ibid.*, pl. 114); and Sir William MacGregor and Sir Hubert Murray, the

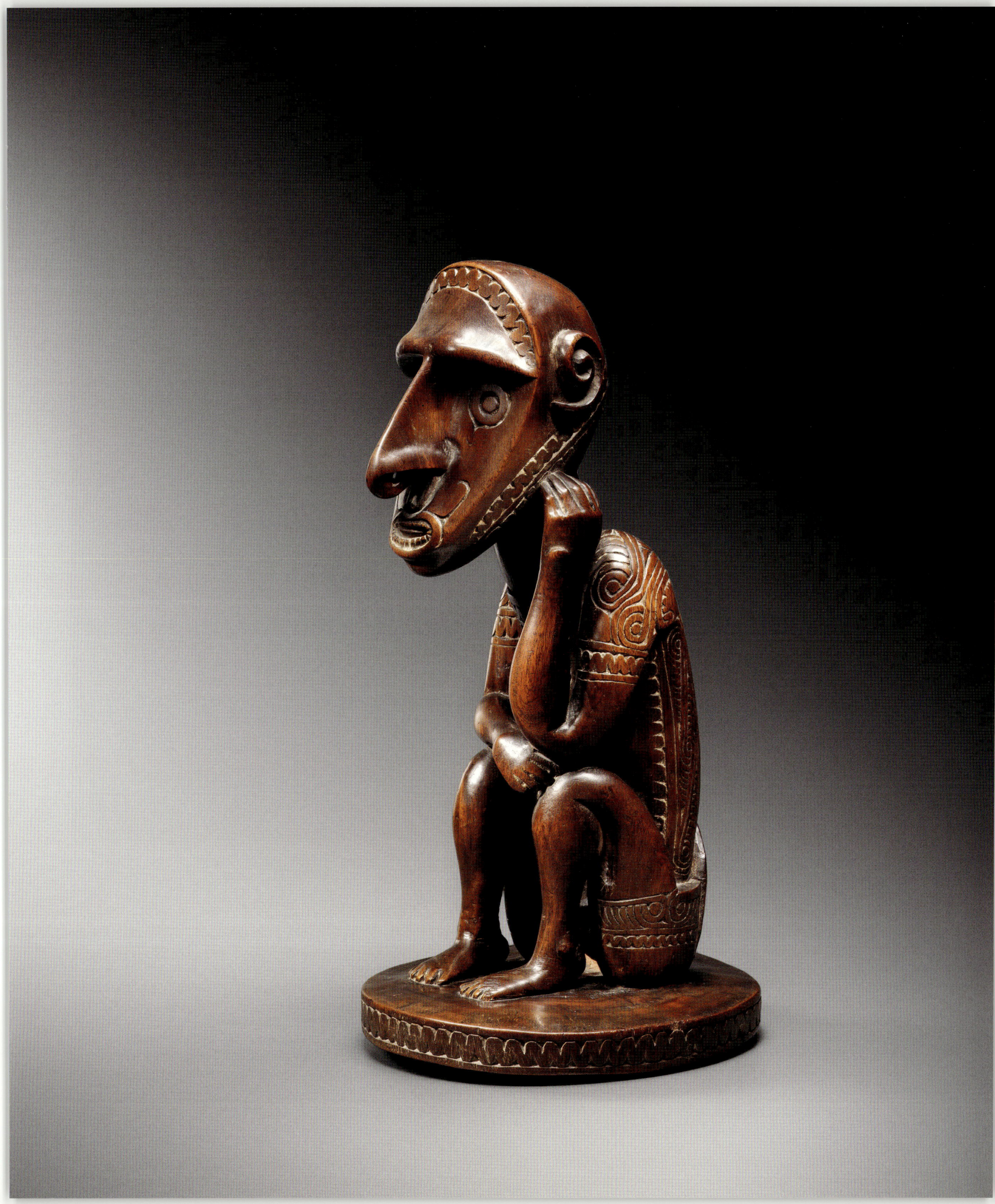

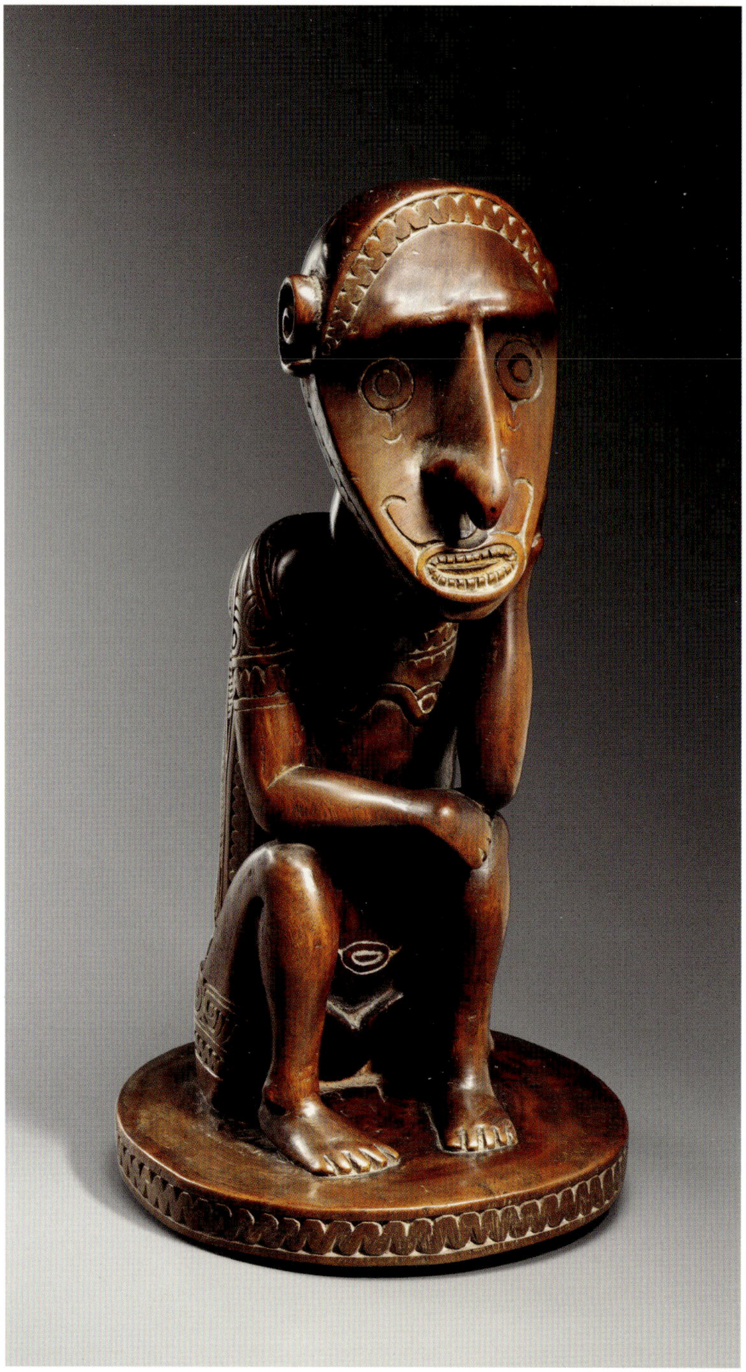

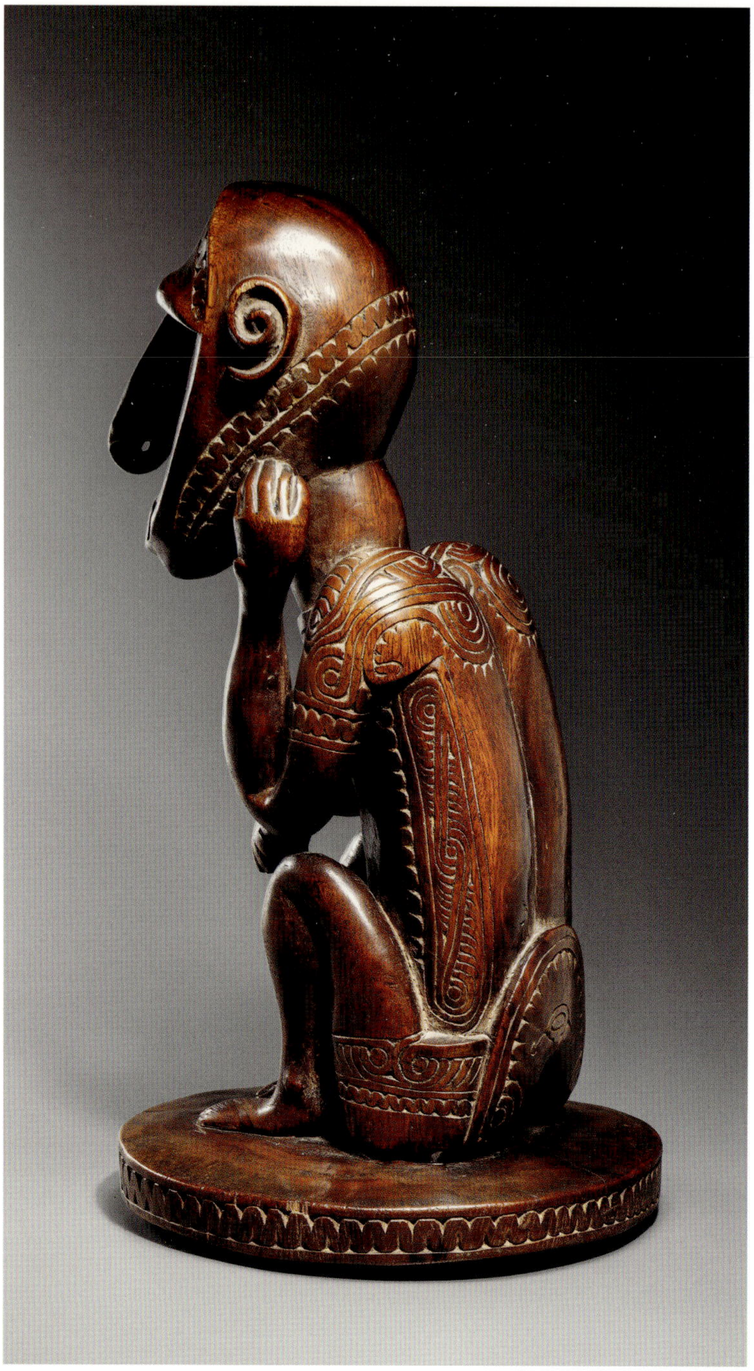

country's most memorable lieutenant-governors (*ibid*., pl. 58, 60, 72, 81, and 84). An entry in the diary of Bronislaw Malinowski, one of the founding fathers of modern anthropology, shows that he met Mutuaga. The entry for 7 December 1914 in *A Diary in the Strict Sense of the Term* (1967, p. 49) includes the following passage: "Lovely landscape at Suau . . . On the shore I sat on a cannibal *gahana* and talked with Imtuaga [sic] master carver." The misspelling of the artist's name is presumably due to a misreading of Malinowski's handwriting by Norman Guterman, who translated the diary from the Polish. It seems that Malinowski did not obtain any carvings by Mutuaga when he met him as there do not seem to be any in the anthropologist's extensive collection of Massim artworks and artefacts. Malinowski stayed with Charles Abel at the Kwato Island mission station and may then have been encouraged to visit the artist by Abel.

Mutuaga was a New Guinea artist working in a changing world. He started his artistic career carvings artworks for local use but after meeting Charles Abel increasingly made carvings for Westerners as gifts in the expectation of a gift in return. The large number of works by him provide a unique opportunity to study the creativity of a New Guinea woodcarver and to see how a New Guinea artist's style can change over time. [HB]

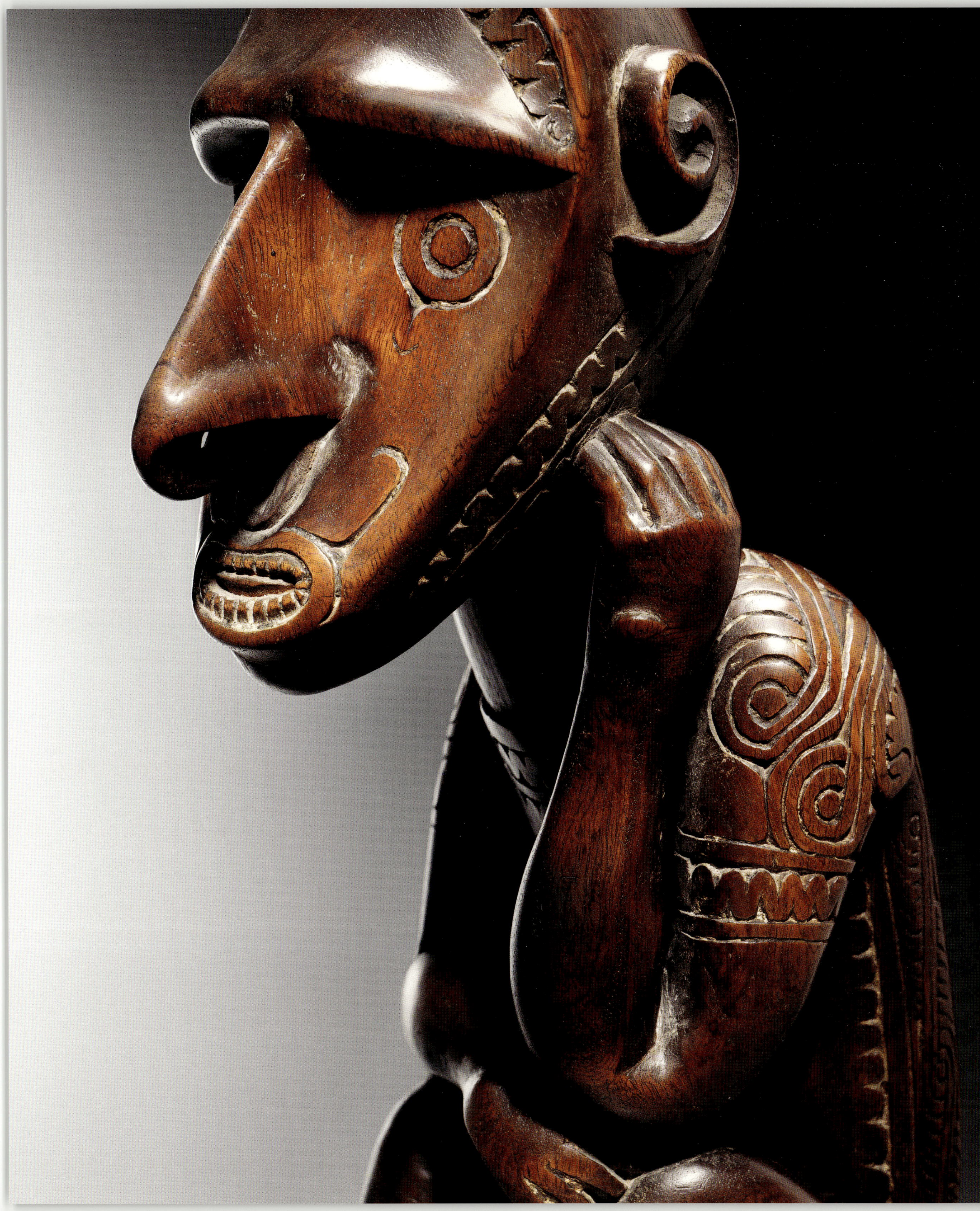

Hook

Tami islands, Morobe Province, Papua New Guinea, H. 30.5 cm

Hooks like this are very rare and most if not all were collected in a short period encompassing the end of the nineteenth and early twentieth century. The Weill hook is an old example and dates from an earlier generation than its possible collection date. It was probably made by a senior carver and likely represents the spirit associated with the carver's *Tago* allegiance.[1] It is a minimalist masterpiece from an ancient pre-literate society.

In those days the main Tami Island, Wonam, where this hook most likely came from, had a population of about 120,[2] perhaps only 30 adult men – hardly sufficient to service three or four ocean-going canoes, yet their products and designs were widespread and influenced a whole region.

Persons, spirits, obligations and things merge in this hook and the designs have to some extent to be inferred.

The holed attachment for a hanging rope is probably circumscribed by two green tree lizard (*kabulisat*) heads, one resting on each figures topknot but the form actually looks like a two headed snail.[3] The topknot appears to be an image of the type of hairstyle drawn by Hans Vogel[4] but extended by artistic licence or peak shift to give it more authority, it equally might be a depiction of a widow's head piled high with domestic *bilum* bags as was a custom in the region following a death, or it might be a bark hat headdress. The extended topknot allowed the artist an opportunity to add long extended earlobes (*talingalau*) with a shell hanger (*taling baniobo*) resting on the joint shoulders of the figures. They give some structural stability to the hook when loaded.

The faces of each of the figures are decorated with *Tago* symbols with peaks (*matasi*) above and below the eye.[5] Georg Bamler[6] notes that only the most senior man (*Kumali lanqa*) of the most senior Mayongal clan (*sib*) displays Janus *Tago* masks. This hook's two-sided figure may be a signal of the same importance, however the Moyangal clan *Tago* has three *matasi* above the eye and this has only one. It might therefore signify a subsidiary of the Moyangal clan called *Elemun*, or, because of especially long ears, might be from a *Tago* called *Nding* that eats the flesh of dead bodies. The Tami, who were not headhunters, had a practice before contact to house the dead in an especially constructed shelter next to the dwelling so they could watch the melting of flesh as the dead slowly departed to an amorphous spirit world of *Kani*.

The base is decorated with bands that Bodrogi records as *kalikali* (centipede)[7] but the Tami call it *matimuat*—a type a caterpillar or grub that arches it's back, moving one step at a time.

It can safely be inferred that no marking is wasted on this hook including the markings on the head (fish or shark teeth - *iliniu*, or alternatively a ray's tail- *aipa*) and the *matimuat* band working its way all around the base and up the prongs. Concepts are being conveyed.

The round marks are nearly always prominent as joint marks. The belly button is the last join at birth.

Although the figures are clearly female they have the angularity of males and lack breasts. This might be deliberate, as the Tami respected duality in symbolism. Moon/Sun, Black/Red, Female/Male; the hook could originally have been painted with black and red ochre in quadrants to accentuate this duality. Incisions were highlighted in white. [EC]

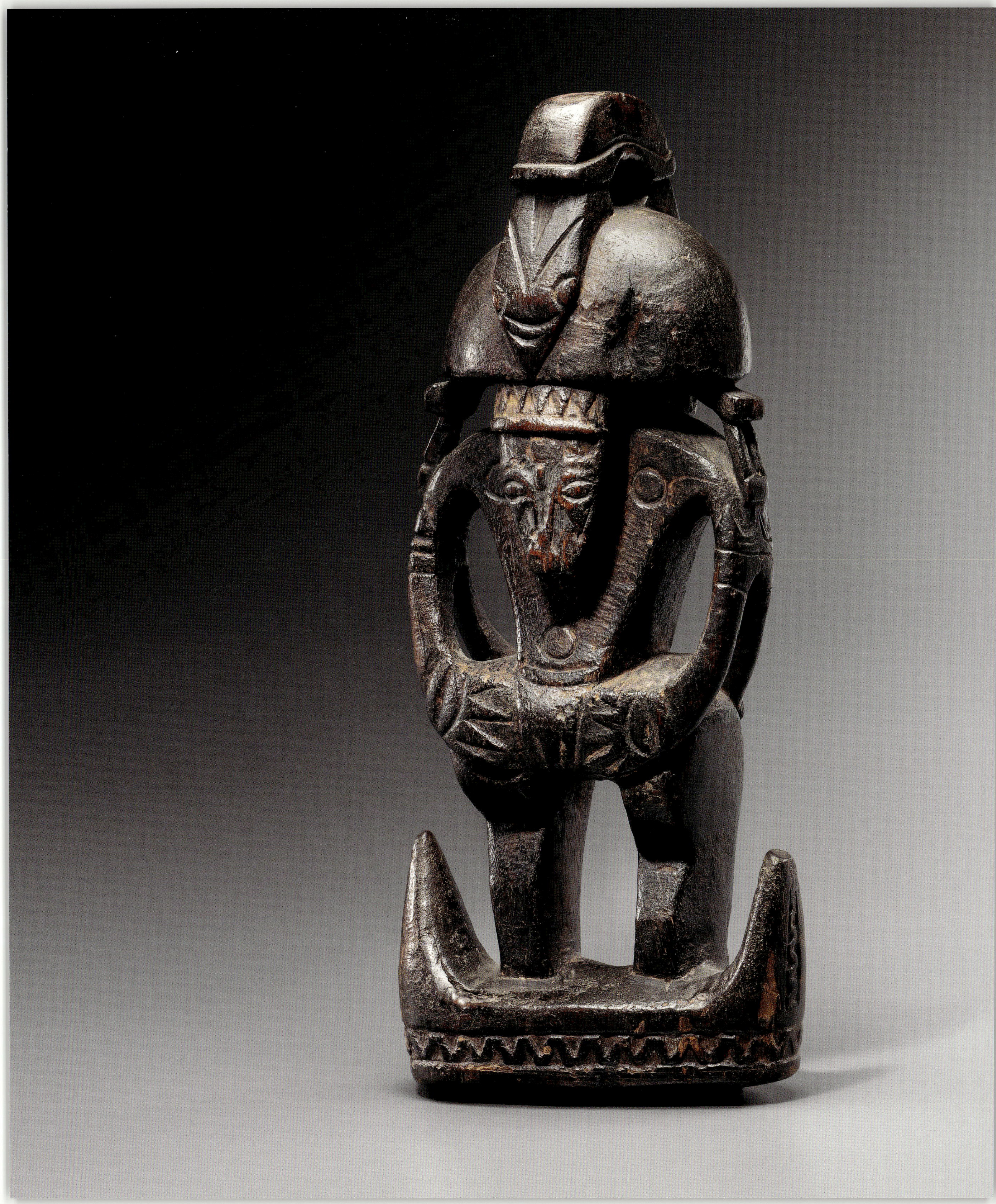

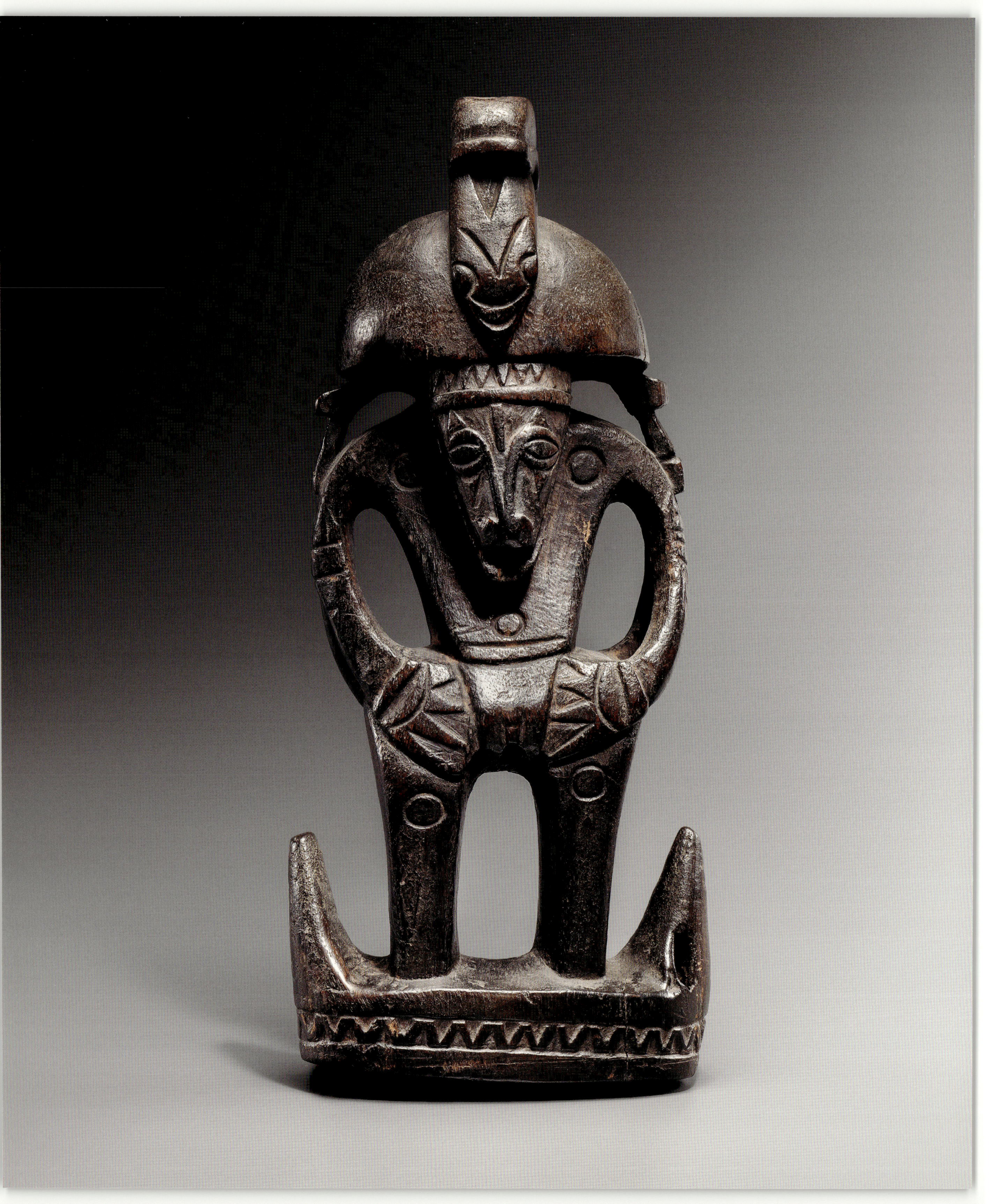

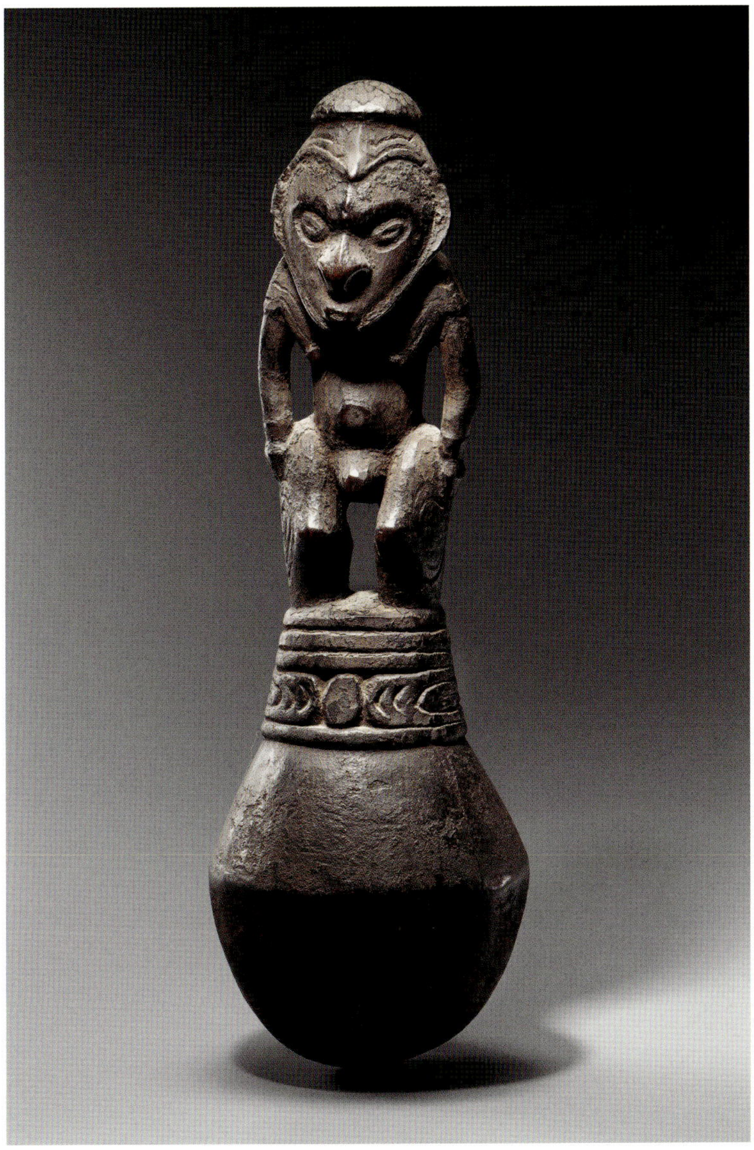

Pestle
Murik Lake, Papua New Guinea, H. 30 cm

The most highly appreciated food on the northwest coast of Papua New Guinea is taro, a tuber that is a major crop in the area. It is a woman's job to mash the cooked taros with pestles.
The handle of these pestles is often given human form. In this case, the style of the figure makes it possible to assert that it probably comes from one of the coastal villages in the Lake Murik region. This male figure bears facial scarification whose meanings are now impossible to determine. One of the most common depicts a spider, an animal much admired for its cunning in capturing its food in a web. [PP]

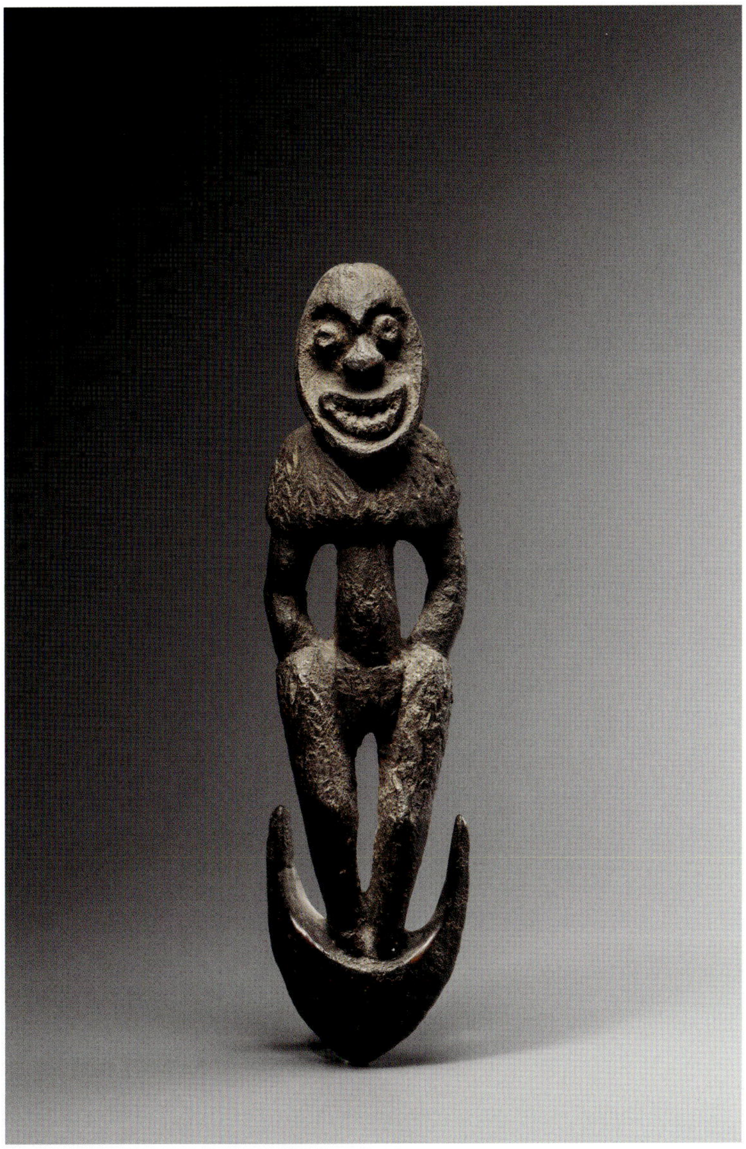

Hook
Sepik River, Papua New Guinea, H. 20 cm

This charming object shows a woman carefully balanced on a crescent moon. The effectiveness of this poetic image is due to a composition where curves and straight lines, troughs and swells achieve a degree of perfection that is rarely equalled.
These small hooks were probably used in family homes. The figure with scarification on the shoulders and thighs represents a clan ancestor. Offerings would have been hung from it when seeking the figure's intervention in time of need. [PP]

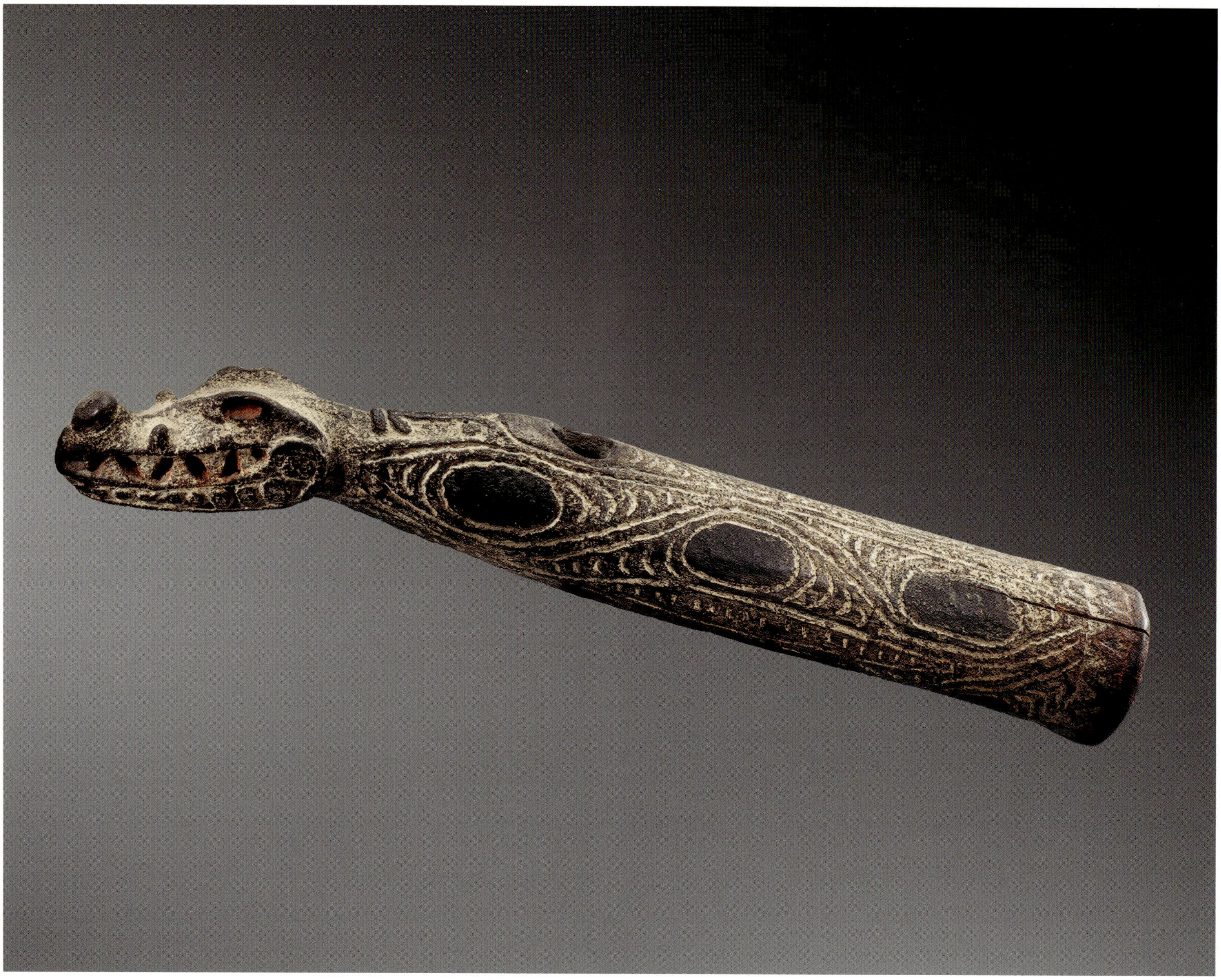

Iatmul trumpet
Sepik River, Papua New Guinea, L. 49 cm

Returning from a headhunting expedition, men would blow on these trumpets to announce their victory and to specify how many heads they would be bringing. They might also be played at festivals. The animal head depicted at one end combines the features of pigs' teeth and a crocodile head. This deliberate ambiguity refers to the ancestors' notorious ability to take multiple forms. The spiral pattern on the animal's body symbolizes a river's swirling waters, which reveal the ancestors' presence.
This particular piece belonged to Pierre Loeb. Like his Surrealist friends, he, too, must have appreciated this double figure alluding to the ancestors' powers of metamorphosis. [PP]

Iatmul mask
Sepik River, Papua New Guinea, H. 47 cm

Mwai masks are emblematic objects in Iatmul culture. When young men finally leave the men's house where they have been held for several months during their initiation period, they wear showy costumes made of leaves, flowers, and feathers, in the middle of which appears the *mwai* mask. While wearing this mask, the young initiates themselves become their clan's ancestor.
Variations of the *mwai* mask are manifold, but they all feature a long nose that stretches down to the chin. This motif is associated with the myth of the origin of speech. Hidden under their costumes, the dancers play a short flute, adding a strange, piercing sound to their striking appearance. [PP]

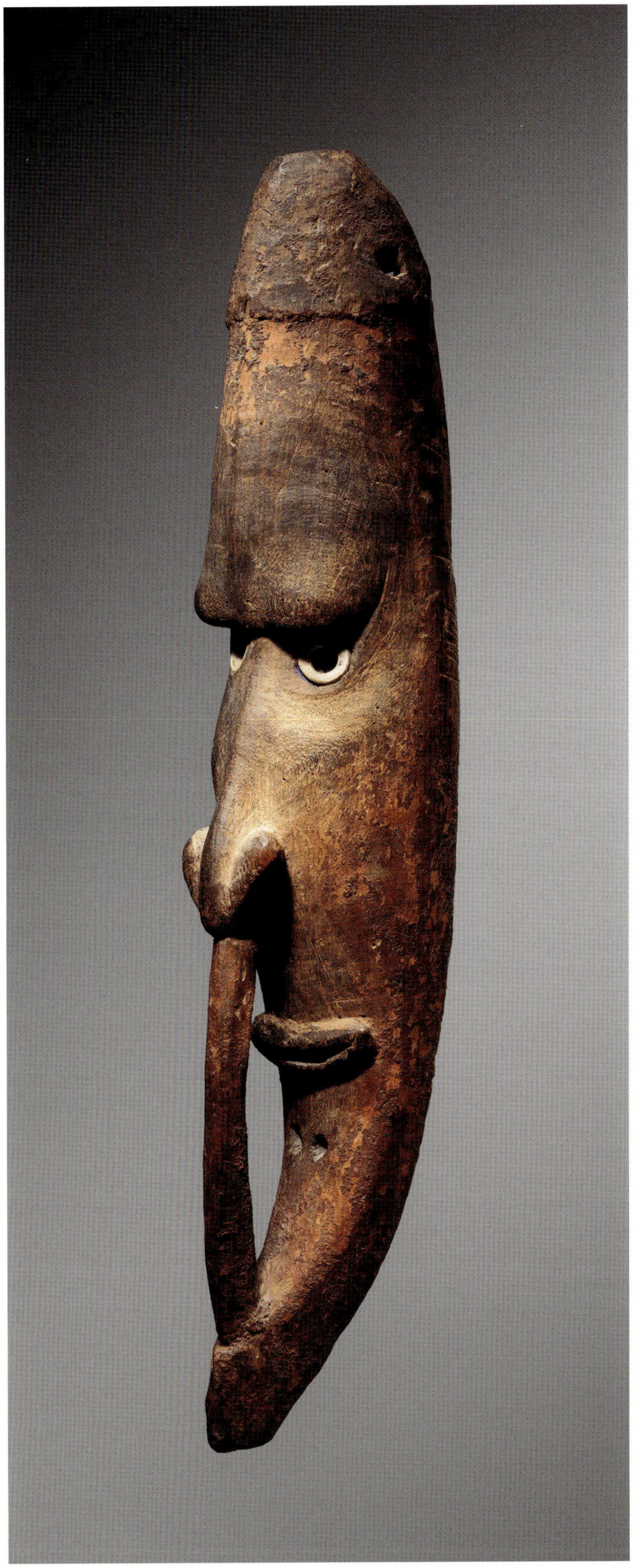

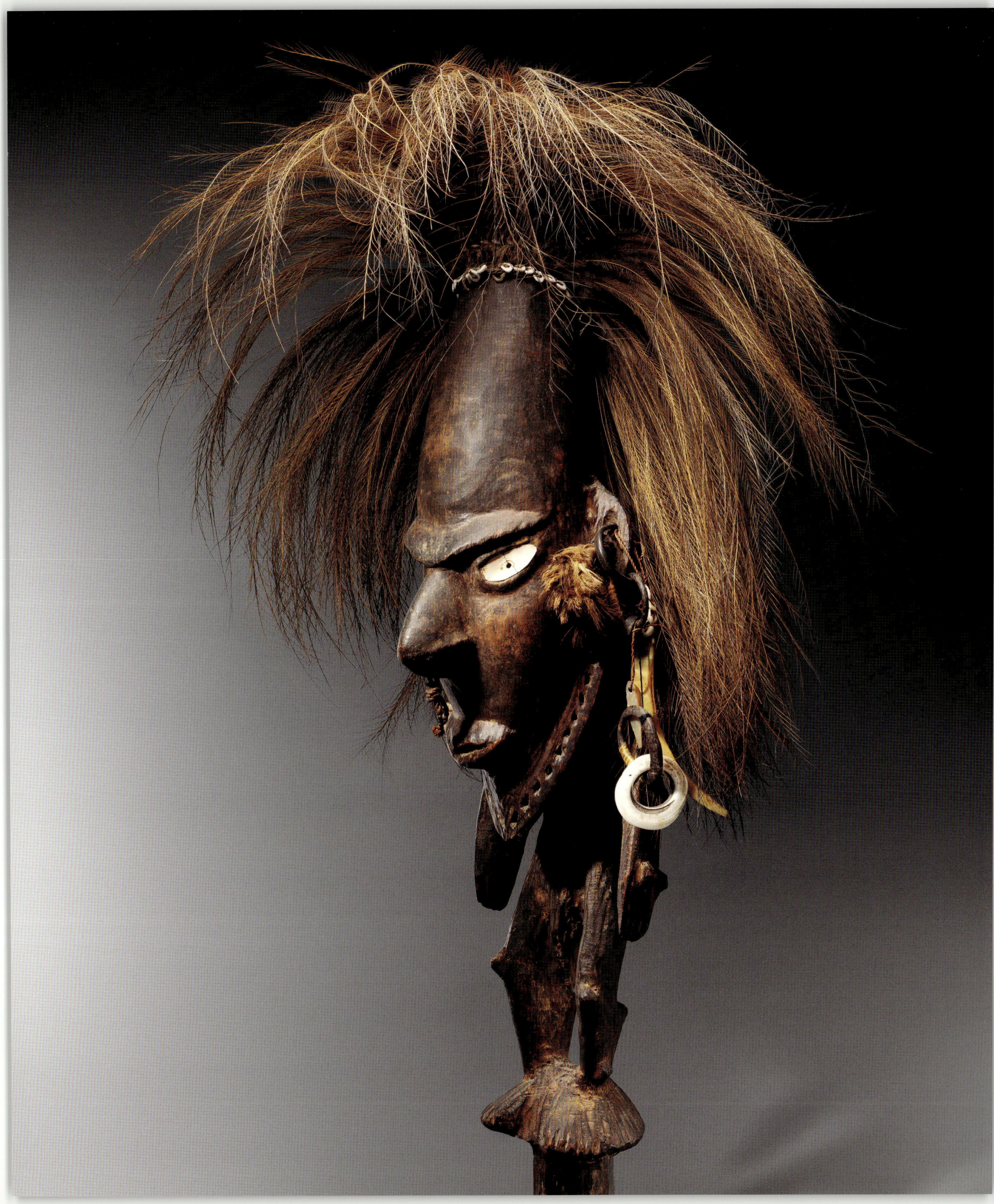

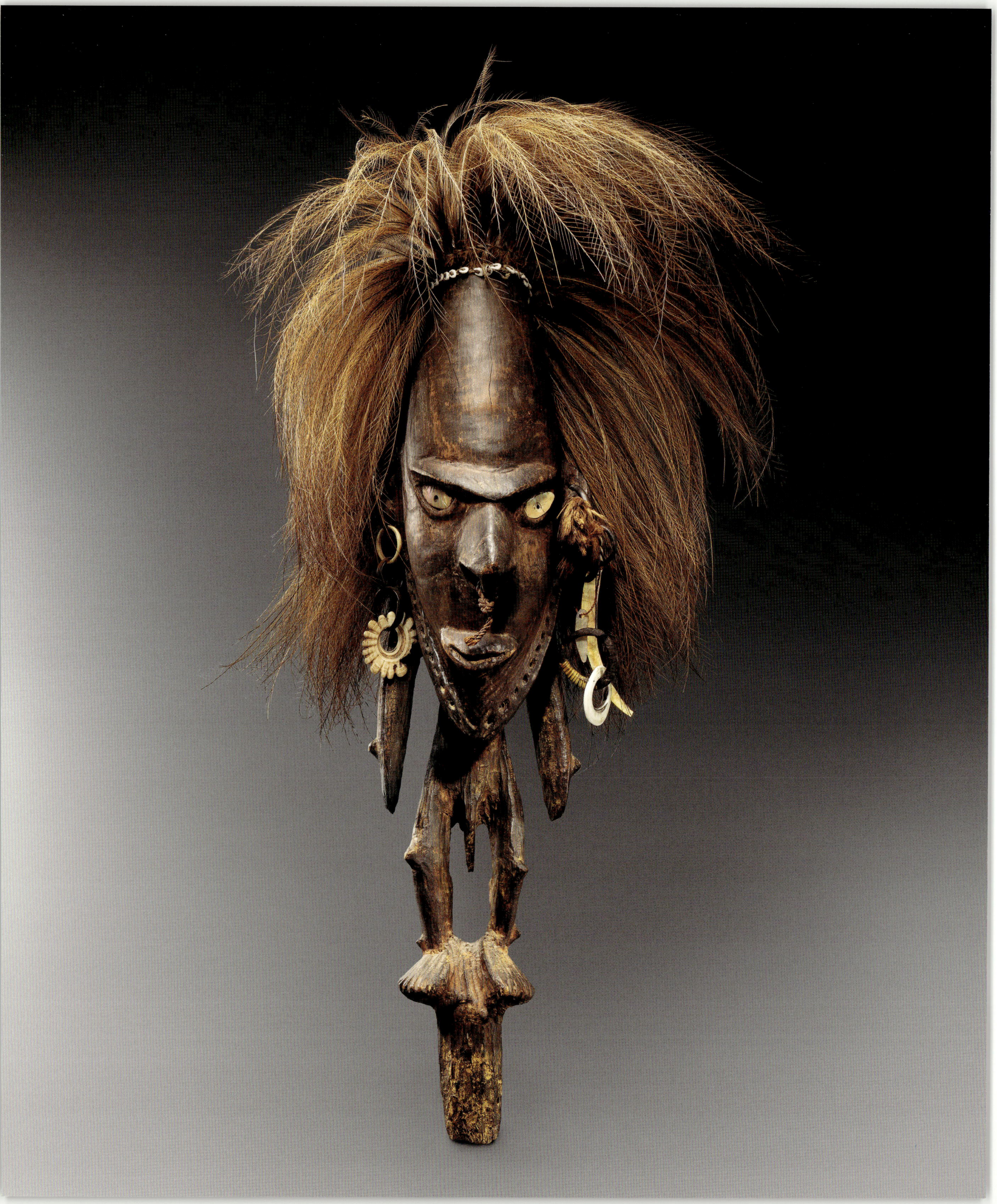

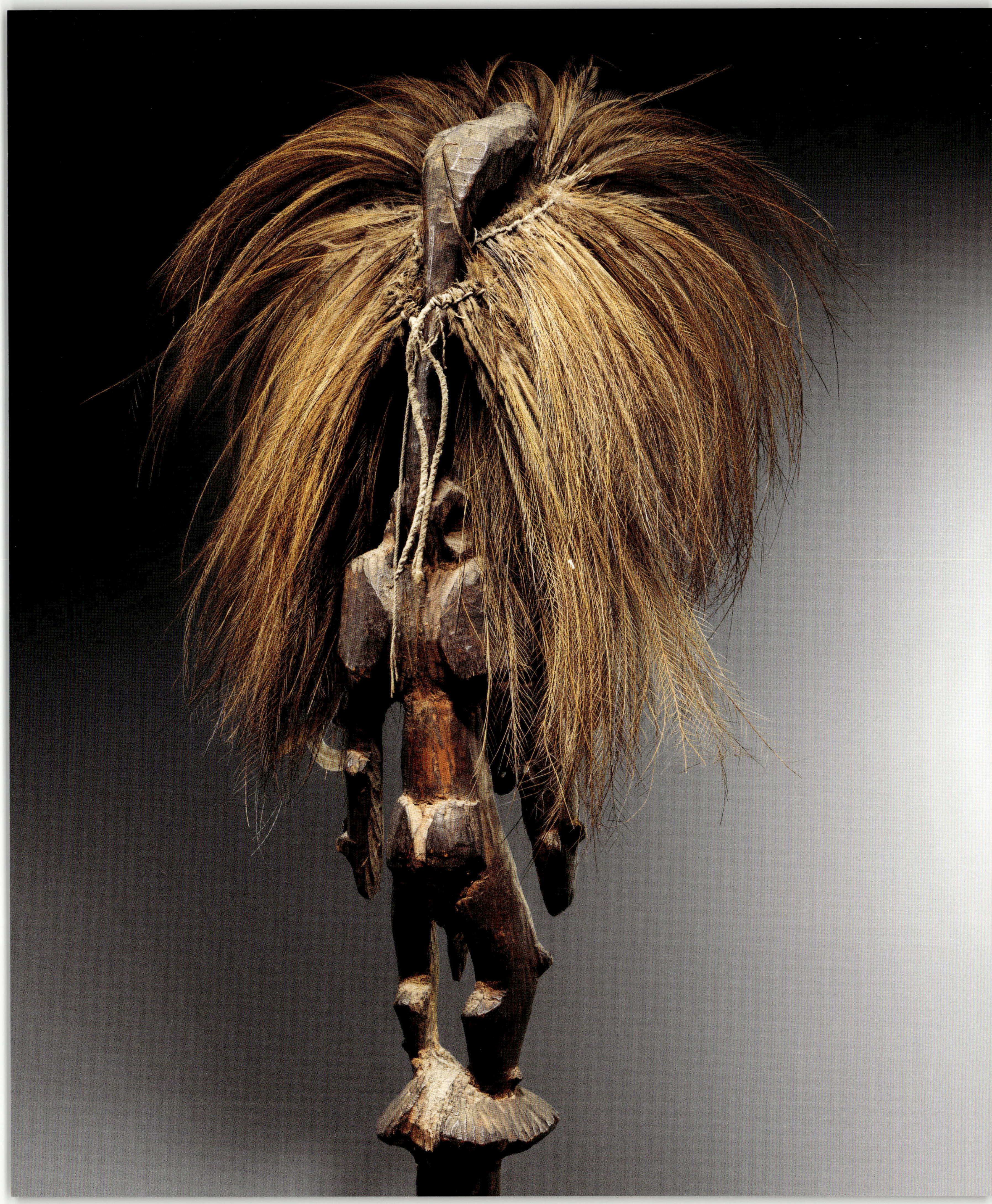

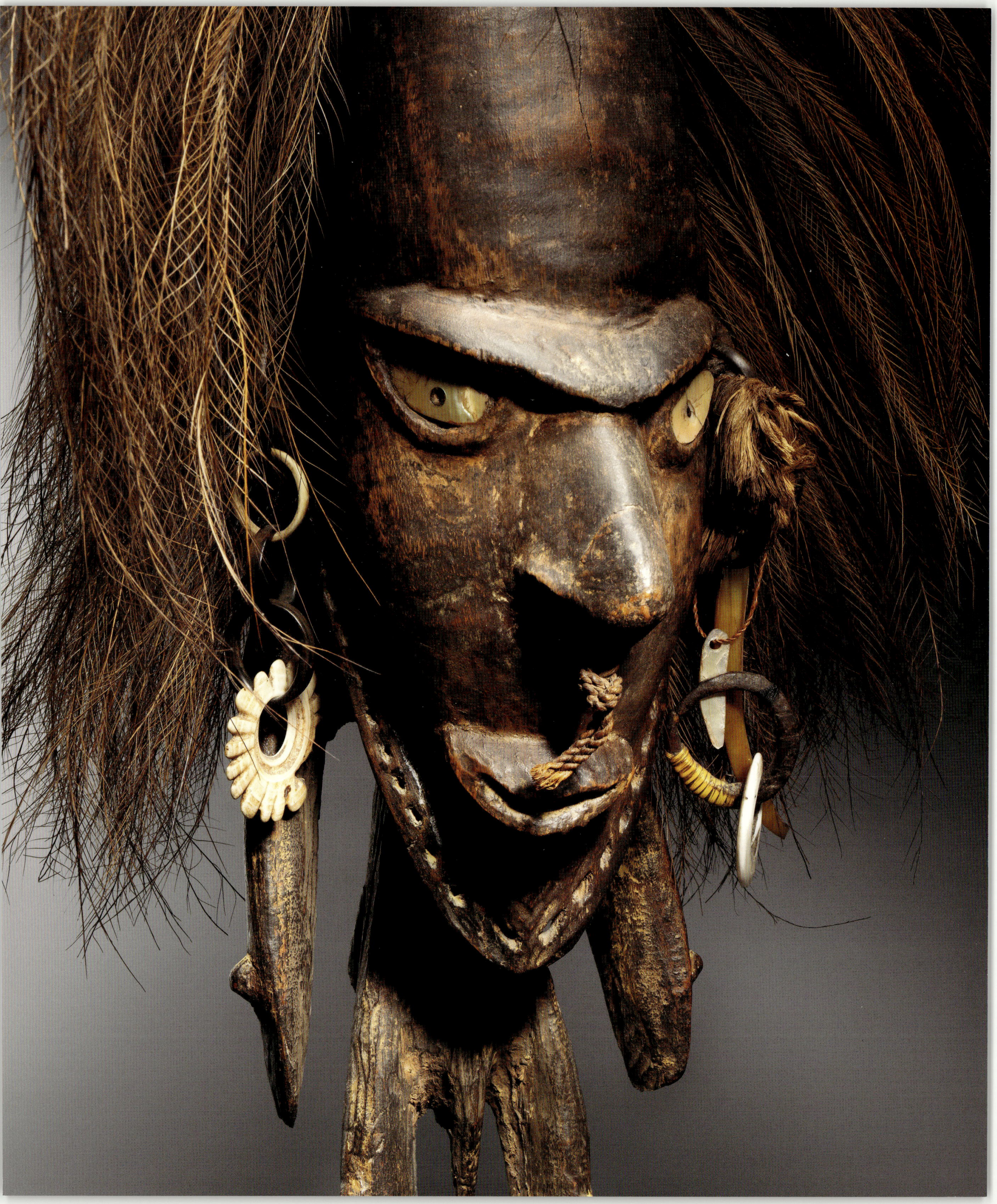

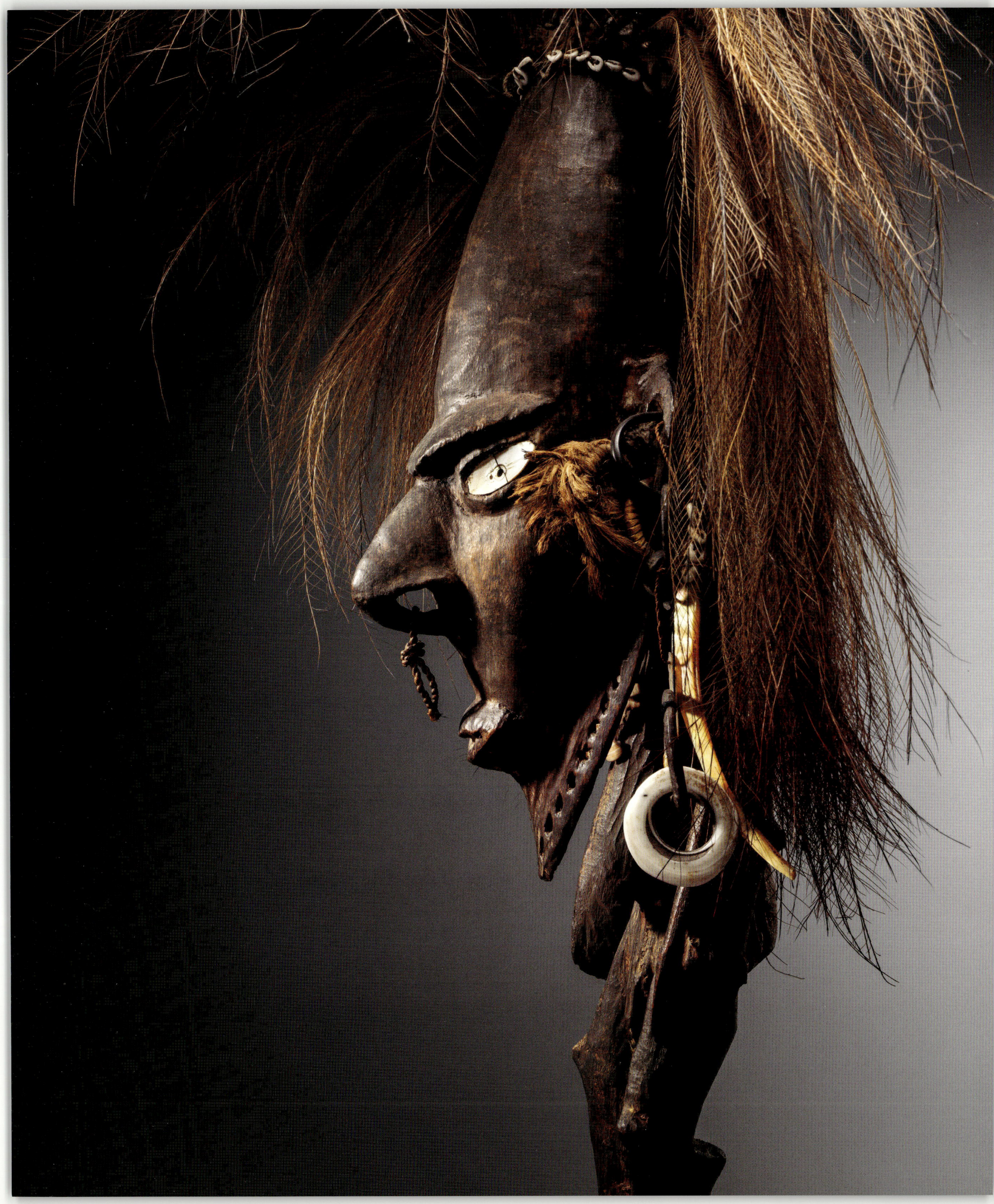

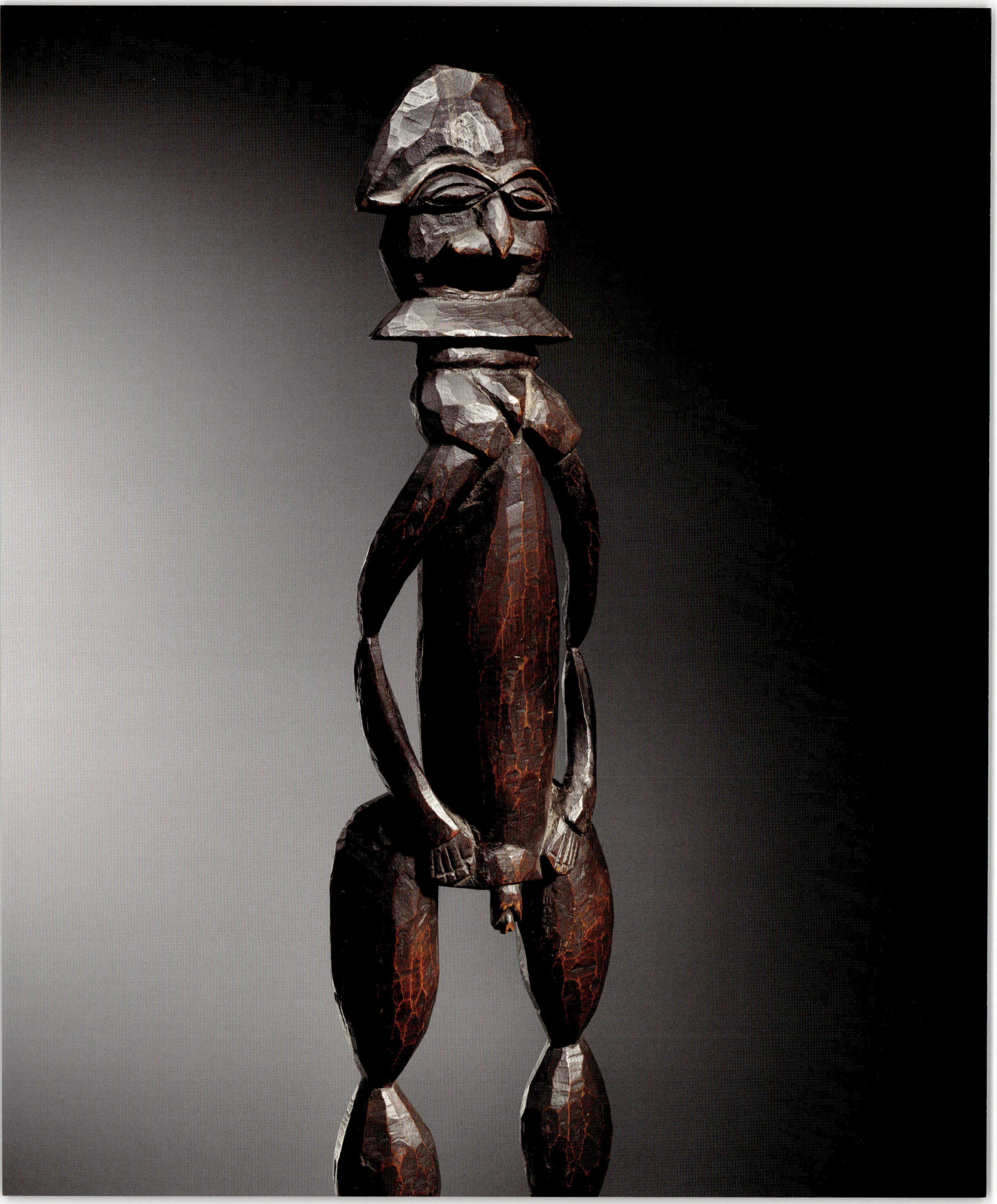

Kanak statue
New Caledonia, H. 86 cm

At exchange ceremonies in New Caledonia, large ancestor figures would be placed in front of the large communal house of the chiefdom, where they ensured that each member performed his duties.
Unfortunately, the early literature has nothing to say about the distribution of these figures. Even so, the features of this particular specimen—a sort of ruff under its face, extremely stylized limbs, highlighted joints—enable it to be attributed to the central coastal region on the eastern side of the island, more specifically the area stretching from Canala to Koné. [PP]

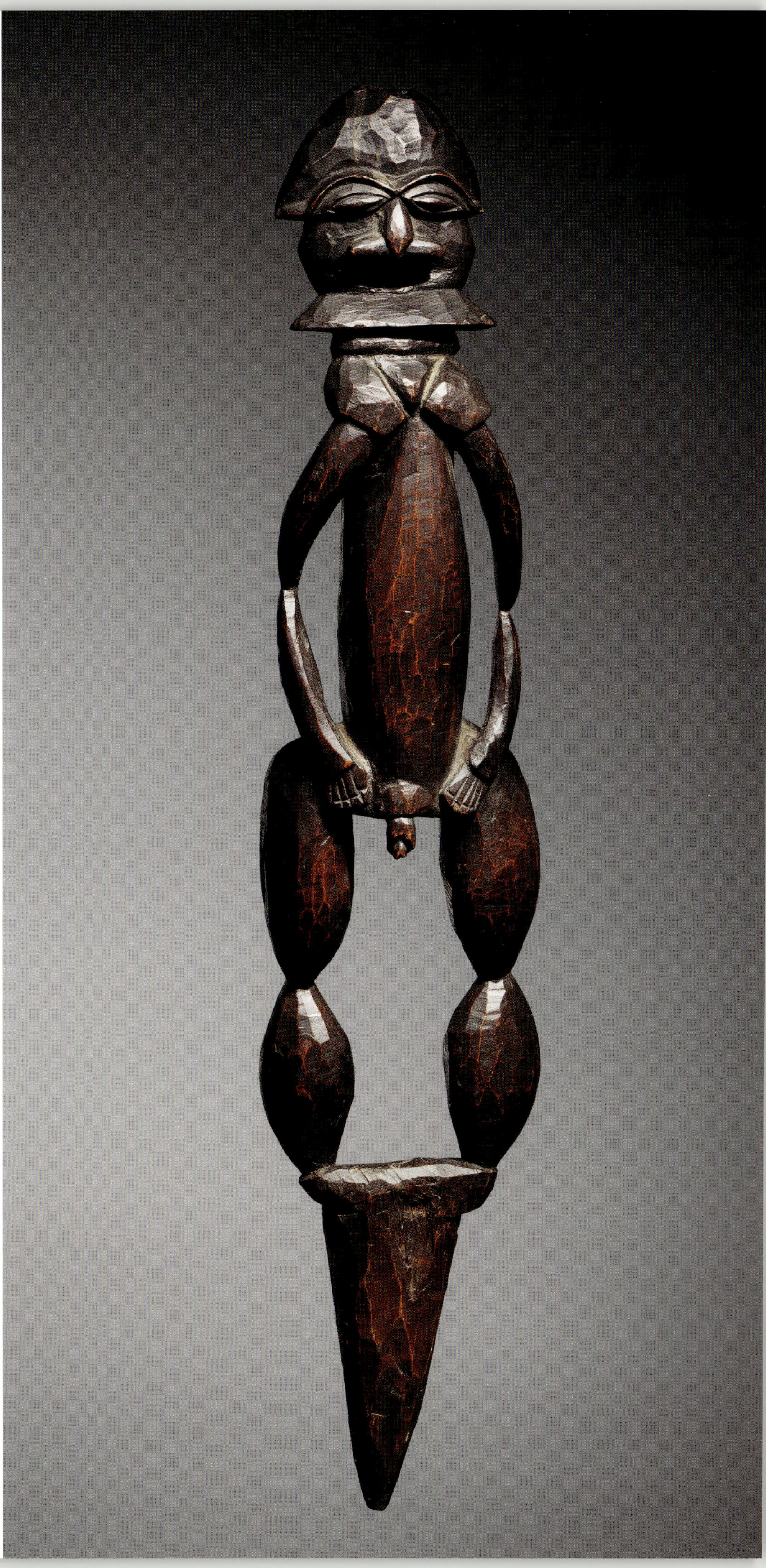

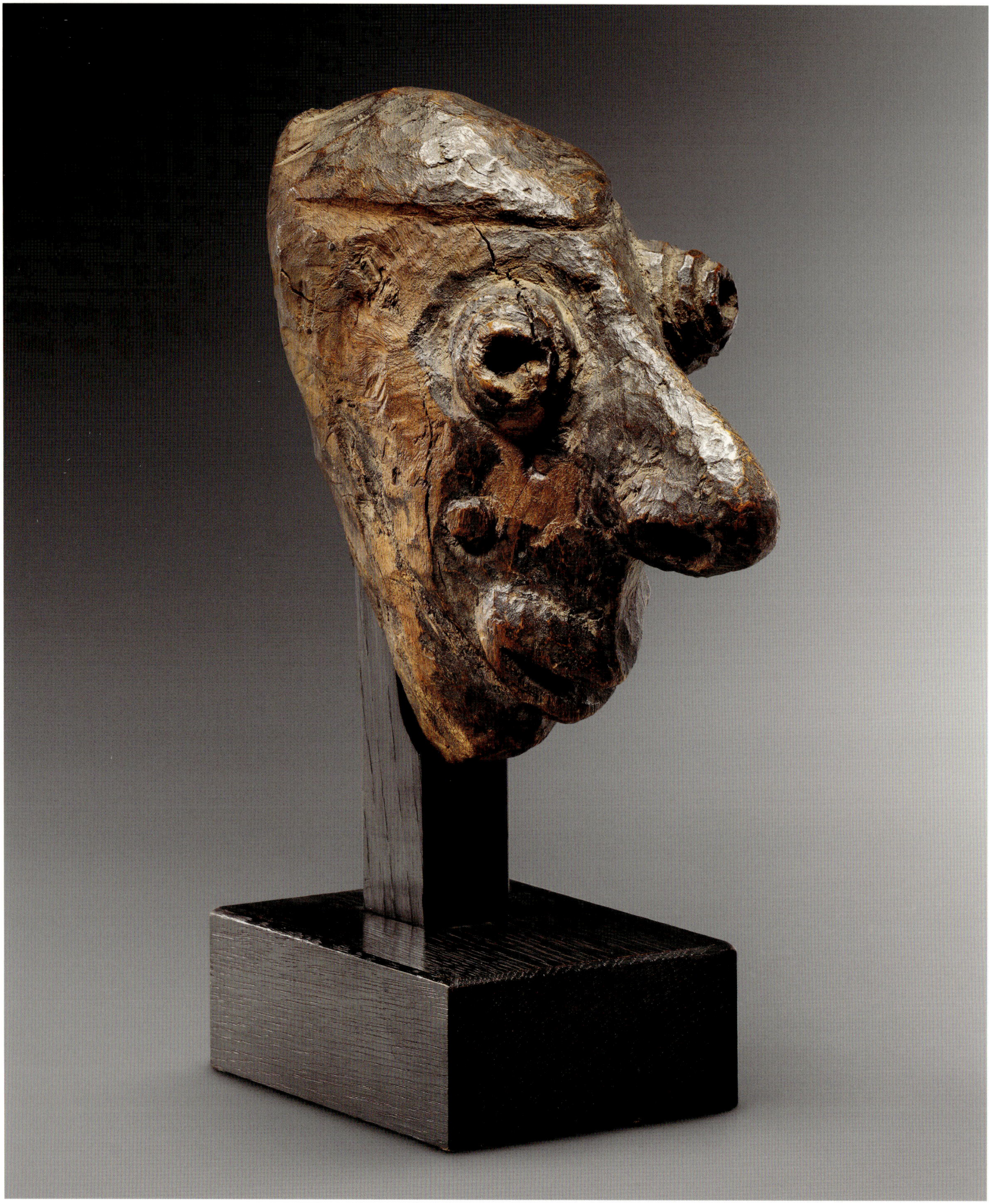

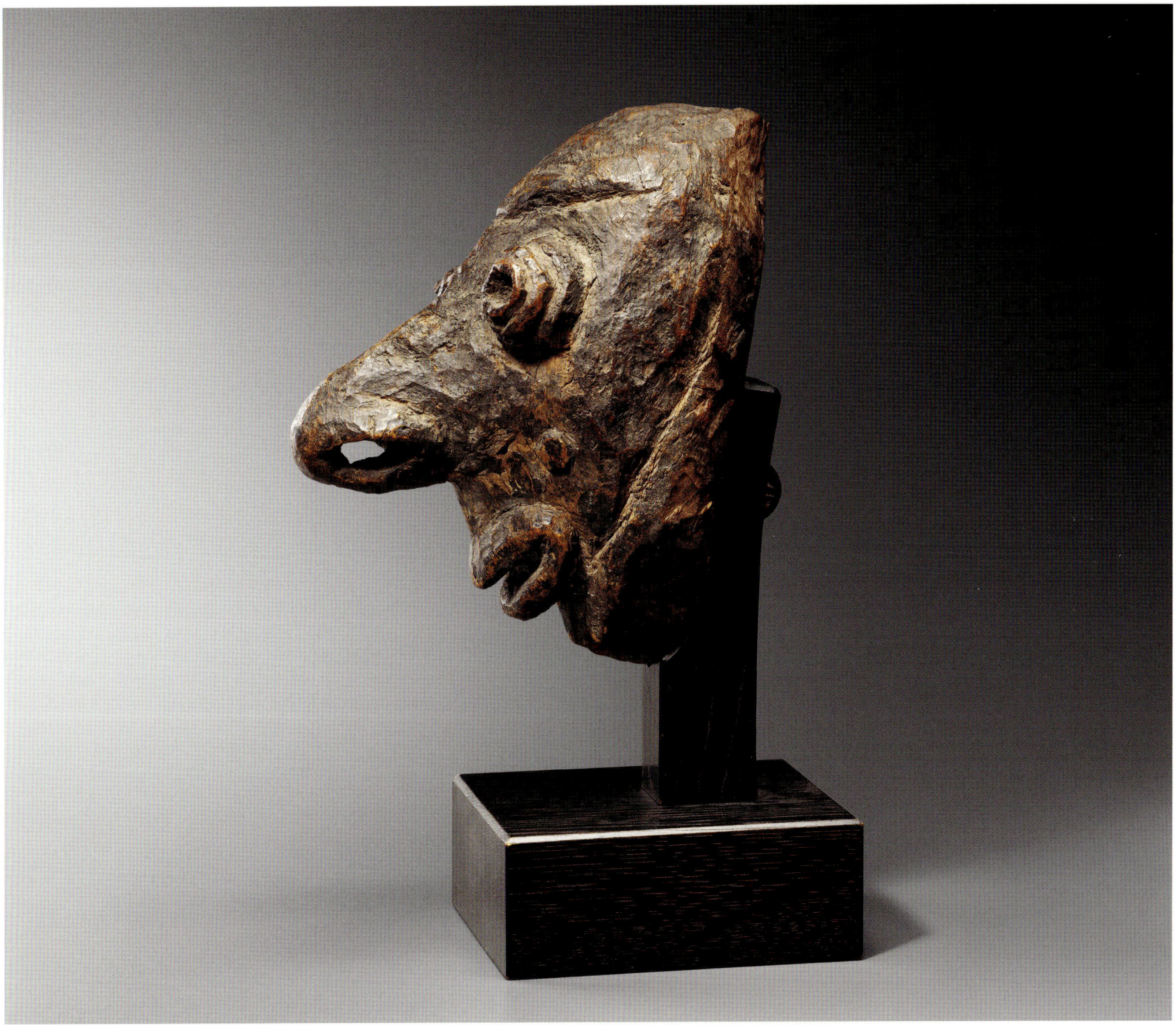

Small mask
Malekula, Vanuatu, H. 16 cm
Stand by Kichizô Inagaki

This wild-eyed, captivating head once belonged to René Gaffé, a Belgian journalist and experienced collector who was close to the Surrealists. In the sale catalogue for his collection of tribal art, it is attributed to the lower Sepik valley. However this cannot be right: it was undoubtedly made by an inhabitant of the area to the north of the Port Sandwich region on the island of Malekula. It is probably the only example of an artistic tradition that died out very early and is otherwise known from just a handful of photographs (my thanks go to Kirk Huffman for identifying them). [PP]

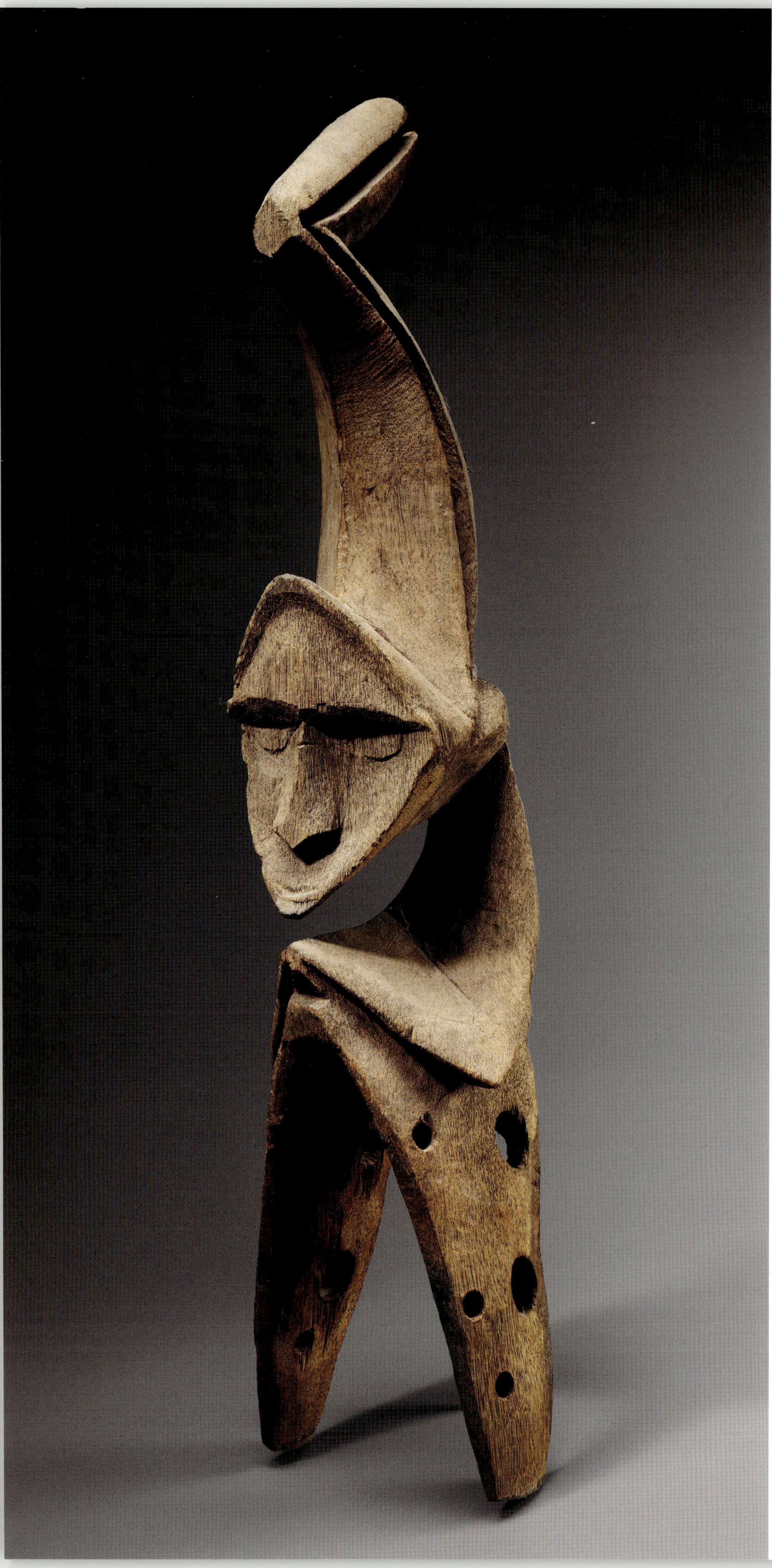

Canoe prow
Vanuatu, H. 63 cm

Atchin is a tiny island off the northeast coast of the island of Malekula. There is a village on the island but families till their plots on the much larger neighbouring island, which men and women reach in dugout canoes. The figures carved on the prows of the male canoes can vary considerably, with the designs reflecting the rank each man has reached in a strict hierarchy.
In this case, the body of the object consists of an elegant, airy figure of a bird with a human head on its back. The bird is probably a frigate, which is admired for its skill in catching fish and its agility when in flight. [PP]

Canoe prow
Solomon Islands, H. 25 cm

Most often known as *musumusu* (the name varies according to the region), these prow figures were attached just above the water line on large ceremonial canoes in the Western Solomon Islands.
Blackened and inlayed with mother-of-pearl, the figure holds a tiny head in its hands. The figure's face combines human and canine features, its jaws especially taking the form of a dog's snout. In this way, through the logic of sympathetic magic, the figure acquires a dog's ability to flush out game or sniff approaching enemy canoes in time of war. [PP]

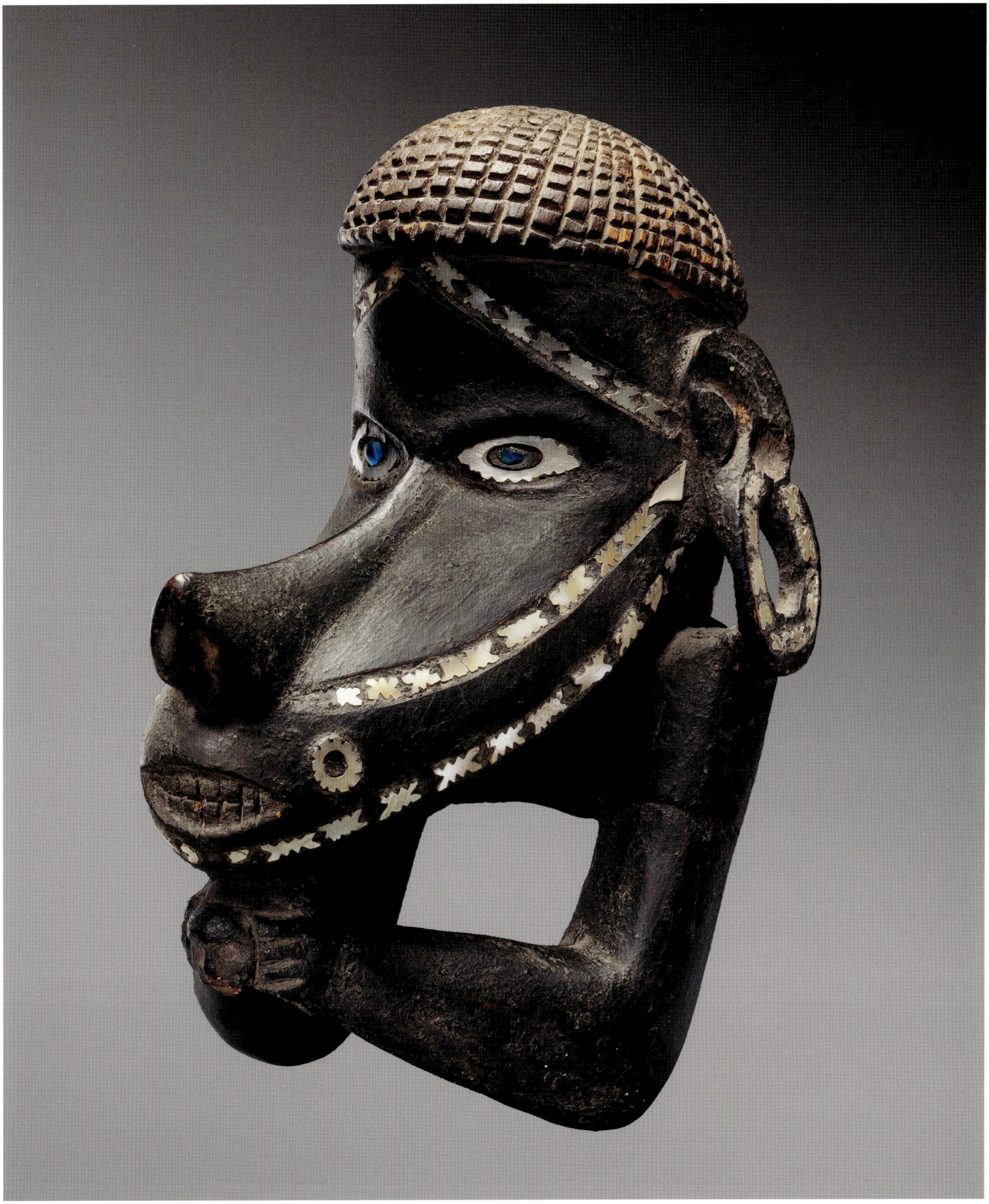

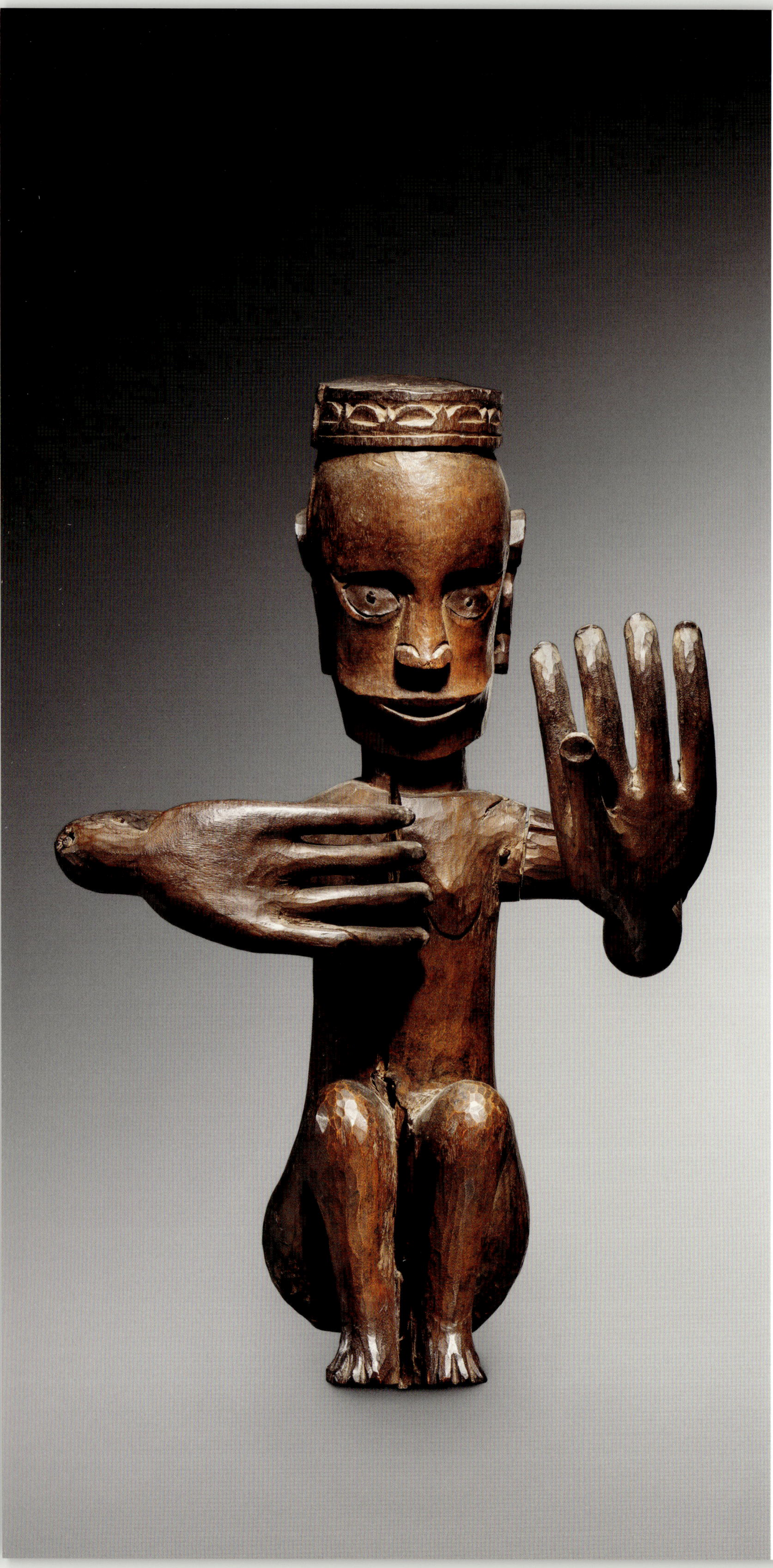

Batak statue
Sumatra, Indonesia, H. 34 cm

The Batak of northern Sumatra are extraordinary sculptors. Carved with articulated arms, enormous hands and a hypertrophied head, this sculpture portrays a man in dancing position. Ancient photos of masquerades show men adopting similar stances. One can make a guess that the artist intended through the concentrated expression of the face and the position of the hands to convey the desire to keep the viewer at a distance in order to ensure the distancing necessary in contacting the ancestors or spirits. Through the skilfully judged circular movement of the arms and hands, the sculptor has managed masterfully to establish a balance in this figure sitting on its haunches. [CDM]

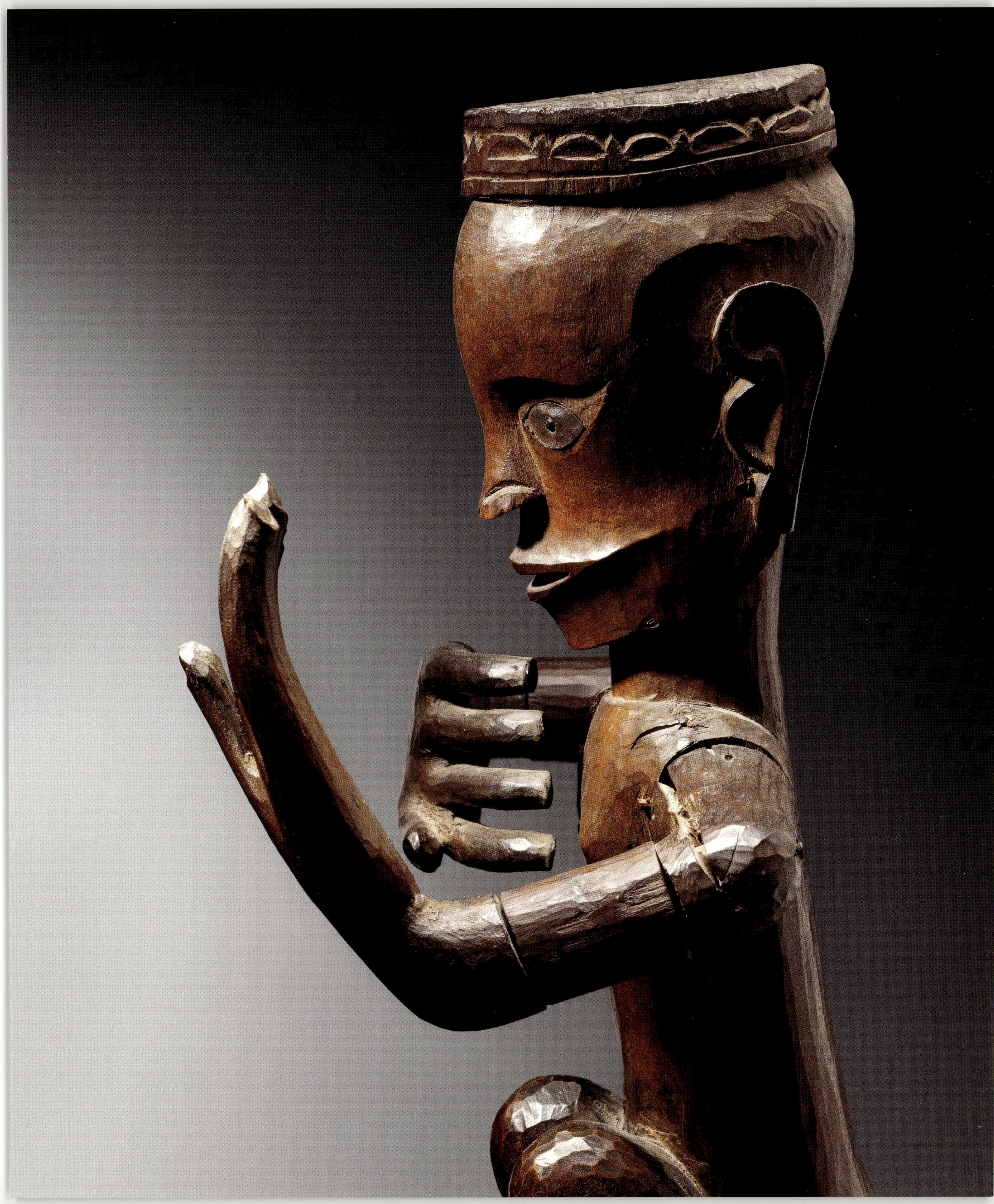

Dayak architectural element
Borneo, Indonesia, H. 51 cm

The mountainous island of Borneo straddles the equator and is the largest island in southeast Asia. It is covered in dense jungle and crossed by numerous rivers, which are the main means of communication. Some of the most important sculpture on the island actually involves architectural elements. These works are often associated with the themes of protection and the journey made by the souls of the departed. This crouching anthropomorphic figure, which seems ready to leap forward, portrays a supernatural being. Everything about it—its striking body, its face, and its jutting, diamond-shaped mouth showing its teeth—expresses the power of a tutelary spirit. The style is reminiscent of certain Modang sculptures from the River Mahakam, to the east of Kalimantan. [CDM]

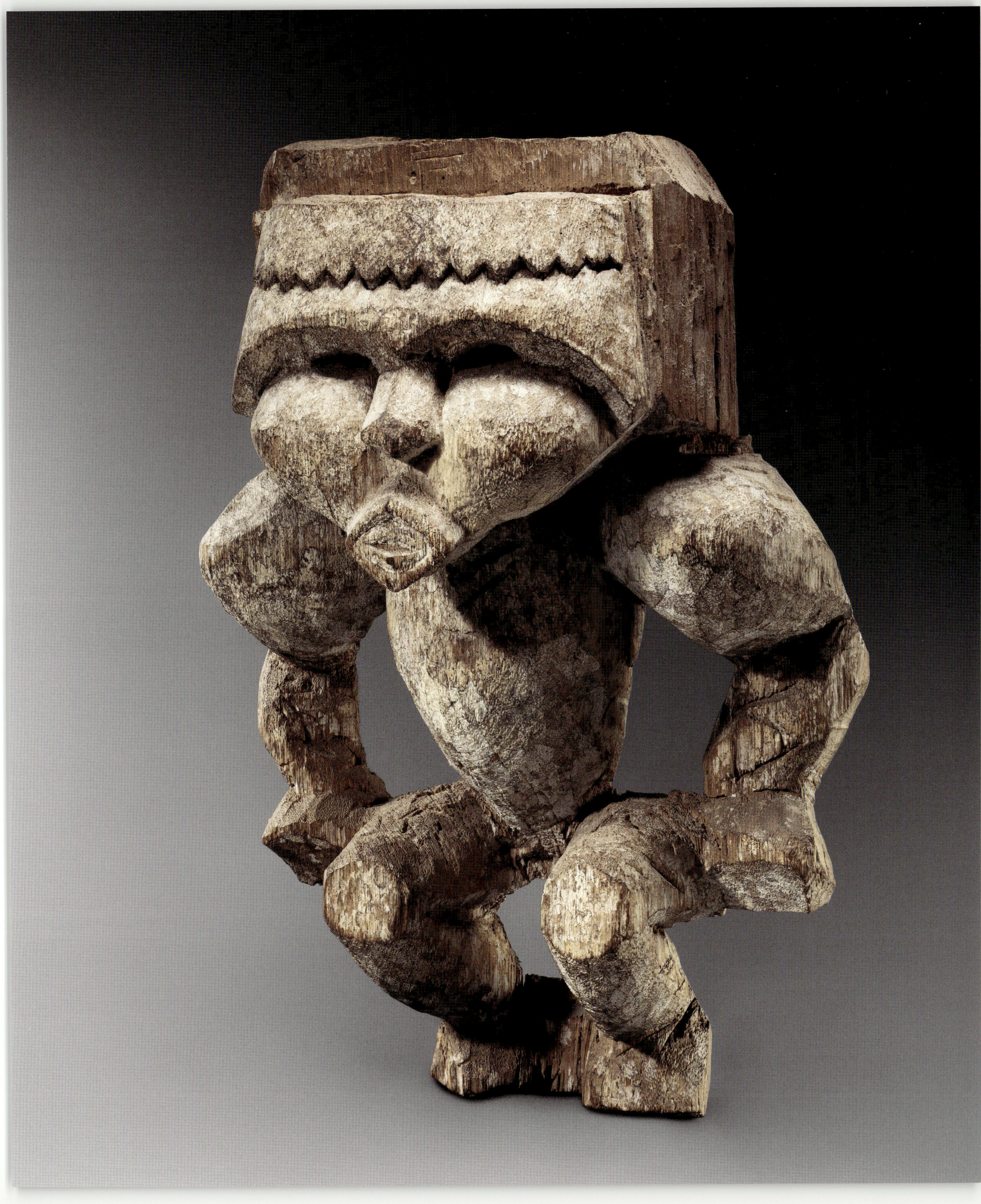

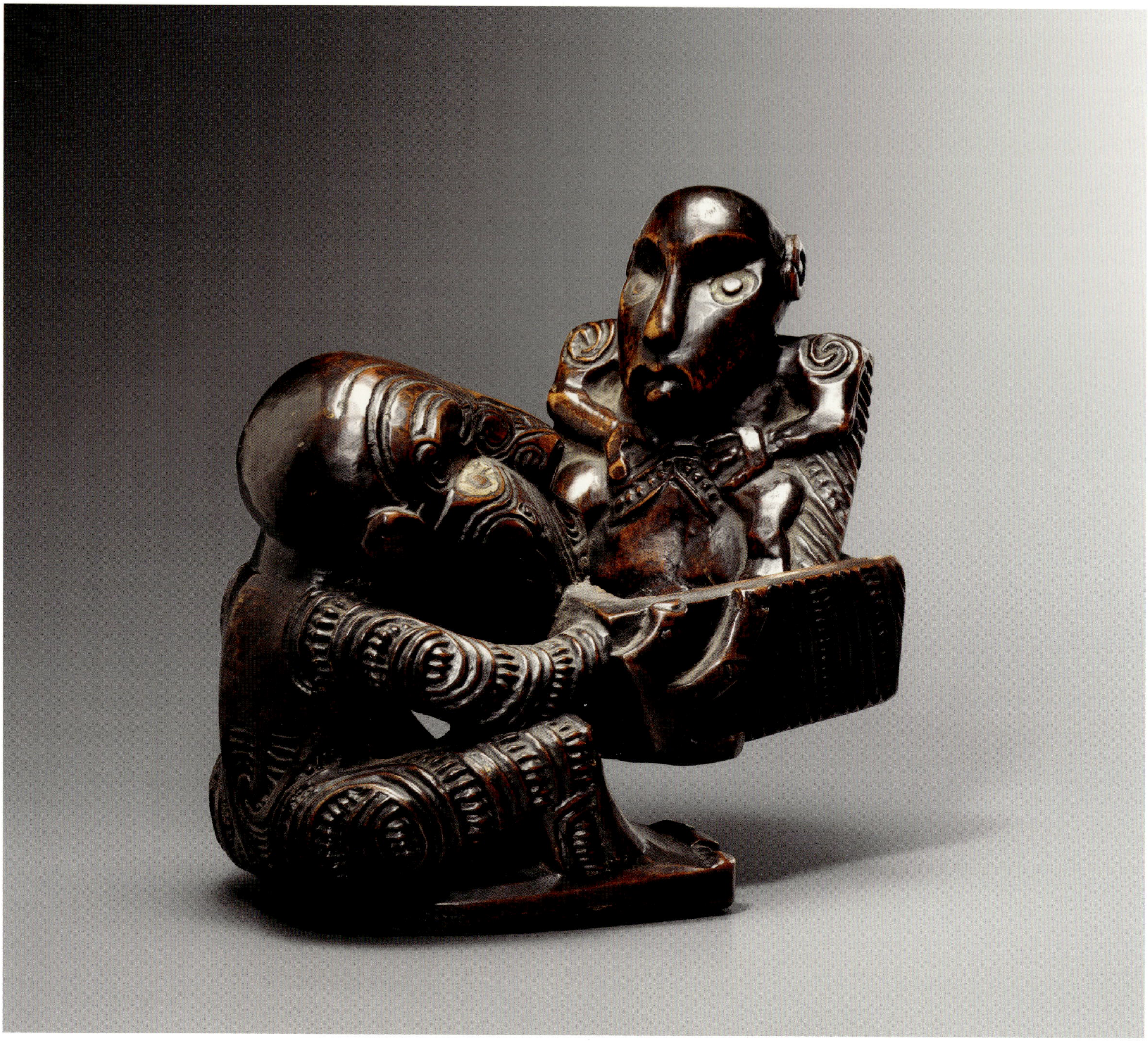

Maori box
New Zealand, H. 12 cm

In this sculpture a crouching figure seems to hold in its mouth a box whose lid is carved in the form of another figure. Swirling tattoos cover all the surfaces.
In order to meet foreign demand, Maori sculptors began in the 1860s to produce objects whose forms, while derived from traditional models, reveal an extraordinary inventiveness. In this instance, the entire conception of the box is unusual and illustrates the sculptor's total mastery of his art. [PP]

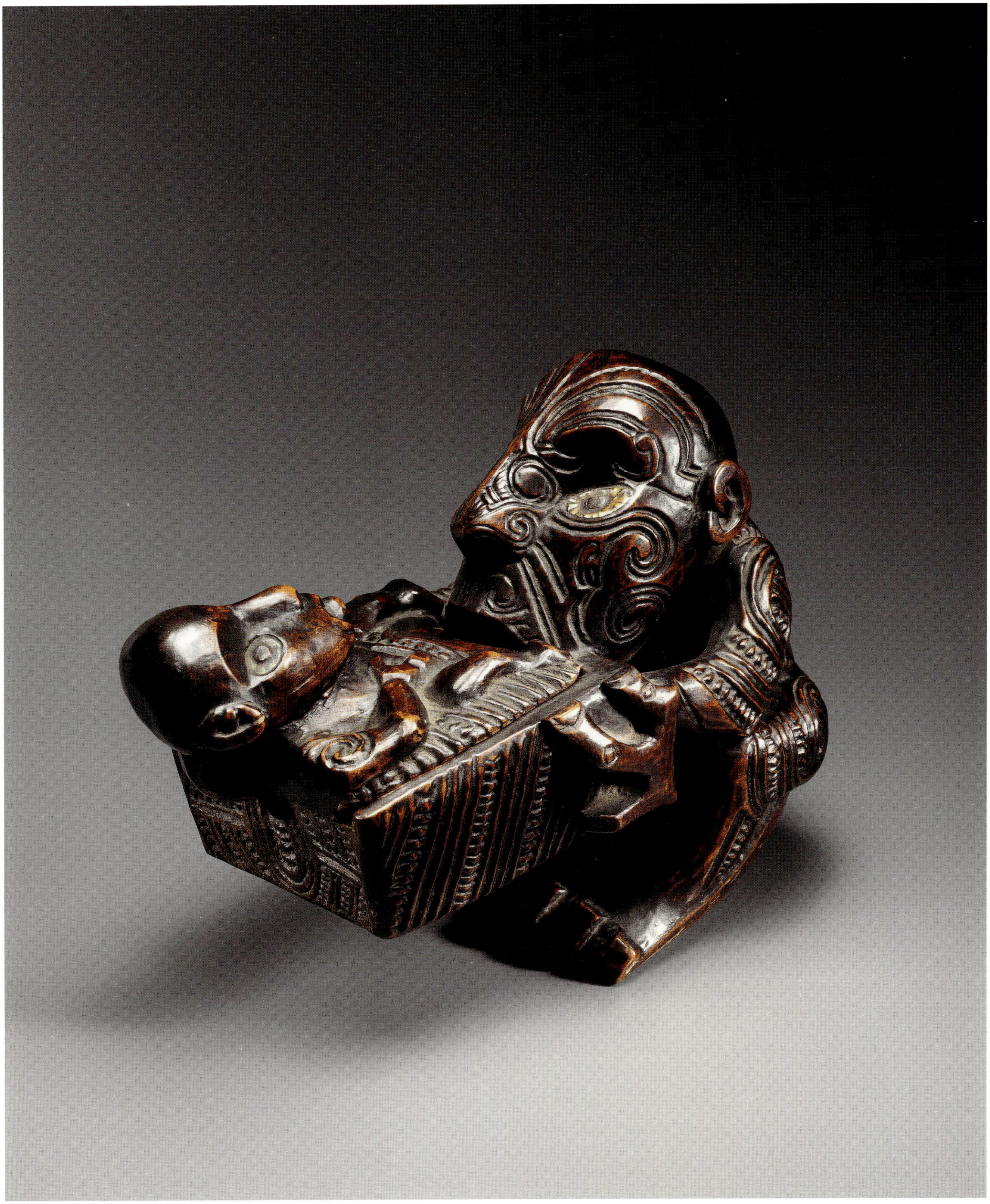

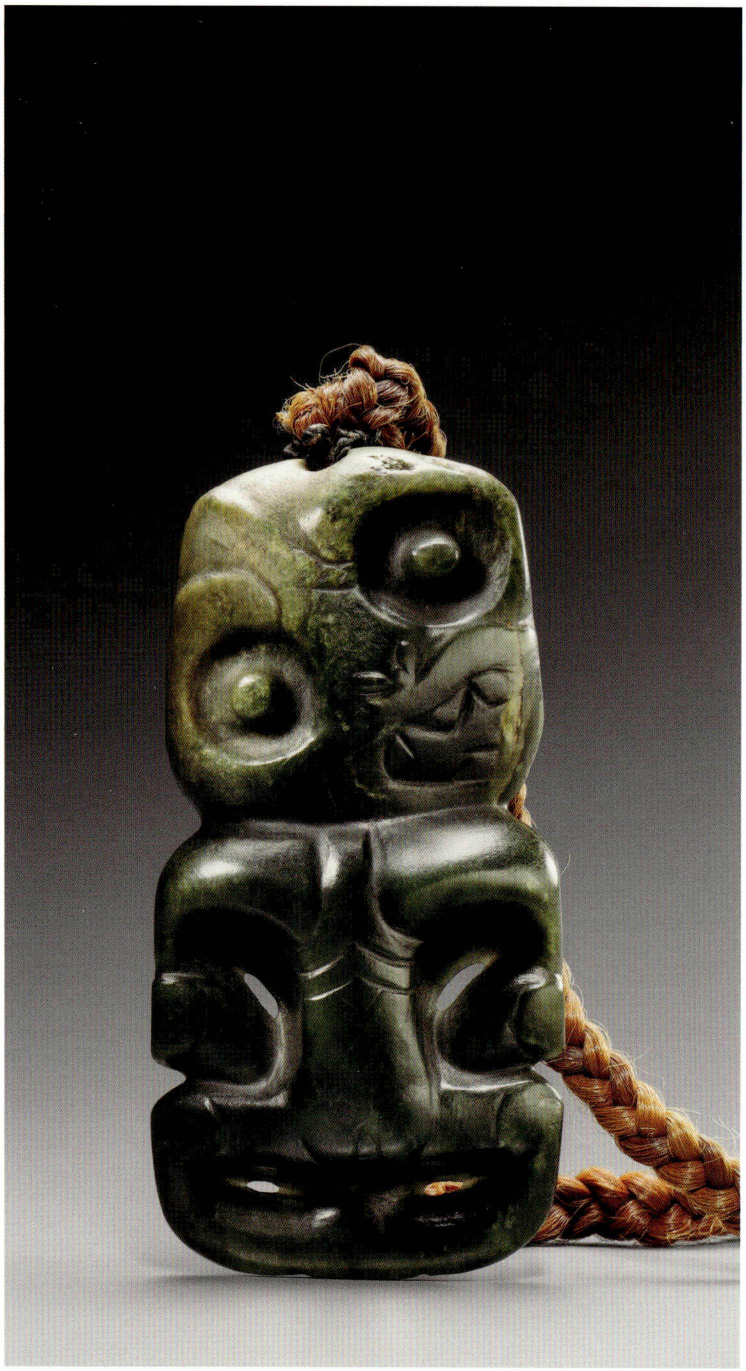

Maori pendant
New Zealand, H. 12 cm

Hei tiki are the most popular type of pendant in New Zealand – Aotearoa. They are sculpted out of nephrite, an extremely hard stone that requires considerable polishing after the object has been crafted. Maoris name and evaluate the stones according to their colour and appearance. All are iridescent and translucent.
The meaning of the object, depicting a small figure crouching with its hands resting on its thighs, is still a matter of debate. Every pendant is a precious heirloom handed down from generation to generation, accumulating the memory and power of each successive owner. [PP]

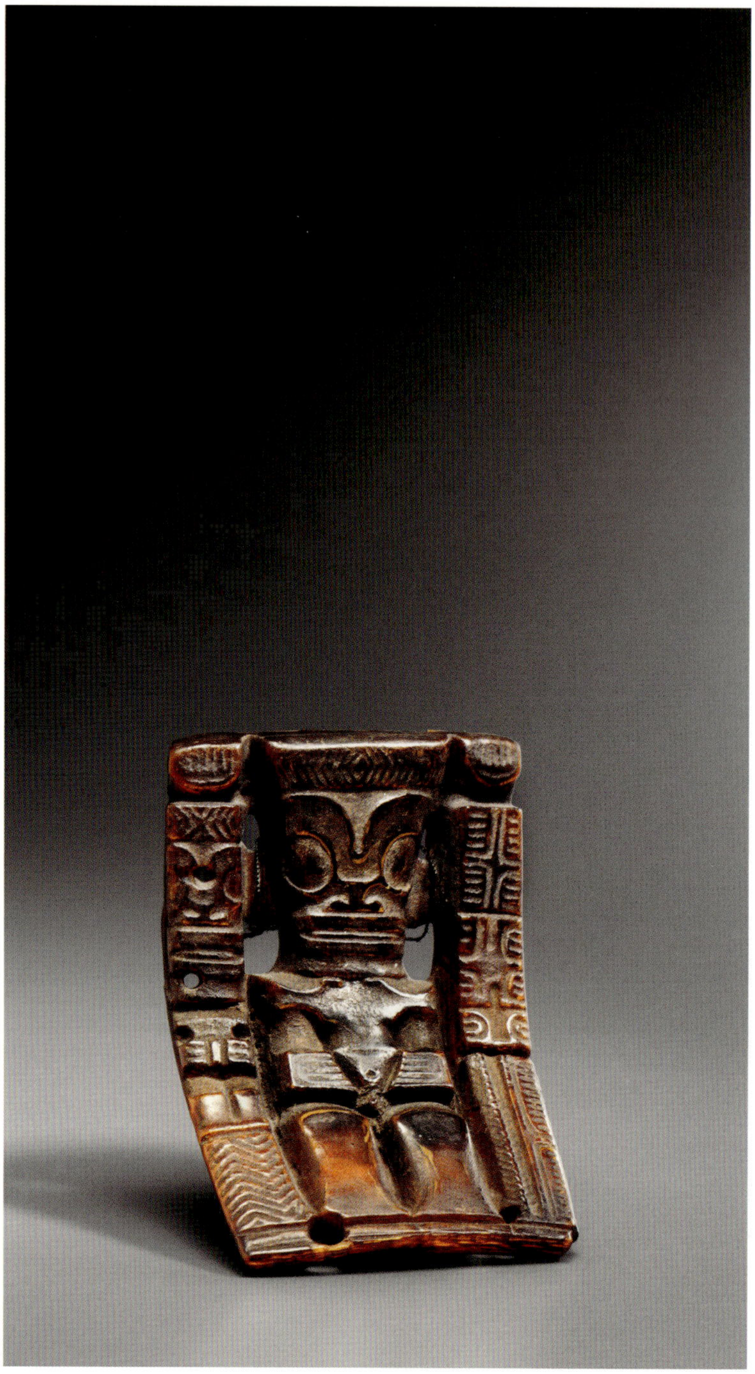

Ornament
Marquesas Islands, H. 5.3 cm

This object depicts a *tiki*—the first man in the world—carved in the middle of a thick piece of tortoiseshell. The figure is framed by tattoo motifs, which might refer to legendary events.
The holes at the sides and top prove this piece was once attached to a crown (*paè kea*) made up of alternating translucent tortoiseshell plates and opaque pieces of shell. A *paè kea* would be a particularly precious item in the family treasure and worn by girls and boys during festivals. [PP]

Maori sculpture
New Zealand, H. 14 cm
Stand by Kichizô Inagaki

This small figure sporting a spiral tattoo has a hand in its mouth and was sculpted under the footpiece (*teka*) of a digging stick (*ko*), an article that was used during the gardens ceremonial opening. The gesture symbolizes the abundance of food.
The object used to be in the distinguished Roland Tual Collection. Tual was the first director of the Surrealist gallery in 1925, and over the 1920s he assembled a considerable collection of Oceanic objects. The quality of this particular piece earned it a place in the Galerie Pigalle in 1930. [PP]

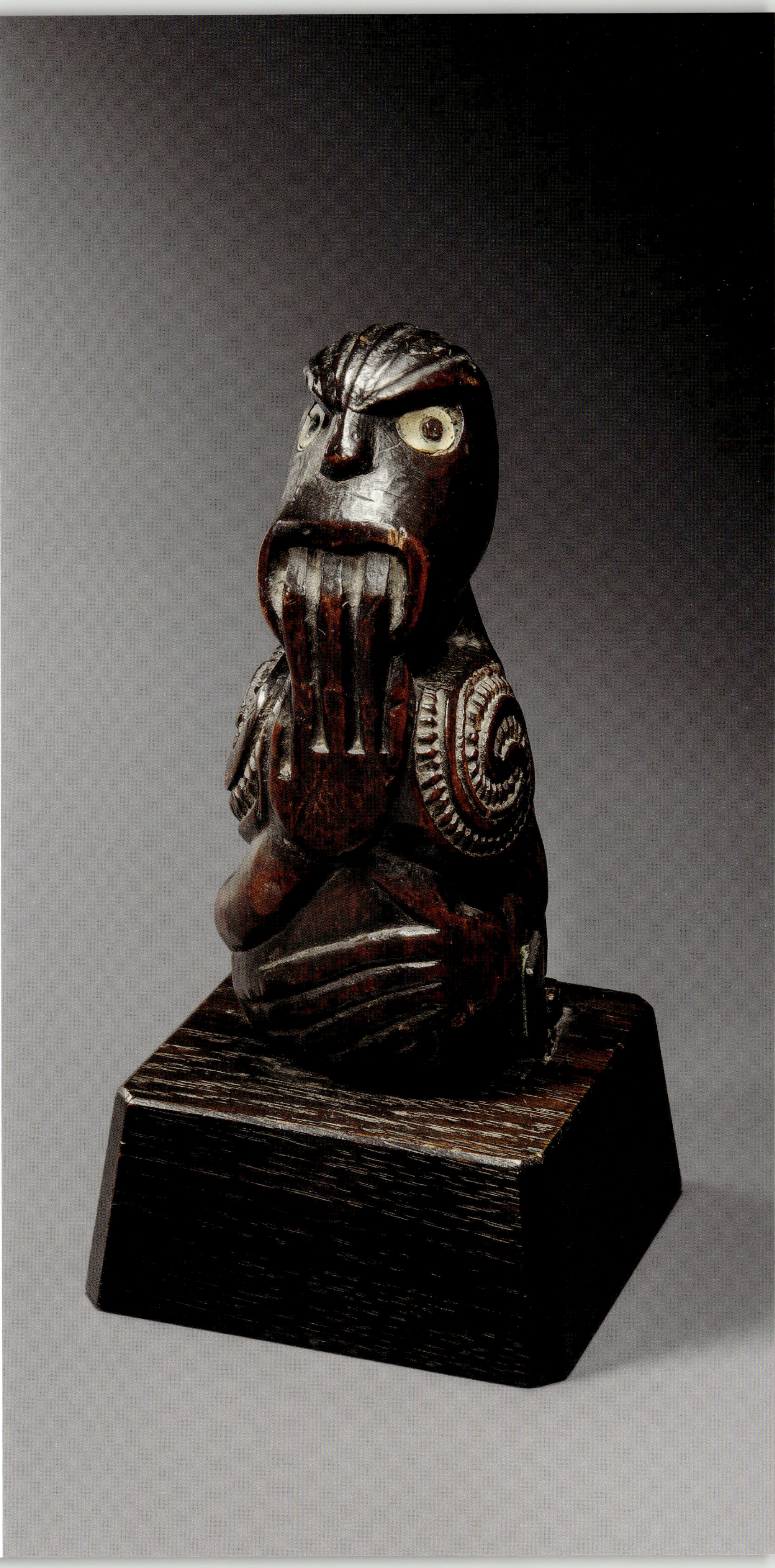

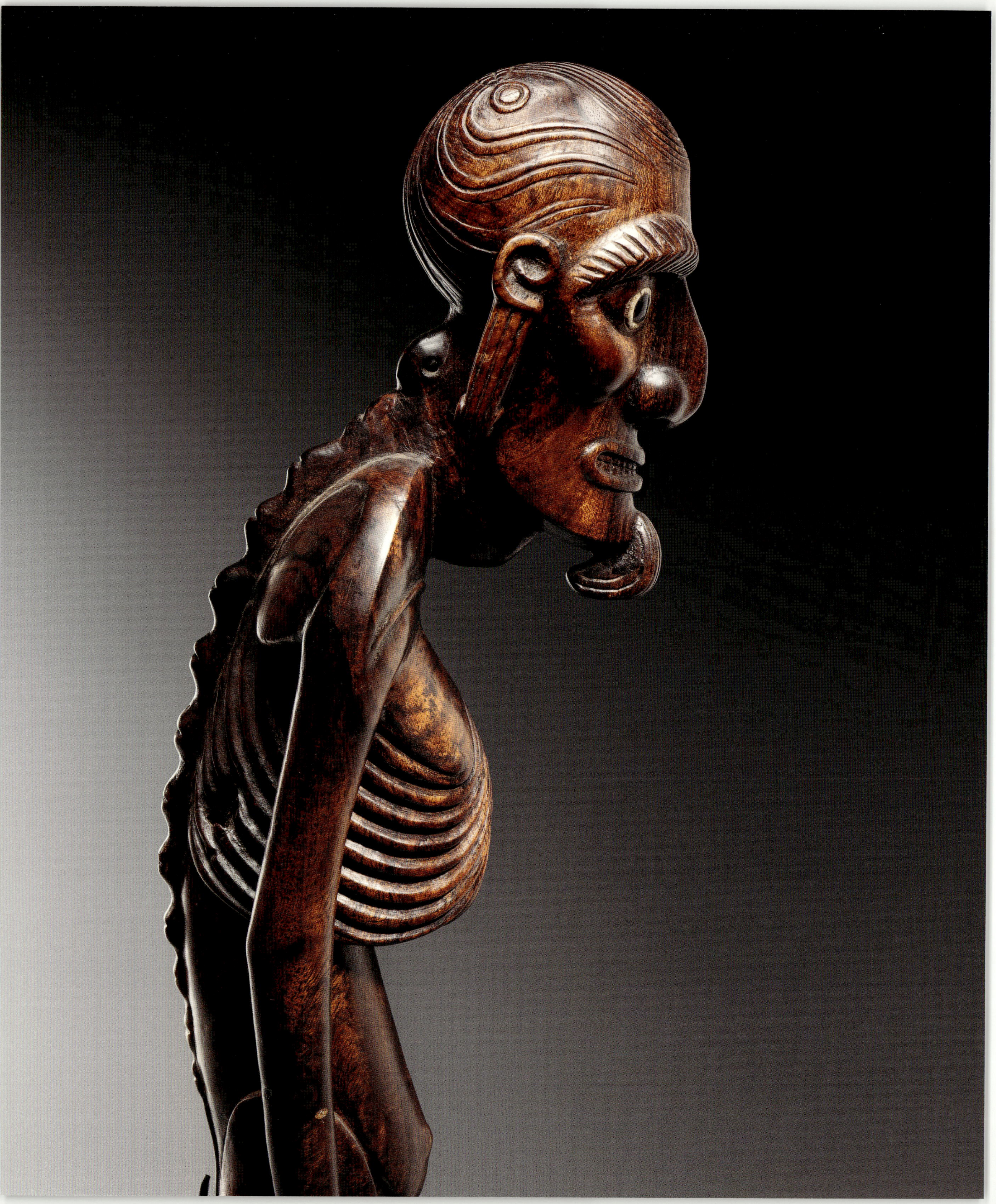

Statue
Easter Island, H. 43 cm

The most talented Easter Island sculptors observed living creatures with the precision of our zoology textbooks, as can be seen in the octopus in Vienna and the chiton in Oslo. They represented in a rational manner various supernatural beings in their multiple metamorphoses. The islanders shared their world with these visible or invisible polymorphic beings that were able to change sex and bring messages from the gods of the earth (lizards), the sky (birds), and the sea (whales, fish, and molluscs).

Gathered too late, the remaining fragments of Rapanui mythology provide a rare insight into an afterlife inhabited by numberless beings and a countless crowd of ancestors, who as ghosts could be either benevolent or malicious. Around one thousand years ago, Tuu ko Ihu, one of the first Polynesian nobles to reach the island, caught two of these frightening ghosts in their sleep: "just ribs and bones, with no body." Hurrying home, he quickly carved their likeness in a stump of the sacred *toromiro* shrub. This was the origin of the *moai kavakava*, carved figures (*moai*) with an overdeveloped rib cage (*kavakava*). Tuu ko Ihu's creations were admired and envied; everyone wanted to have one. But there was a further marvel: people said they had secretly spied on the sculptor and seen him cause the statues to walk in his house.

As a result, the Rapanui always took care to hang *moai kavakavas*, as well as several other statuettes, on the frames of their homes. They would be taken down and used in private rituals to treat their illnesses or to bring harm to their enemies. Carried in clusters on their bodies, these figures would be proudly displayed during ceremonies in the tribe's ceremonial enclosure.

This particular *kavakava*, acquired by able seaman George Harvey when HMS Topaze reached Easter Island in November 1868, combines this illustrious origin with the quality of an exceptional piece of sculpture. This is the work of a renowned *tahunga*, an artist-priest trained by a master craftsman, who, being inspired by the gods, was admired by their descendants, the holders of power in the Easter Island microcosm. [MO]

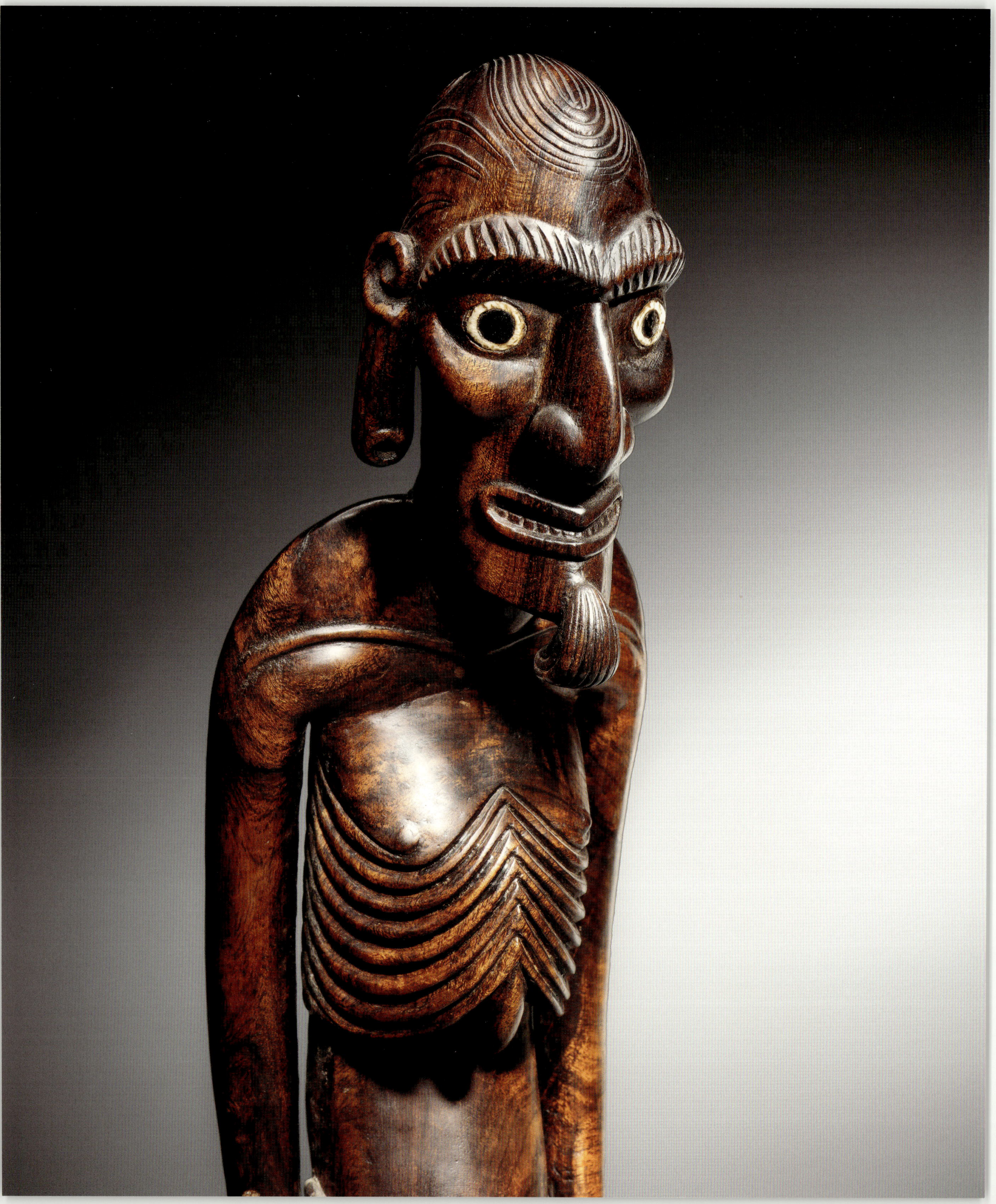

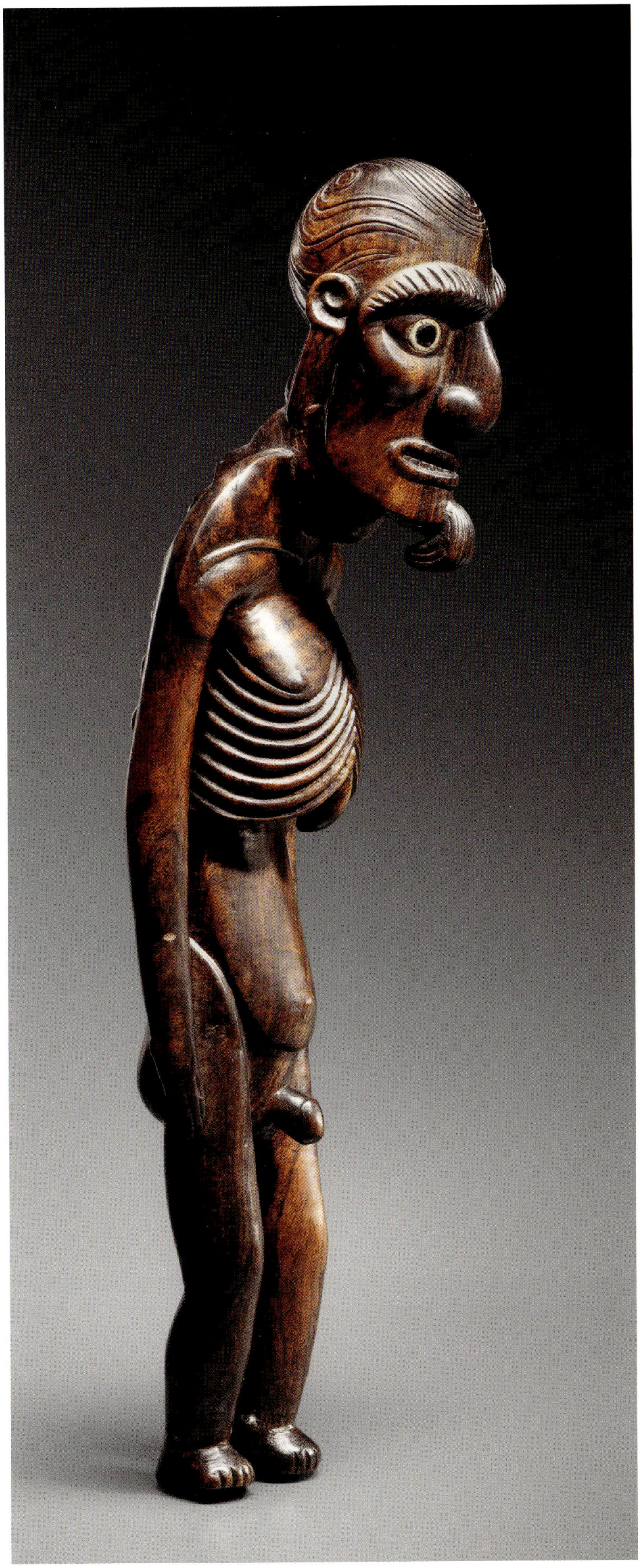

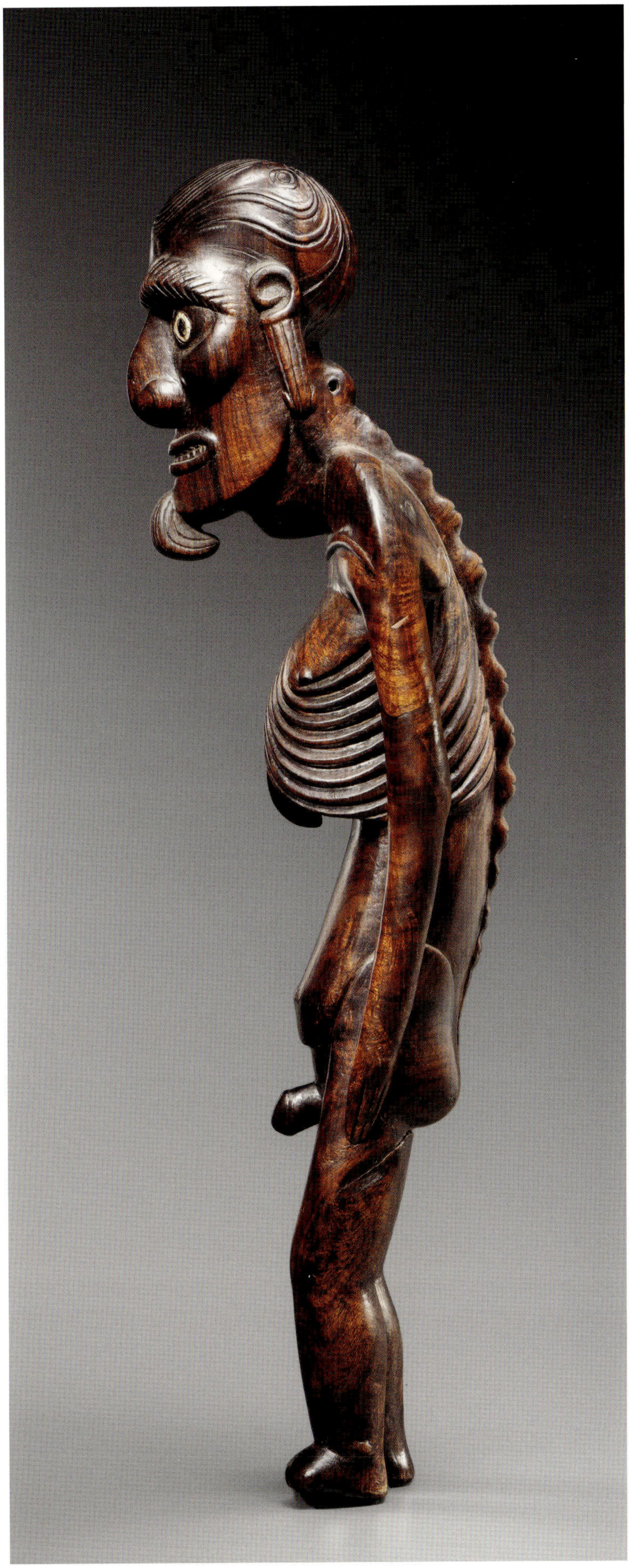

AMERICA

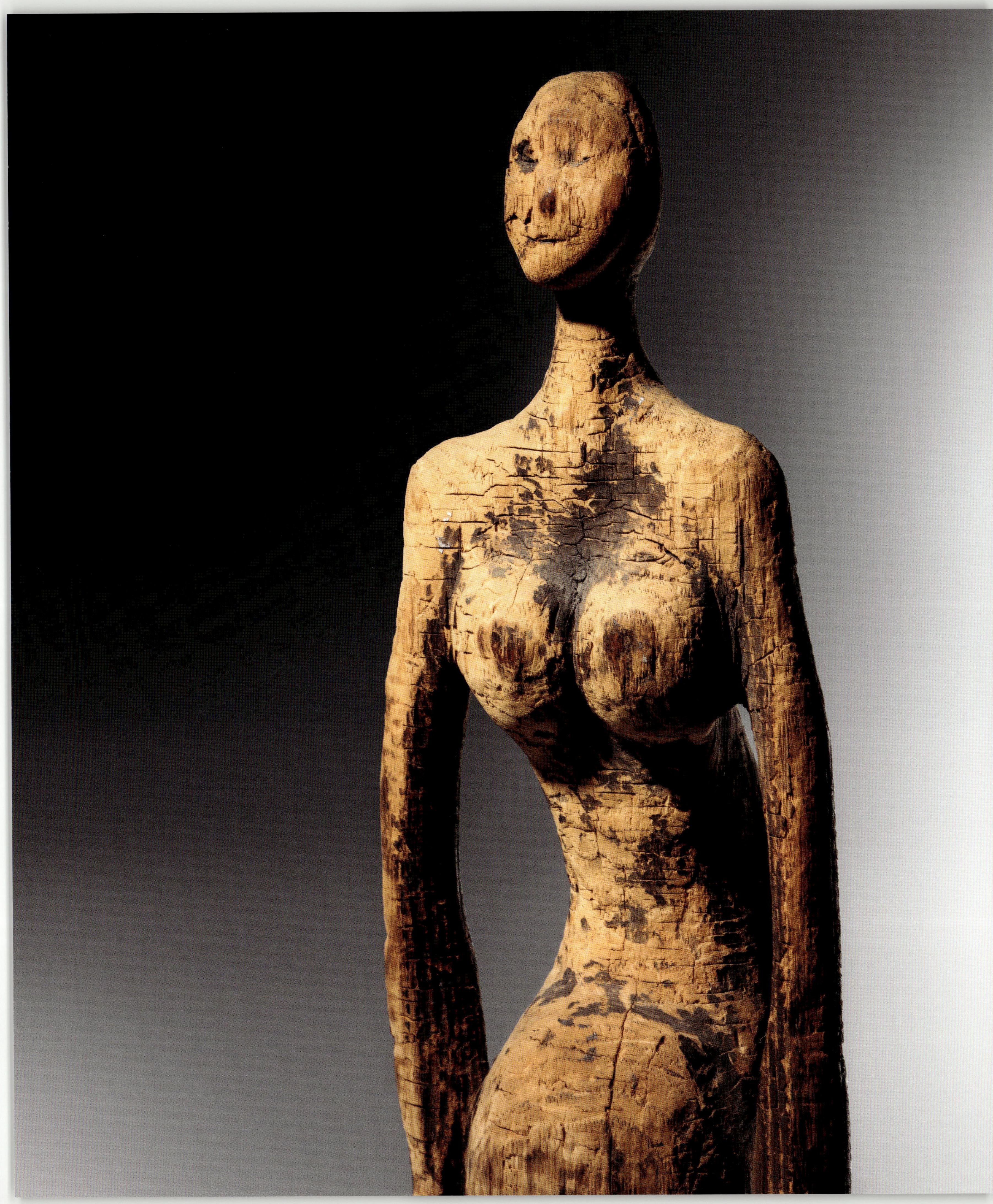

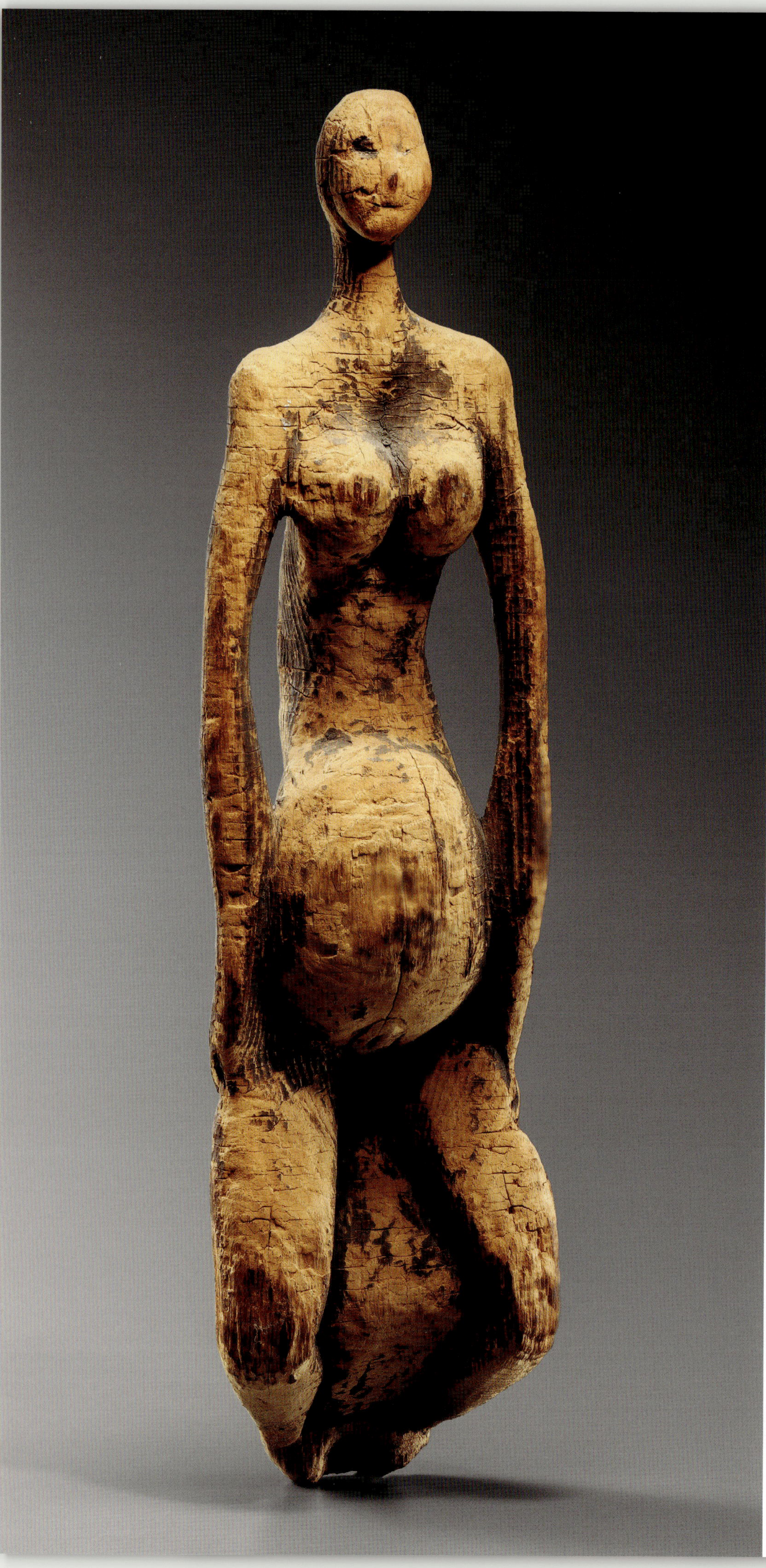

Statue
Pre-Inuit culture, Western Thule, Alaska, H. 40 cm
Circa 1500–1800

This very unusual sculpture is rare, not only for being an example carved in driftwood, a material which does not survive well in the Arctic, but also because of its highly articulated form. While the head is characteristic of Arctic carving, comporting with the style of modeling from the Old Bering Sea, the fully modeled arms, belly, bending legs, and elongated neck are unlike most other dolls. At the same time, it expresses the commonly carved subject of other examples in ivory: the fertility figure.

The late anthropologist Edmund Carpenter often emphasized the use of multiple orientations among Arctic carvings, and the lack of a "correct" viewpoint. He also repeatedly noted the many visual puns enjoyed by Arctic carvers, where a carving turned upside-down might reveal a completely different figure, or the presence of a hidden animal. Janus-type figures abound in numerous examples.

Here, this pregnant female expresses a curious posture, where her head appears almost backwards on her torso. Seen frontally, she is clearly in the position of childbirth. But seen from the side, her arching back becomes a stomach, her swollen belly become buttocks, flowing into properly curving legs and knees. Indeed, we note how seen this way, her hands are oriented correctly, albeit to exaggeratedly elongated arms that reach almost the entire length of her body. All of these qualities combine to create a mysterious figure of dreamlike, supernatural capabilities. She seems at once to embody "before and after," the important moment of childbirth, and the independent ancestral spirit meant to be invoked during this rite of passage. [SM]

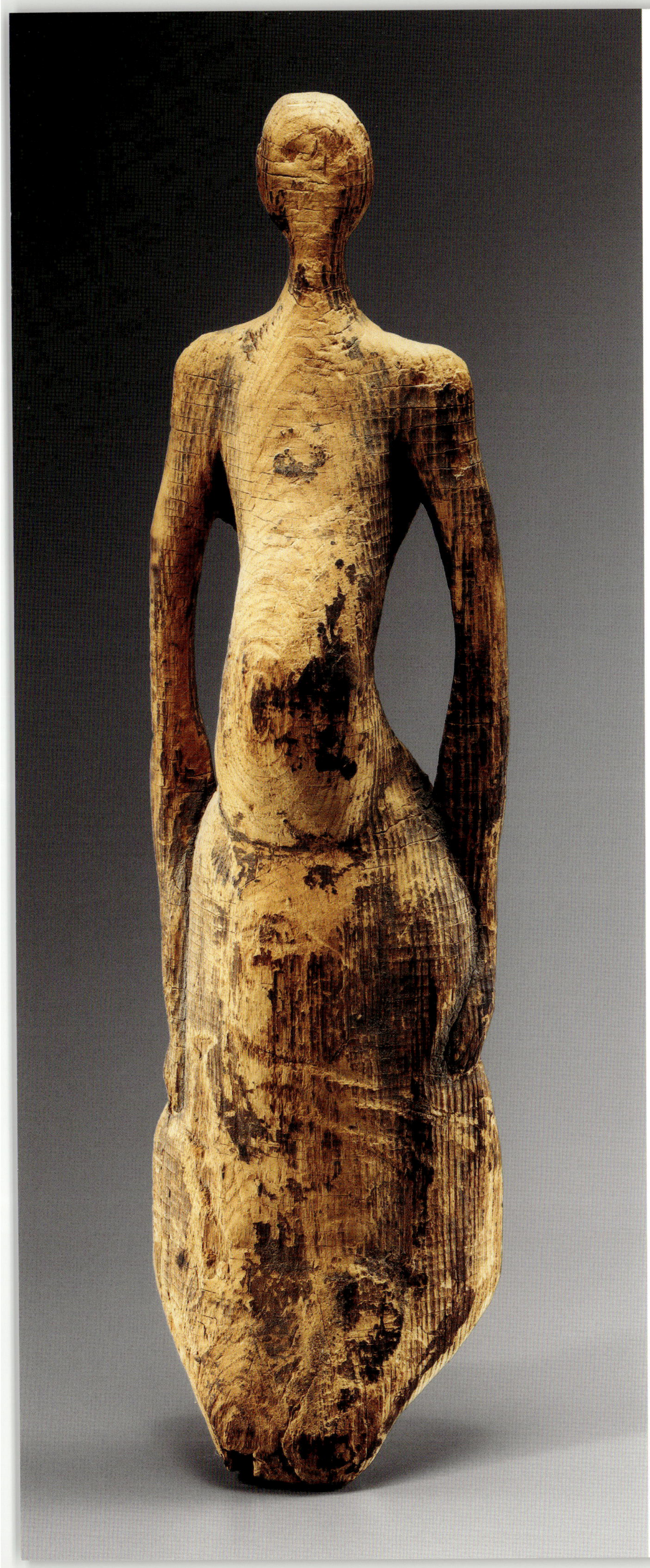
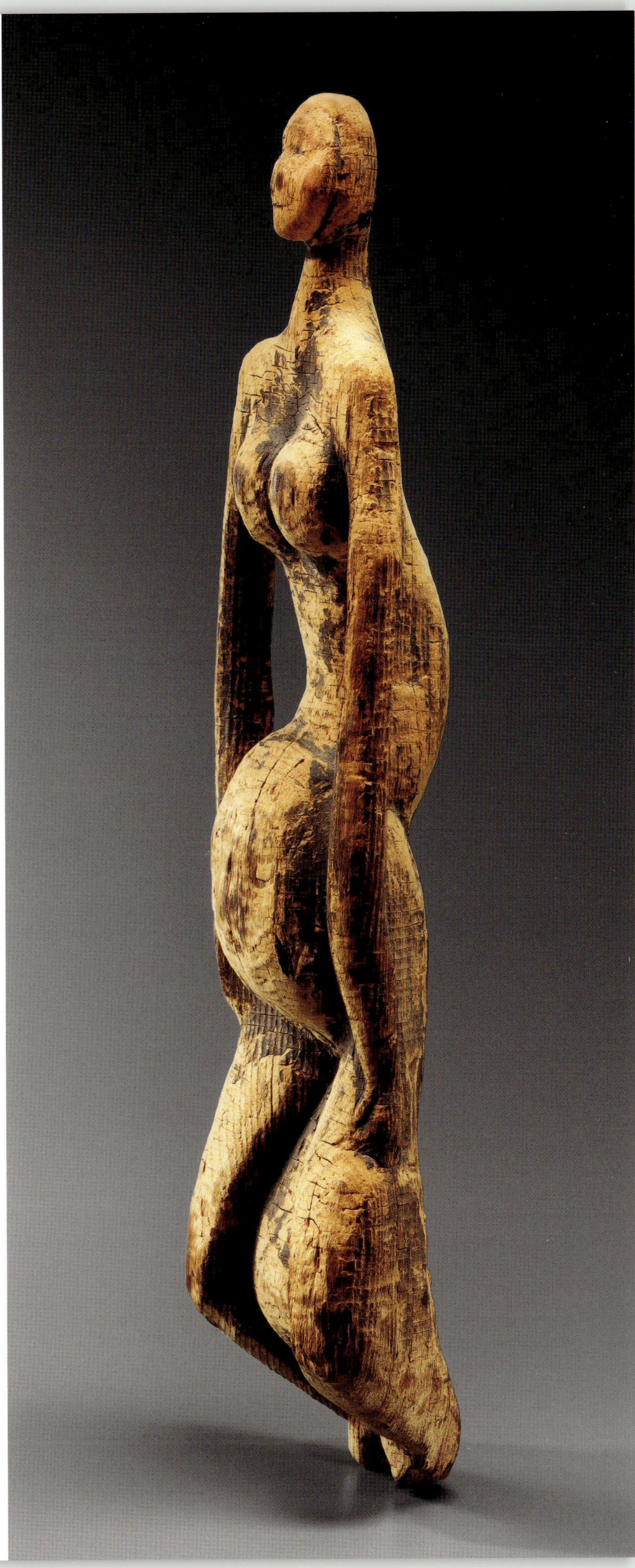

Yup'ik mask
Goodnews Bay, Alaska, H. 22 cm
Circa 1890–1900

Surrealist artists, writers, and philosophers were drawn to indigenous arts, especially those of Native Americans, since the early days of the movement. They were especially intrigued by masks and "shamanistic paraphernalia," which they understood to be critical to native people's engagement with the spirit world. While they looked to these objects to fulfill their own concepts of artistic reinvention, seeking non-European models of expression, the Surrealists almost by accident discovered the masks of the Yup'ik peoples of Alaska. Their interpretations of these masks' meaning merged two main concepts: transformation and dream imagery. While they were somewhat off the mark in thinking that the masks represented the inner psychological world expressed in dreams, they correctly saw in them the creative work of the act of dreaming. For in many cases, by Yup'ik tradition, masks would be created to fulfill the requirements of the village shaman, who would have a dream or vision, which would then form the basis of a song, dance, and mask.

During their time as refugees in New York during WWII, André Breton and his associates—among them, Claude Lévi-Strauss, Georges Duthuit, Max Ernst, Roberto Matta, Robert Lebel, *et al.*—had opportunities to collect masks and other objects made by Yup'ik and Pacific Northwest Coast peoples. They returned to Europe after the war with prized collections. Today, masks collected by Breton and Lebel are displayed in the Louvre and Quai Branly museums, recognized as masterpieces of material culture. The fact that they were admired and collected by Surrealists and other artists seems to add to their influence and power, for they emphasized not only aesthetic characteristics, but the philosophical basis for seeing life through a different logic than the ones created by Western civilizations.

In this example, we can see what attracted Surrealists like Breton to Yup'ik masks. Consistent with Surrealist fascination with inner psychology, occult transformations, and dream imagery, this mask appears to represent a twisting, changing human face, agonized with conflict. We can see, however, that the mask's left and right halves are distinctly oppositional: each part of the mouth, nose, eyes, and cheeks seem to represent a different expression, almost a different creature. In fact, this is consistent with Yup'ik practices and philosophies, whereby all creatures are expected to demonstrate dualistic properties: earthly and spiritual. Most Yup'ik masks will exhibit an animal form, and simultaneously depict the *yua*[1] (personal spirit) of that animal.

The means of representing the dualistic nature of masks will vary from place to place. In the villages of the Kuskokwim River, for example, the *yua* expression is sometimes composed as a separate human face residing within the belly of another creature. On other occasions, these are expressed by the presence of two separate masks, therefore the symbiotic pairing of groups of masks is integral to their understanding. However, in places like Nunivak Island, masks are often created to bisect the face vertically, somewhat akin to what we see in this example. On Nunivak, these bisected faces often refer to *irci*, spiritualized creatures who are half-human, half-animal. The separate halves of the mask, and its spiritual duality, are usually emphasized by painting the two halves in different colours. Given that Goodnews Bay is in relatively close proximity to Nunivak Island, and the tradition of Nunivak's Messenger Feast is to invite villagers from the mainland to participate in reciprocal dances, some blending of local traditions and carving styles is to be expected. Although it would be impossible to reconstruct the narrative that this mask was intended to perform, we see in it the presence of a human spirit who is existing simultaneously in two planes of reality. [SM]

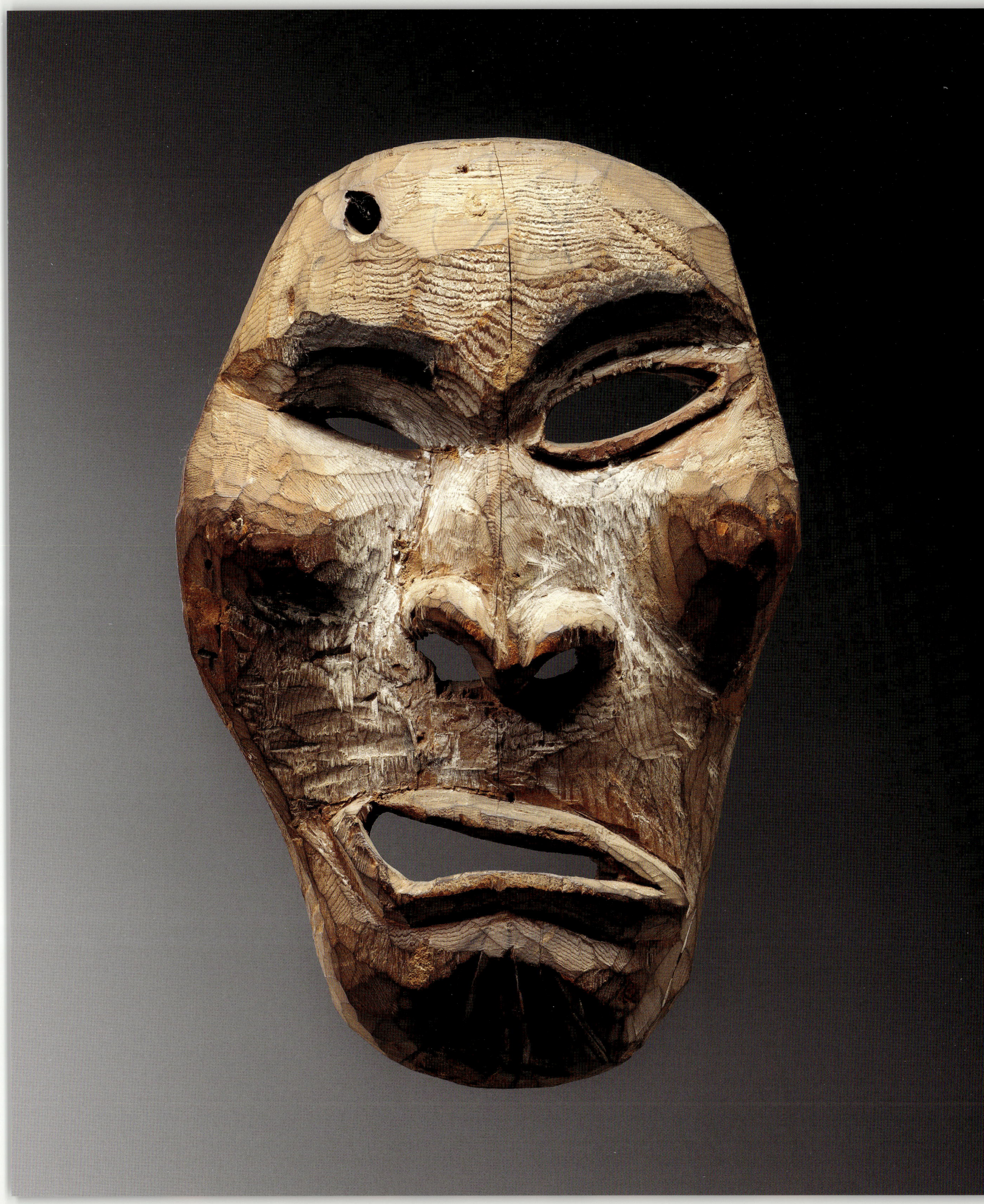

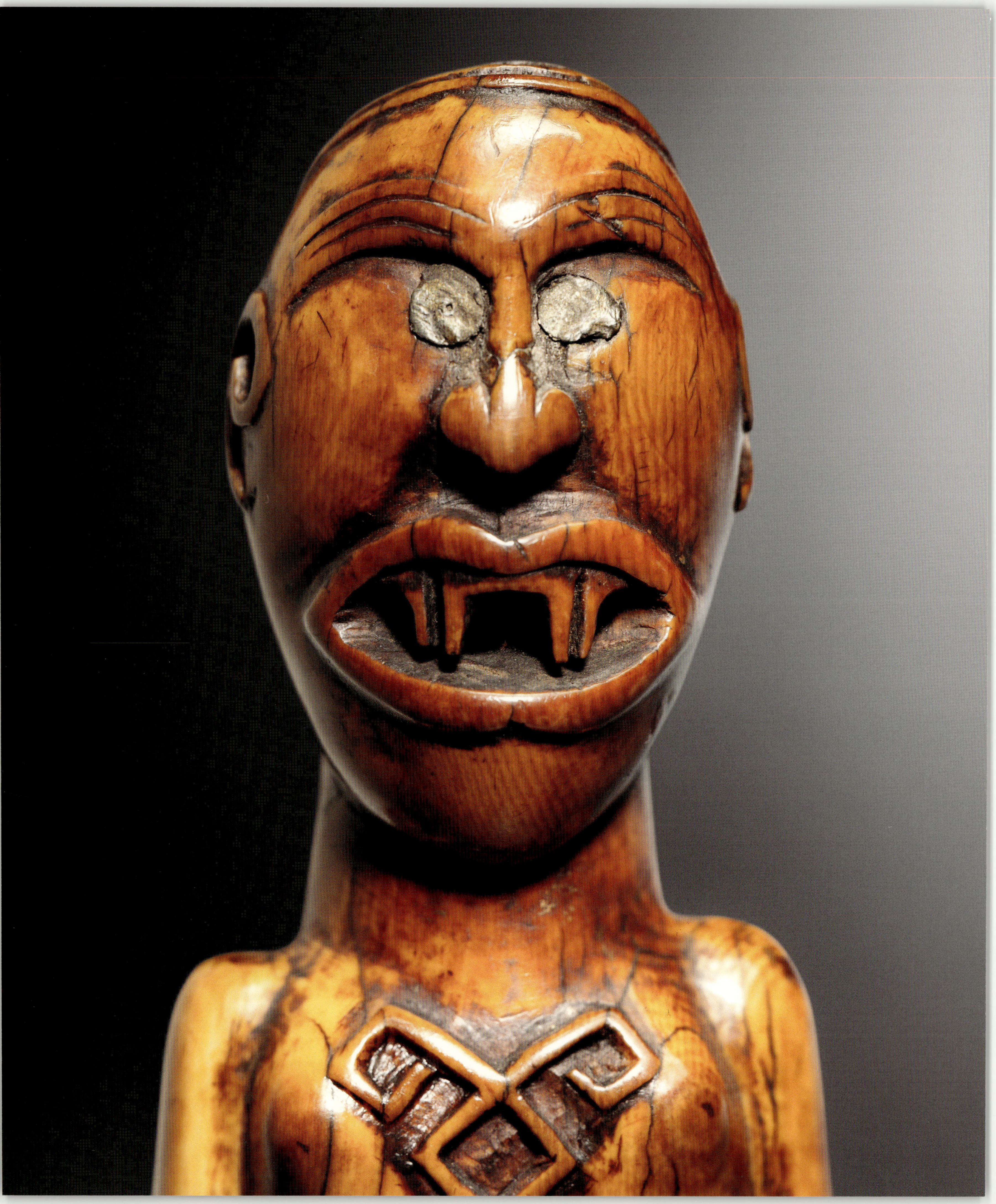

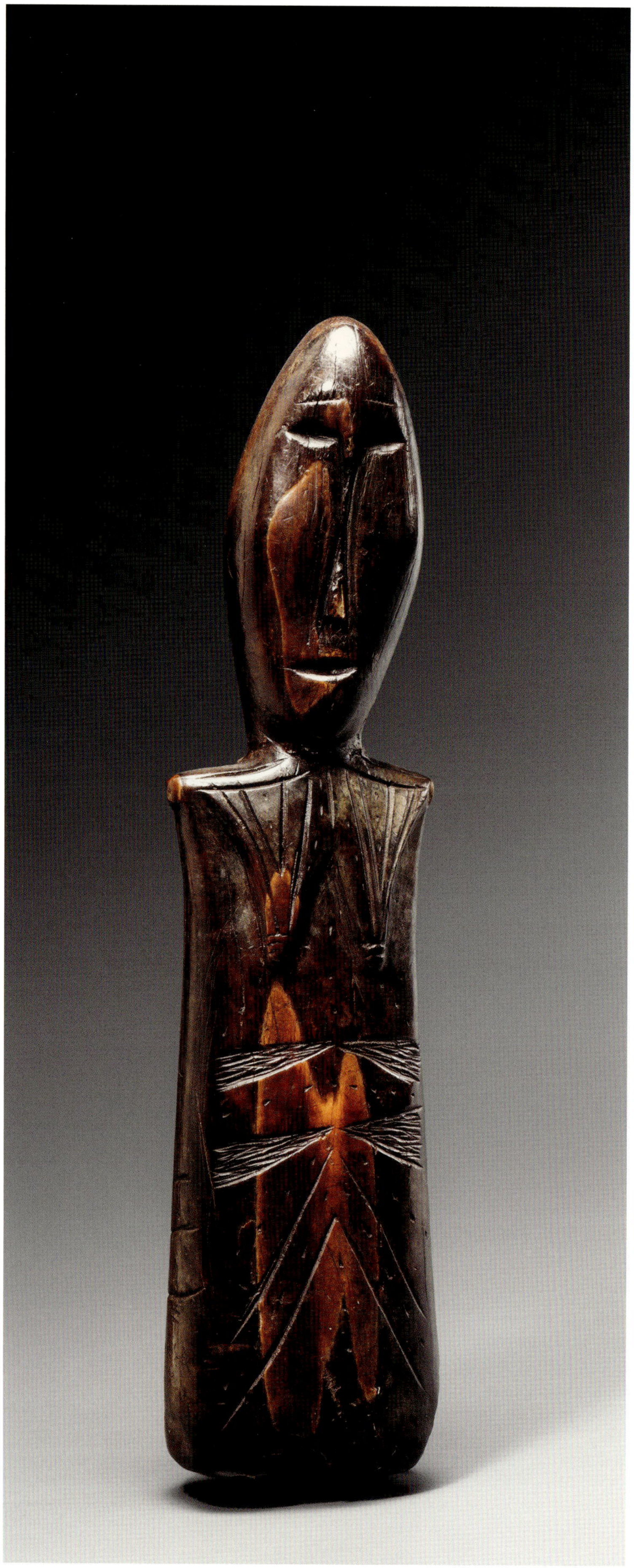

Statuette
Paleo-Eskimo culture, St Lawrence Island (*Sivuqaq*), Alaska (Siberian Yup'ik)
Old Bering Sea I (Okvik period), H. 17 cm
Circa 250 BC – 100 AD

This complete doll from the Okvik period has the distinctive qualities of the classic type: an elongated head, coming nearly to a point at the top; a truncated torso, devoid of limbs. It also has some decorative details that define it simultaneously as a female fertility amulet and a highly spiritualized emblem of ancestral worship. The doll's pointed breasts, with their tattoo patterns, indicate a respected female elder, perhaps a memorialized ancestor. The torso, significantly, is decorated with deeply incised lines that radiate outwards from the stomach, mimicking the shape and direction of the breasts, but also suggestive of the inner spirit that is the *inua* of the figure. In Arctic cosmology, all animals are believed to possess an *inua*, a personal spirit, typically located residing in the belly of the person or animal it belongs to, like an infant in the womb.
Often, human dolls are symbolic of fertility and ancestor worship simultaneously, as they demonstrate the possession of *inua*, represented in numerous ways. In this example, the *inua* remains hidden, but is pointed to by linear patterns on the torso and breasts. Notable, too, are the highly articulated skeletal patterns on the rear of the torso. Skeletal designs often were utilized to indicate ancestral continuity in Arctic art, since they symbolize the survival of the body beyond death. When the physical being ceases to live, its *inua* departs (in order to return in another animal form), but the skeleton remains as evidence that life continues, but is fragile and fleeting. [SM]

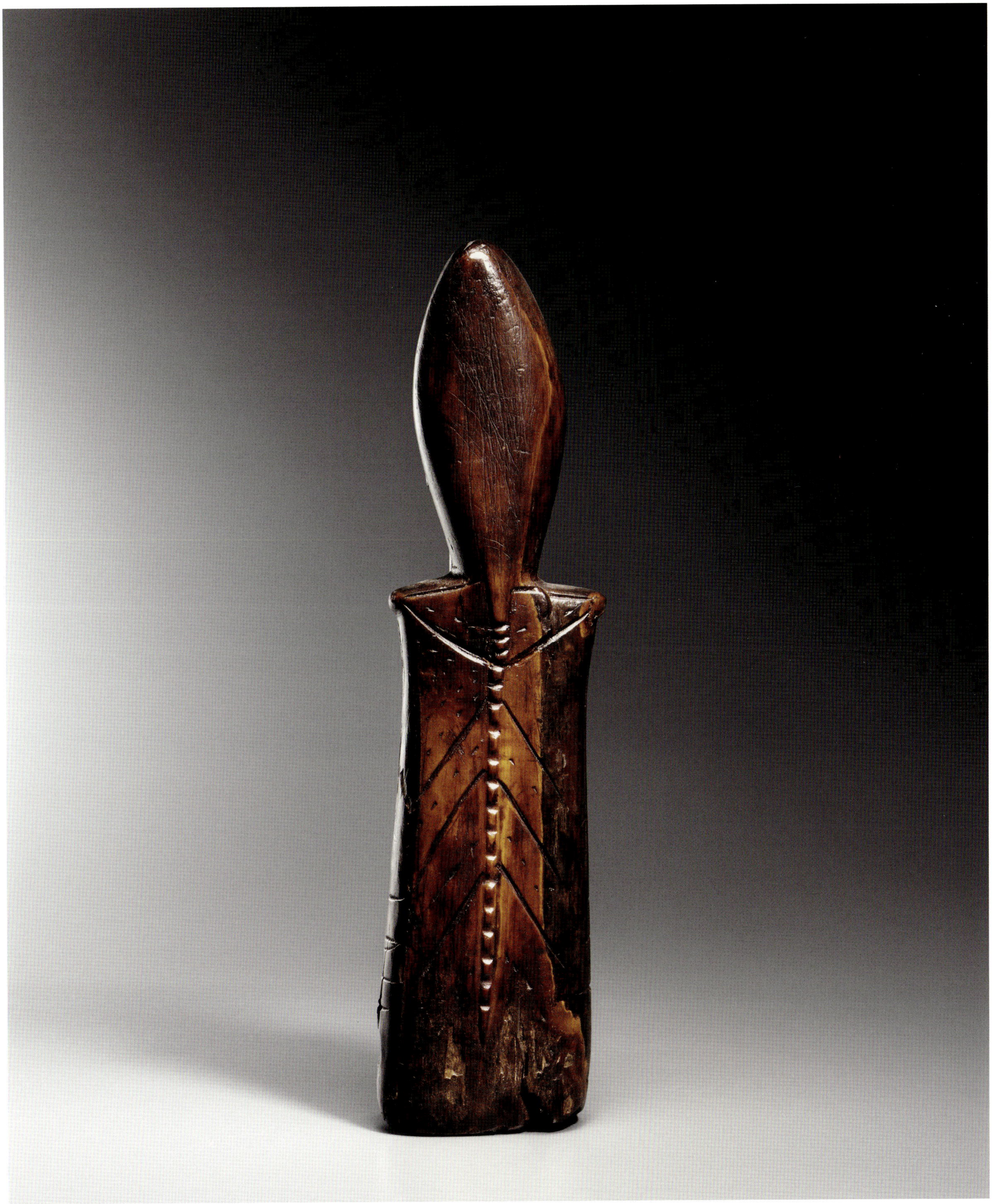

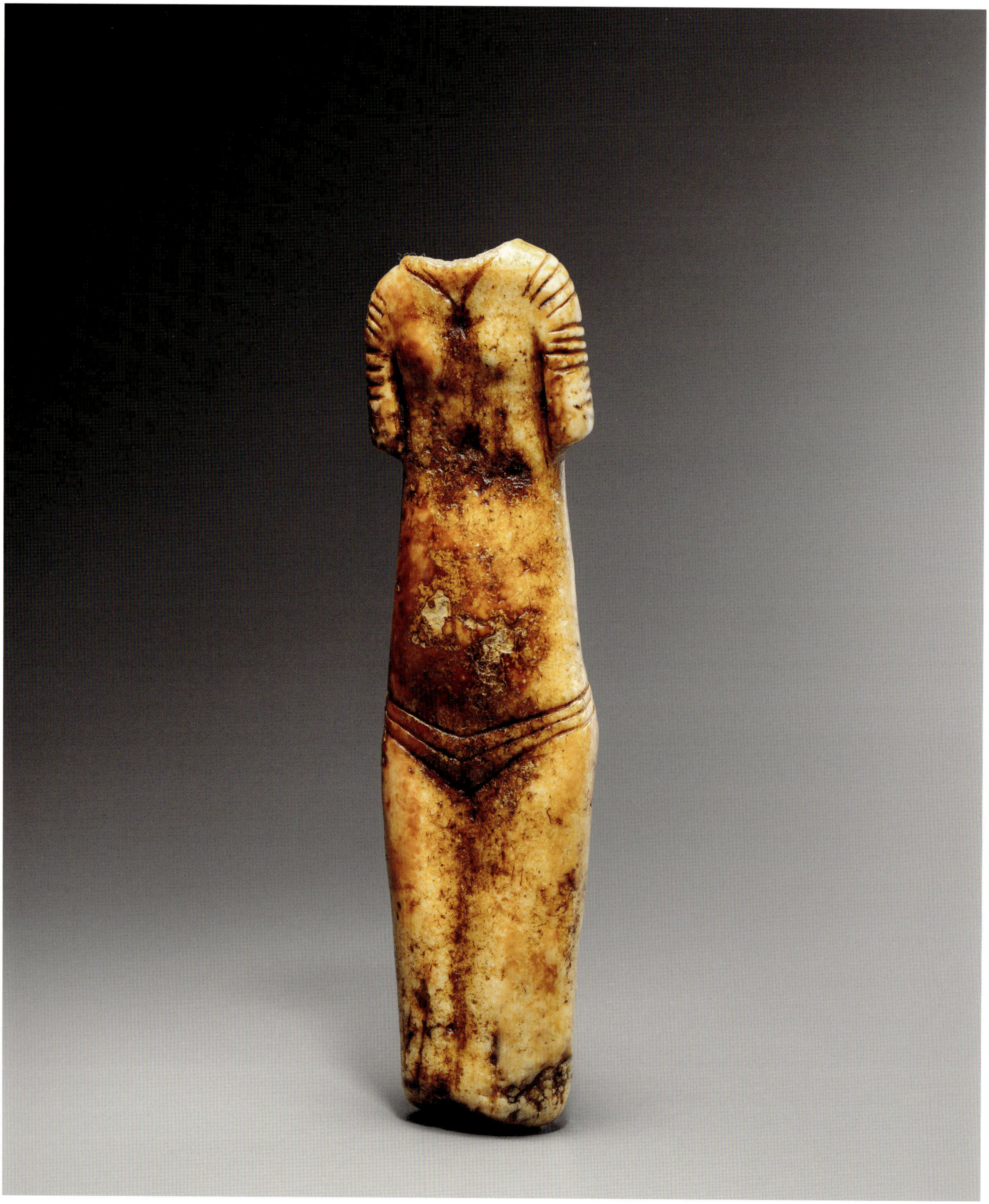

Torso
Paleo-Eskimo culture, St Lawrence Island (*Sivuqaq*), Alaska (Siberian Yup'ik)
Archaic Punuk, H. 17 cm
Circa 500–800

Upon close examination, many ivory carvings of human figures appear to have been designed to be dressed with clothing. Often, a head will show a rough groove carved along the vertical perimeter, hiding the missing ears, suggesting that the head once wore a hooded parka. At other times, articles of clothing are modelled into the ivory carving itself, which appears to be the case with this figure. Note how the areas surrounding the waist have double lines tracing them, as if it wears a delicate garment. And the neck incorporates a v-shaped opening of a shirt or perhaps a necklace. While the figure remains naked, it very likely had been dressed with skins or furs when it was first made.

In any case, this elegant female torso, now missing its head, suggests the carving of an altogether different sculpture tradition, that of ancient Rome. It seems almost to wear a diaphanous cloth, with legs joined and tattooed shoulders slightly tilting into a *contrapposto* gesture. It would be stretching the point to note that the Old Bering Sea era was contemporary to that of classical Rome, but this does not lessen the fascination of what Arctic carvers managed to accomplish. It is worth remembering that their remarkable art was created not only at the same time, but under the harsh conditions of Arctic winters, using stone tools and severely limited resources, and that their village communities contained populations of no more than 200 people, at most. [SM]

Torso
Paleo-Eskimo culture, St Lawrence Island (*Sivuqaq*), Alaska (Siberian Yup'ik)
Old Bering Sea I (Okvik period), H. 21 cm
Circa 250 BC – 100 AD

This extraordinary Okvik figure is an example of the great creative range of expression among the earliest known carvers of Arctic art. While examples with articulated legs are not unknown, they are quite rare, and somewhat enigmatic in what they symbolize. Here, the thin, finely modelled legs emanate from a large, blocky body, which contains a host of expressive details. The fact that the figure is headless is also significant. Everything about this figure suggests that it was functionally used as a fertility amulet, perhaps a birthing figure, used during the act of childbirth or the traditional naming ceremonies associated with birth.
The figure is clearly female, with pronounced vagina and youthful breasts. But it also has a curiously concave belly, carved to exaggerate the cavity below the ribs, as though the figure has been expunged of its child-burden. Below the breasts are seen two engraved eye patterns, mimicking the vagina but most likely carved to suggest the all-seeing consciousness of the *inua*. In Arctic cosmological beliefs, the outer universe, and all that is known and unknown, is conceived as a form of consciousness, or awareness (in Yup'ik language, *ella*). The possession of *inua* is an expression of this awareness, which connects earthly existence to the spirit world. One may interpret in the presence of eyes upon this torso that this figure is meant to be a witness, on behalf of ancestors, that the family continues, and that it follows the rites and rituals required of it for harmonious balance with the universe.
The highly articulated spinal designs on the rear side also suggest ancestral awareness, and I also interpret the missing head as symbolic. Cleanly broken, with relatively little material worn away after two thousand years, the missing head was likely removed purposefully, although we can only surmise why. Nonetheless, it differs greatly from the missing leg, but this, too, may have a reason, lost to us now. [SM]

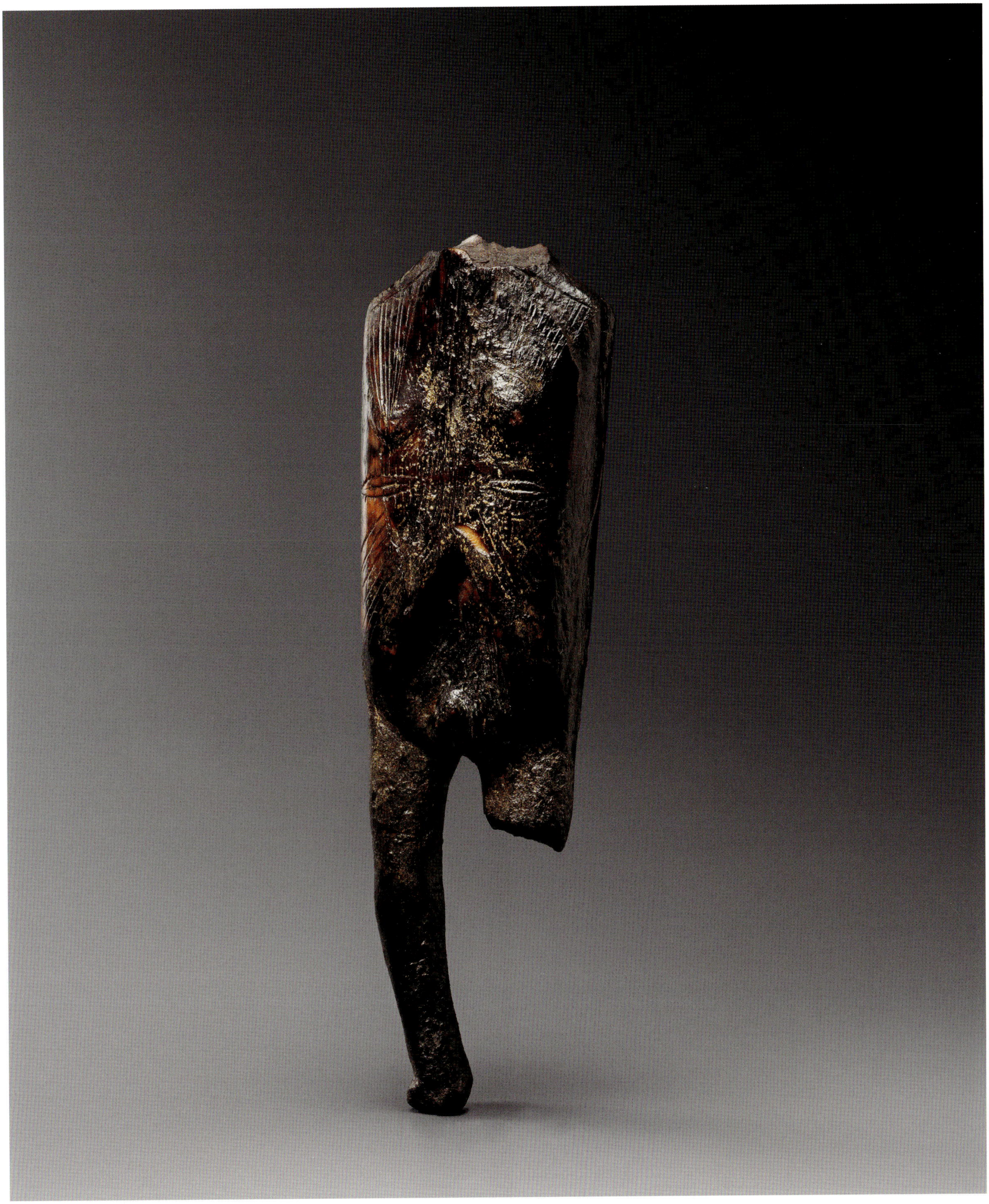

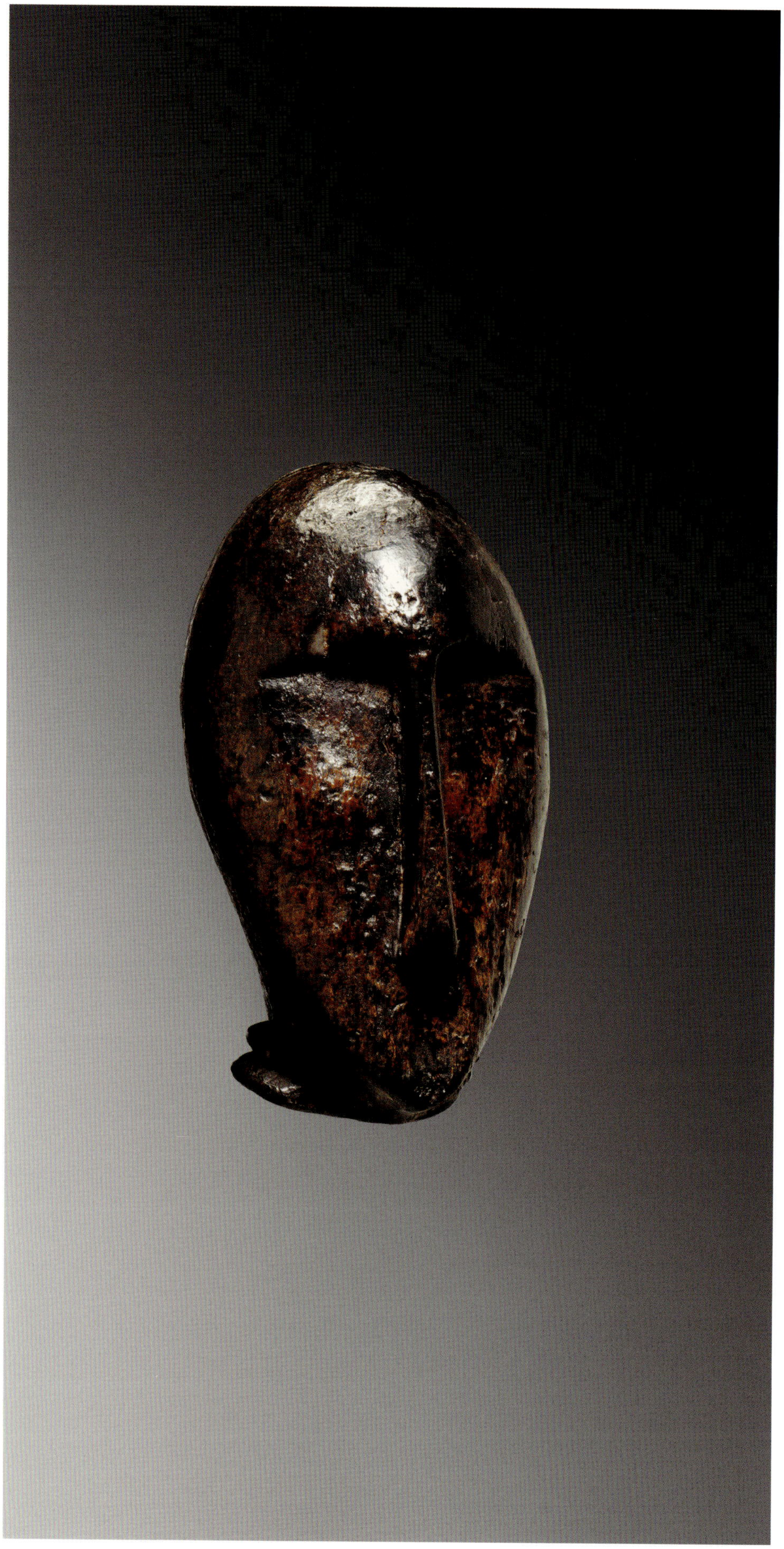

Head
Paleo-Eskimo culture, St Lawrence Island (*Sivuqaq*), Alaska (Siberian Yup'ik)
Old Bering Sea I (Okvik period), H. 7.5 cm
Circa 250 BC – 100 AD

Okvik sculpture is typified by a remarkable style of human figure, usually no larger than 15 cm tall, which display a refined stylistic reduction of form. The figures are often modelled monolithically, without arms or legs, and exhibit symbolic surface markings to express the skeleton, genitals, and other somewhat mystical details. The heads of these figures are perhaps their most distinctive feature, with elongated nose and face, resembling more the works of modern artists than any other works of antiquity. The head seen here is a typically elegant example, rather classical in the extended proportions of its minimal features.
Okvik human figures are largely interpreted as dolls, and have numerous associations. One such interpretation is that they were used as protective house dolls, representing an ancestor who would act as family guardian. Many times, the dolls are carved with open mouths, as if singing, and there is evidence that these dolls may have been ritualistically fed, as a sign of ancestral respect. Often, the heads from these dolls were removed from their torsos, as we see here. There is some evidence that the heads may have been ritualistically broken off from the bodies, rather than by accident, as examples have been found at excavation sites where heads were cleanly removed and the two parts discovered some meters apart from each other. One theory from this is that the dolls may have represented actual living people, and that they may have been ritualistically broken upon the death of that person, perhaps to assist in the release and transmigration of their *inua*, or spirit. Numerous taboos regarding the *inua* persist into modern times, and it is logical that the family would wish to encourage the departure of the ancestor's *inua*, to avoid its haunting presence and to foster the spirit's return to another child at a later time. [SM]

Head
Paleo-Eskimo culture, St Lawrence Island (*Sivuqaq*), Alaska (Siberian Yup'ik)
Archaic Punuk, H. 8.5 cm
Circa 500 – 800

This remarkable doll head represents a female figure, as it expresses the dramatic facial tattoo patterns traditionally worn by Arctic women from earliest times. Anthropologist Lars Krutak (Smithsonian Institution) has published widely on the subject of native tattooing, and notes that the earliest written descriptions of women's tattoos in the Arctic come from Martin Frobisher, who explored the Arctic in 1576. Other European explorers recorded similarly on the practice, describing also the methods of tattooing, which were administered with special bone sewing needles, caribou skin sinew threads, and soot from oil lamps as pigment. William Gilder wrote in 1881 an account that closely describes the pattern seen on this doll, carved more than 1,000 years before: "*. . . The forehead is decorated with a letter V in double lines, the angle very acute, passing down between the eyes almost to the bridge of the nose, and sloping gracefully to the right and left before reaching the roots of the hair . . .*" [1]

The method of inserting pigmented sinew into the skin and tracing linear patterns through it may account for the striking linear designs, but they are also consistent with other skeletal markings, which had important symbolic value among early Arctic peoples. These, and especially the facial tattoos worn by women, offered protection from harmful spirits, as well as connections to ancestors. On St Lawrence Island, women received their first tattoos after the event of their first menstruation, typically straight lines below the mouth pointing to the chin. The complex patterns seen on this doll head would indicate that the subject is a respected elder, who wears the advanced symbols of an entire life's experience. [SM]

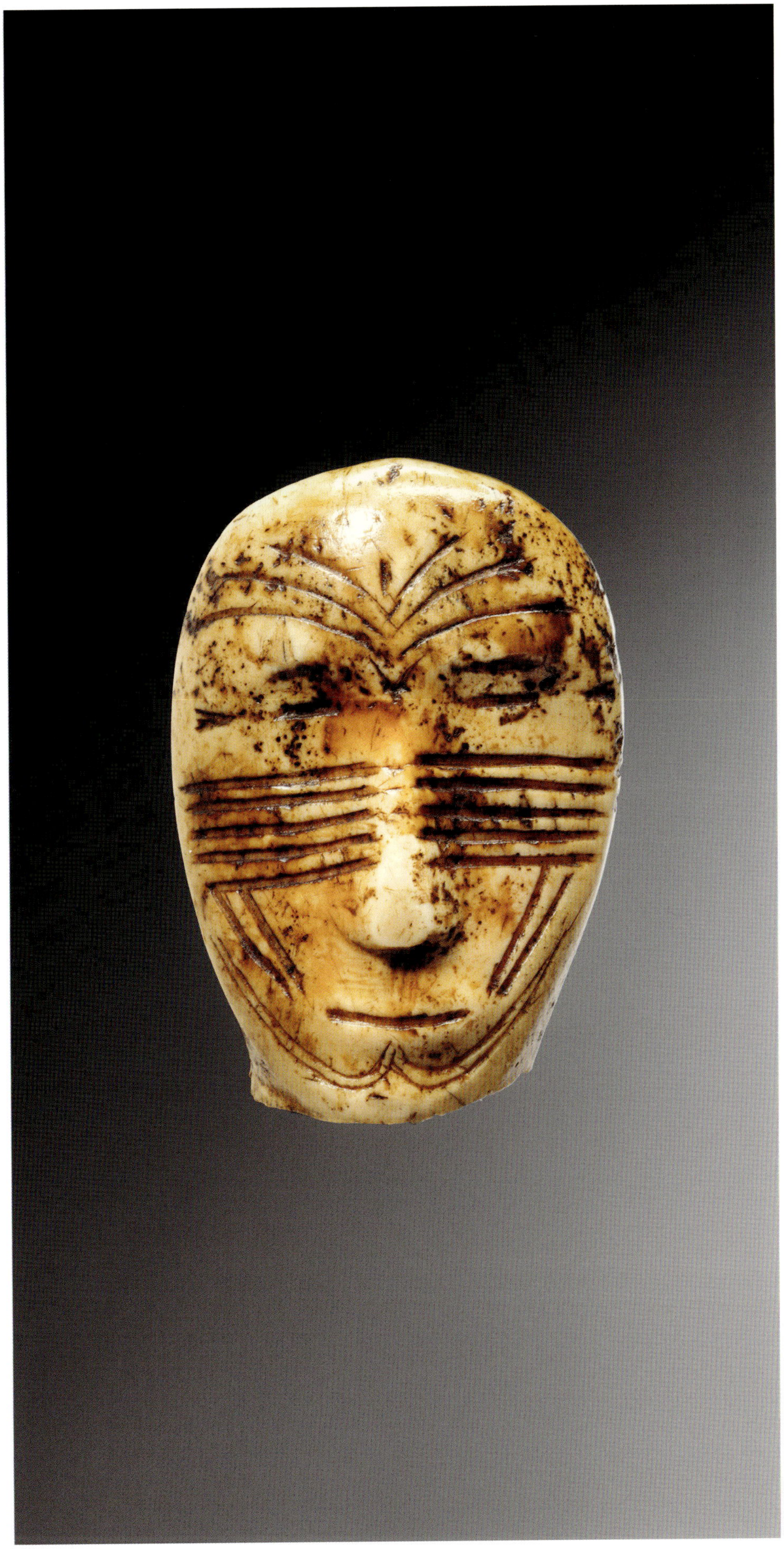

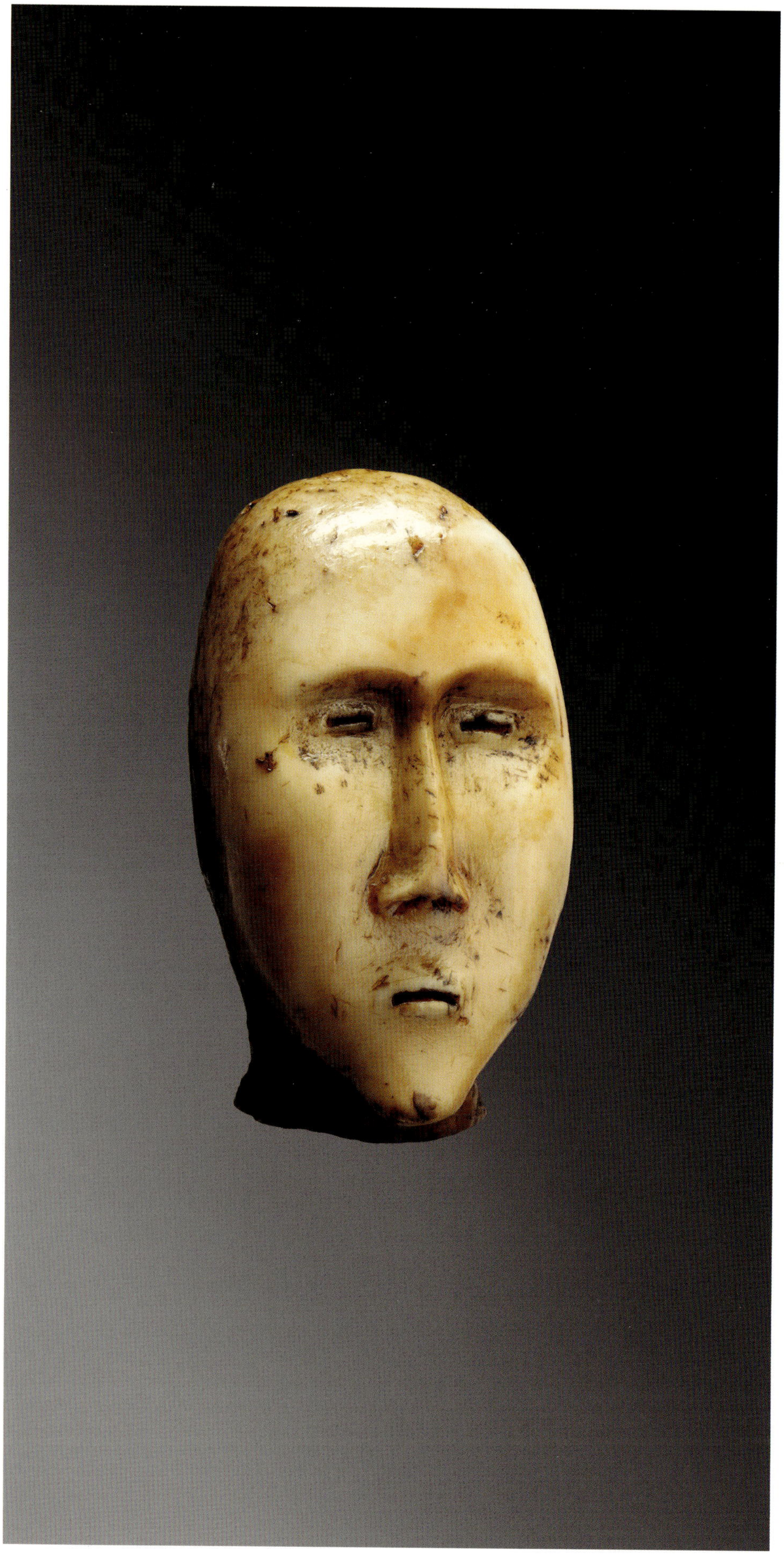

Head
Paleo-Eskimo culture, St Lawrence Island (*Sivuqaq*), Alaska (Siberian Yup'ik)
Late Punuk or archaic Western Thule, H. 6 cm
Circa 600 – 1200 or 1200 – 1500

By contrast to the previous female doll's head, this slightly later period human head is without decorative patterning, and its modelling is almost portrait-like. It likely represents a male figure, although the lack of facial tattoos is not enough to definitively identify its gender. Still, the serenity of expression, denoted by the almost closed eyes and mouth, and the naturalistically carved nose and forehead, suggest that this may represent a specific family member.
The deeply engraved eyes and mouth also suggest that they may have originally been inlaid with another material, which has fallen out over time. The dark-coloured whalebone baleen, taken from the jaw of the Bowhead whale, is a soft keratin substance (like human fingernails), easily carved and inserted into ivory to contrast with its light colour. Just as a European oil painter might add highlights of colour to enliven the eyes and lips of the subject, the skilful carver of Arctic ivories utilized the limited palette of white walrus ivory and black whale baleen to accentuate details and create contrasting patterns. [SM]

Wrist guard
Paleo-Eskimo culture, St Lawrence Island (*Sivuqaq*),
Alaska (Siberian Yup'ik)
Archaic Punuk, H. 7.5 cm
Circa 500 – 800

This decorated plaque is very likely to be a wrist guard, utilized when hunting with bow and arrow. Wrist guards are strapped onto the inside of the arm just below the first digit of the thumb, to protect the interior veins at their most vulnerable point, during the repeated volleys of arrows during hunting. Some wrist guards are designed to fit snugly over the thumb (better known as "thumb guards") and also act as guides for the arrow fletching, helping the hunter take aim.

This fine example is without visible points of attachment, and as such can be considered fragmentary, although hunting aids such as this were carved individually to fit a specific hunter. Therefore, wrist guards are highly specialized, and take a variety of ingenious forms. This one may have had a piece of sinew tied over it to secure it to the hunter's arm, or a clever pocket may have been sewn into his parka sleeve.

More importantly, the decorations on the wrist guard mark it in almost heraldic fashion. Shaped in a shield-like manner, it has the typical linear patterns at its border, with the distinctive "dot and thorn" pattern within the shield area, a notable decoration of the Punuk era. Most prominent on the heraldic form is the human face carved in high relief, dominating the slightly convex lower half of the guard. Symmetrically arranged double-line marks radiate outward from the cheeks, in a common tattoo pattern seen on representations of ancestors. We may interpret this image, then, as a protective amulet, akin to others used in hunting, wherein the spirit of a respected ancestor is invoked to inspire success in hunting, at a most critical place of the hunter's arm. [SM]

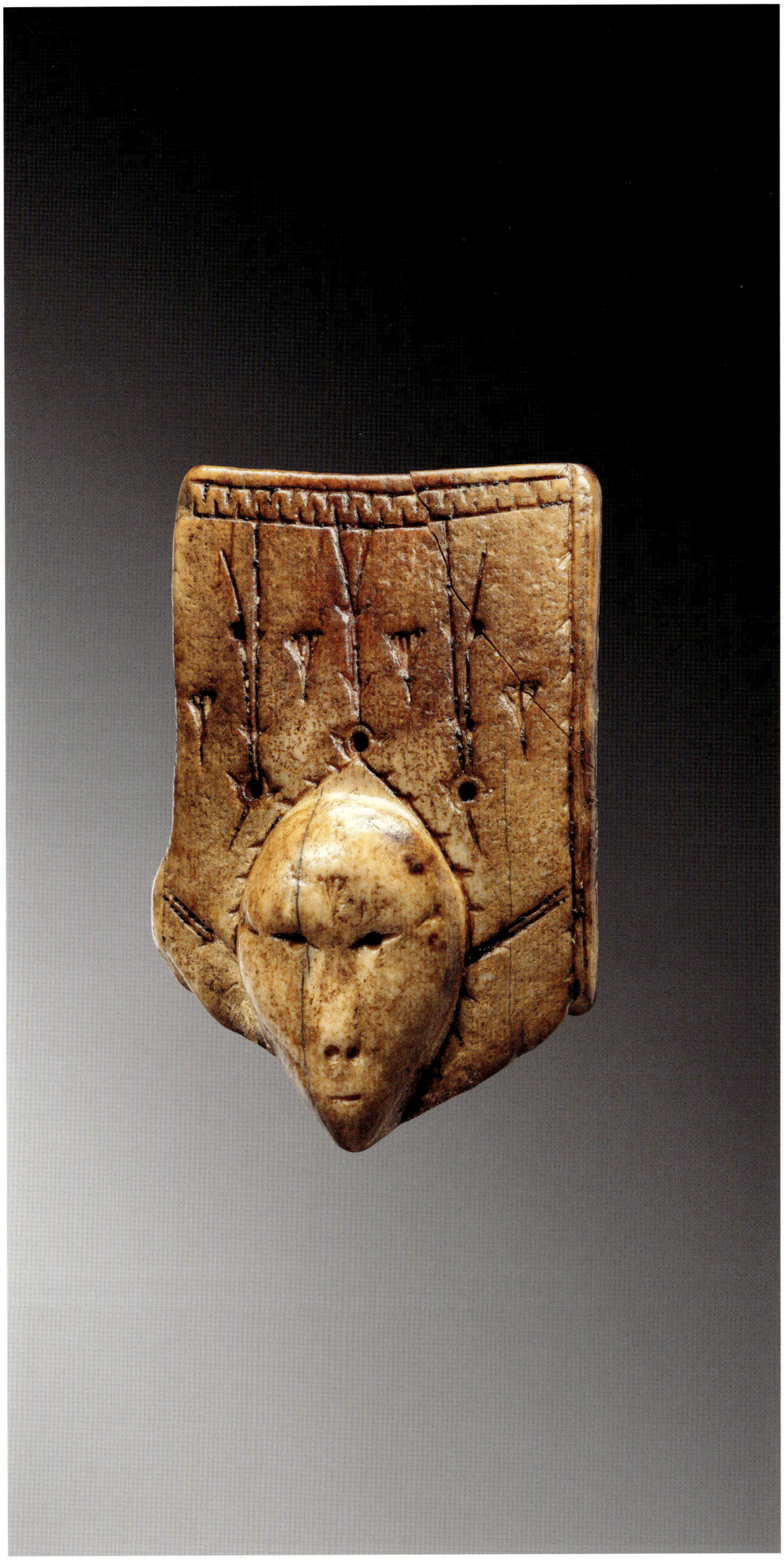

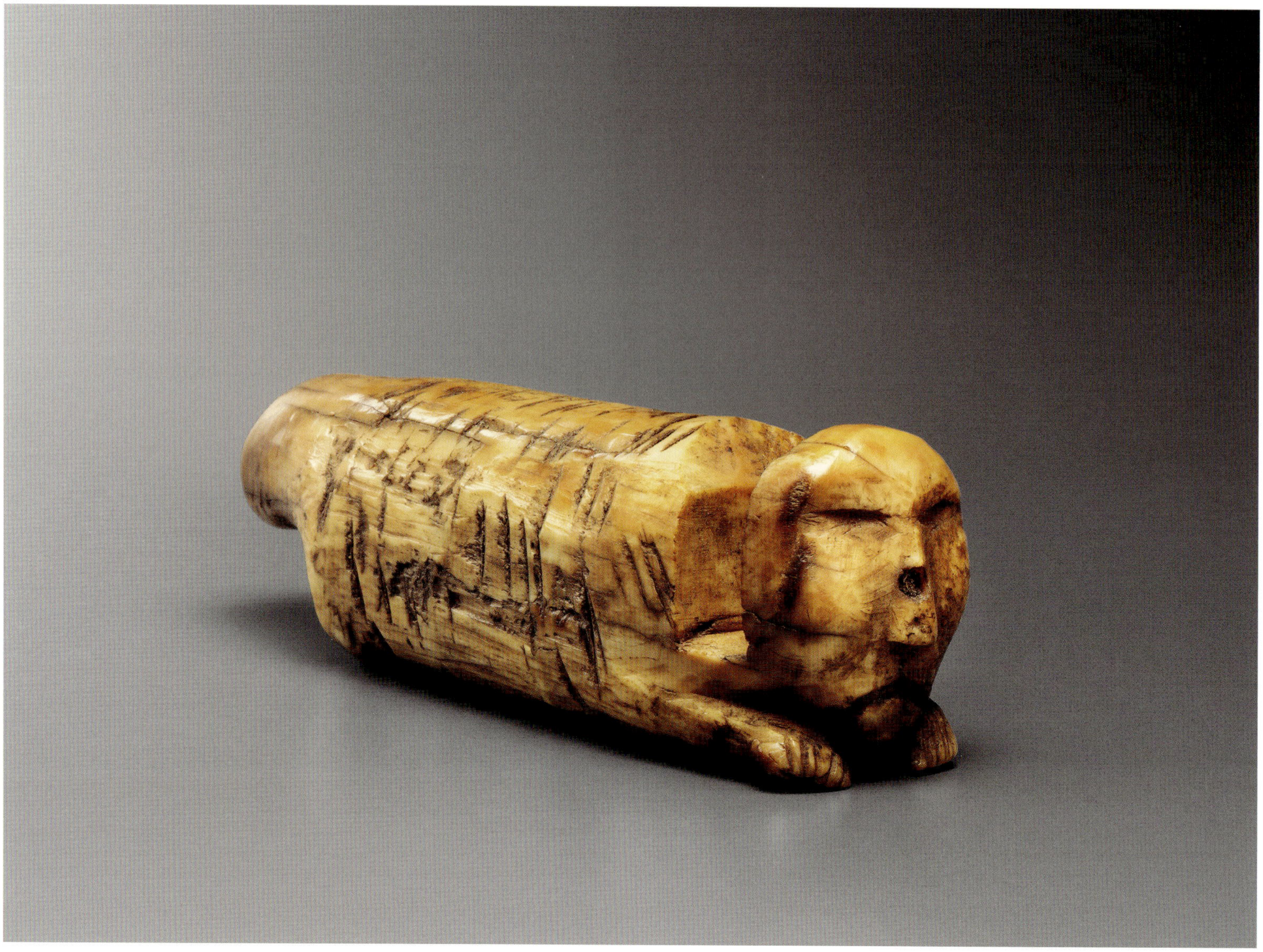

Drum handle
Paleo-Eskimo culture, St Lawrence Island (*Sivuqaq*), Alaska (Siberian Yup'ik)
Late Punuk or archaic Western Thule, H. 10.5 cm
Circa 800 – 1400

Throughout the Arctic, traditions of storytelling, singing and dancing have existed since earliest times. In much of Alaska, especially in coastal areas, large hoop drums stretched with sealskin are used to set the rhythm of the festival dances and songs. The handle of the drum, the point of contact between the drummer and the sealskin, is usually decorated and carved from ivory or driftwood. This curious example exhibits the dualism that is symbolic of the mediating nature of the winter dance festivals.
While most ceremonial dances in the Arctic are secular, often comic—a form of village entertainment—some were performed by the shaman (*angalkuq*) to assist in mediating between the village and the spirit world. In the late winter ceremonies, for example, dances would be held in advance of the spring hunting season, where songs would be performed to formally appeal to the *inua* of the animals, pleading for their return. As such, the drums were important vehicles for the song and dance, to help propel the sound of village singing outward, and ensure it would be heard by the spirits.
It has been noted that Arctic carvings often contain visual puns, in which an animal's body might reveal a human's head, and vice versa. Here, we see a classic example, where a seal representation, when turned to the opposite side, reveals a Sphynx-like human. We may interpret this carving in several ways, each following the dualistic nature of the drum handle. First, it shows both the seal—the animal whose *inua* is being addressed in the song—and also the seal's human *inua* emblem. For we must remember that the *inua* is always represented in human form, as the "personal human" of the animal. This is expressed in the very word itself: *Inua* comes from the root *Inu-* which is the common identifier for "man" in many Arctic languages. Inuit simply means "the People," plural form of *Inu* (person).

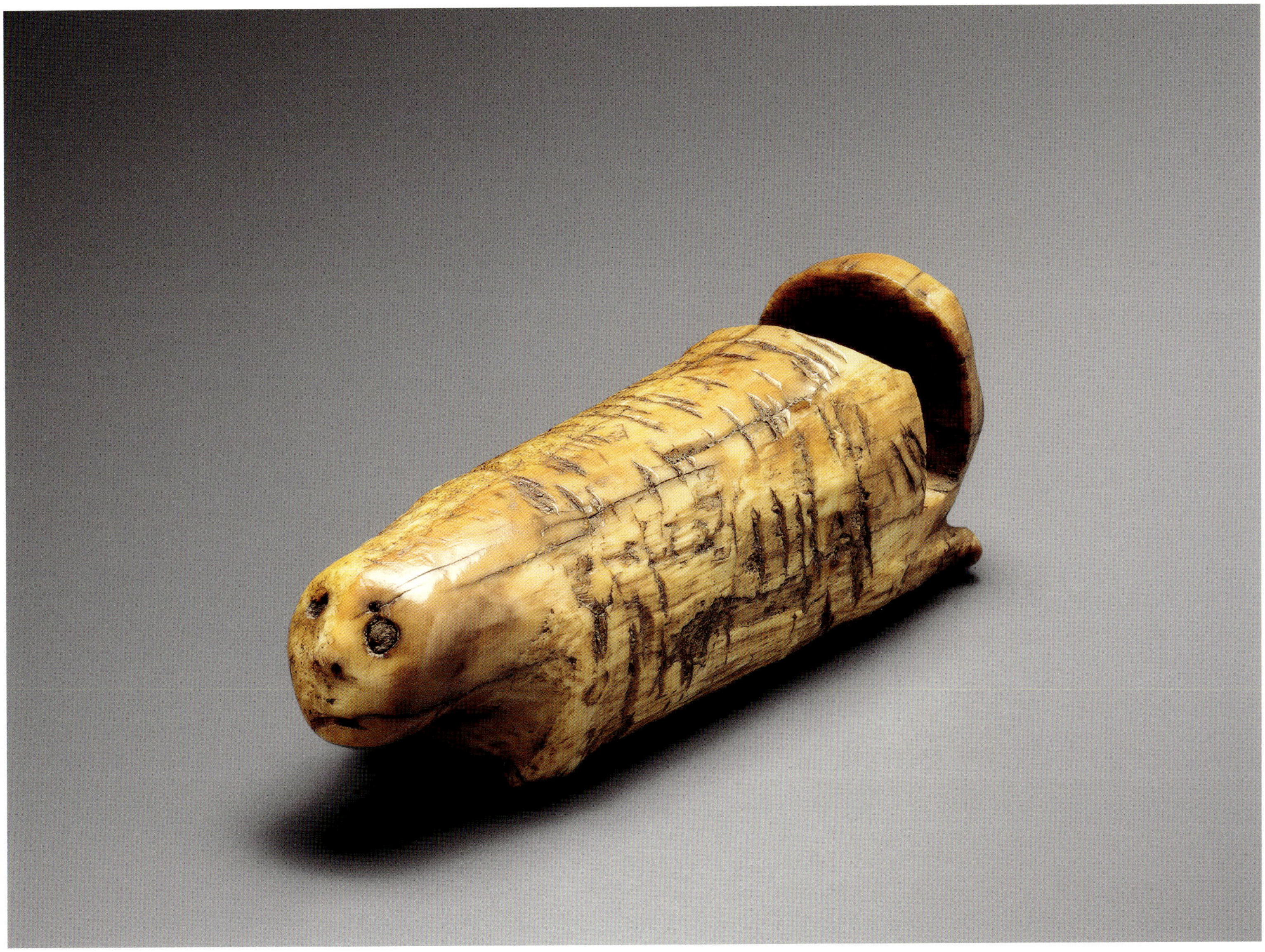

Secondly, drum handles often are made to represent the *angalkuq* himself, as the chief mediator with the drum, and therefore with the spirit world. Among the shaman's talents is to occasionally transform himself into another animal in order to travel to convene with the *inua* of that creature, and it is common to see images of shamans composed to express this dualistic nature. Here, we have a figure who is half-human, half-seal, as if in the process of transforming. Notably, the *angalkuq's* head faces upward, towards the centre of the drum, which becomes during the dance a vehicle for the conveyance of the *inua*, encouraging its movement. The deeply carved notch behind his head would capture the edge of the drum hoop, directing the handle's human face to witness the surface of the skin, the central place for spiritual and musical conveyance. [SM]

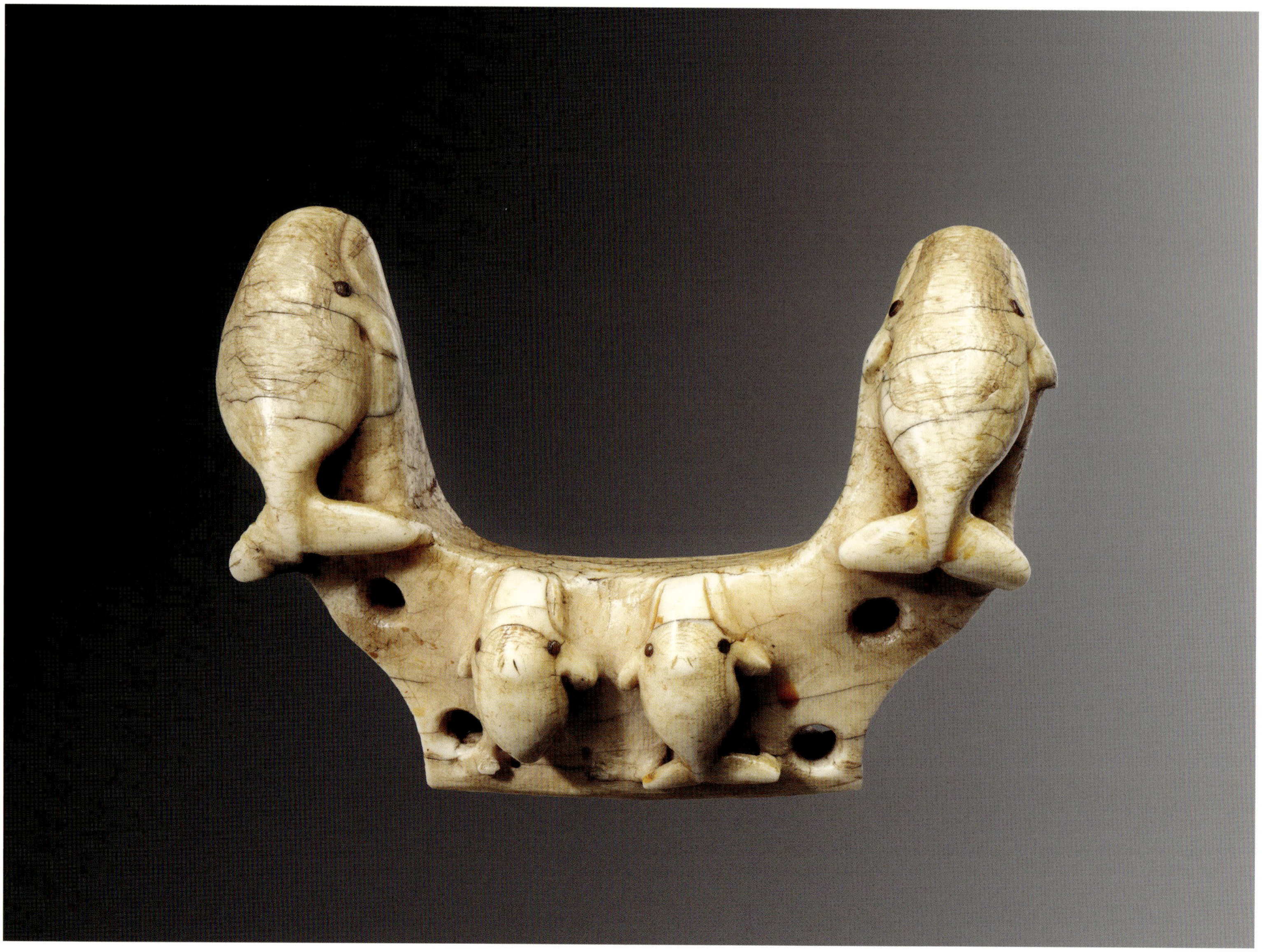

Harpoon rest
Pre-Inuit culture, Alaska (Iñupiat), late Western Thule, L. 12 cm
Circa 1500 – 1800

The traditional hunting boat for whaling in the Arctic is the *umiak*, a skin-covered open boat large enough to accommodate as many as eight hunters. The *umiak* differs from the kayak or *bidarka* in that these smaller boats, for one, two or three persons, would be completely covered with skins, leaving only a round hole for the hunter to insert his legs. The large, open *umiak* is more like a modern boat, capacious enough for harpoons, lines, and a crew, but leaving them more vulnerable to the dangers of hunting whale in open sea. More than any other activity, whale hunters needed all the assistance they could get from a harmonious relationship to the spirit world.
Among the apparatus of the *umiak* there was usually one or more ivory harpoon rests, mounted near the prow of the boat, to provide secure and ready access to the striker, who rode in front. Like the hunting charm on page 223, these harpoon rests were often carved with the effigies of helping animals, usually seals or walruses, or figures of the whales themselves. Not only do these effigies provide spiritual guidance to the hunter, but they also act as a sort of labelling system: a harpoon rest used on a small kayak when hunting seal might be carved with seal effigies, for example. This ivory harpoon rest is decorated with five figures of bowhead whales, carved in high relief. Four of them appear to dive forward in a common direction, flowing with the chase. The fifth, on the reverse side, appears motionless and flattened, as if evidence of the successful hunt itself. [SM]

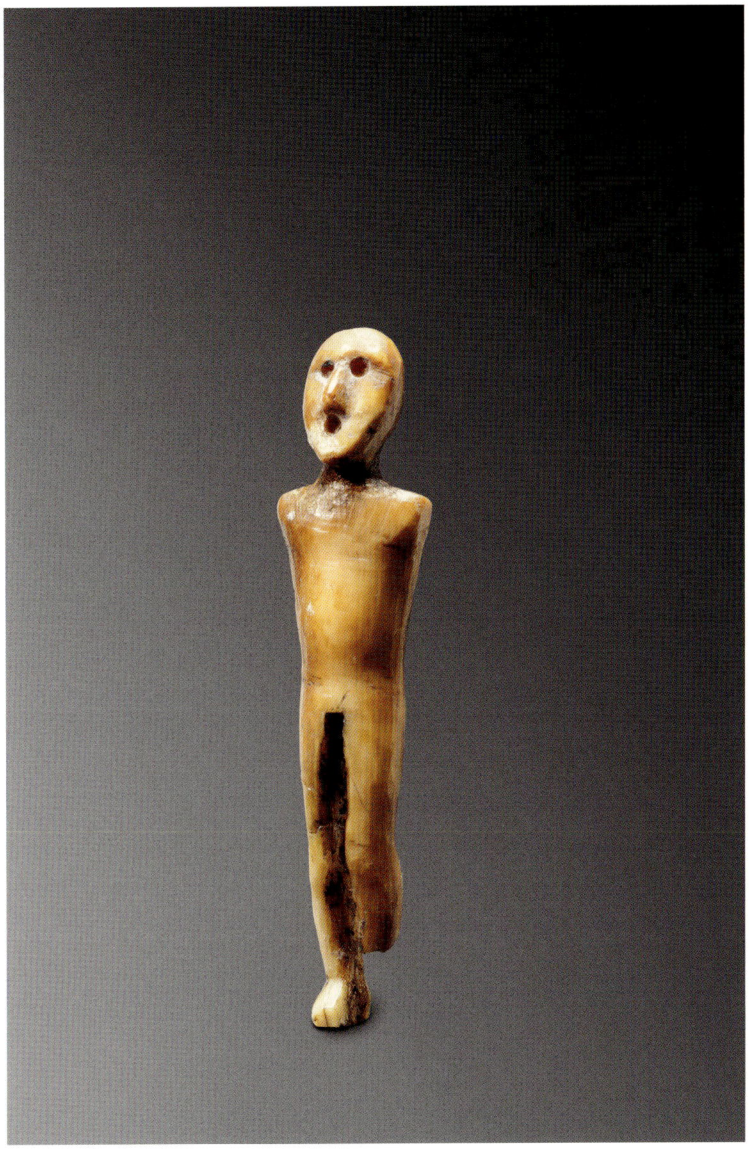

Statuette
Pre-Inuit culture, Coast of Alaska (Siberian Yup'ik or Iñupiat)
Archaic Western Thule, H. 4 cm
Circa 1200 – 1500

This much smaller human figure, like the previous example (see pp. 212-13), demonstrates remarkable compositional uniformity after more than 1,000 years. Like the other, it has an armless torso but articulated legs. Curiously, it too is missing part of its left leg, although I take this as a coincidence.
While miniaturized, this doll's head retains the classic modelling of previous epochs. The Punuk and subsequent early Thule periods represented somewhat of a return to earlier traditional styles, closely adhering to the Old Bering Sea after the end of the Okvik period. Like on the head of page 216, the eyes and mouth may have once been inlaid with black baleen material, as their deeply engraved sockets suggest. [SM]

Amulet in the form of a sea otter
Pre-Inuit culture, Alaska (Iñupiat), late Western Thule, H. 11.2 cm
Circa 1500 – 1800

In Arctic traditional beliefs, all beings are expected to possess an *inua*, the personal spirit of that creature. In hunting, the *inua* of the prey is invoked, in a process of appealing to the animal's spirit, asking for its readiness to sacrifice itself for service to the human community. The consciousness of the *inua* of both hunter and prey is considered to be reciprocal; if the hunter pays attention to the *inua* of the animal, that animal's *inua* will be aware of the hunter as well. It is this act of silent communication that ensures harmonious existence among all Arctic creatures, in the traditional way of life. Too, since all creatures are believed to possess an *inua*, which is by default considered to be human and interchangeable, there is little hierarchy among the order of species. As such, then, other creatures, known as skilled hunters in their own right, may be called upon to assist the human hunter in his pursuits.
This small amulet of a sea otter is one such example of the type of "charm" figure that a hunter might carry with him during the pursuit of hunting or fishing. Note how its tail has been cleverly hollowed into a tube, for attachment to an article of clothing, or perhaps to a chain link of ivory, now lost. Known to be expert fish-catchers, this sea otter may have been carried as an assistant to the fisherman, to encourage success. Or perhaps it was carried during the process of hunting other sea otters, as a means of helping the hunter appeal to their own *inua*, to bring them forth to a worthy friend.
The presence of three small inlaid dots of whale baleen on the stomach is notable, for creating a triangular pattern, commonly seen especially during the Western Thule period. This further indicates the spiritualized nature of the amulet, as it makes clear the locus of the *inua* in the belly of the animal. [SM]

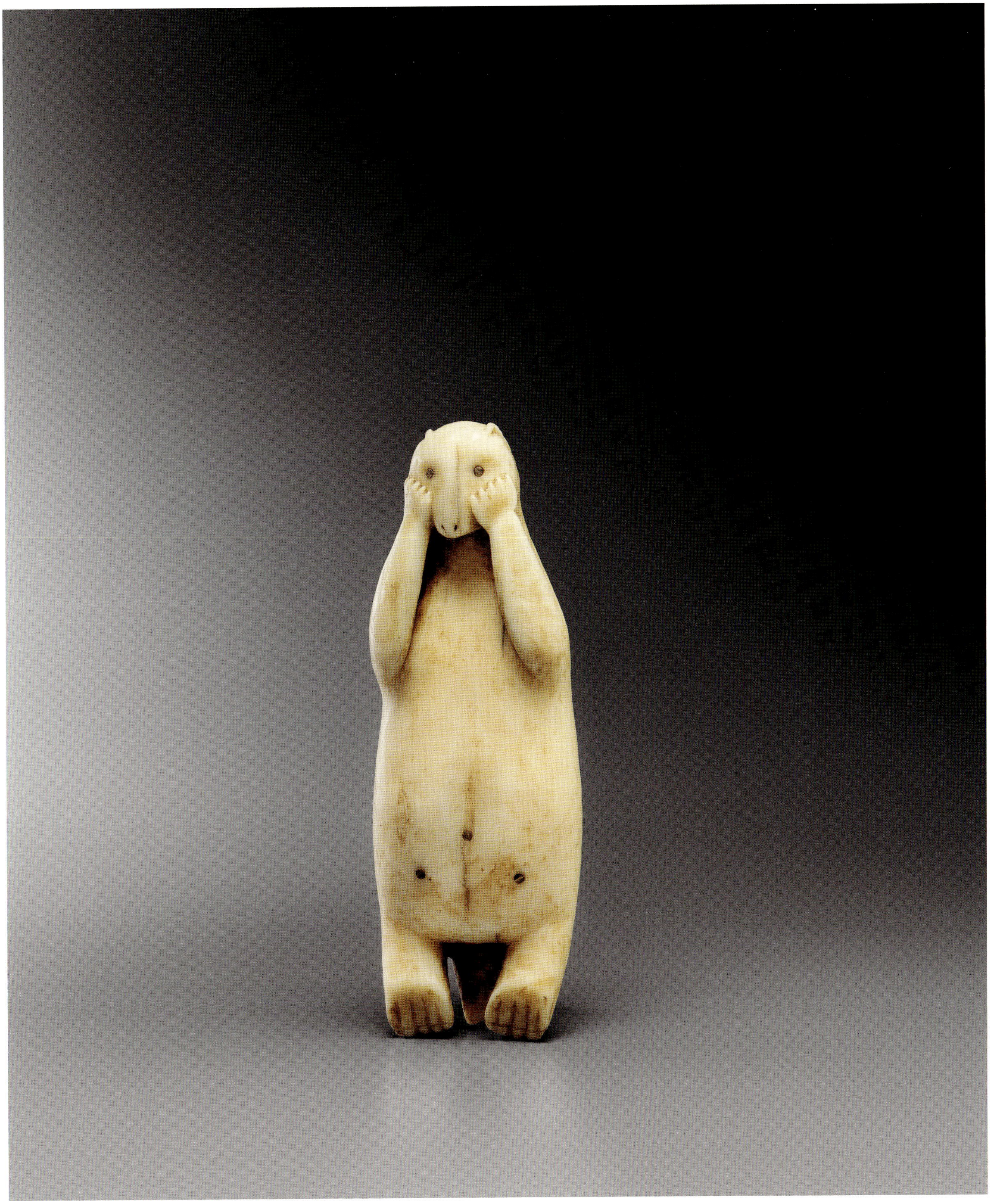

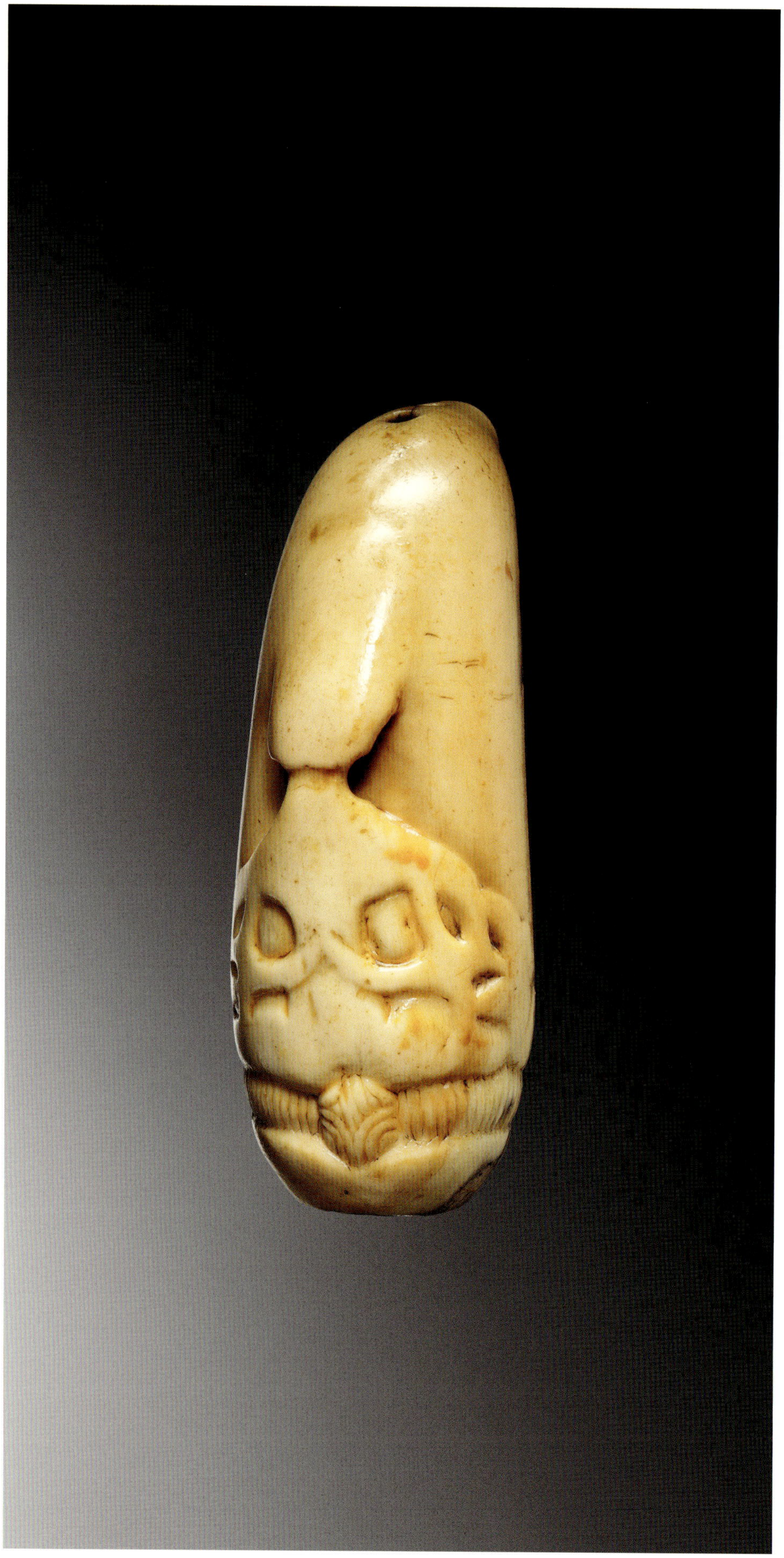

Maori whistle
New Zealand, H. 11.5 cm

The *nguru*, one end of which is curved, is a type of whistle that is peculiar to New Zealand. The material used is usually wood, but very occasionally they are made out of sperm whale teeth, as here.
The wear on the sculpture is testimony to the object's age. The repeated use of this flute has turned the figure into a touching ghost-like apparition. *Ngurus* were often worn by their owners around the neck (three holes to accommodate a strap can be seen above the figure) and were the instruments most commonly played by Maori communities. [PP]

Maori club
New Zealand, H. 33 cm

The word *patu* in Maori stands for a short-handled weapon. The weapons were used in close combat and in traditional duels (*wero*), for those with a proud history to defend. There was a special version of these clubs known as a *kotiate* with two notches arranged symmetrically in the middle of the blade.
This ancient *kotiate*, with its tight, closely packed forms, was carved out of a sperm whale jaw. The end of the handle is embellished with the head of the mythical *manaia*, whose eye is here fashioned by the addition of a piece of top shell mother-of-pearl. [PP]

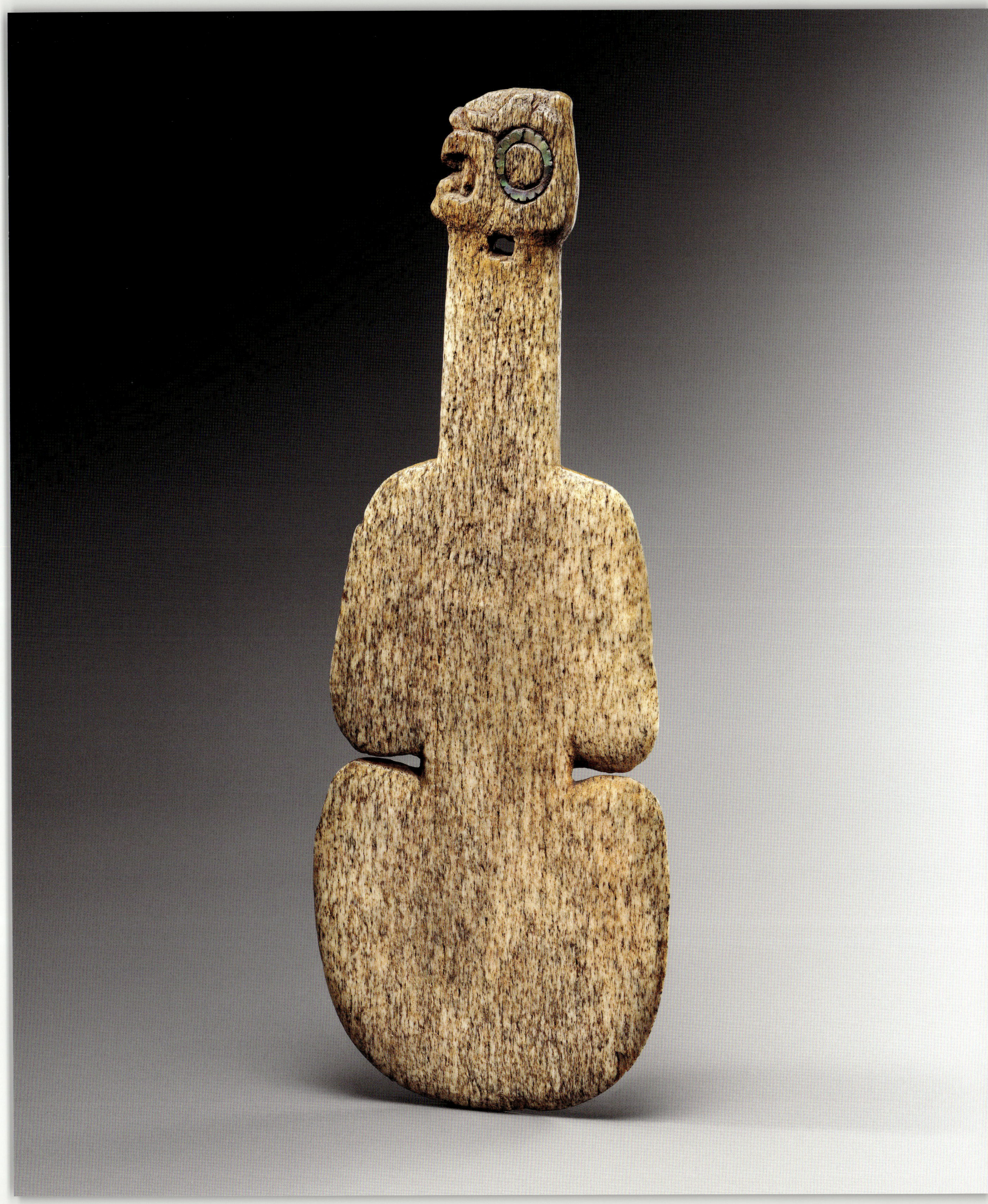

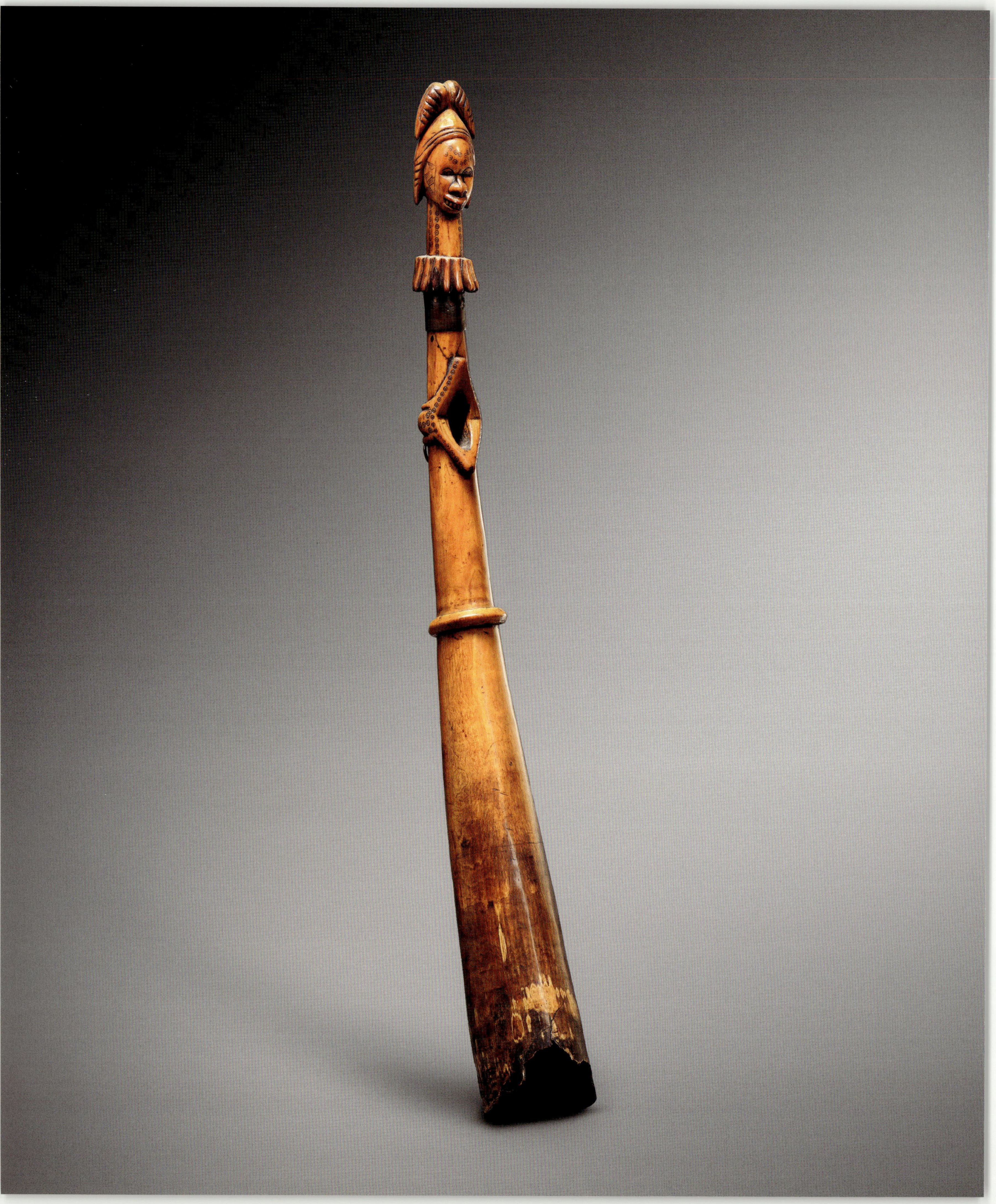

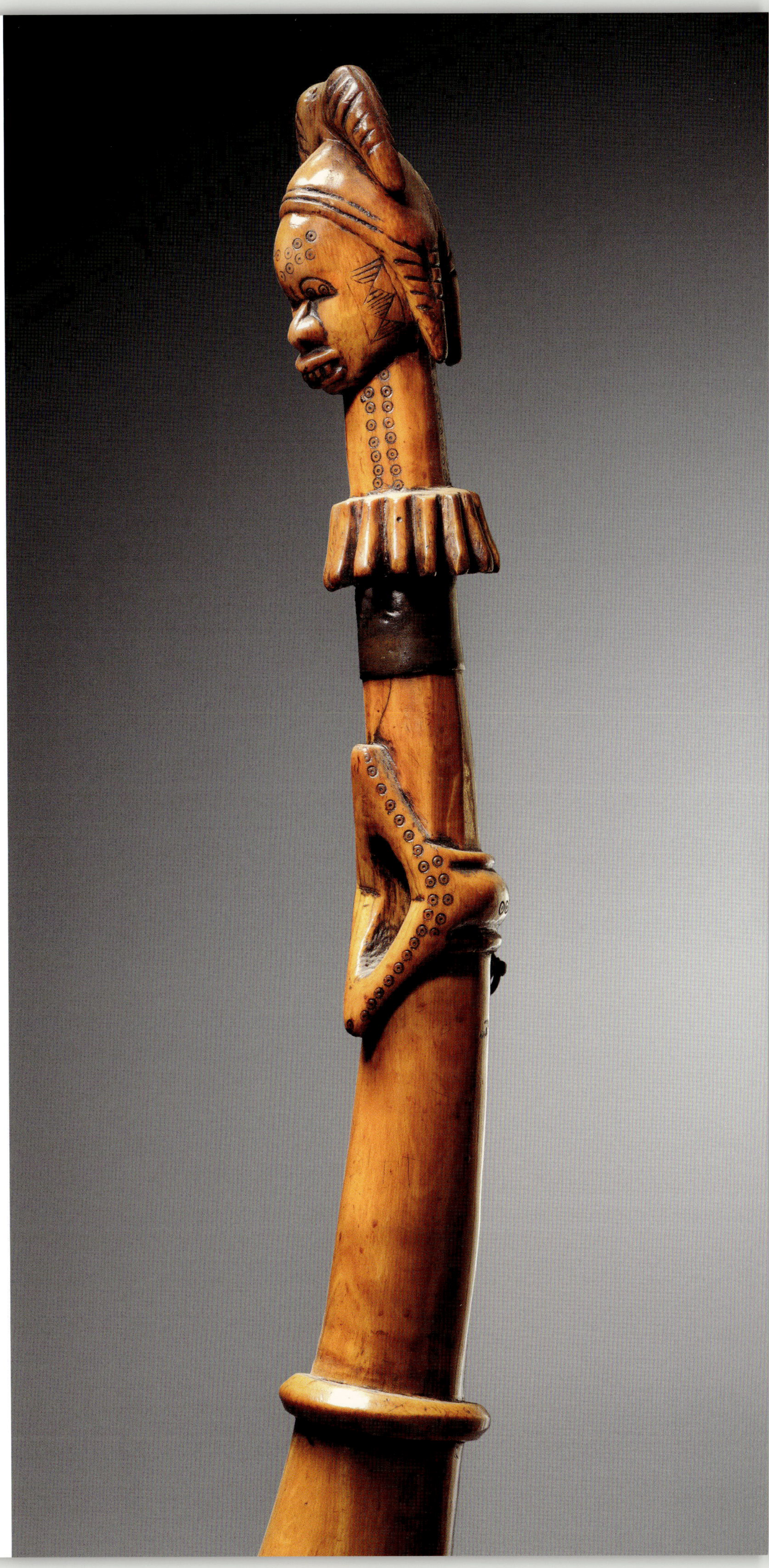

Mende olifant
Sierra Leone, L. 83 cm

Ivory trumpets are sacred prestige objects and are known to have existed on the coasts of Guinea and Sierra Leone since the fifteenth century. The style of the face sculpted on the end, towards the tip, brings to mind the ancient soapstone works from the region that were used until the seventeenth century. A ring placed between the mouthpiece and the head is reminiscent of the small cone-shaped animal horns filled with magical protective substances, a typical feature found on numerous masks and other objects associated with initiation rites and power. [AG]

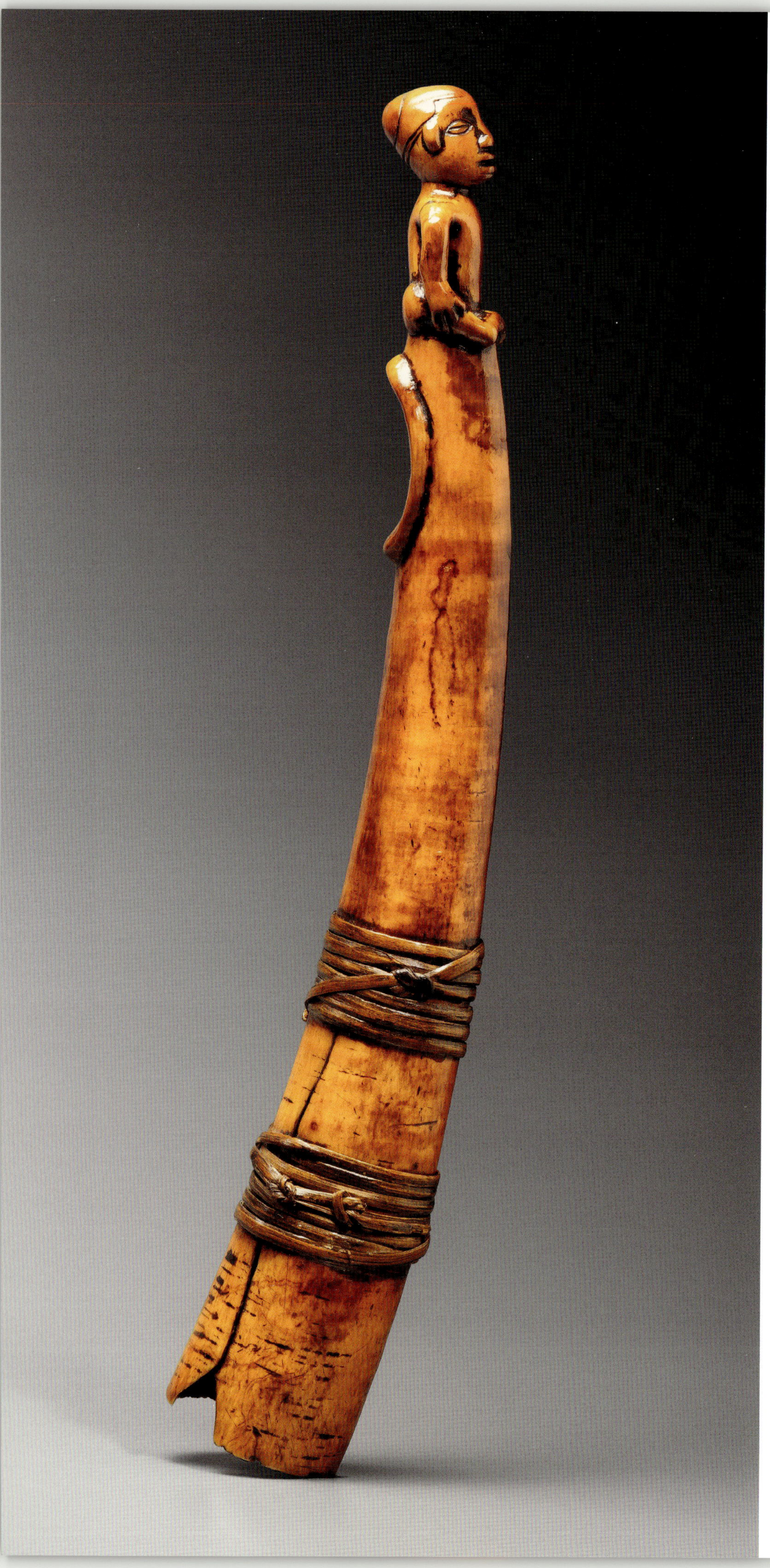

Kongo olifant
Democratic Republic of the Congo, L. 35.5 cm

According to the customs of the Kongo people, ivory olifants were the prerogative of the chiefs. Wearing them in front of them during official travel, they were exposed at their feet during ceremonies and were an integral part of the *regalia* associated with the representation of their power. The powerful sound they produced symbolically punctuated important political investitures, funeral and initiation rites.

Many of the pieces in this corpus are raw: the presence of a decoration, engraved or sculpted, shows a particular refinement. The olifant on this page presents a male character at the top. Sculpted with its back to the almond-shaped opening through which the instrument was played, it is depicted kneeling, his hands on the side of his thighs. This posture indicates that he is probably a man of power. [MC]

Mende container
Sierra Leone, L. 25.5 cm

This container, with marks on the bottom showing where the fastening mechanism used to be, is a unique object. It is also a symbol of power that bears the signs of its owner's standing: the female head displays the classic criteria of beauty, wealth, and respectability in Mende society in Sierra Leone. The folds in the neck, the high forehead and the extremely sophisticated hairstyle suggest this is a powerful woman, a chief's wife or a woman with an important role in the Sande initiation society. The straw hat decorated with a ribbon reveals a decided taste for goods imported from Europe. This type of headdress was extremely popular from the seventeenth century. [AG]

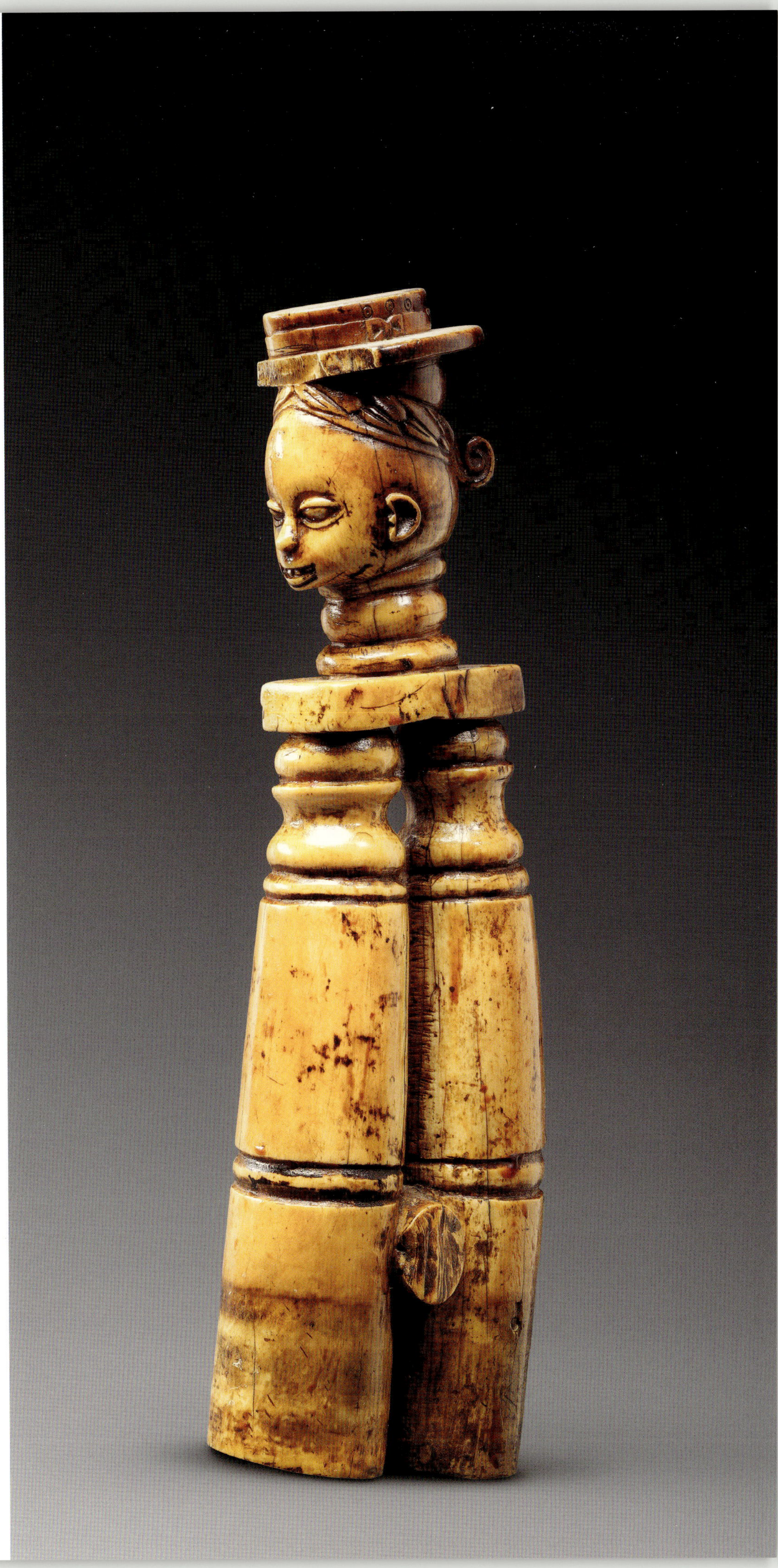

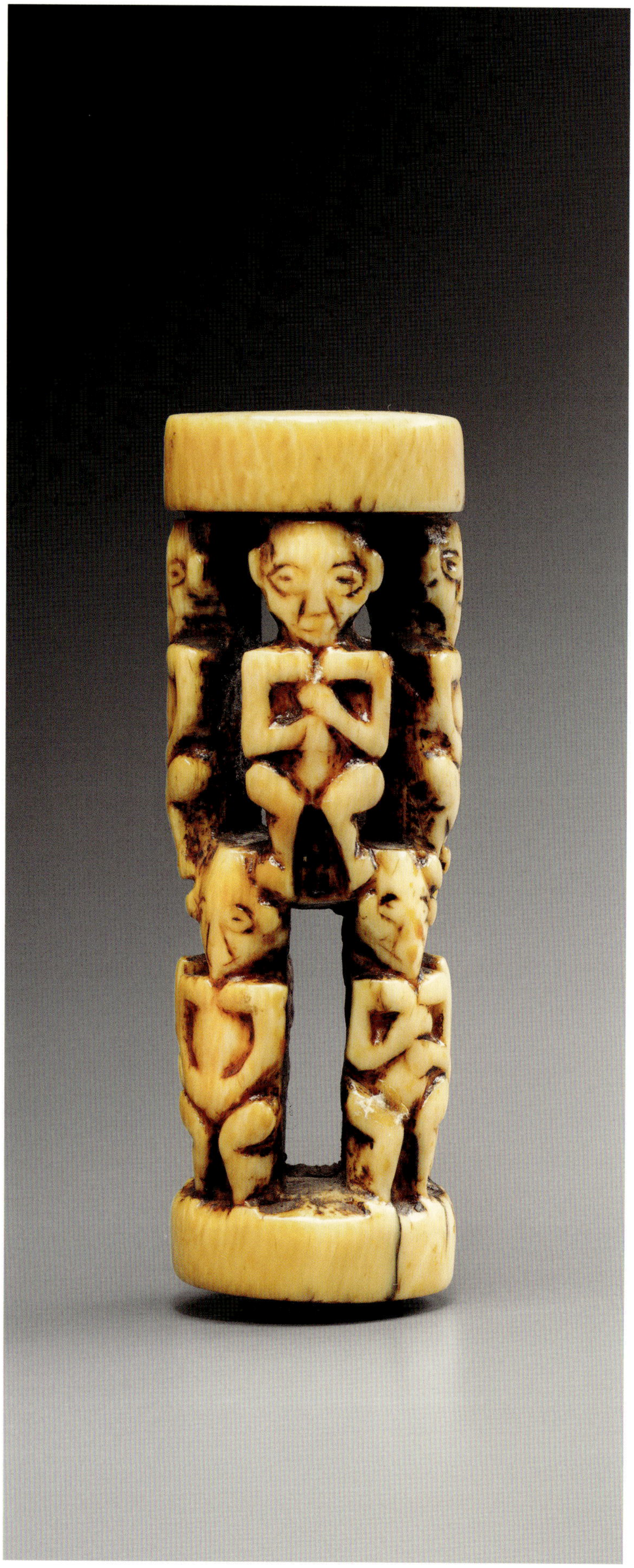

Bamileke pipe ornament
Cameroon, H. 11.5 cm

In Cameroon's Grassland, pipes are both cultural objects and symbols of social status. At the time of sowing or the harvest festival, they were used to spread a ritual smoke on the earth. In addition, the status of individuals—women and men—could be identified by their pipes. A pipe which used to be adorned with ivory elements could only belong to a high ranking individual, because ivory was an insignia in itself. The motif of the small anthropomorphic figures also emphasizes the idea of the community. [BVL]

Bangwa olifant
Cameroon, L. 30 cm

The olifants are a little smaller than the ivory trumpets that were used to celebrate a festive event. The elephant being a royal animal like the leopard, ivory was, like the skin of this feline, considered as a mark of honour.
The telling design of two back to back figures with oval heads and with their hands reaching to their chin, is observed in slightly varied forms not only on Bangwa olifants and double figures but also among the Kundu (see Museum für Völkerkunde in Berlin, Inv. no. III C 6282) and the Bafo in the forest area. [BVL]

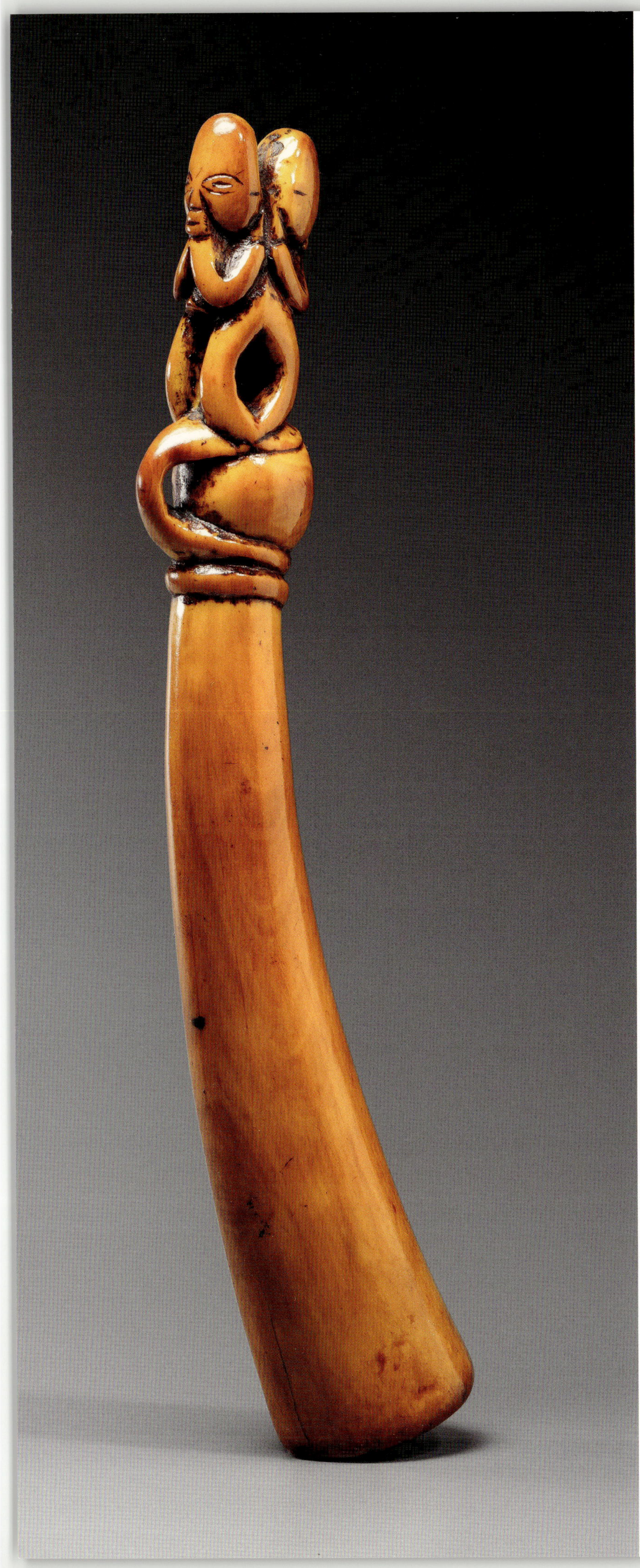
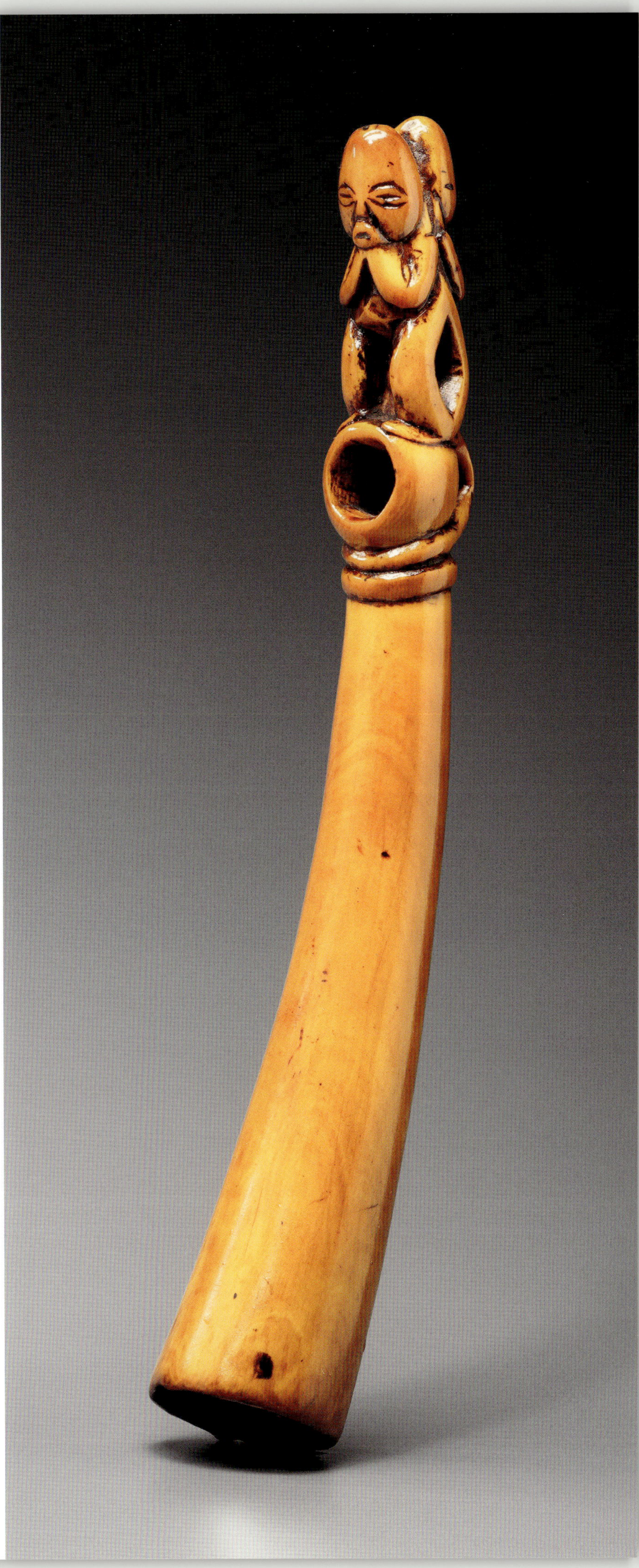

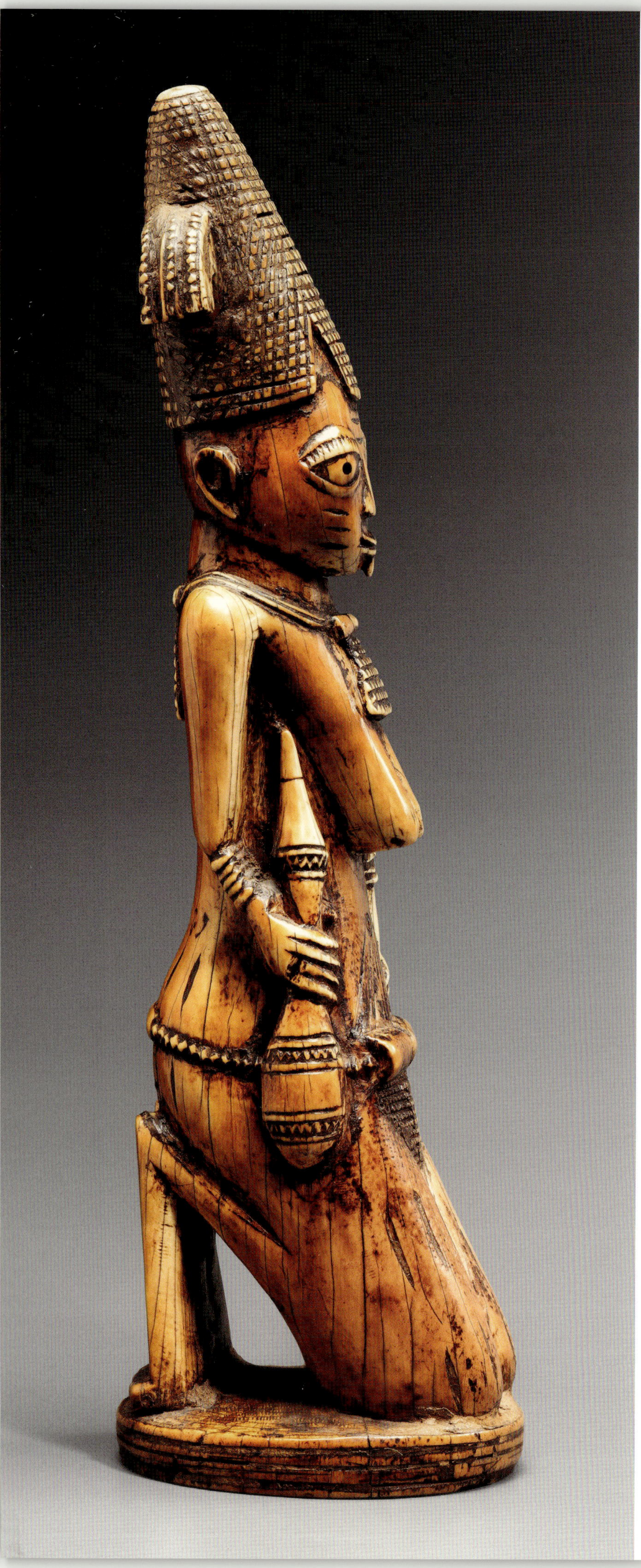
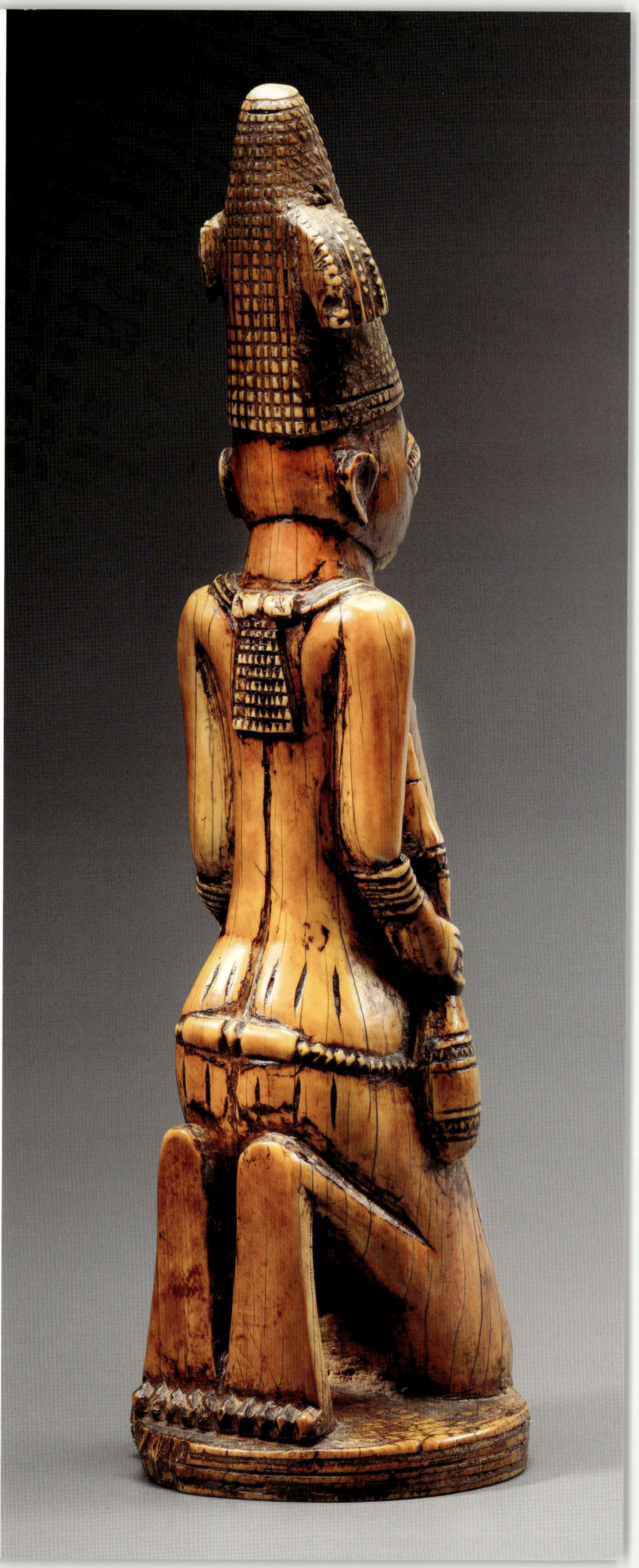

Yoruba statuette
Owo, Nigeria, H. 31 cm

The finest Yoruba ivory pieces (sixteenth–seventeenth century) are said to come from the town of Owo, a city-state lying between Ife and Benin. The highest ranking *babalawo*, Ifa-Orunmila priests, *orishas* of divination, have an exclusive right to objects sculpted in this precious material and rubbed to a smooth finish with palm oil: *iroke Ifa* tappers, *agere Ifa* bowls for palm nuts.[1]
This kneeling female figure is depicted holding a large gourd filled with ritual ingredients and her size is exceptional. She is adorned with a double amulet and wears a tall headdress with wing-like projections that allude to, and highlight, her *ori inu* (destiny). The figure is a feminine archetype expressing welcome and respect—a frequent iconography in Ifa worship.
[HJ]

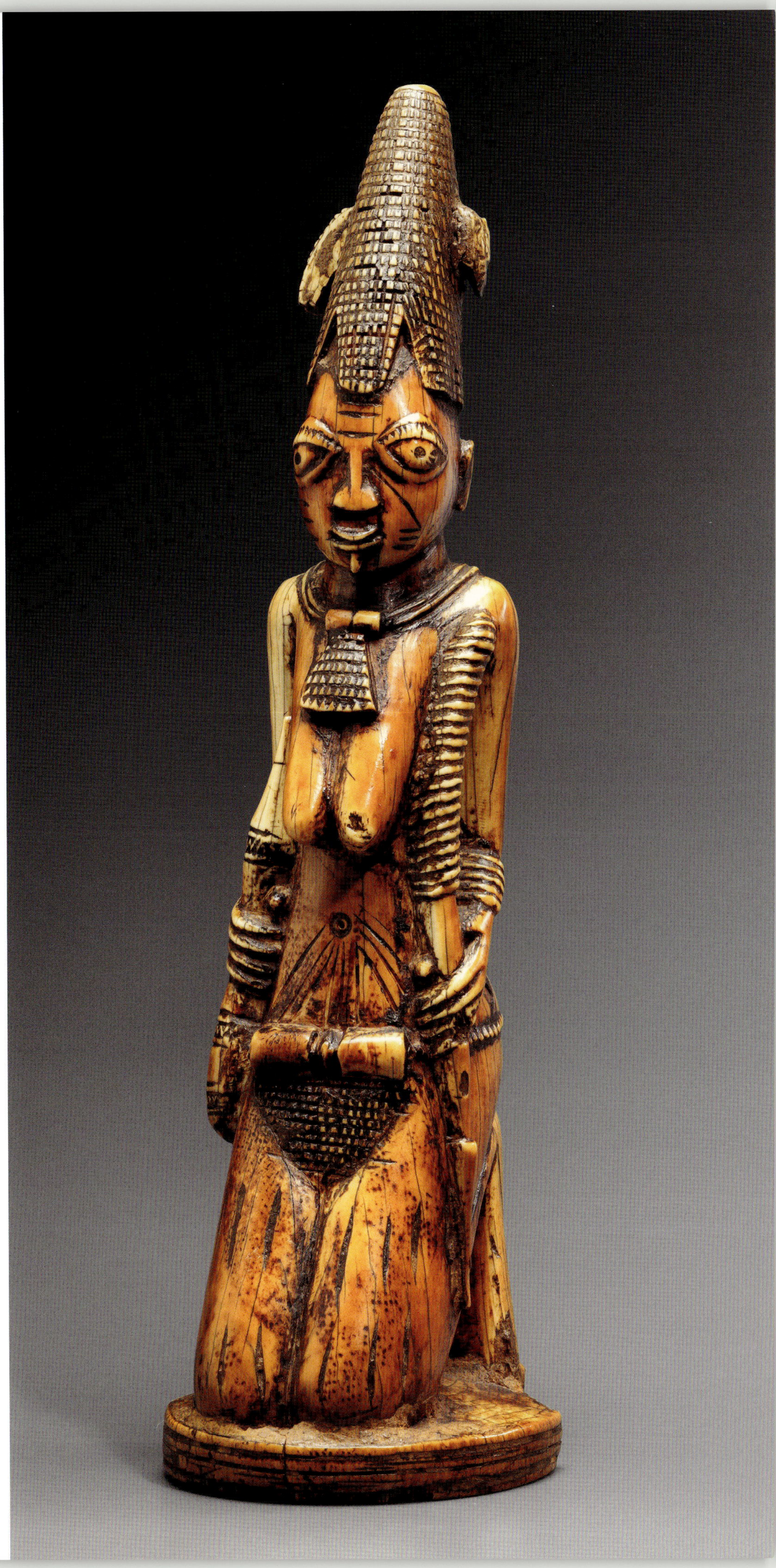

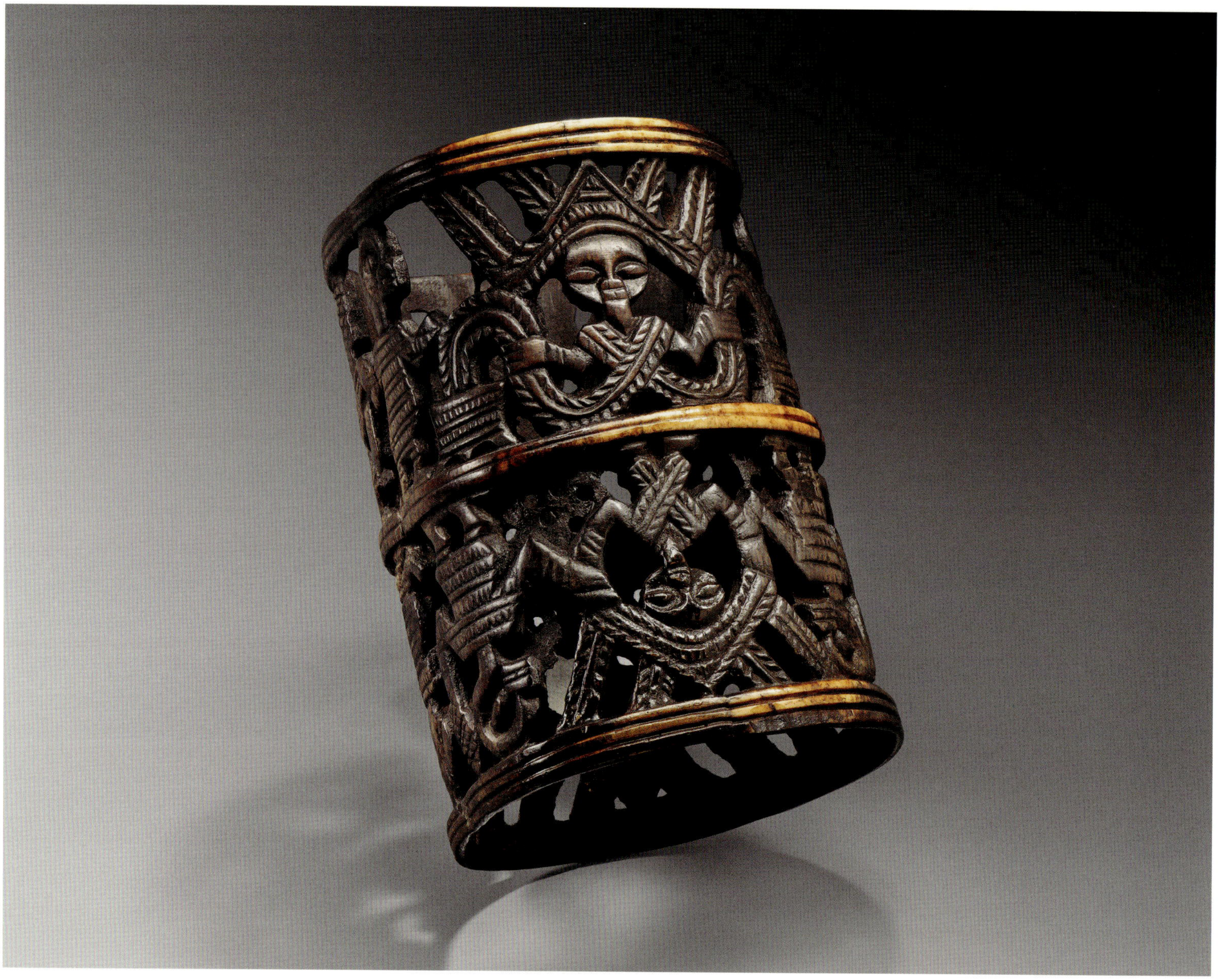

Yoruba bracelet
Owo, Nigeria, H. 12 cm

This elegant adornment, with its dark finish typical of Owo pieces,[1] probably belonged to the *Olowo* who had the exclusive right to wear ivory. The pattern consists of two almost specular registers separated by a band, each containing different kinds of figures, particularly *abraxas*,[2] with fish tail legs held in the hand, which is related to the concept of mediating divine royalty. The frieze of personages, kings and chiefs, viewed from the front or in profile, develops over a thin, perforated strip of ivory that has broken off at some points. [HJ]

Yoruba statuette
Nigeria, H. 15 cm

This figure represents a titled woman sitting on a stool that proclaims her status. She is wearing a pointed headdress encircled by a beaded headband suggesting a royal crown, numerous bracelets, a string of beads at the waist and a labret in her lower lip. This small sculpture resembles the *Olori Ikin*, miniature heads with tall headdresses who personify Exhu, an *orisha* interceding between heaven and earth, and a friend of Ifa, who opens the way for Ifa in the divination procedures. [HJ]

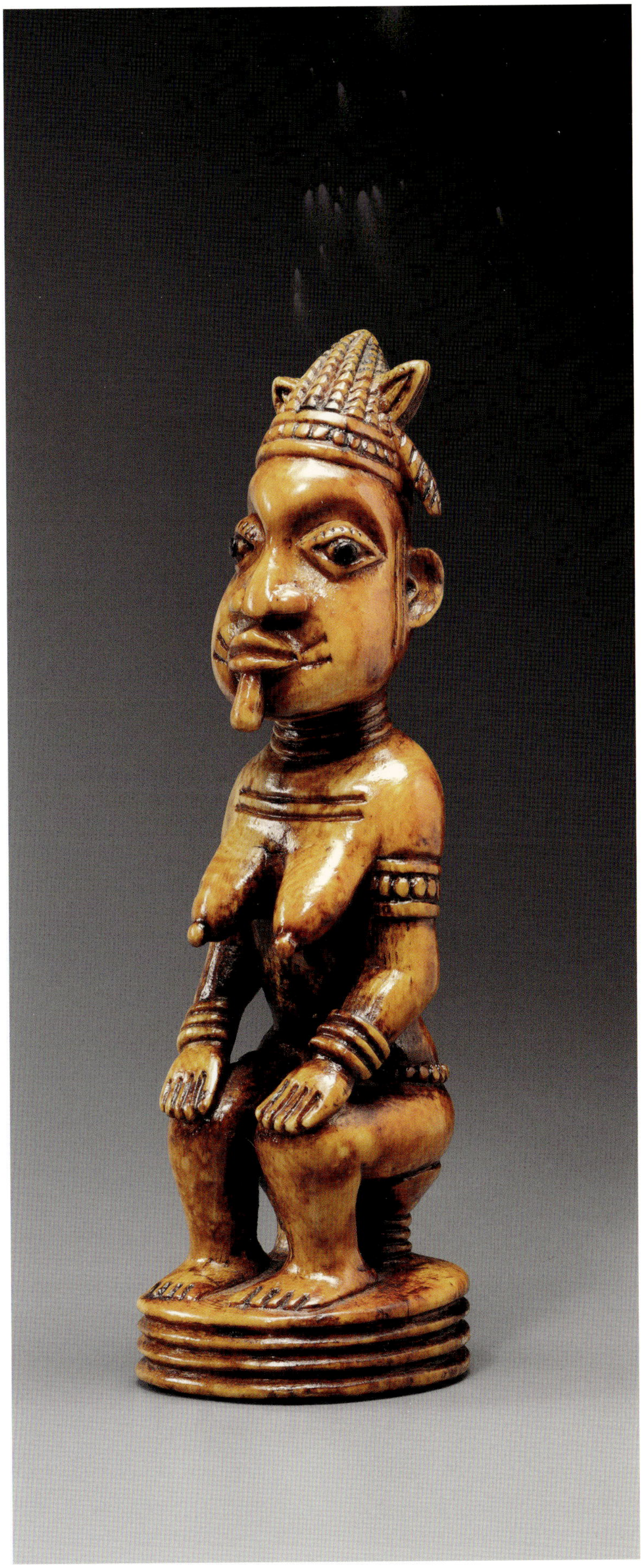

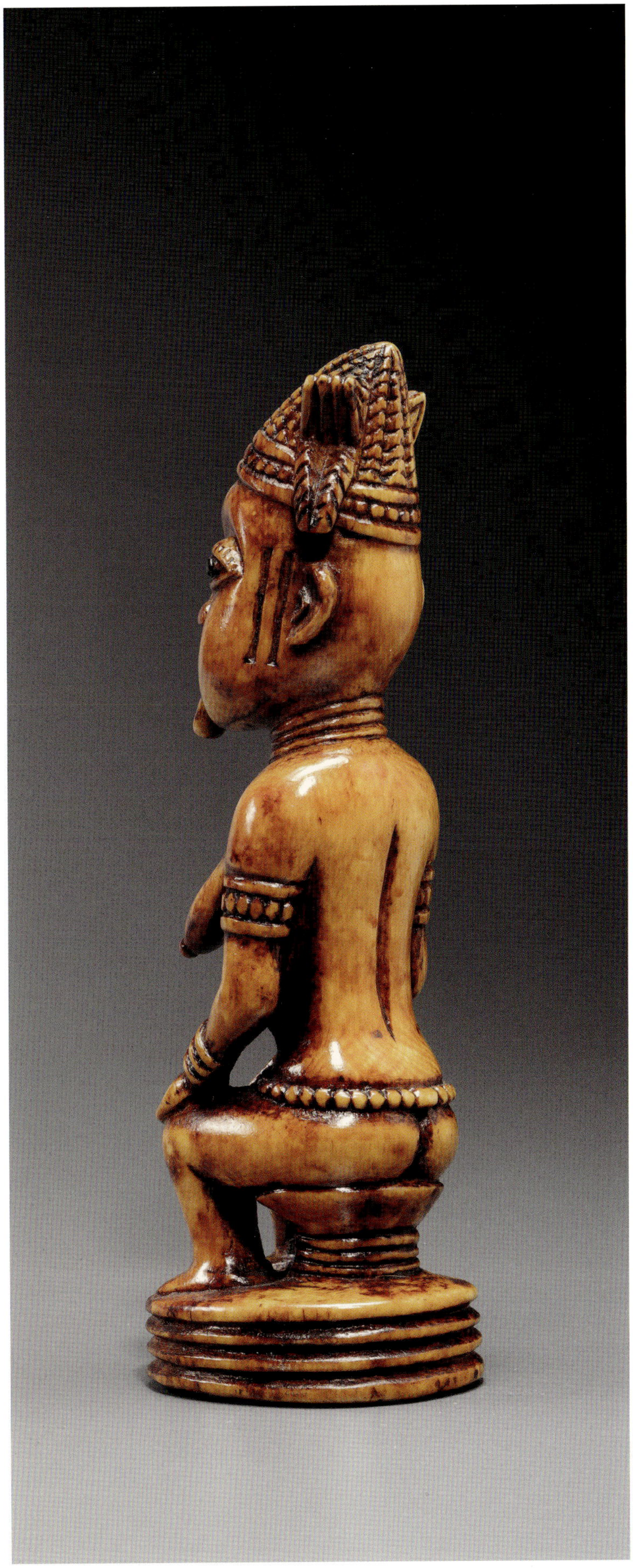

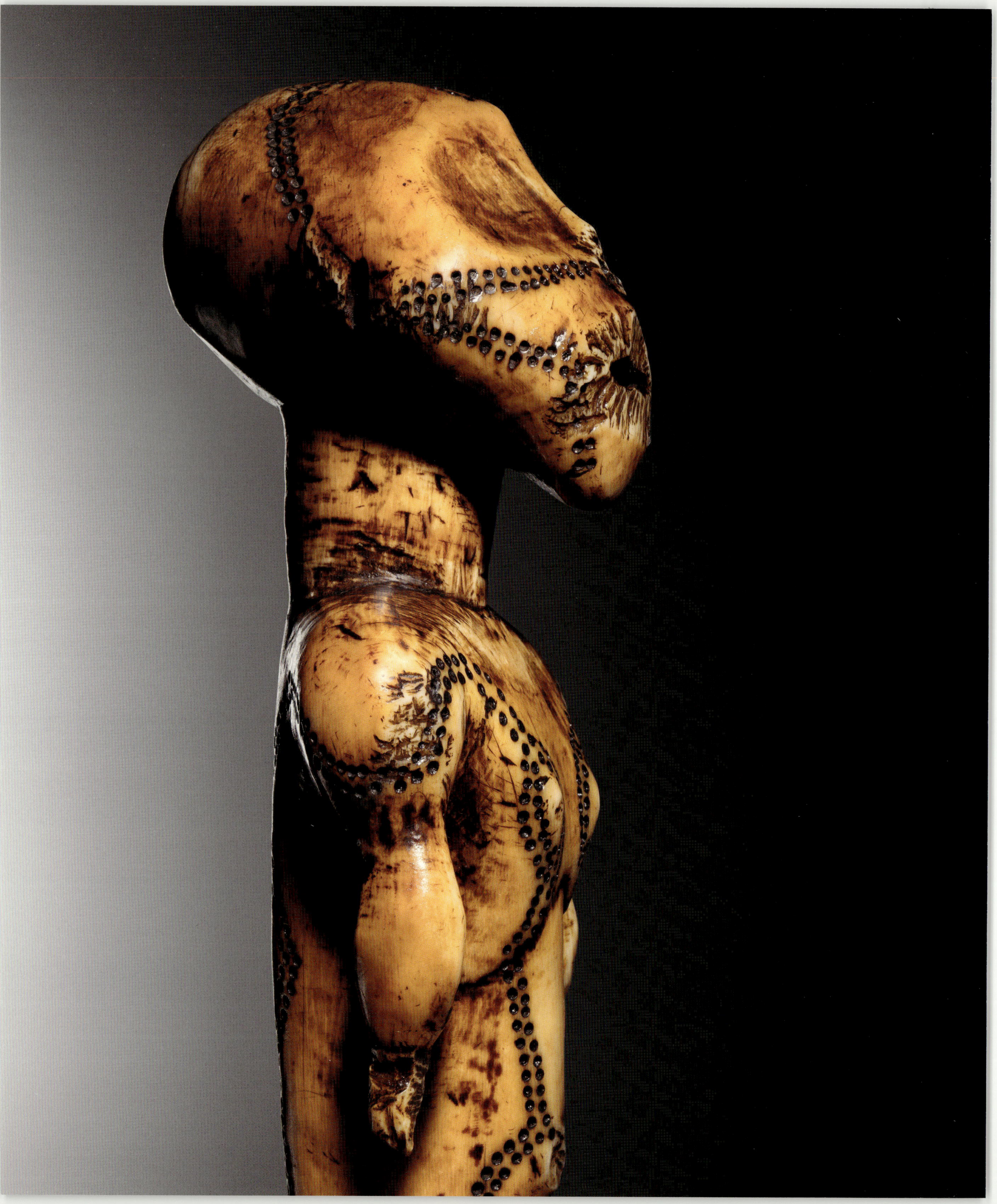

Lega statuette
South-Kivu Province, Democratic Republic of the Congo, H. 26.5 cm

The Lega have always proudly turned their backs on any attempts to centralize power; their communities were always essentially regulated by the *bwami*, an initiation society which also admitted women as the wives of initiates. There were several different grades in the *bwami* and although almost 80% of men reached the first stage, only a small proportion achieved the highest ranks, the *kindi* grade for the men and the *bunyamwa* for the women. The influence of the initiates, or *bami* (sing. *mwami*), was far-ranging and included the fields of ethics, rituals, medicine, law, and politics.
Whether masks, figurines made of wood or ivory, headdresses, or spoons, virtually all Lega art was in some way associated with the *bwami*. As soon as it was introduced into the association, each object was given the name *isengo* (plur. *masengo*). Of all these various different objects, only the anthropomorphic works were called *iginga* (plur. *maginga*), such as this exceptional ivory figure, at present on display in the Louvre.[1] It is decorated with a series of curves made up of sequences of dots that encircle the barely outlined breasts and describe graceful arabesques over the whole body, right to the top of the head. Bernard de Grunne compares it with other pieces known as the Master of Pareyn figurines,[2] all sharing the same highly naturalistic approach, which is rather unusual among the Lega, as Kellim Brown points out.[3]
However, several other traits set it apart, starting with its great size, which is extremely rare in an *iginga* ivory figure. The figure is covered in scars: on the lips, on the nose, around the navel, on the right hand and the left heel, showing that a little "flesh" has been removed on several occasions to make a powerful protective or healing charm. The absence of a patina on the head and neck suggests resin was added to cover the nape of the neck and that the head used to be adorned by a fibre or resin headdress set with cowrie shells, a sign of its important ritual status.
The figure's prognathous features, with the face upturned, the mouth open and deeply hollowed out, as well as the shape of the nose and eyes, clearly echo a *nina*-type stone head in the musée royal de l'Afrique centrale; according to M. Zographakis, who collected it in the former Shabunda Territory 1931, it copies the old way of burying high-ranking *bami* and represents "the head of a great Moami chief (*kindi*). Great *kindi* are buried upright, with the head sticking out of the ground."[4] Daniel Biebuyck corroborates this information and points out that it was hung from a bent pole stuck firmly in the ground by a liana passed through a hook attached to the upper jaw, until the deceased's head came off the body several weeks later. This funerary practice, known as *kwanga idumba*, "arrange the tomb," was designed to create a climate of harmony and to eliminate all discord.[5] The skull, *lukungu*, was then cleaned, coated with oil and powdered *padouk*, and carefully preserved by the eldest member of the deceased's lineage.[6]
These details enable us to understand how the body language displayed by these works—the upturned head and wide open mouth[7] jutting outwards—alludes to the singular funerary fate that awaits the great initiates. Just like the *bwami* bone and ivory masks, these figures and heads underline the constant presence of the foremost dead initiates among the living. [VB]

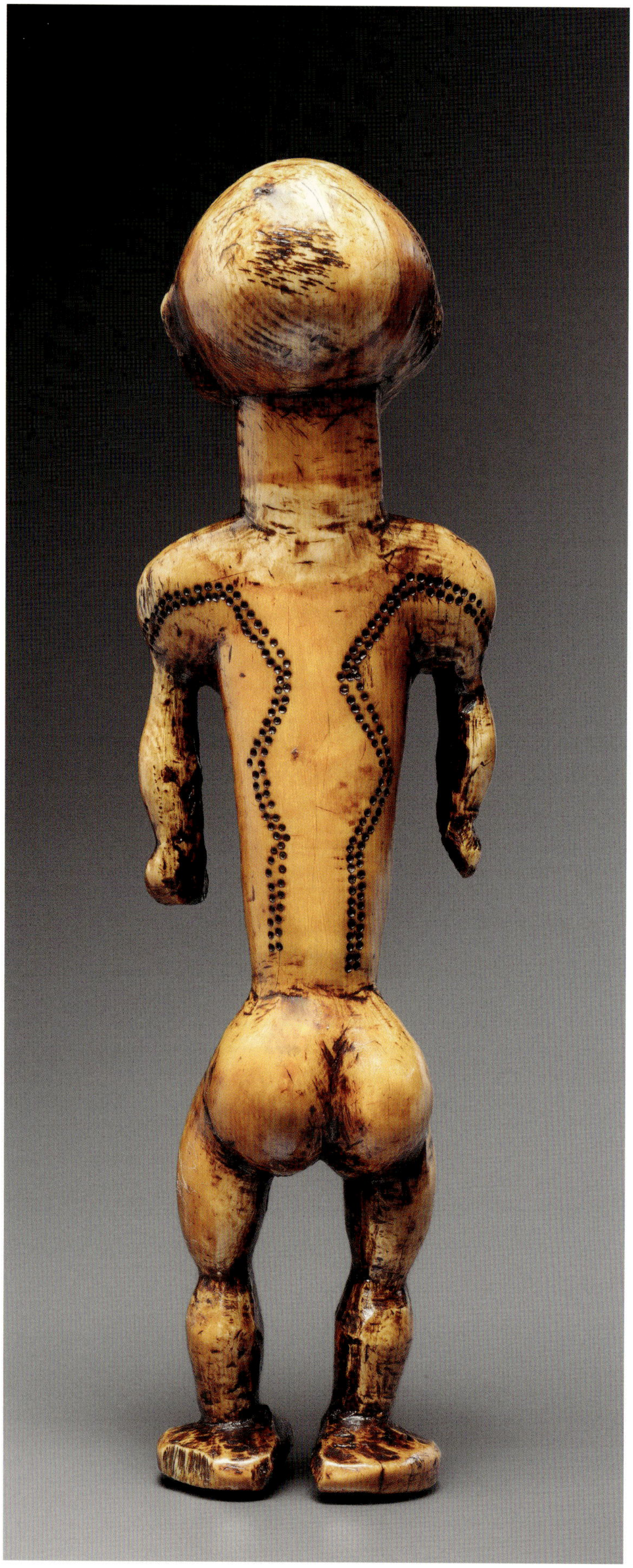

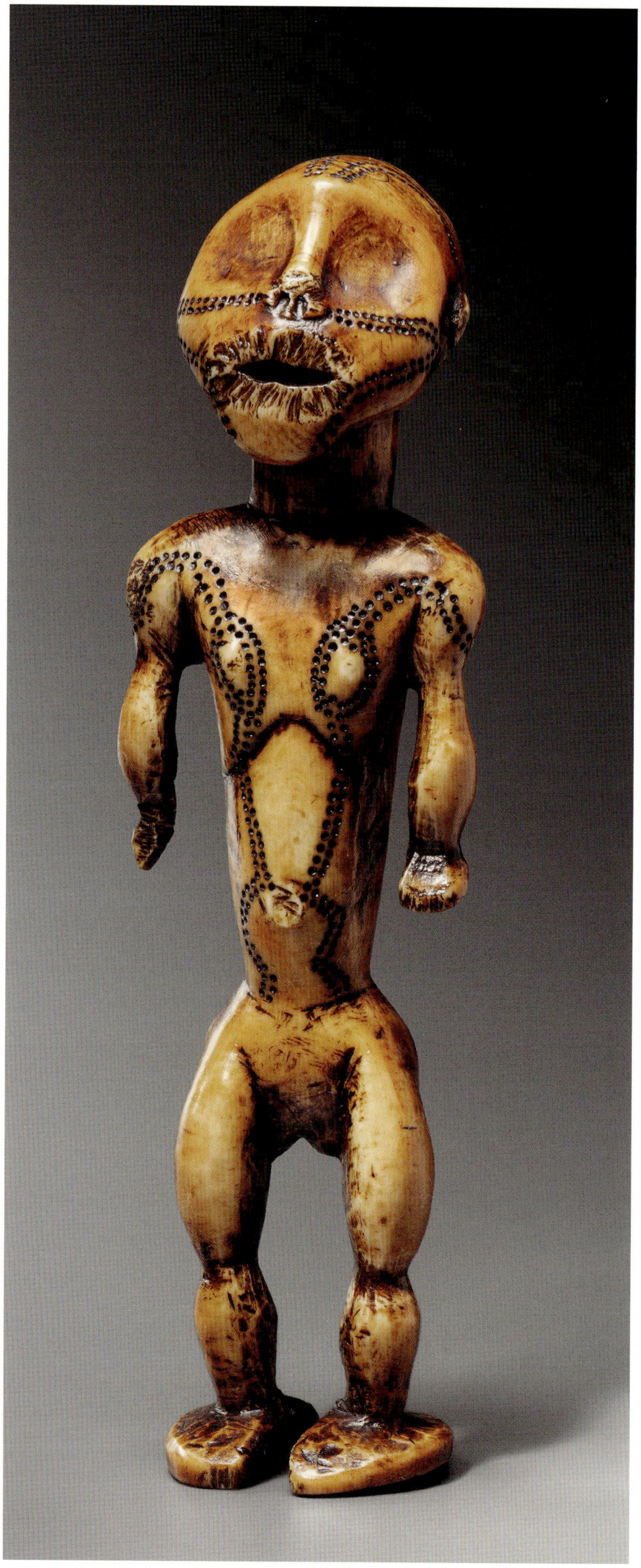

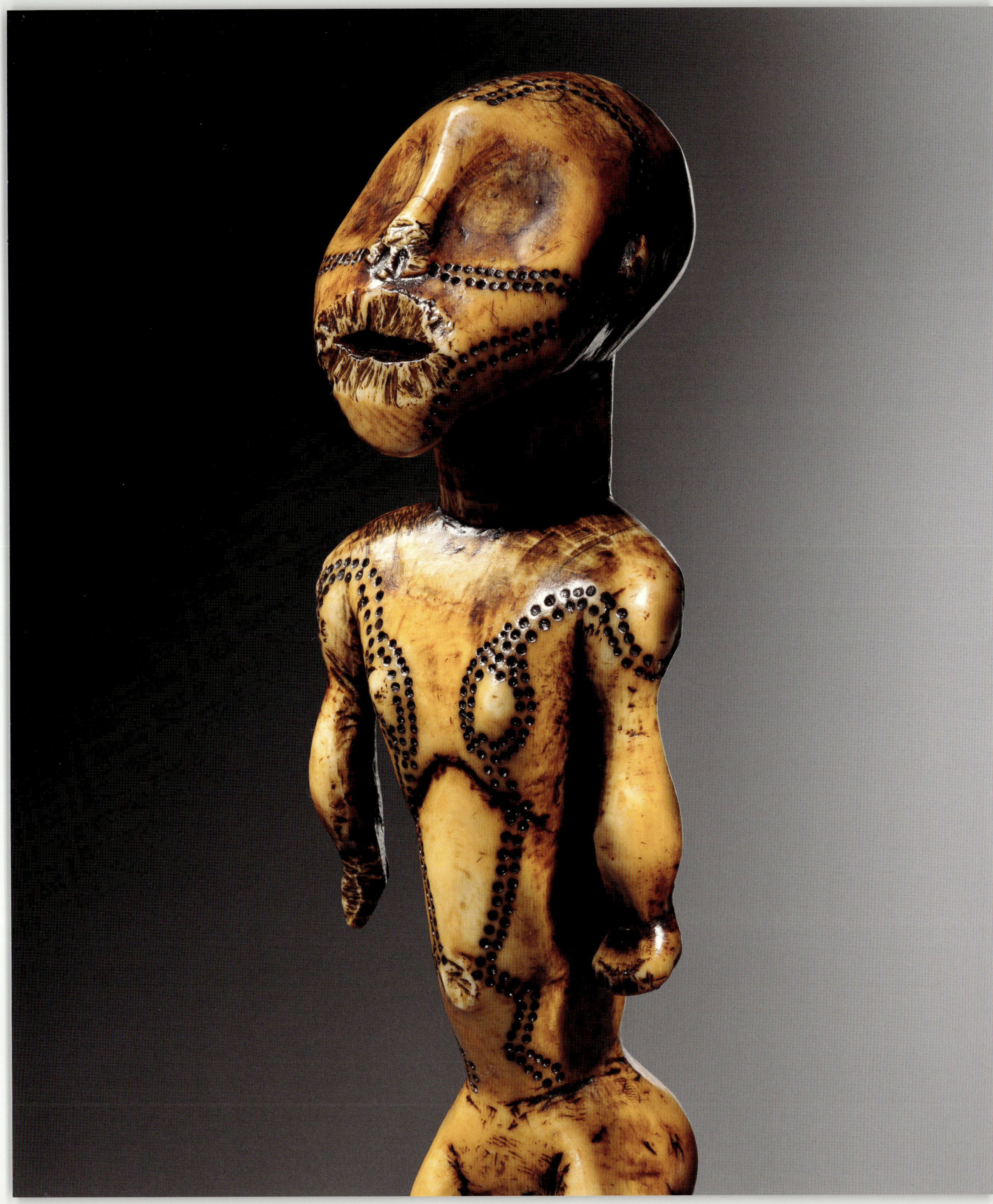

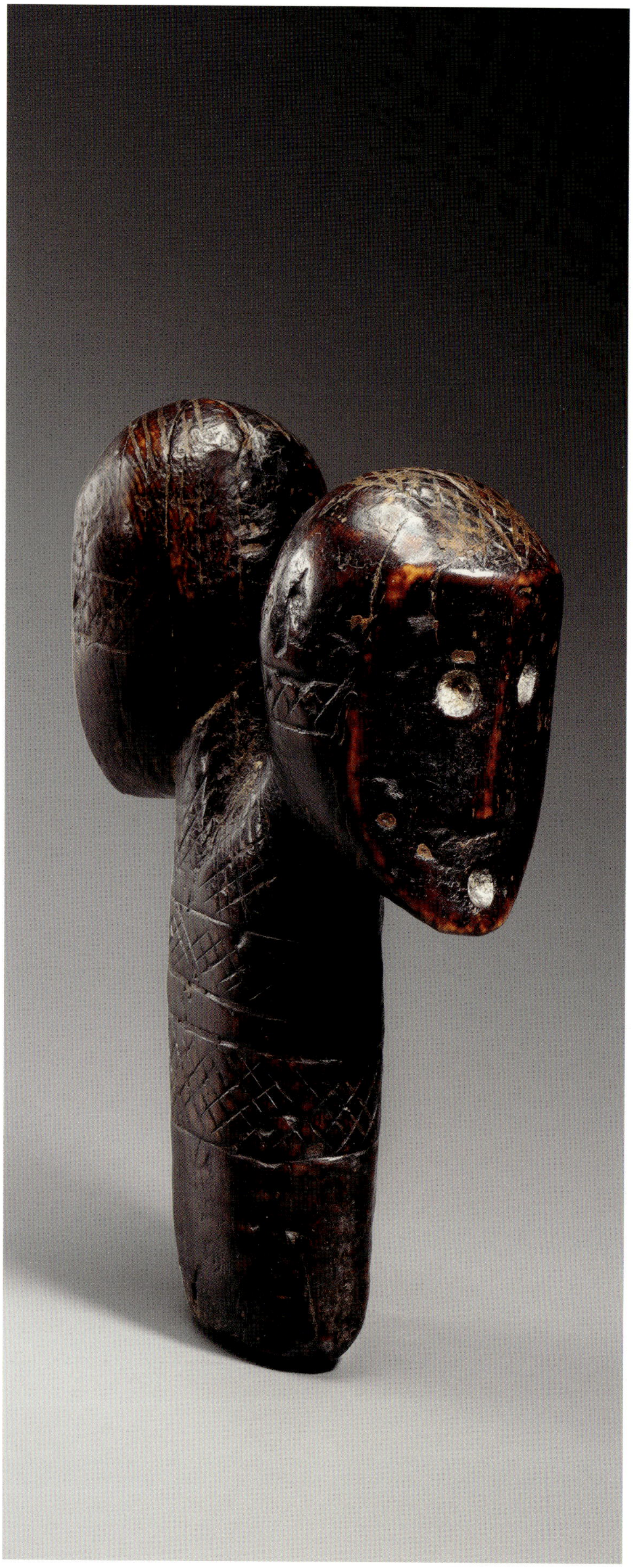

Lega Janus head
South-Kivu Province, Democratic Republic of the Congo, H. 15.5 cm

---

The massive *nina* ivory sculptures, which were the preserve of the highest-ranking initiate of a regional *bwami* lodge, often also included Janus busts or faces, as well as double-headed figures like this rather extraordinary work. Its dark patina, made of *ngula* blackened by time, reveals its great age, while the multitude of motifs decorating it is unusual in Lega art. It might be a representative of a period before the one to which the vast majority of known Lega figures belong, as Kellim Brown suggests.[1] The depiction of two figures joined to each other along their backs generally symbolises the unbreakable bond between a *kindi* initiate and his *bunyamwa* ranked wife.[2] Some of these *nina* figures were given personal names, such as *Nyeitutu*, a term applied to a woman who has performed the supreme rite with her *kindi* spouse"[3]; this epithet shows how these important figures could indeed symbolise a couple of initiates who had reached the highest rank. [VB]

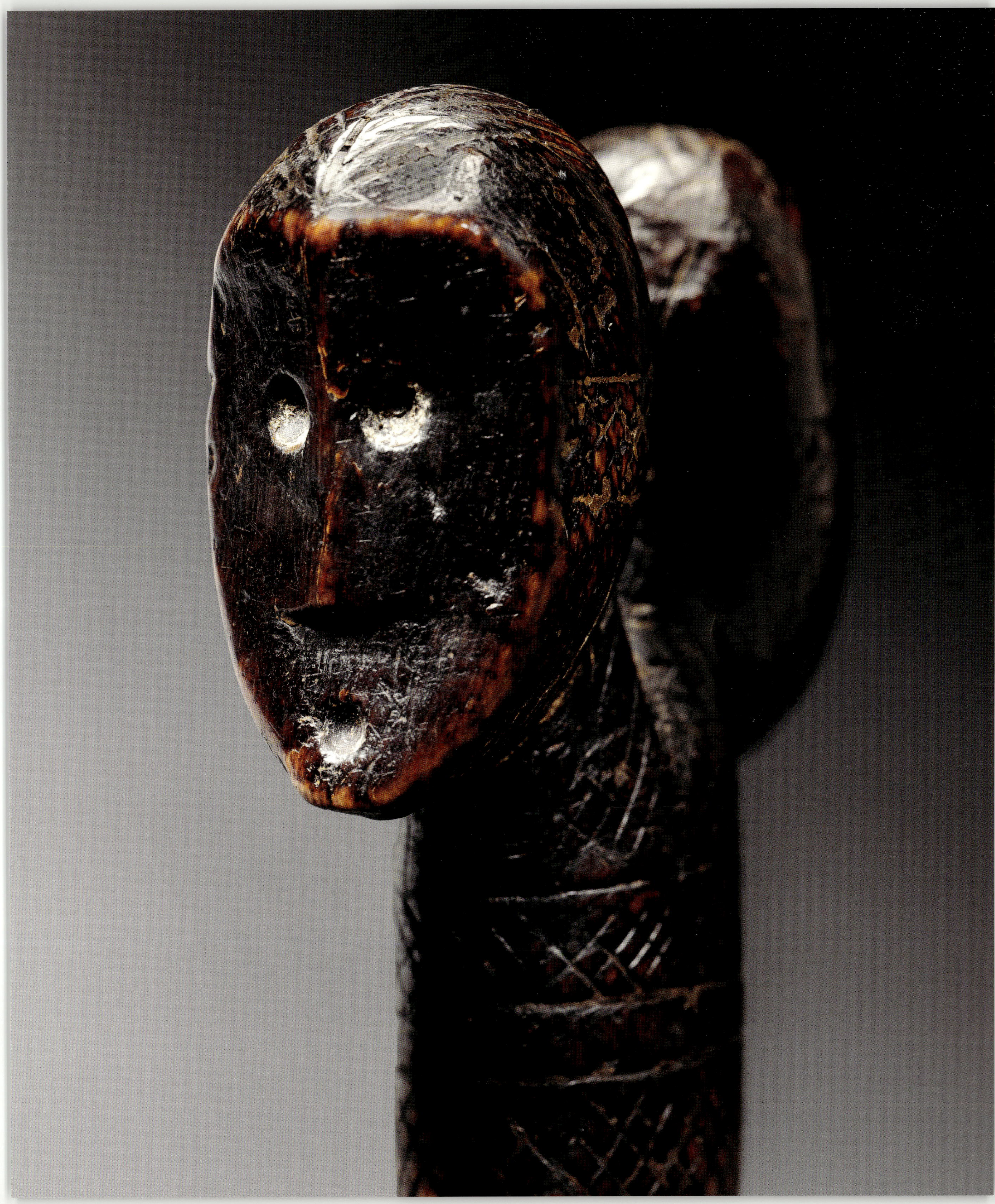

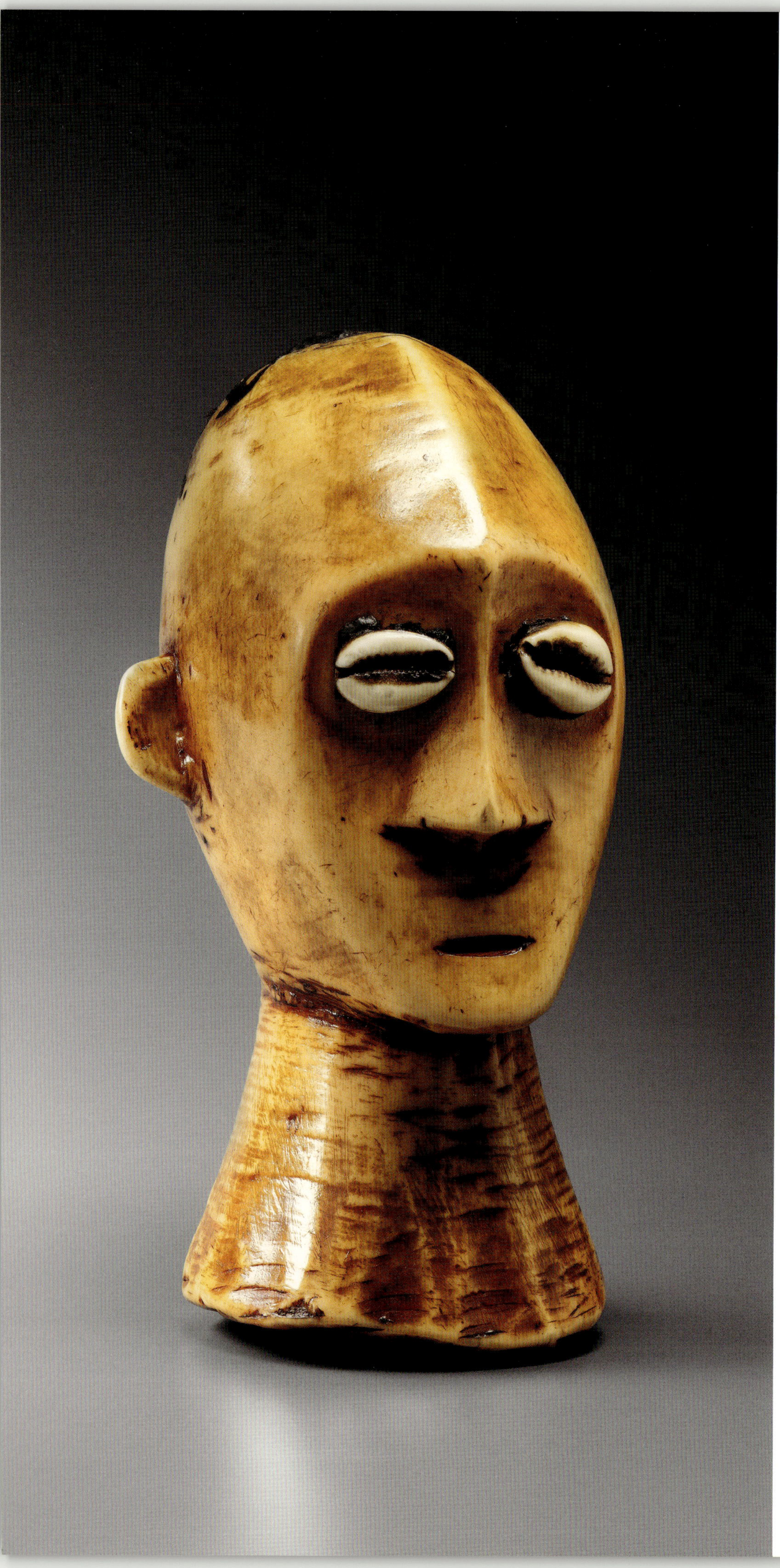

Lega head
South-Kivu Province, Democratic Republic of the Congo, H. 18.5 cm

A number of ivory, or more rarely stone, sculptures stand out from the various anthropomorphic *maginga* figures used during *bwami* rites. They are much larger and also frequently, but not exclusively, take the form of a head, as in this case. This kind of figure was known as a *nina*, "the life-giving mother," sometimes with the added epithet *mukota*, "high-ranking initiate."[1] It would be given to the highest-ranking initiate by all the members of a regional lodge gathered together. Traces of dark residual material and the difference in the patina at the top of the head are the tell-tale signs that this head used to be adorned by a headdress made of fibre or resin, which would undoubtedly have been studded with cowrie shells, a headdress figuring a *bwami* cap. [VB]

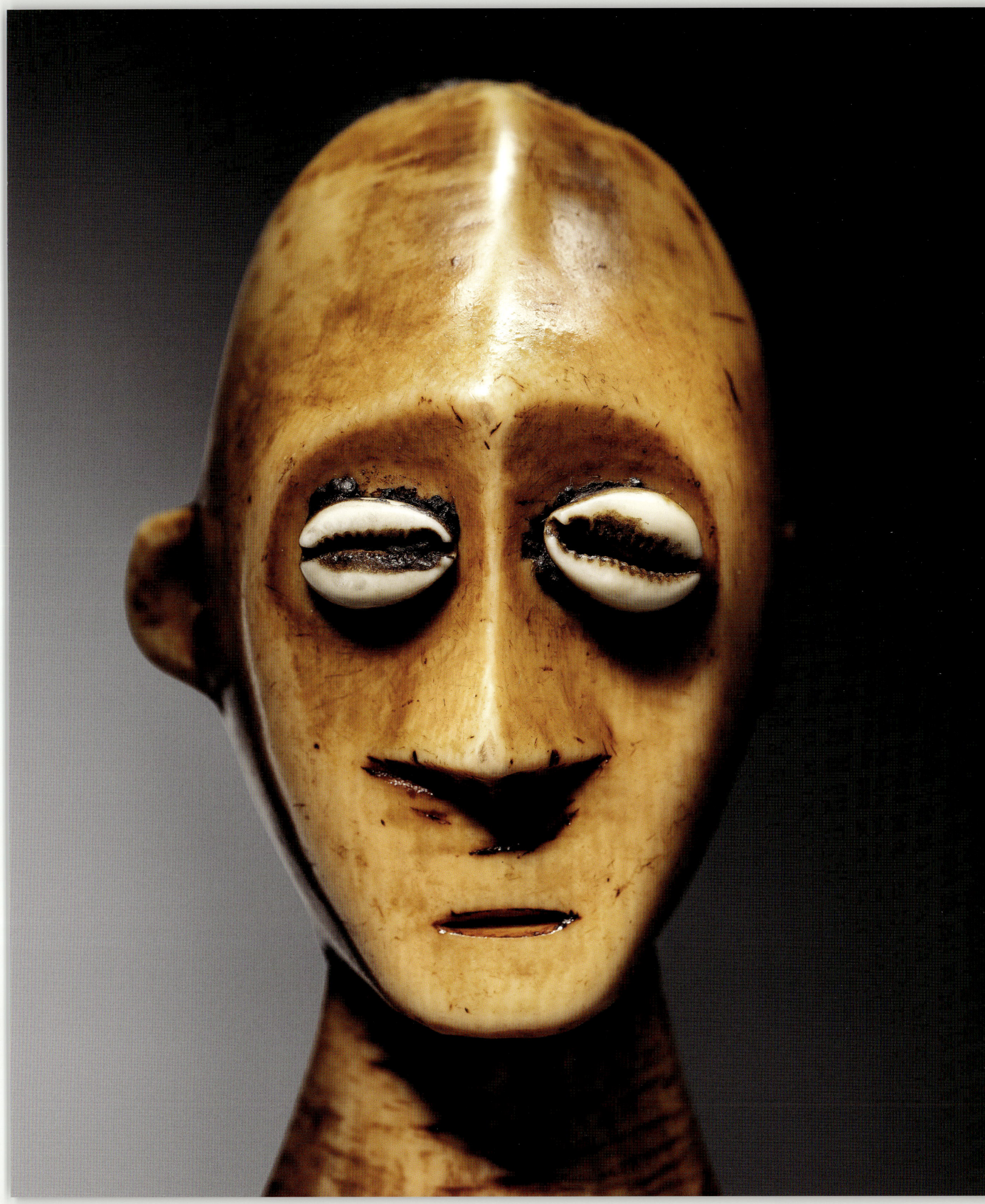

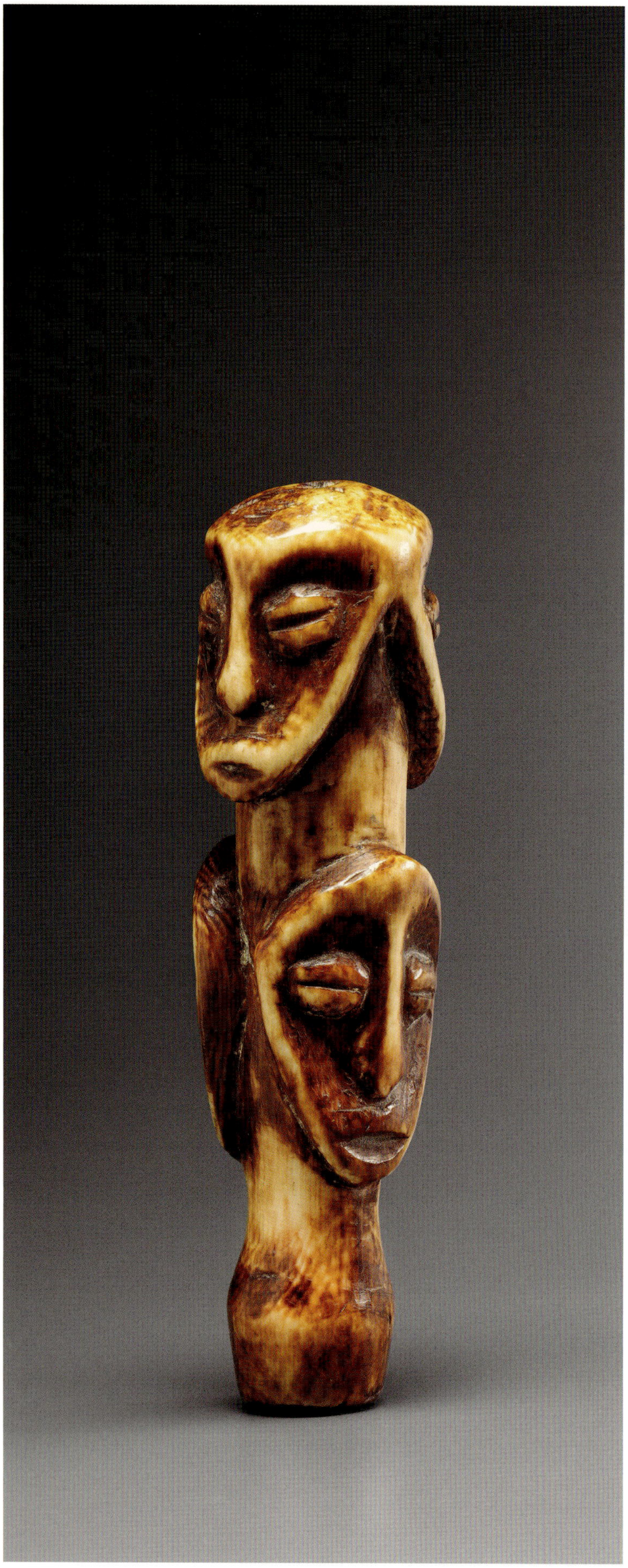

Lega head
South-Kivu Province, Democratic Republic of the Congo, H. 12.5 cm

Every anthropomorphic *inginga* figurine used in the *bwami* depicted a figure designed to illustrate the society's moral code and would be brought out during initiation rites. However, it is not always a simple matter to establish exactly what a given figure was meant to stand for judging just by its formal characteristics. This particular multiple-headed figure belongs to a group of Lega *maginga* figures that are actually the easiest to identify. This is Sakimatwematwe, "Multiple-headed Lord." Endowed with four faces looking in different directions, this figurine represents a great omniscient initiate who will never be caught out because nothing escapes his ever-vigilant eyes. This *iginga* would be taken out during initiations to the highest grades, accompanied by the aphorism "Sakimatwematwe has seen with one eye Elephant on the other bank of the large river."[1] [VB]

Pinda statuette
Angola, H. 11 cm

Little is known about the Pinda. They live in an area to the north of the river Cambalo in Angola, near the coastal town of Sumbe (the present-day region of Southern Kwanza). Although José de Oliveira Ferreira Diniz recorded their existence on the map accompanying his 1918 book *Populações indígenas de Angola*, he published no details about them. In 1998, Marie-Louise Bastin described a fine and rare set of ivory works attributed to the Pinda that are now in Lisbon museum. The miniature in the Weill Collection has a splendid patina that has developed over the years, enhanced by the addition of red "tukula" (*Pterocarpus*) powder. Limited to just a torso, the small female figure has powerful stylized shoulders, a ringed necklace and a hairstyle with several bunches held in place by headbands. There is a hole in the top that would certainly have housed a relic. [MC]

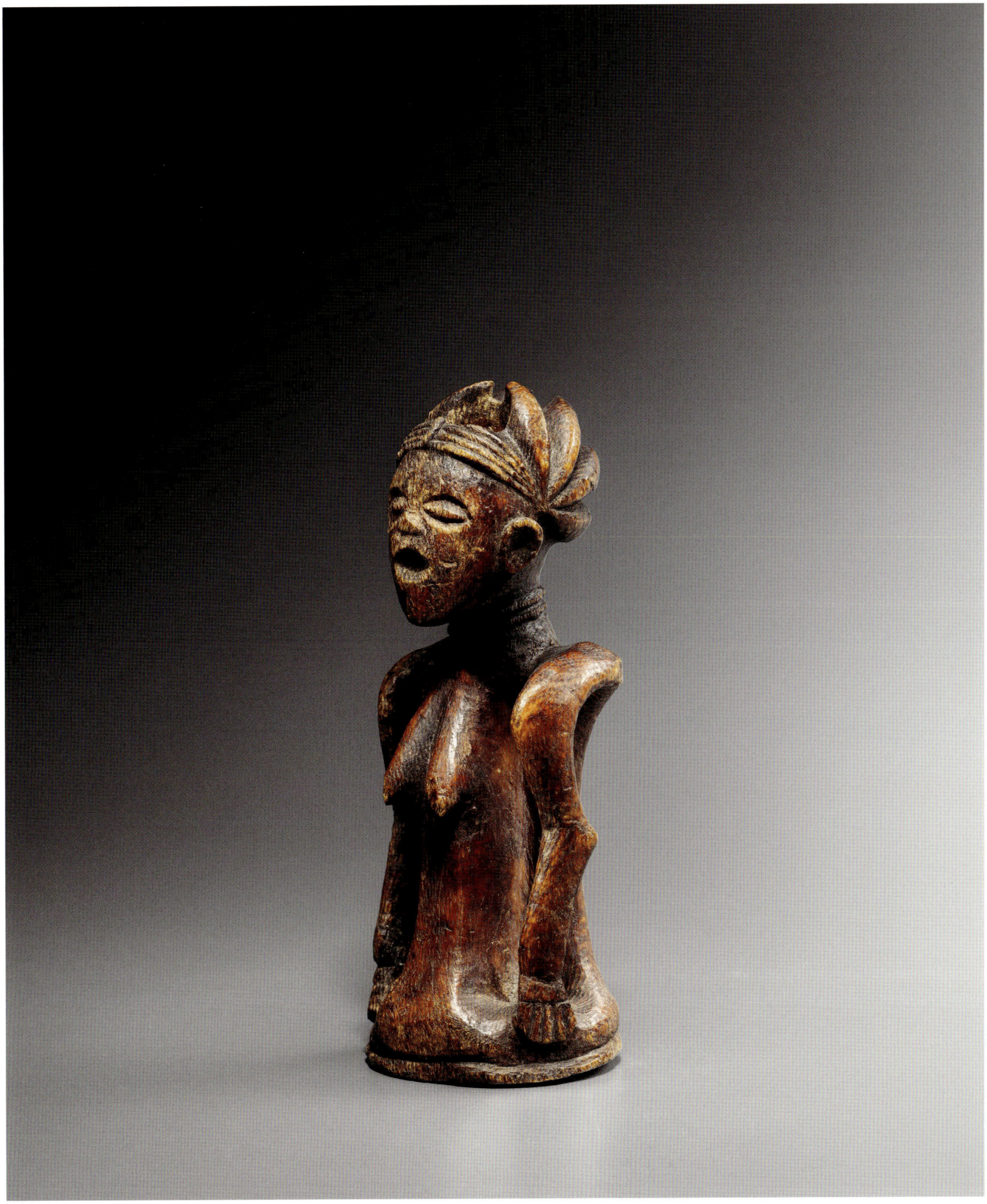

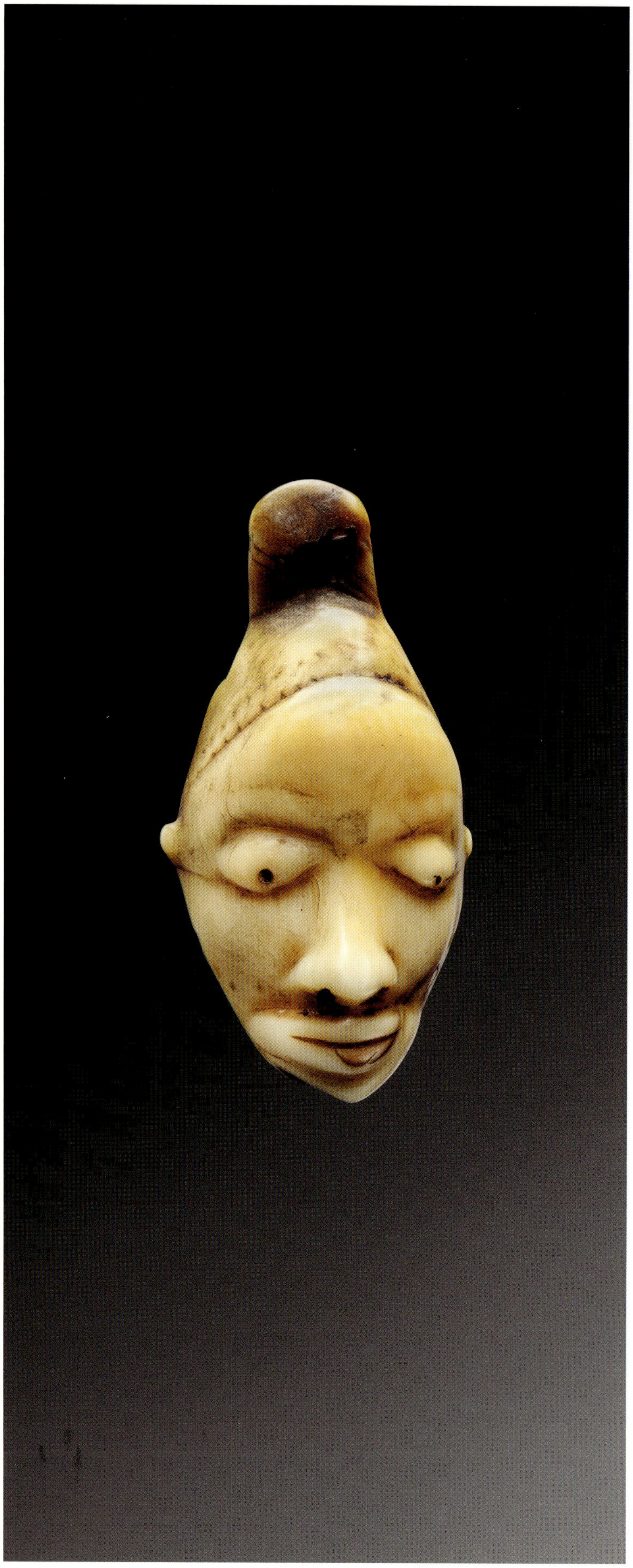

Pende pendant
Kwilu Province, Democratic Republic of the Congo, H. 5.5 cm

At the celebrations marking the closing of the *mukanda* circumcision camps, young initiates would be ritually presented with an ivory *gikhoko* (plur. *ikhoko*) pendant representing one of the numerous *mbuya* masks that would dance during the festivities.
This wonderful specimen is adorned with a crown headdress surmounted by a small diadem. This type of ornament is unusual for the central Pende and resembles the one that surmounts the *pota*, *kinjinga*, and *munyangi* masks of the eastern Pende.[1] This peculiarity, along with the long face, which is more emaciated than in most *katundu*-style *ikhoko*, suggests the piece was fashioned to the east of the central Pende, close to the territory of the eastern Pende.
This fine-featured face probably depicts Pota, one of the masks that according to Léon de Sousberghe were reproduced in the form of *ikhoko* pendants because they were "believed to be powerful healers."[2] Pota is a complex personage, who according to several Pende researchers[3] is supposed to have been created by the husband of a late-bearing first-time mother in order to celebrate her restored fertility. The male figure mimes his spouse, who, on the brink of her menopause, dreams of the recipe for a magic potion that will make her conceive.
A hole was made in this pendant well after it was created in order to replace the horizontal hanging mechanism that gradually got worn away, then broke altogether after constant friction, thus providing further evidence of the object's great age. [VB]

Yaka/Suku pendant
Democratic Republic of the Congo, H. 14.5 cm

Discovered by Pierre Loos at the end of the 1970s, this exceptional ivory pendant does not have its equal in any collection (Felix M.L., *White Gold, Black Hands. Ivory Sculpture in Congo*, vol. III, 2012, p. 93, ill. 018a). It was probably made by a Yaka or Suku artist and depicts a generously proportioned woman, with one hand offering her left breast and the other covering her groin. A zoomorphic figure sculpted on the top of her head probably represents a totemic animal. A rectangular hole with a lid has been dug into the figure's back and probably contained relics or magic substances. [MC]

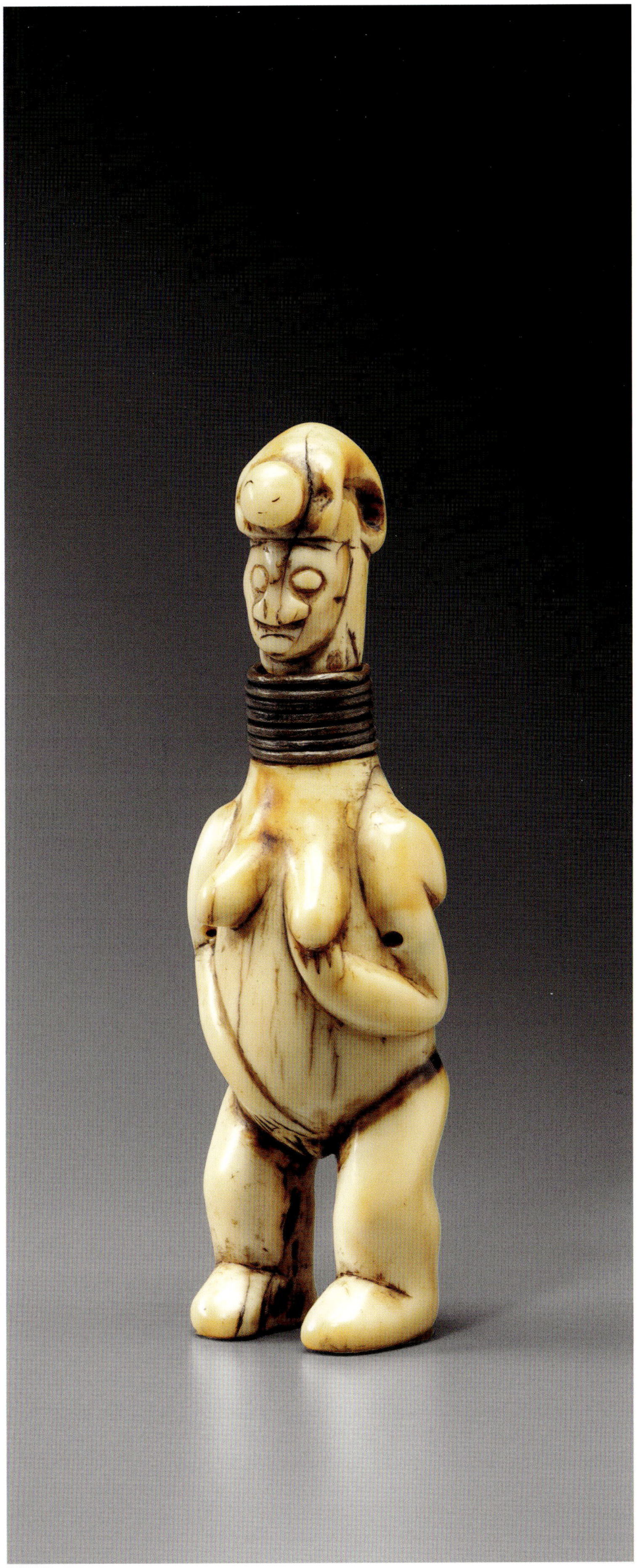
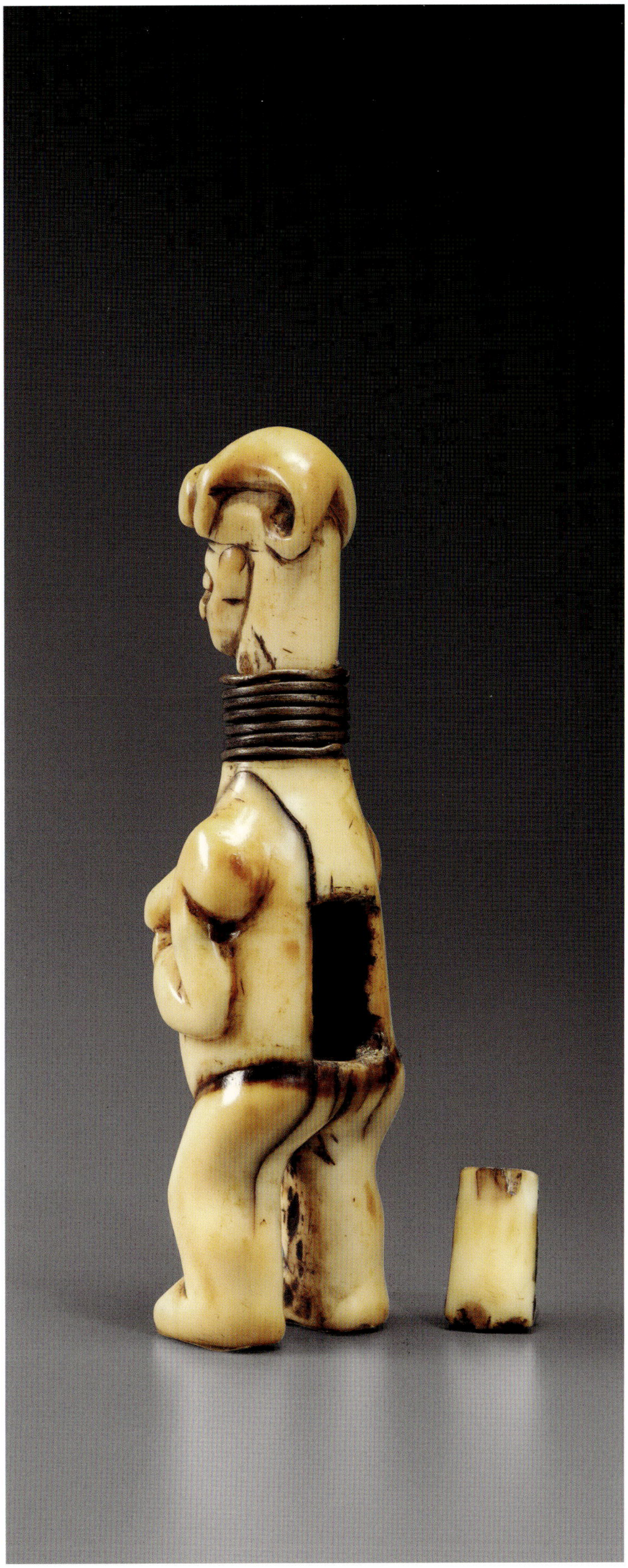

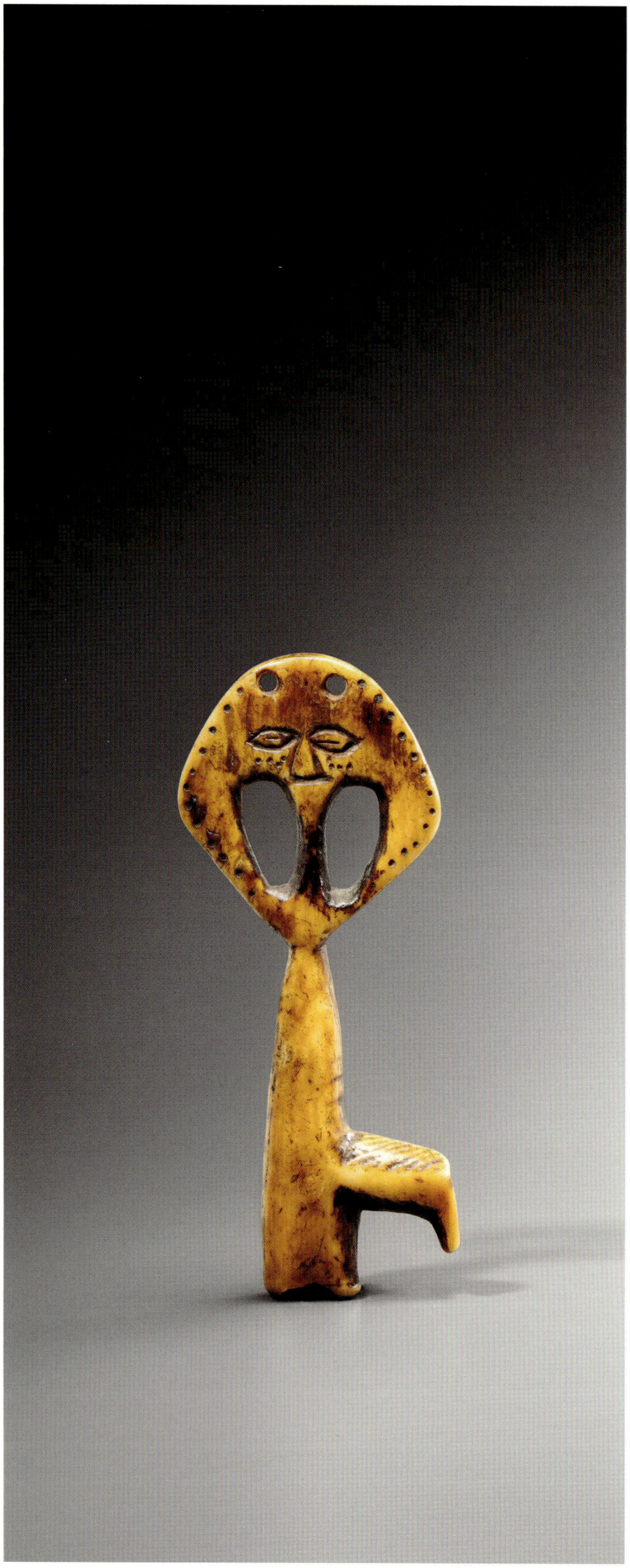

Two Kwilu whistles

Mbuun or Pende whistle
Extreme northwest, Kwilu Province, Democratic Republic of the Congo, H. 9.5 cm

Pende whistle
Western Pende, Kwilu Province, Democratic Republic of the Congo, H. 11.5 cm

---

The role that ivory whistles used to play in the Kwilu region depended essentially on their shape, on the number of finger holes they had and, in whistles with a single hole, on the type of melodic interval between the two notes they produced.

These two whistles have just one finger hole and as a consequence they produce just two notes. The melodic interval between these two sounds is thus the determining factor as regards the function the two whistles can perform. In the case of an interval of a minor third, known as an "imperfect consonance" (3 semi-tones), the whistle might accompany dances and songs, for example during the *minganji* or *mbuya* masked circumcision dances. On the other hand, if the melodic interval was a minor second, "dissonant" (2 semi-tones), the aerophone was more useful for the "spoken" language used particularly by hunters, amongst each other or with their dogs.[1]

A U-shaped whistle in the Tervuren museum has been analysed and the interval was found to be a major second; it can therefore be deduced that it was used mainly in "spoken" communication. A comparative analysis of the ethnographic material collected from the Pende as a whole leads to the conclusion that these U-shaped, "dissonant" instruments played a role during the enthronement of a new chief, when battle-hardened men, wearing a *minganji* mask, left on an expedition to capture an enemy who would be sacrificed for the occasion.[2]

The right one here is prettily decorated with zig-zag motifs. Circular patterns that are still visible but completely covered by a patina produced by the passing of time reveal the instrument's great age and its constant use in more day-to-day activities, such as hunting.

As for the Mbuun figurative whistle on the left, the form will provide the necessary clues. This whistle actually belongs in the so-called "key" whistle category: they look like a key whose stem is hollow. Examining the sound emitted by several Pende key whistles in Tervuren shows that the *figurative* specimens, most of which are head-shaped, produced minor thirds. The present example, decorated with a face, was therefore probably present during the masked dances, with which the Mbuun, like the Pende, were very familiar. [VB]

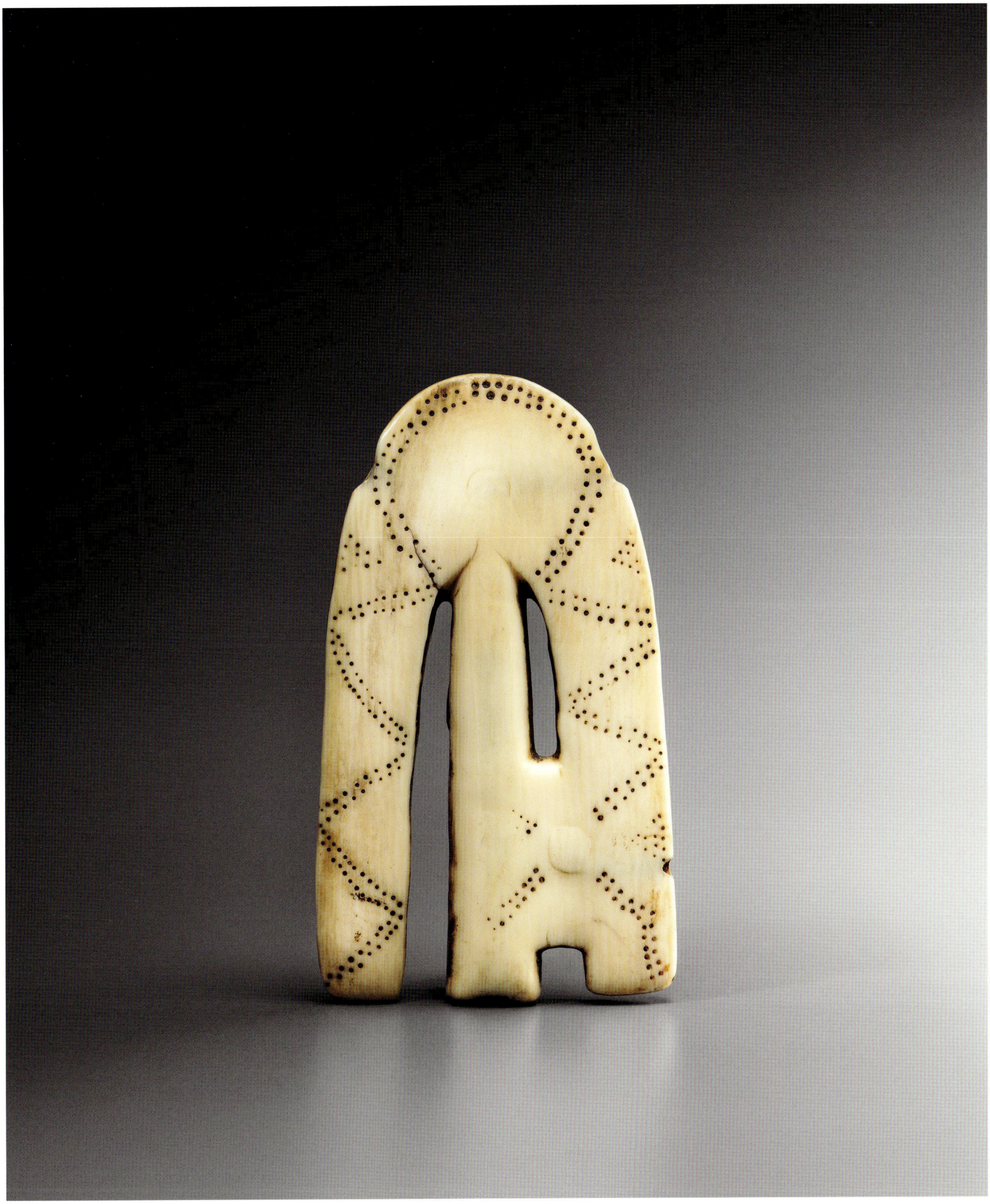

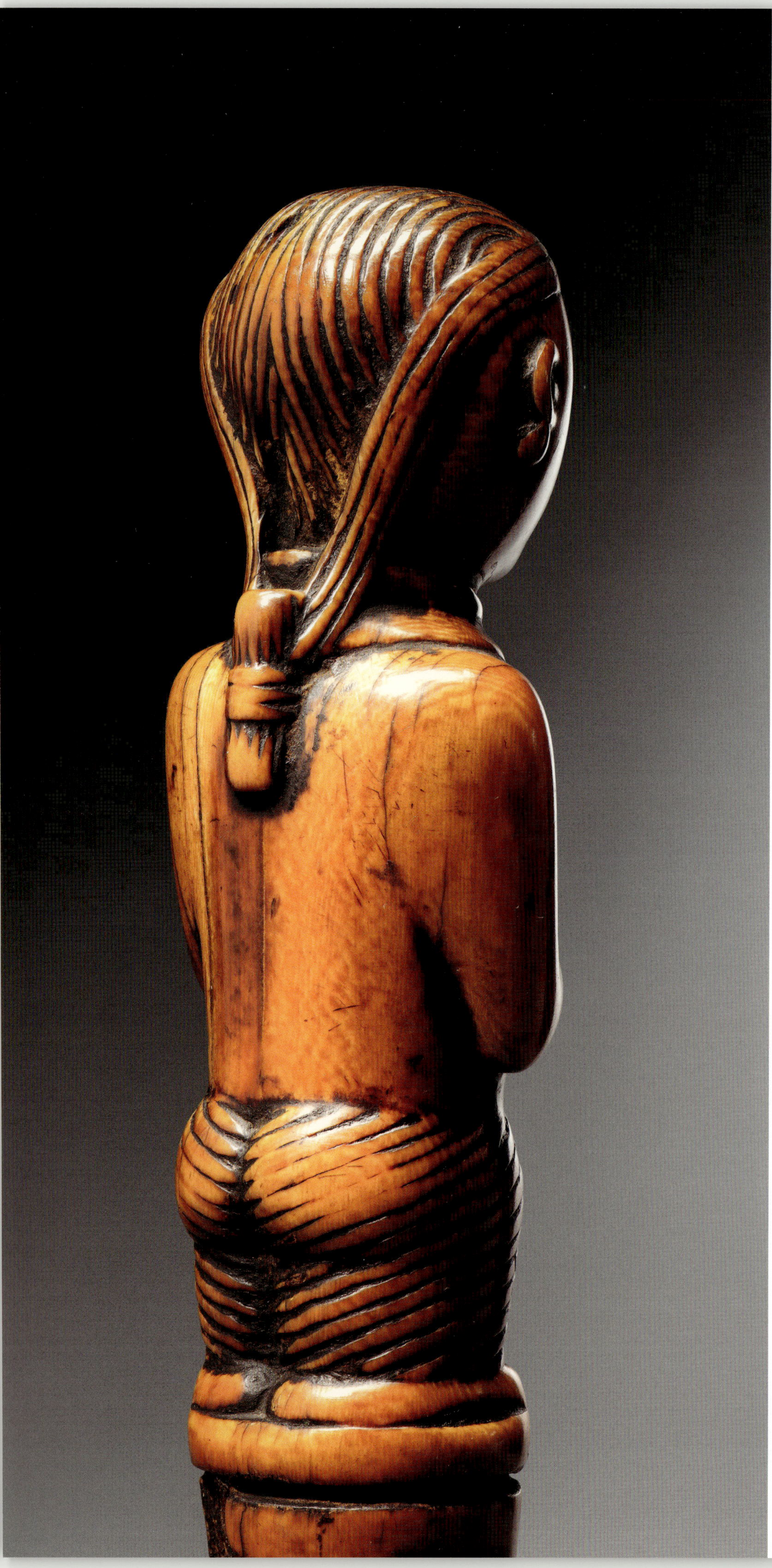

Kongo prestige emblem finial
Democratic Republic of the Congo, H. 18 cm

This figurine, which used to act as the handle of a *mvwala* prestige staff, is a real goldmine of ethnohistoric information for those who can decipher its details, a task that Marc Felix has admirably performed. While the figure's sex is uncertain, some for example seeing a woman carrying a manioc pestle, the author suggests that this stick with a striped and rounded tip, looks much more like the war clubs used in Angola in the nineteenth century. In this case, the figure depicted would be a war chief, a theory that is further reinforced by the wholly male handling of the long, pleated (imported) cloth, separating both legs.[1]
[VB]

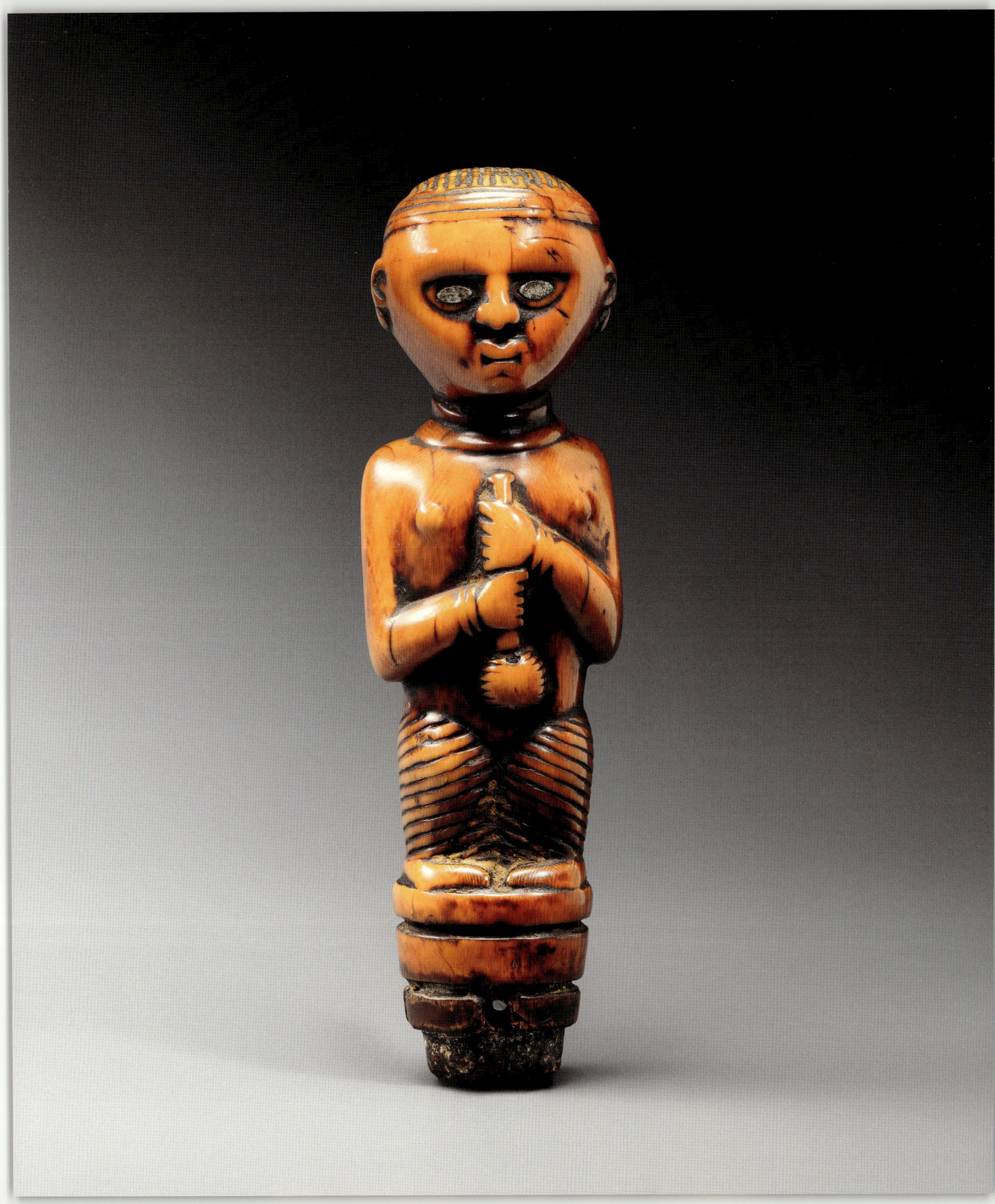

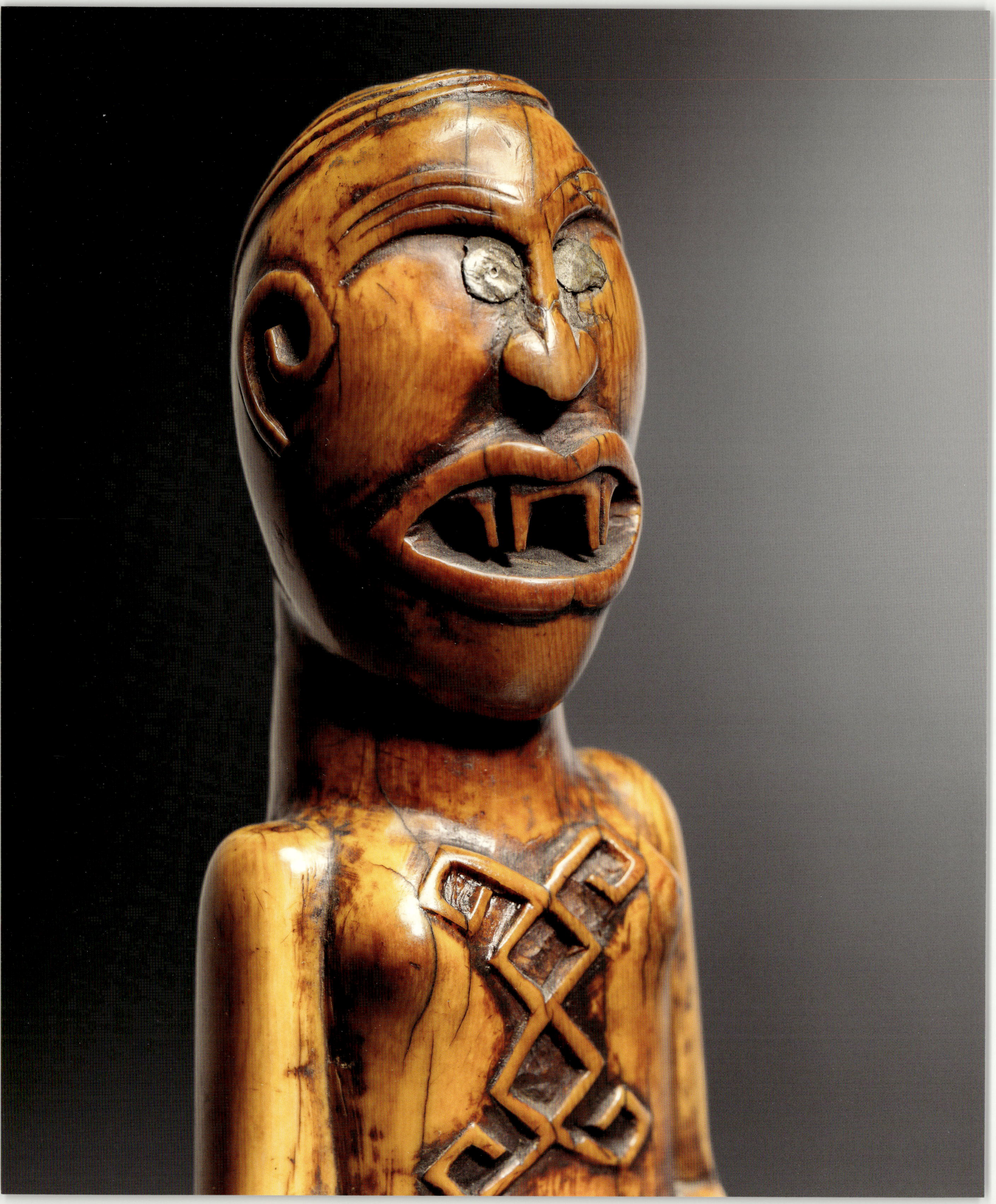

Kongo prestige emblem finial
Republic of the Congo or DRC, H. 15.5 cm

This female figure is one of a group of ten or so works that seem to have been made in the same workshop or by the same artist. They all depict a figure with a wide-open mouth displaying long teeth filed down to a point, lending their faces a threatening and rather feline appearance. Four of these ivory figures with filed teeth, including the present specimen, are distinguished by their very unusual gestures: they are portrayed kneeling, with their forearms held out in front of them, hands open and palms turned upwards. Some authors have interpreted this as a gesture of offering, but I agree with Marc Felix's view that this is an example of a woman in an act of supplication and giving the little statues the charming name "supplication ladies."[1]

This figurine used to adorn a prestige emblem—the top of a staff, the handle of a flywhisk or the pommel of a sword or dagger—as is substantiated by the hole that goes right through the base of the object and which still contains an iron nail.[2] There is no way of knowing exactly what kind of object this carving graced, but it must have belonged to a king, a chief or a dignitary of some kind, or a ritual performer. Whether emblems of power or symbols of ritual status, these eloquent signs legitimized in everyone's eyes the holder's political entitlement or confirmed his knowledge of arcane initiation practices.

The emblems of political power of a titled man (or woman) were generally conferred upon him at his enthronement. According to Lutete Esaya, one of Karl Laman's collaborators, a chief's investiture in northeastern Mayombe would take place in a sacred enclosure known as *lulombe*, which was also the cemetery where all the previous chiefs were buried. In the same space there would also be a *mbalala* tree, which provided the wood from which the new chief's *mvwala* staff would be sculpted. It was also there that the *nkisi nsi*,[3] an important protective charm, was buried and reactivated at every investiture; on this occasion the new chief was coated with white paint and he would then roll around on the sacred soil, thus absorbing the powers of the spirits of the earth. He then laid down his newly forged "sword of power" (*mbeele a lulendo*). Possession of this ceremonial sword gave the power to order certain people to be executed. However, the notable who had to carry out the sentence actually used another such weapon, the *mbeele ya makenda*, "the beheading sword." Both these weapons might be adorned with an ivory figurine, just like the *mvwala* staff.[4]

The *nkisi nsi* charm was made up of natural ingredients and was the symbol of life, the *mbeele a lulendo* sword was associated with death, and the *mvwala* staff ensured social harmony. [VB]

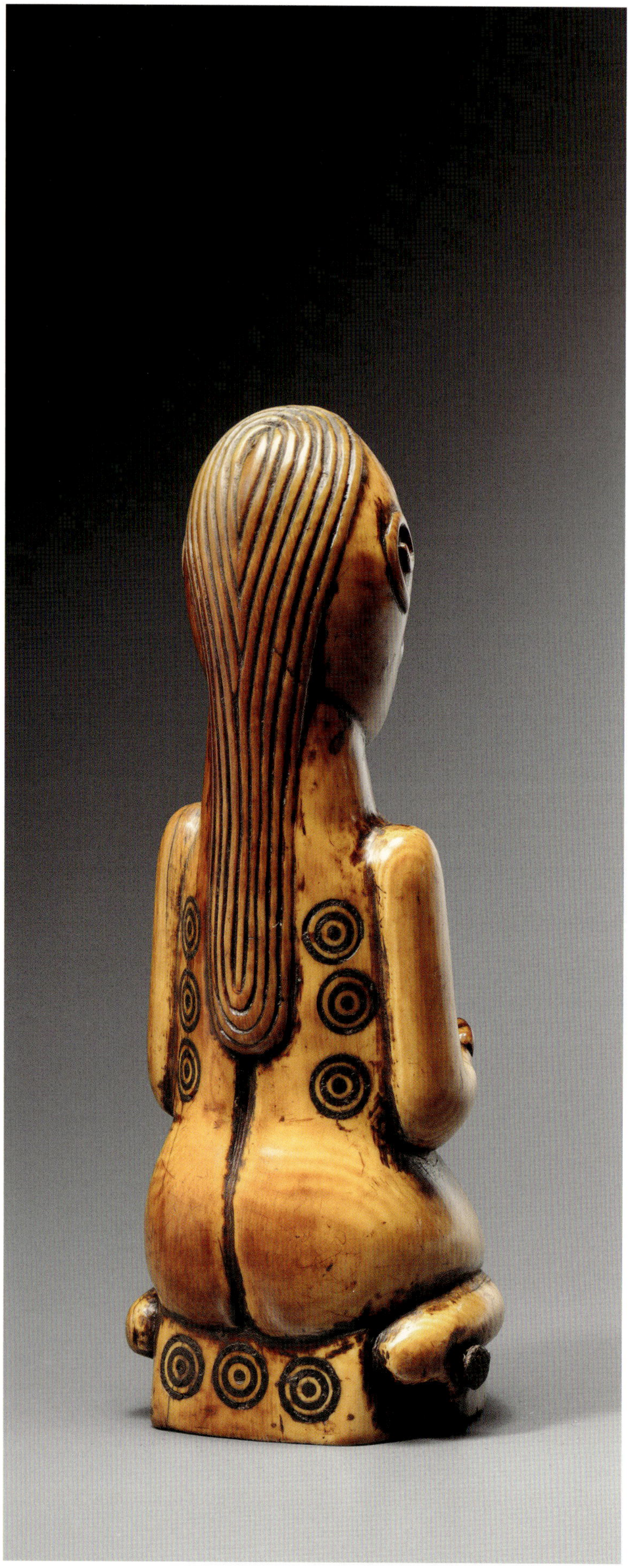

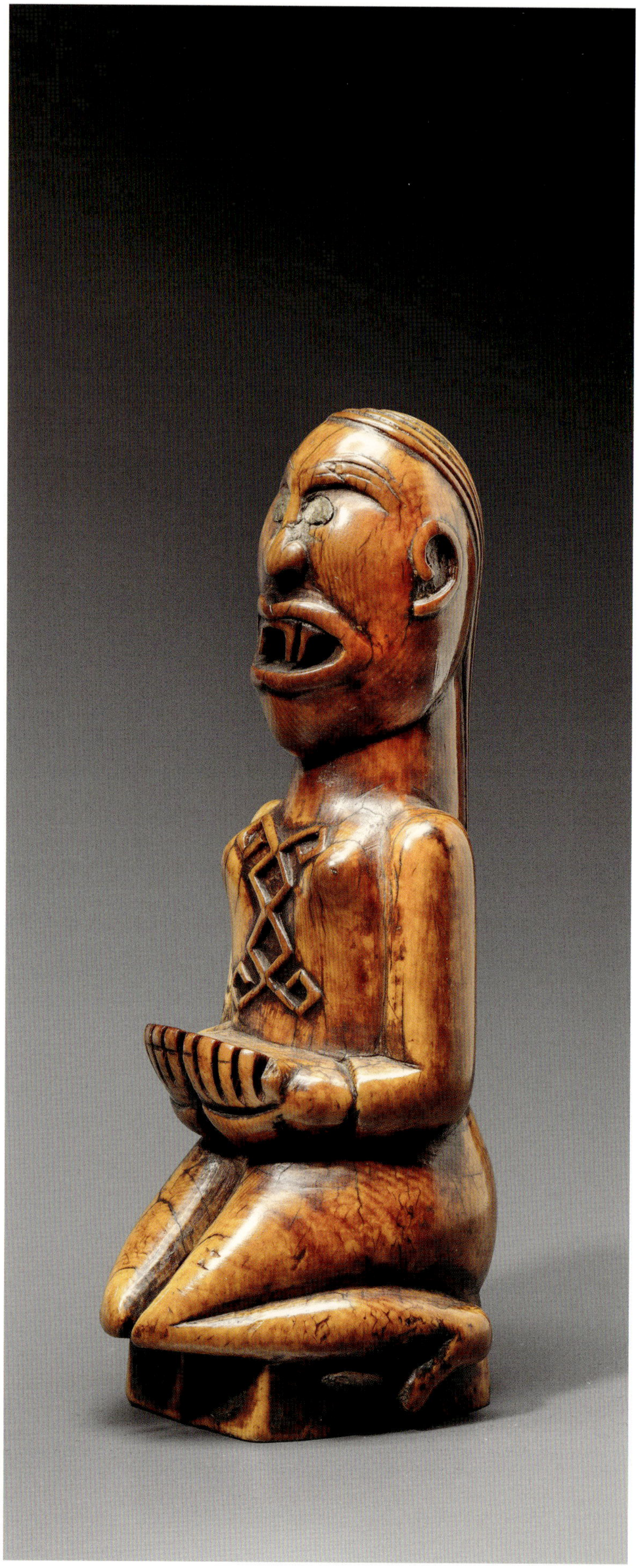

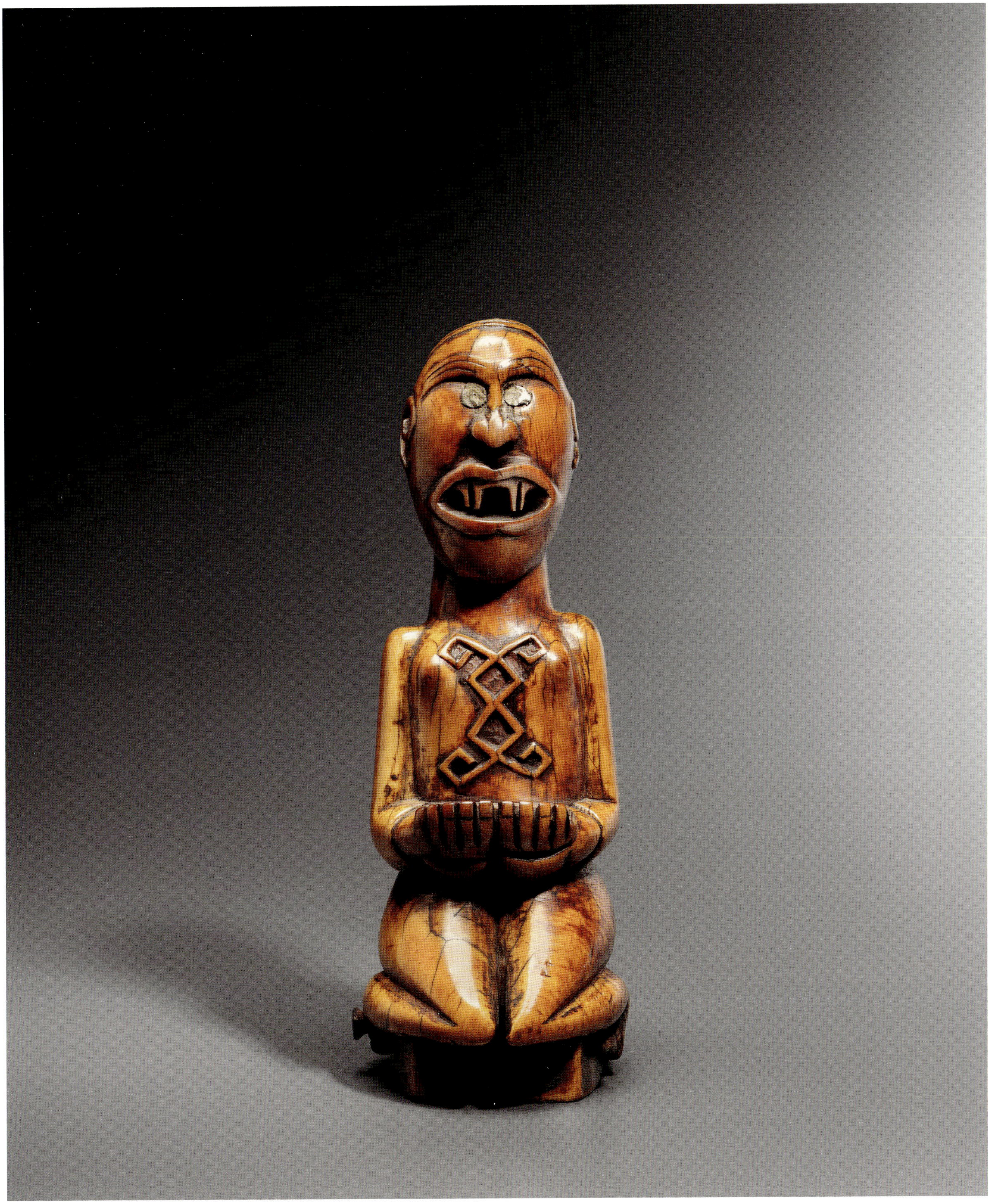

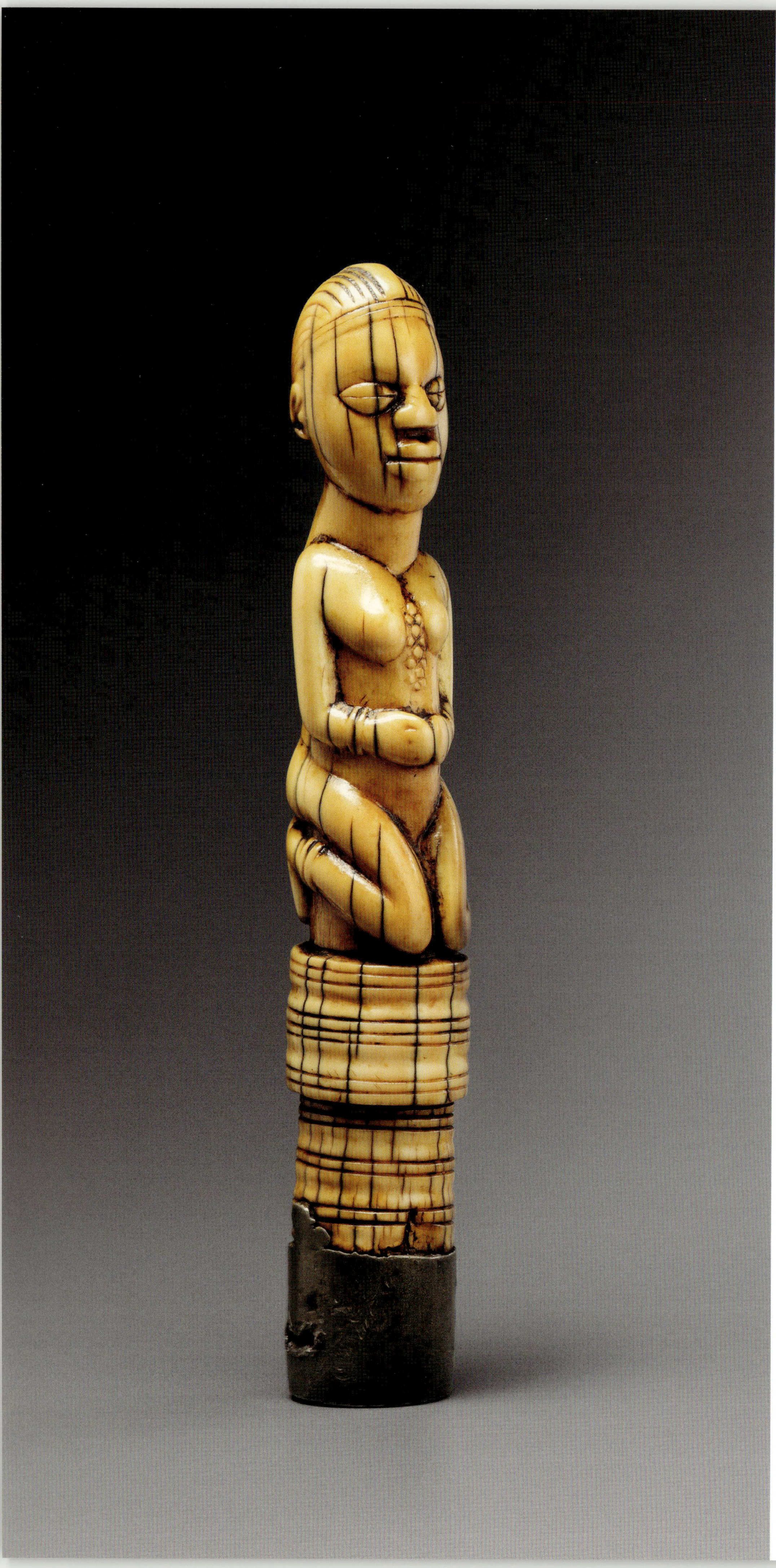

Kongo prestige emblem finial
Republic of the Congo or DRC, H. 20.5 cm

This female figurine used to adorn the top of a *mvwala* prestige staff, an emblem reserved for chiefs and certain performers of rituals. Its chest and back are decorated with scarifications. The *mpu* cap and the bracelets and anklets she wears indicate that this was an important dignitary.
Since the Kongo are matrilineal, the female figures fitted to the tops of the staffs usually symbolise the original ancestor, who ensures the fertility of the entire clan, but may also represent a powerful woman in her own right. In northeastern Mayombe, women could attain the *kayi* stage just below the full status of chief and in consequence possess a *mvwala* staff.
[VB]

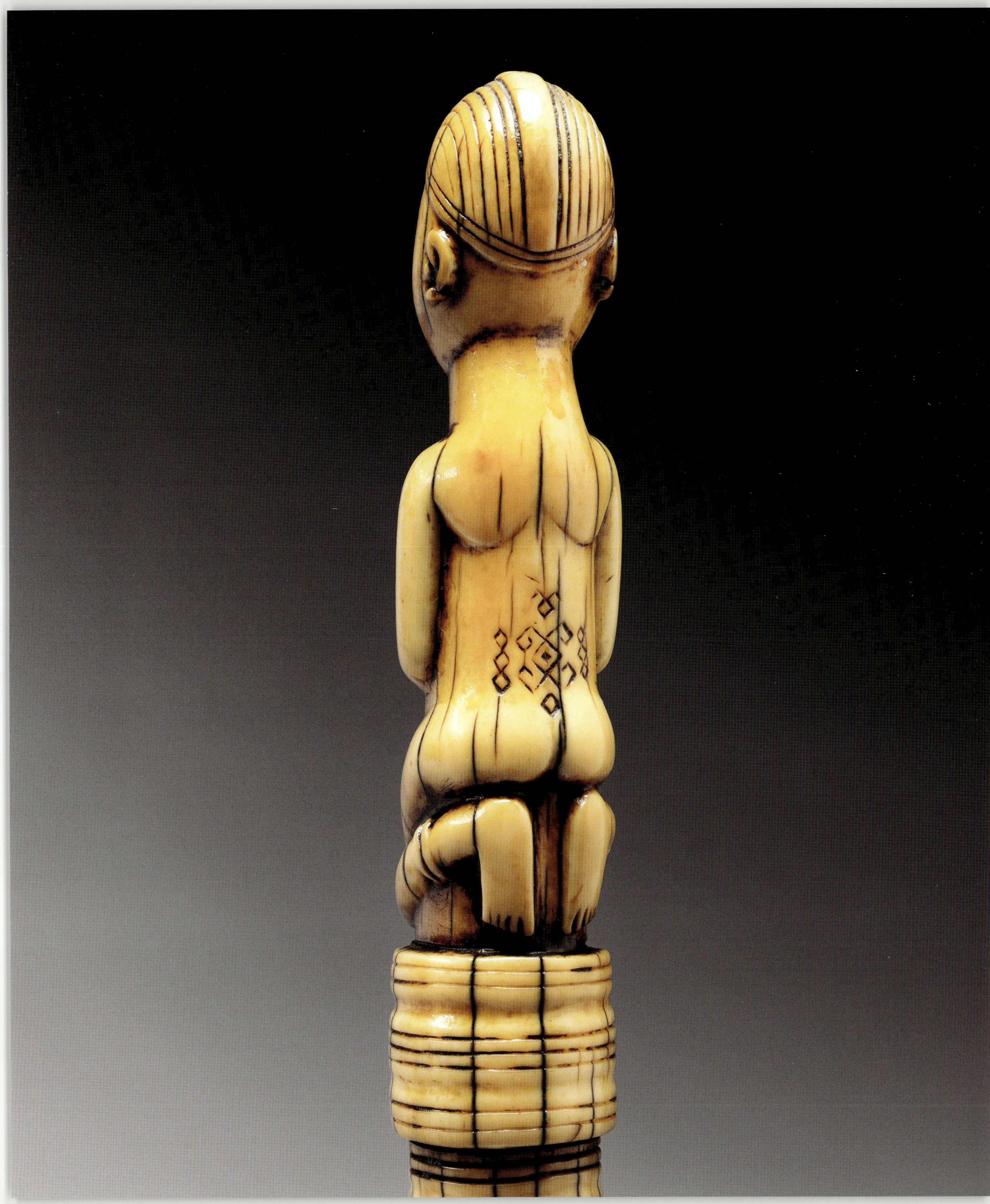

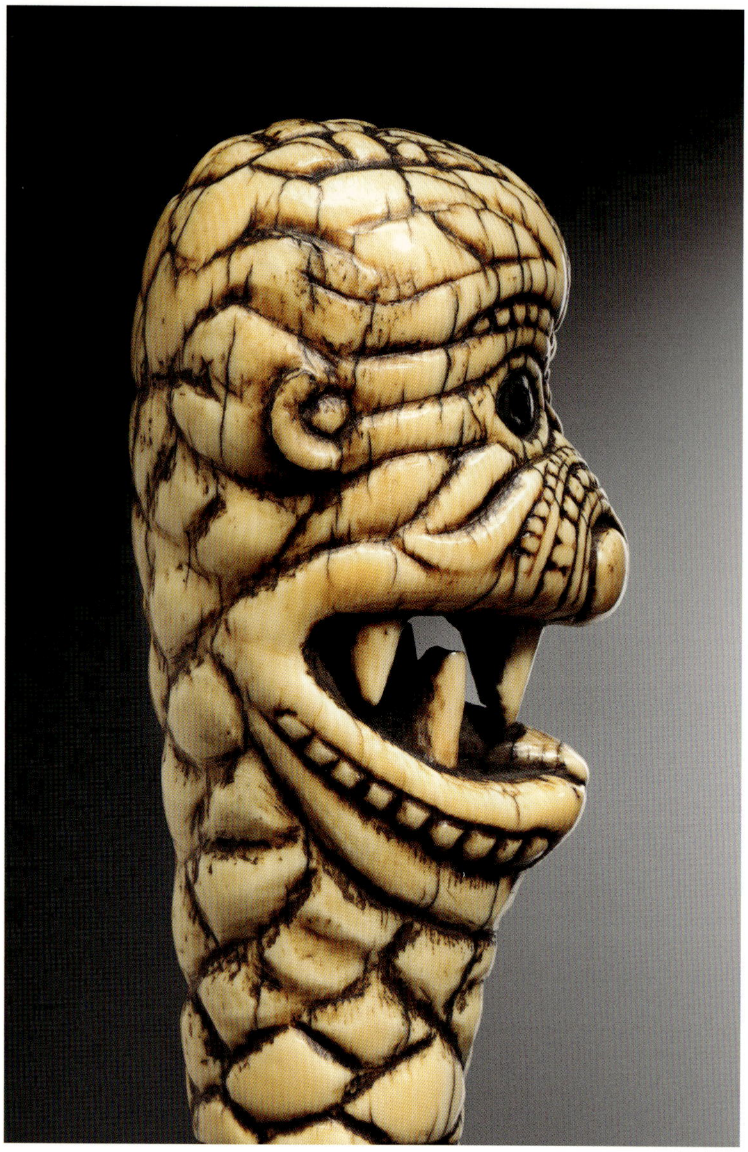

Kongo prestige emblem finial
Democratic Republic of the Congo, H. 12 cm

The total absence of big cats in the Lower Kongo explains the extreme rarity of this motif in this region's art. Only four examples are known to exist in the entire body of ivory sculpture. The first is a statue formerly in the Paul and Ruth Tishman Collection and now in the National Museum of African Art (Smithsonian Institution, Washington, inv. no. 2005-6-33) and depicts a human body with a lion's head. The second and third are reproduced in *White Gold Black Hands* de Marc Leo Felix (Felix M.L., *White Gold, Black Hands. Ivory Sculpture in Congo*, vol. II, 2011, pp. 184–85, fig. 904 and 907). Lastly, the fourth is the subject of the present entry. This type of ivory used to decorate prestige objects, such as sceptres, trumpets, staffs, flywhisks, swords, etc. Most of these have become detached from their original housings and there is now no way of knowing how they were used. According to M.L. Felix, Kongo artists were certainly inspired to adorn their regalia with lion heads by the pommels on eighteenth- and nineteenth-century European swords (see Felix M. L., *Ibid.*, fig. 906). [MC]

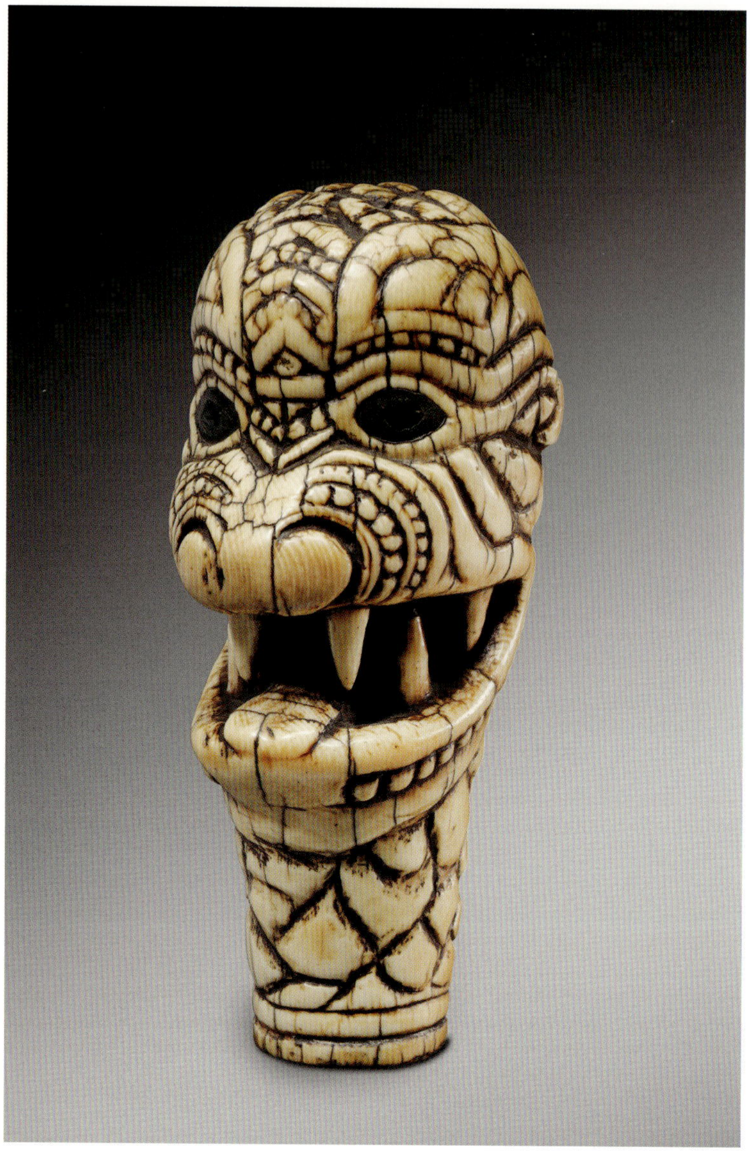

Kongo prestige emblem finial
Republic of the Congo or DRC, H. 13 cm

This statuette used to adorn a prestige emblem. However, there is no sign of jewellery or scarification on the figure; only the mitre-shaped headdress alludes to the fashion among the Mayombe Kongo in former times. Seated in a highly asymmetrical, albeit very graceful casual pose,[1] this lady seems to be looking up at the sky. The sculptor has very skilfully incorporated the left breast in the shoulder, a detail that is only noticed when the figure is seen from the front. This is quite evidently the work of an imaginative artist, who is confident and skilled enough to break free of the conventions imposed by tradition. [VB]

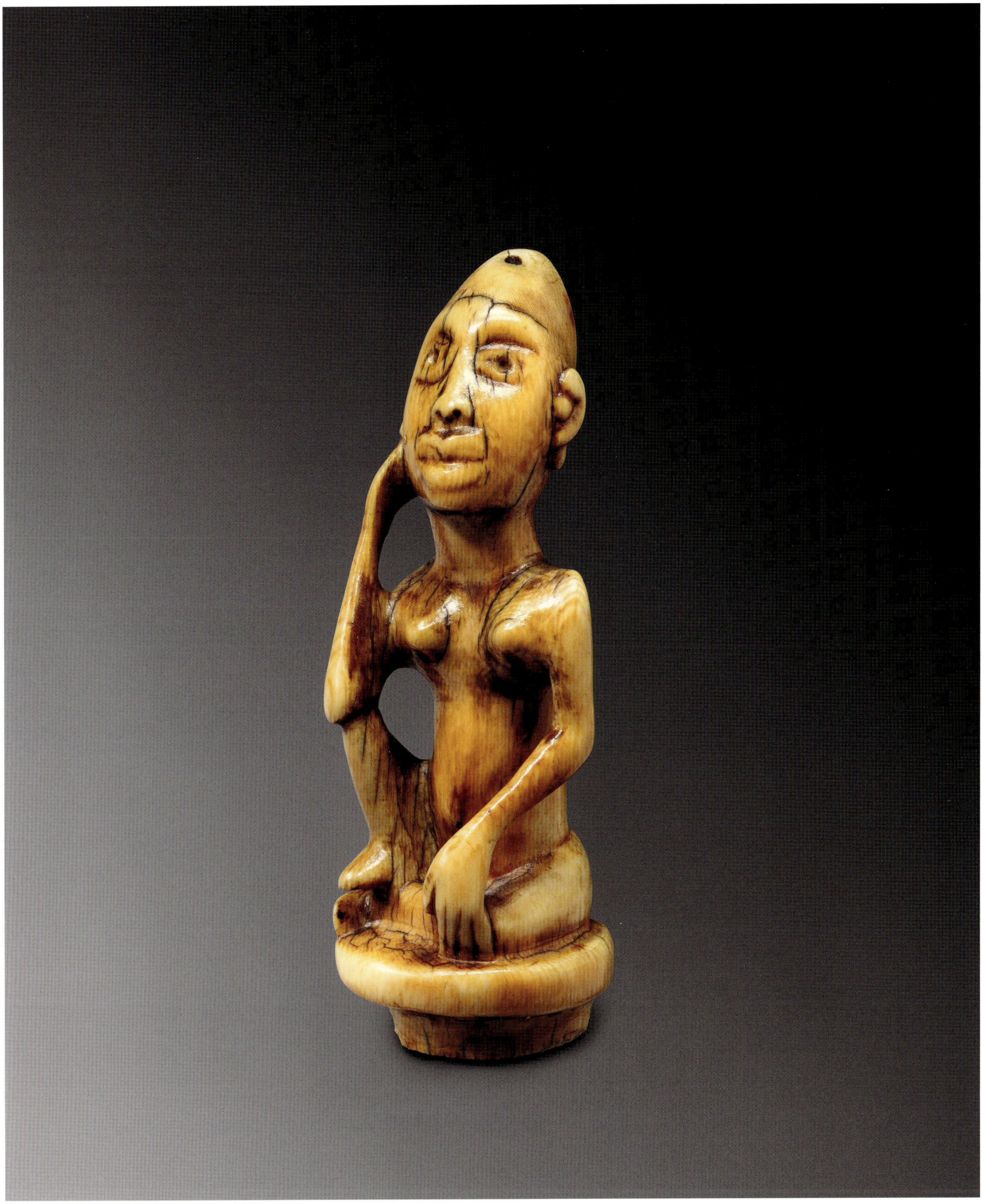

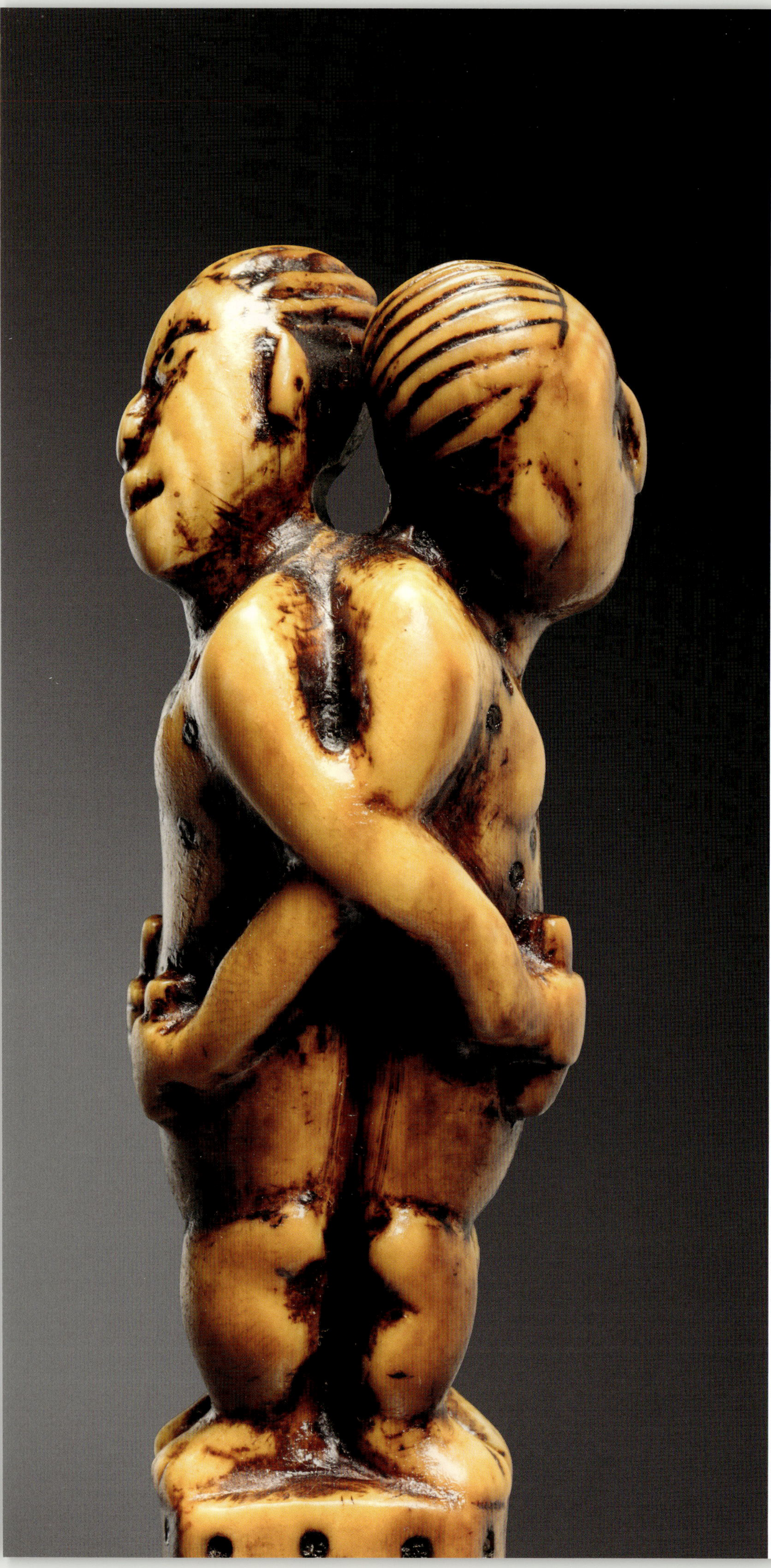

Kongo prestige emblem finial
Republic of the Congo or DRC, H. 11 cm

This staff top was probably sculpted before 1850. It depicts two entwined figures standing back to back with their head leaning to the right, each resting his hands on his partner's belly. The chest of one is decorated with a pattern forming a circle made up of eight dots resembling the rosette symbol of the Lemba,[1] an initiation society whose important members carried a staff and wore a brass bracelet.[2] This association performed the key role of preserving law and order for almost 300 years across the enormous trading network between the interior of the country and the coastal ports to the north of the River Congo. The Lemba also put the spotlight on marriage bonds and a man generally underwent his initiation at the same time as his chief spouse. Each spouse was then given miniature short paddles[3] as tokens of their faithfulness and integrity. Could it be that the small objects that the entwined spouses hold in their hands are these very symbols? [VB]

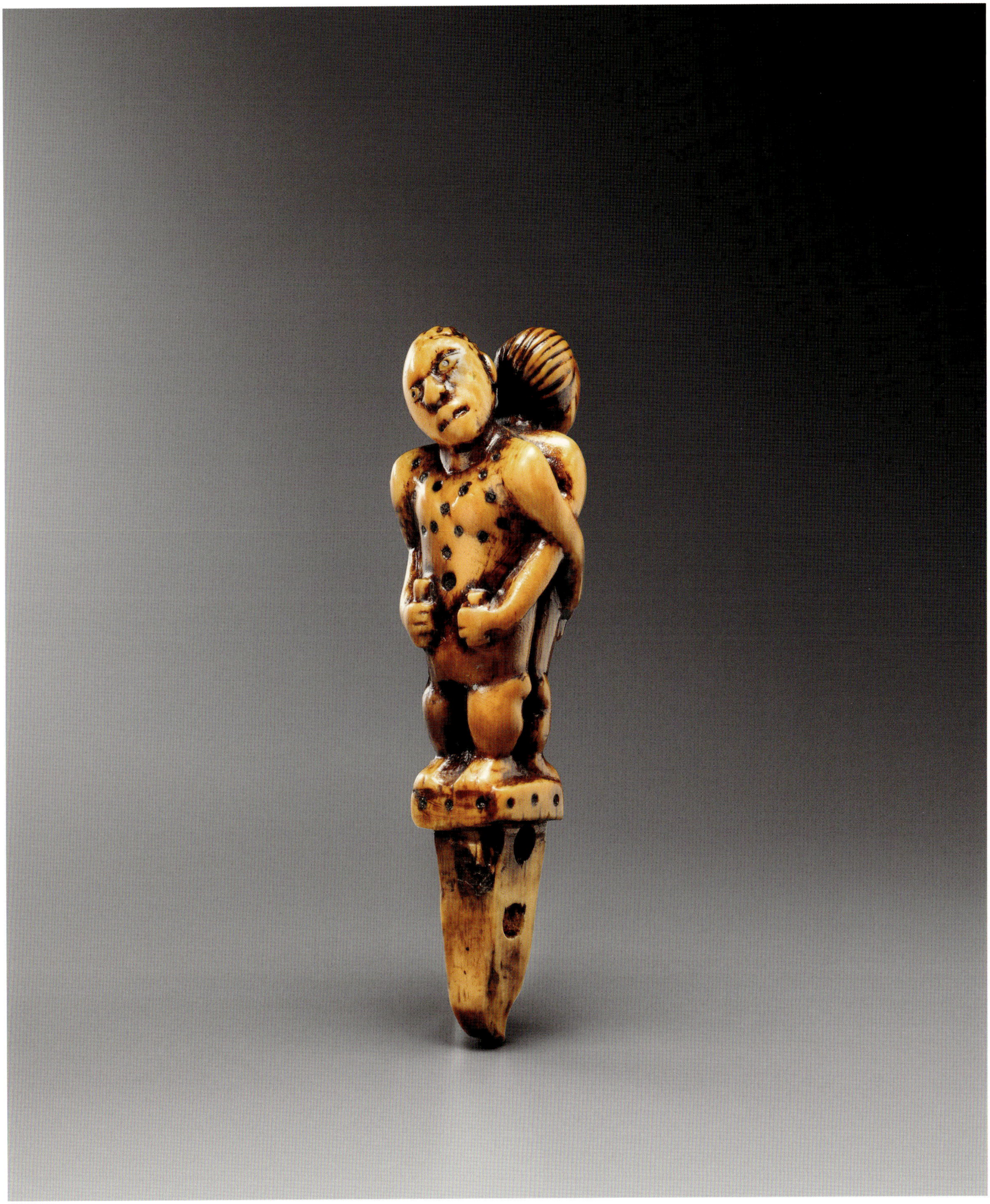

CAPTIONS

AFRICA

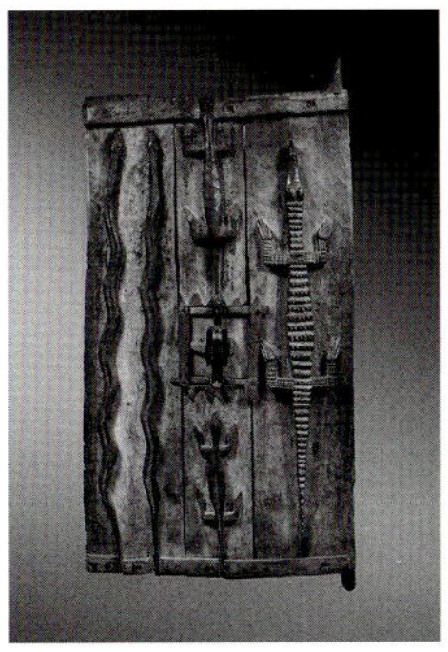

Page 24
Bamana door
Mali, H. 185 cm

Provenance
Hélène Leloup, Paris
John Houston, USA
Hélène Leloup, Paris

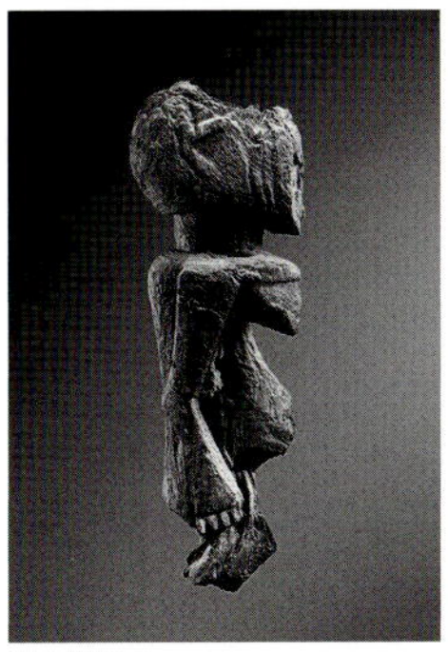

Page 26
Niongom bust
Mali, H. 76 cm

Provenance
Pierre Loeb, Paris
Robert Burawoy, Paris

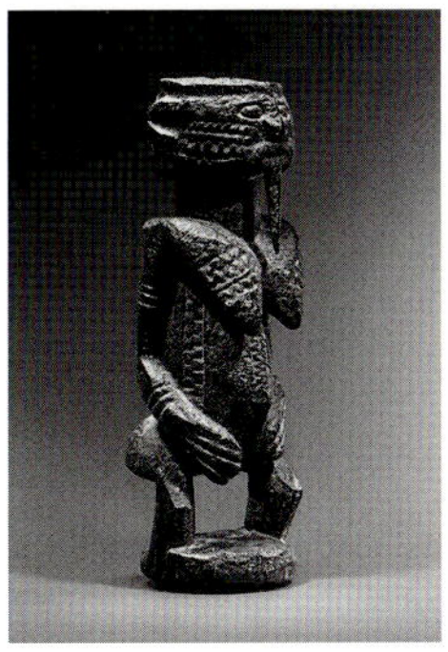

Page 28
Djennenke statue
Mali, H. 29.5 cm

Provenance
Calmels, Paris, 29 May 1996, lot 17

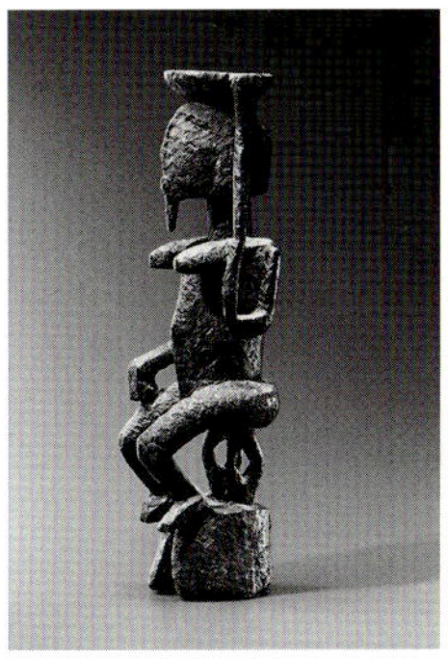

Page 29
Bombou Toro statue
Mali, H. 37.5 cm

Provenance
Galerie Lemaire, Amsterdam
Sotheby's, New York, 19 November 1999, lot 29

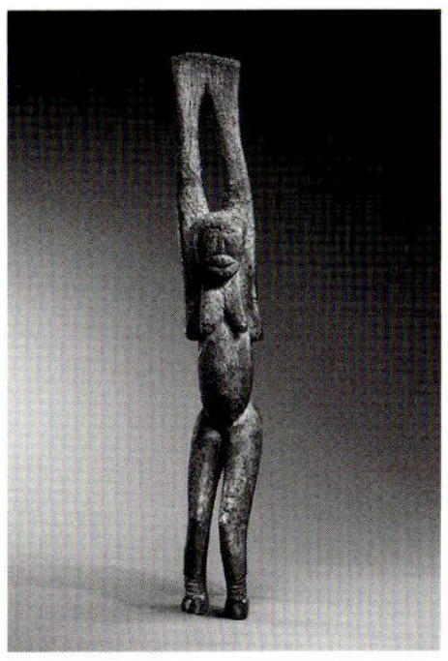

Page 30
Tellem statue
Mali, H. 74 cm
1304 – 64 (70.2%, C14 test by CIRAM, Bordeaux)

Provenance
Musée Barbier-Mueller, Geneva (inv. no. BMG 10004-12)
Hubert Goldet, Paris
Ricqlès, Paris, *Collection Hubert Goldet*,
30 June – 1 July 2001, lot 94

Published
Homberger L. (ed.), Ezra K., *Die Kunst der Dogon*, Zurich, 1995, p. 77, fig. 36
Dulon B., Gay B., *Lumière noire : arts traditionnels*, Tanlay, 1997, pp. 14, 80
Leloup H., *Dogon*, Paris, 2011, p. 175

Exhibited
Zurich, *Die Kunst der Dogon*, Museum Rietberg, 7 May – 3 September 1995
Tanlay, *Lumière noire : arts traditionnels*, Château de Tanlay – Centre d'Art Contemporain, 7 June – 5 October 1997
Dogon:
– Paris, Musée du quai Branly – Jacques Chirac, 5 April – 24 July 2011
– Bonn, Ausstellungshalle der Bundesrepublik Deutschland, 14 October 2011 – 22 January 2012
– Milan, Palazzo Reale, 21 February – 3 June 2012

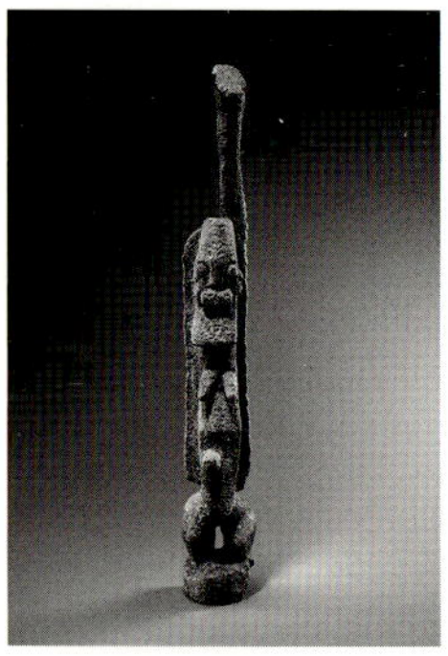

Page 37
Tellem statue
Mali, H. 63.5 cm
1416–46 (95.4%, C14 test by CIRAM, Bordeaux)

Provenance
Hélène Leloup, Paris

Published
Leloup H., Rubin W., Serra R., Baselitz G., *Statuaire Dogon*, Strasbourg, 1994, cat. 46

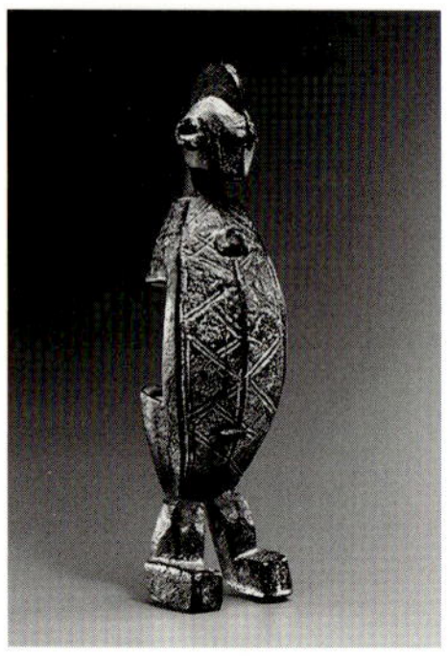

Page 38
Part of a Bamana doorlock
Mali, H. 25.5 cm

Provenance
Harmer Johnson, New York
Nicole and John Dintenfass, New York
Sotheby's, New York, 19 November 1999, lot 32

Note
1 See Imperato, 2001

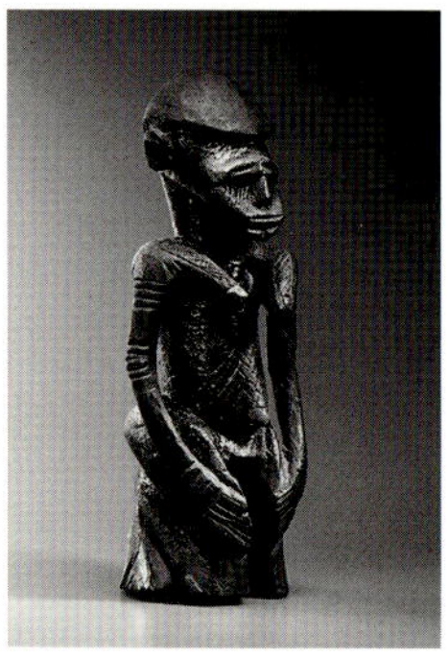

Page 38
Turka statue
Burkina Faso, H. 27.5 cm

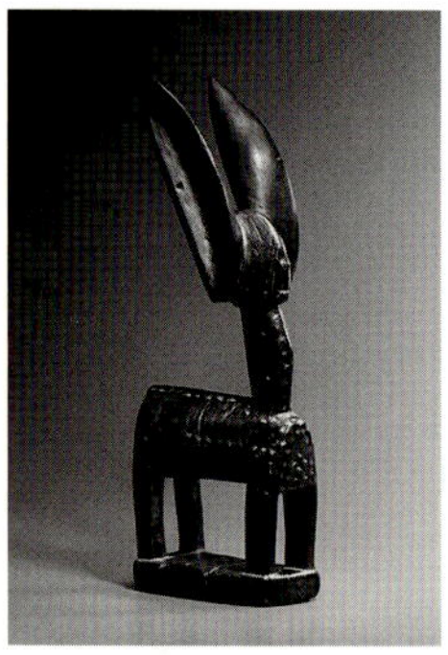

Page 39
Bamana head crest
Mali, H. 24.5 cm

Provenance
Hélène Leloup, Paris

Published
Leloup H., *Bambara*, Paris, 2000, pp. 92–3, fig. 14

Exhibited
Paris, *Bambara*, Galerie Leloup, June 2000

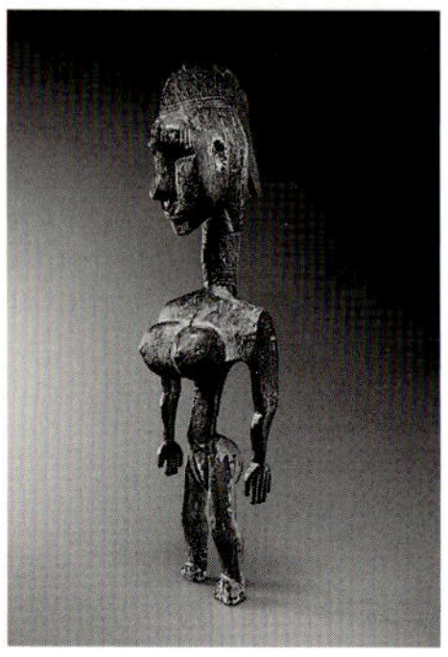

Page 40
Bamana statue
Mali, H. 70 cm

Provenance
Hélène Leloup, Paris

Published
Meauzé P., *L'Art nègre*, Paris, 1967, p. 146, fig. 1
Leloup H., *Bambara*, Paris, 2000, pp. 74–5, fig. 27 and invitation card

Exhibited
Paris, *Bambara*, Galerie Leloup, June 2000

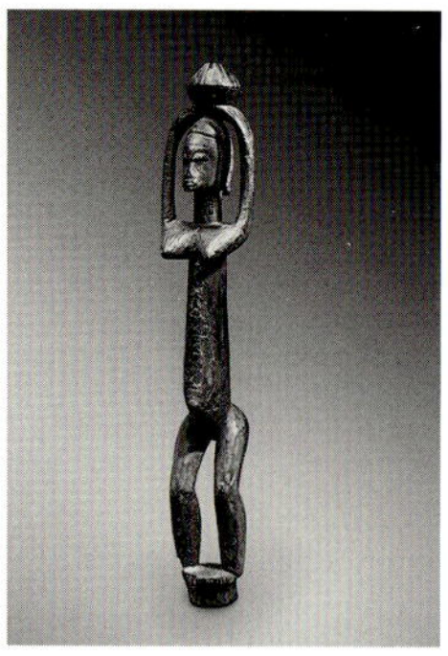

Page 42
Bamana statue
Mali, H. 54.5 cm

Provenance
Merton D. Simpson, New York, 1965
Allen et Matty Alperton, New York
Sotheby's, New York, 18 May 1992, lot 2
Sotheby's, New York, 21 November 1996, lot 56
Hélène Leloup, Paris

Published
Leloup H., *Bambara*, Paris, 2000, pp. 92–3, fig. 35

Exhibited
Paris, *Bambara*, Galerie Leloup, June 2000

Note
1 See Ezra K., "L'art de la société du Jo" *in* Colleyn J.-P., 2002, pp. 131–42; Malé S. *in* Colleyn J.P., 2002, pp. 143–60 ; Malé S., 1995

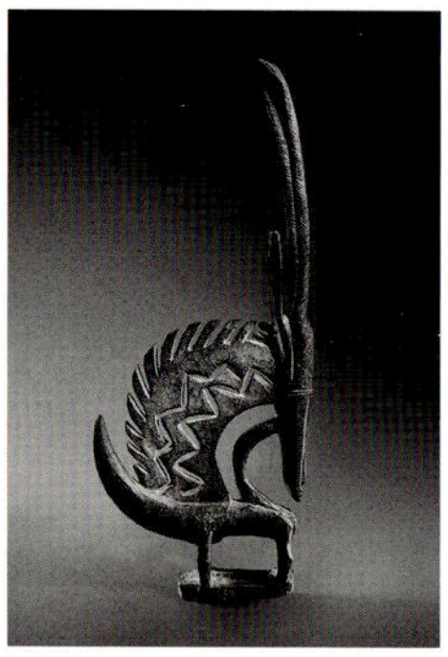

Page 44
Bamana head crest
Mali, H. 112 cm

Provenance
Acquired in Kenedugu by Frédéric-Henri Lem
Paul Chadourne, Garches
Tajan, Paris, 8 November 1996, lot 30 and cover

Published
Lem F.H., *Sculptures soudanaises/Sudanese Sculpture*, Paris, 1948/1949, p. 65, pl. 19
Lem F.H., "Réalité de l'Art nègre" *in Tropiques*, 4th quarter, no. 327, Paris, December 1950, p. 31
Diop A. (ed.), *L'Art nègre*, Paris, 1951, fig. 1
Elisofon E., Fagg W., *The Sculpture of Africa*, London, 1958, p. 45, fig. 35
Goldwater R., *Bambara Sculpture of the Western Sudan*, New York, 1960, p. 36, fig. 51
Zahan D., *Antilopes du soleil, arts et rites agraires d'Afrique noire*, Vienna, 1980, pl. 27, fig. IM76

Exhibited
New York, *Antelopes and Queens: Bambara Sculpture from the Western Sudan,* Museum of Primitive Art, 17 February – 8 May 1960

Note
1 See Zahan, 1980, pl. 27, drawing IM 76; Colleyn, 2006; LaGamma, 2002, pp. 78–127

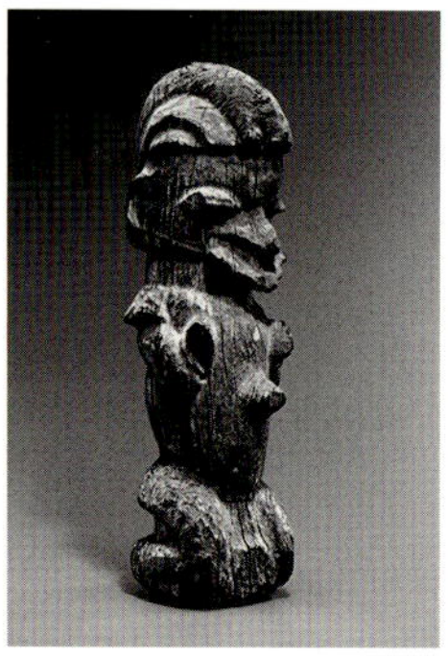

Page 46
Kissi statuette
Sierra Leone, H. 24 cm

Provenance
Vittorio and Marina Mangiò, Monza
Ralph Brienen, Hasselt
Sotheby's Parke Bernet, New York, 23 April 1974, lot 21

Published
Tagliaferri A., *Stili del potere: Antiche sculture in pietra dalla Sierra Leone e dalla Guinea*, Milan, 1989, pp. 106–7, figs 84–5

Phillips T., *Africa: The Art of a Continent*, Munich/London/New York, 1995, p. 471, fig. 5.134B

Exhibited
London, *Africa: The Art of a Continent*, Royal Academy of Arts, 4 October 1995 – 21 January 1996

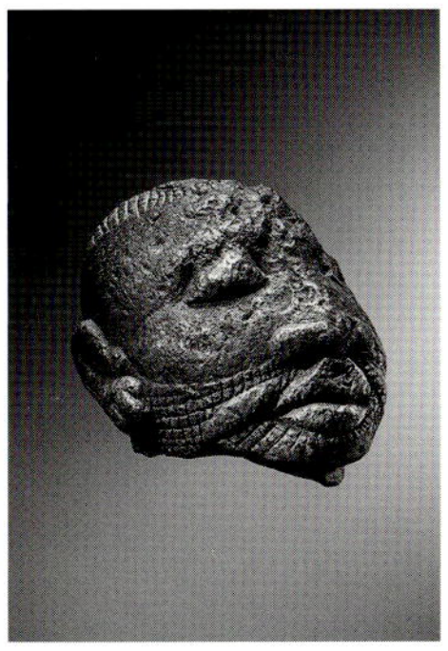

Page 47
Kissi head
Sierra Leone, H. 15.5 cm

Provenance
Laura and Mario Meneghini, Comabbio
Johann Levy, Paris

Published
Tagliaferri A., Hammacher A., *Fabulous ancestors: Stone carvings from Sierre Leone & Guinea*, Milan, 1974, fig. 20
Tagliaferri A., *Pomdo Mahen Yafe et Nomoli*, Paris, 2003, fig. 29

Exhibited
Paris, *Pomdo Mahen Yafe et Nomoli*, Galerie Johann Levy, September – October 2003

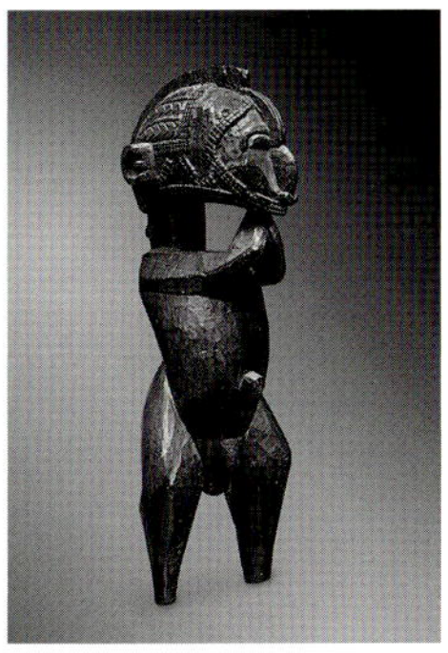

Page 48
Baga statue
Republic of Guinea, H. 57 cm

Provenance
Maurice de Vlaminck, Paris
Loudmer, Paris, 2 July 1987, lot 175
Hélène Leloup, Paris

Published
Lamp F.J., *Art of the Baga: a drama of cultural reinvention*, New York, 1996, p. 15, fig. 4
Vallès-Bled M. (ed.), *Vlaminck: un instinct fauve*, Paris, 2008, p. 168, ill. 1 and p. 176, fig. 2

Exhibited
Paris, *Vlaminck : Un instinct fauve*, Musée du Luxembourg, 20 February – 20 July 2008

Notes
1 Coffinières de Nordeck A., "Voyage en pays baga," *Le Tour du monde*, 1st semester 1886, pp. 273–304
2 *Voix de Notre-Dame 1930, 1932*. The manuscripts of the letters written by Fathers Lerouge, Mell, and Balez are held in the archives of the Congregation of the Fathers of the Holy Spirit
3 Chevrier M.A., "Notes relatives aux coutumes des adeptes de la société des Scymos," *L'Anthropologie*, no. 27, 1906, pp. 359–76
4 Sarro R., *The Politics of Religious Change on the Upper Guinea Coast: Iconoclasm Done and Undone*, Edinburgh University Press for the International African Institute, Edinburgh, 2009
5 Curtis M.Y., Sarró R., "The Nimba Headdress: Art, Ritual and History of the Baga and Nalu Peoples of Guinea," *Museum Studies*, Publication of the Art Institute of Chicago, 1997
6 Lamp F., *The Art of Baga: A Drama of Cultural Reinvention*, The Museum for African Art, Prestel Verlag, New York, 1996, p. 15, fig. 4
7 Berliner D., *Baga – Mémoires religieuses*. Catalogue de l'exposition du musée Barbier-Mueller, Somogy éditions d'art, Geneva, 2014

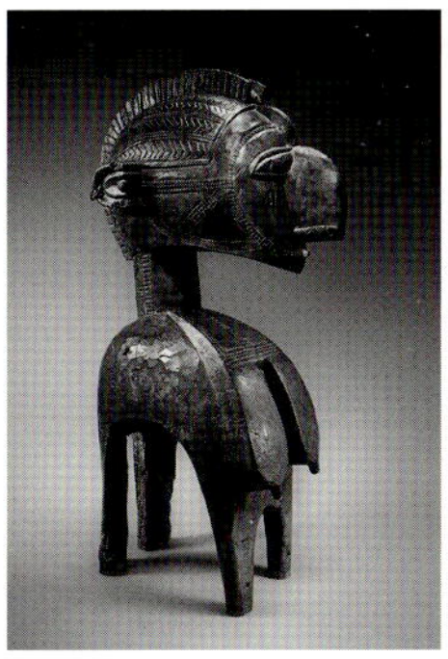

Page 50
Baga shoulder mask
Republic of Guinea, H. 116 cm

Provenance
Millon, Paris, 22 June 2012, lot 451
Alain de Monbrison, Paris

Published
Falgayrettes-Leveau C., Cutsem-Vanderstraete (van) A., *L'Art de manger : rites et traditions en Afrique, Insulinde et Océanie*, Paris, 2014, p. 37
Geoffroy-Schneiter B., "Agapes des antipodes" *in L'Œil*, no. 676, 1 February 2015, p. 100

Exhibited
Paris, *L'Art de manger : rites et traditions en Afrique, Insulinde et Océanie*, Musée Dapper, 15 October 2014 – 12 July 2015

Notes
1 Coffinières de Nordeck A., "Voyage en pays baga," *Le Tour du monde*, 1st semester 1886, pp. 273–304
2 Archives G. Mols
3 Paudrat J.-L., "From Africa," *in* Rubin W. (ed.), *Primitivism in 20th Century Art: Affinity of the Tribal and the Modern*, The Museum of Modern Art, New York, 1984, vol. I, pp. 125–75
4 Musée du Quai Branly picture library, photographs by Béatrice Appia
5 Sarro R., *The Politics of Religious Change on the Upper Guinea Coast: Iconoclasm Done and Undone*, Edinburgh University Press for the International African Institute, Edinburgh, 2009
6 Vogel S.M., *Africa Explores: 20th Century African Art*, exhibition catalogue, Museum for African Art, New York, 1991
7 Van Geertruyen G., "Le style nimba," *Arts d'Afrique noire*, n°. 31, 1979, pp. 20–37
8 Chevrier M.A., "Notes relatives aux coutumes des adeptes de la société des Scymos," *L'Anthropologiee*, no. 27, 1906, pp. 359–76
9 Coffinières de Nordeck A., "Voyage en pays baga," *Le Tour du monde*, 1st semester 1886, pp. 273–304
10 Curtis M.Y., *Sculptures, Afrique, Asie, Océanie, Amériques*, musée du Louvre, Pavillon des sessions, RMN, musée du Quai Branly, Paris, 2000, pp. 68–72
11 Curtis M.Y., Sarró R., "The Nimba Headdress: Art, Ritual and History of the Baga and Nalu Peoples of Guinea," *Museum Studies*, Publication of the Art Institute of Chicago, 1997
12 Curtis M.Y., op. cit., musée du Louvre, Pavillon des sessions, RMN, musée du Quai Branly, Paris, 2000, pp. 68–72, and Lamp F., *The Art of Baga: A Drama of Cultural Reinvention*, The Museum for African Art, Prestel Verlag, New York, 1996, p. 5, fig. 4

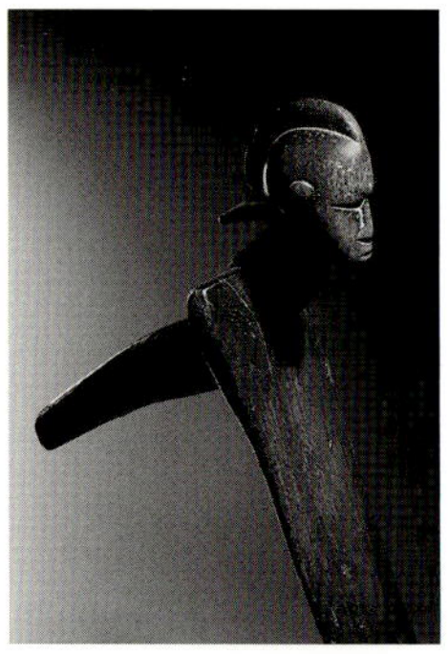

Page 54
Lobi stool
Burkina Faso, L. 62 cm

Provenance
Alain de Monbrison, Paris

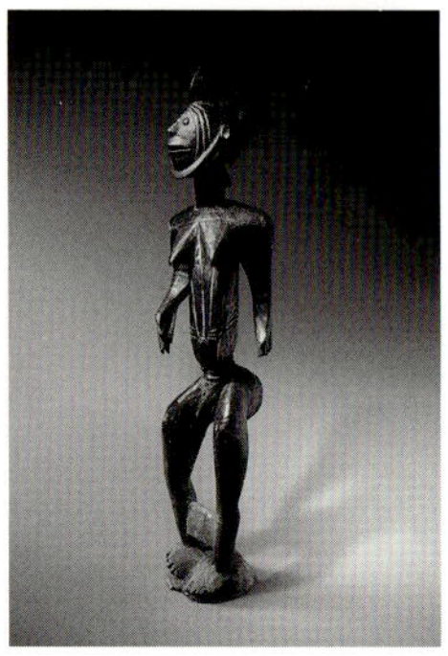

Page 55
Mossi statue
Burkina Faso, H. 94 cm

Provenance
Alain de Monbrison, Paris

Published
Breton S. (ed.), *Qu'est-ce qu'un corps?*, Paris, 2006, p. 42, fig. 23

Exhibited
Paris, *Qu'est-ce qu'un corps?*, Musée du quai Branly-Jacques Chirac, 1 January 2006 – 30 June 2007

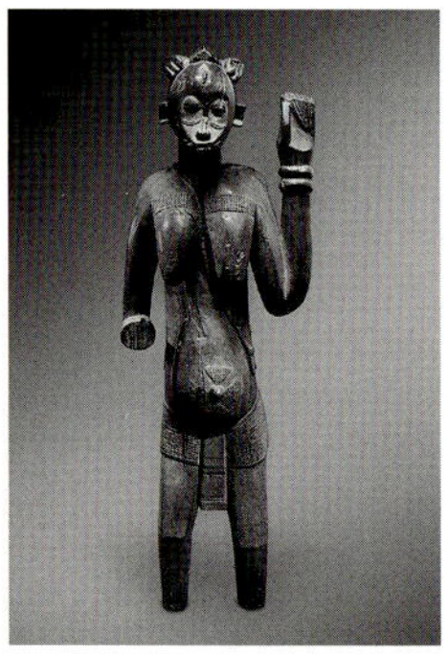

Page 58
Senufo statue
Côte d'Ivoire, H. 102 cm

Provenance
René Rasmussen, Paris
Loudmer-Poulain, Paris, 3 and 5 December 1977, lot 53

Published
Kerchache J., Paudrat J.-L., Stephan L., *L'Art africain*, Paris, 1988, p. 374, fig. 320
Gohr S., Heymer K., *Afrikanische skulptur. Die Erfindung der Figur/ African sculpture. The Invention of the figure*, 1990, p. 95, no. 10
Collective, *Passions privées : art moderne et contemporain dans les collections particulières en France*, Paris, 1995, p. 367 (view of apartment)

Exhibited
Afrikanische skulptur. Die Erfindung der Figur/ African sculpture. The Invention of the figure:
– Cologne, Museum Ludwig Köln, 27 July – 30 September 1990
– The Hague, Gemeente Museum Den Haag, November 1990 – January 1991
Paris, *Passions privées : art moderne et contemporain dans les collections particulières en France*, musée d'art moderne de la ville de Paris, 14 December 1995 – 24 March 1996

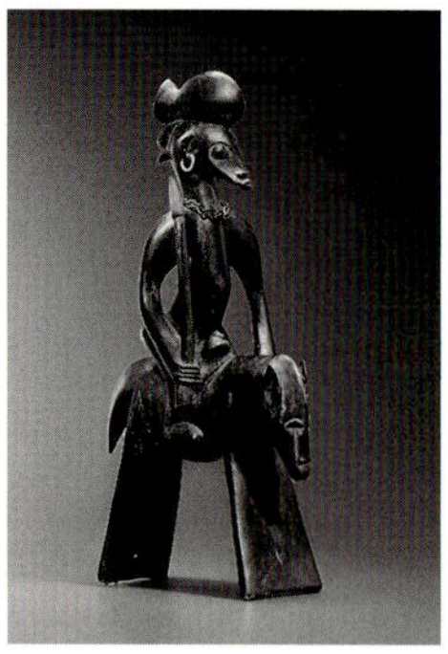

Page 64
Senufo horseman
Côte d'Ivoire, H. 29 cm

Provenance
Paul Wirz, Basle
Private collection
Sotheby's, Paris, 16 June 2010, lot 39

Published
Schneckenburger M., *Resonanzen: Naturvolkkunst – Modern Kunst/Resonances: Tribal Art – Modern Art*, Basle, 1984, fig. 1
Magazine *Arts d'Afrique Noire*, no. 51, 1984, cover
Gagliardi S.E., *Senufo Unbound. Dynamics and Identity in West Africa/Sénufo sans frontières. La dynamique des arts et des identités en Afrique de l'Ouest*, Cleveland, 2014/Milan, 2015, fig. 158
Neyt F., *Trésors de Côte d'Ivoire*, Brussels, 2014, p. 164, fig. 112

Exhibited
Basle, *Resonanzen: Naturvolkkunst – Modern Kunst/ Resonances: Tribal Art – Modern Art*, Galerie Greub, January – June 1984
Senufo Unbound. Dynamics and Identity in West Africa/ Sénufo sans frontières. La dynamique des arts et des identités en Afrique de l'Ouest :
– Cleveland, The Cleveland Museum of Art, 22 February – 31 May 2015
– Saint Louis, Saint Louis Art Museum, 28 June – 27 September 2015
– Montpellier, Musée Fabre, 28 November 2015 – 6 March 2016

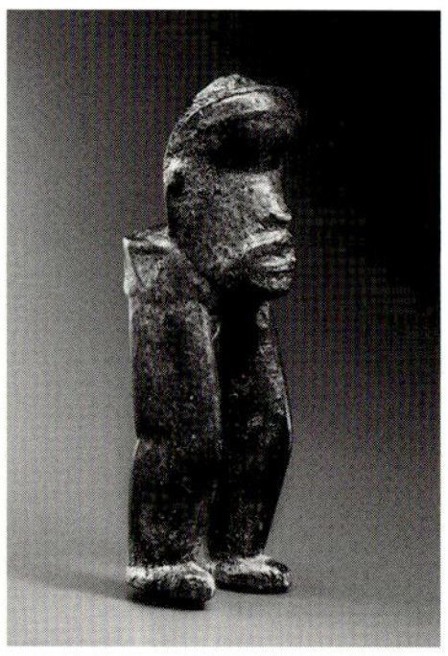

Page 68
Dan sculpture
Côte d'Ivoire, H 18.5 cm

Provenance
Bernard Dulon, Paris
Christine Valluet, Paris

Published
Ferrandin Y., Valluet C., *Arts anciens de Côte-d'Ivoire et régions limitrophes*, Paris, 2002, p. 71

Exhibited
Paris, *Arts anciens de Côte-d'Ivoire et régions limitrophes*, Galerie Valluet-Ferrandin, November – December 2002

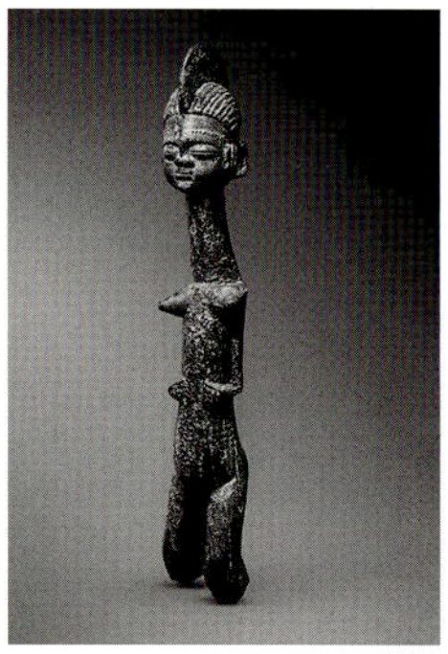

Page 69
Koulango statue
Côte d'Ivoire, H. 55 cm

Provenance
Arman, Paris/New York
Bernard Dulon, Paris

Published
Sourrieu M. (ed.), *Arman & l'art africain*, Marseille/Paris, 1996, p. 123, fig. 96
Herreman F. (ed.), *African faces, African figures, The Arman Collection*, New York, 1997, p. 62, fig. 11

Dulon B., *Arman l'africain*, Paris, 2002, fig. 7
Neyt F., *Trésors de Côte d'Ivoire*, Brussels, 2014, pp. 280–81, fig. 203

Exhibited
Arman & l'art africain:
– Marseille, Musée d'Arts africains, océaniens, amérindiens, chapelle de la Vieille Charité, 23 June – 30 October 1996
– Paris, Musée National des arts d'Afrique et d'Océanie, 3 December 1996 – 17 February 1997
– Cologne, Rautenstrauch-Joest-Museum, Museum für Völkerkunde, March – August 1997
New York, *African faces, African figures, The Arman Collection*, The Museum for African Art, 9 October 1997 – 19 April 1998
Paris, *Arman l'africain*, Galerie Bernard Dulon, 1 9 September – 31 October 2002

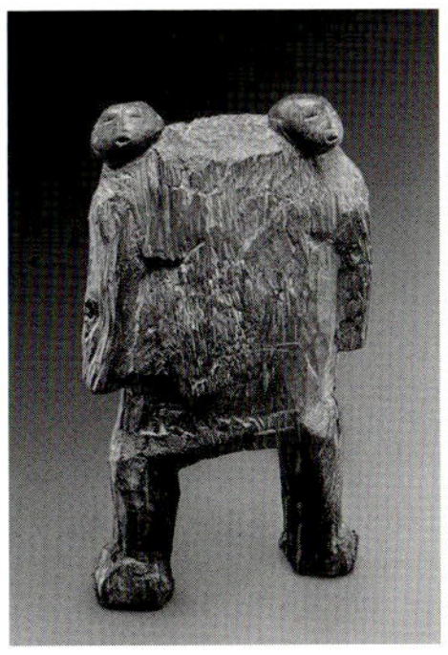

Page 72
Lamba-Naodem statue
Northern Togo, H. 31 cm

Provenance
Ousman Abdoulaye, Lomé
Pierre Amrouche, Paris
Alain de Monbrison, Paris

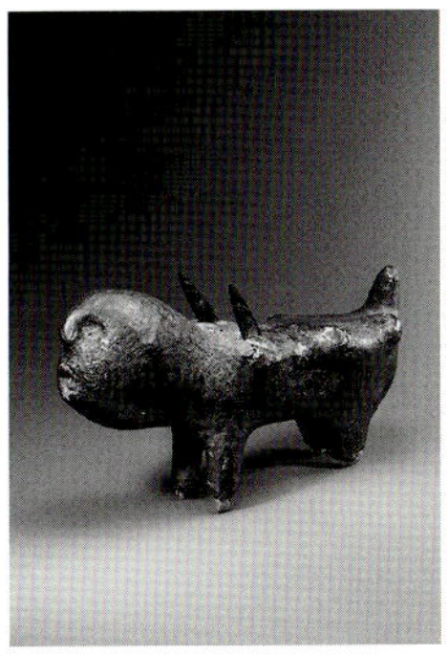

Page 73
Bamana sculpture
Mali, L. 35 cm

Provenance
Hélène Leloup, Paris

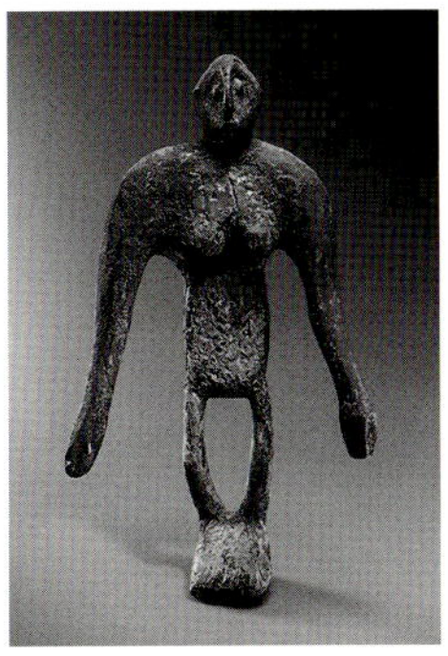

Page 74
Statue
Nigeria (?), H. 58 cm

Provenance
Alain de Monbrison, Paris

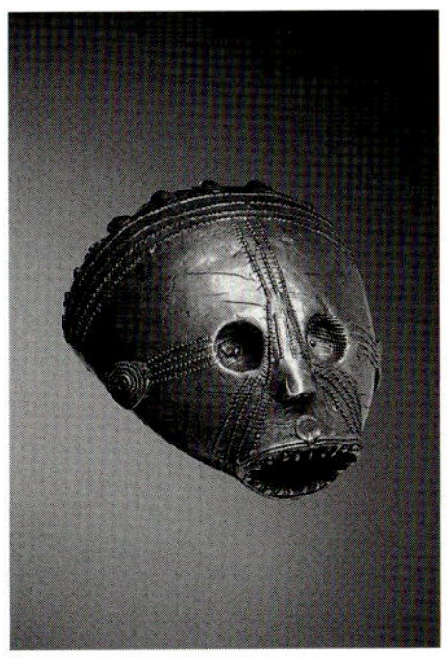

Page 76
Votive head
Cross River, Nigeria, H. 17.5 cm

Provenance
Alain Dufour, Saint-Maur
Alain de Monbrison, Paris

Published
Berjonneau G., Sonnery J.-L., *et al.*, *Rediscovered Masterpieces of African Art/Chefs-d'oeuvre inédits de l'Afrique noire/Onbekende meesterwerken uit zwart Afrika,* Boulogne, 1986/Paris, 1987/Tielt, 1987, p. 109, fig. 40
Falola T., Joubert H., Lebas A., *Arts du Nigeria dans les collections privées françaises*, Milan, 2012, p. 269, fig. 56

Exhibited
Paris, *Chefs-d'oeuvre inédits de l'Afrique noire*, Musée Dapper, 23 October 1987 – 23 April 1988
Quebec, *Arts du Nigeria dans les collections privées françaises*, musée de la Civilisation, 24 October 2012 – 21 April 2013

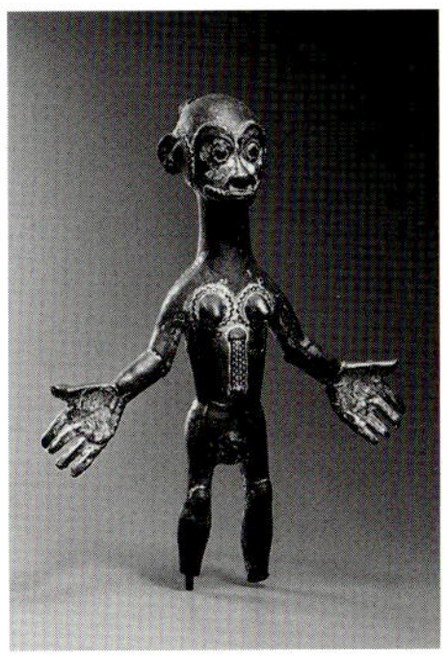

Page 78
Tiv (?) statue
Nigeria, H. 30.5 cm

Provenance
Samir Borro, Brussels
Bernard Dulon, Paris
Lance and Roberta Entwistle, Paris/London

Published
Rivière M. (ed.), *Image de la Femme dans l'art africain*, Tours, 2000, fig. 60

Exhibited
Image de la Femme dans l'art africain:
– Tours, Château de Tours, 21 October – 3 December 2000
– Nogent-le-Rotrou, Château Saint-Jean, 9 December 2000 – 29 January 2001

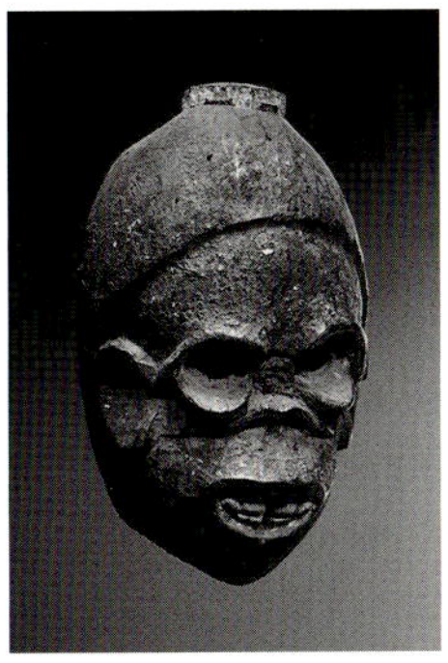

Page 80
Ibibio mask
Nigeria, H. 25.5 cm

Provenance
René Rasmussen, Paris
Loudmer-Poulain, Paris, Succession René Rasmussen, 19 March 1980, lot 52
Paolo Morigi, Lugano
Sotheby's, Paris, Collection Paolo Morigi, 6 December 2005, lot 84

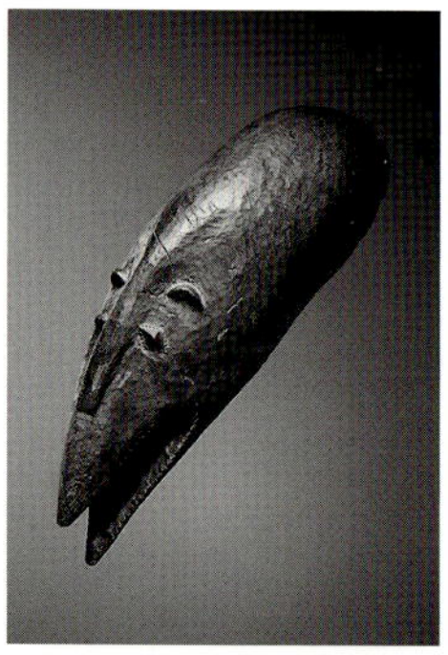

Page 81
Mask
Middle Benue (?), Nigeria H. 41.5 cm

Provenance
Acquired *in situ* by Dr Dodd, 1950
Christie's, Paris, 20 June 2006, lot 151

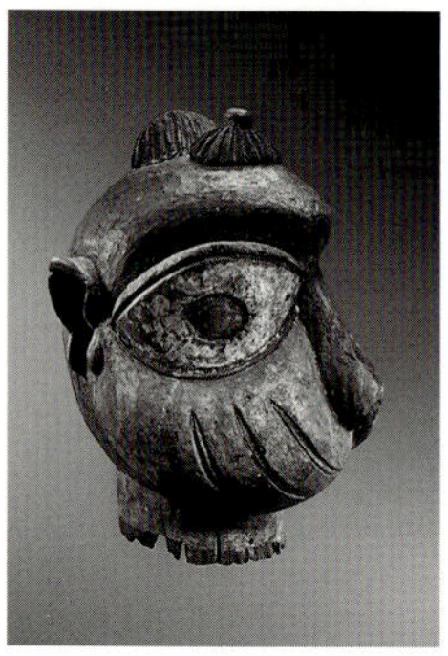

Page 82
Yoruba head
Nigeria, H. 33 cm

Provenance
Robert Duperrier, Paris
Hubert Goldet, Paris
Ricqlès, Paris, Hubert Goldet Collection,
30 June – 1 July 2001, lot 148

Note
1 A very similar *egungun* crest is listed in the Van Gelder Collection published *in* Lebas A. (ed.), *Arts du Nigéria dans les collections privées françaises,* 5 Continents Editions, Milan, 2012, fig. 10, pp. 79, 262

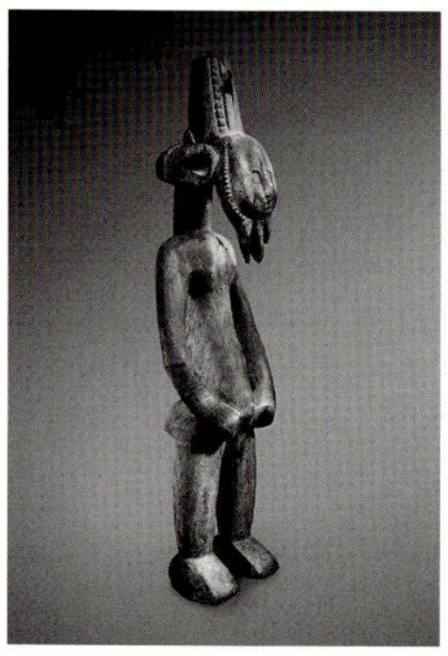

Page 85
Jukun Wurbo statue
Middle Benue, Nigeria, H. 82 cm

Provenance
Jacques Kerchache, Paris
Prince Sadruddin Aga Khan, Geneva
Sotheby's, London, *The Prince Sadruddin Aga Khan Collection of African Art*, 27 June 1983, lot 28

Published
Kerchache J., Paudrat J.-L., Stephan L., *L'art africain*, Paris, 1988, p. 410, fig. 513
Bacquart J.-B., *The Tribal Arts of Africa/L'Art tribal d'Afrique Noire* London/Paris, 1998, p. 79 (right)

Exhibited
Rome, *Sculpture africaine*, Villa Medici,
7 March – 15 June 1986
Paris, *Passions privées : art moderne et contemporain dans les collections particulières en France*, musée d'art moderne de la ville de Paris, 14 December 1995 – 24 March 1996

Notes
1 Arnold Rubin's field notes, 1964–65, Fowler Museum Archives at UCLA
2 The oldest specimens have been dated by the C14 method to the mid-fifteenth/seventeenth centuries.
3 Photo Arnold Rubin in Berns M.C., Fardon R., Kasfir S.L., *Central Nigeria unmasked, arts of the Benue river valley*, UCLA, Fowler Museum, 2011, p. 296

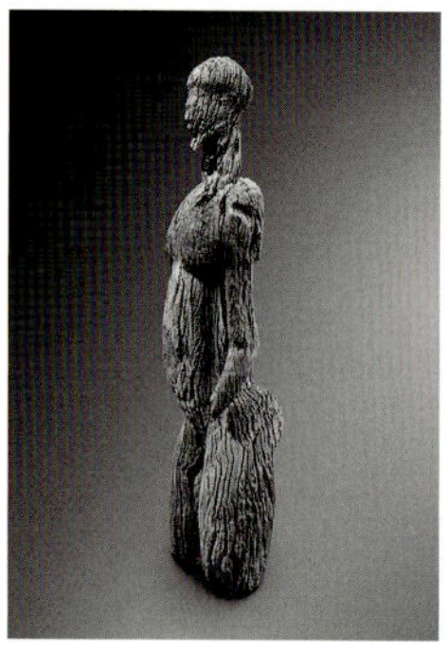

Page 88
Mboye statue
East of the Gongola valley, Nigeria, H. 118 cm
1309–61 (64.8%, C14 test by CIRAM, Bordeaux)

Provenance
Alain Dufour, Saint-Maur
Lucien Van de Velde, Antwerp, circa 1970
Loed Van Bussel, Amsterdam
Robert Burawoy, Paris

Published
Berns M. *et al.*, *Central Nigeria Unmasked: arts of the Benue River Valley*, Los Angeles, 2011, p. 552, fig. I.4
Tribal Art Magazine, spring 2012, no. 63, p. 57, fig. 14
LaGamma A., "Silenced Mbembe Muses," *in Metropolitan Museum Journal*, vol. 48, New York, 2013, p. 148, fig. 24

Exhibited
Central Nigeria Unmasked: arts of the Benue River Valley:
– Los Angeles, Fowler Museum,
13 February – 24 July 2011
– Washington, DC, National Museum of African Art,
14 September – 4 March 2012
– Stanford, Cantor Arts Center,
16 May – 2 September 2012
– Paris, Musée du Quai Branly – Jacques Chirac,
12 November 2012 – 27 January 2013
New York, *Warriors and Mothers. Epic Mbembe Art*,
The Metropolitan Museum of Art,
9 December 2014 – 15 September 2015

Notes
1 Monumental male statue from the Menil Collection, Houston
2 Berns M.C., "Vestiges in wood: ancestor sculptures of the Eastern Gongola valley," *in* Berns M.C., Fardon R., and Kasfir S.L., *Central Nigeria Unmasked: arts of the Benue river valley,* Fowler Museum at UCLA, 2011, pp. 550–59

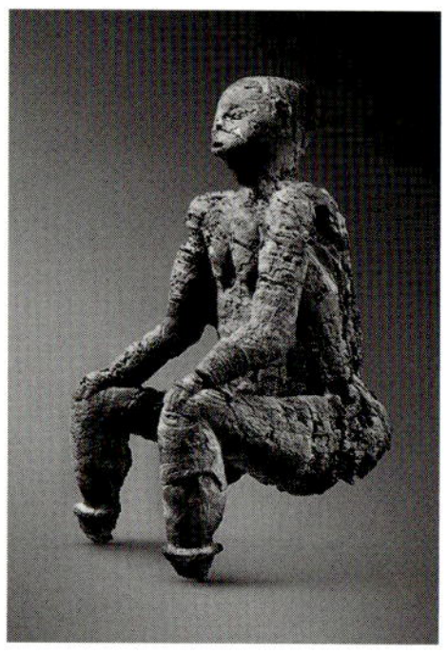

Page 93
Mbembe drum figure
Nigeria, H. 71 cm
seventeenth–eighteenth century

Provenance
Ousman Traoré, Lomé
Hélène Leloup, Paris
Josette and Jean-Claude Weill Collection, Paris
Private Collection, Unites States

Published
Leloup H., *Ancêtres M'bembé,* Paris, 1974, no. 6
Bassani E., *Arts of Africa. 7000 ans d'art africain*, Monaco, 2005, p. 213, fig. 85a
LaGamma A., "Silenced Mbembe Muses," *in Metropolitan Museum Journal*, vol. 48, 2013, p. 153, fig. 16

Exhibited
Paris, *Ancêtres M'bembé*, Galerie Hélène Kamer,
28 May – 22 June 1974
Monaco, *Arts of Africa. 7000 ans d'art africain*, Grimaldi Forum Monaco, 16 July – 4 September 2005

New York, *Warriors and Mothers, Epic Mbembe Art*, The Metropolitan Museum of Art, 9 December 2014 – 15 September 2015

Notes

1 The sculpture in the Weill Collection belongs to a small body of around a dozen pieces, fragments of impressive drums that were never recorded as they were being used *in situ*, which were gathered together for the *Ancêtres mbembé* exhibition organized by Hélène Kamer in her Paris gallery in 1974. This set was brought to France by Ousman Traoré, an antiquarian from Mali based in Lome, after two collecting expeditions in 1972/73. Unfortunately, this was a one-off event

2 The German ethnologist Max von Stefenelli added two specimens dated to the fifteenth/sixteenth century by the C14 method to the collection of the Ethnographic Museum of Berlin in 1907

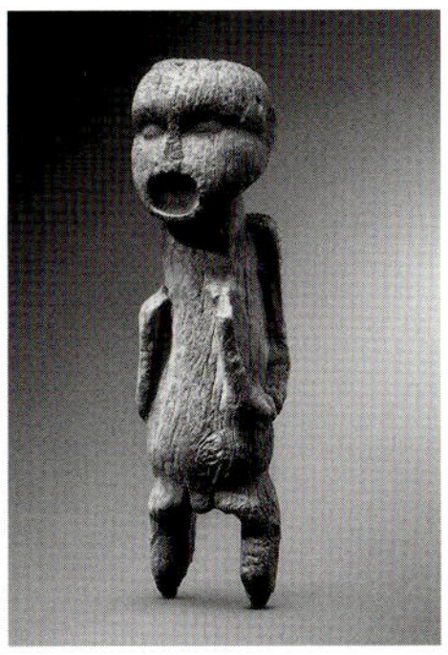

Page 94

Mbembe statue

Nigeria, H. 62 cm

1646–1800 (84.7% – Test C14 by CIRAM, Bordeaux)

Provenance

Mathias Komor, New York

Christie's, New York, 7 May 1980, lot 80

Lance and Roberta Entwistle, Paris/London

Published

Falola T., Joubert H., Lebas A., *Arts du Nigeria dans les collections privées françaises*, Milan, 2012, p. 273, fig. 86

Exhibited

Quebec, *Arts du Nigeria dans les collections privées françaises*, Musée de la Civilisation, 24 October 2012 – 21 April 2013

Note

1 Kamer H., *Ancêtres mbembe*, catalogue of Galerie Kamer exhibition, Paris, 1974

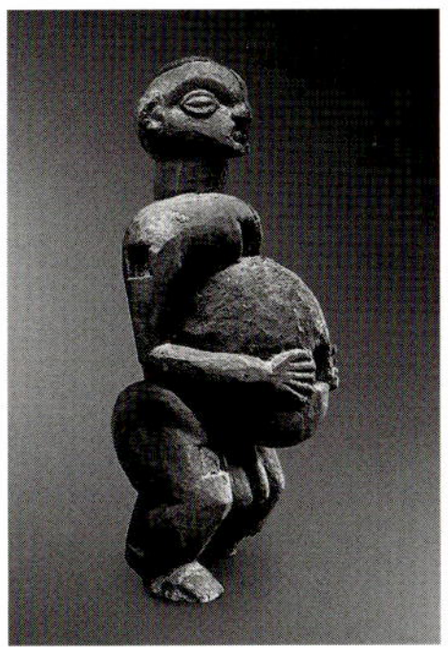

Page 96

Bangwa statue

Western Bangwa, Cameroon, H. 68 cm

Provenance

Pierre Langlois, Paris

Hubert Goldet, Paris

Ricqlès, Paris, *Hubert Goldet Collection*, 30 June – 1 July 2001, lot 154

Published

Harter P., *Arts anciens du Cameroun,* Arnouville, 1986, p. 337, no. 361

Lintig (von) B., *Die bildende Kunst der Bangwa*, Munich, 1994, p. 236, fig. 59

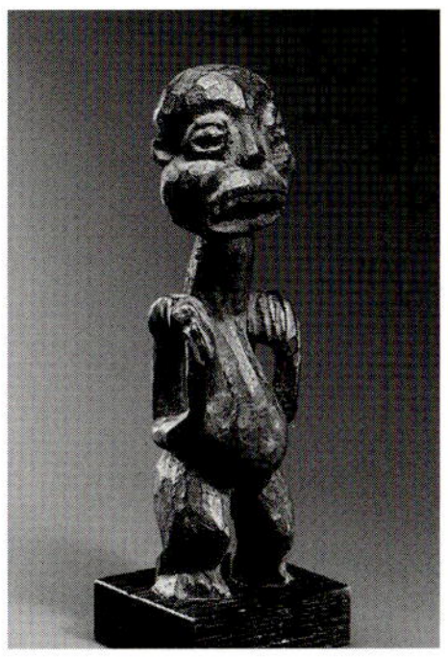

Page 98

Bangwa statuette

Eastern Bangwa, (Bangwa-Batoufam Bamileke region), Cameroon, H. 19 cm

Stand by Kichizô Inagaki

Provenance

Joseph Herman, London

Sotheby's, New York, 21 November 1996, lot 125

Tajan, Paris, 21 December 2000, lot 31

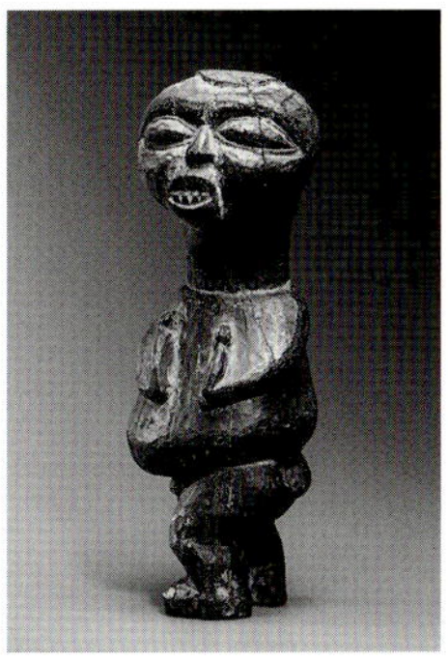

Page 98

Bamileke-Batie statuette

Cameroon, H. 19 cm

Provenance

Galerie Flak, Paris

Alexandre Bernand, Paris

Bernard Dulon, Paris

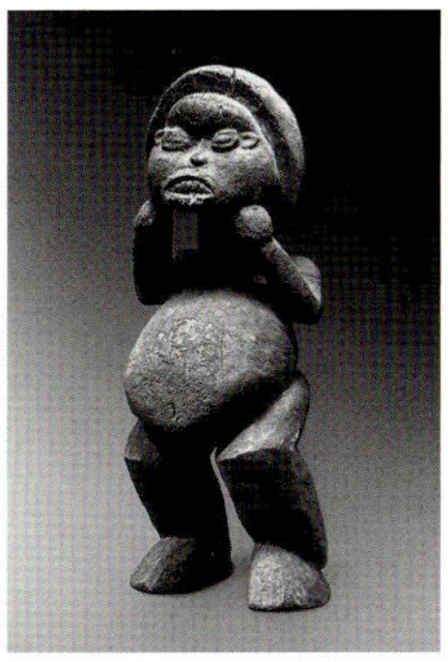

Page 99

Bamileke-Batie statue

Cameroon, H. 38 cm

Provenance

Alain Dufour, Saint-Maur/Ramatuelle, 1982

Lucien Van de Velde, Antwerp, 1983

Alain de Monbrison, Paris

Published

African Arts, vol. XVIII, no. 2, February 1985, p. 23 (Monbrison advertisement)

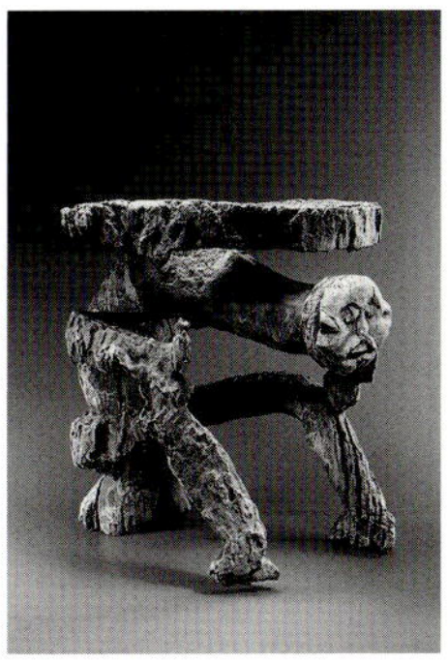

Page 100

Fragment of Bamileke-Batie throne

Cameroon, H. 46 cm

Provenance

Acquired *in situ* in 1965

Private Collection, Brussels

Bernard Dulon, Paris

Johann Levy, Paris

Published

Lecoq R., *Les Bamiléké – une Civilisation Africaine*, Présence Africaine (ed.), Paris/Dakar, 1957, p. 97, fig. 66

Lintig (von) B., *Cameroun : arts traditionnels,* Paris, 2006, p. 49

Exhibited

Cameroun : arts traditionnels:

– Paris, Galerie Bernard Dulon, 16 June – 30 September 2006

– New York, Friedman & Vallois Gallery, 20 October – 30 November 2006

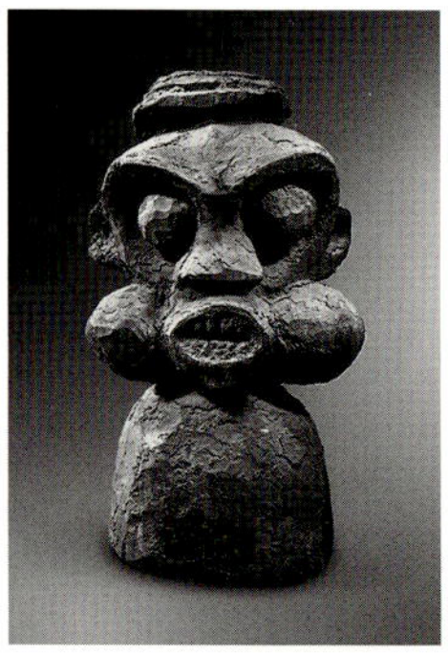

Page 103
Bangwa crest
Bangwa occidental, Cameroon, H. 42 cm

Provenance
Jacques Kerchache, Paris
Christie's, Paris, *Intérieurs. Collection Anne et Jacques Kerchache*, 29 October 2008, lot 111

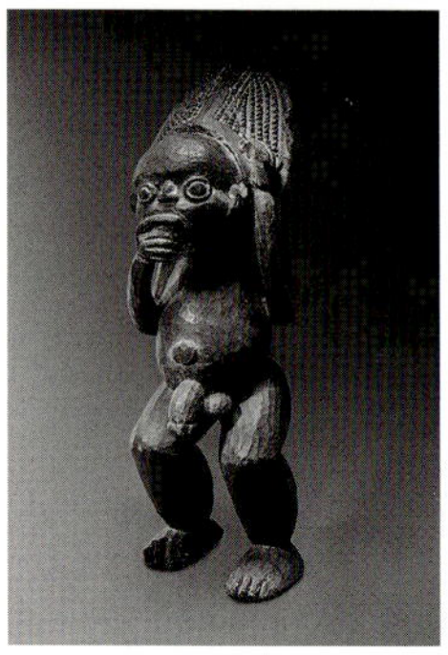

Page 104
Bamileke statue
Cameroon, H. 51 cm

Provenance
Alain de Monbrison, Paris

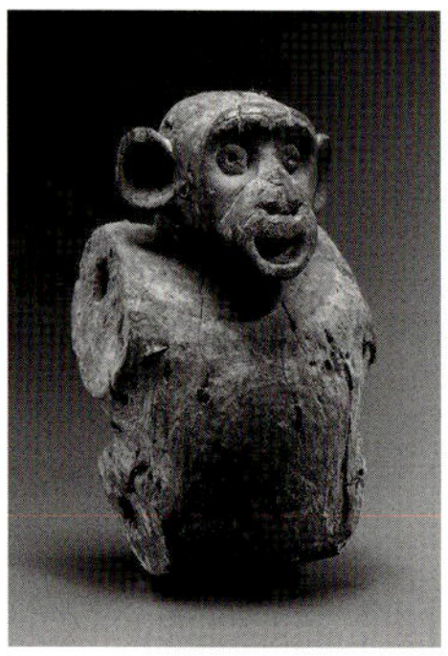

Page 106
Fang bulu-beti monkey
Ebolowa region, southern Cameroon-northern Gabon, H. 32 cm

Provenance
Christian Duponcheel, Pietrebas
Jacques Kerchache, Paris

Published
Leuzinger E., *Die Kunst von Schwarz-Afrika*, Zürich, 1970, p. 260, fig. Q20
Kerchache J., Paudrat J.-L., and Stephan L., *L'Art africain*, Paris, 1988, p. 557, no. 971

Exhibited
Zürich, *Die Kunst von Schwarz-Afrika*, Kunsthaus Zürich, 31 October 1970 – 17 January 1971

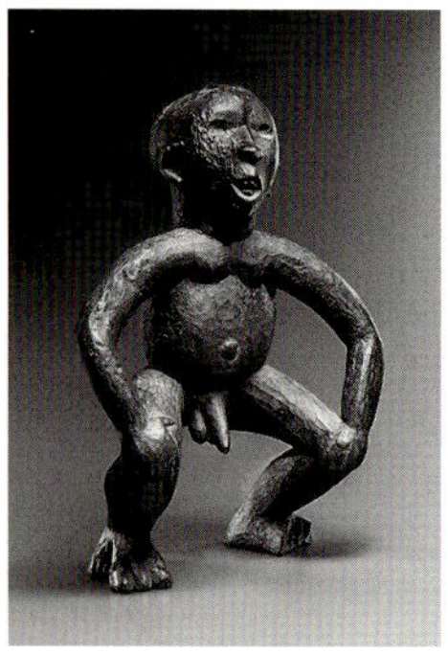

Page 108
Bamileke statue
Cameroon, H. 37 cm

Provenance
Merton D. Simpson, New York
Pace Primitive, New York
Béatrice and Patrick Caput, Paris
Bernard Dulon, Paris

Published
Dulon B., Laurquin A., *Objetos-Signos de Africa*, Saragozza, 2000, p. 78, fig. 42
Lintig (von) B., *Cameroun : arts traditionnels*, Paris, 2006, pp. 70–1

Exhibited
Saragozza, *Objetos-Signos de Africa*, Centro de Exposiciones y Congresos, 11 April – 24 June 2000
Cameroun: arts traditionnels:
– Paris, Galerie Bernard Dulon, 16 June – 30 September 2006
– New York, Friedman & Vallois Gallery, 20 October – 30 November 2006

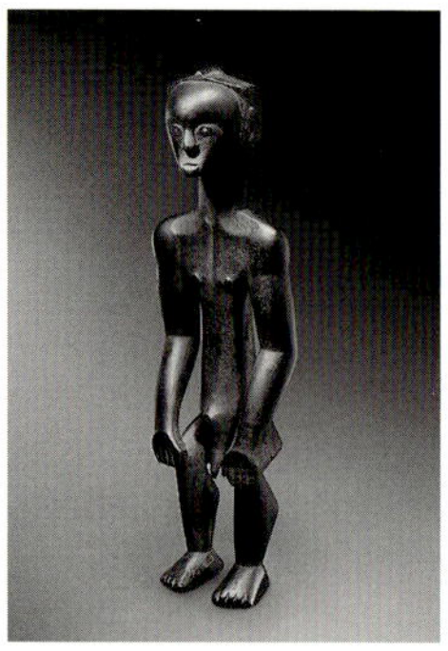

Page 111
Fang reliquary figure
Ngumba or Ntumu group, South Cameroon, H. 51 cm

Provenance
Lance and Roberta Entwistle, Paris/London

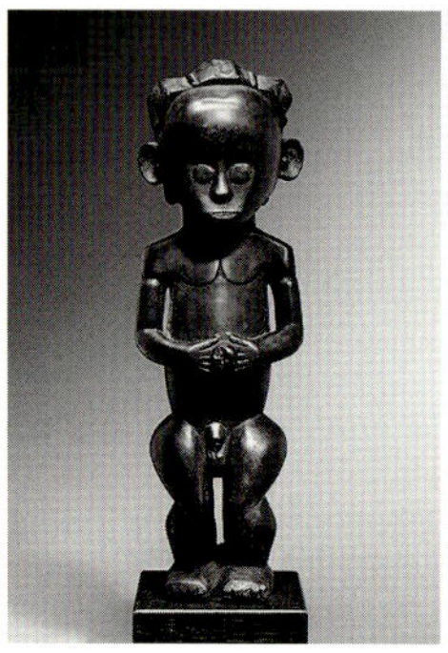

Page 115
Fang reliquary figure
Betsi-Nzaman group, South Cameroon, H. 43.5 cm

Provenance
Charles Ratton, Paris
Edward Goldberg Robinson, Los Angeles
Jane Robinson Sidney, Los Angeles
Sotheby's, London, *Primitive Art from the Edward G. Robinson Collection,* 10 July 1973, lot 186
James H. Kirkman, London
Patricia Ann Withofs, Sydney/London
Oliver et Pamela Cobb, Seattle, 1975
Sotheby's, Paris, *Collection Oliver et Pamela Cobb*, 12 June 2012, lot 13

Published
Perrois L., *Arts du Gabon. Les Arts plastiques du Bassin de l'Ogooué*, Arnouville, 1979, p. 79, fig. 65
Clarke C., *African Art in the Barnes Foundation. The Triumph of L'Art nègre and the Harlem Renaissance*, Philadelphie, 2015, p. 198, fig. 2
Le Fur Y., *Les Forêts natales : Arts d'Afrique équatoriale atlantique*, Paris, 2017, pp. 57 and 228, fig. 72

Exhibited
Paris, *Les Forêts natales : Arts d'Afrique équatoriale atlantique,* musée du quai Branly – Jacques Chirac, 3 October 2017 – 21 January 2018

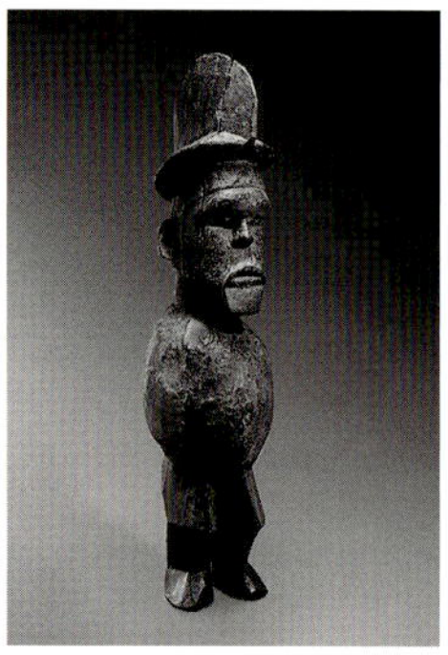

Page 120
Teke statue
Malebo Pool region, Democratic Republic of the Congo, H. 56 cm

Provenance
Maurice de Vlaminck, Paris
Loudmer, Paris, 2 July 1987, lot 169
Michel Perinet, Paris
Alain de Monbrison, Paris
Hélène Leloup, Paris

Published
Monbrison (de) A., *Biennale des Antiquaires*, Paris, 2002, n.p.

Vallès-Bled M. (ed.), *Vlaminck : un instinct fauve*, Paris, 2008, p. 168, ill. 1, p. 175, fig. 1

Exhibited
Paris, Biennale des Antiquaires, Grand Palais, 20 – 29 September 2002
Paris, *Vlaminck : un instinct fauve*, Musée du Luxembourg, 20 February – 20 July 2008

Notes
1 Marc Felix suggests that the crest on this type of headdress symbolizes a dugout canoe, a theory that is well worth considering since the Malebo Pool Teke were the "masters of the river" during the slave trade between the coast and the inland areas; besides, miniature dugouts are frequently associated with ritual statues. Lastly, there is no record in the known photographic archives of a similar headdress worn by men (Felix M., 2011, pp. 16–20)
2 The very names of the different spiritual beings that may inhabit these statues and the different categories to which they belong differ considerably depending on whether they are involved in the ritual systems of the western Teke (Laadi, Ntsaye), the Kukuya of the eastern Teke (Mbe, Mfunu), or the Mfinu (Vansina J., 1973, pp. 11–2)
3 Vansina J., 1973, p. 40 and p. 42, fig 1
4 Lema G.M., 1978, p. 170, quoted by Volper J., 2016, pp. 17, 41–3, ill. 21, p. 42

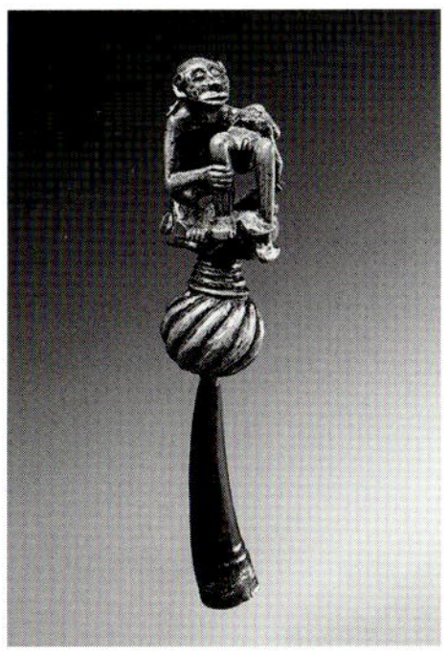

Page 122
Kongo whistle
Democratic Republic of the Congo, H. 18 cm

Provenance
Charles Ratton, Paris
Merton D. Simpson, New York
Ernst et Ruth Anspach, New York
Johann Levy, Paris
Sotheby's, New York, 15 May 2003, lot 70
Marceau Rivière, Paris
Philippe Ratton, Paris
Lucas Ratton, Paris

Published
Rachewitz (de) B., *Eros noir/Black Eros*, Milan, 1963/New York, 1964, p. 104
Lehuard R., Lecomte A., *Les sifflets Bakongo*, Paris, 2013, p. 78

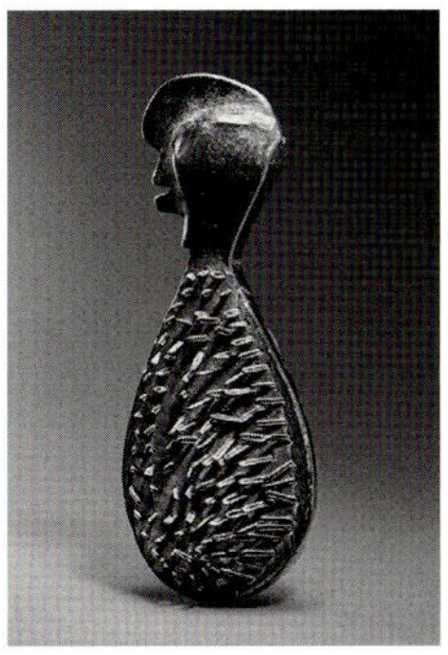

Page 124
Songye comb
Democratic Republic of the Congo, H. 11 cm

Provenance
John D. Graham, New York
Michael Rhodes, New York
Nicole and John Dintenfass, New York
Sotheby's, Paris, *Collection Nicole et John Dintenfass*, 23 June 2006, lot 37

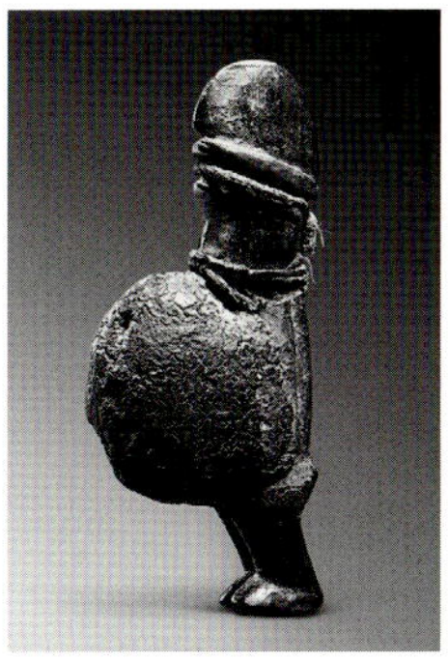

Page 124
Teke statuette
Malebo Pool region, Democratic Republic of the Congo, H. 11 cm

Provenance
Général Germain Mennerat, acquired *in situ* between 1925 and 1927
By descent
Sotheby's, Paris, 4 December 2008, lot 139

Notes
1 On the right bank of the river, statues all have the generic name *itio*, except the smallest, which are called *ititio* (Vansina J., 1973, pp. 40, 176)
2 Lehuard R., 1996, p. 209
3 Ibid., p. 19 quoting Lema Gete 1978, pp. 394, 432
4 Vansina J., 1973, p. 180

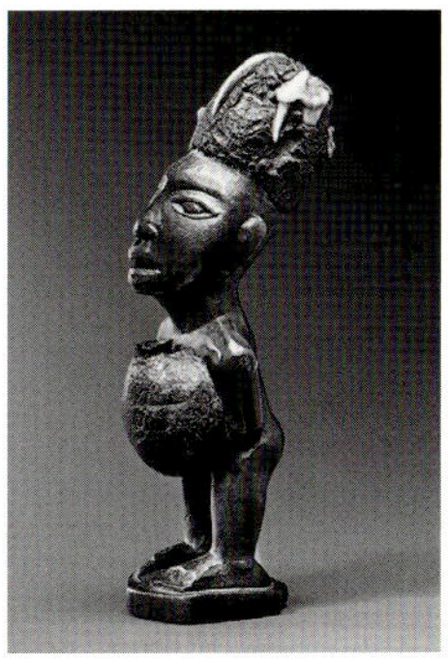

Page 125
Vili statuette
Democratic Republic of the Congo, H. 14 cm

Provenance
Paul Rupalley, Paris
Flagel-Portier, Paris, *Collection Paul Rupalley*, 17–18 March 1930, lot 137
Robert and Raoul Lehuard, Arnouville
Galerie Ratton-Hourdé, Paris

Published
Lehuard R., *Art Bakongo – Les Centres de style*, vol. I, Arnouville, 1989, p. 241, fig. D 5-1-4
Lehuard R., *Kongo. Collection de Robert et Raoul Lehuard*, Paris, 1999, p. 13
Felix M.L., *White Gold, Black Hands. Ivory Sculpture in Congo*, vol. I, Qiqihar, 2010, p. 36

Exhibited
Paris, *Kongo. Collection de Robert et Raoul Lehuard*, Galerie Ratton-Hourdé, December 1999 – January 2000

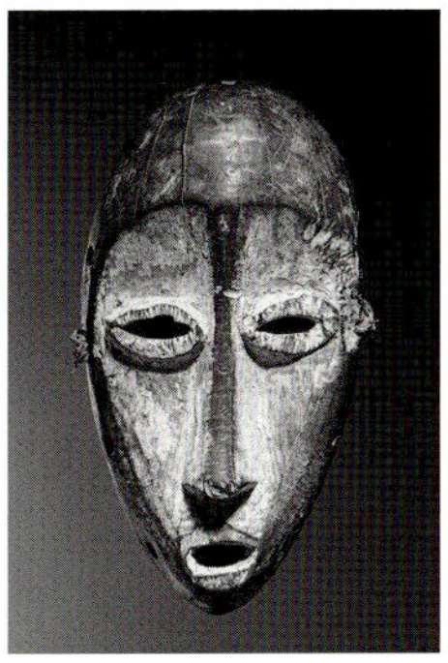

Page 125
Lega mask
Democratic Republic of the Congo, H. 16 cm

Provenance
Arman, Paris/New York
Bernard Dulon, Paris

Published
Dulon B., *Arman l'Africain*, Paris, 2002, fig. 1

Exhibited
Paris, *Arman l'Africain*, Galerie Bernard Dulon, 19 September – 31 October 2002

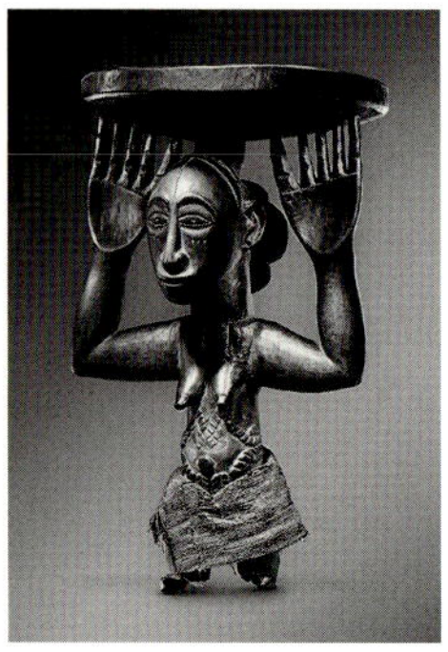

Page 127
Hemba caryatid stool
Nkuvu or Muhona, Tanganyika, Democratic Republic of the Congo, H. 45.5 cm

Provenance
Jacques Kerchache, Paris

Published
Kerchache J., Paudrat J.-L., Stephan L., *L'art africain*, Paris, 1988, p. 444, fig. 680

Notes
1 Nooter R., and Roberts M., 1996, pp. 154–55
2 All these titles are clearly of Luba origin (cf. in Luba *twite*, *bulopwe*, etc.)
3 Neyt F., 1977, pp. 491–95
4 Baeke V., 2017, pp. 69–77
5 The verb *úbatízha* means, "to look at someone or something until one has acquired a profound knowledge of it" (Blakely T.D., Blakely P.A.R., 1987, pp. 31–2; Blakely T.D., 1981, pp. 6–7, quoted by Baeke V., 2017, p. 72

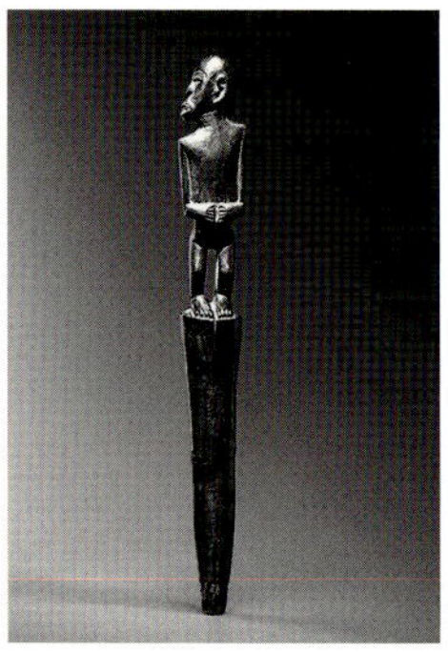

Page 130
Vili sceptre
Democratic Republic of the Congo, H. 38 cm

Provenance
William Downing Webster, Bicester (inv. no. 6576)
Mathias Komor, New York
Hélène Leloup, Paris
Jean-Pierre Weill Collection, Paris

Published
Cornet J.A., *Kongo : objets de bois, objets d'ivoire*, Paris, 1998, cover and p. 11, no. 1

Exhibited
Paris, *Kongo : objets de bois, objets d'ivoire*, Galerie Hélène et Philippe Leloup, June 1998

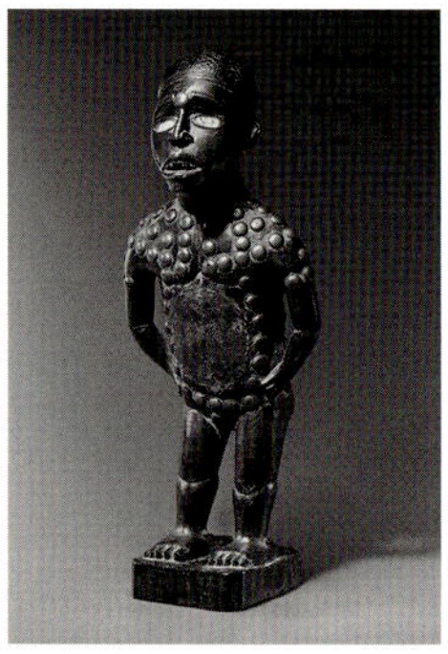

Page 132
Yombe statue
Central Kongo Province, Democratic Republic of the Congo, H. 34 cm

Provenance
Pace Primitive, New York
Arman, Paris/New York
Jacques Kerchache, Paris

Published
African Arts magazine, vol. X, no. 4, July 1977, p. 57 (Pace Primitive advertisement)
Arts d'Afrique Noire magazine, no. 62, summer 1987, p. 57 (Pace Primitive advertisement)
Lehuard R., *Art Bakongo – Les Centres de style*, vol. II, Arnouville, 1989, p. 469, fig. J 1-3-2
Kerchache J., Paudrat J.-L., Stephan L., *L'art africain*, Paris, 1988, p. 429, fig. 601
Herreman F. (ed.), *African Faces, African Figures. The Arman Collection*, New York, 1997, p. 150, fig. 139
Sourrieu M. (ed.), *Arman & l'art africain*, Marseille/Paris, 1996, p. 136, fig. 109

Exhibited
Arman & l'art africain:
– Marseille, Musée d'Arts africains, océaniens, amérindiens, chapelle de la Vieille Charité, 23 June – 30 October 1996
– Paris, Musée National des arts d'Afrique et d'Océanie, 3 December 1996 – 17 February 1997
– Cologne, Rautenstrauch-Joest-Museum, Museum für Völkerkunde, March – August 1997
New York, *African faces, African figures, The Arman Collection*, The Museum for African Art, 9 October 1997 – 19 April 1998

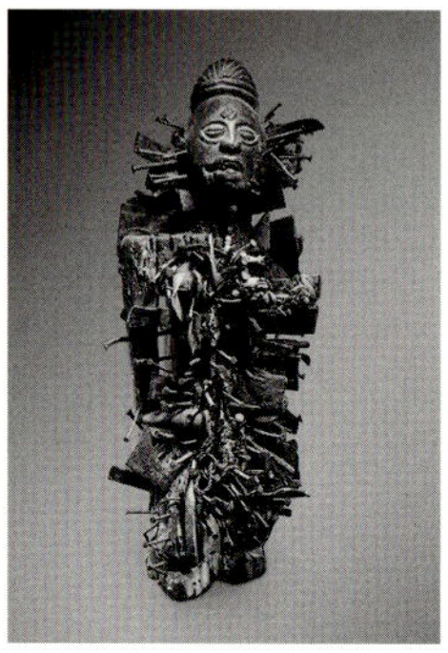

Page 134
Kongo-Mayanga statue
Central-Kongo Province, Democratic Republic of the Congo, H. 51 cm

Provenance
Reportedly Dr Giovanni Trolli
Pierre Dartevelle, Brussels
Belgian private collection
Christie's, Paris, 11 December 2012, lot 74

Published
Arts d'Afrique Noire magazine, Index, no. 1–57, 1986 (Impasse St-Jacques advertisement)
Heusch (de) L. *et al.*, *Utotombo. Kunst uit Zwart-Afrika in Belgisch prive-bezit/Utotombo. L'Art d'Afrique noire dans les collections privées belges,* Brussels, 1988, p. 9, no. XXVI
Lehuard R., *Art Bakongo. Les Centres de style*, vol. II, Arnouville, 1989, p. 446, fig. I 3-1-1
Tribal Art Magazine, spring 2013, no. 67, p. 23 (Christie's advertisement)

Exhibited
Brussels, *Utotombo. Kunst uit Zwart-Afrika in Belgisch prive-bezit/Utotombo. L'Art d'Afrique noire dans les collections privées belges*, Palais des Beaux-Arts, 25 March – 5 June 1988

Notes
1 Lehuard R., 1989 (vol. II), *Le style mayanga*, pp. 440–51 and ill. I.3.1.1, p. 446
2 MacGaffey W., 2000, pp. 80–1
3 Probably a reflection of the fact that, "in the Kong-speaking area in general, the world was traditionally depicted according to a binary concept that opposed the earth to the sky" (de Heusch L., 2000, p. 265, quoted by Baeke V., 2016, p. 126

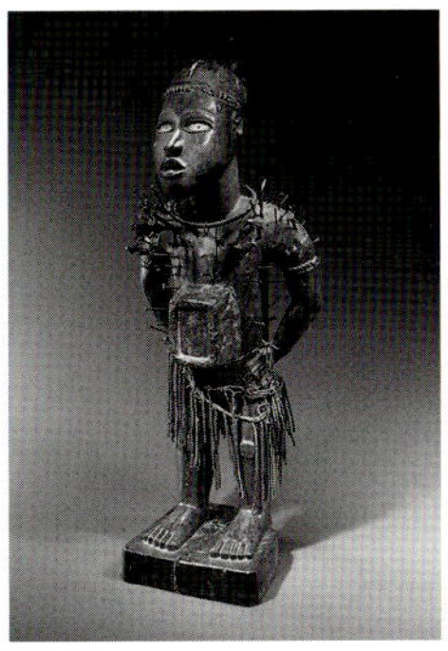

Page 139
Vili statue
Democratic Republic of the Congo/Cabinda,
H. 76 cm

Provenance
Robert Burawoy, Paris

Published
Lehuard R., *Fétiches à clous du Bas-Zaïre,* Arnouville, 1980, p. 197, fig. 109

Notes
1 As Luc de Heusch expertly points out, the Vili and the Woyo have no interest in their ancestors and prefer to worship the *bakisi basi* spirits of the earth, whereas to the south of the River Congo the pantheon of the Southern Kongo includes both the *bakulu* ancestors and the *basimbi* and *bankita* spirits of nature. As for the Yombe, this people have a place for these spirits as well as the *bakisi tsi* earth spirits (de Heusch L., 2000, pp. 217–21)
2 *Nkobe di Lemba* basket, Musée royal de l'Afrique centrale (EO.0.0.43040), collected by Rev. Bittremieux in 1937, and published by Janzen J.M., 1982, p. 253 and photo 5 (between p. 257 and p. 258)
3 Berg en Dal, Afrika Museum collection, inv. 177, no date, published in Janzen J.M., 1982, photo 19 (between p. 257 and p. 258), MRAC, EO.0.0.43040 (24 x 20.4 cm)

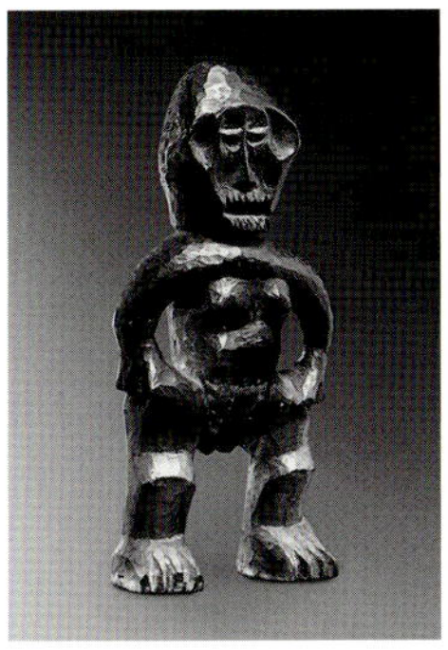

Page 142
Metoko (?) statue
Democratic Republic of the Congo, H. 29 cm

Provenance
Thomas Alexander III, Saint Louis
Hélène Leloup, Paris

Published
Leloup H., *Féminité. Sa diversité dans l'Afrique traditionnelle,* Paris, 2003, p. 93, no. 44

Exhibited
Paris, *Féminité. Sa diversité dans l'Afrique traditionnelle,* Galerie Hélène Leloup, June 2003

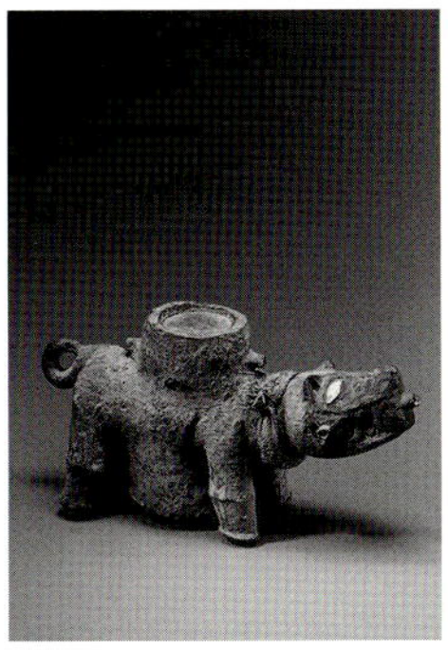

Page 143
Kongo dog
Democratic Republic of the Congo, L. 23 cm

Provenance
MM. Delory and Grunevald
Bernard Dulon, Paris
Robert and Raoul Lehuard, Arnouville
Galerie Ratton-Hourdé, Paris

Published
Dennett R.E., *Seven years among the Fjort. An English trader's experiences in the Congo district/Sept ans parmi les Bavili. Les expériences d'un marchand anglais dans la région du Congo*, Arnouville, 1991, p. 85
Dulon B., *Kongo*, Paris, 1991, p. 31
Lehuard R., *Kongo. Collection de Robert et Raoul Lehuard*, Paris, 1999, p. 21 and invitation card

Exhibited
Paris, *Kongo*, Galerie Bernard Dulon, 1991
Paris, *Kongo. Collection de Robert et Raoul Lehuard,* Galerie Ratton-Hourdé, December 1999 – January 2000

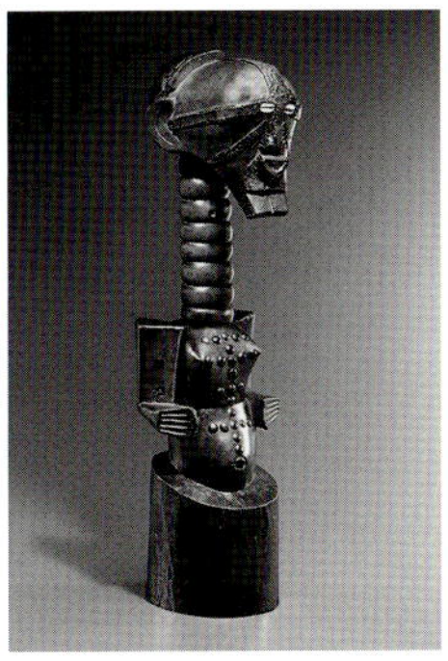

Page 144
Songye statue
Lomami Province, Democratic Republic of the Congo, H. 53.5 cm

Provenance
Sandro Volta, Milan
Rheims, Paris, *Collection Monsieur Sandro Volta,* 17 May 1957, lot 210
Lance and Roberta Entwistle, Paris/London

Published
Allemand M., *L'Art de l'Afrique Noire et " l'époque nègre" de quelques artistes contemporains*, Saint-Étienne, 1956, no. 27, cat. 160

Exhibited
Saint-Étienne, *L'Art de l'Afrique Noire et " l'époque nègre" de quelques artistes contemporains,* Musée d'Art et d'Industrie, 20 March – 10 May 1956
Milan, *L'Illustrazione Italiana, Sculture dell'Africa Tenebrosa*, September 1956

Notes
1 Wauters G., 1949, pp. 231–46
2 Neyt F., 2004, ill. 200, p. 234
3 Baeke V., 2004, pp. 22–3
4 Wauters G., 1949, p. 145 and drawings pp. 136–7. According to the author, inductors adamantly confirm the importance of the objects present during initiation rites as symbols rather than as *bwangas*, thus suggesting that this statue was in fact not equipped with any ritual charge (*Idem*, pp. 154 and 182)
5 Stappers L., 1950, p. 89

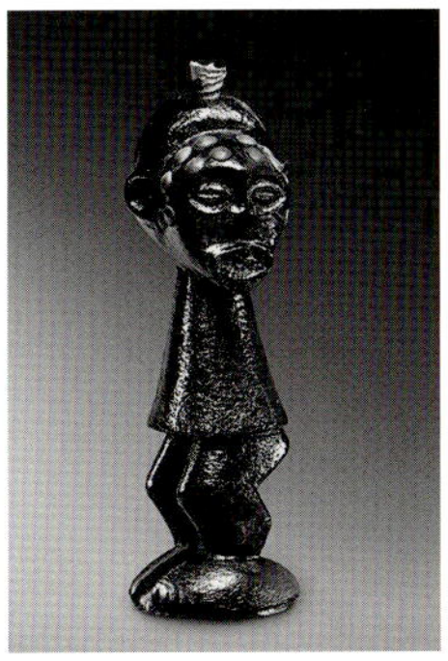

Page 146
Songye statuette
Ilande or Milembwe region, Lomami Province, Democratic Republic of the Congo, H. 24 cm

Provenance
Ernst and Ruth Anspach, New York
Alain de Monbrison, Paris, 1998
Jeff Soreff, New York
Sotheby's, Paris, *A New York Collection*, 30 November 2010, lot 3

Published
Robbins W.M., Nooter N.I., *African Art in American Collections, Survey 1989,* Washington, DC /London, 1989, p. 468, no. 1204
Anderson M.G., Kreamer C.M., *Wild Spirits Strong Medecine: African Art and the Wilderness,* New York/ Seattle, 1989, pl. 85
Bacquart J.-B., *The Tribal Arts of Africa/L'Art tribal d'Afrique Noire*, London/Paris, 1998, p. 170, ill. B

Exhibited
Wild Spirits Strong Medecine: African Art and the Wilderness:
– New York, Center for African Art,
10 May – 20 August 1989
– Evanston, Block Art Gallery,
21 September – 22 November 1989
– Coral Gables, Lowe Art Museum,
14 December 1989 – 28 January 1990
– Columbus, The Columbus Museum of Art,
18 February – 30 April 1990
– Worcester, The Worcester Art Museum,
15 September – 1 December 1990

Notes
1 Merriam A.P., 1974, p. 147
2 Like two other Songye figures (Neyt F., 2004, ill. 264 and 266)

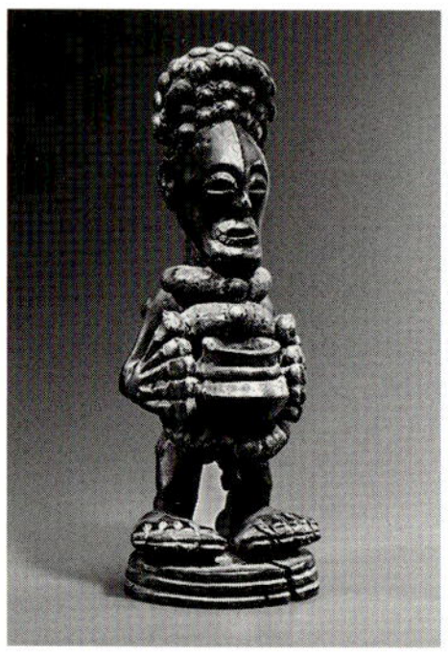

Page 148
Kalundwe statuette
Democratic Republic of the Congo, H. 25 cm

Provenance
Bernard Dulon, Paris

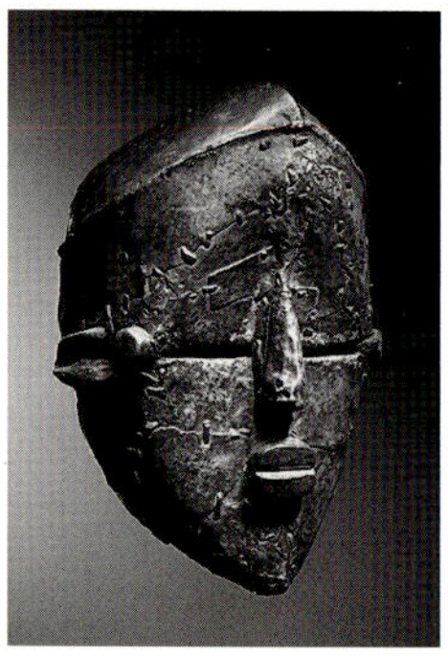

Page 150
Lwalu mask
Democratic Republic of the Congo, H. 29 cm

Provenance
Photographed in the village of Kangambu
by Rik Ceyssens in 1971 (MRAC, inv. no. EPH9122)
Marc Leo Felix, Brussels, acquired *in situ*
in the early 1980s
Myron Kunin, Minneapolis, acquired on
10 December 1989
Alain de Monbrison, Paris, 1992
Sotheby's, Paris, 12 June 2012, lot 100

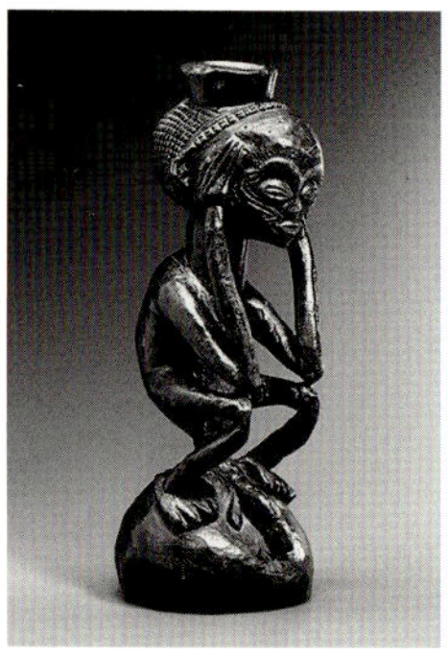

Page 153
Luluwa statuette
Democratic Republic of the Congo, H. 27 cm

Provenance
Jacques Kerchache, Paris
Pierre Bergé, Paris, *Collection Anne et Jacques Kerchache*, 12 and 13 June 2010, lot 337

Published
Kerchache J., *Chefs d'oeuvres de l'art africain*, Grenoble, 1982, n.p.
Kerchache J., Paudrat J.-L. et Stephan L., *L'art africain*, Paris, 1988, p. 582, fig. 1035

Exhibited
Grenoble, *Chefs d'oeuvres de l'art africain*, musée
de Grenoble, 4 November – late December 1982

Note
1 Further reading: Petridis C., 2018

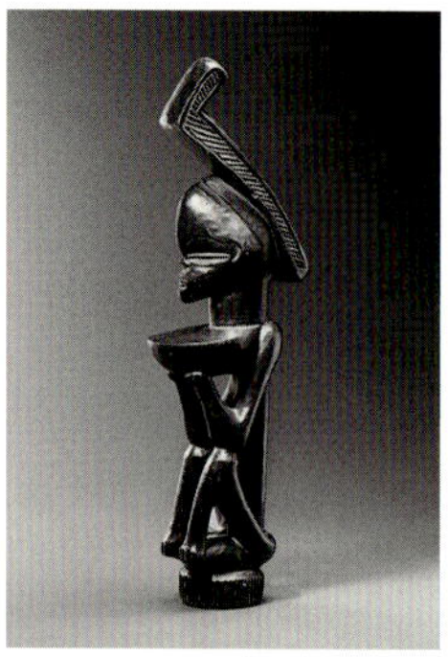

Page 159
Songo statue
Angola, H. 26 cm

Provenance
Charles Ratton, Paris
Private Collection, California, acquired in 1948
Sotheby's, New York, 22 November 1998, lot 357

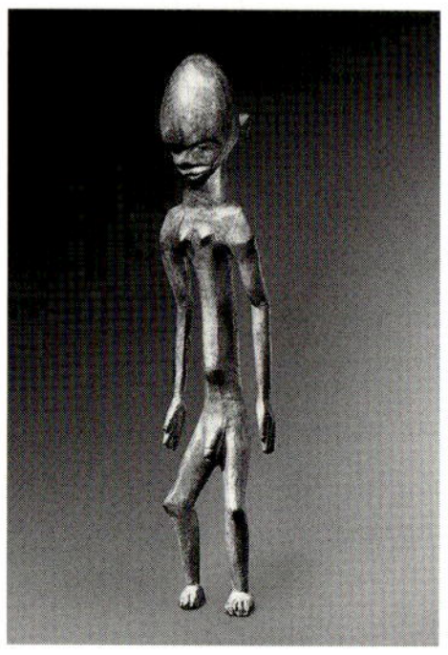

Page 161
Bari statue
Sudan, H. 63.5 cm

Provenance
Alain de Monbrison, Paris

Published
Monbrison (de) A., *Biennale des Antiquaires*, Paris, 2002, n.p.

Exhibited
Paris, Biennale des Antiquaires, Grand Palais,
20 – 29 September 2002

OCEANIA

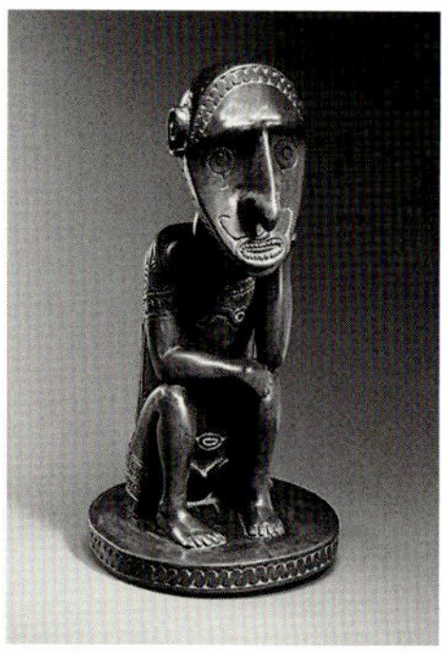

Page 167
Massim Statue
Sculpted by Mutuaga, village of Dagodagoisu, Suan Region, Papua New Guinea
H. 39 cm

Provenance
Jacques Kerchache, Paris

Published
Meyer A., *Art Océanien*, Cologne, 1995, p. 52, fig. 30
Beran H., *Mutuaga, a nineteenth-century New Guinea master carver*, Wollongong, 1996, pl. 79

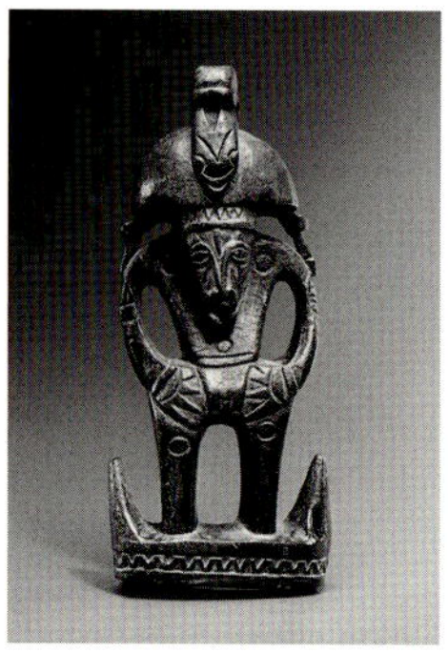

Page 171
Hook
Tami Islands, Morobe Province, Papua New Guinea,
H. 30.5 cm

Provenance
Walter Randel, New York
Wayne Heathcote, Miami
Marcia and John A. Friede, Rye
Collection Masco Corporation, Detroit
Luciano Lanfranchi, Milan
Bruce Frank, New York
Anthony Meyer, Paris
Collection Lambert, Brussels
Anthony Meyer, Paris

Published
Wardwell A., *Island Ancestors, Oceanic Art from the Masco Collection*, Detroit, 1994, p. 89, fig. 29
Falgayrettes-Leveau C., van Cutsem-Vanderstraete A., *L'art de manger : rites et traditions en Afrique, Insulinde et Océanie*, Paris, 2014, p. 271

Exhibited
Island Ancestors, Oceanic Art from the Masco Collection:
– The Kimbell Museum, Fort Worth,
24 September – 4 December 1994
– Honolulu Academy of Arts, Honolulu,
2 February – 26 March 1995
– The Detroit Institute of Art, Detroit,
11 June – 6 August 1995
– North Carolina Museum of Art, Raleigh,
9 March – 5 May 1996
Paris, *L'Art de manger : rites et traditions en Afrique, Insulinde et Océanie*, musée Dapper,
15 October 2014 – 12 July 2015

Notes
1 Bamler G., "Die Tago" *in* Neuhauss R., 1911, Deutsche Neu Guinea, Vol III, pp. 507–13
2 Bodrogi T., *Art in North East New Guinea*, Budapest, 1961, p. 31
3 There is a local legend of a two-headed lizard that walks one way at night and the other way during the day but this may not apply here. My Tami informants always referred to a green tree lizard but the facial motifs on the lizard heads were different to this hook.
4 *Eine Forschvgreise im Bismarck-Archipel*, Hamburg, 1911, p. 171. Vogel was impressed by the Tami men.
5 According to the Tami informants of Georg Bamler around 1900s many of the *Tago* marks go back to Maligep in West New Britain (WNB) and predate the Kani/Balum cult of the current Tami and coastal communities of the Huon Gulf—indicating perhaps that some if not all the Tami are migrants from WNB. There is also evidence of a Tami family on Arop. Island (Neuhauss, 1911, vol. I p. 338)
6 Bamler G., *in* Neuhauss R., 1911
7 Tibor Bodrogi's information was from Lajos Biro and Tibor decided to use names from the Yabim speakers. He followed the precedent of the Lutherans that adopted Yabim as the lingua franca of the nearby mainland. A decision had to be made because of the wide variability of names for similar symbols all around the Huon Gulf (Tami) style area.

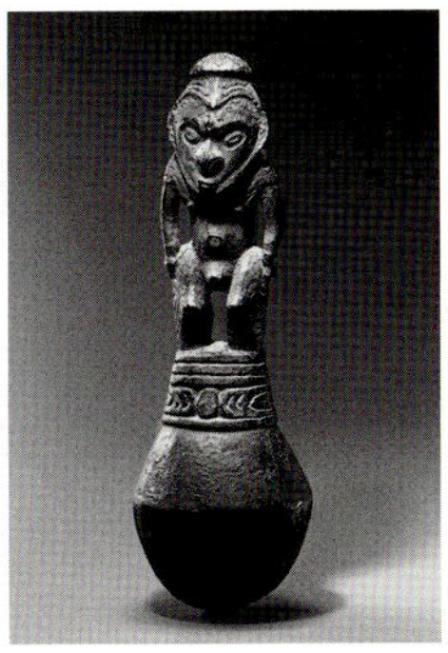

Page 173
Pestle
Murik Lake, Papua New Guinea, H. 30 cm

Provenance
De Quay & Lombrail, Paris, *Arts Primitifs – Collection Jean-Claude Bellier et à divers amateurs*, 21 June 1995, lot 76

Published
Falgayrettes-Leveau C., van Cutsem-Vanderstraete A., *L'art de manger : rites et traditions en Afrique, Insulinde et Océanie*, Paris, 2014, p. 262

Exhibited
Paris, *L'Art de manger : rites et traditions en Afrique, Insulinde et Océanie*, musée Dapper, 15 October 2014 – 12 July 2015

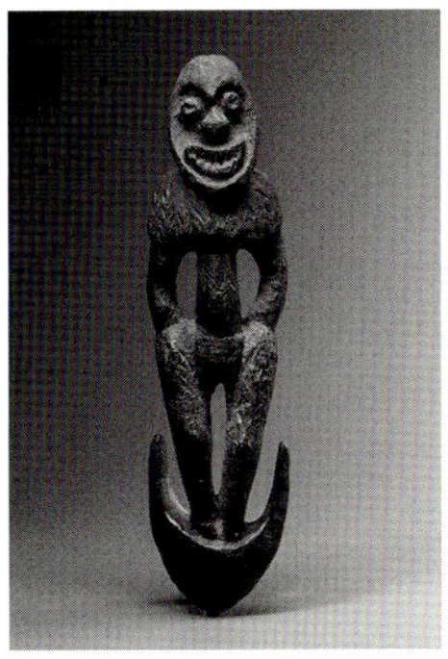

Page 173
Hook
Sepik River, Papua New Guinea, H. 20 cm

Provenance
Marcia and John A. Friede, Rye
Collection Jolika, Fine Arts Museums, De Young Museum, San Francisco (inv. no. 2007.44.43)
Christie's, Paris, *Collection Jolika, chefs-d'oeuvre de Nouvelle-Guinée provenant des Fine Arts Museums de San Francisco*, 19 June 2013, lot 4

Published
Friede J. A. *et al*, *New Guinea Art Masterpieces from the Jolika Collection of Marcia and John Friede*, San Francisco, 2005, vol. 1, p. 189, cat. 157 and vol. 2, p. 107, cat. 157

Exhibited
San Francisco, Fine Arts Museum of San Francisco, de Young Museum, 15 October 2005 – 14 February 2013

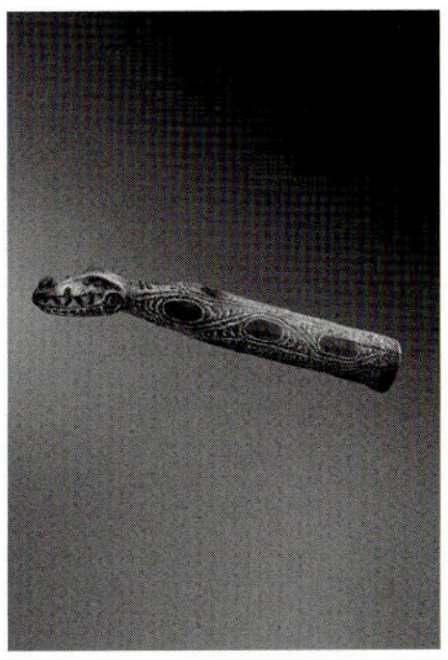

Page 174
Iatmul trumpet
Sepik River, Papua New Guinea, L. 49 cm

Provenance
Pierre Loeb, Paris
Loudmer-Poulain, Paris, 1977, lot 32

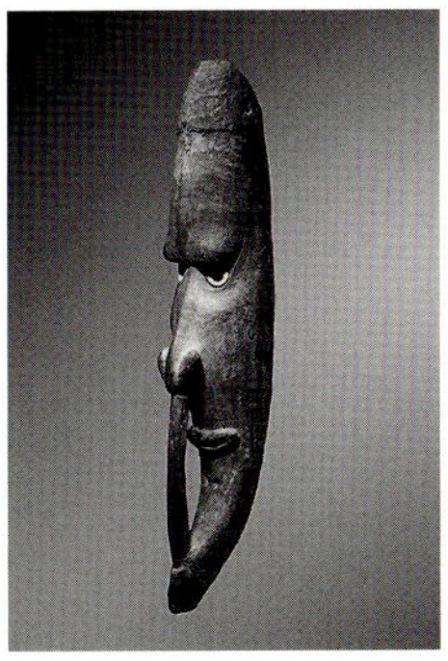

Page 175
Iatmul mask
Sepik River, Papua New Guinea, H. 47 cm

Provenance
Alain Schoffel, Plouguiel
Christie's, Paris, 15 June 2002, lot 31

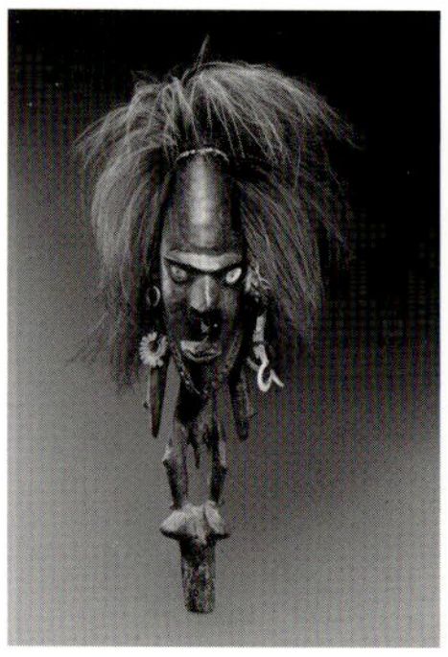

Page 177
Biwat flute stopper
Yuat River, Papua New Guinea, H. 59 cm

Provenance
Probably Museum für Völkerkunde, Berlin
Arthur Speyer I, Berlin
Arthur Speyer II, Berlin
Matthias L.J. Lemaire, Amsterdam
Sotheby's, Paris, 12 December 2012, lot 17

Published
Kooten (van) T., Heuvel (van den) G., *Sculptuur uit Afrika en Oceanië/Sculpture from Africa and Oceania*, Otterlo, 1990, p. 247, no. 93
Meyer A., *Art Océanien*, Cologne, 1995, p. 210, no. 220, and cover
Schindlbeck M., *Gefunden und Verloren, Arthur Speyer, Die Dreissiger Jahre und die Verluste der Sammlung Südsee des Ethnologischen Museums Berlin*, Bönen, 2012, ill. 52 and 55
Revue *Tribal Art Magazine*, spring 2013, no. 67, p. 32, no. 2

Exhibited
Otterlo, *Sculptuur uit Afrika en Oceanië/Sculpture from Africa and Oceania*, Rijksmuseum Kröller-Müller, 17 November 1990 – 20 January 1991

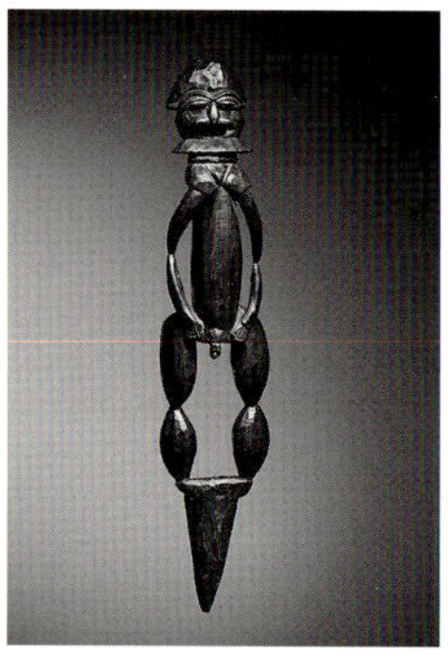

Page 183
Kanak statue
New Caledonia, H. 86 cm

Provenance
Maurice Bonnefoy, Paris
Ader Picar Tajan, Paris, 18 December 1990, lot 2
Lewis Wara Gallery, Seattle / New York
Pierre Bergé, Brussels, 5 June 2007, lot 593
Pierre Bergé, Brussels, 7 November 2008, lot 299
Yann Ferrandin, Paris

Published
Bühler A., Gabus J., *Art Océanien*, 1970, Neuchâtel, p. 95, no. 1938 (listed)

Exhibited
Neuchâtel, *Art Océanien,* musée d'Ethnographie, 27 June – 31 December 1970

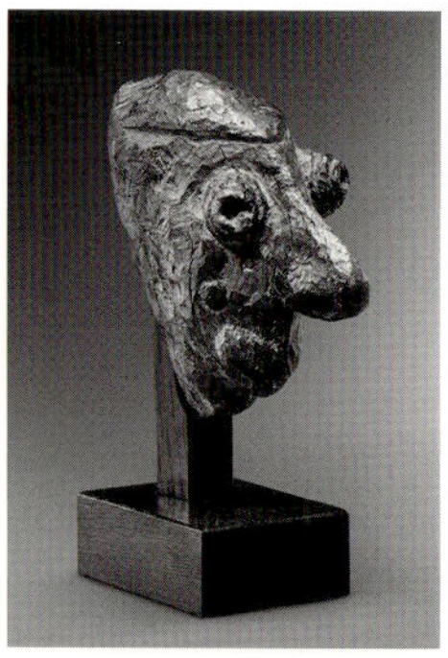

Page 184
Small mask
Malekula, Vanuatu, H. 16 cm
Stand by Kichizô Inagaki

Provenance
René Gaffé, Paris
Christie's, *Collection René Gaffé*, 8 December 2001, lot 6

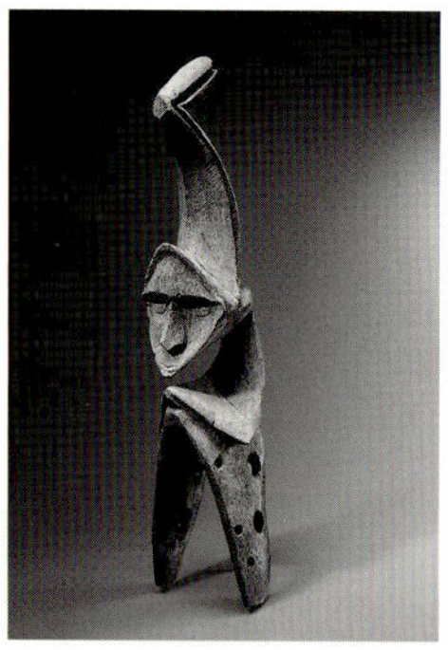

Page 186
Canoe prow
Vanuatu, H. 63 cm

Provenance
Sotheby's, Paris, 11 June 2008, lot 54

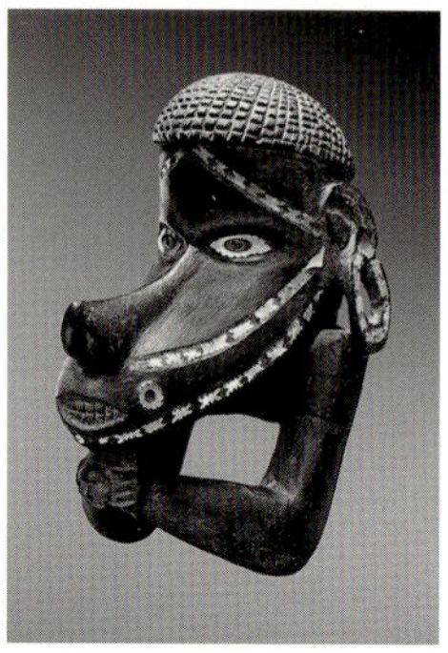

Page 187
Canoe prow
Solomon Islands, H. 25 cm

Provenance
Acquired *in situ* between 1905 and 1908, Captain E.L. Cardale, lieutenant on *H.M.S. Torch*
By descent
Christie's, London, 26 April 1977, lot 73
Lance and Roberta Entwistle, Paris/London
Oliver Cobb, Seattle
Lance and Roberta Entwistle, Paris/London

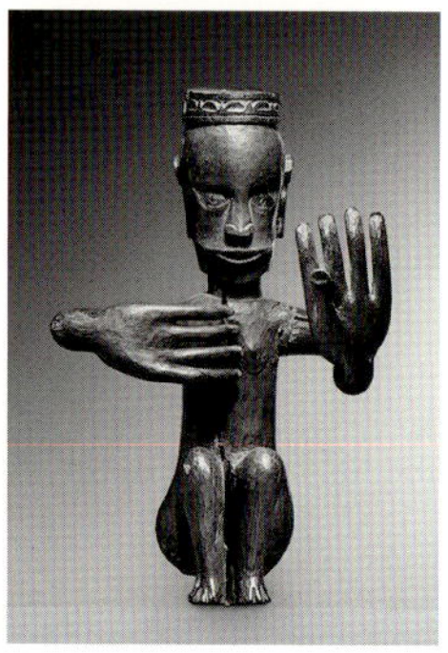

Page 188
Batak statue
Sumatra, Indonesia, H. 34 cm

Provenance
Lecorneur-Roudillon gallery, Paris
Hélène Leloup, Paris

Published
Rousseau M., *L'Art océanien, sa présence*, Paris, l'APAM, 1951, p. 48, fig. 71

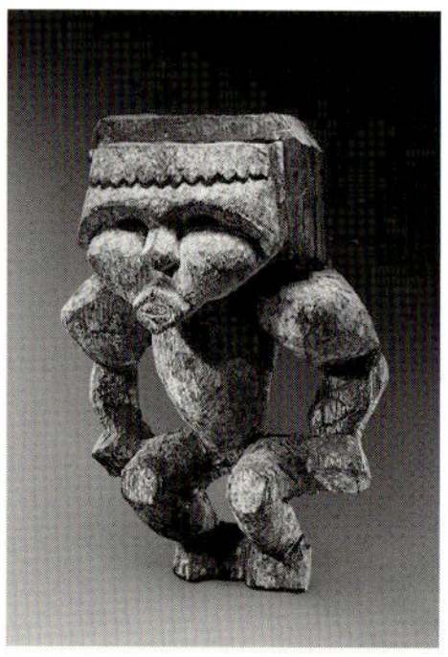

Page 191
Dayak architectural element
Borneo, Indonesia, H. 51 cm

Provenance
Bernard Dulon, Paris

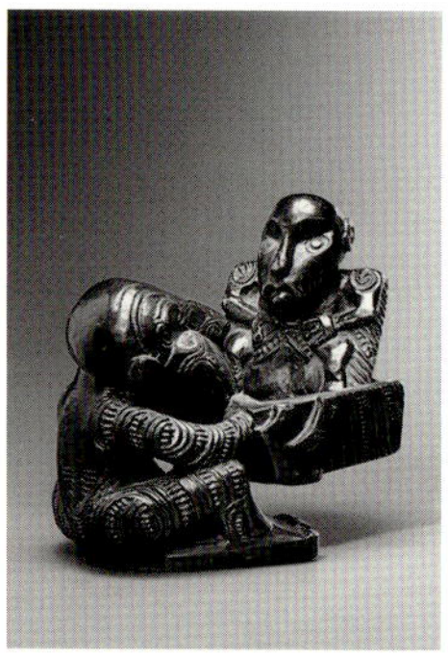

Page 192
Maori box
New Zealand, H. 12 cm

Provenance
Carlo Monzino, Castagnola
Sotheby's, Paris, 12 December 2012, lot 21

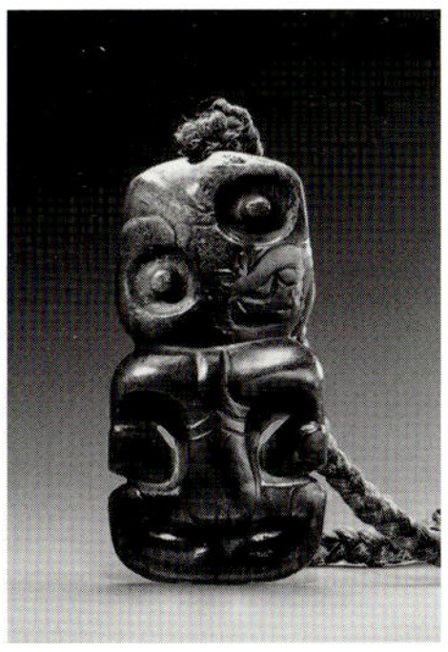

Page 194
Maori pendant
New Zealand, H. 12 cm

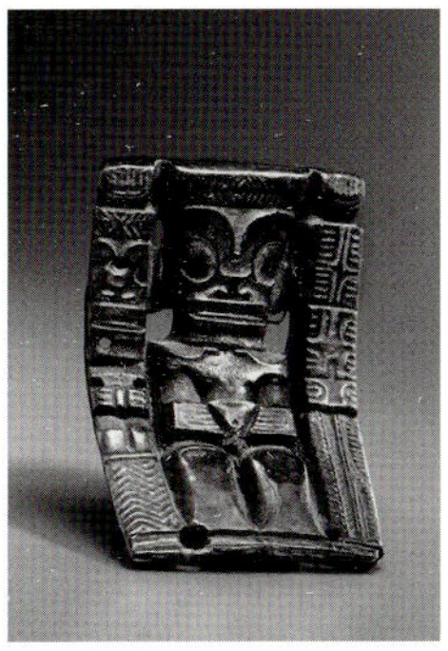

Page 194
Ornament
Marquesas Islands, H. 5.3 cm

Provenance
Henri Kamer, Paris
Philippe Bourgouin, Paris
Anthony Meyer, Paris

Published
Meyer A., *Art Océanien,* Cologne, 1995, p. 501, fig. 572

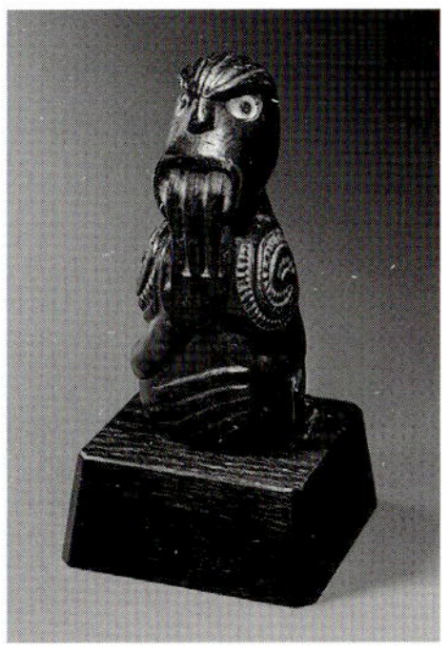

Page 195
Maori sculpture
New Zealand, H. 14 cm
Stand by Kichizô Inagaki

Provenance
Roland Tual, Paris
Loiseau-Schmitz-Digard, Saint-Germain-en-Laye, 5 October 1997, lot 84A
Anthony Meyer, Paris
Daniel Masson
Calmels-Cohen, Paris, 8 June 2005, lot 388

Published
Marquetty M.V., *Galerie Pigalle : Afrique, Océanie*, Paris, 1930, p. 27, cat. 391
Hourdé C.-W., Rolland N., *Galerie Pigalle : Afrique, Océanie. 1930. Une exposition mythique*, Paris, 2018, p. 311, cat. 391

Exhibited
Paris, *Exposition d'art africain et d'art océanien*, Galerie Pigalle, 1930
Paris, *Pigalle 1930, retour sur une exposition mythique*, espace Tribal, 11 – 16 September 2018

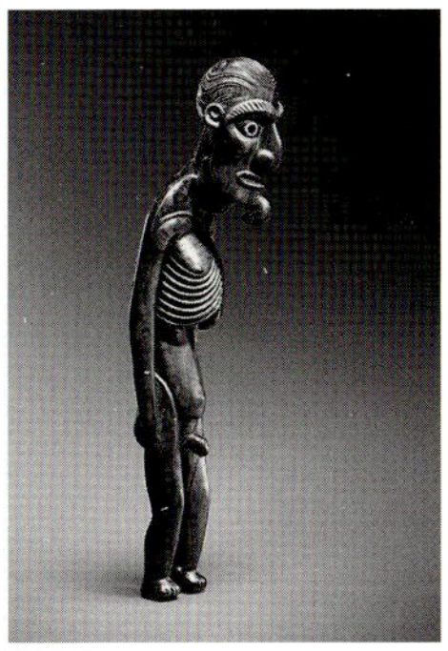

Page 196
Statue
Easter Island, H. 43 cm

Provenance
Acquired *in situ* by George Harvey, a sailor in the sixth company of the Royal Marine Artillery when HMS Topaze made landfall at Easter Island, between 1 and 7 November 1868
By descent
Christie's, South Kensington, London, 28 June 1988, lot 163
Lance and Roberta Entwistle, Paris/London
Michel Perinet, Paris
Alain de Monbrison, Paris
Collection Rosenthal, Paris
Sotheby's, Paris, *Collection Rosenthal, Art d'Océanie*, 24 March 2010, lot 12

Published
Monbrison (de) A., *XXe Biennale des Antiquaires*, Paris, 2000, no. 11
Arts d'Afrique Noire magazine, winter 2000, no. 116, p. 47

Exhibited
Paris, *XXe Biennale des Antiquaires, Carrousel du Louvre*, 15 September – 1 October 2000

AMERICA

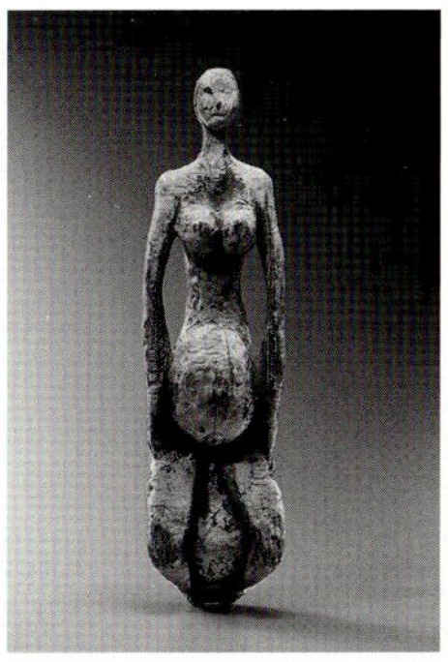

Page 202
Statue
Pre-Inuit culture, Western Thule, Alaska, H. 40 cm
Circa 1500–1800

Provenance
Walter Randell, New York
Alain de Monbrison, Paris

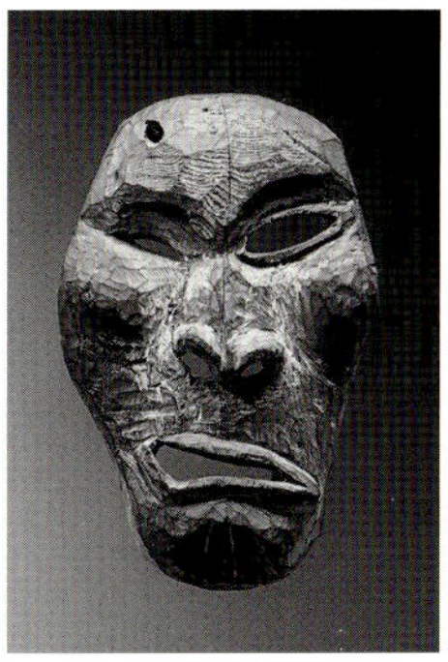

Page 205
Yup'ik mask
Goodnews Bay, Alaska, H. 22 cm
Circa 1890–1900

Provenance
Acquired in 1923 by the Museum of the American Indian, Heye Foundation, New York (inv. no. 12/898)[2]
Julius Carlebach, New York, 1945
André Breton, Paris
Calmels Cohen, Paris, *Collection André Breton*, 17 April 2003, lot 6162

Notes
1 The Central Yup'ik word *yua* is equivalent to the Siberian Yupik and Iñupiat word *inua*, and both are taken from the root word for person in each language. Whereas Inu is the root for person, therefore Inuit is the plural "People," so also is Yukthe root for person, and thus "Yup'ik" translates to "The Real People" [the apostrophe providing vocal emphasis to the word Yupik, in a boasting fashion: Real People].
2 "Purchased by MAI from an unknown source in 1923." So are described a series of dance masks and dance objects (hand fans, etc.) collected by George Heye for his Museum of the American Indian. Heye's

cataloguing system, each number painted by hand onto the rear side of each object by Heye personally, typically grouped objects together sequentially, by order of acquisition. This system often allows us to identify the village origin of the object. Breton acquired a group of at least seven Yup'ik masks from Heye's collection, and four of them were recorded to come from the Yup'ik village of Goodnews Bay.

IVORIES

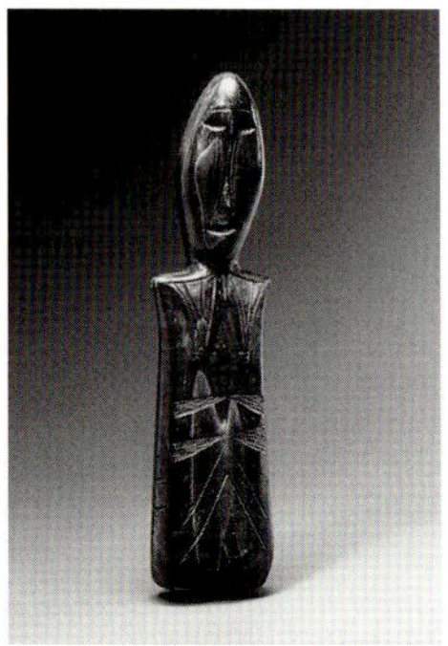

Page 208
Statuette
Paleo-Eskimo culture, St Lawrence Island (*Sivuqaq*), Alaska (Siberian Yupik)
Old Bering Sea I (Okvik period), H. 17 cm
Circa 250 BC – 100 AD

Provenance
Baron Frédéric Rolin, Brussels/New York

Published
Wardwell A., *Ancient Eskimo Ivories of the Bering Strait*, New York, 1986, pp. 38–9, fig. 3

Exhibited
New York, *Ancient Eskimo Ivories of the Bering Strait*, The American Federation of Arts, July 1986 – January 1988

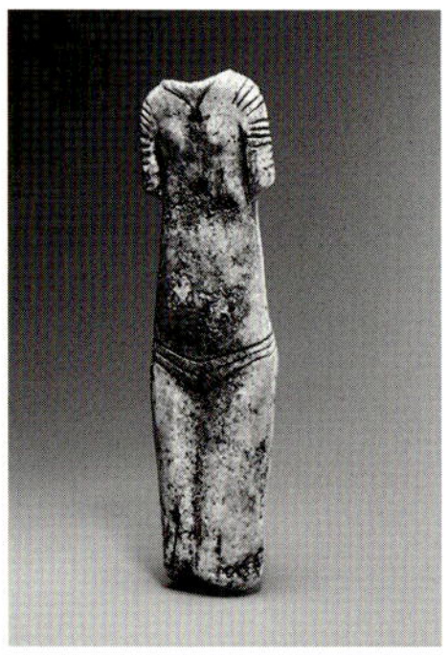

Page 210
Torso
Paleo-Eskimo culture, St Lawrence Island (*Sivuqaq*), Alaska (Siberian Yupik)
Archaic Punuk, H. 17 cm
Circa 500–800

Provenance
Baron Frédéric Rolin, Brussels/New York

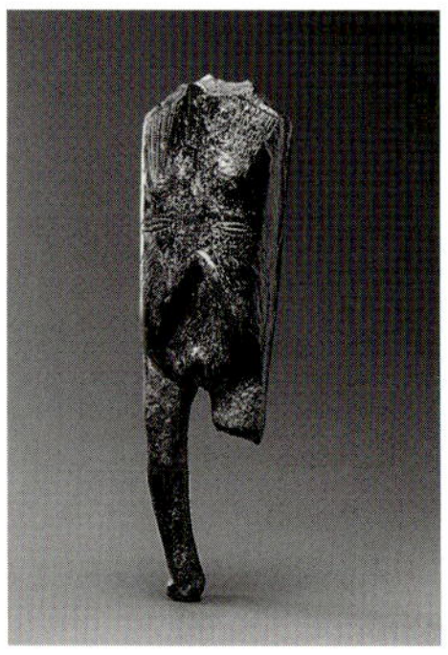

Page 213
Torso
Paleo-Eskimo culture, St Lawrence Island (*Sivuqaq*), Alaska (Siberian Yupik)
Old Bering Sea I (Okvik period), H. 21 cm
Circa 250 BC – 100 AD

Provenance
Baron Frédéric Rolin, Brussels/New York

Published
Wardwell A., *Ancient Eskimo Ivories of the Bering Strait*, New York, 1986, p. 39, fig. 6

Exhibited
New York, *Ancient Eskimo Ivories of the Bering Strait*, The American Federation of Arts, July 1986 – January 1988

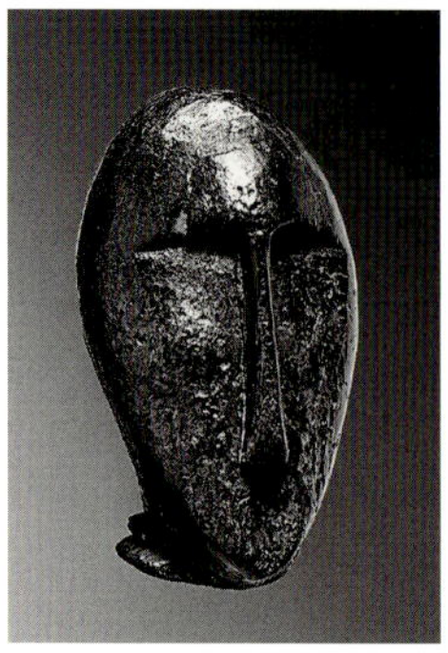

Page 214
Head
Paleo-Eskimo culture, St Lawrence Island (*Sivuqaq*), Alaska (Siberian Yupik)
Old Bering Sea I (Okvik period), H. 7.5 cm
Circa 250 BC – 100 AD

Provenance
Christie's, London, 13 June 1978, lot 226
Jean-Claude Bellier, Paris

Published
Wardwell A., *Ancient Eskimo Ivories of the Bering Strait*, New York, 1986, p. 51, fig. 35

Exhibited
New York, *Ancient Eskimo Ivories of the Bering Strait*, The American Federation of Arts, July 1986 – January 1988

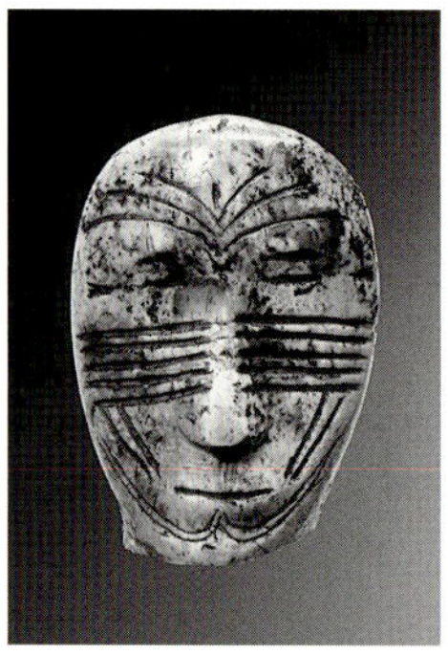

Page 215
Head
Paleo-Eskimo culture, St Lawrence Island (*Sivuqaq*), Alaska (Siberian Yupik)
Archaic Punuk, H. 8.5 cm
Circa 500 – 800

Provenance
Christie's, London, 13 June 1978, lot 227
Jean-Claude Bellier, Paris

Published
Wardwell A., *Ancient Eskimo Ivories of the Bering Strait*, New York, 1986, p. 99, fig. 118

Exhibited
New York, *Ancient Eskimo Ivories of the Bering Strait*, The American Federation of Arts, July 1986 – January 1988

Note
1 Quoted from: Krutak L., *Tattoos of the Hunter-Gatherers of the Arctic*, 2000; ref. cited 28 March 2019: https://www.larskrutak.com/tattoos-of-the-hunter-gatherers-of-the-arctic/

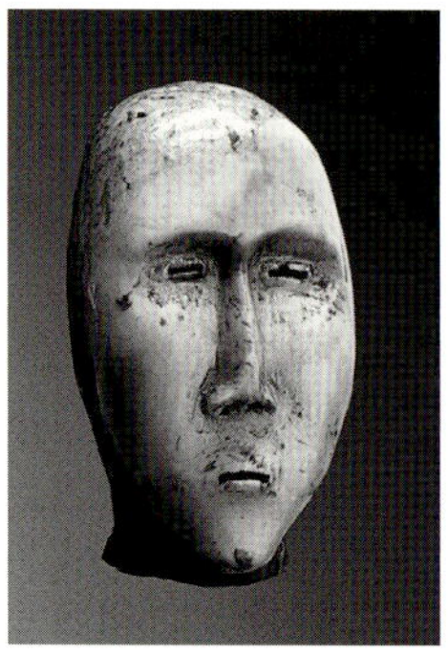

Page 216
Head
Paleo-Eskimo culture, St Lawrence Island (*Sivuqaq*), Alaska (Siberian Yupik)
Late Punuk or archaic Western Thule, H. 6 cm
Circa 600 – 1200 or 1200 – 1500

Provenance
Baron Frédéric Rolin, Brussels/New York

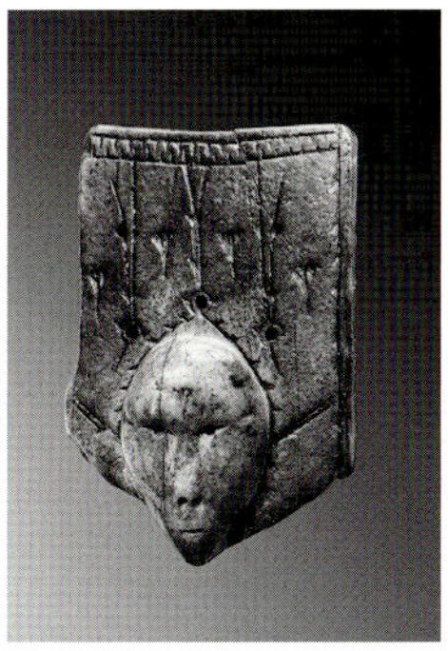

Page 217
Wrist guard
Paleo-Eskimo culture, St Lawrence Island (*Sivuqaq*), Alaska (Siberian Yupik)
Archaic Punuk, H. 7.5 cm
Circa 500 – 800

Provenance
Baron Frédéric Rolin, Brussels/New York

Published
Wardwell A., *Ancient Eskimo Ivories of the Bering Strait*, New York, 1986, p. 105, fig. 135

Exhibited
New York, *Ancient Eskimo Ivories of the Bering Strait*, The American Federation of Arts,
July 1986 – January 1988

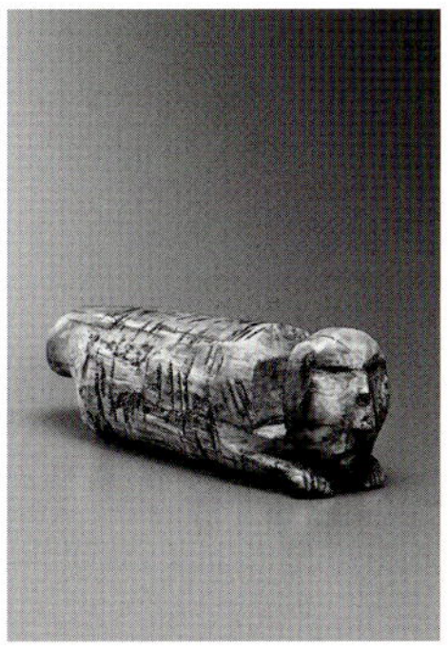

Page 218
Drum handle
Paleo-Eskimo culture, St Lawrence Island (*Sivuqaq*), Alaska (Siberian Yupik)
Late Punuk or archaic Western Thule, H. 10.5 cm
Circa 800 – 1400

Provenance
Anthony Meyer, Paris

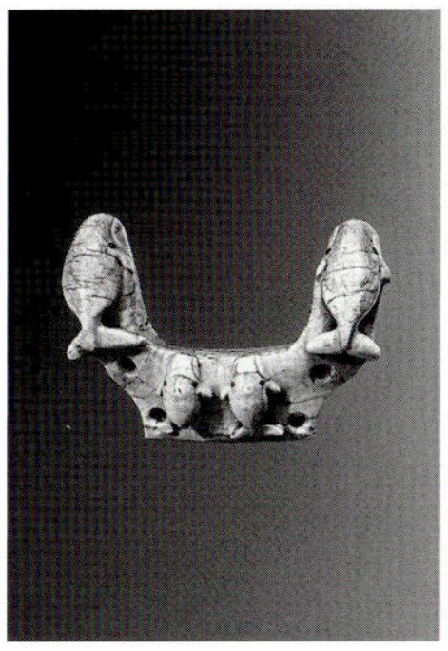

Page 220
Harpoon rest
Pre-Inuit culture, Alaska (Iñupiat), late Western Thule, L. 12 cm
Circa 1500 – 1800

Provenance
Private Collection, Los Angeles
Rita and Oscar Meyer, Los Angeles, in the 1960s
Boisgirard & Heeckeren, Paris, *Collection Meyer*, 29 and 30 November, 1 December 1977, lot 322

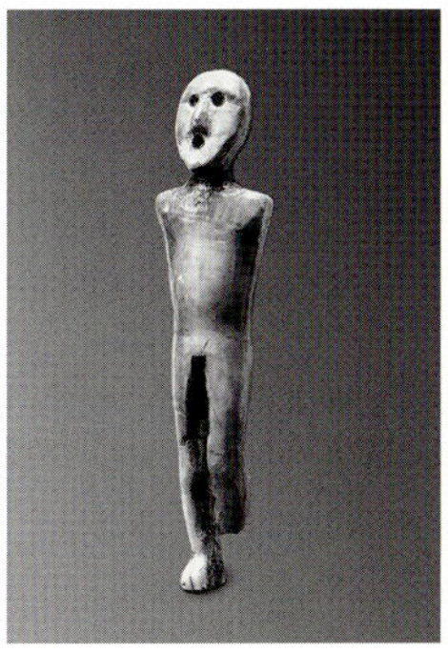

Page 221
Statuette
Pre-Inuit culture, Coast of Alaska (Siberian Yupik or Iñupiat)
Archaic Western Thule, H. 4 cm
Circa 1200 – 1500

Provenance
Private Collection, Los Angeles
Rita and Oscar Meyer, Los Angeles, in the 1960s
Boisgirard & Heeckeren, Paris, Collection Meyer, 29–30 November, and 1 December 1977, lot 322

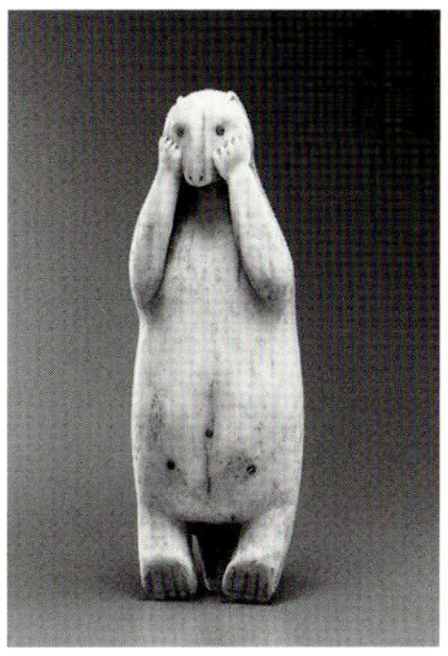

Page 223
Amulet in the form of a sea otter
Pre-Inuit culture, Alaska (Iñupiat), late Western Thule, H. 11.2 cm
Circa 1500 – 1800

Provenance
Raymond Grandin, Paris
Christie's, Paris, 11 December 2012, lot 23

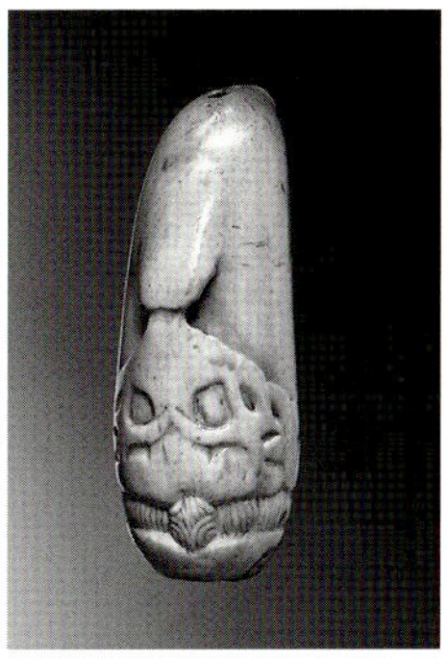

Page 224
Maori whistle
New Zealand, H. 11.5 cm

Provenance
Alexander Martin, London
George Ortiz, Geneva
Sotheby Parke Bernet, London, *The George Ortiz Collection of Primitive Works of Art*, 29 June 1978, lot 147

Published
Martin A., *Art of the South Seas*, 1970, cat. 18

Exhibited
London, *Art of the South Seas*, Gallery Alexander Martin, 20 October – 10 November 1970

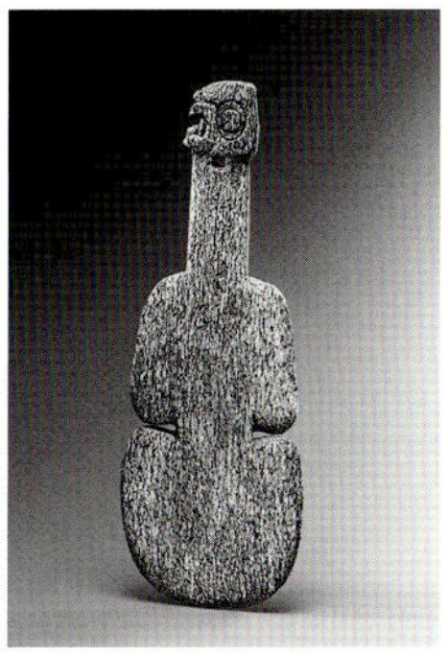

Page 225
Maori club
New Zealand, H. 33 cm

Provenance
William O. Oldman, London
Picard, Paris, 14 February 1994, lot 51

Published
Bühler A., Gabus J., *Art Océanien*, 1970, Neuchâtel, no. 992

Exhibited
Neuchâtel, *Art Océanien*, musée d'Ethnographie, 27 June – 31 December 1970

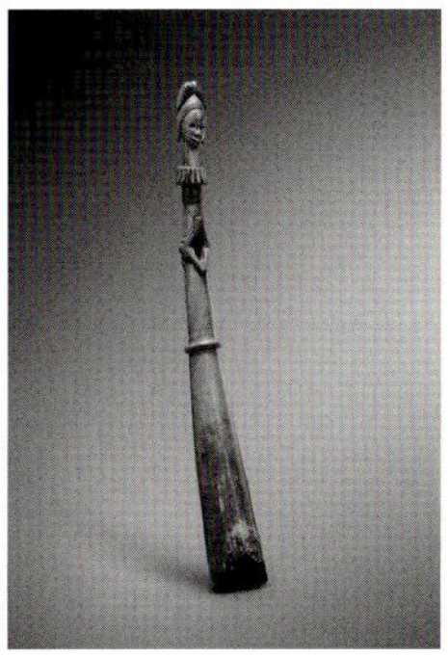

Page 226
Mende olifant
Sierra Leone, L. 83 cm

Provenance
James Hooper, Arundel
Charles Ratton, Paris
Guy Ladrière, Paris
Alain de Monbrison, Paris

Published
Monbrison (de) A. (ed.), *Monbrison. 1997,* Paris, 1997, pl. III–IV
Falgayrettes-Leveau C., *Aethiopia, Vestiges de Gloire*, Paris, 1987, p. 26, no. 15
Brincard M.-T. (ed.), *Sounding Forms. African Musical Instruments*, New York, 1989, p. 160, no. 120

Brincard M.-T. (ed.), *Afrique: formes sonores*, Paris, 1990, p. 153, no. 115

Exhibited
Paris, *Aethiopia, Vestiges de Gloire*, musée Dapper, 3 July – 3 October 1987
Sounding Forms: African Musical Instruments:
– Washington, DC, The National Museum of African Art, 26 April – 18 June 1989
– Richmond, The Virginia Museum of Fine Arts, 16 July – 10 September 1989
– Kansas City, The Nelson-Atkins Museum of Art, 7 October – 5 December 1989
Paris, *Afrique: formes sonores*, musée National des Arts d'Afrique et d'Océanie, 25 January – 20 March 1990

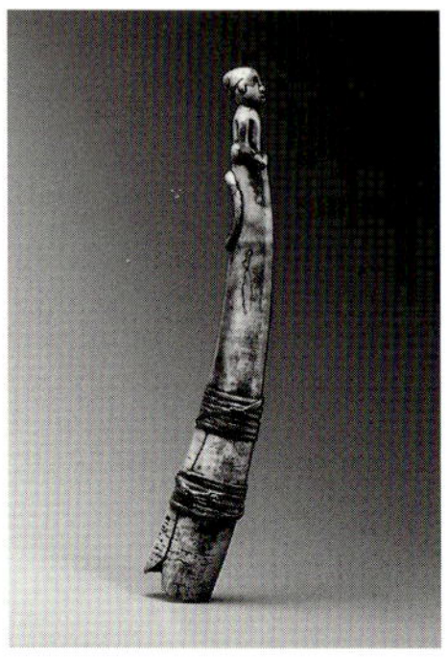

Page 228
Kongo olifant
Democratic Republic of the Congo, L. 35.5 cm

Publication
Felix M. L., *White Gold, Black Hands. Ivory Sculpture in Congo*, vol. I, Qiqihar, 2010, p. 194, fog. 287

Provenance
Jean-Claude Bellier, Paris

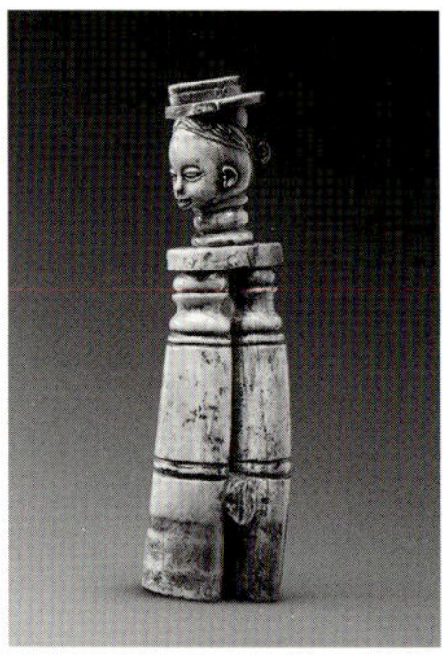

Page 229
Mende container
Sierra Leone, L. 25.5 cm

Provenance
Lucien Van de Velde, Antwerp
Vittorio and Marina Mangiò, Monza
Jacques Kerchache, Paris

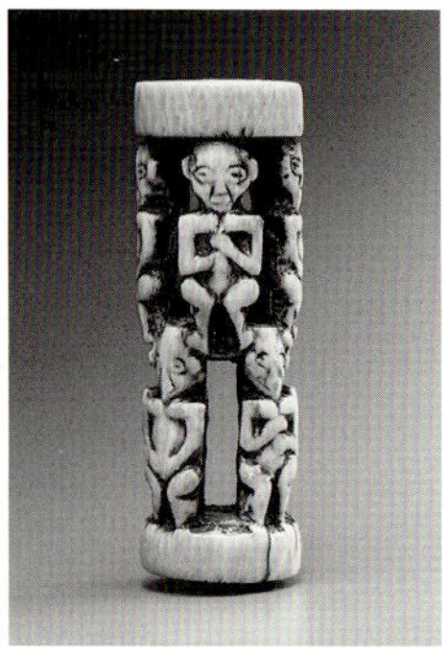

Page 230
Bamileke pipe ornament
Cameroon, H. 11.5 cm

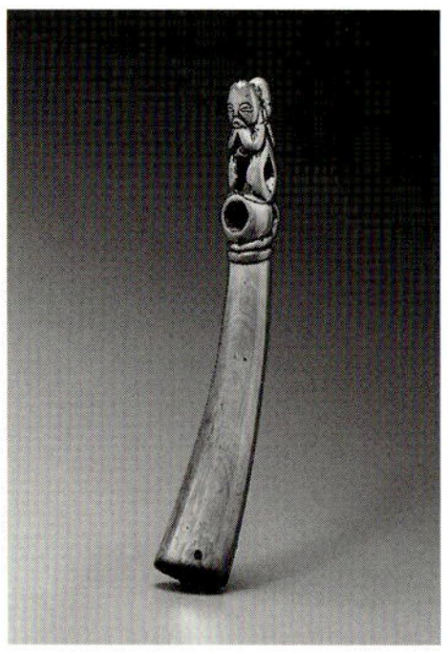

Page 231
Bangwa olifant
Cameroon, L. 30 cm

Provenance
Jean-Claude Bellier, Paris

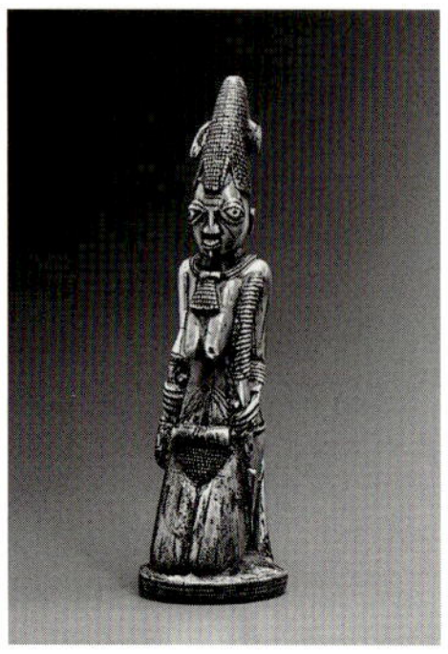

Page 232
Yoruba statuette
Owo, Nigeria, H. 31 cm

Provenance
Ian Auld, Halstead
Entwistle-Plowright, London
John K. Hewett, Bog Farm
Baron Frédéric Rolin, Brussels/New York
Lance and Roberta Entwistle, Paris/London

Published
Rolin F., *African Ivories,* New York, 1978, cover, no. 55

Exhibited
New York, *African Ivories,* 10 May – 20 June 1978, Frédéric Rolin Gallery

Note
1 Drewal H. J., Pemberton III, J., Abiodun R., *Yoruba; nine centuries of art and thought,* The Center for African Art/Harry N. Abrams Inc Publishers, New York, 1989

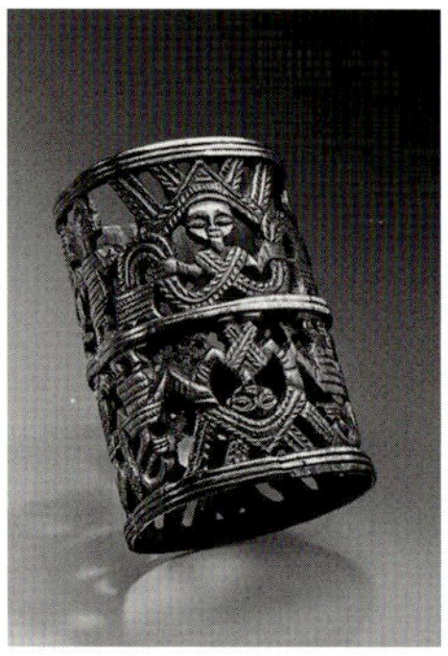

Page 234
Yoruba bracelet
Owo, Nigeria, H. 12 cm

Provenance
Alain de Monbrison, Paris

Notes
1 There is a very similar specimen in the musée du quai Branly (73.1997.17.1), published in Bassani E., *Ivoires d'Afrique dans les anciennes collections françaises*, musée du quai Branly, 19 February – 11 May 2008, Paris, Actes Sud, musée du quai Branly, 2008
2 William Fagg, in 1951, was the first to discover the origin of the Owo ivories, which had long been attributed to the *Igbesanwan* in the Kingdom of Benin. He also employed the term *abraxas* to refer to the mythical fish-tail legged figures, which can also be found in Edo iconography.

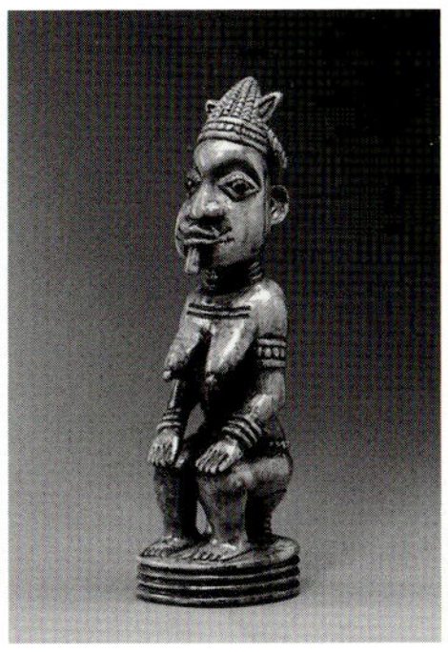

Page 235
Yoruba statuette
Nigeria, H. 15 cm

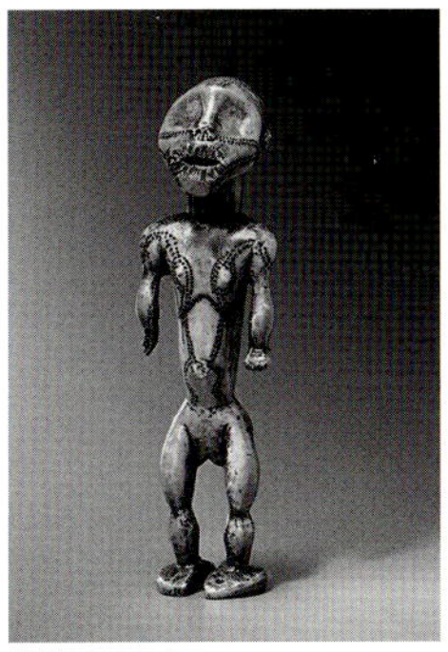

Page 236
Lega statuette
South-Kivu Province, Democratic Republic of the Congo, H. 26.5 cm

Provenance
Lucien Van de Velde, Antwerp, bought together with Loed van Bussel, Amsterdam
Walter Randell, New York
Wayne Heathcote, Miami
Lance and Roberta Entwistle, Paris/London
Jean-Claude Bellier, Paris
Josette and Jean-Claude Weill Collection, Paris
Musée du Quai Branly – Jacques Chirac, Paris (inv. no. 70.2018.41.1)

Published
African Arts magazine, 1978, vol. XII, no. 1, November 1978, back cover (Entwistle advertisement)
Gillon W., *Collecting African* Art, London, 1979, pl. XXIII
Kerchache J., Paudrat J.-L., Stephan L., *L'Art africain*, Paris, 1988, p. 265, fig. 176
Neyt F., *Fleuve Congo. Arts d'Afrique centrale. Correspondances et mutations des formes*, Paris, 2010, p. 91, fig. 49
Felix M.L., *White Gold, Black Hands. Ivory Sculpture in Congo*, vol. 5, Qiqihar, 2013, pp. 237, fig. A26, 260, fig. A28, 272–273, fig. A27
Felix M.L., *White Gold, Black Hands. Ivory Sculpture in Congo*, vol. 6, Qiqihar, 2013, p. 220, fig. 82a

Exhibited
Paris, *Fleuve Congo. Arts d'Afrique Centrale. Correspondances et mutations des formes,* musée du quai Branly – Jacques Chirac, 22 June – 3 October 2010
Paris, on permanent display, Pavillion des sessions, Musée du Louvres, 2018

Notes
1 Certain figurines and figurative pendants stand out, such as the *kalimbangoma* or *katimbitimbi*; more closely linked to the personal history of each high-ranking initiate, both male and female, who possessed them, they either marked their moral commitements or guaranteed loyalty within couples (Baeke, 2013*b*, pp. 21–23).
2 de Grunne B., 2013, p. 220, fig. 82
3 Brown K., 2013a, p. 272
4 Baeke V., 2013*a*, pp. 93–7, ill. p. 95; Dossier Ethnographique no. 561: M. Zographakis, 10 August 1931, Service du Patrimoine du MRAC archives
5 Biebuyck D., 1973, p. 104
6 Ibid., pp. 104–5
7 Kellim Brown rightly wonders why the mouth is quite so deeply hollowed out (Brown K., 2013*a*, p. 260); I think the answer lies in the treatment meted out to the deceased during this funerary episode, which this figure so graphically depicts.

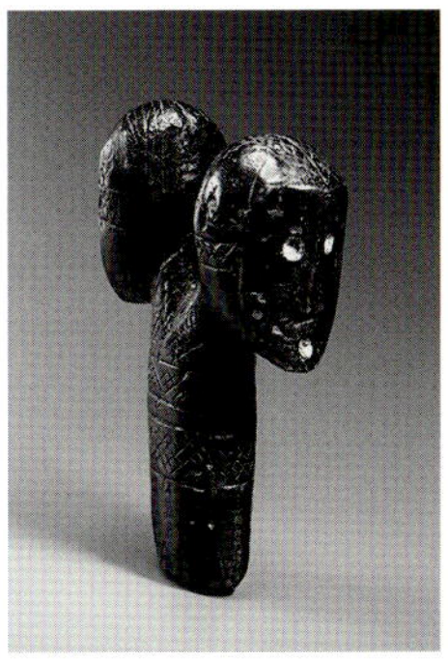

Page 240
Lega Janus head
South-Kivu Province, Democratic Republic of the Congo, H. 15.5 cm

Provenance
Jean-Pierre Lepage, Brussels
Pierre Dartevelle, Brussels
Merton D. Simpson, New York
George and Rosemary Lois, New York
Lance and Roberta Entwistle, Paris/London

Published
Felix M.L., *White Gold, Black Hands. Ivory Sculpture in Congo*, vol. VI, Qiqihar, 2013, p. 59, fig. A153

Notes
1 Brown K., 2013 p. 60 and fig. A153, p. 59
2 Biebuyck D., 1986, p. 76 and ill. 15; Baeke V., 2013*a*, p. 82 and ill. p. 81; Baeke V., 2013*b*, p. 15, fig. 14; Brown K., 2013 p. 24, fig. A87–A89 and pp. 58–60, ill. A153 and A154
3 Biebuyck D., 2002, p. 130-131.

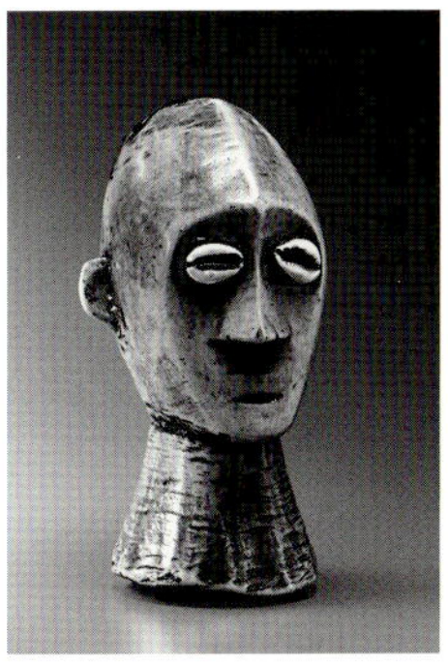

Page 242
Lega head
South-Kivu Province, Democratic Republic of the Congo, H. 18.5 cm

Provenance
Hélène Leloup, Paris

Note
1 Biebuyck D., 2002, p. 129

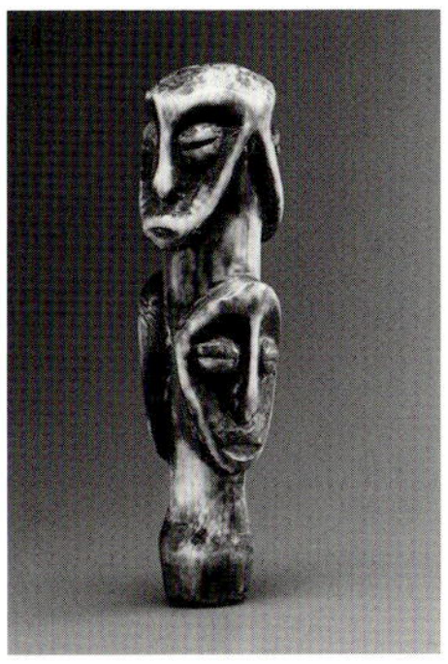

Page 244
Lega head
South-Kivu Province, Democratic Republic of the Congo, H. 12.5 cm

Provenance
Fernand Stradiot, colonial administrator in the Belgian Congo in the 1930s
By descent
Binoche and Giquello, Paris, 19 May 2016, lot 72

Note
1 Biebuyck D., 1986, pp. 85–6

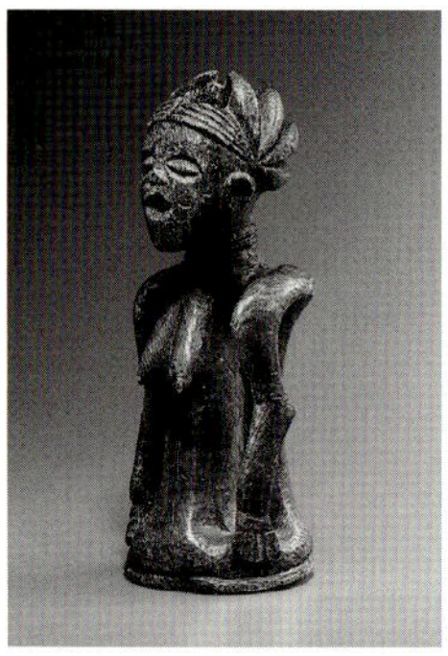

Page 245
Pinda statuette
Angola, H. 11 cm

Provenance
Private collection, acquired in Angola in around 1955
Sotheby's, 2 December 2015, lot 78

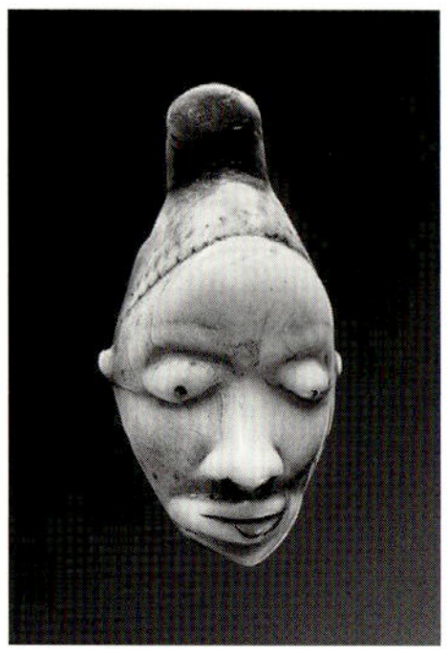

Page 246
Pende pendant
Kwilu Province, Democratic Republic of the Congo, H. 5.5 cm

Provenance
Galerie Ratton-Ladrière, Paris
M. Haury Collection, Paris, circa 1990
Yann Ferrandin, Paris
Sotheby's, 2 December 2015, lot 78

Notes
1 Strother Z. S., 1998, ill. 86, p. 202, ill. 87, p. 203 and ill. 88, p. 204
2 de Sousberghe L., 1960, p. 74
3 Ndambi-Munamuhega, 1975, p. 35; Mudiji, 1981, p. 101; Baeke V., 2011, pp. 256–59

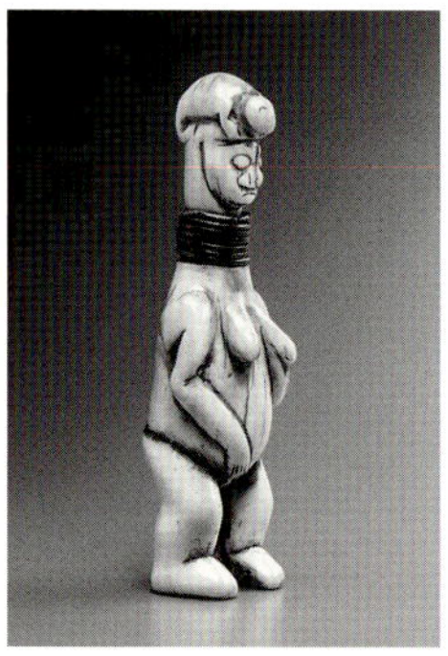

Page 247
Yaka/Suku pendant
Democratic Republic of the Congo
H. 14.5 cm

Provenance
Pierre Loos, acquired at the end of the 1970s
Marc Leo Felix, Brussels
Hélène Leloup, Paris

Published
Felix M. L., *White Gold, Black Hands. Ivory Sculpture in Congo*, vol. III, Qiqihar, 2012, p. 93, ill. 018a

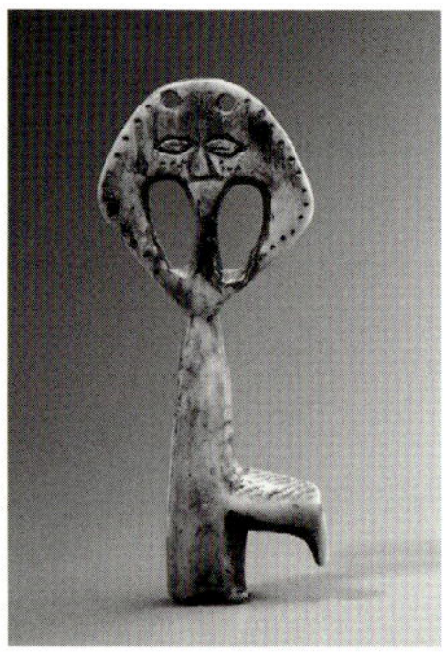

Page 248
Mbuun or Pende whistle
Extreme northwest, Kwilu Province, Democratic Republic of the Congo, H. 9.5 cm

Provenance
Acquired *in situ* in Kikwit in 1983
Françoise and Jean Corlay, Paris
Sotheby's, Paris, *Collection Françoise et Jean Corlay*, 18 June 2013, lot 2

Published
Felix M. L., *White Gold, Black Hands. Ivory Sculpture in Congo*, vol. III, 2012, Qiqihar, p. 113, ill. 083 and 170, ill. 67

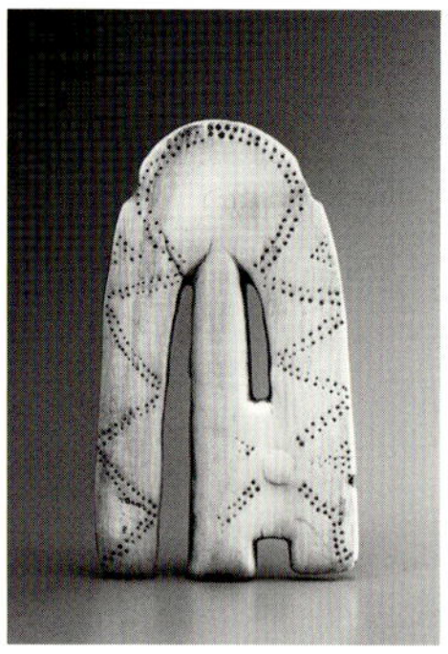

Page 249
Pende whistle
Western Pende, Kwilu Province, Democratic Republic of the Congo, H. 11.5 cm

Provenance
Émile Lejeune (1883–1920), Liège, acquired *in situ* between 1906 and 1914
Boris de Starowietsky, Brussels,
By descent
Sotheby's, Paris, 12 December 2012, lot 1

Notes
1 Baeke V., 2011, p. 34
2 Baeke V., 2011, p. 44-88

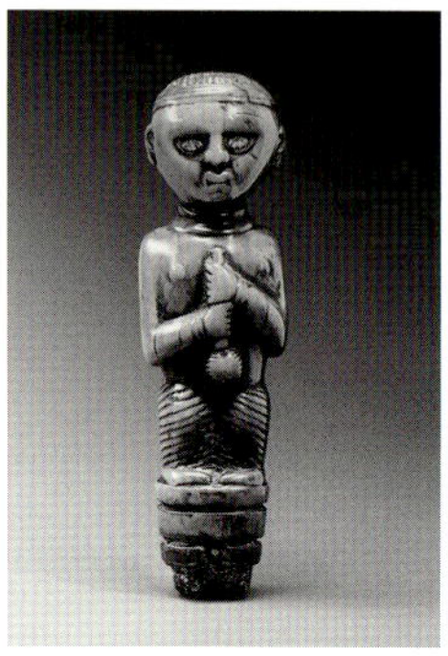

Page 250
Kongo prestige emblem finial
Democratic Republic of the Congo, H. 18 cm

Provenance
Hélène Leloup, Paris

Published
Cornet J.A., *Kongo : objets de bois, objets d'ivoire*, Paris, 1998, pp. 50–1, no. 20
Felix M.L., *White Gold, Black Hands. Ivory Sculpture in Congo*, vol. I, Qiqihar, 2010, pp. 162–63, fig. 204
Felix M.L., *White Gold, Black Hands. Ivory Sculpture in Congo*, vol. II, Qiqihar, 2011, pp. 152–53, fig. 821 a, b and 813 a, b

Exhibited
Paris, *Kongo : objets de bois, objets d'ivoire*, Galerie Hélène Leloup, June 1998

Note
1 Felix M., 2010, p. 162 and 2011, p. 152

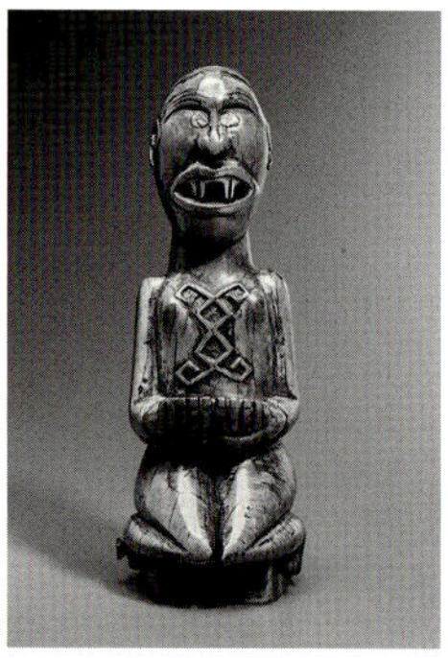

Page 252
Kongo prestige emblem finial
Republic of the Congo or DRC, H. 15.5 cm

Provenance
Hélène Leloup, Paris

Published
Cornet J.A., *Kongo : objets de bois, objets d'ivoire*, Paris, 1998, cover and p. 11, fig. 23
Felix M.L., *Le Geste kôngo*, Paris, 2002, p. 113
Felix M.L., *White Gold, Black Hands. Ivory Sculpture in Congo*, vol. II, Qiqihar, 2011, p. 174, fig. 882a, b, and c

Exhibited
Paris, *Kongo : objets de bois, objets d'ivoire*, Galerie Hélène Leloup, June 1998
Paris, *Le geste kôngo*, Musée Dapper, 18 September 2002 – 9 February 2003

Notes
1 Felix M., 2011, p. 74
2 One of these figures, a virtual twin of the present statuette, has a third hole between her thighs that was probably designed to ensure a firmer coupling at

the top of the emblem (see Bergé, 9 December 2009, lot 15).
3 This charm would activate the protective powers of the *bankisi be nsi*, the spirits of the earth, who were linked to the territory the chief administered.
4 MacGaffey W., 2000, chapter 9: Lutete's chiefs, pp. 160–81

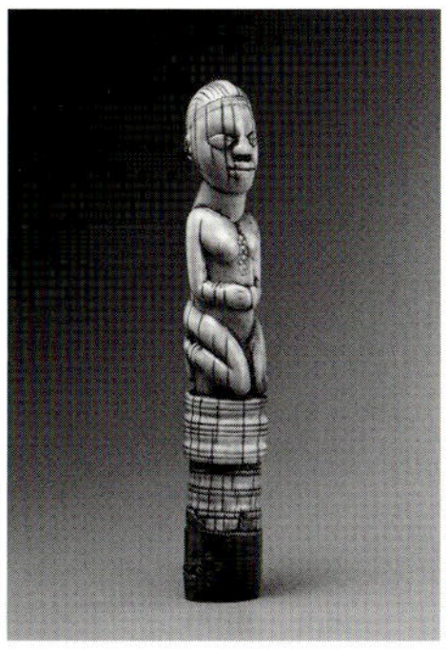

Page 256
Kongo prestige emblem finial
Republic of the Congo or DRC, H. 20.5 cm

Provenance
George Ortiz, Geneva
Loudmer-Poulain-Cornette de Saint-Cyr, Paris, *Arts Primitis – Collection du M. George Ortiz*, 6 June 1973, lot J
Sotheby Parke Bernet, London, *The George Ortiz Collection of Primitive Works of Art*, 29 June 1978, lot 57

Published
Felix M.L., *White Gold, Black Hands. Ivory Sculpture in Congo*, vol. I, Qiqihar, 2010, p. 142, fig. 175a, b and c

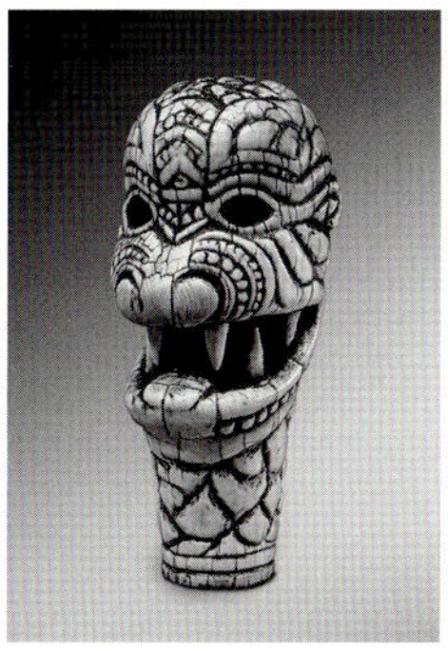

Page 258
Kongo prestige emblem finial
Democratic Republic of the Congo, H. 12 cm

Provenance
Joseph Bard, Paris
Christie's, Paris, 11 December 2012, lot 85

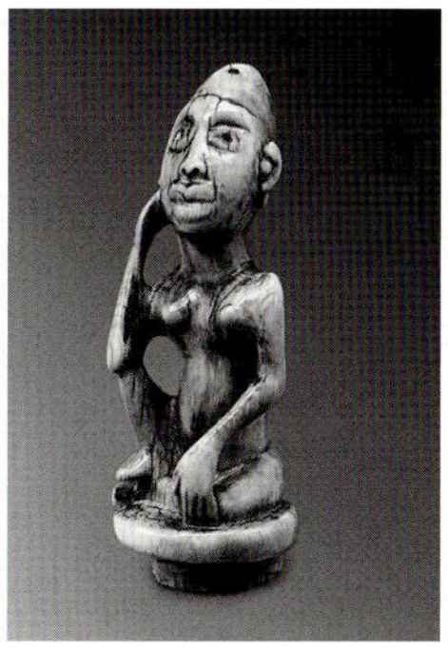

Page 259
Kongo prestige emblem finial
Republic of the Congo or DRC, H. 13 cm

Provenance
Hélène Leloup, Paris

Published
Felix M. L., *White Gold, Black Hands. Ivory Sculpture in Congo*, vol. II, Qiqihar, 2011, p. 164, fig. 858a

Note
1 Marc Felix, includes it among the rare representations of seated women, while stressing the originality of her posture (Felix M., 2011, p. 164)

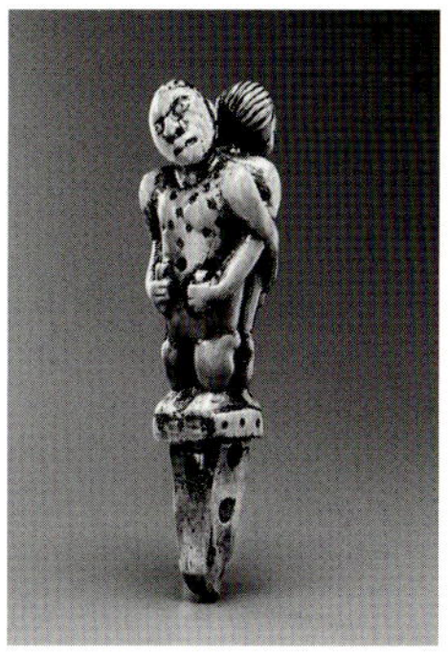

Page 260
Kongo prestige emblem finial
Republic of the Congo or DRC, H. 11 cm

Provenance
Simon Kouello, Loango
George Ortiz, Geneva
Sotheby Parke Bernet, London, *The George Ortiz Collection of Primitive Works of Art*, 29 June 1978, lot 56

Published
Felix M. L., *White Gold, Black Hands. Ivory Sculpture in Congo*, vol. I, Qiqihar, 2010, p. 172, fig. 219

Notes
1 Felix M., 2010, p. 170; Janzen J.M., 1982 p. 253, fig. 21 and p. 257, ill. 5 and 8, which show this motif on the lid of the ritual basket containing the *nkisi lemba*, as well as on the copper bracelet.
2 Janzen J.M., p. 124
3 Ibid., p. 126. The small paddles drawn by the author seem to correspond to the small objects the two figures are holding

BIBLIOGRAPHY

African Faces, African Figures. The Arman Collection. New York: Museum for African Art, 1997.

Baeke V. "Quand les formes informent. Codes esthétiques et normes éthiques du *bwami* lega," *in* Felix, Marc Leo (ed.), *Joyaux lega. D'ivoire, d'Os et de Bois*. Brussels: BRUNEAF, 2013*b*, pp. 9–29.

Baeke V. "La force. Statuaire rituelle songye," *in* Baeke V., Bouttiaux A.-M., and Dubois H. (eds.), *Le Sensible et la Force. Photographies de Hughes Dubois et sculptures songye*. Tervuren: Musée royal de l'Afrique centrale, 2004, pp. 13–37.

Baeke V. "Les sculptures en ivoire des Pende. Première partie: Les *ikhoko* démasqués?," *in* Felix M. (ed.), *White Gold, Black Hands: Ivory Sculpture in Congo*, vol. 2. Grand Rapids: Gemini Sun, 2011, pp. 193–307.

Baeke V. "Les sculptures en ivoire des Pende. Seconde partie: Quand l'ivoire chante avec les masques et chasse avec les chiens," *in* Felix M. (ed.), *White Gold, Black Hands: Ivory Sculpture in Congo*, vol. 3. Grand Rapids: Gemini Sun, 2012, pp. 11–79.

Baeke V. "Rites de passage et savoirs d'initiés en République Démocratique du Congo," *in* Falgayrettes-Leveau C. (ed.), *Initiés. Bassin du Congo*. Paris: Éditions Dapper, 2013*a*, pp. 48– 115.

Baeke V. "Et Dieu dans tout ça ? Objets de culte thérapeutiques et cynégétiques inspirés par l'iconographie chrétienne," *in* Volper J. (ed.), *Du Jourdain au Congo : Art et Christianisme en Afrique central*. Paris: Musée du Quai Branly-Jacques Chirac, 2016, pp. 117–137.

Baeke V. "Figures de pouvoir, figures de mémoire (sud-est de la DRC)," *in* Serge Schoffel (ed.) *Finalité sans Fin,* exh. cat., BRUNEAF (6 – 11 June 2017), Brussels, 2017, pp. 45–98.

Baeke V. "La mort n'est pas une fin. Le rôle de la statuaire songye dans le cycle de la vie," *in* Serge Schoffel (ed.) *Finalité sans Fin,* exh. cat., BRUNEAF (6 – 11 June 2017), Brussels, 2017*b*, pp. 99–116.

Beran H. *Mutuaga: A Nineteenth-Century New Guinea Master Carver*. Wollongong: Wollongong University Press, 1996.

Beran H. *More Mutuagas: further woodcarvings by the nineteenth-century master carver of the Massim region, Papua New Guinea*, unpublished.

Bergé (Pierre & associés). Brussels, *Arts premiers. Ivoires africains*, 9 December 2009, lot 15.

Biebuyck D., *Lega Culture. Art, initiation and Moral Philosophy among a Central African People*. Berkeley: University of California Press, 1973.

Biebuyck D. *The Art of Zaïre, vol II: Eastern Zaire*. Berkeley: University of California Press, 1986.

Biebuyck D. *Lega. Ethique et beauté au cœur de l'Afrique*. Ghent: KBC Banque & Assurance, Snoeck-Ducaju & Zoon, 2002.

Blakely T.D. "To gaze or not to gaze: visual communication in Eastern Zaïre," *Sociolinguistic Working Papers*, 87, Austin, Texas, 1981.

Blakely T. D. and Blakely P.A.R. "So'o Masks and Hemba Funerary Festival," *African Arts*, vol. XXI, 1, 1987, pp. 30–7 and 84–6.

Brown K. "Crossing the Lega Ivory Spectrum. A contemporary Ride trough 'Heavy Things' (part one) in Maniema (part one)," *in* Felix M. (ed.), *White Gold, Black Hands: Ivory sculpture in Congo*, vol. 5. Grand Rapids: Gemini Sun, 2013*a*, pp. 236–99.

Brown K. "Crossing the Lega Ivory Spectrum. A contemporary Ride trough 'Heavy Things,'" *in* Felix M. (ed.), *White Gold, Black Hands: Ivory sculpture in Congo*, vol. 6. Grand Rapids: Gemini Sun, 2013*b*, pp. 10–159.

Colleyn J.-P. *Bamana: un art et un savoir-vivre au Mali,*. Zurich: Museum Rietberg, 2002.

Cornet J.-A. *Kongo, Objets de bois et objets d'ivoire*. Paris: Galerie Leloup, 1998.

de Grunne B. "On Leg Styles," *in* Felix M. (ed.), *White Gold, Black Hands: Ivory sculpture in Congo*, vol. 6. Grand Rapids: Gemini Sun, 2013, pp. 160–249.

de Heush L. *Le roi de Kongo et les monstres sacrés*. Paris: Gallimard, 2000.

de Sousberghe L. *L'art pende*. Brussels: Académie royale de Belgique, 1960.

Doutreloux A. *À l'ombre des Fétiches. Société et culture yombe*. Louvain: Publication of the Université Lovanium in Léopoldville, Nauelaerts Editions, 1967.

Fagg W. and Plass M. *African Sculpture. An anthology*. Studio Vista Limited, 1964 (revised edition 1966).

Felix M. "Ivory sculptures in the Kongo Kingdom: 4. Staffs," *in* Felix M. (ed.), *White Gold, Black Hands: Ivory sculpture in Congo*, vol. 1. Grand Rapids: Gemini Sun, 2010, pp. 124–77.

Felix M. "La crête de la vague," *Ngonge. Carnets de Sciences Humaines*. Rhode St Genèse, 2011.

Felix M. "Ivory sculptures in the Kongo Kingdom: 11. Finials," *in* Felix M. (ed.), *White Gold, Black Hands: Ivory sculpture in Congo*, vol. 2. Grand Rapids: Gemini Sun, 2011, pp. 144–89.

Gebauer, P. *Art of Cameroon; With a Catalog of the Gebauer Collection of Cameroon Art at the Portland Art Museum and the Metropolitan Museum of Art*, Portland/New York, 1979.

Hahner-Herzog I. *Afrika – Kult und Visionen. Unbekannte Kunst aus deutschen Völkerkundemuseen. Ausstellungskatalog.* Detmold: Lippisches Landesmuseum, 1999.

Harter p. *Les Rois Sculpteurs. Art et Pouvoirs dans le Grasland Camerounais*. Paris: Musée national des Arts d'Afrique et d'Océanie, 1993.

Hersak D. *Songye. Masks and Figure Sculpture*. London: Ethnographica Ltd, 1985.

Homberger L. (ed.). *Kamerun. Kunst der Könige. Ausstellungskatalog*. Zurich: Museum Rietberg, 2008.

Janzen J. M. *Lemba 1650–1930. A Drum of Affliction in Africa and the New World*. New York: Garland Publishing Inc., 1982.

Kerchache J., Paudrat J.-L., and Stéphan L. *L'Art africain*. Paris: Mazenot, 1988.

LaGamma A. *Genesis: ideas of origin in African Sculpture*. New York: Metropolitan Museum of Art, 2002.

Lehuard R. *Statuaire du Stanley-Pool*. Arnouville: Arts d'Afrique noire, 1974.

Lehuard R. *Fétiches à clous du Bas-Zaïre*. Arnouville: Arts d'Afrique noire, 1980.

Lehuard R. *Art Bakongo. Les Centres de Style* (vol. I- II). Arnouville: Arts d'Afrique noire, 1989.

Lehuard R. *Les Arts bateke*. Arnouville: Arts d'Afrique noire, 1996.

Leloup H. *Statuaire Dogon,* Amez (ed.), Strasbourg, 1994

Lema G. *La statuaire dans la société teke : morphologie et contexte culturel*, doctorate thesis, KU Leuven, 1978.

Lutete E. (1915–19). *Cahiers 216-237, notes de terrain*, in Laman Karl 1953-–68, *The Kongo*, vol. I -IV, Uppsala.

MacGaffey W. *Kongo Political Culture*. Bloomington: Indiana University Press, 2000.

Malé, S. *Le culte Jo en pays Baninko (Mali) : objets et rites initiatiques*, Nanterre, 1995.

Malgras G-J. "Ivoires d'Afrique de d'orient," *in ABC Décor*, no. 89, March 1972, p. 48.

Malinowski B. *A Diary in the Strict Sense of the Term*. New York: Harcourt, Brace & World, 1957.

Merriam A.P. *An African World. The Basongye Village of Lupupa Ngye*. Bloomington: Indiana University Press, 1974.

Newton D. *Massim: Art of the Massim Area, New Guinea*. New York: Museum of Primitive Art, 1975.

Neyt F. *La grande statuaire Hemba du Zaïre*. Louvain-la-Neuve: Publications d'Histoire de l'Art et d'Archéologie de l'Université catholique de Louvain, 1977.

Neyt F. *Luba. Aux sources du Zaïre*. Paris: Musée Dapper, 1993.

Neyt F. *Songye. La redoutable statuaire songye d'Afrique Centrale*. Antwerp: Fonds Mercator, 2004.

Nooter R.M. and Roberts A.R. (eds.). *Memory. Luba Art and the Making of History*. New York: The Museum for African Art, 1996.

Petridis C. *Luluwa: Central African Art Between Heaven and Earth*. Brussels: Fonds Mercator, 2018.

Ramona A. Introduction and entries to the *mvwala* staffs, cat. 31–38, *in* Verswijver G., De Palmenaer E., Baeke V., and Bouttiaux A.-M. (eds.), *Trésors d'Afrique. Musée de Tervuren*. Tervuren: Musée royal de l'Afrique centrale, 1995, pp. 292–97.

Stappers, L. "De geheime sekte van de bukisi bij de Beena Milembwe," *Kongo-Overzee*, XVI, 2–3, 1950, pp. 73–96.

Strother Z. *Pende*. Milan: 5 Continents Editions, "Visions of Africa" series, 2008.

Thomson R.F. *The Four Moments of the Sun*. Washington, DC: National Gallery of Art, 1981.

Vansina J. *The Tio Kingdom of The Middle Congo 1880-1892*. London: Oxford University Press, 1973.

Wauters, G. *L'ésotérie des Noirs dévoilée*. Brussels: Éditions Européennes, 1949.

Zahan, D. *Antilopes du soleil: arts et rites agraires d'Afrique Noire*, Vienne, 1980.

THE AUTHORS

Philippe Dagen
Art historian and critic

Charles-Wesley Hourdé
Expert in arts from Africa, Oceania and the Americas

Pierre Amrouche
Antique dealer, author, photographer and expert in African art

Viviane Baeke
Doctor in Social Anthropology and collaborator with the Heritage Department of the Royal Museum of Central Africa, where she has been curator for twenty-six years

Harry Beran
Author specialised in Melanesian art

Maëva Chanoine
Art historian

Jean-Paul Colleyn
Anthropologist, documentary filmmaker, director of studies at the École des Hautes Études en Sciences Sociale and member of the Institut des Mondes Africains

Eric Coote
Founding member of the Oceanic Art Society in Sydney and an author specialising in art of the Tami Islands

Marie Yvonne Curtis
Art historian, doctor of ethno-aesthetics at Université Paris 1, author and member of the Société des Africanistes, Paris

Aurélien Gaborit
Curator of the African collections – Musée du quai Branly – Jacques Chirac and Scientific Supervisor of the Pavillon des Sessions – Musée du Louvre, Paris

Bertrand Goy
Historian, author, member of the Société des Africanistes and of the Société de géographie in Paris

David Henrion
Antique dealer and expert in African art

Hélène Joubert
Chief Curator, responsible of the Africa Heritage Unit at Musée du quai Branly –Jacques Chirac, Paris

Alisa LaGamma
Art historian, Ceil and Michael E. Pulitzer Curator in charge of the Department of Arts of Africa, Oceania and the Americas at the Metropolitan Museum of Art de New York

Hélène Leloup
Antique dealer and expert in African art, specialist in Dogon art, accomplished many expeditions in Africa leading to exhibitions with catalogues, and author of the work *Statuaire Dogon* (Amez, 1994), considered as the thesis about Dogon people

Bettina von Lintig
Historian, anthropologist with a specialty in art, writer

Constance de Monbrison
Art historian and responsible of the Insulinde collections at Musée du quai Branly – Jacques Chirac, Paris

Sean Mooney
Chief Curator of the Rock Foundation, and supervisor of the private collections of Adelaide de Menil and of the anthropologist Edmund Carpenter

Michel Orliac
Archaeologist, former CNRS researcher and prolific author on the art of Easter Island

Philippe Peltier
Ethnologist and art historian, former head of the heritage unit
Oceanic-Insulinde at the Musée du quai Branly – Jacques Chirac in Paris

Constantine Petridis
Chair of the department of the arts of Africa and the Americas and curator of African Art at the Art Institute of Chicago

ACKNOWLEDGMENTS

We would like to thank all the authors who contributed to the production of this book as well as the various personalities who assisted us and without whom nothing would have been possible, in particular:

Bernard Dulon
Lance Entwistle
Marc Leo Felix
Julien Flak
Yves Le Fur
Anthony Meyer
Alain de Monbrison
François de Ricqlès

5 Continents Editions

Editorial Coordination
Laura Maggioni

Art Direction
Annarita De Sanctis

Lay-out
Daniela Meda

Translation
Julian Comoy
Robert McInnes

Editing
Emily Ligniti

Colour Separation
Pixel Studio, Bresso, Italy

5 Continents Editions
Piazza Caiazzo 1 – 20124 Milan, Italy
www.fivecontinentseditions.com

978-88-7439-898-0

Distributed by ACC Art Books throughout the world,
excluding Italy.
Distributed in Italy and Switzerland by Messaggerie
Libri S.p.A.

Printed and bound in Italy in July 2019
by Tecnostampa – Pigini Group Printing Division,
Loreto – Trevi, for 5 Continents Editions, Milan